AN EXEGETICAL SUMMARY OF
MARK 9–16

AN EXEGETICAL SUMMARY OF
MARK 9–16

Richard C. Blight

SIL International®
Dallas, Texas

©2014 by SIL International®

ISBN: 978-1-55671-379-8

Library of Congress Control Number: 2014951720
Printed in the United States of America

All Rights Reserved

No part of this publication may be reproduced, stored in a retrieval system, or transmitted in any form or by any means—electronic, mechanical, photocopy, recording, or otherwise—without the express permission of SIL International®, with the exception of brief excerpts in journal articles or reviews.

Copies of this and other publications of SIL International® may be obtained through distributors such as Amazon, Barnes & Noble, other worldwide distributors and, for select volumes, www.sil.org/resources/publications:

SIL International Publications
7500 West Camp Wisdom Road
Dallas, TX 75236-5629, USA

General inquiry: publications_intl@sil.org
Pending order inquiry: sales_intl@sil.org
www.sil.org/resources/publications

PREFACE

Exegesis is concerned with the interpretation of a text. Exegesis of the New Testament involves determining the meaning of the Greek text. Translators must be especially careful and thorough in their exegesis of the New Testament in order to accurately communicate its message in the vocabulary, grammar, and literary devices of another language. Questions occurring to translators as they study the Greek text are answered by summarizing how scholars have interpreted the text. This is information that should be considered by translators as they make their own exegetical decisions regarding the message they will communicate in their translations.

The Semi-Literal Translation

As a basis for discussion, a semi-literal translation of the Greek text is given so that the reasons for different interpretations can best be seen. When one Greek word is translated into English by several words, these words are joined by hyphens. There are a few times when clarity requires that a string of words joined by hyphens have a separate word, such as "not" (μή), inserted in their midst. In this case, the separate word is surrounded by spaces between the hyphens. When alternate translations of a Greek word are given, these are separated by slashes.

The Text

Variations in the Greek text are noted under the heading TEXT. The base text for the summary is the text of the fourth revised edition of *The Greek New Testament,* published by the United Bible Societies, which has the same text as the twenty-sixth edition of the *Novum Testamentum Graece* (Nestle-Aland). The versions that follow different variations are listed without evaluating their choices.

The Lexicon

The meaning of a key word in context is the first question to be answered. Words marked with a raised letter in the semi-literal translation are treated separately under the heading LEXICON. First, the lexicon form of the Greek word is given. Within the parentheses following the Greek word is the location number where, in the author's judgment, this word is defined in the *Greek-English Lexicon of the New Testament Based on Semantic Domains* (Louw and Nida 1988). When a semantic domain includes a translation of the particular verse being treated, **LN** in bold type indicates that specific translation. If the specific reference for the verse is listed in *A Greek-English Lexicon of the New Testament and Other Early Christian Literature* (Bauer, Arndt, Gingrich, and Danker 1979), the outline location and page number is given. Then English equivalents of the Greek word are given to show how it is translated by commentators who offer their own translations of the whole text and, after a semicolon, all the versions in the list of abbreviations for translations. "All versions" refers only to those versions used in the lexicon. "All translations" refers to both the versions and the commentaries used in the lexicon. Sometimes further comments are made about the meaning of the word or the significance of a verb's tense, voice, or mood.

The Questions

Under the heading QUESTION, a question is asked that comes from examining the Greek text under consideration. Typical questions concern the identity of an implied actor or object of an event word, the antecedent of a pronominal reference, the connection indicated by a relational word, the meaning of a genitive construction, the meaning of figurative language, the function of a rhetorical question, the identification of an ambiguity, and the presence of implied information that is needed to understand the passage correctly. Background information is also considered for a proper understanding of a passage. Although not all implied information and background information is made explicit in a translation, it is important to consider it so that the translation will not be stated in such a way that prevents a reader from arriving at the proper interpretation. The question is answered with a summary of what commentators have said. If there are contrasting differences of opinion, the different interpretations are numbered and the commentaries that support each are listed. Differences that are not treated by many of the commentaries often are not numbered, but are introduced with a contrastive 'Or' at the beginning of the sentence. No attempt has been made to select which interpretation is best.

The Use of This Book

This book does not replace the commentaries that it summarizes. Commentaries contain much more information about the meaning of words and passages. They often contain arguments for the interpretations that are taken and they may have important discussions about the discourse features of the text. In addition, they often have information about the historical, geographical, and cultural setting. Translators will want to refer to at least four commentaries as they exegete a passage. However, since no one commentary contains all the answers translators need, this book will be a valuable supplement. It makes more sources of exegetical help available than most translators have access to. Even if they had all the books available, few would have the time to search through all of them for the answers.

When many commentaries are studied, it soon becomes apparent that they frequently disagree in their interpretations. That is the reason why so many answers in this book are divided into two or more interpretations. The reader's initial reaction may be that all of these different interpretations complicate exegesis rather than help it. However, before translating a passage, a translator needs to know exactly where there is a problem of interpretation and what the exegetical options are.

Acknowledgements

I am grateful for the help I received in preparing this book for publication. Dr. J. Harold Greenlee researched the variant readings of the Greek text and helped with the text notes. My son, Thomas C. Blight, read this book for its literary style and made many helpful suggestions.

ABBREVIATIONS

COMMENTARIES AND REFERENCE BOOKS

An asterisk (*) indicates a book that translators may find especially helpful as they study the text of Mark.

AB1	Mann, C. S. *Mark.* The Anchor Bible. New York: Doubleday, 1986.
AB2	Marcus, Joel. *Mark 1–8.* The Anchor Bible. New York: Doubleday, 1999.
AB2	Marcus, Joel. *Mark 8–16.* The Anchor Yale Bible. New Haven: Yale University Press, 2009.
BAGD	Bauer, Walter. *A Greek-English Lexicon of the New Testament and Other Early Christian Literature.* Translated and revised from the 5th ed., 1958 by W. F. Arndt and F. W. Gingrich; 2nd edition, revised and augmented by F. W. Gingrich and F. W. Danker. Chicago: University of Chicago Press, 1979.
BECNT*	Stein, Robert H. *Mark.* Baker Exegetical Commentary on the New Testament. Grand Rapids: Baker, 2008.
BNTC	Hooker, Morna D. *The Gospel According to Saint Mark.* Black's New Testament Commentary. Peabody, MA: Hendrickson, 1991.
CBC	Bock, Darrell L. *The Gospel of Mark.* Cornerstone Biblical Commentary, Vol. 11. Carol Stream, IL: Tyndale, 2005.
CGTC	Cranfield, C. E. B. *The Gospel According to St. Mark.* The Cambridge Greek Testament Commentary. Cambridge: Cambridge University Press, 1959.
EBC*	Wessel, Walter W. "Mark," in *The Expositor's Bible Commentary*, vol. 8. Grand Rapids: Zondervan, 1984.
EGT	Bruce, Alexander Balmain. *The Synoptic Gospels.* Expositor's Greek Testament, vol. 1. 1910. Reprint. Grand Rapids: Eerdmans, 1980.
Gnd	Gundry, Robert H. *Mark.* Grand Rapids: Eerdmans, 1993.
Hb	Hiebert, D. Edmond. *The Gospel of Mark.* Revised edition. Greenville, SC: Bob Jones University Press, 1994.
ICC	Gould, Ezra P. *The Gospel According to St. Mark.* The International Critical Commentary. Edinburgh: T & T Clark, 1896.
LN	Louw, Johannes P., and Eugene A. Nida. *Greek–English Lexicon of the New Testament Based on Semantic Domains.* New York: United Bible Societies, 1988.
Lns	Lenski, R. C. H. *The Interpretation of St. Mark's Gospel.* Minneapolis, MN: Augsburg, 1946.

My	Meyer, Heinrich August Wilhelm. *Critical and Exegetical Handbook to the Gospels of Mark and Luke.* Translated from the fifth edition by Robert Wallas and revised by William Dickson. NY: Funk and Wagnalls, 1884.
NAC	Brooks, James A. *Mark.* The New American Commentary. Nashville, TN.: Broadman, 1991.
NCBC	Anderson, Hugh. *The Gospel of Mark.* The New Century Bible Commentary. Grand Rapids: Eerdmans, 1976.
NICNT	Lane, William L. *The Gospel of Mark.* The New International Commentary on the New Testament. Grand Rapids: Eerdmans, 1974.
NIGTC*	France, R. T. *The Gospel of Mark.* The New International Greek Testament Commentary. Grand Rapids: Eerdmans, 2002.
NTC	Hendriksen, William. *The Gospel of Mark.* New Testament Commentary. Grand Rapids: Baker,
PNTC	Edwards, James R. *The Gospel According to Mark.* The Pillar New Testament Commentary. Grand Rapids: Eerdmans, 2002.
Sw	Swete, Henry Barclay. *The Gospel According to St. Mark.* Reprinted from 3rd edition, 1909. Grand Rapids: Eerdmans, 1956.
Tay	Taylor, Vincent. *The Gospel According to St. Mark.* Second edition. New York: St. Martin's Press, 1966.
TH*	Bratcher, Robert G., and Eugene A. Nida. *A Translator's Handbook on the Gospel of Mark.* London: United Bible Societies, 1961.
TRT*	Carlton, Matthew E. *The Gospel of Mark.* Translator's Reference Translation. Dallas, TX: SIL International, 2001.
WBC	Guelich, Robert A. *Mark 1–8:26.* Word Biblical Commentary. Dallas, TX: Word, 1989.
WBC	Evans, Craig A. *Mark 8:27–16:20.* Word Biblical Commentary. Nashville, TN: Nelson, 2001.

GREEK TEXT AND TRANSLATIONS

GNT	The Greek New Testament. Edited by B. Aland, K. Aland, J. Karavidopoulos, C. Martini, and B. Metzger. Fourth ed. London, New York: United Bible Societies, 1993.
CEV	The Holy Bible, Contemporary English Version. New York: American Bible Society, 1995.
ESV and ESVfn	ESV Study Bible, English Standard Version. Wheaton, IL: Crossway Bibles, 2008.
GW	God's Word. Grand Rapids: World Publishing, 1995.
KJV	The Holy Bible. Authorized (or King James) Version. 1611.

NASB	New American Standard Bible. La Habra, CA: Lockman Foundation, 1995.
NCV	New Century Version. Dallas: Word Publishing, 1991.
NET and NETfn	The NET Bible, New English Translation. Version 6r,715, Biblical Studies Press, 2006.
NIV and NIVfn	NIV Study Bible, New International Version. Grand Rapids: Zondervan, 1995.
NLT and NLTfn	NLT Study Bible, New Living Translation. Second edition. Carol Stream, Ill.: Tyndale House, 2008.
NRSV	The Holy Bible: New Revised Standard Version. New York: Oxford University Press, 1989.
REB	The Revised English Bible. Oxford: Oxford University Press and Cambridge University Press, 1989.
TEV	Good News Bible, Today's English Version. Second edition. New York: American Bible Society, 1992.

GRAMMATICAL TERMS

act.	active	mid.	middle
fut.	future	opt.	optative
impera.	imperative	pass.	passive
imperf.	imperfect	perf.	perfect
indic.	indicative	pres.	present
infin.	infinitive	subj.	subjunctive

EXEGETICAL SUMMARY OF MARK 9–16

DISCOURSE UNIT—9:1–13 [NASB]. The topic is the transfiguration.

9:1 And he-was-saying to-them, "Truly[a] I-say to-you that there-are some of-the (ones) standing here who will- not -taste[b] death until they-see the kingdom of-God having-come with power.[c]"

LEXICON—a. ἀμήν (LN 72.6) (BAGD 2. p. 45): 'truly' [AB1, BAGD, BECNT, BNTC, LN, WBC; ESV, NASB, NRSV, REB], 'verily' [KJV], 'amen' [AB2, Lns]. The phrase 'truly I say to you' is translated 'I tell you the truth' [NCV, NET, NIV, NLT], 'indeed, it is true that' [LN], 'I tell you' [TEV], 'I can assure you' [CEV], 'I can guarantee this truth' [GW], 'I solemnly declare to you' [NTC]. This particle makes a strong affirmation of what is being declared [LN]. It is an assertive particle that begins a solemn declaration' [BAGD]. The phrase 'truly I say to you' occurs at 3:28; 8:12; 9:1, 41; 10:15, 29; 11:23; 12:43; 13:30; 14:9, 18, 25, 30.

  b. aorist mid. (deponent = act.) subj. of γεύομαι (LN 90.78) (BAGD 2. p. 157): 'to taste' [AB1, AB2, BNTC, Lns, NTC, WBC; ESV, KJV, NASB, NIV, NRSV, REB], 'to experience' [LN], 'to come to know something' [BAGD]. The phrase 'will not taste death' is translated 'will not experience death' [NET], 'will not die' [CEV, GW, NLT, TEV], 'will by no means die' [BECNT]. The phrase 'will not taste death until they see' is translated 'will see…before they die' [NCV]. This verb means to experience something, usually focusing on personal involvement [LN]. 'Taste' is a figurative expression for experiencing or coming to know something [TH]. To experience death means to die [NTC].

  c. δύναμις (LN 76.1) (BAGD 1. p. 207): 'power' [BAGD, LN]. The phrase 'to come with/in power' [all translations except GW, NLT] is also translated 'to arrive with/in power' [GW, NLT]. This noun denotes the potentiality to exert force in performing some function [LN].

QUESTION—How is this verse related to its context?

  1. This verse is a paragraph in itself [AB1, BNTC, EBC, Lns, NTC; all versions except KJV, NASB, NET, NRSV]. It serves as the conclusion to the discourse unit that began at 8:34 with the words 'And having summoned the crowd along with his disciples he said to them' [AB1, AB2, BECNT, BNTC, CBC, CGTC, EBC, Gnd, Hb, ICC, Lns, NAC, NCBC, NICNT, NIGTC, NTC, PNTC, Sw, Tay, TH, WBC; CEV, ESV, GW, NCV, NET, NIV, NLT, NRSV, TEV]. So the words 'And he was saying to *them*' could mean that Jesus was still speaking to that same crowd [Gnd, NICNT, TH]. The last verse of chapter 8 spoke of the coming of the kingdom as the coming of the Son of Man in the glory of his Father, and this verse adds that the time of that coming would be after many of them were dead [ICC]. However, some think that the crowd had

left and the twelve disciples were privately asking Jesus to explain what he meant about his disciples losing their lives [EBC, Sw].
2. This verse begins a new discourse unit consisting of verses 1–13 [NASB].

QUESTION—What is meant by the statement that those people will not die *until* they see that the kingdom has come with power?

1. The perfect tense of the participle ἐληλυθυῖαν 'having come' indicates that this is not talking about seeing the arrival of the kingdom, but that they will witness the fact that it *has come* [Lns, NIGTC, TH; ESV, NASB, NRSV]. The focus is not on its arrival, but on the time afterwards when its reality is visible and displayed with power [NIGTC]. Not only will they see it in the act of its coming, but also after it has come [Lns]. This does not imply that they will die as soon as they see the kingdom come. It simply means that they will still be alive to see the kingdom present ('having come') in power [TH].
2. Many do not emphasize the perfect tense of the verb and simply focus on the time when the arrival of the kingdom occurs [all versions except ESV, NASB, NRSV].

QUESTION—When will they see that the Kingdom of God has come in power?

1. This refers to what the three disciples will see at the transfiguration (BECNT, BNTC, CBC, CGT, ESVfn, Gnd, Hb, My, NETfn, NICNT, NIGTC, NLTfn, Tay, WBC). The transfiguration is to be regarded as the enthronement of Jesus that anticipates the glory that is to come. It was a momentary manifestation of the sovereign power of Jesus that pointed to the end-time when he will return in power [Hb, NICNT]. This happened just six days later when Jesus took three of his disciples with him to the mount of transfiguration. There they saw Jesus transfigured and heard God announce that Jesus is his beloved Son, the one whom the disciples are to obey [Gnd]. The transfiguration offered dramatic proof that the kingdom had come in the preaching and ministry of Jesus [WBC]. Mark understood the event on the mountain to be at least a partial fulfillment of Jesus' words even though the reality of the coming was not yet visible [NIGTC].
2. All of the disciples will see this power in the resurrection and ascension of Jesus [PNTC].
3. This refers to the establishment of the church as a spiritual kingdom [ICC, NTC, Sw, Tay]. Since some of the present disciples would see this happen, this refers to a spiritual kingdom and the agencies in its establishment will be the Holy Spirit and the providence of God in human affairs [ICC].

DISCOURSE UNIT—9:2–13 [CBC; CEV, ESV, GW, NCV, NET, NIV, TEV]. The topic is the transfiguration [ESV, NET, NIV, TEV], Jesus' transfiguration [CBC], the true glory of Jesus [CEV], Moses and Elijah appear with Jesus [GW], Jesus talks with Moses and Elijah [NCV].

DISCOURSE UNIT—9:2–10 [NLT]. The topic is the transfiguration.

DISCOURSE UNIT—9:2–8 [EBC, Hb, NICNT; NRSV]. The topic is the transfiguration [EBC; NRSV], transfiguration on the mount [Hb], the transfiguration: the glory of the Son of Man [NICNT].

9:2 **And after six days Jesus takes[a] Peter and James and John and leads-them -up[b] to a-high mountain by-themselves.[c] And he was transfigured[d] before them,**

LEXICON—a. pres. act. indic. of παραλαμβάνω (LN 15.168) (BAGD 1. p. 619): 'to take' [AB2, BECNT, BNTC; GW, NCV, NLT], 'to take along' [BAGD, LN, Lns, WBC], 'to take with (him)' [AB1, NTC; CEV, ESV, KJV, NASB, NET, NIV, NRSV, REB, TEV], 'to bring along' [LN]. The verb means that someone takes or brings someone along with him [LN].

b. pres. act. indic. of ἀναφέρω (LN 15.176) (BAGD 1. p. 63): 'to lead up, to bring up' [BAGD, LN]. The phrase 'leads them up to' is translated 'led them up' [AB2, BNTC, NTC; ESV, GW, NET, NIV, NLT, NRSV, REB, TEV], 'leads them up into' [BECNT; similarly KJV], 'takes them up into' [WBC], 'brings them up into' [Lns], 'led them to' [AB1], 'brought them up on' [NASB], 'they went up on' [CEV], not explicit [NCV]. This verb means to bring or lead someone up to some place [LN].

c. The idiom κατ' ἰδίαν 'according to that which is private' (LN 28.67) is translated 'by themselves' [BNTC, NTC; ESV, NASB, NCV, REB], 'privately by themselves' [AB2, BECNT], 'apart, by themselves' [KJV, NRSV], 'in private alone' [Lns], 'alone...privately' [NET], 'to be alone' [NLT], 'where they were alone' [AB1; TEV; similarly NIV], 'where they could be alone' [CEV, GW]. This idiom pertains to what occurs in a private context or setting and has the sense of not being made known publicly [LN]. The four of them were together, alone by themselves [TH]. This idiom occurs at 4:34; 6:31; 7:33; 9:2, 28; 13:3.

d. aorist pass. indic. of μεταμορφόομαι, μεταμορφόω (LN 58.16) (BAGD 1. p. 511): 'to be transfigured, to be transformed, to be changed in form' [BAGD], 'to be changed in appearance' [LN]. The phrase 'he was transfigured' [AB1, BECNT, Lns; ESV, KJV, NASB, NET, NIV, NRSV, REB] is also translated 'he was transformed' [AB2, BNTC, Lns, NTC, WBC], 'Jesus' appearance was transformed' [NLT], 'Jesus' appearance changed/was-changed' [GW, NCV], 'Jesus was completely changed' [CEV], 'a change came over Jesus' [TEV]. This verb means to take on a different physical form or appearance [LN]. It means to change into another form [EBC]. The passive verb 'was transfigured' indicates that Jesus was transfigured by God [Gnd, Hb, Lns].

QUESTION—What is meant by Jesus being μετεμορφώθη 'transfigured'?

The text indicates that the physical appearance of Jesus was changed [Hb, NICNT, Lns, NIGTC, NTC, TH]. Luke 9:29 says 'the appearance of his face changed' and Matthew 17:2 says 'his face shone like the sun' [Lns, NCBC, NIGTC, PNTC]. His appearance was temporarily changed from that of an ordinary human being to a divine being in all his glory [NAC]. This was not a change in his nature, but an outward transformation of his appearance to reflect his true nature [PNTC]. The transfiguration gave a preview of the coming of the Son of Man 'in the glory of his Father' (8:38) [BECNT, Gnd, WBC].

9:3 and his clothes became shining,[a] exceedingly white such-as no bleacher[b] on earth is-able to-whiten them.

TEXT—Manuscripts reading λευκὰ λίαν 'exceedingly white' are followed by GNT which does not mention a variant reading. A variant reading is λευκὰ λίαν ὡς χιών 'exceedingly white as snow' and it is followed by KJV.

LEXICON—a. pres. act. participle of στίλβω (LN **14.47**) (BAGD p. 768): 'to shine, to be radiant' [BAGD], 'to glisten, to dazzle, to gleam, to flash' [LN]. The description 'became shining, exceedingly white' [KJV] is also translated 'became glistening, intensely/very white' [BECNT, Lns], 'became radiant and exceedingly white' [NASB], 'became radiant, intensely white' [ESV], 'became radiantly white' [NET], 'became exceedingly white' [WBC]; 'became shining white' [NCV, TEV], 'became dazzling white' [AB1, AB2, NTC, BNTC, **LN**; GW, NIV, NLT, NRSV, REB], 'became much whiter (than any bleach could make them)' [CEV]. This verb means to give off or to reflect a very bright light [LN].

b. γναφεύς (LN **48.7**) (BAGD p. 162): 'bleacher, fuller' [BAGD, LN]. The clause 'such as no bleacher on earth is able to whiten them' is translated 'such as no one on earth could bleach them' [NRSV; similarly ESV], 'as no launderer on earth can whiten them' [NASB; similarly AB2, WBC], 'more so than any launderer in the world could bleach them [NET], 'so white as no bleacher on earth could make them' [**LN**; similarly REB], 'so as no fuller on earth can white them' [KJV], 'whiter than anyone in the world could wash them' [TEV], 'whiter than any person could make them' [NCV], 'whiter than any bleacher on earth could bleach them' [NTC], 'whiter than anyone on-earth/in-the-world could bleach them' [GW, NIV], 'such as no earthly bleacher is able to whiten' [BECNT], 'much whiter than any bleach on earth could make them' [CEV, similarly NLT], 'with a whiteness no bleacher on earth could achieve' [BNTC], 'with a brightness no cleaner anywhere could equal' [AB1]. This noun denotes a person who cards, cleans, and bleaches cloth. The reference is obviously pointing to the bleaching process even though a bleacher would also be engaged in the cleaning and carding of cloth where the nap of the cloth was somewhat raised and softened by combing it with bristles [LN].

9:4 And appeared[a] to-them Elijah with[b] Moses and they-were talking-with[c] Jesus.

LEXICON—a. aorist pass. indic. of ὁράω (LN 24.1) (BAGD 1.a.δ. p. 578): 'to appear' [BAGD, BECNT, BNTC, Lns, NTC, WBC; all translations except CEV, TEV], 'to be seen' [LN], 'to become visible' [BAGD]. The phrase 'and appeared to them Elijah with Moses' is translated 'then the

three disciples saw Elijah and Moses' [TEV], 'then Moses and Elijah were there' [CEV].
- b. σύν (LN 89.107): 'with' [AB1, AB2, BECNT, BNTC, LN, Lns, WBC; ESV, KJV, NRSV, REB], 'along with' [NASB, NET], 'together with' [LN], 'and' [NTC; CEV, GW, NCV, NIV, NLT, TEV]. This preposition indicates an associative relationship that often involves joint participation in some activity [LN].
- c. pres. act. participle of συλλαλέω (LN 33.157) (BAGD p. 776): 'to talk with' [AB1, AB2, BAGD, BNTC, LN; all versions], 'to converse with' [BAGD, LN, WBC], 'to speak with' [BECNT, LN, Lns], 'to be engaged in conversation with' [NTC]. This verb means to converse with someone [LN].

QUESTION—How could Elijah and Moses suddenly appear before the three disciples and how would the disciples recognize who they were?

Elijah and Moses came from the presence of God in heaven [ESVfn, TRT]. The three disciples saw Elijah and Moses with their physical eyes [Lns, NTC, NCBC]. The saints in heaven do not need to be introduced since they are known at once through a God-given intuition of the beholder [Hb. Lns, Sw]. Peter could have figured out the identity of the two men from their conversation with Jesus [ICC].

QUESTION—What is significant about the appearance of Elijah?

Elijah was to come back before the Day of the Lord (Mal. 4:5–6) [AB2, BECNT, Gnd, Hb, NETfn]. He was the illustrious representative of the prophets [ESVfn, Hb, Lns, NAC, NIGTC, Sw, Tay]. Perhaps Elijah is named first because verses 8:28 and 9:11 indicate that Elijah was already in their thoughts [Sw].

QUESTION—What is significant about the appearance of Moses?

Moses was the great representative of the Law [BECNT, ESVfn, Hb, Lns, NETfn, NAC, NIGTC, Sw, Tay]. He represented the prophetic office [NETfn]. He represented the old covenant [NICNT].

QUESTION—What was the discussion about?

Even though Mark and Matthew apparently thought it was not important to reveal what they talked about, we learn in Luke 9:31 that they talked about the imminent departure of Jesus in Jerusalem [BECNT, ICC, Tay].

9:5 And speaking,[a] Peter says to-Jesus, "Rabbi,[b] it-is good[c] for-us to-be here, and let-us-make three tents,[d] one for-you and one for-Moses and one for-Elijah."

LEXICON—a. aorist pass. (deponent = act.) participle of ἀποκρίνομαι (LN 33.28) (BAGD 2. p. 93): 'to speak' [LN; TEV], 'to speak up' [NTC], 'to declare, to say' [LN], 'to begin' [BAGD], 'to answer' [AB2, Lns, WBC; KJV], 'to respond' [BECNT], not explicit [AB1, BNTC; all versions except KJV, TEV]. This verb introduces or continues a somewhat formal discourse and it regularly occurs with λέγω 'to say' [LN]. It means to continue a discourse [BAGD]. This verb is redundant and it is not necessary to translate it [NETfn].

b. ῥαββί (LN 33.246) (BAGD p. 733): 'rabbi' [AB1, AB2, BECNT, BNTC, LN, Lns, NTC, WBC; ESV, GW, NASB, NCV, NIV, NLT, REB, NRSV], 'teacher' [LN; CEV, NET, TEV], 'master' [KJV]. This noun is borrowed from Aramaic to denote a Jewish teacher and scholar who is recognized for his expertise in interpreting the Jewish Scriptures [LN]. It is an honorary title for an outstanding teachers of the law [BAGD]. This title means the same as the title Διδάσκαλε 'teacher' in 4:38, but here Mark uses 'Rabbi' to give an OT feeling to the occasion in which Moses appears as the prototype Teacher of the Law [NIGTC]. In the two parallel passages, Peter addresses Jesus as 'Lord' in Matt. 17:4 and as 'Master' in Luke 9:33. In each of these three passages, the writer offered his own translation of the Aramaic word that Peter must have used, so the three terms they used can be considered synonyms [Lns, NTC]. This noun occurs at verses 9:5, 11.21, and 14:45.

c. καλός (LN **66.2**) (BAGD 3.c. p. 400): 'good' [BAGD, **LN**], 'fitting' [LN]. The clause καλόν ἐστιν ἡμᾶς ὧδε εἶναι 'it is good for us to be here' [AB2, BECNT; CEV, KJV, NASB, NET, NIV, NRSV] is also translated 'how good it is for us to be here' [NTC], 'it's wonderful for us to be here' [NLT], 'excellent it is for us to be here' [Lns]. Some change the infinitive form of the verb to present tense: 'it is good that we are here' [AB1, BNTC, WBC; ESV, GW, NCV, REB], 'how good it is that we are here' [TEV]. This adjective describes something as being fitting, and at the same time probably good [LN].

d. σκηνή (LN 7.9) (BAGD p. 754): 'tent' [BAGD, LN, WBC; ESV, GW, NCV, TEV], 'dwelling' [NRSV], 'shelter' [AB1, AB2, NTC; CEV, NET, NIV, NLT, REB], 'tabernacle' [KJV, NASB], 'booth' [BECNT, BNTC, Lns]. This noun denotes a portable dwelling of cloth and/or skins. It is held up by poles and fastened to stakes by cords [LN]. The material used for the shelters in this setting would have to be obtained there on the mountain side [ICC], so they probably used leafy tree branches [BNTC, CGTC, Hb, NIGTC, Tay, TRT] and twigs [CGTC, TRT].

QUESTION—Why did Peter join the conversation?

As Peter listened, he impulsively felt the situation called for a response from him [Hb]. Peter was responding to what the disciples had just seen and heard [Gnd, ICC, Lns, NIGTC]. It was his first reaction to what he thought was needed by Jesus and the two men who had suddenly arrived from heaven [NTC].

QUESTION—Who was Peter referring to when he told Jesus, "It is good for *us* to be here"?

1. The pronoun 'us' is an exclusive first person plural pronoun that does not include the person addressed. It includes only Peter, James, and John [AB2, BECNT, CGTC, Gnd, Lns, NICNT, NIGTC, Sw, Tay]. The reason

why it was good for the disciples to be there is unclear [BECNT, Hb, Tay].
- 1.1 Peter meant that it was good that the disciples were available to build three shelters for Jesus and the two heavenly visitors [CGTC, NICNT, NIGTC, NTC]. It was good that they were present to serve Jesus and the two men from heaven [NICNT].
- 1.2 Peter meant that it was a good thing for the disciples to be present and see the kingdom come in power as Jesus was transfigured in their presence and then see him conversing with the great men of history, Elijah and Moses [Gnd, Hb]. The presence of these three disciples at the transfiguration was good because they were seeing 'the kingdom of God having come with power' just as Jesus had predicted in verse 1 [Gnd].
- 2. The pronoun 'us' is an inclusive first person plural pronoun that includes the person addressed. It includes Jesus along with the three disciples [Lns; perhaps TH]. The interpretation that 'we' includes all six persons (or at least the three disciples and Jesus) has been preferred by many who take this to describe the blessedness of the experience for all those present [TH]. Because the three disciples and Jesus were together on the mountain at the time of both Jesus' transfiguration and the appearance of Elijah and Moses, the disciples were filled with awe as they realized that they were truly in the presence of the divine majesty of Jesus [Lns].

QUESTION—Who was Peter referring to when he said to Jesus, "Let us make three tents"?

When Peter addressed Jesus with the first person plural verb ποιήσωμεν 'let us make' he was excluding Jesus and only intended the 'us' to refer to himself, James, and John [CBC, Gnd, Hb, Lns, NICNT, NIGTC, NTC, TH, TRT]. Peter was not suggesting that Jesus, Moses, and Elijah should join in making the three shelters [Gnd].

QUESTION—Why did Peter suggest making a shelter for Jesus and the two heavenly visitors?

Instead of Jesus, Moses, and Elijah merely standing out in the open for their meeting, Peter thought it would be more dignified if they were sheltered from the sun by a 'tent' [NIGTC]. Because Luke 9:33 says that Peter made this suggestion just prior to the departure of Moses and Elijah, it is possible he was trying to encourage the consultation to continue indefinitely [ESVfn, Lns, NIGTC, WBC]. It was the custom for the Jews to build such types of shelters every year for the celebration of the Feast of Tabernacles [BECNT, NETfn, NIGTC, Tay, TH], so Peter may have been thinking of making the 'booths' used in the Feast of Booths (Tabernacles) (Lev. 23.42) [NETfn, NIVfn]. But he could have been thinking of making 'tents of meeting' (Exodus 29:42) where God would communicate with his people [NIVfn]. Judaism kept alive the hope that God would again tabernacle with his people as he had in the Exodus [PNTC] and some think Peter was referring to building three *tabernacles*, that is, three 'tents of meeting' where God would again communicate with his people [NICNT; KJV, NASB]. However, the suggestion of building *three* such shelters ignores the fact that only Jesus was transfigured and it would seem to be placing Moses, Elijah, and Jesus all on the same level [BECNT, NLTfn].

9:6 Because^a he-had- not -known^b what he-said since they-were terrified.^c

LEXICON—a. γάρ (LN 89.23) (BAGD 1.e. p. 152): 'because' [LN], 'for' [AB2, BNTC, LN, Lns, NTC, WBC; ESV, KJV, NASB, NET, REB], 'but' [CEV], not explicit [AB1; GW, NCV, NIV, NRSV, TEV]. The implied clause is made explicit: 'He said this because' [BECNT; NLT]. This conjunction indicates the cause or reason between events [LN].
  b. pluperfect act. indic. of οἶδα (LN 32.4) (BAGD 1.f. p. 556): 'to know, to understand, to comprehend' [LN]. The clause 'had not known what he said' is translated 'did not know what to say' [AB1, BNTC; ESV, NCV, NET, NIV, NRSV, REB, TEV; similarly NTC], 'wist not what to say' [KJV], 'did not know what he should say/reply' [BECNT, WBC], 'did not know what to answer' [AB2; NASB], 'knew not what he answered' [Lns], 'didn't know how to respond' [GW], 'did not really know what to say' [NTC], 'didn't really know what else to say' [NLT], 'did not know what he was talking about' [CEV]. This verb means to comprehend the meaning of something [LN].
  c. ἔκφοβος (LN 25.256) (BAGD p. 247): 'terrified' [BECNT, BNTC, LN; ESV, GW, NASB, NLT, NRSV, REB], 'so afraid' [**LN**], 'so frightened' [AB1, NTC; NCV, NIV, TEV], 'terribly frightened' [CEV], 'very frightened, very much afraid' [LN], 'sore afraid' [KJV], 'greatly afraid' [WBC], 'afraid' [AB2, Lns; NET]. This adjective pertains to being extremely afraid [LN].

QUESTION—What relationship is indicated by the initial conjunction γάρ 'because'?

This conjunction indicates the reason Peter had spoken as he did in the previous verse [BECNT, Hb, TH; NLT]. It introduces a parenthetical note by Mark [AB1, AB2, NTC, NETfn, NICNT] and this is shown by enclosing the verse with parentheses [AB1, AB2; NET]. This editorial comment by Mark keeps the readers from overlooking Peter's error when he foolishly acted as though Moses and Elijah were on a par with Jesus [BNTC, Gnd]. It was also foolish to think that in their exalted state the three would need shelter for the night as ordinary men do [Lns]. Such crude earthly tabernacles would not be fitting for them [Hb]. If Peter had known what to say, he would not have made such a foolish suggestion [ICC].

QUESTION—What relationship is indicated by the second γάρ '*since* they were terrified'?

This conjunction indicates the reason why Peter did not know what to say [Hb, TH]. The fear felt by all three disciples was the reason for Peter's inappropriate idea of making shelters [NIGTC]. Their fear was an appropriate response to the overpowering glory of God's rule that they were seeing in fulfillment of verse 1 [Gnd]. Such a fear often accompanies a theophany since it is then that human weakness and sin stand in sharp contrast to the holiness and omnipotence of God [BECNT]. In the presence of the glorious persons before them, Peter could not control his thoughts and just babbled whatever came to his tongue [Lns].

9:7 And a-cloud appeared, overshadowing[a] them, and a-voice came out-of the cloud, "This is my Son, the beloved,[b] listen[c] to-him."

LEXICON—a. pres. act. participle of ἐπισκιάζω (LN 14.62) (BAGD 2. p. 298): 'to overshadow' [AB2, BECNT, BNTC, Lns, WBC; ESV, GW, KJV, NASB, NET, NLT, NRSV], 'to cover' [BAGD, NTC; NCV], 'to envelop' [NIV], 'to cast a shadow upon' [LN]. The phrase 'a cloud appeared, overshadowing them' is translated 'a cloud appeared, casting its shadow over them' [REB], 'a cloud appeared and covered them with its shadow' [AB1; TEV], 'the shadow of a cloud passed over and covered them' [CEV]. This verb means to cause a shadow by interposing something between an object and a source of light [LN].

b. ἀγαπητός (LN 58.53) (BAGD 1. p. 6): 'beloved' [BAGD], 'only dear, only' [LN]. The phrase 'my Son, the beloved' [AB1, Lns, WBC; NRSV] is also translated 'my Son, my Beloved' [NTC], 'my beloved Son' [AB2, BECNT, BNTC; ESV, KJV, NASB, REB], 'my Son, whom I love' [GW, NCV, NIV], 'my Son, and I love him' [CEV], 'my own dear Son' [TEV], 'my one dear Son' [NET], 'my dearly loved Son' [NLT]. This adjective pertains to someone who is the only one of his class and at the same time is particularly loved and cherished [LN]. It means 'beloved,' but inclines strongly toward the meaning 'only beloved' [BAGD].

c. pres. act. impera. of ἀκούω (LN 36.14): 'to listen to' [AB1, AB2, BNTC, LN, NTC; all versions except KJV], 'to hear' [BECNT, Lns, WBC; KJV], 'to pay attention to and obey' [LN]. This verb means to listen or pay attention to a person in order to conform to what is advised or commanded [LN]. This present imperative indicates their continuing duty to obey Jesus [EBC, Hb, Lns].

QUESTION—What was the cloud like and how did the cloud cover them?

It is called a 'bright cloud' in Matthew 17:5 [Lns, NAC, NTC]. This reminds some of the Shekinah glory of the OT that signaled the presence of God [BNTC, CBC, Hb, NAC, NIGTC, Sw].

1. This cloud remained above them and overshadowed them [AB1, AB2, BNTC, TH; REB, TEV; probably BECNT, WBC; ESV, GW, KJV, NASB, NET, NLT NRSV which say that the cloud 'overshadowed' them]. Since the voice of God came *out* of the cloud, the disciples at least must have remained outside of it [AB2, BNTC].
2. This cloud enveloped Jesus, Moses, and Elijah, but not the disciples [CGTC, EBC, NICNT]. The word ἐπισκιάζω 'covered' means that the cloud enveloped and concealed Jesus, Moses, and Elijah. God addressed the disciples from the cloud while they stood outside the cloud [CGTC].

3. This cloud enveloped all those present [Gnd, Hb, Lns, NIGTC]. It was a luminous cloud (Matt. 17:3) that suddenly appeared over them and then enveloped them all, causing fear among the disciples (Luke 9:34) [Hb]. Probably the cloud covered the whole mountain and enveloped all six persons [NIGTC]. In this cloud they could no longer see Jesus or anyone else, they could only hear God's voice [Gnd].

QUESTION—What is implied by God's command ἀκούετε αὐτοῦ 'Listen to him'?

The expression 'listen to him' comes from the words of Moses to the Israelites in Deut. 18:15 when he said, 'The Lord your God will raise up for you a prophet like me from among you…you must listen to him'. This identifies Jesus as a leader-prophet like Moses and points out that they still have much to learn from him [NETfn]. It means that Jesus is now God's authorized spokesman instead of Moses and Elijah [Hb, WBC]. The disciples were to pay attention solely to Jesus since God's rule has come with power only in the person of Jesus [Gnd]. Peter's plan to build three tent-tabernacles implied that Peter thought of all three being equal, each deserving his own tabernacle, but God's command to listen only to his Son Jesus showed how mistaken he was [NIGTC, PNTC, WBC]. This command also rebukes Peter for refusing to accept what Jesus had said concerning his suffering and rejection in 8:32 [BECNT, NAC, NLTfn, PNTC].

9:8 And suddenly^a looking-around they- no longer -saw anyone but Jesus alone with them.

LEXICON—a. ἐξάπινα (LN **67.113**) (BAGD p. 273): 'suddenly' [BAGD, LN; all translations except CEV, NASB, TEV], 'immediately' [**LN**], 'at once' [LN; CEV], 'all at once' [NASB], not explicit [TEV]. This adverb indicates an extremely short period of time between a previous state or event and a subsequent state or event [LN].

QUESTION—What happened ἐξάπινα 'suddenly'?

1. The adverb 'suddenly' modifies the only active verb in the sentence, εἶδον 'they saw' [AB1, AB2, BECNT, BNTC, EGT, Hb, Lns, NIGTC, NTC, Sw, Tay, TRT, WBC; ESV, GW, KJV, NET, NIV, NLT, NRSV, REB]: *suddenly they no longer saw*. Many translate the participial phrase περιβλεψάμενοι 'looking around' [BECNT, Lns] as a temporal circumstance: 'when they looked around' [AB2, NTC, KJV, NET, NIV, NLT, NRSV, REB], 'as they looked around' [AB1; GW]. Matthew 17:6–8 says that when the disciples heard God speak they were terrified and fell face downward. When Jesus touched them and told them not to be afraid, they suddenly looked around and saw only Jesus [Hb, Lns, Sw]. They had hidden their faces while God spoke from the cloud. When they opened their eyes they found that Elijah, Moses, and the cloud were no longer there [NIGTC].

2. 'Suddenly' is treated as though it modifies the participle περιβλεψάμενοι 'looking around' [ICC, Gnd, LN, TH; CEV, NASB, NCV, TEV]:

'suddenly Peter, James, and John looked around, but they saw only Jesus there alone with them' [NCV], 'they immediately looked around but did not see anybody but Jesus' [**LN**], 'at once the disciples looked around, but saw only Jesus' [CEV], 'all at once they looked around and saw no one with them anymore, except Jesus alone' [NASB], 'they took a quick look around but did not see anyone else; only Jesus was with them' [TEV]. There is a difference of opinion about whether the adverb 'suddenly' belongs with the participle 'looking around' or with the verb 'they saw.' Since 'looking' and 'seeing' are parts of the same action, the adverb should be connected with the participle 'looking' in order to avoid separating the two closely related aspects of the same act [ICC].

QUESTION—How did Jesus appear when they saw him?

When they looked at Jesus, his appearance was now normal [Hb, Lns, NIGTC, Sw]. Some think his garments were still glistening white from the transfiguration [Gnd, WBC].

DISCOURSE UNIT—9:9–13 [EBC, Hb, NICNT; NRSV]. The topic is a discussion concerning Elijah [Hb], the coming of Elijah [EBC, NICNT; NRSV].

9:9 And (as) they were coming-down from the mountain, he-gave-orders to-them that they-should-tell no-one what they-had-seen except[a] when the Son of-Man[b] had-risen[c] from (the) dead.

LEXICON—a. εἰ μή (LN 89.131): The phrase εἰ μή 'if not' means 'except, but, however, instead, but only'.[LN]. The phrase εἰ μή ὅταν 'except when' [Lns] is also translated 'until' [AB1, AB2, BECNT, BNTC, WBC; all versions except NET, NRSV], 'until after' [NTC; NET, NRSV]. The phrase εἰ μή 'except' indicates a contrast by designating an exception [LN].

b. υἱὸς τοῦ ἀνθρώπου (LN 9.3) (BAGD 2.e. p. 835): This title of Jesus is translated 'the Son of Man' [BAGD, LN; all translations except AB1], 'The Man' [AB1]. It is a title with Messianic implications that Jesus used concerning himself [LN]. At that time Jewish teaching included a heavenly being who was looked upon as a 'Son of Man' or 'Man' who exercised Messianic functions such as judging the world [BAGD]. See 2:10 for a discussion of this title.

c. aorist act. subj. of ἀνίσταμαι, ἀνίστημι (LN 23.93) (BAGD 2.a. p. 70): 'to arise' [BAGD], 'to come back to life, to live again, to be resurrected' [LN]. The phrase 'had risen from the dead' [NTC; ESV, NCV, NET, NIV, NLT, NRSV, REB; similarly KJV] is also translated 'should have risen from the dead' [BNTC], 'should arise/rise from the dead' [BECNT, Lns, WBC], 'has risen from death' [TEV], 'had been raised from the dead' [AB1; CEV], 'rose from the dead' [NASB], 'had come back to life' [GW]. This verb means to come back to life after having died [LN]. The phrase ἐκ νεκρῶν 'from dead' lacks an article with the noun 'dead,' which indicates that the phrase refers to the condition of being dead and means 'arising from death' [Lns].

QUESTION—Why were the three disciples told not to tell anyone about what they had seen at the transfiguration?

The disciples could not understand the true significance of what they had seen and heard until after the resurrection when they would truly understand the person of Jesus [CGTC, Hb]. The disciples did not yet understand that the vindication and glory for the Son of Man would be through his dying on the cross. So if they told others about what happened at the transfiguration it would only cause more confusion when Jesus was put to death [BECNT]. People were already excited with their own hopes about the Messiah, and the story of the transfiguration would only intensify these false hopes. The death and resurrection of Jesus would put an end to their false expectations and enable them to accurately report the account of Jesus' earthly glory and power [ICC].

9:10 And they-kept[a] the word to themselves discussing[b] what to-rise from the dead means.

LEXICON—a. aorist act. indic. of κρατέω (LN 13.34) (BAGD 2.e.δ. p. 448): 'to keep, to hold' [LN], 'to hold back' [BAGD]. The clause τὸν λόγον ἐκράτησαν 'they kept the word' is translated 'they scrupulously kept the charge' [NTC], 'they kept in mind what he said' [GW], 'they obeyed his order' [TEV], 'the followers obeyed Jesus' [NCV], 'they seized on this saying' [BNTC], 'they seized upon that statement' [NASB], 'they seized upon those words' [REB], 'they fastened on this saying' [AB1], 'they fastened on the word' [Lns], 'they latched onto this saying' [AB2]. Some connect the following phrase πρὸς ἑαυτούς 'to themselves with the verb 'they kept' in this clause: 'they kept this saying/statement to themselves' [WBC; NET; similarly KJV], 'they kept the matter to themselves' [BECNT; ESV, NIV, NRSV], 'they kept it to themselves' [CEV, NLT]. This verb means to cause the continuation of some state on the basis of one's authority or power [LN]. Here it means to keep a saying to oneself in order to consider it later [BAGD].

b. pres. act. participle of συζητέω (LN 33.157) (BAGD 1. p. 775): 'to discuss, to carry on a discussion about something' [BAGD], 'to talk with, to speak with, to converse' [LN]. The participle 'discussing' [NET, NIV] is also translated 'debating' [WBC], 'questioning' [BECNT; ESV, NRSV], 'questioning one with another' [KJV], 'but they often asked each other' [NLT], 'but they wondered' [CEV]. Some connect the preceding phrase πρὸς ἑαυτούς 'to themselves' with this verb: 'discussing among themselves' [AB1, BNTC], 'and discussed among themselves' [REB], 'discussing with one another' [NASB], 'but they discussed' [NCV], 'meanwhile questioning among themselves' [NTC], 'by disputing with each other' [Lns], 'arguing among themselves' [AB2], 'but argued among themselves' [GW]. 'but among themselves they started discussing the matter' [TEV]. This verb means to converse with someone [LN]. This verb occurs at 1:27; 8:11; 9:10, 14, 16; 12:28.

QUESTION—What is meant by the statement 'the word they kept to themselves discussing'?
1. The phrase πρὸς ἑαυτούς 'to themselves' belongs with the preceding verb ἐκράτησαν 'they kept.' They kept the matter of the transfiguration to themselves and only discussed the meaning of 'rising from the dead' with each other [BECNT, CBC, EGT, WBC; CEV, ESV, KJV, NET, NIV, NLT, NRSV]. They kept their knowledge of what occurred at the transfiguration to themselves and did not speak about it to others [EGT]. If the disciples had told people how God had confirmed Jesus' messiahship before Jesus had died and was resurrected, it would only have caused confusion and misunderstanding since the role of Jesus as Messiah was so different from popular expectations [BECNT]. They didn't even share the experience with the other disciples [BECNT, WBC].
2. The phrase πρὸς ἑαυτούς 'to themselves' belongs with the following participle 'discussing' and there are two interpretations of the meaning of the verb κρατέω 'they kept'.
2.1 They kept (obeyed) what Jesus had said about not telling others what they had seen, but they did discuss among themselves what Jesus had meant about his 'rising from the dead' [CBC, CGTC, Gnd, NICNT, NTC, TH; NCV, TEV]. They understood what the words 'rising from the dead' meant, but they were puzzled why the Son of Man should have to rise from the dead [TH].
2.2 They kept (in mind) what they had seen and heard at the transfiguration, and they discussed among themselves what Jesus had meant about his 'rising from the dead' [AB1, AB2, BNTC, Hb, ICC, Lns, My, NIGTC, Sw; NASB]. They retained in their memory what the Lord had said and they were especially puzzled about what he could have meant about rising from the dead [ICC, Sw].

QUESTION—What puzzled the disciples about the Son of Man rising from the dead?
They wondered what death and resurrection had to do with the Son of Man [NICNT]. Questions of all sorts would come to mind: Were Jesus' statements literal or figurative? If Jesus wanted to rise again, why would he ever let himself be killed? How was it possible for the Son of God to be killed, and if he could not be killed, how could he rise from the dead? [Lns].

DISCOURSE UNIT—9:11–13 [NLT]. The topic is Jesus discusses Elijah.

9:11 **And they-were-questioning him saying, "Why do the scribes[a] say that it-is-necessary-for Elijah to-come[b] first[c]?"**
LEXICON—a. γραμματεύς (LN 53.94): 'scribe' [AB1, AB2, BECNT, BNTC, Lns, NTC, WBC; ESV, GW, KJV, NASB, NRSV, REB], 'a person learned in the Law [LN], 'an expert in the Law' [LN; NET], 'a teacher of the law/Law' [NCV, NIV, TEV], 'a teacher of religious law' [NLT], 'a teacher of the Law of Moses' [CEV]. This noun denotes a recognized expert in Jewish law [LN]. The noun 'scribe' originally referred to a

copyist of the law, but by NT times it especially designated a biblical scholar who was an interpreter of the law and an expounder of tradition [TH]. The scribes studied, interpreted, and taught the Old Testament laws and the traditions that had developed from those laws [TRT]. This word occurs at 1:22; 2:6, 16; 3:22; 7:1, 5; 8:31; 9:11, 14; 10:33; 11:27; 12:28, 32, 38; 14:1, 43, 53; 15:1, 31.
  b. aorist act. infin. of ἔρχομαι (LN 15.81) (BAGD I.1.a.θ. p. 311): 'to come' [BAGD, LN; all translations], 'to appear' [BAGD]. This verb means to move toward or up to the reference point of the viewpoint character or event [LN]. In regard to forerunners of the Messiah, it means 'to appear' [BAGD].
  c. πρῶτος (LN 67.18) (BAGD 2.a. p. 726): 'first' [all translations except CEV, NLT], 'before' [BAGD, LN]. The phrase 'to come first' is translated 'come before the Messiah comes' [CEV], 'return before the Messiah comes' [NLT]. This adjective pertains to a point of time in a sequence that is earlier than something else [LN]. The coming of Elijah was a required event before something else takes place [TH].

QUESTION—What was behind the disciples' question about Elijah coming first?

The question about the coming of Elijah was prompted by Elijah's presence on the mountain of transfiguration [CBC, Sw]. That Elijah would come first is probably the scribal interpretation of Malachi 4:5–6 [AB1, AB2, BECNT, BNTC, CBC, CGTC, Lns, NCBC, NTC, PNTC, Sw, Tay, TRT, WBC] where it is prophesied "See, I will send you the prophet Elijah before that great and dreadful day of the Lord comes. He will turn hearts of the fathers to their children, and the hearts of the children to their fathers; or else I will come and strike the land with a curse" (NRSV). In the Septuagint Greek translation, 'turn the hearts' is translated '*restore* the hearts' [WBC]. This must mean that the scribes expected Elijah to come before the appearance of the Messiah [AB2, ICC, NLTfn, Sw, TRT; CEV, NLT]. Yet the disciples already recognized Jesus to be the coming Messiah. So how did the appearing of Elijah at the transfiguration accord with the scribal teaching? [Hb]. If the disciples are referring to a question raised by the scribes, it probably means that the scribes had objected to Jesus' statement in 1:14–15 where he preached that the kingdom of God was already near. The scribes argued that Elijah had not yet come to restore all things before the coming of the kingdom [AB2, BECNT, WBC]. The disciples wanted to know how the prophecy in Malachi related to Jesus' proclamation of God's kingdom and his prediction of his own death, resurrection, and return (8:31, 38; 9:9) [NLTfn]. If Elijah's appearance on the mountain was the expected return of Elijah to teach the Jews and restore all things, it seems that Jesus would want the disciples to tell everyone rather than being silent about it [BNTC, Lns, NCBC]. The appearance of Elijah on the mountain could only indicate the coming of the restoration that would include leading the people to repentance. So the disciples were perplexed by what Jesus said about the people being so unprepared that they will reject the Son of Man and kill him [EBC, NTC]. Perhaps the disciples wanted to counteract Jesus' statement about his coming death by arguing that Elijah's return to restore all things would make it unnecessary for Jesus to go to the cross [PNTC].

9:12 And he-said to-them, "Indeed[a] Elijah having-come first restores[b] all (things).

LEXICON—a. μέν (LN 91.6) (BAGD 1.a.β. p. 502): 'indeed' [LN], 'to be sure' [BAGD]. The phrase 'indeed Elijah having come first' is translated 'Elijah indeed comes/will-come first' [AB1, BECNT; NET; similarly BNTC], 'Elijah is indeed coming first' [NLT, NRSV, TEV], 'Elijah certainly will come' [CEV], 'to be sure, Elijah does come first' [NIV], 'Elias verily cometh first' [KJV], 'Elijah does come first' [NTC; ESV, REB; similarly BNTC; NASB], 'they are right to say that Elijah must come first' [NCV], 'Elijah is coming first' [GW], 'Elijah, coming first, does (restore all things)' [WBC; similarly Lns]. Instead of treating this as a statement, one translation makes this a counter-question that denies that Elijah comes first to restore all things: 'Is it really the case that Elijah, when he comes first, restores all things?' [AB2]. This particle indicates a relatively weak emphasis and frequently it is just reflected in the word order and not translated [LN]. The word μέν 'indeed' means 'it is true,' so Jesus confirms that the scribes are right that Elijah does come first [BECNT, CGTC, EBC, Hb, NIGTC].

b. pres. act. indic. of ἀποκαθίστημι (LN 13.65) (BAGD 1. p. 91) 'to restore' [AB1, AB2, BECNT, BAGD, LN, Lns, NTC, WBC; ESV, KJV, NASB, NET, NIV, NRSV], 'to reestablish' [BAGD]. The phrase 'restores all things' is translated 'to get everything ready' [CEV, NLT, TEV], 'will put everything in order again' [GW], 'puts everything in order' [BNTC], 'to set everything right' [REB], 'and make everything the way it should be' [NCV]. This verb means to change to a previous good state [LN].

QUESTION—When does 'Elijah restore all things'?

In the book of Malachi there are two prophesies concerning Elijah: 'I am about to send my messenger before me who will clear the way before me' (3:1) and 'I will send you Elijah the prophet before the great and terrible day before the Lord arrives. He will encourage fathers and mothers and their children to return to me' (4:5–6) [NET]. It is clear that when John the Baptist appeared just before the ministry of Jesus in Mark's account at 1:4 he was the *spiritual* fulfillment of those prophecies about Elijah. However, there is a difference of opinion about whether or not there will also be a literal fulfillment with Elijah himself appearing in the end times before the second coming of the Messiah [Hb].

1. The reference to Elijah 'restoring all things' refers exclusively to the ministry of John the Baptist [BECNT, BNTC, ESVfn, Lns, NICNT, NIGTC, NTC, Sw, WBC]. The scribes were wrong in thinking that it refers to a still future event. Elijah had come in the form of John the

Baptist who had brought about a spiritual restoration by bringing people back to God in repentance and faith [Lns]. They were correct about the scribal teaching about 'the end time' coming of Elijah, but actually Elijah's coming had already taken place in the ministry of John the Baptist [BECNT, NIGTC]. Elijah has already restored the people through calling Israel to repentance, and it is reported in 1:3 that all Jerusalem and Judea went out to be baptized by him in preparation for the coming of the kingdom of God [BECNT]. John restored all things by initiating the new order [Sw]. The restoration of all things promised in Malachi 4:6 was fulfilled in the ministry of John the Baptist. Since John had suffered as Elijah did, John's ministry showed that the fulfillment of all things was at hand [NICNT]. This is about a spiritual restoration and it concerns turning the hearts of the people by repentance and faith to the scriptural principles and practices of the fathers [Lns].
2. The reference to Elijah 'restoring all things' in Malachi 4:5–6 refers to a literal appearance of Elijah still in the future at the end of this age [AB2, Gnd, Hb, PNTC]. Elijah will ultimately return to restore righteousness and harmony before the day of Yahweh [PNTC]. Instead of the usual translation, it should be translated 'Is it really the case that Elijah, when he comes first, restores all things?' If Elijah had already restored everything before the Messiah arrived, there would be no need for the Son of Man to suffer [AB2]. The present tense 'restores' rules out a reference to the work of John the Baptist who had already been martyred without restoring all things. It does not refer to Elijah's appearance at the transfiguration since the Son of Man still must suffer. Therefore the present tense must be a futuristic coming before the end of the age [Gnd]. John the Baptist was the *spiritual* fulfillment of the Elijah prophecy, but there will yet be a *literal* return of Elijah at the second advent. This explains why John the Baptist denied that he was Elijah in John 1:21 [Hb].

And how[a] has-it-been-written concerning the Son of-Man that he-must-suffer[b] many (things) and be-treated-with-contempt[c]?

LEXICON—a. πῶς (LN 92.16) (BAGD 1.a. p. 732): 'how' [LN], 'for what reason' [LN], 'in what sense, with what right' [BAGD]. The phrase 'and how is it written' [ESV; similarly Lns; KJV] is also translated 'how is it, then, that the scriptures say' [REB], 'how then is it written' [NRSV], 'how then has it been written' [AB2], 'and yet how is it written' [WBC; NASB], 'and yet how is it that it is written' [NTC], 'yet/and how is it that the Scriptures say' [AB1, BNTC], 'yet how come it is written' [BECNT], 'and why is it written' [NET], 'why then is it written' [NIV], 'yet why do the Scriptures say' [NLT, TEV], 'but why does the Scripture say' [NCV], 'but don't the Scriptures also say' [CEV], 'but in what sense was it written' [GW]. This interrogative particle refers to the reason for something [LN]

b. aorist act. subj. of πάσχω (LN 24.78) (BAGD 3.b. p. 634): 'to suffer' [BAGD, LN], 'to endure suffering' [BAGD]. The phrase 'must/should/will suffer many things' [BECNT, Lns, NTC, WBC; ESV, KJV, NCV, NET] is also translated 'must suffer terribly' [CEV], 'must suffer greatly' [NLT], 'must/will suffer much' [NIV, TEV], 'must suffer a lot' [GW], 'he is to suffer many things' [AB2], 'he is to go through many sufferings' [NRSV], 'is to endure much/great suffering' [AB1, BNTC; REB], 'will suffer many things' [NASB]. This verb means to suffer pain [LN].

c. aorist pass. subj. of ἐξουδενέω (LN 88.133) (BAGD p. 277): 'to be treated with contempt' [AB2, BAGD, BECNT, BNTC, NTC, WBC; ESV, NASB, NRSV, REB], 'to be treated with utter contempt' [NLT], 'to be despised' [WBC; NET], 'to be set at naught' [Lns; KJV], 'people will treat him as if he were nothing' [NCV], 'to be rejected' [CEV, NIV, TEV], 'to be treated shamefully' [GW], 'to be ill-treated, to be ill-treated and to be looked down upon' [LN]. This verb means to ill-treat someone with contempt [LN].

QUESTION—What is the function of the conjunction καί 'and'?

Jesus is now adding an additional problem [Hb]. It has the sense 'and yet it has been written' [Lns]. Whatever is said about Elijah does not preclude the suffering of the Son of Man [EBC]. This introduces a rhetorical question [BECNT, NIGTC] that reminds his disciples of the necessity of his death [BECNT] and expands their understanding beyond what the scribes have taught [NIGTC].

QUESTION—Where does this question end?
1. The question extends to the end of the verse [AB1, AB2, BECNT, BNTC. Lns, NTC; all versions]: Why has it been written concerning the Son of Man that he must suffer many things and be treated with contempt?
2. The first clause is a rhetorical question that Jesus then answers with the portion of what has been written about the Son of Man that he wants them to think about [WBC; Hb, My]: How is it written about the Son of man? It is written that he must suffer many things and be treated with contempt.

QUESTION—Where was this written about the Son of Man?

Instead of being a quotation of one particular text in the OT, it gives the import of many passages such as Psalms 22:1–18; 69:9, 11, 20, 21; 118:22, Isaiah 53:37 [Hb, NTC]. It especially refers to the Suffering Servant passage in Isaiah 52:13–53:12 [EBC].

QUESTION—What was the point of bringing up the prophesies about his suffering and rejection?

Jesus was reminding them of the OT predictions of his suffering and rejection that would soon lead to his death [Hb]. Whatever the coming of Elijah involves, it does not preclude the suffering of the Son of Man [EBC. NICNT].

9:13 But I-say to-you that Elijah indeed^a has-come and^a they-did^b to-him whatever they-wanted, just-as it-had-been-written concerning him."

LEXICON—a. καί (LN 89.102) (BAGD I.6. p. 393): The combination of καί...καί is translated 'both...and' [BAGD, LN], 'not only...but also' [BAGD]. The first καί 'both' is translated 'indeed' [NTC; GW, KJV, NASB], 'certainly' [NET], 'already' [CEV, NCV, NLT, REB, TEV], not explicit [AB1, AB2, BECNT, BNTC, Lns, WBC; ESV, NIV, NRSV]. This combination connects two closely related elements or sentences [BAGD, LN].

b. aorist act. indic. of ποιέω (LN 41.7) I.1.d.γ. p. 682): 'to do to' [BAGD, LN], 'to behave toward, to deal with' [LN]. The phrase 'and they/people did to him' [BECNT, Lns, WBC; ESV, NASB, NCV, NET, NRSV] is also translated 'and they have done to him' [AB2, BNTC; KJV, NIV, REB], 'and they treated him' [NLT]. The clause 'and they did to him whatever they wanted' is translated 'and people treated him just as they wanted to' [CEV], 'yet/and people treated him as they pleased' [GW, TEV], 'and they have had their way with him' [AB1], 'and they chose to abuse him' [NLT]. This verb means to behave or act in a particular way with respect to someone [LN].

QUESTION—Who was Jesus referring to when he said Elijah has come and they did to him whatever they wanted?

Even though Jesus does not mention John the Baptist by name, it is obvious that he means that Elijah had come in the person of John the Baptist [all commentaries]. Jesus and the NT writers often had to interpret OT prophecy in a non-literalistic way because the prophets often used metaphorical and impressionistic language to proclaim their prophetic messages. The prophecy in Malachi 4:5 refers to a person who would fulfill the role of the prophet Elijah, and this turned out be John the Baptist [BECNT]. Jesus thus contradicted the popular expectation that hoped for the literal return of Elijah [ESVfn].

QUESTION—What did 'they' do to John the Baptist?

The disciples would recognize that this refers to John's imprisonment and execution that had been ordered by Herod and Herodias [EBCfn, NICNT].

QUESTION—Where was it written about what they did to Elijah?

Since the prophesied coming of Elijah was fulfilled in the person of John the Baptist, the OT accounts of what happened to Elijah are applied to what had happened to John. This refers to what had been written about Elijah in regard to Elijah's relationship to Ahab and Jezebel in 1 Kings 19:1–2 [BECNT, BNTC, CBC, EBC, EGT, Hb, Lns, NAC, NICNT, NIGTC, Sw, Tay]. The account in 1 Kings is only about an attempt to kill Elijah, whereas John had actually been killed, but the wording 'they did as many things as they wanted' implies that what the enemies of Elijah wanted and failed to do was what the enemies of John succeeded in doing [Gnd, Hb]. The fate of both Elijah and John is in keeping with an overall picture of suffering and death [WBC].

QUESTION—What is the purpose of this final comment by Jesus?

John the Baptist was a *type* of Elijah and both of them had suffered rejection by the people of Israel. The fate of both Elijah and John points to the suffering and death in which Jesus will share [WBC]. John's death was a pointer to what Jesus must suffer [BECNT, CBC, CGTC], and the disciples should be prepared for it [CBC, CGTC]. The parallel account in Matt. 17:12 ends with Jesus saying, 'In the same way the Son of Man is going to suffer at their hands' [Lns].

DISCOURSE UNIT—9:14–32 [NIV]. The topic is the healing of a boy with an evil spirit.

DISCOURSE UNIT—9:14–29 [CBC, EBC, Hb, NICNT, NIGTC; CEV, ESV, GW, NASB, NCV, NET, NLT, NRSV, TEV]. The topic is Jesus heals a boy [CEV], Jesus heals a sick boy [NCV], the healing of a possessed boy [NICNT], Jesus cures a demon-possessed boy [GW], the healing of a boy with a spirit [NRSV], Jesus heals a boy with an unclean spirit [ESV], healing a boy with an evil spirit [EBC], Jesus heals a boy with an evil spirit [TEV], Jesus heals a demon-possessed boy [NLT], the cure of the demoniac boy [Hb], Jesus performs an exorcism after the disciples' failure [CBC], success and failure in exorcism [NIGTC], the disciples' failure to heal [NET], all things possible [NASB].

9:14 **And having-come to the disciples they-saw a-great crowd around them and scribes arguing**[a] **with them.**

TEXT—Manuscripts with the plural forms ἐλθόντες…εἶδον 'having come… they saw' are given a B rating by GNT to indicate it was regarded to be almost certain. A variant reading is the singular forms ἐλθών…εἶδεν 'having come…he saw' and it is followed by KJV.

LEXICON—a. pres. act. participle of συζητέω (LN **33.440**) (BAGD 2. p. 775): to argue' [AB1, AB2, BAGD, BECNT, BNTC, LN, NTC; all versions except KJV], 'to dispute' [BAGD, **LN**, Lns], 'to debate' [WBC], 'to question' [KJV]. This verb means to express forceful differences of opinion without necessarily having a presumed goal of seeking a solution [LN]. Since it is the scribes who are arguing, this carries the hostile sense of 'disputing' with them [NIGTC]. This verb occurs at 1:27; 8:11; 9:10, 14, 16; 12:28.

QUESTION—Who came to which disciples?

Jesus and his three disciples Peter, James, and John came to the other disciples who had been surrounded by the crowd [BECNT, CGTC, Gnd, Hb, Lns, NLTfn, NTC, TH, TRT; CEV, NCV]. The disciples surrounded by the crowd were the other nine of the twelve disciples [Hb, NTC, Sw]. Instead of coming to 'the disciples' some translations say that they came to 'the other disciples' [NTC; CEV, GW, NCV, NIV, NLT] or 'the rest of the disciples' [TEV].

QUESTION—Who were the scribes arguing with?

The scribes were arguing with the disciples who had been waiting for Jesus to return [Hb, NTC, Sw]. The scribes had probably come to monitor the teaching and preaching of Jesus [EBC]. They were arguing with the disciples about why they had failed to exorcise the demon that possessed the boy who had been brought to them. Probably the argument was about the disciples' authority to even make an attempt to exorcise demons [NICNT]. The scribes were delighted with the failure of the disciples and were taunting them about it [EGT, NTC].

9:15 And immediately all the crowd having-seen him were-greatly-amazed[a] and running-up-to (him) they greeted[b] him.

LEXICON—a. aorist pass. indic. of ἐκθαμβέομαι, ἐκθαμβέω (LN **25.210**) (BAGD p. 240): 'to be greatly amazed' [Lns, NTC, WBC; ESV, KJV], 'to be utterly amazed' [BECNT], 'to be amazed' [BAGD, LN; NASB, NET], 'to be astounded' [BNTC, **LN**], 'to be awestruck' [AB2], 'to be very/greatly surprised' [GW, TEV], 'to be overcome with surprise' [AB1], 'to be really surprised' [CEV], 'to be surprised' [NCV], 'to be overwhelmed with wonder' [NIV], 'to be overwhelmed/overcome with awe' [NLT, NRSV, REB]. This verb means to be greatly astounded [LN]. The prefix ἐκ- intensifies the verb [Lns]. This verb occurs at 9:15; 14:33; 16:5, 6.

b. mid./pass. (deponent = act.) indic. of ἀσπάζομαι (LN **33.20**) (BAGD 1.a. p. 116): 'to greet' [AB1, BAGD, BECNT, BNTC, **LN**, WBC; CEV, ESV, NASB, NET, NIV, NLT, NRSV, TEV], 'to welcome' [NTC; GW, NCV, REB], 'to hail' [AB2], 'to salute' [Lns; KJV]. This verb means to employ certain set phrases as a part of the process of greeting [LN].

QUESTION—Why were the people amazed to see Jesus?

1. The people were amazed at the sudden and unexpected appearance of Jesus [BECNT, CGTC, EBC, EGT, ICC, Lns, NAC, NTC, PNTC, Sw, Tay, TH, WBC]. The crowd had been so intent on the argument that they hadn't seen Jesus approaching and were amazed at his sudden appearance [Hb]. They hadn't been expecting Jesus to return so soon [AB1, Sw]. This refers to their surprise and excitement at his appearance [CBC]. He had arrived at the very time he could meet a critical need [EBC]. Since he had instructed his three disciples to keep the transfiguration event a secret, it is unlikely that his garments would still be glistening and be the cause of the crowd's amazement [BECNT, EBC, Hb, NICNT, NIGTC, PNTC, Sw, Tay].

2. Their great amazement was an extreme awe at seeing his still glistening white garments from the transfiguration [Gnd, WBC].

9:16 And he-asked them, "What are-you-arguing-about with them?"

TEXT—Manuscripts reading ἐπηρώτησεν αὐτούς 'he asked them' are followed by GNT which does not mention any variant reading. A variant reading is ἐπηρώτησεν τοὺς γραμματεῖς 'he asked the scribes' and it is followed by KJV.

QUESTION—Who was Jesus talking with?
1. Jesus was addressing his disciples [TH, WBC; TEV]. In verse 14 it says that Jesus came to the disciples who were surrounded by the crowd as they were arguing with the scribes. Now Jesus asks those disciples what they were arguing about with the scribes. It is not strange that one of the men in the crowd answered the question since it was the action of that man that had prompted the discussion [TH].
2. Jesus was addressing the people in the crowd [AB1, BECNT, BNTC, CGTC, EGT, ICC, My, Sw, Tay]. He asked the people in the crowd who came to greet him [BECNT, EGT], and it is one of those men who answers Jesus in the next verse [AB1, BNTC, CGTC, Tay].
3. Jesus was addressing the scribes [Lns, NICNT, NIGTC, NTC, PNTC; GW, KJV]. In verse 14, the scribes were arguing with the disciples while the crowd stood around and listened. In this verse Jesus asked those scribes why they had been arguing with his disciples [Lns]. Jesus wanted the scribes to direct their questions to him instead of to his disciples [PNTC]. However, they were not anxious to answer Jesus and were silent [NTC].

QUESTION—Who are the people referred to by 'them' in the question, "What are you arguing about with *them*?"

If Jesus was speaking to his disciples, then the disciples had been arguing with the scribes. If Jesus was speaking to the crowd or to the scribes, then either the crowd or the scribes had been arguing with the disciples [TH].

9:17 **And from the crowd someone answered him, "Teacher, I-brought my son to you, having a-mute[a] spirit.[b]**

LEXICON—a. ἄλαλος (LN 33.106) (BAGD p. 35): 'mute, unable to speak' [BAGD, LN], 'dumb, incapable of talking' [LN]. The participial clause ἔχοντα πνεῦμα ἄλαλον 'having a mute/dumb spirit' [Lns; similarly KJV] is also translated 'who has a mute spirit' [WBC], 'who is possessed by a spirit that makes him mute' [NET; similarly NASB], 'who is possessed by a spirit that has robbed him of speech' [NIV]. Some include a conjunction to indicate that this is a *causal* participial phrase: 'because he has a mute spirit' [AB2, BECNT], 'for he has a spirit that makes him mute' [ESV], 'because he is possessed by a spirit, which makes him speechless' [AB1], 'because he has an evil spirit in him and cannot talk' [TEV], 'for he is possessed by a spirit that has deprived him of the ability to speak' [NTC]. Some translate this participial clause as a separate clause or sentence: 'he has a dumb spirit' [BNTC], 'he has a spirit that makes him unable to speak' [NRSV], 'He has an evil spirit in him that stops him from talking' [NCV], 'He is possessed by a spirit/evil-spirit that won't let him talk' [GW, NLT], 'He is possessed by a spirit that makes him dumb' [REB], 'A demon keeps him from talking' [CEV]. The adjective ἄλαλος 'mute' pertains to not being able to speak or talk [LN]. It describes a spirit that robs men of their speech [BAGD]. This word occurs at 7:37, 9:17, 25.

b. πνεῦμα (LN 12.33, 12.37) (BAGD 4.c p. 676): 'spirit' [BAGD, LN; all translations except NLT, TEV], 'evil spirit' [NLT, TEV]. This noun denotes a supernatural and non-material entity, and the word itself does not indicate whether the spirit is good or evil [LN (12.33)], but in this context it denotes an evil supernatural being or spirit [LN (12.37)].

QUESTION—What is meant by the father's words 'I brought my son to you'?

It had been the man's intention to bring his son to Jesus [CGTC, Hb, NTC, Sw]. But he hadn't brought his son directly to Jesus. He actually brought his son to the disciples who had not accompanied Jesus to the mountain [WBC]. When he said 'I brought my son πρὸς σέ 'to you', he indicated that he had intended to enlist Jesus' help in person. Since Jesus had been absent when he arrived, some of the disciples had tried to help the boy but failed [NIGTC]. It is not until verse 20 that some people actually bring the boy into Jesus' presence.

QUESTION—What is meant by πνεῦμα ἄλαλον 'a mute spirit'?

This evil spirit is called 'a mute spirit' because the spirit had caused the boy to become mute [AB1, AB2, BAGD, BECNT, EBC, Hb, ICC, Lns, My, NICNT, NTC, Sw, TH, WBC; CEV, ESV, GW, NASB, NCV, NET, NIV, NLT, NRSV, REB, TEV].

QUESTION—What was wrong with the boy?

The boy did not have the power of speech [Hb]. He had a speech loss [EBC] and was unable to speak [CBC]. When Jesus addresses this demon as a 'dumb and deaf' spirit in verse 25, we learn that the boy was a deaf mute, one who could neither hear nor speak [BECNT, Lns, NICNT, NTC]. It is unclear whether the muteness was continuous or occurred only during the demonic attacks [BECNT]. Although most commentaries give the impression that this was a permanent condition, some suggest that this muteness might have happened only during the demonic attacks described in the next verse, and between seizures the boy was able to speak [Gnd, My].

9:18 And wherever it-seizes[a] him it-throws- him -down,[b] and he-foams-at-the-mouth[c] and grinds[d] (his) teeth and he-becomes-stiff.[e]

LEXICON—a. aorist act. subj. of καταλαμβάνω (LN **39.48**) (BAGD 1.b. p. 413): 'to seize' [BAGD, BECNT, Lns, NTC, WBC; ESV, NASB, NET, NIV, NLT, NRSV], 'to bring on a seizure' [GW], 'to attack' [AB1, **LN**; CEV, NCV, REB, TEV], 'to overpower' [LN], 'to grab' [AB2], 'to take hold of' [BNTC], 'to take' [KJV]. This verb means to attack in order to gain control over someone [LN]. This happened wherever the boy might be when the spirit seized him [TH]. Verse 22 reveals that the seizures frequently occurred [TH].

b. pres. act. indic. of ῥήγνυμι, ῥήσσω (LN **23.168**) (BAGD 2.b. p. 735): 'to throw down' [BAGD; ESV, NET], 'to throw to/on the ground' [BECNT, BNTC; CEV, GW, NCV, NIV, TEV], 'to throw violently to the ground'

[NLT], 'to hurl to the ground' [AB1], 'to fling to the ground' REB], 'to knock down' [WBC], 'to dash down' [Lns], 'to dash to the ground' [BAGD, NTC; similarly NRSV], 'to slam to the ground' [NASB], 'to throw down in convulsions' [**LN**], 'to throw into a fit' [LN], 'to tear' [AB2; KJV]. This verb means to cause someone to fall to the ground in convulsions [LN].
  c. pres. act. indic. of ἀφρίζω (LN 14.28) (BAGD p. 127): 'to foam at the mouth' [AB1, AB2, BAGD, BECNT, BNTC, LN, NTC, WBC; all versions except ESV, KJV, NRSV], 'to foam' [Lns; ESV, KJV, NRSV]. This verb means to cause or to produce the foaming up of a liquid, and in the NT it refers to the foaming at the mouth of a person who is experiencing an epileptic seizure [LN]. In Matt. 17:15 the father says that his son is epileptic [TH].
  d. pres. act. indic. of τρίζω (LN **23.41**) (BAGD p. 826): 'to grind the teeth' [AB2, BAGD, BECNT, BNTC, **LN**, NTC, WBC; ESV, GW, NASB, NCV, NET, NLT, NRSV, REB], 'to gnash the teeth' [LN, Lns; NIV; similarly KJV], 'to grit the teeth' [AB1; TEV], 'to grit the teeth in pain' [CEV]. This verb means grinding or gnashing one's teeth because of an illness, or in order to express an emotion such as anger, pain, or suffering [LN].
  e. pres. pass. indic. of ξηραίνομαι, ξηραίνω (LN **23.172**) (BAGD 2.b. p. 548): 'to become/go rigid' [AB1, AB2, BECNT, BNTC, WBC; ESV, NIV, NLT, NRSV, REB], 'to become stiff' [BAGD, **LN**, NTC; CEV, NCV], 'to become stiff all over' [TEV], 'to stiffen out' [NASB], 'to become paralyzed' [LN], 'to become exhausted' [GW], 'to be thrown into a convulsion' [NET], 'to waste away' [Lns], 'to pine away' [KJV]. This verb is a figurative extension of the meaning of 'to dry up' and means to become stiff to the point of not being able to move [LN].
QUESTION—Who are the subjects of the verbs in this sentence?
The mute spirit seizes the boy and throws him down. The boy then foams at the mouth, grinds his teeth, and becomes stiff [TH]. The evil spirit attacks and convulses the boy wherever the boy might be [AB2].

And I-told your disciples in-order-that they-might-cast- it -out,[a] and they-were- not -able-to.[b]"
LEXICON—a. aorist act. subj. of ἐκβάλλω (LN 53.102) (BAGD 1. p. 237) 'to cast out' [AB2, BECNT, LN, Lns, NTC, WBC; ESV, KJV, NASB, NET, NLT, NRSV], 'to make go out, to exorcise' [LN], 'to force out' [CEV, GW, NCV], 'to drive out' [AB1, AB2, BAGD, BNTC; NIV, REB, TEV], 'to expel' [BAGD]. This verb means to cause a demon to no longer possess or control a person [LN]. In reference to 'casting' out demons, this verb occurs at 1:34, 39; 3:15, 22, 23; 6:13; 7:26; 9:18, 28, 38; 16:9, 17.
  b. aorist act. indic. of ἰσχύω (LN 74.9) (BAGD 2.b. p. 383): 'to be able' [BAGD, LN], 'to be strong enough' [BAGD], 'to have the strength to do

34   MARK 9:18

something, to be very capable of doing something' [LN]. The phrase 'they were not able' [WBC; ESV] is also translated 'they could not' [AB1, BECNT, BNTC, NTC; KJV, NIV, REB, TEV], 'they could not do it/so' [CEV, NASB, NCV, NLT, NRSV], 'they were not able to do so' [NET], 'they didn't have the power to do it' [GW], 'they didn't have the strength' [AB2, Lns]. This verb means to have a special personal ability to do something [LN].

QUESTION—Why did this man think the disciples could cast out the demon?
Apparently the boy's father had heard reports that the disciples of Jesus were able to cast out demons. The disciples had been given authority over evil spirits in 6:7, and they cast out evil spirits in 6:12–13 when Jesus sent them out two by two to preach in the various villages [EBC, BNTC, Hb, Sw].

9:19 **And answering[a] them he-says, "O unbelieving[b] generation, how long[c] shall-I-be with you? How long shall-I-put-up-with[d] you? Bring him to me."**

TEXT—Manuscripts reading ἀποκριθεὶς αὐτοῖς 'answering them' are given an A rating by GNT to indicate it was regarded to be certain. A variant reading is ἀποκριθεὶς αὐτῷ 'answering him' and it is followed by KJV.

LEXICON—a. aorist passive (deponent = act.) participle of ἀποκρίνομαι (LN 33.28) (BAGD 1. p. 93): 'to answer, to reply' [BAGD], 'to speak, to declare, to say' [LN (33.28]. The phrase 'answering them he says' [WBC; similarly BECNT, Lns] is also translated 'he answered them and said' [NASB; similarly AB2, NTC; KJV], 'he answered them' [ESV, NET, NRSV], 'Jesus answered' [AB1, BNTC; NCV, REB], 'Jesus replied' [NIV], 'Jesus said to them' [GW, NLT, TEV], 'Jesus said' [CEV]. This verb introduces or continues a somewhat formal discourse and occurs regularly with λέγω 'to say'. A literal translation such as 'Jesus *spoke and said*' may sound redundant in many languages [LN 33.28].

  b. ἄπιστος (LN **31.98**) (BAGD 2. p. 85): 'unbelieving' [BAGD, LN], 'faithless' [BAGD], 'refusing to believe' [LN]. The phrase ῏Ω γενεὰ ἄπιστος 'O unbelieving generation' [NASB, NIV' similarly Lns] is also translated 'O faithless generation' [AB2, BECNT, NTC, WBC; ESV, KJV], 'You unbelieving generation!' [GW, NET], 'What an unbelieving generation!' [REB], 'Unbelieving generation!' [AB1], 'How unbelieving you people are' [**LN**; TEV], 'You faithless generation' [BNTC; NRSV], 'You faithless people' [NLT], 'You people don't have any faith!' [CEV; similarly NCV]. This adjective means to be in a state of not believing as a result of refusing to believe [LN]. It means 'unbelieving, not having faith, faithless' rather than being unfaithful [TH].

  c. ἕως (LN 67.119) (BAGD II.1.e. p. 335): 'until' [BAGD, LN], 'up to' [BAGD]. The question ἕως πότε πρὸς ὑμᾶς ἔσομαι? literally, 'until when with you shall I be?' is translated 'how long shall/will I be with you?' [AB2, BNTC, Lns, NTC, WBC; KJV, NASB, REB], 'how long am I to be with you?' [AB1; ESV], 'How much longer will I be with you?' [BECNT], 'how long shall I stay with you? [NIV], 'How long must I stay with you?' [NCV, TEV], 'How long must I be with you?' [GW, NLT], 'How much longer must I be with you?' [CEV, NET], 'how much longer must I be among you?' [NRSV]. This preposition refers to a continuous extent of time up to some point [LN].

d. fut. mid. indic. of ἀνέχομαι, ἀνέχω (LN 25.171) (BAGD 1.a. p. 65): 'to endure, to bear with, to put up with' [BAGD], 'to be patient with' [LN]. The question ἕως πότε ἀνέξομαι ὑμῶν literally, 'until when shall I put up with you?' is translated 'How long shall/will I put up with you?' [AB2, NTC; NASB, NIV], 'How long must I put up with you?' [GW, NCV, NLT], 'How long do I have to put up with you?' [TEV], 'How long am I to bear with you?' [WBC; ESV; similarly Lns], 'How long shall I suffer you?' [KJV], 'How long must I endure you?' [AB1; REB], 'How much longer shall/must I put up with you?' [BECNT; NRSV; similarly BNTC], 'How much longer must I endure you?' [NET], 'Why do I have to put up with you?' [CEV]. This verb means to be patient with someone by enduring a possible difficulty [LN].

QUESTION—Who were the people of the 'unbelieving generation' Jesus was addressing when he answered αὐτοῖς 'them'?

The noun γενεά 'generation' applies to the people of Jesus' time as a whole, a generation that deserved to be described as faithless and unbelieving [Hb, Lns]. This emphasizes Jesus' distress over all the unbelieving people among whom he ministered everywhere [AB1, Tay, WBC]. He was addressing 'You people who do not believe' [TH]. Jesus was deeply dissatisfied with the people of his own generation, and in this context he was particularly dissatisfied with the boy's father, the scribes, the crowd in general, and even his nine disciples [BECNT, NTC]. The antecedent of the αὐτοῖς 'them' whom Jesus addressed is not clear and it is not clear what brought about this exclamation. It could be addressed to particular groups within the crowd such as the father and his son, the disciples, the scribes, the crowd in general, or perhaps it was a more general expression of exasperation addressed to his whole human environment [NIGTC]. Since the boy's father has been introduced as 'one from the crowd,' the 'unbelieving generation' probably refers to the people in the crowd [BECNT, Gnd, PNTC, Sw], either including the disciples [BECNT, Sw] or not including the disciples [Gnd, PNTC]. Some think that the words 'unbelieving generation' were expressly directed at the nine disciples who had failed to cast out the evil spirit due to their lack of faith [AB2, CGTC, EBC, Hb, ICC, Lns, My, NAC, NICNT], thus causing this painful situation [AB2, BECNT, Hb]. That would imply that those disciples had remained indistinguishable from the unregenerate men who were fundamentally untrue to God [NICNT].

QUESTION—What did Jesus mean when he asked the rhetorical questions, "How long shall I be with you? How long shall I put up with you?"

The two questions indicate that Jesus felt that his surroundings had become almost unbearable and he was wondering how long it would last [ICC]. The questions suggest that Jesus was longing to be with his heavenly Father because he was weary with the spiritual obtuseness of his disciples [EBC], and his disappointment with them is apparent as he asks how long it will be before his mission with them is realized [Hb]. It expresses his frustration and exasperation [AB2, BECNT, Gnd, PNTC], his pain and indignation [NTC]. This expression of exasperation showed that the crowd had brought him to the point of weariness and heart-break [NICNT]. His questions imply 'How long must I remain with you in order for you to have faith?' [TH].

QUESTION—Who was it that Jesus told to bring the boy to him?

The subject of the verb is plural, so he was still addressing the crowd, which included the disciples [AB2]. Probably Jesus was speaking directly to his disciples who would carry out this command [Lns]. He had to ask them to bring the boy because the boy probably had been taken to some place of safekeeping while the father went to talk with Jesus [Hb].

9:20 And they brought him to him. And having-seen him the spirit[a] immediately convulsed[b] him. And having-fallen[c] on the ground he-was-rolling-around[d] foaming-at-the-mouth.

LEXICON—a. πνεῦμα (LN 12.37) (BAGD 4.c. p. 676): 'spirit' [AB1, AB2, BAGD, BECNT, BNTC, Lns, NTC, WBC; all versions except CEV, NCV, NLT], 'evil spirit' [BAGD, LN; NCV, NLT], 'demon' [BAGD, LN; CEV]. This noun refers to an evil supernatural being or spirit [LN]. In contrast to a reference to God or good spirits, this verse refers to an evil spirit, that is, a demon [BAGD].

b. aorist act. indic. of συσπαράσσω (LN 23.167) (BAGD p. 794): 'to throw into a-convulsion/convulsions' [AB1, BECNT, BNTC, LN, Lns, NTC; GW, NASB, NET, NIV, REB], 'to throw into a violent convulsion' [NLT], 'to throw into a fit' [LN; TEV], 'to convulse' [AB2, WBC; ESV, NRSV], 'to make (the boy) shake all over' [CEV], 'to make (the boy) lose control of himself' [NCV], 'to tear' [KJV]. This verb means to cause a person to shake violently in convulsions [LN].

c. aorist act. participle of πίπτω (LN 15.119) (BAGD 1.b.α. p. 659): 'to fall' [AB1, AB2, BECNT, BNTC, LN, Lns, NTC, WBC; all versions except CEV, NCV], 'to fall down' [LN; CEV, NCV]. This verb means to fall down to the ground from a standing or upright position [LN].

d. imperf. mid./pass. indic. of κυλίομαι, κυλίω (LN 16.17) (BAGD 2. p. 457): 'to roll around' [AB2, BECNT, Lns, NTC; GW, NASB, NET, NIV, TEV], 'to roll about' [AB1, BNTC, LN, WBC; ESV, NRSV, REB], 'to roll on the ground' [CEV, NCV], 'to writhe' [NLT], 'to wallow' [KJV]. This verb means to roll back and forth or to roll about. It is used in the sense of a chaotic and uncontrolled rolling on the ground of a person in an epileptic fit [LN]. The imperfect tense indicates that the boy continued to twist and roll about [Hb].

QUESTION—Who saw αὐτὸν 'him' (Jesus)?
   The verb ἰδών 'having seen' is a masculine participle and 'spirit' is a neuter noun, so grammatically the subject seems to be a person instead of a spirit [Hb].
   1. The evil spirit saw Jesus [BECNT, CGTC, EGT, Hb, ICC, Lns, TH; CEV, ESV, GW, NCV, NET, NIV, NLT, NRSV, REB, TEV]. Even though the word 'spirit' is neuter in gender, the actor of the verb is probably the spirit regarded as a person [Hb, Sw]. This is confirmed by the fact that the mention of the spirit is in the nominative case [Gnd].
   2. The boy saw Jesus [My].
QUESTION—Who was the αὐτόν 'him' convulsed by the evil spirit?
   The evil spirit saw him (Jesus) and immediately convulsed him (the boy). Some translations avoid the ambiguity by translating the pronoun 'him' as 'the boy' [AB2, BECNT, BNTC, WBC; CEV, ESV, GW, NCV, NET, NIV, NRSV, REB, TEV] or 'the child' [NLT]. When the evil spirit saw Jesus and realized he would soon lose control of the boy, he immediately vented his rage on that boy [Hb]. The spirit wanted to show its contempt for Jesus by destroying the boy [NICNT]. It was demonstrating its power in order to intimidate Jesus [Gnd].

9:21 And he-asked the father of-him, "How-long a-time is-it since this happened[a] to-him?" And he-said, "From childhood.
LEXICON—a. perf. act. indic. of γίνομαι (LN 13.107) (BAGD 1.3.b.γ. p. 159): 'to happen' [BAGD, LN], 'to occur' [LN], 'to take place' [BAGD]. The phrase 'since this happened to him' is translated 'since this has come to him' [Lns], 'since this came unto him' [KJV], 'has he been like this' [AB1, AB2, BNTC; CEV, GW, NIV, REB, TEV], 'has this been happening to him' [BECNT, NTC, WBC; ESV, NASB, NET, NRSV], 'has this been happening' [NCV, NLT]. This verb means to happen and implies that what happens is different from a previous state [LN].
QUESTION—Whose father was Jesus addressing?
   The phrase 'and he asked the father of him' is often translated 'he asked his father,' but the translation must not be ambiguous as to whether Jesus was addressing his own father God or the father of the boy possessed by the evil spirit [TH, TRT]. Some translations eliminate any ambiguity by translating it 'and he asked the boy's father' [NTC; CEV, NCV, NIV, NLT].
QUESTION—What does the adjective τοῦτο 'this' refer to in the clause, 'since this happened to him'?
   The word 'this' refers to the pathetic scene before their eyes [Hb]. The word 'this' could be made specific: 'has he suffered this way,' 'has he been afflicted,' 'has he had the demon in his heart' [TH].
QUESTION—Why did Jesus ask this question?
   This had no special bearing on the cure, but it does indicate the compassionate interest of Jesus. The question brings out the seeming hopelessness of the boy's condition [Hb]. The demonic possession of this

boy was nearly lifelong and therefore harder to break [Gnd]. Since Luke 9:42 calls him a παῖς 'child' at the time of this question, the answer 'from childhood' must mean that he was a little boy when it first happened to him [CBC, Sw].

9:22 And it also often threw[a] him into fire and into waters[b] in order-to destroy[c] him. But if you-can-do[d] anything, having-compassion[e] on us help[f] us."

LEXICON—a. aorist act. indic. of βάλλω (LN 15.215) (BAGD 1.b. p. 131): 'to throw' [AB1, AB2, BAGD, BNTC, LN, Lns, NTC; all versions except ESV, KJV, NRSV], 'to cast' [BECNT, WBC; ESV, KJV, NRSV]. This verb means to throw something [LN].
- b. ὕδωρ (LN 2.7) (BAGD 1. p. 833): This plural form 'waters' [AB2, Lns; KJV] is also translated 'water' [AB1, BECNT, BNTC, NTC, WBC; all versions except KJV]. This noun denotes water [BAGD, LN]. In this context, the plural form 'waters' probably means any sized bodies of water [ICC, TRT], such as pools and streams [EBC], or rivers and the sea [AB2]. The evil spirit had tried to drown the boy [BECNT].
- c. aorist act. subj. of ἀπόλλυμι (LN 20.31): 'to destroy' [AB2, BECNT, BNTC, LN, Lns, NTC, WBC; ESV, GW, KJV, NASB, NET, NRSV, REB], 'to kill' [AB1; CEV, NCV, NIV, NLT, TEV]. This verb means to destroy or to cause the destruction of persons, objects, or institutions [LN].
- d. pres. mid./pass. (deponent = act.) indic. of δύναμαι (LN 74.5) (BAGD 3. p. 207): 'can do' [BAGD, LN], 'to be able to' [LN]. The clause 'if you can do anything' [AB2, BNTC, NTC; ESV, KJV, NASB, NIV] is also translated 'if you are able to do anything' [NET, NRSV], 'if you can' [AB1, WBC; CEV, NLT], 'if you are able' [BECNT], 'if you possibly can' [TEV], 'if you can do anything for him' [NCV], 'if it's possible for you' [GW], 'if it is at all possible for you' [REB], 'if thou art able in any way' [Lns]. This verb means to be able to do something [BAGD, LN]. When he brought his boy to the disciples, he probably thought they would heal him. But after their failure, he was not even sure that Jesus could do it [BECNT, BNTC, EBC, Gnd, Hb, NAC, NICNT, NIGTC, NLTfn, Sw, WBC], yet he hadn't quite given up hope [BNTC]. The father thought Jesus might be able to help, yet he wasn't sure [NTC].
- e. aorist pass. (deponent = act.) participle of σπλαγχνίζομαι (LN 25.49) (BAGD p. 762): 'to have compassion on' [Lns; ESV, KJV], 'to feel compassion for/on' [LN; NET], 'to have mercy' [NLT], 'to have/take pity [AB1, AB2, BAGD, BECNT, NTC, WBC; CEV, NASB, NCV, NIV, NRSV, REB, TEV], 'to feel sympathy' [BAGD]. The phrase 'having compassion on us' is translated 'put yourself in our place' [GW]. This verb means to experience great affection and compassion for someone [LN]. The participle takes its mode from the main verb, so here it is imperatival: 'be merciful and help us,' and the imperative in this context

expresses a petition, not a command [TH]. Jesus would express his compassion by helping them [Hb].

f. aorist act. impera. of βοηθέω (LN **35.1**) (BAGD 2. p. 144): 'to help' [AB1, AB2, BAGD, BECNT, **LN**, Lns, NTC, WBC; all versions], 'to come to the aid of' [BAGD]. This verb means to assist in supplying what may be needed [LN].

9:23 And Jesus said to-him, "The[a] 'If you can!' All (things) (are) possible[b] for-the (one) believing.[c]"

TEXT—Manuscripts reading Τὸ Εἰ δύνῃ 'The *If you can*' are given a B rating by GNT to indicate it was regarded to be almost certain. A variant reading is τὸ εἰ δύνασαι πιστεῦσαι 'the *If you can believe*' and it is followed by KJV. Other variant readings are τοῦτο Εἰ δύνῃ 'this *If you can*', Εἰ δύνῃ 'If you can', εἰ δύνασαι πιστεῦσαι 'If you can believe', and εἰ δύνῃ πιστεῦσαι 'If you can believe'.

LEXICON—a. ὁ (BAGD II.8.a. p. 552): 'the' [BAGD]. The clause 'Τὸ Εἰ δύνῃ 'The "If you can."' is enclosed within quote marks to show that Jesus is quoting what the boy's father had just said to him '"If you can"?' [AB2; NASB, NIV], '"If you are able"?' [BECNT; NET], 'You said, "If you can"!' [WBC; NCV], 'as far as your words, "If you can" are concerned' [BAGD], 'As to that *if you can*' [NTC; similarly Lns], 'Why do you say "if you can"?' [CEV], 'What do you mean, "If I can"?' [NLT]. Others translate it 'If it is possible!' [REB], 'As far as possibilities go' [GW]. Some turn the question back on the man: 'Yes, if you yourself can!' [TEV], 'If you can!' [AB1, BNTC; ESV], 'If you are able!' [NRSV]. This neuter article before whole sentences or clauses indicates that the words following it are being quoted [BAGD, TH].

b. δυνατός (LN 71.2) (BAGD 2.b. p. 209): 'possible' [BAGD, LN]. The clause 'all things are possible for the one believing' is translated 'all things are possible for the-one/him who believes' [BECNT, BNTC, NTC; ESV, NCV, NET; similarly AB2, Lns; KJV, NASB], 'everything is possible for him/the-person who believes' [GW, NIV; similarly AB1, BNTC; REB], 'all things can be done for the one who believes' [NRSV], 'Anything is possible if a person believes' [NLT], 'all things are possible for the one who has faith' [WBC], 'Anything is possible for someone who has faith!' [CEV; similarly TEV]. This adjective refers to being possible, and implies having the power or ability to alter or control circumstances [LN].

c. pres. act. participle of πιστεύω (LN 31.85) (BAGD 2.c. p. 662): 'to believe' [AB2, BECNT, BNTC, LN, Lns, NTC; all versions except CEV, TEV], 'to have faith' [LN, WBC; CEV, TEV], 'to trust' [LN], 'to have confidence' [BAGD, LN]. This verb means to believe to the extent of having complete trust and reliance [LN]. It refers to a special kind of faith that is confident that God or Christ is in a position to help the supplicant out of his distress [BAGD].

QUESTION—Who is the referent of the pronoun in the statement, 'if *you* can'?
1. Jesus makes his point by repeating the words the boy's father had said to him: 'If you can' [BAGD, BECNT, BNTC, CGTC, EBC, EGT, Gnd, Hb, ICC, Lns, My, NAC, NCBC, NICNT, NIGTC, NTC, PNTC, Sw, Tay, TH; CEV, NASB, NCV, NET, NIV, REB]. Jesus is challenging the father's words 'As to your "if you can",…' [CGTC], 'Why do you say, "If you can"?' [TH]. 'With respect to your phrase, "If you are able"' [Gnd], 'As regards your remark about my ability to help your son, I tell you everything depends upon your ability to believe, not on mine to act' [NICNT].
2. Jesus quotes the words of the boy's father, but applies it to the father: 'If you yourself can' [Sw; ESVfn, NRSV, TEV]. It depends not upon Jesus, but upon the boy's father to determine whether it will be done [Sw].

QUESTION—What are the things that are possible for the one believing'?
There should be no question about Jesus having the power to heal the man's son. The real question was whether the father had faith to believe that Jesus could do so [EBC, Hb, NAC, NCBC, NIGTC, NTC]. This calls attention to the man's doubt that was expressed when he spoke to Jesus and said 'If you can do anything' [CGTC, ICC]. The focus has shifted from Jesus' ability to do something for the boy to the belief of the one who asks. The point is that 'all things (are) able (to be done) for the person who believes' and 'all things' includes the difficult exorcism at hand [BECNT, Gnd]. A man who has faith will not set any limit to what Jesus can do [CGTC]. All things can be done for the one who has faith, but such a faith will submit to the will of God in making its petitions [Hb, TRT].

QUESTION—What is it that a person must believe?
The father must believe that Jesus has the power to heal his boy [BNTC, EBC, Gnd, Lns, PNTC]. He must believe that God has unlimited power [Hb, NIGTC]. This faith is in Jesus through whom the power of God is released [NICNT]. Another interpretation is that 'the one believing' includes both Jesus and the boy's father. Jesus has the ability to heal because of his faith, and the man can expect healing to be granted in response to his own faith [AB2, BNTC, NIGTC].

9:24 Immediately the father of-the child crying-out,[a] said "I-believe.[b] Help[c] my unbelief."

TEXT—Manuscripts reading τοῦ παιδίου 'of the child' are given an A rating by GNT to indicate it was regarded to be certain. A variant reading is παιδίου μετὰ δακρύων 'of the child with tears' and it is followed by KJV.

TEXT—Manuscripts reading Πιστεύω 'I believe'. are given an A rating by GNT to indicate it was regarded to be certain. A variant reading is Πιστεύω κύριε 'I believe, Lord'. and it is followed by KJV.

LEXICON—a. aorist act. participle of κράζω (LN 33.83) (BAGD 2.a. p. 447): 'to cry out' [BAGD], 'to shout' [LN]. The phrase 'crying out, said' is translated 'cried out and said' [AB2, WBC; ESV, KJV, NASB, NET],

'cried out and was saying' [BECNT], 'with a yell went on to say' [Lns], 'cried out' [AB1, BNTC, NTC; GW, NCV, NLT, NRSV, TEV], 'cried' [REB], 'shouted' [CEV], 'exclaimed' [NIV]. This verb means to shout or cry out [LN].
  b. pres. act. indic. of πιστεύω (LN 31.85): 'to believe, to have faith, to trust' [LN], 'to have confidence' [BAGD, LN]. The clause 'I believe' [AB2, BECNT, BNTC, WBC; ESV, GW, KJV, NET, NRSV, REB] is also translated 'I do believe' [Lns, NTC; NASB, NCV, NIV, NLT], 'I do have faith' [CEV], 'I have faith!' [AB1], 'I do have faith, but not enough' [TEV]. This verb means to believe to the extent of having complete trust and reliance [LN].
  c. aorist act. impera. of βοηθέω (LN 35.1) (BAGD 2. p. 144): 'to help' [BAGD, LN; all versions], 'to come to the aid of' [BAGD]. The clause βοήθει μου τῇ ἀπιστίᾳ 'help my unbelief' [AB2, BECNT, BNTC, NTC, WBC; ESV, KJV, NASB, NET, NRSV, REB] is also translated 'be helping my unbelief' [Lns], 'help me overcome my unbelief' [NIV, NLT], 'help my lack of faith' [GW], 'Help me have more!' [TEV], 'Help me to believe more!' [NCV], 'Please help me to have even more (faith)' [CEV], 'Help me where faith is lacking!' [AB1]. This verb means to assist in supplying what may be needed [LN]. This is the same verb the father used when he said 'help us' in 9:22.

QUESTION—What is meant by the father's plea 'Help my unbelief'?

Many readers of literal translations of this plea have wrongly understood it to be a plea for assistance to have even less faith! But this is a plea for help to overcome a lack of faith' [TH].

  1. The father asked Jesus to help him overcome his unbelief by having more faith [BECNT, BNTC, CBC, CGTC, EBC, EGT, ESVfn, Gnd, Hb, NCBC, NICNT, NTC, Sw, Tay, TH, TRT; CEV, GW, NCV, NIV, NLT, TEV; probably ESV, KJV, NASB, NET, NRSV, REB]. The father's growing faith was shown when he openly declared his faith while still acknowledging the weakness of that faith. Now he calls for the Lord's continued help in rising to a stronger faith by removing his remaining unbelief [Hb]. It seems that the father had brought his son there with faith that Jesus was able to cast out the demon, but then he had that faith crushed when the disciples of Jesus failed. After this rebuke, however, his faith revived, although still accompanied with a bit of unbelief [Gnd, WBC]. If Jesus would heal his son, it would result in him having more faith [BECNT].
  2. The father asked Jesus to help him in spite of his unbelief [ICC, Lns, My]. This man had faith, but he acknowledged the weakness of that faith by calling it unbelief. Instead of saying 'help me, free me from my unbelief,' he acknowledges his weakness of faith and his request is 'help me in my unbelief' [Lns]. He asks, 'Help me out of my trouble in spite of any unbelief that you may find in me' [ICC].

9:25 And Jesus having-seen a-crowd rapidly gathering,[a] rebuked[b] the unclean spirit saying to-it, "Mute and deaf[c] spirit, I command you, come-out of him and never[d] enter him again!"

LEXICON—a. pres. act. indic. of ἐπισυντρέχω (LN 15.134) (BAGD p. 301): 'to rush together to a place, to throng to' [LN]. The participial phrase 'having seen a crowd rapidly gathering' is translated 'when Jesus saw that a crowd was rapidly gathering' [NASB], 'when Jesus saw that a crowd was quickly gathering' [NCV, NET], 'when Jesus saw that a crowd was gathering fast' [CEV], 'when Jesus saw that a crowd came running together' [ESV, NRSV; similarly Lns, NTC], 'when Jesus saw that the people came running together' [KJV], 'when Jesus saw that a crowd was running to the scene' [GW, NIV], 'because Jesus saw that a crowd was running together toward him' [BECNT], 'seeing that the crowd was closing in on them' [AB1], 'noticed that the crowd was thronging toward him' [LN], 'when Jesus saw that the crowd of onlookers was growing' [NLT], 'seeing that a crowd was gathering together rapidly' [AB2], 'seeing that a crowd was gathering' [WBC], 'seeing a crowd gathering' [BNTC], 'when Jesus saw that the crowd was closing in on them' [REB], 'Jesus noticed that the crowd was closing in on them' [TEV]. This verb means to come together hurriedly to, toward, or at a particular location [LN]. This could refer to a crowd converging on a single location from one or more directions [Tay].

b. aorist act. indic. of ἐπιτιμάω (LN 33.331, 33.419) (BAGD 1. p. 303): 'to rebuke' [AB1, AB2, BAGD, BECNT, LN (33.419), NTC, WBC; ESV, KJV, NASB, NET, NIV, NLT, NRSV], 'to reprove' [BNTC], 'to speak sternly to' [CEV, REB], 'to command' [LN (33.331), Lns], 'to give a command to' [TEV], 'to order' [NCV], 'to give an order to' [GW], 'to warn' [BAGD]. This verb means to express strong disapproval of someone [LN (33.419)] or to command someone with the implication of a threat [LN (33.331)]. The separate pronoun ἐγώ 'I' with the verb emphasizes his authority and power [NLTfn].

c. κωφός (LN 24.68) (BAGD 2. p. 462): 'deaf' [BAGD, LN]. The phrase Τὸ ἄλαλον καὶ κωφὸν πνεῦμα 'The mute and deaf spirit' is translated 'You mute and deaf spirit' [ESV; similarly AB2; NET], 'Thou spirit, dumb and deaf' [Lns; similarly KJV], 'Mute and deaf spirit' [BECNT, WBC], 'You spirit that keeps this boy from speaking and hearing' [NRSV], 'the evil spirit that had kept the boy from speaking or hearing' [CEV]. Some reverse the order of the two adjectives: 'You deaf and dumb spirit' [NTC], 'Deaf and dumb spirit' [AB1, BNTC; REB, TEV], 'You deaf and mute spirit' [NASB, NIV], 'You spirit that makes people unable to hear or speak' [NCV], 'Listen, you spirit that makes this boy unable to hear and speak' [NLT], 'You spirit that won't let him talk' [GW]. This adjective pertains to being unable to hear [LN].

d. μηκέτι (LN 67.130) (BAGD 5.a. p. 518): 'no longer' [BAGD, LN], 'not from now on' [BAGD]. The clause 'never enter him again' [AB1, WBC;

ESV, GW, NCV, NET, NIV, NLT, NRSV; similarly BECNT] is also translated 'do not enter him again' [NASB], 'don't ever enter him again [AB2, NTC], 'never return' [BNTC], 'enter no more into him' [KJV], 'no longer enter into him' [Lns], 'never go into him again' [TEV], 'never go back' [REB], 'Don't ever bother him again' [CEV]. This adverb indicates an extension of time up to a point but not beyond [LN].

QUESTION—What is the function of the participial phrase, 'having seen a crowd rapidly gathering'?
1. The participle signals a temporal relationship [Lns; all versions except TEV]: *when he saw the crowd rapidly gathering*. It is not causal since Jesus had already determined to deliver the boy [Lns].
2. The participle signals a causal relationship [BECNT, Hb, ICC, Tay, TEV]: *because he saw the crowd rapidly gathering*. Jesus didn't want to attract a larger crowd and proceeded with the cure without further delay [ICC].

QUESTION—What crowd was gathering?
This crowd was a still larger group of people or simply an addition of new people to the crowd identified in verse 14 [TH]. Either this crowd was an addition to the crowd mentioned in verse 14, or else the original crowd had withdrawn while Jesus spoke with the father and it was now hurrying back to see what was going to take place [AB1, Hb]. This is the same crowd mentioned in verses 14 [EGT, Gnd, NTC, TRT, Sw]. Although it is natural to think that this was the same crowd that ran to Jesus in verse 14, there has been no mention of it withdrawing while he talked with the boy's father. It is possible that the gathering crowd refers to other people that had begun to gather as word of Jesus' presence had spread [EBC, ICC, NICNT, Tay].

QUESTION—Why is the unclean mute spirit now called the mute and deaf spirit?
It means that the evil spirit that prevented the boy from being able to speak also prevented him from being able to hear [BECNT, Hb, NTC, TH].

QUESTION—What is implied by the command 'never enter him again'?
1. This indicates that there had been intermittent possessions of the boy by the demon [EGT]. Each time the demon entered the boy it caused the boy to have a seizure, and the seizure would stop when the demon left him [EGT, Sw].
2. This command simply ordered the demon to come out and never return [EBC, Lns]. This command prevented the demon from returning at a future time [BECNT, Hb, NIGTC]. It reassures the father that the condition that had persisted for such a long time would no longer affect the boy [NIGTC].

9:26 And having-cried-out[a] and having-convulsed (him) severely[b] it-came-out. And (the boy) became like[c] a-corpse, so-that most[d] said that he-had-died.

LEXICON—a. aorist act. participle of κράζω (LN 33.83) (BAGD 1. p. 447): 'to cry out' [BAGD, BECNT; ESV, NASB, NRSV], 'to cry' [WBC; KJV], 'to scream' [BAGD, LN; CEV, GW, NCV, NLT, TEV], 'to shriek' [NTC; NET, NIV, REB], 'to shriek out' [AB1], 'to yell' [Lns], 'to shout' [AB2, LN], 'with a loud cry' [BNTC]. This verb means to shout or cry out [LN].
  b. πολύς (LN **78.3**) (BAGD I.2.b.β. p. 688): 'severely, greatly' [LN (78.3)], 'violently' [BAGD]. The phrase πολλὰ σπαράξας 'having convulsed him severely' is translated 'caused him to convulse severely' [**LN**], 'convulsing him greatly' [AB2], 'having convulsed him much' [Lns], 'having caused much convulsing' [BECNT], 'convulsed him violently' [NIV; similarly WBC], 'convulsing him terribly' [ESV, NRSV], 'sending him into severe convulsions' [AB1], 'throwing him/the-boy into terrible convulsions' [NTC; NASB, NET], 'threw the boy into another violent convulsion' [NLT], 'threw the boy into a bad fit' [TEV], 'rent him sore' [KJV], 'shook the child violently' [GW], 'made the boy shake all over' [CEV], 'threw the boy into repeated convulsions' [REB], 'with many convulsions' [BNTC], 'caused the boy to fall on the ground again' [NCV]. This adverb indicates the upper range of a scale of extent [LN].
  c. ὥστε (LN 64.12) (BAGD 1. p. 899): 'like, as' [BAGD, LN]. The clause ἐγένετο ὡσεὶ νεκρός 'he became like a corpse' [AB2] is also translated 'the boy looked like a corpse' [BNTC, TEV; similarly NET, NIV], 'he/the-boy was like a corpse' [AB1, WBC; ESV, NRSV], 'leaving him looking like a corpse' [REB], 'the boy looked as if he were dead' [GW, NCV], 'he was like one dead' [KJV], 'he became like dead' [Lns], 'he became as if he were dead' [BECNT], 'the boy looked dead' [CEV], 'the boy appeared to be dead' [NLT], 'the boy became so much like a corpse' [NASB], '(To such an extent) did the boy resemble a corpse' [NTC]. This particle indicates a relationship between events or states [LN]. It indicates a comparison [BAGD].
  d. πολύς (LN 59.1) (BAGD I.2.a.β. p. 688): 'many, a great number of' [LN]. The phrase τοὺς πολλούς 'the many' is translated 'most of them' [BNTC; ESV, NASB, NRSV], 'most people' [NTC; NLT], 'the majority' [Lns], 'almost everyone' [CEV], 'many' [BECNT, WBC; KJV, NCV, NET, NIV, REB], 'many people' [AB2], 'everyone' [GW, TEV], 'the whole crowd' [BAGD]. The clause is translated 'A murmur ran through the crowd as people said, "He's dead."' [NLT]. This adjective indicates a relatively large quantity of objects or events [LN].

QUESTION—What is the function of the adverb πολλά 'severely' in the phrase 'having convulsed him severely'?
  1. The adverb describes the severity of the convulsions [BAGD, Gnd, Hb, LN, Lns, NICNT, NIGTC, NTC, WBC; CEV, ESV, GW, KJV, NASB, NET, NIV, NLT, NRSV, TEV].

2. The adverb refers to a repetition of convulsions [BECNT, BNTC, TH; NCV, REB].

QUESTION—What was significant about the boy lying there like a corpse?

The stillness of the boy lying there gave additional proof of the eviction of the demon that had manifested itself by throwing the boy into water and fire and violently convulsing him [WBC]. After the demon had revealed its great strength, Jesus then showed his own greatness [NLT].

QUESTION—How many of the people are referred to by the adjective πολλοὺς 'most, many' in the phrase '*the many* were led to say that he died'?

1. Many of the people said the boy had died [AB2, BECNT, WBC; KJV, NCV, NET, NIV, REB].
2. Most of the people there said that the boy had died [BNTC, Hb, Lns, NICNT, NTC, Tay, TH; CEV, ESV, NASB, NRSV].
3. All of the many people who were there said that the boy had died [BAGD, CGTC, Gnd; GW, TEV].

9:27 But Jesus having-grasped[a] his hand lifted- him -up[b], and he-stood-up.

LEXICON—a. aorist act. participle of κρατέω (LN 18.6) (BAGD 1.b. p. 448): 'to grasp, to take hold of' [BAGD], 'to hold on to, to retain in the hand, to seize' [LN]. The participial phrase 'having grasped his hand' [Lns] is also translated 'grasped his hand' [BECNT, BNTC, NTC], 'taking him by the hand' [WBC], 'took him by the hand' [AB1; ESV, KJV, NASB, NIV, NLT, NRSV], 'took hold of his hand' [CEV, REB], 'took his hand' [GW], 'gently took his hand' [NET], 'seized his hand' [AB2], 'took the boy by the hand' [TEV], 'took hold of the boy's hand' [NCV]. This verb means to hold on to an object [LN].

b. aorist act. indic. of ἐγείρω (LN 17.10) (BAGD 1.a.β. p. 214): 'to raise, to help to rise' [BAGD], 'to cause to stand up [LN]. The phrase ἤγειρεν αὐτόν 'lifted him up' [BNTC; ESV, KJV, NRSV] is also translated 'raised him up' [BECNT, Lns, WBC], 'raised him' [AB2; NASB], 'helped him rise' [TEV], 'raised him to his feet' [NET; REB], 'lifted him to his feet' [NIV], 'helped him to his feet' [AB1; NLT]. The clauses 'lifted him up, and he stood up' are translated 'helped him stand up' [CEV; similarly GW, NCV], 'lifted him to his feet' [NTC]. This verb means to cause to stand up, possibly implying there was some previous incapacity [LN].

QUESTION—What happened when Jesus took the prone boy's hand and lifted him up?

This was not a resurrection. Jesus restored the boy to normality after his traumatic experience of exorcism [NIGTC]. The completely exhausted boy responded to the touch of Jesus [EBC, Hb]. This touch of Jesus' hand infused a reviving energy into the prostrate body of boy and his normal strength and health were restored [Hb].

9:28 And (when) he had-entered into a-house, his disciples privately[a] were-asking him, "Why were we not able to-cast- it -out[b]?"

LEXICON—a. The idiom κατ' ἰδίαν means 'according to that which is private' (LN 28.67). The phrase 'privately were asking him' [BECNT] is also translated 'privately asked him' [WBC], 'asked him privately' [AB1, AB2, BNTC, NTC; GW, ESV, KJV, NET, NIV, NRSV, REB, TEV; similarly NCV], 'began questioning him privately' [NASB], 'went on to inquire of him in private' [Lns], 'when Jesus was alone...with his disciples, they asked him' [NLT], 'after...Jesus and the disciples were alone, they asked him' [CEV]. This idiom pertains to what occurs in a private context or setting and it has the sense of not being made known publicly [LN]. It means 'privately' in the sense of being 'alone' when no one else was there [TH]. This idiom occurs at 4:34; 6:31; 7:33; 9:2, 28; 13:3.

    b. aorist act. infin. of ἐκβάλλω (LN 53.102) (BAGD 1. p. 237): 'to cast out' [AB1, AB2, BECNT, LN, Lns, NTC, WBC; ESV, KJV, NET, NLT, NRSV], 'to drive out' [BAGD, BNTC; NASB, NIV, REB, TEV], 'to expel' [BAGD], 'to force out' [CEV, GW, NCV], 'to exorcise' [LN]. This verb means to cause a demon to no longer possess or control a person [LN]. In reference to 'casting' out demons, this verb occurs at 1:34, 39; 3:15, 22, 23; 6:13; 7:26; 9:18, 28, 38; 16:9, 17.

QUESTION—Why did the disciples ask this question?

Jesus had given the disciples authority over evil spirits in 6:7 and they had already successfully cast out many demons, so they couldn't understand why they had not been able to cast the evil spirit out of this boy [EBC].

9:29 And he-said to-them, "This kind[a] can come-out[b] by nothing except by prayer."

TEXT—Manuscripts reading ἐν προσευχῇ 'by prayer' are given an A rating by GNT to indicate it was regarded to be certain. A variant reading is ἐν νηστείᾳ καὶ προσευχῇ 'by fasting and prayer' and it is followed by KJV.

LEXICON—a. γένος (LN 58.23) (BAGD 4. p. 156): 'kind' [BAGD, LN], 'type' [LN], 'class' [BAGD]. The phrase τοῦτο τὸ γένος 'this kind' [AB1, Lns, NTC, WBC; all versions except CEV, GW, NCV] is also translated 'this/that kind of spirit' [GW, NCV], 'this sort' [BNTC], 'this sort of spirit' [AB2], 'this/that kind of demon' [BECNT; CEV]. This noun denotes a category or class based upon an implied derivation or lineage [LN].

    b. aorist act. infin. of ἐξέρχομαι (LN 15.40) (BAGD 1.a.δ. p. 274): 'to come out' [BAGD], 'to go out' [BAGD, LN], 'to depart out of, to leave from within' [LN]. The whole statement is translated 'This kind is able to come out by nothing save by prayer' [Lns], 'This kind can come forth by nothing, but by prayer (and fasting)' [KJV], 'This kind cannot come out by anything but prayer' [NASB], 'This kind can come out only by/through prayer' [NTV; NET, NIV, NRSV], 'This kind cannot come out by any means except by prayer' [WBC], 'This kind cannot be driven out by anything but prayer' [ESV], 'This sort cannot be cast out by anything except prayer' [BNTC], 'This kind can be cast out only by prayer' [NLT], 'This kind of spirit can be forced out only by prayer' [GW; similarly NCV], 'This kind cannot be driven out except by prayer' [REB], 'There is no way of casting out this kind but by prayer' [AB1], 'This sort of spirit can't be gotten out in any way except by prayer' [AB2], 'Only prayer can force out that kind of demon' [CEV], 'Only prayer can drive this kind out, nothing else can' [TEV], 'This kind of demon is not able to be cast out by anything except prayer' [BECNT]. This verb means to move out of an enclosed or well-defined two or three-dimensional area [LN].

QUESTION—What does τοῦτο τὸ γένος 'this kind' refer to?
1. This refers to a type of demon that is different from other types of demons [CGTC, Hb, Lns, My, NIVfn, NTC, Sw, Tay, WBC; CEV, GW, NCV]. It suggests that there are different kinds of demons [NIVfn]. Some demons are more powerful and more malignant than others [Lns]. When a demon leaves and reenters a man in Mathew 12:45, it is accompanied by seven *worse* demons than itself [Hb].
2. This refers to demons as a whole [ICC, TH]. Instead of meaning that a particular kind of demon had possessed the boy, it is probably referring to demons considered as whole [TH]. It means 'this kind of thing,' that is, this genus called demons or evil spirits [ICC].

QUESTION—How would someone cast out a demon by prayer?
When a demon stubbornly refuses a command to leave a person, the disciple must resort to prayer for God's power to overcome that demon. It seems that they had not maintained their continued sense of dependence upon God's power through continued prayer [Hb]. The disciples apparently had taken it for granted the power to cast out demons was inherent in themselves and they had no longer prayerfully depended on God for that power [EBC]. It seems that the disciples believed the authority to cast out demons they had received from Jesus in 6:7 was now under their own control and so they had not relied on the unlimited power of God by praying with a sincere faith [NICNT]. They must persevere in prayer [NTC]. This is a general statement that miracles of any kind are possible only to those who pray [ICC].

DISCOURSE UNIT—9:30–10:52 [REB]. The topic is learning what discipleship means.

DISCOURSE UNIT—9:30–50 [NIGTC, PNTC]. The topic is mere discipleship [PNTC], more lessons about the way of the cross [NIGTC].

DISCOURSE UNIT—9:30–37 [NASB]. The topic is death and resurrection foretold.

DISCOURSE UNIT—9:30–32 [CBC, EBC, Hb, NICNT; CEV, ESV, GW, NCV, NET, NLT, NRSV, TEV]. The topic is a renewed teaching about the cross

[Hb], Jesus again foretells that he will die and come back to life [GW], Jesus again foretells his death and resurrection [ESV, NRSV], Jesus predicts his death again [CBC], Jesus again predicts his death [NLT], Jesus talks about his death [NCV], Jesus again speaks about his death [CEV, TEV], a second prediction of the Passion [EBC], the second major prophecy of the passion [NICNT], a second prediction of Jesus' death and resurrection [NET].

9:30 And having-gone-forth^a from-there they-were-passing^b through Galilee, and he did- not -want that anyone should-know.^c

LEXICON—a. aorist act. participle of ἐξέρχομα (LN 15.40): 'to go out of, to depart out of' [LN]. The clause 'having gone forth from there/thence' [Lns] is also translated 'having departed from there' [BECNT], 'from there they went out' [NASB], 'they went on from there' [ESV, NET, NRSV], 'they departed thence' [KJV], 'going out from there' [AB2], 'leaving there' [WBC], 'they left that area/place' [AB1, BNTC; GW, NIV], 'after they left that place' [NTC], 'they left that district' [REB], 'leaving that region' [NLT], 'Jesus and his followers left that place' [NCV, TEV], 'Jesus left with his disciples' [CEV]. This verb means to move out of an enclosed or well-defined two or three-dimensional area [LN].

b. imperf. mid./pass. (deponent = act.) indic. of παραπορεύομαι (LN 15.28) (BAGD 2. p. 621): 'to pass by, to go by' [LN], 'to go (through)' [BAGD]. The phrase 'they were passing through' [GW] is also translated 'and began to go through' [NASB], 'and started through' [CEV], 'and went on through' [AB1; TEV; similarly AB2, WBC; NCV], 'and passed through' [ESV, KJV, NET, NIV, NRSV], 'they were passing along through' [Lns], 'they were proceeding through' [BECNT], 'they were making a trip through' [NTC], 'and made their way through' [BNTC; REB], 'they traveled through' [NLT]. This verb means to move past a reference point [Lns]. The imperfect tense indicates that they traveled through Galilee without any prolonged stays at any one place [Hb]. It implies that Jesus did not stop to preach or minister to the people in the towns of that area [TH].

c. aorist act. subj. of γινώσκω (LN 27.2) (BAGD 2.c. p. 161): 'to learn (of), 'to find out' [BAGD, LN]. The phrase 'to know' [AB1, BNTC, Lns; ESV, NET, REB] is also translated, 'to know it' [AB2, BECNT, NTC, WBC; KJV, NRSV], 'to know about it' [CEV, NASB], 'to obtain knowledge of it' [BAGD], 'to know he was there' [NLT], 'to know where he was' [GW, NCV, TEV], 'to know where they were' [NIV]. This verb means to acquire information by whatever means [LN]. He didn't want anyone to know it [TH].

QUESTION—From where did they go forth?

They left the house mentioned in verse 28 [BECNT, CGTC, Gnd, Hb, NAC, WBC] or they left the neighborhood in which the healing of the boy took place [CGTC, EGT, Hb, NAC]. They left the vicinity of Caesarea Philippi [ICC, Lns, My].

QUESTION—What didn't Jesus want anyone to know?

Jesus didn't want anyone to know about his presence as he passed through Galilee [TH]. He avoided the areas of population in order to keep from being recognized [NIGTC]. The time of his public ministry in Galilee was over [BNTC, Tay]. Jesus didn't want anyone to know that he was in their vicinity because he wanted to be alone with his disciples as he instructed them [EBC, Gnd, NICNT, NIGTC, NTC, Tay]. This was a time for an intense training of the Twelve as Jesus prepared them for the end [Lns]. The next verse about his approaching death and resurrection describes what he wanted to instruct his disciples about [BECNT, CGTC, EBC, EGT, ESVfn, Gnd, ICC, My, NAC, NLTfn, Tay, WBC].

9:31 Because he-was-teaching his disciples and was-saying to-them, "The Son of-Man[a] is-going-to-be delivered[b] into (the) hands of-men, and they-will-kill[c] him, and having-been killed, after three days he-will-rise.[d]"

TEXT—Manuscripts reading μετὰ τρεῖς ἡμέρας 'after three days' are followed by GNT which does not mention any variant reading. A variant reading is τῇ τρίτῃ ἡμέρα 'on the third day' and it is followed by KJV.

LEXICON—a. υἱὸς τοῦ ἀνθρώπου (LN 9.3) (BAGD 2.e. p. 835): This title is translated 'the Son of Man' [BAGD, LN; all translations except AB1], 'The Man' [AB1]. It is a title with Messianic implications that Jesus used concerning himself [LN]. Jewish thought at that time knew of a heavenly being who was looked upon as a 'Son of Man' or 'Man' who exercised Messianic functions such as judging the world [BAGD]. See 2:10 for a discussion of this title.

b. pres. pass. indic. of παραδίδωμι (LN 37.12, 37.111) (BAGD 1.b. p. 614): 'to be handed over to, to be turned over to' [BAGD, LN (37.111)], 'to be betrayed' [LN (37.111)], 'to be delivered to the control of, to be handed over to' [LN (37.12)]. The phrase 'is going to be delivered into the hands of men' [ESV; similarly BNTC; NASB] is also translated 'is being delivered into the hands of men' [Lns; similarly KJV], 'is delivered into human hands' [WBC], 'will be turned over to the hands of human beings' [AB2], 'would/will be handed over to people' [CEV, NCV], 'will be handed over to men' [AB1], 'will be delivered into human hands' [BECNT], 'is now to be handed over into the power of men' [REB], 'will/is-going-to be betrayed into the hands of men' [NET, NIV], 'is to be betrayed into human hands' [NRSV], 'is about to be betrayed into the hands of men' [NTC], 'is going to be betrayed into the hands of his enemies' [NLT], 'will be betrayed and handed over to people' [GW]. This verb means to deliver a person into the control of someone else, and it refers to either the handing over of a presumably guilty person for punishment by authorities or the handing over of an individual to an enemy who will presumably take undue advantage of the victim [LN

(37.111)]. The idiom 'to give into the hands' means to hand someone over into the control of others [LN (37.12)]. Here the present tense of the verb has a future force [BECNT, CGTC, EBC, ICC, Lns, Tay, TH]. The passive voice hints that someone will betray Jesus [Hb].
- c. fut. act. indic. of ἀποκτείνω (LN 20.61) (BAGD 1.a. p. 94): 'to kill' [BAGD, LN; all translations]. This verb means to cause someone's death, normally by violent means [LN].
- d. fut. mid. indic. of ἀνίστημι (LN 23.93) (BAGD 2.a. p. 70): 'to rise' [WBC; ESV, KJV, NASB, NET, NIV, NLT], 'to arise' [AB2], 'to rise again' [Lns, NTC; NRSV, REB], 'to rise up' [BNTC], 'to come back to life' [BAGD, LN; GW], 'to rise from the dead' [BECNT; NCV], 'to rise to life' [CEV, TEV], 'to be raised up' [AB1], 'to live again, to be resurrected' [LN]. This verb means to come back to life after having once died [LN].

QUESTION—What relationship is indicated by the beginning conjunction γάρ 'because'?

This conjunction indicates the reason why the preceding verse says that Jesus didn't want anyone to know of his trip through Galilee [EGT, Hb, ICC, My, Sw, TH]. Jesus was now fully occupied with training the Twelve [Sw]. The reason for the need for secrecy was that Jesus was telling his disciples about his pending arrest, death, and resurrection [EGT, ICC, WBC].

QUESTION—In what way will Jesus be delivered into the hands of men?
1. The passive voice hints that an agent will be involved in delivering him into the hands of the Sanhedrin [Lns]. It probably refers to Judas delivering Jesus into the power of the Sanhedrin, and then the Sanhedrin delivering Jesus into the power of Pilate, who delivers Jesus into the power of the soldiers [CGTC, Lns].
2. This probably refers to God delivering Jesus into the power of men [AB1, BECNT, BNTC, EBC, Hb, NAC, NICNT, PNTC, Tay, TRT]. This is the divine passive which indicates that God would do this [EBC, NAC, NICNT, WBC]. It centers on the eschatological action of God [NICNT]. God took the initiative in providing salvation for men [EBC]. If this only referred to what Judas did, the words 'into the hands of men' would be superfluous [NAC].

QUESTION—How are the three days to be counted?

The phrase 'after three days' [ESV, NCV, NET, NIV] is also translated 'three days after being killed' [NRSV, REB], 'the third day' [KJV], 'three days later' [CEV, NASB, NLT, TEV], 'on the third day' [GW]. The resurrection was really on the third day [ICC]. His body rested in the grave during three day-night periods: part of Friday, all of Saturday, and part of Sunday [NTC].

9:32 But they were-not-understanding[a] the statement,[b] and they-were-afraid[c] to-ask him.

LEXICON—a. imperf. act. indic. of ἀγνοέω (LN (**32.7**) (BAGD 1. p. 735): 'to not understand' [BAGD, **LN**; all translations except Lns, NTC], 'to not grasp' [Lns], 'to not know what to make of it' [NTC]. This verb means to fail to understand [LN].

b. ῥῆμα (LN 33.98) (BAGD 1. p. 735): 'statement' [LN], 'saying, word, that which is said' [BAGD, LN]. The phrase 'the/this statement' [NTC; NASB] is also translated 'the/that/this saying' [AB2, BECNT, WBC; ESV, KJV, NET], 'the utterance' [Lns], 'what he said' [BNTC; REB], 'what he was saying' [NLT, NRSV], 'what was being said' [AB1], 'what he/Jesus meant' [CEV, GW, NCV, NIV], 'what this teaching meant' [TEV]. This noun denotes that which has been stated or said, and the primary focus is on the content of the communication [LN].

c. imperf. pass. indic. of φοβέομαι, φοβέω (LN 25.252) (BAGD 1.a. p. 863): 'to be afraid' [BAGD, LN; all translations]. This verb means to be in a state of fear [LN].

QUESTION—Why couldn't the disciples understand?

Jesus had spoken too explicitly for them to be in any doubt about what he was saying, but they could not understand why he said that it was necessary for all of this to take place [EGT]. Jesus' words weren't consistent with their views of a reigning Messiah [Hb].

QUESTION—Why were the disciples afraid to ask Jesus?

They were afraid to know the worst by asking for further clarification [BECNT, ESVfn, ICC, Lns, My, NAC, NICNT1, SW]. They also remembered Jesus' rebuke to Peter in 8:33 [ESVfn, Hb, NAC, Sw] and were afraid that any critical question they might ask would draw another sharp reprimand [Hb].

DISCOURSE UNIT—9:33–50 [Hb]. The topic is teaching in Capernaum to the disciples.

DISCOURSE UNIT—9:33–37 [CBC, EBC, Hb, NICNT; CEV, ESV, GW, NCV, NET, NIV, NLT, NRSV, TEV]. The topic is greatness in the kingdom [GW], the greatest in the kingdom [CBC; NLT], a question about greatness [EBC, Hb; NET], true greatness [NICNT], who is the greatest? [CEV, ESV, NCV, NIV, NRSV, TEV].

9:33 And they-came into Capernaum. And being[a] in the house he-asked them, "What were-you-discussing[b] on the way[c]?

TEXT—Manuscripts reading ἦλθον 'they came' are followed by GNT which does not mention any variant reading. A variant reading is ἦλθεν 'he came' and it is followed by KJV.

TEXT—Manuscripts reading διελογίζεσθε 'were you discussing' are followed by GNT which does not mention any variant reading. A variant reading is πρὸς ἑαυτοὺς διελογίζεσθε 'were you discussing among yourselves' and it is followed by KJV.

LEXICON—a. aorist mid. (deponent = act.) participle of γίνομαι (LN 85.6): 'to be' [LN]. The participial phrase ἐν τῇ οἰκίᾳ γενόμενος 'being in the house' [KJV] is also translated 'when he was in the house' [AB2, BECNT; NTC, WBC; ESV, NASB, NIV, NRSV], 'when they went into a house there' [NCV], 'after Jesus was inside the house' [NET], 'after they were inside the house' [CEV], 'when he had gone indoors' [BNTC], 'when they were indoors' [AB1], 'after going indoors' [TEV], 'after he got into the house [Lns], 'when he had gone indoors' [REB], 'while Jesus was at home' [GW], 'and settled in a house' [NLT]. This verb means to be in a certain place and sometimes it implies 'having come to be in such a place' [LN].

b. imperf. mid./pass. (deponent = act.) indic. of διαλογίζομαι (LN 33.158) (BAGD 2. p. 186): 'to discuss' [AB2, BECNT, LN, NTC, WBC; ESV, NASB, NET, NLT], 'to consider and discuss' [BAGD], 'to converse' [LN], 'to reason about' [Lns], 'to argue about' [AB1, BAGD, BNTC; CEV, GW, NCV, NIV, NRSV, REB, TEV], 'to dispute' [KJV]. This verb means to engage in some relatively detailed discussion of a matter [LN]. The imperfect tense indicates that they did this for some time [Hb, ICC, Lns]. This was a discussion [AB2, BECNT, NCBC, Sw, Tay, TH, WBC; ESV, NASB, NET, NLT]. It had turned into an argument [AB1, BAGD, BNTC, EBC, Gnd, ICC, NICNT, NIGTC, PNTC; CEV, GW, KJV, NCV, NIV, NRSV, REB, TEV].

c. ὁδός (LN 15.19) (BAGD 1.b. p. 554): 'way, journey' [LN (15.1)]. The phrase ἐν τῇ ὁδῷ 'on the way' [AB1, AB2, BNTC, WBC; ESV, NASB, NET, NRSV, REB] is also translated 'on the road' [Lns, NTC; GW, NCV, NIV], 'out on the road' [NLT, TEV], 'in the way' [BECNT], 'by the way' [KJV], 'along the way' [CEV]. This noun denotes a journey [LN]. Here it refers to an action such as being on a journey rather than to a place such as a road or highway [BAGD, TH]. In some languages it might have to be translated with a verb such as 'as you walked along the road' [TH].

QUESTION—Whose house was Jesus in?

It may have been the house owned by Peter and Andrew (1:29) [AB1, AB2, CGTC, EBC, Gnd, Hb, NAC, NIGTC, PNTC, Tay, TH, TRT, WBC] or perhaps Jesus had acquired his own house for a headquarters by then [Hb, Lns]. The focus is not on the house but on what takes place in the house [BECNT].

QUESTION—What was the purpose of Jesus' question?

Jesus asked the question in order to give his disciples some needed teaching [Hb, NICNT, NTC]. He already knew what they had been discussing before he asked them, but he asked the question so they might reflect on what they had done and feel ashamed [NTC]. He wanted to bring out how little they had understood [NIGTC]. Mark doesn't say whether Jesus knew what their discussion had been about because he had overheard them or because he knew through supernatural insight, but Luke 9:47 implies it was the latter [AB1, Gnd, Hb, Lns].

9:34 **But they were-silent,[a] because they-had-argued[b] with one-another on the way (about) who (was) greatest.[c]**

LEXICON—a. imperf. act. indic. of σιωπάω (LN 33.117) (BAGD 1. p. 752): 'to be silent' [AB1, AB2, BECNT, BNTC, LN, Lns, WBC; GW, NET, NRSV, REB], 'to keep silent' [ESV, NASB], 'to keep quiet' [LN; NIV], 'to keep still' [NTC], 'to hold one's peace' [KJV], 'to not answer' [CEV, NCV, NLT, TEV]. This verb means to refrain from speaking or talking [LN]. The force of the imperfect tense is shown by a translation such as 'they *kept* silent' [ICC, TH], 'they *continued* silent' [Lns].

  b. aorist pass. (deponent = act.) indic. of διαλέγομαι (LN **33.446**) (BAGD 1. p. 185): 'to argue' [AB1, **LN**, Lns; CEV, GW, ESV, NET, NIV, NLT, NRSV, TEV], 'to dispute' [BNTC, LN, NTC; KJV], 'to discuss' [AB2, BAGD, BECNT, WBC; NASB, NRSV]. The phrase 'they had argued with one another...about' is translated 'their argument...was about' [NCV]. This verb means to argue about differences of opinion [LN]. It concerns controversies with someone [BAGD]. In this context, the aorist tense should be translated as a past perfect, 'they had argued' [TH].

  c. μέγας (LN 87.22) (BAGD 2.b.α. p. 498): 'greatest' [all translations except Lns], 'greater' [BAGD, LN, Lns], 'better, superior to' [LN]. This comparative adjective pertains to being great in terms of status [LN]. This was a question of who was the most important [TRT].

QUESTION—What relationship is indicated by the conjunction γάρ 'because'?

This conjunction indicates the reason why they kept silent. They were ashamed that they had been arguing about which of them was the greatest [EBC, EGT, Gnd, ICC, NICNT]. They knew that Jesus would not have approved of their discussion if they had told him [BECNT, WBC].

QUESTION—Where were the disciples arguing before Jesus questioned them?

The disciples had been arguing among themselves while they were on the way back to Capernaum. Apparently Jesus had been walking ahead of them while the disciples followed along at a distance [Hb].

QUESTION—What is meant by being μείζων 'greatest'?

  1. 'Greatest' has the superlative sense of which one of the Twelve will be the greatest one of them all [AB1, AB2, BECNT, BNTC, CGTC, EBC, Gnd, Hb, ICC, NAC, NICNT, NTC, PNTC, Sw, Tay, TH, TRT; all versions]. They wanted to know which one of the Twelve was the greatest [ICC]. Perhaps the argument centered on the privileges given to Peter, James, and John when Jesus selected them to be present at the transfiguration, and the argument was about which of those three would have the chief place in the messianic kingdom [Hb, NIGTC, Sw]. Evidently they did not regard Peter to have been assigned the position of primacy among the twelve disciples [Hb] and there will be a bid for leadership by James and John at 10:35–45 [BECNT, NIGTC, NLTfn].

2. 'Greatest' has the comparative sense of how each disciple would rank in comparison with the other disciples [ESVfn, Lns]. Expecting Jesus to be a political liberator, all of the disciples were dreaming of their own status, honor, and power [ESVfn]. The argument was not which one would be greater than the other eleven. All twelve of the disciples would be great, but some will be greater than others [Lns].

9:35 And having-sat-down[a] he-called[b] the twelve and he-says to-them, "If someone desires to-be first,[c] he-must-be last[d] of-all and servant[e] of-all."

LEXICON—a. aorist act. participle of καθίζω (LN 17.12) (BAGD 2.a.α. p. 390): 'to sit down' [BAGD, LN]. The participial phrase 'having sat down' [BECNT, Lns] is also translated 'sitting down' [AB2, WBC; NASB, NIV], 'he/Jesus sat down' [AB1, BNTC; ESV, GW, KJV, NCV, NLT, NRSV, TEV], 'so he sat down' [NTC; REB], 'after he/Jesus sat down' [CEV, NET]. This verb means to be in a seated position or to take such a position [LN].

b. aorist act. indic. of φωνέω (LN 33.307) (BAGD 2.b. p. 870): 'to call' [BAGD, LN], 'to call to oneself' [BAGD], 'to summon' [LN]. The phrase 'he called the twelve/Twelve' [AB1, AB2, BECNT, BNTC, Lns, WBC; NASB, NET, NIV, NRSV, REB; similarly ESV, KJV], is also translated 'called the twelve to him' [NTC, WBC], 'called the twelve apostles' [GW], 'called the twelve apostles to him' [NCV], 'called the twelve disciples' [TEV], 'called the twelve disciples over to him' [NLT], 'and told the twelve disciples to gather around him' [CEV]. This verb means to communicate directly or indirectly to someone in order to tell that person to come [LN]. Since the disciples were already there, it means that Jesus called for their attention [NAC]. It could be that after sitting down he called them to where he was seated, or there may have been an interval between this verse and the previous one and he again gathered them around him. Or perhaps only some of the disciples had been present before and now he wanted them all to hear what he had to say [CGTC].

c. πρῶτος (LN 65.52) (BAGD 1.c.β. p. 726): 'first, foremost' [BAGD], 'most important' [BAGD, LN]. The phrase Εἴ τις θέλει πρῶτος εἶναι 'If any man desire to be first' [KJV] is also translated 'If anyone would be first' [NTC], 'If anyone wants to be first' [AB1, AB2, WBC; NASB, NET, NIV, REB], 'If anyone wishes/wills to be first' [BECNT, BNTC, Lns], 'Whoever wants to be first' [NLT, NRSV, TEV], 'Whoever wants to be the most important' [NCV], 'If anyone would be first' [ESV], 'If you want the place of honor' [CEV], 'Whoever wants to be the most important person' [GW]. This adjective pertains to exceeding everyone else in importance [LN]. In their Jewish culture, 'first' referred to rulers, aristocrats, ruling priests, and other persons of authority and influence [WBC].

d. ἔσχατος (LN 87.66) (BAGD 2. p. 313): 'last' [BAGD, LN], 'least, most insignificant' [BAGD], 'lowest, least important' [LN]. The clause ἔσται πάντων ἔσχατος 'he must be last of all' [BECNT, NTC; ESV, NCV, NET, NRSV] is also translated 'he must make himself last of all' [REB], 'he must himself be last of all' [AB1], 'he must be the very last' [NIV], 'must take the last place' [GW; similarly NLT], 'must place himself last of all' [TEV], 'he/the-same shall be last of all' [WBC; KJV, NASB; similarly AB2], 'let him be last of all' [BNTC], 'he will be last of all' [Lns], 'you must become a slave and serve others' [CEV]. This adjective pertains to being of the lowest status [LN]. In their Jewish culture, 'last' and 'servant' meant someone without rank, authority, or privilege [WBC].

e. διάκονος (LN 35.20) (BAGD 1.a. p. 184): 'servant' [BAGD, LN]. The clause καὶ πάντων διάκονος 'and servant of all' [AB1, BECNT, BNTC, NTC, WBC; ESV, KJV, NASB, NCV, NET, NRSV, REB] is also translated 'and the servant of all' [AB2, NIV], 'and be servant of all' [TEV], 'and be the servant of everyone else' [NLT], 'and be a servant to everyone else' [GW], 'and a minister of all' [Lns], 'and serve others' [CEV]. This noun denotes a person who renders service [LN]. It defines what being 'last of all' involves [Lns].

QUESTION—Why does it say that Jesus sat down and called the twelve disciples even though they had entered the house together in verse 33 and he had already been talking with them?

At this point Jesus deliberately assumed the recognized position of a Jewish teacher [AB1, AB2, BECNT, BNTC, CGTC, EBC, ESVfn, Gnd, Hb, NAC, NCBC, NLTfn, NTC, PNTC, Sw, Tay, TH, WBC]. It implies that this would be a formal time of instruction, and as teacher he summons his pupils to gather around him and listen [NIGTC]. An important lesson was going to be taught [Hb, NTC].

QUESTION—What is meant by the disciples being the first and the last?

'First and last' is a matter of rank among the disciples [Gnd, TH]. Since this concerns the 'Twelve' gathered about Jesus, the numerical contrast between first and last is a contrast between the first and the twelfth of those apostles who had been arguing about which was the greatest of them [Gnd]. The disciples had been arguing about who would be first among those in their group, but this is presented as a general principle that applies to all who are in the kingdom of God [Hb, Lns, NTC].

QUESTION—Why does the person who desires to be first have to be last?

This is not a threat against those who seek to be first as though Jesus was saying 'This is what will happen if anyone wants to be first.' The future tense of the verb in the phrase ἔσται πάντων ἔσχατος 'he shall be last of all' should not be taken to mean that if the person wants to be first he will end up last of all. This future tense 'shall be' has the force of an imperative: '*he must be* last of all.' It is the way one can really become first [TH]. Most translate the verb as 'must be' [all versions except NASB]. Being last in the kingdom of God is described as being a servant of all [WBC]. Those who took the last place and served others were positioning themselves to be first in Jesus' estimation [CBC]. Jesus determined the rank and standing of a disciple by the way in which he makes himself last, that is, by the character and the amount of service he renders to as many as possible [Lns].

9:36 **And having-taken[a] a-child he-placed[b] him in (the) middle of-them and having-taken- him -in-his-arms[c] he-said to-them,**

LEXICON—a. aorist act. participle of λαμβάνω (LN 18.1) (BAGD 1.a. p. 464): 'to take' [AB1, AB2, BECNT, BNTC, Lns, NTC, WBC; all versions except CEV, NLT], 'to take hold of, to grasp' [BAGD, LN], not explicit [CEV, NLT]. This verb means to take hold of something or someone without any implication on how much force was required [LN]. Jesus took the child by the hand [TH].

b. aorist act. indic. of ἵστημι (LN 85.40) (BAGD I.1.a. p. 382): 'to place, to set' [BAGD, LN], 'to put, to make stand' [LN]. The phrase 'he placed him in the middle of them' is translated 'he put him in the midst of them' [WBC; ESV], 'he set him in their midst' [AB2], 'he set him in the midst of them' [KJV], 'he set him before them' [NASB], 'he placed/set him in front of them' [AB1; REB], 'he put a little child among them' [NLT; similarly NRSV], 'he had him stand in front of them' [TEV], 'he had him stand among them' [GW, NCV, NET, NIV], 'he had him stand in the midst of them' [NTC], 'he stood it in the middle of them' [BECNT; similarly Lns], 'he set it in the center' [BNTC], 'Jesus had a child stand near him' [CEV]. This verb means to cause someone to be in a place, with or without the accompanying feature of a standing position. This verb may very well imply a standing position, but what is in focus is not the stance but the location [LN]. Jesus led the child over in front of the disciples who then crowded around Jesus and the boy [TH].

c. aorist mid. (deponent = act.) participle of ἐναγκαλίζομαι (LN 34.63) (BAGD p. 261): 'to take in one's arms' [BAGD], 'to put one's arms around, to embrace, to hug' [LN]. The phrase 'having taken him/it in his arms' [Lns] is also translated 'taking the child in his arms' [NCV], 'taking the-child/him/it in his arms' [NTC; ESV, NASB, NET, NIV, NLT, NRSV], 'when he had taken him in his arms' [KJV], 'having put his arms around him' [BECNT], 'putting his arms around him' [WBC], 'he put his arms around the child/him' [AB1; GW, TEV], 'he put his arm around the child' [CEV; similarly BNTC; REB], 'embracing him' [AB2]. This verb means to put one's arms around someone as an expression of affection and concern [LN]. Jesus took the child up in his arms and put him on his lap [TH].

QUESTION—Where did this child appear from and why did Jesus pick him out?

Presumably the child lived in the house where Jesus was teaching his disciples [Gnd, NICNT]. Perhaps it was Peter's child [Hb]. The child would have known Jesus, so he readily came when Jesus called to him [Lns]. Jesus planned to use the child to illustrate the principle he had just been teaching his disciples in verse 35 [EBC, NIGTC]. Jesus wanted his disciples to identify themselves with children who have no pretensions to greatness [NICNT]. This child would demonstrate a child's submission and trustfulness [Hb].

QUESTION—How did Jesus put the child in the middle of the disciples?

Jesus had the child stand near him [Hb, Lns, NTC; CEV] so that the child was facing the half circle of disciples seated in front of Jesus [Hb]. Jesus led the child to a spot right in front of the disciples [Hb, Sw, TH].

QUESTION—How did Jesus take the child in his arms?

Jesus was probably already seated again when he lifted the child to his lap [TH, TRT]. Jesus was seated and was able to reach out to hug the boy who was standing next to him [Gnd]. This was a little child, and Jesus embraced him in the crook of his arm [Hb].

9:37 "Whoever receives[a] one of-such[b] children on-account-of[c] my name, receives me. And whoever receives me not[d] (only) receives me but (also) the-one having-sent me."

LEXICON—a. aorist mid. (deponent = act.) subj. of δέχομαι (LN 34.53) (BAGD 1. p. 177): 'to receive' [AB1, AB2, BAGD, BECNT, BNTC, LN, Lns, WBC; ESV, KJV, NASB, REB], 'to welcome' [LN, NTC; CEV, GW, NET, NIV, NLT, NRSV, TEV], 'to accept' [LN; NCV]. This verb means to accept a person into one's presence with friendliness [LN]. To 'receive' someone implies that the person is welcomed and treated as a friend [WBC]. Jesus received the child with a kindly welcome [Hb, NAC]. Jesus received this child by hugging him [Gnd].

b. τοιοῦτος (LN 92.31) (BAGD 2.a.α. p. 821): 'of such a kind, of a kind such as this' [BAGD, LN]. The phrase 'one of such children' [KJV] is also translated 'one of such little children' [Lns, NTC], 'one such child' [AB1, AB2; ESV, NRSV], 'one/a child like this' [BECNT; GW, NASB, NCV, REB; similarly NLT], 'one of these little children' [BNTC; NET, NIV; similarly WBC; TEV], 'even a child' [CEV]. This adjective refers to that which is of such a kind that is identified by the context [LN].

c. ἐπί (LN 89.27) (BAGD II.3. p. 288): 'because of, on the basis of [LN], 'in connection with, by the use of' [BAGD]. The phrase ἐπὶ τῷ ὀνόματί μου 'on account of my name' is translated 'in my name' [AB1, AB2, BNTC, NTC, WBC; all versions except CEV, NLT], 'on my name' [Lns], 'on my behalf' [NLT], 'for my sake' [BECNT], 'because of me' [CEV]. This preposition indicates cause or reason as the basis for a subsequent event [LN].

d. οὐ (LN 69.3): 'not' [LN]. This negative particle signals a negative proposition [LN]. Referring to ὃς ἂν ἐμὲ δέχηται 'whoever receives me', the verse ends with the negative statement οὐκ ἐμὲ δέχεται ἀλλὰ τὸν ἀποστείλαντά με 'does not receive me but the one who sent me' [AB2]. Others also translate this quite literally: 'receives not me but the one who sent me' [BNTC; similarly WBC], 'receives not me but him that commissioned me' [Lns], 'does not welcome me but the one who sent me'

[NET, NIV; similarly NTC; ESV, GW, KJV, NASB, NRSV, REB]. However, the phrase 'does not receive me' probably means 'does not *so much* receive me as receive the one who sent me' [AB2]. 'Not me' means 'not only me' [Hb, NTC]. So others make that meaning clear: 'receives not only me but the one who sent me' [AB1], 'welcomes not only me but also my Father who sent me' [NLT, similarly TEV], 'when you welcome me, you welcome the one who sent me' [CEV], 'whoever accepts me accepts the one who sent me' [NCV].

QUESTION—What is meant by the phrase τῶν τοιούτων παιδίων 'such children'?

1. The position in society that is typical of such children is in focus [AB2, BECNT, EBC, CGTC, EGT, ICC, NIGTC, PNTC, WBC]. A child is the least in the Christian social ladder [BECNT]. The child is insignificant [EBC, NIGTC, PNTC] or lowly and unimportant [BECNT, WBC]. They must forget all about rank and prominence when they receive a child [NTC].
2. The character traits typical of such children are in focus [AB1, BNTC, Gnd, Hb, NTC]. The child before them is representative of the class of children that are simple, trusting, and unassuming disciples of Jesus [Hb]. They are weak, needy, and dependent [NTC].
3. The child's relationship to Jesus is in focus. 'These little ones, the ones believing in me' in verse 42 points back to 'such children' whom the present child represents [Gnd].

QUESTION—Who is 'one of such children' that is to be received by the disciples?

1. Jesus is referring to receiving another little child like the little child Jesus was holding in his arms [AB1, AB2, BECNT, Gnd, Hb, Lns, NTC, Tay, TH, WBC]. The child who was there with Jesus is the representative 'one' of the children to be received on account of Jesus' name [Gnd].
2. Jesus is referring to his disciples receiving any person who is similar in some respects to the little child he was holding in his arms [BNTC, EBC. ICC, NAC, NIGTC, Sw]. This child is representative of the insignificant people of any age [EBC, ICC, NIGTC]. Instead of worrying about their own positions, the disciples should be concerned about the weakest and most humble members of the community who are typified by the little child Jesus was holding [BNTC]. 'Such a one' refers to people who are considered to be insignificant. Instead of ignoring and suppressing such a one, the disciples are to treat that person as really being significant [NIGTC].
3. Jesus is referring to villagers receiving his disciples with hospitality as the disciples travel from town to town. The disciples are like one of such children in that they have no pretensions of greatness. The reason they should be received in a village is because they are representatives of Jesus, and whoever receives the disciples receive Jesus and the Father who sent him [NICNT].

QUESTION—What is meant by receiving one of such children 'on account of my name'?

This ambiguous phrase could mean 'for my sake,' 'because the child believes in me,' or 'because the child is my follower/representative' [TRT]. It could mean receiving the child 'on account of my name,' 'for my sake,' because of me,' 'out of regard for me' [TH]. It could mean 'because the child who is a believer belongs to me,' 'because the child in his need is my representative,' or 'because this action is something I desire' [CGTC]. It means they should receive such a child on the behalf of Jesus [NLTfn]. The phrase is literally 'on the ground of my name' and it specifies the basis for accepting one such child [BECNT, Sw, Tay]. They should accept such a child because Jesus accepts such children [BECNT, EBC, Gnd]. Or they should accept the child because of the child's connection with Jesus [Sw], the child belongs to Christ [Hb]. It means to do this in the name of Jesus, that is, to do as Jesus would do, to do it for Jesus' sake, and to do it as a Christian [NAC]. Or the phrase 'in my name' defines the child as being one who believes in Jesus [ICC, NICNT, Sw].

QUESTION—How can receiving one of such children be an act of receiving Jesus and receiving the God who sent him?

Service done to 'one such little ones' will be accepted as done to Jesus, and service done to Jesus will be accepted by God as rendered to God himself [CGTC]. Since Jesus represents the one who sent him, to receive Jesus is to receive God [NIGTC].

DISCOURSE UNIT—9:38–50 [CBC; NASB, NCV, NET, NLT]. The topic is various teachings of Jesus [NLT], miscellaneous remarks about relationships and accountability [CBC], dire warnings [NASB], anyone not against us is for us [NCV], on Jesus' side [NET].

DISCOURSE UNIT—9:38–42 [EBC, NICNT]. The topic is exorcism through Jesus' name [NICNT], driving out demons in Jesus' name [EBC].

DISCOURSE UNIT—9:38–41 [Hb; CEV, ESV, GW, NIV, NRSV, TEV]. The topic is the mistaken zeal of John [Hb], using the name of Jesus [GW], for or against Jesus [CEV], anyone not against us is for us [ESV], whoever is not against us is for us [NIV, TEV], another exorcist [NRSV].

9:38 John said to-him, "Teacher, we-saw someone casting-out[a] demons in your name[b] and we-were-forbidding[c] him, because he-was- not -following[d] us."

TEXT—Manuscripts reading καὶ ἐκωλύομεν αὐτον, ὅτι οὐκ ἠκολούθει ἡμῖν 'and we were forbidding him, because he was not following us' are given a B rating by GNT to indicate it was regarded to be almost certain. A variant reading is ὃς οὐκ ἀκολουθεῖ ἡμῖν καὶ ἐκωλύσαμεν αὐτον, ὅτι οὐκ ἀκολουθεῖ ἡμῖν 'who does not follow us, and we forbade him, because he does not follow us' and it is followed by Tay; KJV. Another variant reading is ὃς οὐκ ἀκολουθεῖ ἡμῖν καὶ ἐκωλύσαμεν αὐτον 'who does not follow us, and we forbade him'.

LEXICON—a. pres. act. participle of ἐκβάλλω (LN 53.102) (BAGD 1. p. 237): 'to cast out' [AB1, AB2, BECNT, LN, Lns, NTC, WBC; ESV, KJV, NASB, NET, NLT, NRSV], 'to drive out' [BAGD, BNTC; NIV, REB, TEV], 'to force out of people' [CEV, GW], 'to force out of a person' [NCV], 'to make to go out, to exorcise' [LN], 'to expel' [BAGD]. This verb means to cause a demon to stop possessing or controlling a person [LN]. In reference to 'casting out' demons, this verb occurs at 1:34, 39; 3:15, 22, 23; 6:13; 7:26; 9:18, 28, 38; 16:9, 17.

b. ὄνομα (LN 33.126) (BAGD I.4.c.γ. p. 572): 'name' [BAGD, LN] The phrase ἐν τῷ ὀνόματί σου 'in your name' [AB1, AB2, BECNT, BNTC, Lns, NTC, WBC; ESV, KJV, NASB, NET, NIV, NRSV, REB, TEV] is also translated 'using your name' [CEV, NCV, NLT], 'by using the power and authority of your name' [GW]. This noun refers to the proper name of a person or object [LN]. The phrase 'in your name' can mean 'using your name, with mention of your name, while naming you, calling on your name' [My, TH].

c. imperf. act. indic. of κωλύω (LN 13.146) (BAGD 1. p. 461): 'to prevent, to hinder' [BAGD, LN]. The phrase 'we were forbidding him' is translated 'we forbade him' [AB2, WBC; KJV], 'we told him to stop' [CEV, NCV, NIV, NLT, TEV], 'we tried to stop him' [AB1, BNTC, NTC; GW, ESV, NET, NRSV, REB], 'we tried to prevent him' [NASB], 'we tried to hinder him' [Lns], 'we tried to forbid him' [BECNT]. Although the imperfect tense may mean that they repeatedly told the man to stop, it is better take it as a conative imperfect indicating intention: 'We tried to prevent him.' [Hb, NTC].

d. imperf. act. indic. of ἀκολουθέω (LN 15.156): 'to follow, to accompany as a follower, to go along with' [LN]. The phrase 'he was not following us' [BECNT, BNTC, Lns, NTC, WBC; ESV, NASB, NET, NRSV; similarly AB1, AB2; KJV] is also translated 'he was not one of us' [CEV, GW, NIV, REB], 'he wasn't in our group' [NLT], 'he does not belong to our group' [NCV, TEV]. This verb means to follow or accompany someone who takes the lead in determining direction and route of movement [LN].

QUESTION—Who was the unknown exorcist?

Matthew 12:27, 43–45, and Acts 19:13 describe Jews who went around driving out evil spirits [NIGTC]. Jesus had authorized the twelve disciples to cast out demons in 3:15 and 6:7. Now it appears that they considered themselves to be the only ones who had authority to do so [BECNT]. Some think the unknown man in this verse was a true follower of Jesus who carried out his ministry of exorcism outside the circle of the twelve [BECNT, EBC, Gnd, Hb, ICC, Lns, My, NAC, NICNT, NIGTC, NTC]. Another thinks that the man was not a follower of Jesus [AB2].

QUESTION—What is meant by casting out demons 'in Jesus' name'?

It means that the man invoked the power of Jesus' name to cause a demon to leave a person [AB2, EBC, Gnd, Hb, My, NAC, NICNT, NIGTC, Sw, TH, WBC]. John thought that the man should not have used Jesus' name since he was outside the group of disciples [NIGTC]. The name of Jesus was effecting the exorcisms [BNTC, Gnd]. 'In the name' of a person can mean 'in the power of' or 'for the sake of,' but the exorcist in this verse literally pronounced Jesus' name to direct Jesus' spiritual force upon the demons [AB2]. This man had used the authority of Jesus' name to expel demons [Hb, NICNT]. He would say to the demons, 'I command you to come out in Jesus' name!' [NICNT]. Perhaps he said, 'In Jesus' name I command you to come out of this person!' [TRT]. This would have meant that the man was acting with the authority and power given him by Jesus [EBC, ICC].

QUESTION—In what sense was that person not following the disciples who made the complaint?

John told Jesus that the man did not follow 'us (disciples)'. His complaint was that this man was not one of the openly acknowledged followers of Jesus and therefore had no right to use the name of Jesus [Hb, Lns, NTC, PNTC]. These disciples considered themselves to be the only ones who were authorized to do such exorcisms [BECNT]. Their complaint was that the man was doing their work [ICC, NAC]. It is possible that this man had listened to Jesus and given him his allegiance but had not yet established close relationships with the other followers of Jesus [NTC].

9:39 But Jesus said, "Do- not -forbid him. Because there-is no-one who will-do a-miracle[a] 'by-the-use-of[b] my name and soon-afterward[c] be-able to-speak-evil-of[d] me.

LEXICON—a. δύναμις (LN 76.7) (BAGD 4. p. 208): 'miracle' [BAGD, LN], 'mighty deed' [LN], 'deed of power, a wonder' [BAGD]. The phrase ποιέω δύναμιν 'to do a miracle' [BECNT, BNTC, WBC; KJV, NET, NIV] is also translated 'to work a miracle' [CEV, GW], 'to perform a miracle' [NASB, NLT, REB, TEV], 'to do a work/deed of power' [AB1, AB2, Lns; NRSV], 'to do a mighty work' [NTC; ESV], 'to do powerful things' [NCV]. This noun denotes a deed that manifests a power so great that it could only be supernatural [LN]. It refers to an outward expression of power [BAGD]. This word also occurs in the same sense at 6:2.

b. ἐπί (LN 89.27) (BAGD II.3. p. 288): 'by the use of, in connection with, calling upon' [BAGD], 'because of, on the basis of' [LN]. The phrase ἐπὶ τῷ ὀνόματί μου 'by the use of my name' is translated 'in my name' [AB1, AB2, BECNT, BNTC, NTC, WBC; all versions except NCV], 'uses my name' [NCV], 'on my name' [Lns]. This preposition indicates the basis for a subsequent event [LN].

c. ταχύ, ταχύς (LN **67.56**) (BAGD 2.c. p. 807): 'soon afterward' [BAGD, LN, NTC; ESV, NASB, NET, NRSV, TEV], 'soon after' [WBC], 'soon' [AB2, BAGD, LN, Lns; CEV, NLT], 'very soon' [LN], 'in a short time'

[BAGD], 'quickly' [AB1, BECNT], 'in the next moment' [BNTC, NIV; similarly REB], 'can turn around and' [GW], 'can lightly' [KJV], 'easily' [NCV]. This adverb pertains to a point of time subsequent to another point of time with an emphasis upon the relatively brief interval between the two points of time [LN].

d. aorist act. infin. of κακολογέω (LN 33.399) (BAGD p. 397): 'to speak evil of, to insult' [BAGD], 'to revile' [BAGD, LN], 'to denounce' [LN]. The phrase κακολογῆσαί με 'speak evil of me' [AB1, BECNT, BNTC, Lns, WBC; GW, ESV, KJV, NASB, NLT, NRSV, REB] is also translated 'speak ill of me' [NTC], 'say evil things about me' [NCV, TEV], 'say something/anything bad about me' [CEV, NET, NIV], 'to malign me' [AB2]. This verb means to insult in a particularly strong and unjustified manner [LN].

QUESTION—What relationship is indicated by the conjunction γάρ 'because'?

The conjunction indicates the reason for not opposing that man [Hb]. Unlike his disciples, Jesus did not have a restrictive view on who could participate in his mission [EBC]. This unknown person cannot do what he does and then speak as an enemy of Jesus, so there was no reason for the disciples to oppose the man [NIGTC].

QUESTION—Is there a significant difference between the meanings of the prepositions in ἐπὶ τῷ ὀνόματί μου '*by the use* of my name' in this verse and ἐν τῷ ὀνόματί σου '*in* your name' in verse 38?

1. There is no distinction to be made between the two prepositions [Tay, TH, NTC; all translations except Lns]
2. There is a slight distinction involved [Gnd, Hb, Lns; NCV]. In verse 39 the man had understood the power of Jesus' name, so when he cast out demons he told them to leave in (ἐν) the name of Jesus, that is, he was announcing that Jesus had given him the authority to expel them. In this verse the preposition ἐπί has the meaning 'upon' and Jesus explained to his disciples that when anyone does a miracle 'upon' the name of Jesus, that person is depending on the name of Jesus to be the basis for its performance [Hb]. The preposition has the meaning 'on the grounds of.' The man is working a miracle on the grounds of Jesus' name, that is, the man performs a miracle because he used the name 'Jesus' [Gnd].

QUESTION—In the contrast of 'doing a miracle by the use of my name' and 'being able to speak evil of me.' does the inclusion of ταχύ 'soon afterward' imply that later on such a person might speak evil of Jesus?

This means that it would take a considerable time before a person's mind could be so changed that he would speak or think depreciatingly of Jesus [EBC]. Somewhat like a litotes, the reason is given in a negative form and actually implies that such a man will certainly speak well of Jesus [Lns]. It is said with a touch of humor [NICNT]. The word 'later' does leave open the possibility of later apostasy [Gnd].

9:40 Because whoever is not against^a us, is for^b us.
LEXICON—a. κατά (LN 90.31) (BAGD I.2.b.γ. p. 406): 'against' [BAGD, LN; all translations], 'in opposition to, in conflict with' [LN]. This preposition indicates opposition, perhaps including antagonism [LN].
  b. ὑπέρ (LN 90.36) (BAGD 1.a.δ. p. 838): 'for' [AB2, BAGD, BECNT, LN, Lns, NTC, WBC; all versions except KJV, REB], 'be on someone's side' [AB1, BAGD, BNTC; REB], 'be on our part' [KJV]. This preposition indicates a participant who is benefited by an event or on whose behalf an event takes place [LN].
QUESTION—What relationship is indicated by the conjunction γάρ 'because'?
  1. This indicates another reason for the prohibition in verse 39 [CGTC, Gnd, Lns, NICNT, NIGTC, WBC]: *Do not forbid him* because whoever is not against us, is for us.
  2. This gives the reason why the person cannot speak evil of Jesus [NTC].
QUESTION—Why did Jesus say that such a person is for 'us' instead of for 'me'?
  Jesus included his disciples because John had already said in verse 38 that the man 'was not following *us*' [Lns].The man's attitude toward Jesus would also determine his attitude toward the disciples of Jesus [Hb].
QUESTION—What is the logic of the statement 'whoever is not against us, is for us'?
  Once a person has really encountered Christ, neutrality is forever impossible [NTC]. Friendliness and hostility are incongruous and cannot exist together [ICC]. When the man uses Jesus' name, he is demonstrating he is for *us*, so the disciples should not forbid that [Gnd].

9:41 For whoever gives- you(pl) a-cup of-water -to-drink in-view-of the-kind-of-persons-you-are, (namely) that you-belong-to Christ'
TEXT—Manuscripts reading ἐν ὀνόματι 'in name' are given an A rating by GNT to indicate it was regarded to be certain. Variant readings are ἐν ὀνόματί μου 'in my name' and ἐν τῷ ὀνόματί μου 'in my name'.
LEXICON—a. ὄνομα (LN 33.126, **58.22**) (BAGD II. p. 573): 'category' [BAGD, LN (58.23)], 'name' [LN (33.126)]. The clause ἐν ὀνόματι ὅτι Χριστοῦ ἐστε 'in view of the kind of persons you are, namely that you belong to Christ' [LN (58.22)] is also translated 'under the category that you belong to Christ' [BAGD, LN (58.22)], 'on the grounds that you belong to Christ' [BNTC], 'because of your name as followers of Christ' [NASB], 'because you bear the name of Christ' [WBC; NRSV; similarly NET], 'in connection with a name that you are Christ's' (i.e., 'because you are Christ's)' [Lns], 'in the name, because you belong to Christ' [AB2], 'in my name because you belong to Christ' [KJV, NIV], 'in my name, just because you belong to me' [CEV], 'because you belong to Christ' [NTC; ESV, GW], 'because you belong to the Christ' [NCV], 'because you belong to the Messiah' [AB1; NLT], 'because you belong to me' [TEV], 'because you are of Christ' [BECNT], 'because you are

followers of the Messiah' [REB]. This noun denotes the category of something [LN]. It means that the gift of hospitality is given to the Twelve because they belong to Christ [Gnd]

b. Χριστός (LN 53.82) (BAGD 1. p. 887): Without the article in the Greek text this name is translated 'Christ' [AB2, BECNT, BNTC, Lns, NTC, WBC; ESV, KJV, GW, NASB, NET, NIV, NRSV], 'the Christ' [NCV], 'Messiah' [AB1; NLT, REB], 'me' [CEV, TEV]. This noun literally means 'the one who has been anointed'. In the NT it is a title for Jesus who is 'the Messiah, the Christ'. In other contexts, especially when it is without an article, Χριστός functions as part of the name, 'Jesus Christ' [LN]. This word occurs at 1:1; 8:29; 9:41; 12:35; 13:21; 14:61; 15:32.

QUESTION—What relationship is indicated by the initial conjunction γάρ 'for'?

1. This adds a third reason why they should not forbid the independent exorcist [Gnd]. No one who is seeking to serve Jesus is excluded from his circle no matter how seemingly unimportant that service may be [WBC].
2. This gives the reason why his previous reasoning is true [NTC].
3. This explains verse 40 by telling them what it means to 'not be against him' and how much such a man is already for him [Lns].
4. This confirms verse 37. The thread of the teaching in verse 38 is resumed after being interrupted by John's question in verse 39 [Sw].

QUESTION—Why did Jesus talk about giving a cup of water to someone?

This example emphasizes how very small and insignificant a service might be that would be important in God's estimation [CGTC, Sw].

QUESTION—What did Jesus mean by calling himself 'Christ'?

There are seven occurrences of the word Χριστοῦ 'Christ' in Mark (1:1; 8:29; 9:41; 12:35; 13:21; 14:61; 15:32) and all the references except this verse and 1:1 include a definite article that usually indicates the word is being used as the title, 'the Messiah.' The lack of the definite article results in a difference of opinion.

1. 'Christ' is used as a proper name, '(Jesus) Christ' [BNTC, Lns, NAC; possibly AB2, NTC; KJV, NASB, NIV, NET, NRSV which translate this as 'Christ' without an article] or as 'me' [CEV, TEV].
2. 'Christ' refers to Jesus as being the 'Messiah' [AB1, BECNT, Hb, My, PNTC; NCV, NIGTC, NLT, REB]. Jesus didn't freely use this title, but he used it here since that title would be the basis of people's treatment of his disciples after his death [NIGTC].

truly[a] I-say to-you(pl) that in-no-way will-he-fail-to-get[b] his reward.[c]

LEXICON—a. ἀμήν (LN 72.6) (BAGD 2. p. 45): 'truly' [AB1, BAGD, BECNT, BNTC, LN, WBC; ESV, NASB, NRSV, REB], 'verily' [KJV], 'amen' [AB2, Lns], not explicit [CEV]. The phrase 'truly I say to you' is translated 'I tell you the truth' [NCV, NET, NIV, NLT], 'indeed, it is true that' [LN], 'I tell you' [TEV], 'I can assure you' [CEV], 'I can guarantee this truth' [GW], 'I solemnly declare to you' [NTC]. This particle makes a strong affirmation of what is being declared [LN]. It is an assertive particle that begins a solemn declaration' [BAGD]. The phrase 'truly I say to you' occurs at 3:28; 8:12; 9:1, 41; 10:15, 29; 11:23; 12:43; 13:30; 14:9, 18, 25, 30.

b. aorist act. subj. of ἀπόλλυμι (LN **57.67**) (BAGD 1.b. p. 95): 'to fail to get' [**LN**], 'to not obtain' [LN], 'to lose' [BAGD]. The phrase 'in no way will he fail to get his reward' is translated 'will by no means lose his reward' [AB2; ESV], 'will certainly not lose his reward' [NTC, WBC; GW, NIV], 'he shall not by any means lose his reward' [BECNT], 'he shall in no way lose his reward' [Lns], 'he will/shall not lose his reward' [AB1; KJV, NASB], 'will never lose his/the reward' [NET, NRSV], 'will certainly not go unrewarded' [BNTC; REB]. The statement 'in no way will he fail to get his reward' is a litotes in which an emphatic affirmation is made by denying its opposite, so some translate it as an emphatic assertion: 'will certainly receive a reward' [TEV], 'will surely get his reward' [CEV], 'will truly get his reward' [NCV], 'that person will surely be rewarded' [NLT]. This verb means to fail to obtain a valued object [LN]. There have been problems when translators have followed the English phrase 'will not lose his reward' and readers have understood it to mean that after a person receives the reward, he is guaranteed that he will never lose it by misplacing it [TH].

c. μισθός (LN 38.14) (BAGD 2.a. p. 523): 'reward' [BAGD, LN; all translations], 'recompense' [LN]. This noun denotes a recompense that is based upon what a person has earned and thus deserves [LN]. The basic meaning 'pay' is used figuratively of the recompense God gives for the moral quality of an action [BAGD].

QUESTION—Why is the clause ἀμὴν λέγω ὑμῖν ὅτι 'truly I say to you that' moved to the beginning of verse 41 by BNTC; NTC, ESV, GW, NCV, NET, NIV, NRSV, REB, TEV?

It is just for stylish reasons that this clause is moved from the position it occupies in the Greek text to the beginning of the verse [TH].

QUESTION—What is the reward and why would giving a cup of water to someone merit a reward?

Jesus does not specify what the reward is since rewards could depend on various things. A person may be rewarded with special blessings in this life or receive a measure of glory when he enters heaven [Lns]. The reward could be peace of mind in the present time or it could be a public acknowledgement by Christ when he returns [NTC]. The reward is best understood as God's approval [EBC]. The reward would not be given because the act of giving a disciple a cup of water merited it, but because that act shows their faith and obedience [Hb, NICNT]. When someone offers hospitality to the Twelve because they belong to Christ, it is evidence of that person's faith in the gospel and insures his entrance into God's kingdom [Gnd].

DISCOURSE UNIT—9:42-50 [Hb; CEV, ESV, GW, NIV, NRSV, TEV]. The topic is causing others to lose faith [GW], causing to sin [NIV], temptations to sin [CEV, ESV, NRSV, TEV], the seriousness of sin [Hb].

9:42 And whoever causes-to-stumble[a] one of-these little (ones), the ones believing in me, it-is better for-him if a-millstone[b] of-a-donkey is-hung-around[c] his neck and he-be-thrown[d] into the lake.

TEXT—Manuscripts reading πιστευόντων εἰς ἐμέ 'believing in me' are given a C rating by GNT to indicate that choosing it over a variant text was difficult. A variant reading is πιστευόντων 'believing' and it is followed by NASB, REB. Another variant reading is πίστιν ἐχόντων 'having faith'. Although some texts omit εἰς ἐμέ 'in me', the sense remains the same [Lns, NTC, PNTC, TRT] or it could mean to believe the gospel that Jesus and his disciples proclaimed [WBC].

LEXICON—a. aorist act. subj. of σκανδαλίζω (LN 88.304) (BAGD 1.a. p. 752): 'to cause to stumble' [BECNT, WBC; NASB], 'to cause to fall' [BNTC], 'to cause to fall into sin' [NLT], 'to cause to sin' [BAGD, LN, NTC; CEV, ESV, NCV, NET, NIV], 'to cause to lose faith' [GW], 'to cause to lose faith in me' [TEV], 'to put a stumbling block before' [NRSV], 'to cause the downfall of' [REB], 'to cause offense to' [AB1], 'to offend' [AB2; KJV], 'to entrap' [Lns]. This verb is a figurative extension of the verb 'to cause to stumble' and it means to cause someone to sin, with the probable implication of providing some special circumstances that contribute to such behavior [LN]. The sin may be a breach of the moral law, unbelief, or the acceptance of false teachings [BAGD]. This word occurs at 4:17; 6:3; 9:42, 43, 45, 47.

b. μύλος (LN 7.69) (BAGD 2. p. 529): 'millstone' [BAGD, LN]. The phrase μύλος ὀνικὸς 'a millstone of a donkey' is translated 'an ass's millstone' [Lns], 'a millstone' [AB2; KJV, REB], 'a great millstone' [WBC; ESV, NRSV], 'a huge millstone' [NET], 'a large millstone' [AB1, BECNT, BNTC; NIV, NLT, TEV], 'a heavy millstone' [NTC; NASB], 'a heavy stone' [CEV], 'a large stone' [GW, NCV]. This noun denotes either the upper or lower large, round, flat stone used in grinding grain [LN]. The 'millstone of a donkey' means 'a millstone *turned by* a donkey.' It is a large and heavy millstone that a donkey rotates by pulling it around a shaft' [LN 4.32]. It is the largest kind of millstone [Lns].

c. pres. mid./pass. (deponent = act.) indic. of περίκειμαι (LN 85.54) (BAGD 1.a. p. 648): 'to be hung around' [AB2, BAGD, BNTC, NTC, WBC; ESV, GW, KJV, NASB, NLT, NRSV], 'to be tied around' [CEV, NCV, NET, NIV, TEV], 'to be tied to' [AB1], 'to be placed around' [BAGD, BECNT, LN; REB], 'to be put around' [LN], 'to lie around' [Lns]. This verb means to lie around or be placed around something [LN].

d. perf. pass. indic. of βάλλω (LN 15.215) (BAGD 1.b. p. 131): 'to be thrown' [AB1, BAGD, BNTC, LN, NTC; CEV, ESV, GW, NET, NIV, NLT, NRSV, REB, TEV], 'to be cast' [AB2, BECNT, Lns, WBC; KJV,

NASB]. The clause 'and he be thrown into the lake' is translated 'and he be drowned in the sea' [NCV]. This verb means to throw an object [LN]. The perfect tense 'had been thrown' pictures the completed act [Gnd, Hb, Lns].

QUESTION—Who are the 'little ones' believing in Jesus?
1. This refers to children [EGT, Gnd, Lns, TH, WBC]. It refers to the little children represented by the little child in verses 36–37 [Gnd, TH]. The cause of stumbling probably is failing to treat a child as being important and significant [WBC]. Although children are clearly 'the little ones,' the description could also apply to other believers as well [Lns].
2. This refers to any believer [AB1, BECNT, BNTC, CGTC, Hb, ICC, My, NAC, NCBC, NICNT, NTC, Sw, Tay, TRT]. The little child who was still standing next to Jesus symbolizes or represents all believers who are lowly and modest [My], insignificant [AB1]. They are the humblest members of the congregation [Tay]. Although the 'little ones' refers to just children in verse 37, here it includes all followers of Jesus [EBC]. They are those who are immature, weak, and perhaps new believers [NAC]. The appositional addition 'the ones believing in me' indicates that Jesus is thinking not just of the children but of all weak and obscure believers [Hb]. Although some think this points directly back to the disciples' attempt to forbid the work of the unknown exorcist in verses 38–39, it is difficult to see how forbidding him to continue his ministry would of necessity caused him to stumble and lose his faith [BECNT].
3. Since these words were specifically directed toward the twelve disciples, the 'little ones' refer to other followers of Jesus who would be caused 'to sin' because they were pressured to stop acting in Jesus' name and thus end their discipleship [AB2, EBC, NICNT, NIGTC, PNTC]. This warns against inhibiting or destroying the faith of that independent exorcist mentioned in verse 38 or any other simple and ordinary disciple [PNTC]. This warning is the final comment in the section 38–42 [NICNT].

QUESTION—What is meant by causing them to stumble?
Many take this to mean 'to cause them to sin' [BAGD, LN, NTC; CEV, ESV, NCV, NET, NIV]. 'Cause to stumble' means to cause someone to sin, and that is what the disciples are liable to do to believing children if they don't strive to serve the children as well [Gnd]. It means to cause someone to stumble in his faith, to destroy his faith, to cause him to fall away from God [CGTC]. 'Cause to sin' is too specific for this verb [NIGTC, TH] because there are many other ways to wreck another's faith and discipleship [NIGTC]. This is about leading them to disbelief or to transgress God's moral laws [ESVfn].

QUESTION—How would the millstone be hung around the neck of the one who caused one of the little ones to stumble?
Such a millstone had a large hole in the middle of it, thus allowing it to be put over his neck [NTC], and maybe this is meant by those who translate it 'to be hung around his neck' [GW, KJV, NSB, NLT, NRSV] or 'to be placed

around his neck' [REB]. The picture described here is of a man's head stuck through the hole of the millstone so that it hangs around his neck like a collar [BECNT, Gnd, NIGTC, TRT]. Others think the millstone would be tied to the man by a cord around his neck [CEV, NCV, NET, NIV, TEV]. The weight attached to a person's neck would prevent his corpse from rising to the surface so that it could be recovered and buried. Not having a proper burial was a major concern to the people living at that time [Gnd].

QUESTION—Why would it be better for such a person to be drowned?

If such a person had the choice, it would be better for him to die before causing a little one to stumble [TH]. The punishment would be so severe for such a sin that it would have been better if this man had been drowned before he committed such a terrible sin [BECNT, BNTC, CBC, EBC, Gnd, Lns, NICNT, NIGTC]. The actual punishment is described in verse 43 [NIGTC].

DISCOURSE UNIT—9:43–50 [EBC, NICNT]. The topic is the demanding requirements of discipleship.

9:43 **And if your hand causes- you -to-stumble,**[a] **cut- it -off. It-is better for-you to-enter**[b] **into life maimed than having two hands to-go-away**[c] **into Gehenna,**[d] **into the inextinguishable**[e] **fire.**

LEXICON—a. pres. act. subj. of σκανδαλίζω (LN 88.304): 'to cause to stumble' [BECNT, WBC; NASB, NRSV], 'to cause to sin' [AB1, BAGD, LN; CEV, ESV, NCV, NET, NIV, NLT], 'to lure into sin' [NTC], 'to entrap' [Lns], 'to cause to lose one's faith' [GW], 'to make one lose his faith' [TEV], 'to cause one's downfall' [REB], 'to cause to fall' [BNTC], 'to offend' [AB2; KJV]. This is the same verb used in the preceding verse. The present tense σκανδαλίζῃ 'causes' emphasizes the continual nature of the temptations [BECNT].

b. aorist act. infin. of εἰσέρχομαι (LN 90.70) (BAGD 2.a. p. 233): 'to enter (into)' [BAGD], 'to begin to experience, to come into an experience, to attain' [LN]. The phrase κυλλὸν εἰσελθεῖν εἰς τὴν ζωὴν 'to enter/enter-into life maimed' [AB2, BECNT, BNTC, Lns, NTC, WBC; KJV, NIV, NRSV, REB] is also translated 'to enter/go into life crippled' [CEV, NET; similarly ESV, NASB], 'to enter life disabled' [GW], 'to enter eternal life with only one hand' [NLT], 'to enter life without a hand' [AB1, TEV], 'to lose part of your body and live forever' [NCV]. This verb means to begin to experience some event or state [LN].

c. aorist act. infin. of ἀπέρχομαι (LN 15.37): 'to go away, to depart, to leave' [LN]. The phrase ἀπελθεῖν εἰς τὴν γέενναν 'to go away to/into Gehenna' [AB2, Lns] is also translated 'to go into Gehenna' [BNTC], 'to go into hell' [BECNT; KJV, NASB, NCV, NET, NIV], 'to go to hell' [AB1, NTC; ESV, GW, NRSV, REB], 'to go off to hell' [TEV], 'to enter into hell' [WBC], 'to be thrown into (the fires of) hell' [CEV], 'to go into…hell with two hands' [NLT]. This verb means to move away from a reference point with an emphasis upon the departure ' [LN]. Since this

verb is probably functioning as a synonym of the verb βληθῆναι 'to be cast', it could also be translated 'to be cast or thrown into hell' as was done in verses 45 and 47 [TH].
d. γέεννα (LN 1.21) (BAGD. p. 153): 'Gehenna' [AB2, BNTC, LN, Lns], 'hell' [AB1, BECNT, LN, NTC, WBC; all versions]. This noun denotes the place of punishment for the dead [BAGD, LN]. It is the eschatological place of final punishment [TH], the final place of punishment of the lost [Hb].
e. ἄσβεστος (LN **14.71**) (BAGD 1. p. 114): 'inextinguishable' [BAGD], 'unquenchable' [LN]. The phrase εἰς τὸ πῦρ τὸ ἄσβεστον 'to the inextinguishable fire' is translated 'to/into the unquenchable fire/fires' [BECNT, BNTC, NTC, WBC; ESV, NASB, NET, NLT, NRSV, REB; similarly AB1, Lns], 'into the fire that never shall be quenched' [KJV], 'to the fire that never goes out' [TEV], 'to the fire that cannot be put out' [AB2, **LN**; GW], 'into the fires (of hell) that never go out' [CEV], 'where the fire never goes out' [NCV, NIV]. This adjective pertains to a fire that cannot be put out [LN].

QUESTION—How is this verse related to the previous verse?

Verse 42 is about causing someone else to stumble, while verses 43–48 are about causing one's own self to stumble [CGTC, Tay, WBC]. This section is about the self-discipline to prevent sinning and to avoid stumbling from the temptations that come from within a person [BECNT].

QUESTION—How can one's own hand cause him to sin?

The hand is symbolic of the things a person does. One's hand does not act independently of one's will, it is just the instrument for fulfilling the evil desires of a person [Hb].

QUESTION—What is meant by the command to cut off one's hand?

This command is in the form of a metaphoric hyperbole and it is not meant to be taken literally [ESVfn, NAC, PNTC]. It dramatically enhances the teaching that God is more important than even those things that seem most indispensable to us [PNTC]. The hand could serve as a metonymy for sins committed by the hand, such as theft or murder [ESVfn]. This is not a demand for physical self-mutilation [NICNT, Tay]. Cutting off the hand would not cut out the lustful will that caused the hand to act [Hb]. This is a demand for the cessation of the sinful activities associated with the hand since eternal life is at stake [EBC]. The person himself is responsible for the sins he commits and since his hands do not make him sin, the idea is 'If you sin by doing something with your hand, then cut that off.' This hyperbole means that a person must get rid of the source of sin in his heart or mind by repenting of the sin, turning to God, and living according to God's will [TRT]. The three hyperbolic sayings about getting rid of one's hand, foot, and eye are meant to warn people that there is no sin worth going to hell for [BECNT, NLTfn]. No matter how painful repentance might be, it is still better to follow Jesus than to perish in hell [BECNT].

QUESTION—What is meant by 'entering into life maimed'?

This continues the figurative language of being maimed by cutting off one's hand and makes the point that drastic action is necessary in order to avoid missing out on entering heaven [Hb]. Entering life means 'entering God's kingdom' and here God's kingdom is to be taken in its eschatological sense of the new heaven and earth with all of the glory pertaining to it [NTC]. This figurative language presumes that the dead will be resurrected with the same sort of bodily defects that afflicted them during their lifetime [AB2]. It is a thoroughly hyperbolic overstatement that would be recognized by those listening to Jesus. Resurrection to life will actually include full restoration of the body and there will be no lame or blind people going about in heaven [WBC].

QUESTION—What is the life that one would enter?

This refers to 'life with God' as indicted by the parallel phrase 'enter the kingdom of God' in verse 47 [NICNT]. It refers to entering the future life, that eternal blessed life with God [TH]. The contrast between entering life and going away into Gehenna presupposes that there will be a final judgment when God's decision concerning each person is irreversible and has eternal consequences [NICNT].

QUESTION—What is Gehenna?

'Gehenna' was the most common name for the place of eternal punishment in ancient Judaism and early Christianity [AB2]. Gehenna is the Greek transliteration of two Hebrew words that mean 'the valley of Hinnom.' It is a valley that goes along the southwest side of Jerusalem and had become the place where the city's garbage was dumped and burned. Since the fires were always burning, Gehenna became a symbol of the place of divine punishment [EBC, NAC]. Gehenna is a term used in apocalyptic literature for the final place of punishment of the ungodly [NIGTC]. Hades is another term that is also translated hell in the Gospels, but Hades refers to the place that receives the wicked during the intermediate state between death and the resurrection. 'Gehenna' is the place that receives both the body and soul of the wicked after the final judgment [NTC].

QUESTION—What is the inextinguishable fire of Gehenna?

The order of the Greek words, 'the fire, the inextinguishable (one)' stresses the character of that fire [Hb]. The fires of the refuse dumps of Gehenna were said to burn continuously [NIGTC]. Although the fires of the earthly valley of Gehenna could finally burn out, the fires of hell are unquenchable and therefore eternal [Hb, Lns]. Probably Mark added this final clause for the benefit of his Gentile readers who wouldn't know the background behind the Hebrew word 'Gehenna' [CGTC, Tay].

9:44 [[Omitted]]

TEXT—Manuscripts omitting this verse are given an A rating by GNT to indicate the omission was regarded to be certain. A variant reading is identical with verse 48 and it is followed by KJV and placed in brackets by

AB1 and NASB. Apparently a later scribe had inserted the words of verse 48 after verses 43 and 45 to achieve three parallel strophes [NETfn, NLTfn, NTC].

9:45 And if your foot causes- you -to-stumble, cut- it -off. It-is better for-you to-enter into life lame[a] than having two feet to-be-cast[b] into Gehenna.

TEXT—Manuscripts reading εἰς τὴν γέενναν 'into Gehenna' are given an A rating by GNT to indicate it was regarded to be certain. A variant reading is εἰς τὴν γέενναν, εἰς τὸ πῦρ τὸ ἄσβεστον 'into Gehenna, into the unquenchable fire' and it is followed by KJV. Another variant reading is εἰς τὴν γέενναν τοῦ πυρός 'into the Gehenna of fire'.

LEXICON—a. χωλός (LN 23.175) (BAGD p. 889): 'lame' [AB2, BECNT, LN, NTC, WBC; CEV, ESV, GW, NASB, NET, NRSV], 'crippled' [NIV, REB], 'a cripple' [BNTC], 'halt' [Lns; KJV], 'without a foot' [AB1; TEV], 'with only one foot' [NLT], 'to lose part of your body' [NCV]. This adjective describes a disability that involves the imperfect functioning of the lower limbs [LN].

b. aorist act. infin. of βάλλω (LN 15.215): 'to be cast' [AB2, BECNT, Lns, WBC; KJV, NASB, NASB], 'to be thrown' [AB1, BNTC, LN, NTC; CEV, ESV, NCV, NET, NIV, NLT, NRSV, REB, TEV]. This verb means 'to throw' [LN]. The similar warning in verse 43 'to go away into Gehenna' used a much milder verb than the verb βληθῆναι 'to be cast (into Gehenna)' used in this verse and verse 47 [AB1].

QUESTION—How can a person's own foot cause him to sin?

The foot could serve as a metonymy for going somewhere to commit a sinful act [ESVfn] or going to the improper places a person allows himself to go to [Hb].

9:46 [[Omitted]]

TEXT—Manuscripts omitting this verse are given an A rating by GNT to indicate the omission was regarded to be certain. A variant reading is identical with verse 48 and it is followed by KJV and placed in brackets by AB1; NASB.

9:47 And if your eye causes- you -to-stumble, take- it -out.[a] It-is better for-you to-enter into the kingdom of-God one-eyed[a] than having two eyes to-be-cast into Gehenna.

TEXT—Manuscripts reading βληθῆναι εἰς τὴν γέενναν 'to be cast into Gehenna' are followed by GNT which does not mention any variant reading. A variant reading is βληθῆνα εἰς τὴν γέενναν τοῦ πυρός 'to be cast into the Gehenna of fire' and it is followed by KJV.

LEXICON—a. aorist act. impera. of ἐκβάλλω (LN 15.220) (BAGD 3. p. 237): 'to take out' [BAGD; NCV, TEV], 'to remove' [BAGD], 'to tear out' [AB1; ESV, GW, NET, NRSV, REB], 'to pluck out' [BECNT, BNTC, Lns, NTC, WBC; KJV, NIV], 'to gouge out' [NLT], 'to cast out' [AB2],

'to throw out' [LN; NASB], 'to get rid of ' [CEV]. This verb means to throw something out of an object or area [LN].
   b. μονόφθαλμος (LN 24.39) (BAGD p. 528): 'one-eyed' [AB2, BAGD, LN, Lns], 'with one eye' [AB1, BECNT, BNTC, NTC, WBC; CEV, ESV, GW, KJV, NASB, NET, NIV, NRSV, REB], 'with only one eye' [NCV, NLT, TEV]. This adjective describes someone as having only one eye with which he can see [LN].
QUESTION—How can one's own eye cause him to sin?
   The eye may be symbolic of the lusts that are aroused by the sight of forbidden things [Hb, Sw]. The eye could serve as a metonymy for coveting, lust, or adultery [ESVfn].
QUESTION—What is the kingdom that one would enter?
   This is equivalent to the phrase 'entering into life' in verses 43 and 45 [BNTC, Hb, ICC, WBC]. Since entering *life* and entering *the kingdom of God* are contrasted with being cast into Gehenna, this concerns a future event [EBC, Hb, ICC, My, NICNT, NIGTC, NTC, WBC]. This will take place at the final judgment [NICNT]. It appears to refer not simply to God's kingly rule, but also to some kind of territory in which his rule is exercised [AB1].

9:48 **Where their worm^a does- not -die and the fire is- not -extinguished.^b**

LEXICON—a. σκώληξ (LN 4.57) (BAGD p. 758): 'worm' [BAGD, LN], 'maggot' [LN]. The phrase 'their worm does not die' [BECNT, NTC, WBC; ESV, KJV, NASB, NIV] is also translated 'their worm never dies' [BNTC; NET, NRSV], 'their/the worm does not die' [AB2, Lns; NCV], 'the devouring worm never dies' [AB1; REB]. Some use the plural form: 'the worms never die' [CEV], 'the maggots never die' [NLT], 'worms that eat the body never die' [GW], 'the worms that eat them never die' [TEV]. The noun denotes a type of maggot that feeds on refuse [LN].
   b. pres. pass. indic. of σβέννυμι (LN 14.70) (BAGD 1. p. 745): 'to be extinguished, to be put out' [BAGD, LN]. The clause 'the fire is not extinguished' [BECNT] is also translated 'the fire is not quenched' [Lns, NTC, WBC; ESV, KJV, NASB, NIV], 'the fire is never quenched' [NET, NRSV, REB], 'the fire never stops burning' [CEV], 'the fire never goes out' [BNTC; NLT], 'the fire is never put out' [GW, NCV, similarly AB1, AB2], 'the fire that burns them is never put out' [TEV]. This verb means to cause a fire to be extinguished [LN].
QUESTION—Where is this verse found in the OT?
   This is a free quotation from Isaiah 66:24 where it speaks of the dead bodies of those who rebelled against God lying there where 'their worm will not die, and their fire will not be quenched, and they will be an abhorrence to all mankind' [TH].
QUESTION—What is meant by 'their worm never dying'?
   The word 'their' certainly does not mean that the rotting corpses possess the worms. Nor does the singular form 'worm' mean that a single worm is

feeding on all of the dead bodies. The word worm is used generically to designate the kind of worms that will feed on the flesh of the decaying bodies [TH]. The worm and also the fire are symbols of destruction [NAC]. Even though the picture given in Isaiah provides an awful deterrence to committing sin, it is not clear how the two methods of destruction relate to each other or what the function of the worm is [NIGTC].

QUESTION—What is implied by their worm never dying and the fire never being extinguished?

These conditions refer to the never-ending operation of the two destructive forces in Gehenna. The worm perhaps symbolizes some destructive force and the fire may symbolize a punitive force applied from without [Hb]. The fire implies that the torment will be external while the worm implies that it will also be internal [Lns, NTC]. This pictures the punishment in hell as being eternal [AB1, BECNT, CGTC, Hb, Lns, NICNT, NLTfn, NTC]. This verse is the strongest possible warning against rebellion against God [PNTC].

9:49 Because everyone will-be-salted^a with-fire.

TEXT—Manuscripts reading πᾶς γὰρ πυρὶ ἁλισθήσεται 'because everyone will be salted with fire' are given a B rating by GNT to indicate it was regarded to be almost certain. A variant reading is πᾶς γὰρ πυρὶ ἁλισθήσεται καὶ πᾶσα θυσία ἁλὶ ἁλισθήσεται 'for everyone will be salted with fire and every sacrifice will be salted with salt' and it is followed by KJV, TEV. Another variant reading is πᾶσα γὰρ θυσία ἁλὶ ἁλισθήσεται 'for every sacrifice will be salted with salt'.

LEXICON—a. fut. pass. indic. of ἁλίζω (LN 5.28) (BAGD p. 37): 'to apply salt to something, to restore the flavor to salt' [LN]. The phrase πυρὶ ἁλισθήσεται 'will be salted' [AB1, AB2, BECNT, BNTC, WBC; ESV, GW, NASB, NCV, NET, NIV, NRSV, REB] is also translated 'shall be salted' [Lns, NTC; KJV], 'must be salted' [CEV], 'will be tested' [NLT], 'will be purified' [TEV]. This verb means to cause something to taste salty [LN].

QUESTION—What relationship is indicated by the conjunction γάρ 'because'?

This indicates the reason for obeying the command in verses 43–48 [Gnd]. This conjunction should be taken in connection with the whole course of thought in verses 43–48 [EGT, Hb]. Since the only connection with verse 48 is the presence of the word 'fire' and the only connection with verse 50 is the presence of the word salt, verse 49 should be independently interpreted [CGTC].

QUESTION—What does this verse mean?

This is one of the most difficult verses in Mark [EBC] or even in the whole New Testament [ICC]. It is a mixed metaphor without any explanation [NIGTC]. It is not clear what this verse means [AB2, BECNT, BNTC, TH]. Many mention the fact there are many different explanations given for this verse [AB1, EGT, EBC, Lns, NCBC, NETfn, NTC, PNTC, TH, WBC].

Because salt is a purifying element and fire is a destroying element, this means that everyone will be purified either by a self-inflicted loss of parts to preserve the whole or by the destroying fires of Gehenna [ICC]. Because salting is inevitable and indispensable, everyone will be salted by the fire of Gehenna or the fire of severe self-discipline [EGT]. The alternative to the fire which consumes in verse 48 is the salt of the covenant which is the divine fire which purifies, preserves, and consummates a sacrifice [Sw]. With 'fire' representing judgment and everyone being salted indiscriminately, this verse means that the fire of judgment will fall on everyone in order that believers will pass the test of fire and the apostates will suffer the judgment of both eternal fire and decay as described in the preceding verse [Gnd]. If this verse relates to the preceding verse about hell, it could mean 'God will rain fire on everyone in hell like someone sprinkling salt on food as their punishment.' The more probable interpretation is that it relates back to verses 43–48 where everyone is 'salted with fire' to test them and it means that 'God will test everyone with many experiences that are painful like fire is painful' [TRT]. This verse refers to the purifying effect of persecution where salt and fire both symbolize purification and it has nothing to do with the fire of the preceding verse [NAC]. The disciples would be tried and purified by the fires of persecution [NTC, Tay], and once the fiery trial has separated the good people from the bad people, it will then destroy anything that is bad in the believers' hearts and lives so that they can be a preservative force like salt to everything around them [NTC]. Salt refers to the sacrificial salt which purifies a sacrifice, and the fire is either the Holy Spirit or the trials and persecutions that are to be endured by the disciples who sacrifice themselves to God [EBC]. Just as the Jewish sacrifices were salted, the disciples must be seasoned with salt through the fiery trials that will purge everything contrary to God's will [NICNT]. Just like salt was necessary for Temple sacrifices, the fires of trials and persecution are necessary in the lives of the disciples who present themselves as sacrifices to God [CGTC]. The fire of testing has a purifying effect [NLTfn]. Believers are pictured as a sacrifice to God, and salt represents their purification by the fire of suffering and hardship [ESVfn]. All translations except NLT and TEV translate this verse quite literally (with some leaving out the initial conjunction γάρ 'because/for' [AB1; CEV, GW, NCV, NET, NIV, REB, TEV]. The two exceptions are: 'For everyone will be tested with fire' [NLT], 'Everyone will be purified by fire as a sacrifice is purified by salt' [TEV].

9:50 **Salt (is) good.[a] But if the salt becomes unsalty,[b] with what will-you-season[c] it?**

LEXICON—a. καλός (LN 65.22) (BAGD 2.a. p. 400): 'good' [BAGD, LN; all translations except Lns], 'excellent' [Lns], 'useful' [BAGD]. The clause 'salt is good' is translated 'salt is good for seasoning' [NLT]. This adjective 'good' pertains to having acceptable characteristics or to functioning in an agreeable manner [LN]. It refers to the quality of being

in accordance with its purpose [BAGD]. Salt preserves and imparts flavor [NTC]. Here 'good' means valuable, good for something, and useful [TH].
  b. ἄναλος (LN 5.27) (BAGD p. 57): 'without salt' [BAGD, LN], 'saltless' [LN], 'deprived of its salt content' [BAGD]. The clause 'if the salt becomes unsalty' [AB2; NASB] is also translated 'if the salt should/has become saltless [BECNT, LN, WBC; similarly Lns], 'if the salt loses/has-lost its saltiness/saltness' [AB1, NTC; ESV, NET, NIV, NRSV, REB, TEV; similarly KJV], 'if the salt no longer tastes like salt' [LN; CEV], 'if salt loses its salty taste' [NCV], 'if salt loses its taste' [BNTC; GW], 'if it loses its flavor' [NLT]. This adjective pertains to a lack of salt [LN]. Because the process of producing salt by natural evaporation along the shores of the Dead Sea did not produce pure salt, the non-salt residue could decompose due to dampness and nullify the effect of the remaining salt [BAGD].
  c. fut. act. indic. of ἀρτύω (LN 46.14) (BAGD p. 111): 'to season' [BAGD, LN]; 'to salt' [BAGD]. The clause 'with what will you season it' [BECNT, BNTC, Lns] is also translated 'how do/can you make it salty again' [NLT, TEV], 'with what will you make it salty again' [NASB], 'what will you salt it with' [AB2], 'with what will you season it' [AB1, BNTC, WBC; similarly KJV], 'how can/will you season it' [NRSV, REB], 'how will/can you make it salty again' [ESV, NET, NIV], 'how can it be made salty again' [CEV], 'how will you restore its flavor?' [NTC; GW]. This question is translated as a statement: 'you cannot make it salty again' [NCV]. This verb means to add condiments to food [LN]. It refers to restoring its saltness, its capacity to season, and its distinguishing characteristic as salt [TH].
QUESTION—Is it possible for salt to become unsalty?
  1. Some explain how 'salt' could become unsalty [BAGD, BNTC, Gnd, Hb, NAC, NCBC, NICNT, NIGTC, NTC]. The course salt produced by evaporation at the Dead Sea was not pure, and might decompose to leave a useless residue [BAGD, NICNT]. The salt found around the Dead Sea could acquire a stale or alkaline taste [Hb].
  2. Others simply assume this condition is part of the illustration [AB2, NETfn, NICNT]. Scientific explanations are not necessary to understand the message [AB2]. Salt typifies that quality which is the distinctive mark of the disciple that would make him worthless if it is lost, so it can only refer to his allegiance to Jesus and the gospel [NICNT].
QUESTION—What kind of question is 'with what will you season it?'
  It is a rhetorical question that points out the impossibility of restoring the salty effect [Gnd, Hb, NTC].

Have[a] salt in yourselves and be-at-peace[b] with one-another.
LEXICON—a. pres. act. impera. of ἔχω (LN 57.1): 'to have, to own, to possess' [LN]. The clause 'have salt in yourselves' [AB1, AB2, BECNT, BNTC,

WBC; ESV, KJV, NASB, NET, NIV, NRSV] is also translated 'have salt in your own selves' [Lns], 'have salt within yourselves/you' [NTC; GW, REB], 'have salt among you' [CEV], 'be full of salt' [NCV], 'you must have the qualities of salt among yourselves' [NLT], 'have the salt of friendship among yourselves' [TEV]. This verb means to have or possess objects or property in the sense of having control over the use of such objects [LN]. The present imperatives denote a continuing duty [Hb].

b. pres. act. impera. of εἰρηνεύω (LN 88.102) (BAGD 2.b. p. 227): 'to behave peacefully' [LN], 'to live in peace' [BAGD, LN], 'to be at peace, to keep the peace' [BAGD]. The command 'and be at peace with one another' [AB1, BECNT, BNTC, NTC, WBC; ESV, NASB, NRSV, REB] is also translated 'be at peace with each other' [AB2, Lns; NET, NIV], 'have peace with each other' [NCV], 'have peace one with another' [KJV], 'live in peace with one another' [GW, TEV], 'live at/in peace with each other' [CEV, NLT]. This verb means to live in peace with others [LN].

QUESTION—What is meant by the command 'Have salt in yourselves'?

The metaphor of salt has no fixed meaning in the NT and it would be unwise to be too specific in decoding its significance in this sequence of sayings [NIGTC]. It is the salt of a true Christian character [Hb]. Salt is recognized by its taste and the lives of the disciples should enable people to recognize that they are followers of Jesus. If not, they will be as useless as salt that is not salt at all [BNTC]. In the same way salt is recognized by its taste, the followers of Jesus should be recognized by their lifestyles. If they are not, they are just as useless as salt that no longer tastes like salt [BECNT]. Salt symbolizes the attributes of being wise, pure, and gracious [CBC, WBC]. This salt has the qualities that cause them to be at peace with one another [BECNT]. The salt in this verse refers to the quality of allegiance to Jesus and the gospel [NICNT]. They must keep the demanding marks of discipleship [NICNT], have the characters of true disciples [BECNT], and never lose their devotion and spirit of self-sacrifice to Jesus and his gospel [EBC]. It interprets the preceding command and means to hold fast to a peace *in* themselves that will secure peace *among* themselves [AB1]. They must be friendly and agreeable in social relations [TH], behaving in ways that lead to peace [CBC].

QUESTION—What is meant by the command 'and be at peace with one another'?

The connecting conjunction 'and' indicates that this second duty follows as a result of the first [Hb, WBC]. This command interprets the preceding general command by making it specific [BECNT, Gnd]. Instead of taking this final clause as a second command, some mention that it is possible to take it as a result clause: 'Have salt in yourselves, and then you will be at peace with one another' [AB1] or it could be explanatory, 'that is, live in peace with one another' [TRT]. Having these attributes will result in being at peace with one another [CBC, WBC].

DISCOURSE UNIT—10:1–52 [Hb, PNTC; NLT]. The topic is the journey to Jerusalem [Hb], on the way to Jerusalem [NLT], on the way through Judea [PNTC].

DISCOURSE UNIT—10:1–31 [NIGTC]. The topic is the revolutionary values of the kingdom of God.

DISCOURSE UNIT—10:1–12 [CBC, EBC, NICNT; CEV, ESV, GW, NASB, NCV, NET, NIV, NLT, NRSV, TEV]. The topic is a discussion about divorce and marriage [NLT], Jesus teaches about divorce [NCV, TEV], Jesus' teaching about divorce [NASB], Jesus' remarks on divorce [CBC], teaching about divorce [EBC; CEV, ESV, NRSV], the question of divorce [NICNT], a discussion about divorce [GW], divorce [NET, NIV].

DISCOURSE UNIT—10:1 [Hb; NLT]. The topic is the departure from Galilee [Hb], Jesus leaves Galilee [NLT].

10:1 And having-left[a] from-there he-comes into the regions[b] of-Judea and the-other-side-of[c] the Jordan, and crowds come-together[d] to him again, and as he-was-accustomed[e] he-was- again -teaching them.

TEXT—Manuscripts reading καὶ πέραν 'and the other side' are given a C rating by GNT to indicate that choosing it over a variant text was difficult. A variant reading is διὰ τοῦ πέραν 'by the other side' and it is followed by KJV. Another variant reading is πέραν 'the other side'.

LEXICON—a. aorist act. participle of ἀνίσταμαι, ἀνίστημι (LN 15.36, 17.6) (BAGD 2.d. p. 70): 'to leave' [AB1, BNTC, LN (15.36); all versions except ESV, KJV], 'to set out' [BAGD], 'to depart' [LN (15.36), NTC], 'to go away from' [LN (15.36)], 'to arise' [Lns, WBC; ESV, KJV], 'to rise' [AB2, BAGD, BECNT], 'to rise up' [BECNT], 'to get up' [NASB], 'to stand up' [LN (17.6)], 'to get ready' [BAGD]. This verb means to assume a standing position [LN (17.6)] or to move away from a reference point [LN (15.36)]. The verb's basic meaning 'to rise up' has been weakened to indicate the beginning of an action that is expressed by another verb [BAGD]. It means that he was 'leaving that place' [TH].

b. ὅριον (LN 1.79) (BAGD p. 581): 'region' [BAGD, LN], 'boundary' [BAGD], 'territory, land, district' [LN]. The phrase πέραν τοῦ Ἰορδάνου 'Other Side of the Jordan' had become a proper name for the territory that was located east of the Jordan River [Hb] and some translations apparently understand the conjunction καί 'and' to be connecting two separate regions: 'he came into the regions of Judaea and Transjordan' [REB], 'he comes to the regions of Judea and Across the Jordan' [BECNT], 'he came into the districts of Judea and the Far Side of Jordan' [BNTC], 'he comes to the boundaries of Judea and Beyond the Jordan' [Lns]. The noun ὅριον 'region' always occurs as a plural noun even when it refers to one particular region at 5:17; 7:24, 31, and here some translations use the singular form 'region', apparently referring only to the region of Judea: 'region' [AB1, AB2, NTC, WBC; ESV, NASB,

NET, NIV, NRSV], 'province' [TEV], 'area' [NCV], 'territory' [GW]. This noun can denote either a 'region' or some 'regions'. Normally it refers to a geographical center or ethnic group [LN]. It means 'boundary' and always occurs in the plural form to denote a region or district [BAGD].

c. πέραν (LN 83.43) (BAGD 2c. p. 644): 'the other side, opposite, across from' [LN], 'on the other side' [BAGD, LN]. The phrase πέραν τοῦ Ἰορδάνου 'the other side of the Jordan River' [CEV] is also translated 'beyond the Jordan/Jordan-River' [Lns, NTC; ESV, NASB, NET, NRSV], 'across the Jordan/Jordan-River' [BECNT; NCV, NIV], 'across from the Jordan' [WBC], 'along the other side of the Jordan River' [GW], 'the far side of Jordan' [BNTC; similarly KJV], 'the area east of the Jordan River' [NLT], 'Transjordan' [AB1, AB2; REB]. The phrase 'and the other side of the Jordan' is translated 'and crossed the Jordan River' [TEV]. This adjective refers to a position opposite another position with something intervening [LN]. The phrase 'the other side of the Jordan' functioned as the name for the territory on the other (eastern) side of the Jordan River, and that territory was also known as Perea [BAGD, TH].

d. pres. mid./pass. (deponent = act.) indic. of συμπορεύομαι (LN 15.123) (BAGD 2 p. 780): 'to come together' [BAGD, LN], 'to gather together' [LN]. The phrase συμπορεύονται ὄχλοι πρὸς αὐτόν 'crowds come-together to him' is translated 'crowds came to him' [NCV], 'large crowds came to him' [CEV], 'crowds gathered to him' [ESV, NET, REB; similarly BECNT, WBC], 'crowds gathered around him' [GW, NASB, NLT; similarly NRSV], 'crowds collected round him' [BNTC], 'crowds of people came to him' [NIV], 'crowds came flocking to him' [TEV], 'crowds were flocking toward him' [NTC], 'crowds came together to him' [AB2], 'a crowd was gathered around him' [AB1], 'there come together multitudes unto him' [Lns], 'people resort unto him' [KJV]. This verb refers to the movement of two or more objects to the same location [LN].

e. pluperfect. act. indic. of εἴωθα (LN 41.26) (BAGD p. 234): 'to be accustomed' [BAGD], 'to be in the habit of, to carry out a custom' [LN]. The phrase ὡς εἰώθει 'as he was accustomed' [BECNT] is also translated 'as was his custom' [AB2, Lns, WBC; ESV, NET, NIV, NRSV; similarly NTC], 'as was his practice' [REB], 'according to his custom' [NASB], 'as usual' [BNTC; CEV, NLT], 'as he always did' [AB1; TEV], 'as he usually did' [GW, NCV], 'as he was wont' [KJV]. This verb means to carry out a custom or tradition [LN].

QUESTION—Where did Jesus start from?

Jesus had started from Capernaum [Gnd, Hb, ICC, Lns, NTC, PNTC, Sw], leaving the house in Capernaum mentioned in 9:33 [BECNT, Gnd, NAC, NICNT, NIGTC, WBC].

QUESTION—What was the route that Jesus took to teach the people on the other side of the Jordan River?

The account of the route is obscure [BNTC], and a matter of conjecture [NIGTC]. The reason Judea is mentioned first is because the Passion events would be taking place there [Gnd]. Before Jesus continued on to Jerusalem, he wanted to complete his ministry to the Jewish regions to the south of Galilee [PNTC]. This verse is about his journey from Galilee to a public teaching ministry in Judea and Perea [CGTC]. Starting at Capernaum on the northwest shore of the Lake of Galilee, Jesus probably traveled south along the lake to Samaria. He passed through Samaria and partway through Judea. Then he crossed to the east side of the Jordan River to enter the region of Perea [EBC, NIVfn, NICNT]. Jesus resumed his public ministry as he was traveling through Judea and Perea [NICNT].

QUESTION—What is indicated by the use of the plural noun 'crowds' in the statement 'crowds come together to him'?

It is not clear in the Greek text whether the use of the plural form 'crowds' refers to the different crowds that Jesus met as he was traveling about or emphasizes the large size of the crowd that had come together [Gnd, TH]. It means that when he arrived in the different places a crowd would soon gather [EGT, Hb, NICNT, NTC]. Huge crowds of people were traveling together to Jerusalem for the Passover [Gnd]. It doesn't mean that more than one crowd gathered at the same time [TRT].

DISCOURSE UNIT—10:2–12 [Hb; NLT]. The topic is the teaching concerning divorce [Hb], Jesus' teaching about divorce and marriage [NLT].

10:2 **And having-approached**[a] **(some) Pharisees asked him if it-is-lawful**[b] **for- a-husband to-divorce**[c] **(his) wife, testing**[d] **him.**

TEXT—Manuscripts reading καὶ προσελθόντες Φαρισαῖοι ἐπηρώτων 'and having approached, some Pharisees asked him' are followed by GNT, which does not mention any variant reading. A variant reading is καὶ ἐπηρώτων 'and they were asking' [REB]. Other variant readings are καὶ προσελθόντες οἱ Φαρισαῖοι ἐπηρώτων 'and the Pharisees having come to (him) they were asking', οσελθόντες οἱ Φαρισαῖοι ἐπηρώτων 'and the Pharisees having come to (him) they were asking', and also οἱ δὲ Φαρισαῖοι προσελθόντες ἐπηρώτων 'and the Pharisees having come to (him) they were asking'.

LEXICON—a. aorist act. participle of προσέρχομαι (LN 15.77): 'to approach' [BNTC, WBC; LN], 'to move toward, to come near' [LN], 'to come up to' [BECNT, NTC; CEV, ESV, NASB], 'to come' [AB1, Lns; GW, KJV, NCV, NET, NIV, NLT, NRSV, TEV], 'to come forward' [AB2], not explicit [REB]. This verb means to move toward a reference point [LN]. Some of the members of the Pharisee party in Perea came forward from the crowd [Hb].

b. pres. act. indic. of ἔξεστι (LN 71.1) (BAGD 2. p. 275): 'if it is/was lawful' [BECNT, WBC], 'whether it is/was lawful' [Lns; NASB], 'to be permitted' [BAGD], 'to be possible' [BAGD, LN]. The clause 'if it is lawful' is translated 'if it was permissible' [AB2], 'if it was right' [CEV]. Some translate this as a direct question: 'Is it lawful' [AB1, BNTC, NTC; ESV, KJV, NET, NIV, NRSV, REB], 'Does our Law allow' [TEV], 'Is it right' [NCV], 'Can (a husband divorce his wife?)' [GW], 'Should a man be allowed (to divorce his wife?)' [NLT]. This verb means to mark an event as being possible in a highly generic sense [LN].

c. aorist act. infin. of ἀπολύω (LN 34.78) (BAGD 2.a. p. 96): 'to divorce' [BAGD, LN; all translations except Lns; KJV], 'to release' [Lns], 'to put away' [KJV]. This verb means to dissolve the marriage bond [LN].

d. pres. act. participle of πειράζω (LN 27.31, 27.46) (BAGD 2.c. p. 640): 'to test' [AB1, AB2, BECNT, BNTC, WBC; CEV, ESV, GW, NASB, NET, NIV, NRSV, REB], 'to put to the test' [BAGD], 'to trap' [TEV], 'to try to trap' [LN; NLT], 'to attempt to catch in a mistake' [LN], 'to trick' [NCV], 'to tempt' [Lns, NTC; KJV]. This verb means to try to learn the nature or character of someone by submitting him to a thorough and extensive testing [LN (27.46)] or to obtain information to be used against a person by trying to cause him to make a mistake [LN (27.31)]. It means 'to put to the test' and is used in the sense of testing someone in order to bring out something to be used against him. It is not used in the sense of enticing someone to sin [BAGD]. This word occurs at 1:13; 8:11; 10:2; 12:15.

QUESTION—What is the function of the added prepositional phrase πειράζοντες αὐτόν 'testing him'?

Most take this participle to be expressing purpose, 'in order to test him' [PNTC, TH]. They came to question Jesus in order to test him, not to obtain guidance [AB1, BECNT, Hb, LN; ESV, GW, NCV, NLT, NRSV, REB, TEV]. Their question was hostile in nature [BECNT]. It was an attempt to catch Jesus in their trap where any answer would get him into serious difficulties that would discredit him [NAC, NTC].

QUESTION—What was this testing about?

They wanted to test Jesus' claim that he was a Rabbi by presenting one of their puzzles [ICC, NAC, WBC]. They wanted to see where he stood on the much disputed matter of divorce. Either a 'yes' or a 'no' answer would be sure to arouse opposition by some part of the crowd [Hb]. Even though there were provisions for divorce in Deuteronomy 24:1 and most Jews thought divorce should be allowed, there were strong differences of opinion about the permitted grounds for divorce [EBC, NAC, NICNT, NTC]. It was an attempt to bring Jesus' teachings into collision with the Mosaic law [EGT]. By 'tempting' him to get into a party dispute, they thought they would hurt his ministry [Lns].

10:3 And answering he said to-them, "What (did) Moses command[a] you?"

LEXICON—a. aorist mid. (deponent = act.) indic. of ἐντέλλομαι, ἐντέλλω (LN 33.329) (BAGD p. 268): 'to command' [AB1, AB2, BAGD, BECNT,

BNTC, LN, Lns, NTC, WBC; ESV, KJV, NASB, NET, NIV, NRSV, REB], 'to order, to give orders' [BAGD]. The question is translated 'What did Moses command you to do?' [NCV], 'What command did Moses give you?' [GW], 'What law did Moses give you?' [TEV], 'What does the Law of Moses say about that?' [CEV], 'What did Moses say in the law about divorce?' [NLT]. This verb means to give definite orders with authority or official sanction [LN]. Because these Pharisees were not alive during the time of Moses, the question means 'What commandment did Moses give you?' [TH].

QUESTION—How did Jesus answer the question proposed by the Pharisees?

Jesus countered their question with a question of his own. Since Moses was their authority, he asked them what Moses had said about the matter of divorce [EBC]. By asking what Moses had 'commanded', he evidently was asking for some positive instruction found in the Pentateuch about the subject of divorce [BECNT, NICNT], possibly the instruction in Genesis 2:24 where it says, 'For this reason a man shall leave his father and his mother, and be joined to his wife; and they shall become one flesh' (ESV) [NICNT].

10:4 And they-said, "Moses permitted[a] (a husband) to-write a-certificate[b] of-divorce and divorce[c] (his wife)."

LEXICON—a. aorist act. indic. ἐπιτρέπω (LN 13.138) (BAGD 1. p. 303): 'to permit' [AB1, BAGD, BECNT, BNTC, LN, Lns, WBC; NASB, NET, NIV, NLT, REB], 'to allow' [BAGD, LN, NTC; CEV, ESV, GW, NCV, NRSV], 'to give permission' [AB2; TEV], 'to let' [LN], 'to suffer' [KJV]. This verb means to allow someone to do something [LN].

b. βιβλίον (LN **33.38**) (BAGD 2. p. 141): 'certificate, written statement, notice, record' [LN], 'document' [BAGD]. The genitive phrase βιβλίον ἀποστασίου 'a certificate of divorce' [NTC; ESV, NASB, NIV; similarly Lns] is also translated 'a divorce notice' [BAGD, **LN**; TEV], 'divorce papers' [AB1; CEV, NCV], 'a certificate of annulment' [BNTC], 'a bill of divorce' [WBC; similarly KJV], 'a bill of relinquishment' [AB2], 'a certificate of dismissal' [BECNT; NET, NRSV, REB], 'a written notice of divorce' [NLT], 'a written notice to divorce her' [GW]. This noun denotes a relatively short statement in written form [LN].

c. aorist act. infin. of ἀπολύω (LN 34.78) (BAGD 2.a. p. 96): 'to divorce' [AB2, BAGD, BECNT, BNTC, LN; NET, NRSV, REB], 'to release' [Lns, WBC], 'to send away' [BAGD; CEV, ESV, NASB, NCV, NIV, NLT, TEV], 'to put away' [KJV], not explicit [GW]. This verb means to dissolve the marriage bond [LN].

QUESTION—Why did the Pharisees use the word ἐπιτρέπω 'permit' instead of the word ἐντέλλω 'command' that Jesus had used?

Since there is no command in the Pentateuch telling when a man should divorce his wife, the Pharisees could only refer to Deuteronomy 24:1–4 where divorce was permitted [BNTC, CGTC, Lns, PNTC, TH, WBC]. That passage regulates what happens after a divorce has taken place [CBC, NIGTC, Tay]. Even to call this a 'permission' to divorce is an inference from the fact that the divorce is discussed in Scripture without expressing disapproval [NIGTC]. No legal proceedings were necessary for a husband to divorce his wife [Lns]. However, this law said that a Jewish husband had to write a divorce certificate in the presence of a witness, sign it, and then present it to his wife, saying "Here is your bill of divorce" [EBC]. The certificate of divorce that must be given to the wife authenticated her release from the marriage contract and gave her the right to remarry [Hb, NICNT]. It was a means of protection for the woman who had been repudiated by her husband [AB1, BNTC, CGTC, Hb, NICNT, NTC].

10:5 And Jesus said to-them, "Because (of) your hard-heartedness[a] he-wrote you this command.[b] 10:6 But from[c] (the) beginning of-creation he-made[d] them male and female.

TEXT—Manuscripts reading ἐποίησεν αὐτούς 'he made them' are given a B rating by GNT to indicate it was regarded to be almost certain. Variant readings are ἐποίησεν θεό 'God made' and ἐποίησεν αὐτούς ὁ θεός 'God made them'.

LEXICON—a. σκληροκαρδία (LN 88.224) (BAGD p. 756): 'hardness of heart, stubbornness, coldness, obstinacy' [BAGD], 'being stubborn, being completely unyielding' [LN]. The phrase τὴν σκληροκαρδίαν ὑμῶν 'your hard-heartedness' [AB2] is also translated 'the hardness of your hearts/heart' [BNTC; KJV], 'your hardness of heart' [Lns, NTC, WBC; ESV, NASB, NRSV], 'your hard heart/hearts' [BECNT; NET], 'your hearts were hard' [NIV], 'your obduracy' [AB1], 'your stubbornness' [REB], 'you were so stubborn' [NCV], 'you are so hard to teach' [TEV], 'you are so heartless' [CEV; similarly GW], '(only as a concession to) your hard hearts' [NLT]. The idiom 'uncircumcised in heart' means to be obdurate and obstinate [LN]. The singular 'heart' in this compound word is a collective singular that refers to 'hearts' [NETfn]. They were not willing to accept God's will in the matter [TH]. The essence of this particular hardness is their stubborn rebellion against the creation ordinance of marriage given in Genesis 1:27 and 2:24 [NICNT].

b. ἐντολή (LN 33.330) (BAGD 2.a.γ. p. 269): 'command' [BAGD; GW, NCV], 'commandment' [AB1, AB2, BAGD, BECNT, BNTC, LN, NTC, WBC; ESV, NASB, NET, NLT, NRSV], 'order' [BAGD, LN], 'law' [CEV, NIV, TEV], 'rule' [REB], 'precept' [KJV], 'bidding' [Lns]. This noun denotes that which is authoritatively commanded [LN]. Moses did not write this commandment directly to them, but wrote it for their benefit [TH].

c. ἀπό (LN 67.131): 'from, since' [LN]. The phrase ἀπὸ ἀρχῆς κτίσεως 'from the beginning of creation' [AB2, BECNT, BNTC, NTC, WBC; ESV, NASB, NET, NLT, NRSV; similarly KJV] is also translated 'from creation's beginning' [Lns], 'at the beginning of creation' [NIV], 'in the beginning, at the creation' [AB1; GW, REB], 'in the beginning, at the time of creation' [TEV], 'in the beginning' [CEV], 'when God made the world' [NCV]. This preposition marks the extent of time from a point in the past [LN].

   d. aorist act. indic. of ποιέω (LN 42.29) (BAGD I.1.a.β. p. 681): 'to make' [BAGD, LN; all translations], 'to create' [BAGD], 'to fashion' [LN]. This verb means to produce something new with materials that already existed. This contrasts with the verb κτίζω 'to create from nothing' [LN]. Jesus was quoting the last clause of Genesis 1:27 where it says 'male and female he created them' [AB2, Hb, TH]. The Septuagint Greek translation of 'he created them' in that verse is ἐποίησεν αὐτούς 'he made them', which is the same phrase used here [AB2, Hb].

QUESTION—Why did Jesus again use the word ἐντέλλω 'command' instead of the word ἐπιτρέπω 'permit' that the Pharisees had used?

   Jesus corrects their use of 'permission' by calling it a command [Gnd]. Moses had not written a command that a man should divorce his wife, but he had written the command about the restrictions that are to accompany a divorce [Hb]. Their hardheartedness had led them into divorce and that was why Moses had to legislate for such a situation that was not part of God's purpose [NIGTC]. 'This command' refers to the long sentence in Deut. 24:1-4, which is the only relevant legislation in the Pentateuch [NIGTC].

QUESTION—What is the point of contrasting Moses' command in Deut. 24:1 with the reference to what God did at the beginning?

   Jesus goes back in time before human sin to point out God's original intention for marriage [NIVfn]. Although God allowed divorce because of the hard hearts of the people, his will about the matter of divorce is really expressed in Genesis 1:27 and 2:23–24 where it shows that God delights in the institution of marriage. Therefore no one should rebel against God's will by seeking to separate what God has joined together [NLTfn]. The 'beginning of creation' refers to the time when God created Adam and Eve [CGTC]. The nouns in ἄρσεν καὶ θῆλυ 'male and female' occur without articles, which indicates that they are referring to a single pair of people, Adam and Eve [Hb]. The creation of the two sexes is resolved in unity through marriage [NICNT].

10:7 'On-account-of[a] this, a-man shall-leave[b] his father and mother and be-joined[c] to his wife, **10:8** and the two will-be one flesh.[d]' So-then[e] no-longer[f] are they two, but one flesh.

TEXT—Manuscripts reading καὶ προσκολληθήσεται πρὸς τὴν γυναῖκα αὐτοῦ 'and be joined to his wife' are given an C rating by GNT to indicate that choosing it over a variant text was difficult. Some manuscripts omit this phrase and they are followed by NASB, NET.

LEXICON—a. ἕνεκεν, ἕνεκα (LN 89.31) (BAGD p. 264): 'on account of, because of' [BAGD, LN]. The phrase ἕνεκεν τούτου 'on account of this' [AB2, WBC] is also translated 'because of this' [BECNT], 'for this reason' [AB1, BAGD, NTC; NASB, NET, NIV, NRSV, TEV], 'for this cause' [KJV], 'that is why' [BNTC; CEV, GW, REB], 'this explains why' [NLT], 'on this account' [Lns], 'therefore' [ESV], 'so' [NCV]. This preposition indicates cause or reason and it often implies purpose in the sense of 'for the sake of' [LN].

b. fut. act. indic. of καταλείπω (LN 34.40) (BAGD 1.a. p. 413): 'to leave' [LN; all translations], 'to leave behind' [BAGD]. This verb means to cause a particular relationship to cease. It is important to avoid an expression that will suggest abandoning or deserting someone since it only concerns a limitation of a particular relationship [LN]. The verb 'leave' refers to leaving the house of his father and mother, but it does not imply that that he is abandoning or forsaking his parents [TH].

c. fut. pass. indic. of προσκολλάομαι, προσκολλάω (LN 34.22) (BAGD p. 716): 'to be joined to' [AB1, AB2, BAGD, BNTC, LN, WBC; NLT, NRSV], 'to be joined (by God) to' [BECNT], 'to be united to/with' [NCV, NIV, REB, TEV], 'to join oneself to, to become a part of' [LN], 'to hold fast to' [ESV], 'to be glued to' [Lns], 'to cleave to' [NTC; KJV], 'to adhere closely to, to be faithfully devoted to' [BAGD]. The phrase 'and he will be joined to his wife' is translated 'and will remain united with his wife' [GW], 'and gets married' [CEV]. This verb means to begin an association with someone, whether temporary or permanent. It is necessary to avoid an expression that will refer merely to sexual relations. The focus is upon interpersonal relations rather than upon the sexual act [LN].

d. σάρξ (LN 8.4) (BAGD 2. p. 743): 'body' [BAGD, LN], 'physical body' [LN]. The clause 'the two shall/will be/become one flesh' [AB2, BECNT, BNTC, Lns, NTC, WBC; ESV, NASB, NET, NIV, NRSV; similarly REB], 'they twain shall be one flesh' [KJV], 'the two will become one body' [NCV], 'the two will become one' [AB1; TEV], 'the two will be one' [GW], 'the two are united into one' [NLT], 'he becomes like one person with his wife' [CEV]. This noun denotes a living body [LN]. The phrase 'one flesh' is a Semitic expression that simply means 'one' [EBC]. The two independent beings have become 'one flesh', creating a single indivisible unit that not only should not but cannot be separated [NIGTC]. The idea is that the two different people shall be just as though they are one person [TH].

e. ὥστε (LN 89.52) (BAGD 1.a. p. 899): 'so then, accordingly, as a result, so that, and so' [LN], 'for this reason, so' [BAGD], 'therefore' [BAGD, LN]. The last sentence is translated 'So they are no longer two, but one flesh' [ESV, NASB, NET, NRSV; similarly Lns, WBC; KJV], 'So they are no longer two, but one' [GW, NIV, TEV; similarly NCV, NLT], 'So they are no longer two persons, but a single body' [AB1], 'So they are no longer two people, but one flesh' [AB2; similarly BNTC], 'As a result they are no longer two but one flesh' [BECNT; similarly NTC], 'It follows that they are no longer two individuals: they are one flesh' [REB],

'Then they are no longer two people, but one' [CEV]. This conjunction indicates result, often in contexts implying an intended or indirect purpose [LN].

QUESTION—What is the source of the quotation that includes all of verse 7 and the first part of verse 8?

It is a nearly verbatim quotation from the Septuagint Greek translation of Genesis 2:24. [Hb].

QUESTION—What is the reason referred to by the phrase ἕνεκεν τούτου 'on account of *this*' at the beginning of the quotation in verse 7?

The reason had just been given in verse 6 where Jesus quoted 'male and female he made them' from Genesis 1:27 [AB1, AB2, BECNT, EBC, Hb, ICC, Lns, NICNT, PNTC, Sw, Tay, TH, WBC]. In the original context of Genesis 2:21–25a, the words 'on account of this' refer back to the story of the creation of Eve given in detail in Genesis 2:21–23. Jesus evidently took that account concerning the creation of Eve to be just a filling out of the bare statement he used from Genesis 1:27 [CGTC]. That physical relationship results in an even closer union than that between parent and child [ICC].

QUESTION—In what way do the two become one flesh?

This refers to a physical sexual relationship [BECNT, Hb, ICC, Lns, NIGTC, NTC, TH]. They were created as biologically complementary beings, and in their sexual union in marriage their duality gives place to a structural unity [Hb]. It is a relationship more intimate and binding than any other relationship [TH]. The sexual relation in marriage produces a union that involves all other aspects of their lives [Lns]. It not only refers to sexual relations, but also to being faithful to one another and to being united in thought and actions [TRT]. Marriage is to be the closest conceivable bond [NCBC].

QUESTION—What is the function of the last sentence that begins with the conjunction 'so then'?

This is the inference that Jesus makes from the OT quotation [NICNT]. According to God's creative purpose, they are no longer just a male and a female, but one couple, or better, 'a coupled one.' Divorce would then destroy that unity [BECNT, NIGTC]. Their oneness demands that they remain together [Hb]. This deduction is proof of the indissolubility of marriage and rejects the practice of a husband having the right to repudiate his wife [ICC, NICNT]. It means that those who decide to marry must view marriage as a divine institution and make it a true sexual, moral, and spiritual union [NTC].

10:9 **Therefore what[a] God has-joined-together,[b] let- not man[c] -separate.[d]"**

LEXICON—a. ὅς, ἥ, ὅ (LN 92.27): 'who, which, what, the one who, that which' [LN]. The neuter form ὅ is translated 'what' [AB1, AB2, BECNT, BNTC, Lns, NTC, WBC; all versions except CEV, NCV]. The phrase 'what God has joined together' is translated 'God has joined the two together' [NCV], 'a couple that God has joined together' [CEV]. This

pronominal adjective refers to any entity, event, or state that occurs overtly in the immediate context or that is clearly implied in the discourse or setting [LN].
- b. aorist act. indic. of συζεύγνυμι (LN 34.73) (BAGD p. 775): 'to join together' [BAGD, BECNT, BNTC, NTC, WBC; all versions], 'to join together in marriage' [LN], 'to join' [AB1], 'to yoke together' [AB2, Lns]. This verb means to join two persons in a marriage relationship [LN]. Literally 'yoke together', the verb generally has the meaning 'join together' or 'to pair' and it is used specifically for marriage here [BAGD].
- c. ἄνθρωπος (LN 9.1) (BAGD 1.a.β. p. 68): 'man' [AB1, BAGD, BECNT, BNTC, Lns, NTC; ESV, KJV, NASB, NIV, REB], 'human being' [AB2, BAGD; TEV], 'anyone' [GW], '(no) one' [CEV, NCV, NET, NRSV].
- d. pres. act. impera. of χωρίζω (LN 34.78) (BAGD 1. p. 890): 'to separate' [AB1, AB2, BAGD, BECNT, LN, NTC; all versions except KJV, NLT], 'to split apart' [NLT], 'to put asunder' [KJV], 'to divide' [BAGD, BNTC, WBC], 'to divide apart' [Lns]. This verb means to dissolve the marriage bond [LN].

QUESTION—What relationship is indicated by οὖν 'therefore'?

This conjunction indicates the deduction to be made from all that God has said concerning the permanency of marriage [Lns]. This is the conclusion to be made from the divine revelation concerning the marriage bond [NTC].

QUESTION—What is the reason for the use of the neuter adjectival pronoun ὅ 'what'?

1. This pronoun should be translated with its neuter form 'what' [AB1, AB2, BECNT, Hb, Lns, TH; all versions except CEV, NCV]. This pronoun doesn't directly refer to the two people whom God has joined together, but to that condition, that state of affairs, that union which God has effected [TH]. It isn't being applied to specific cases where two individuals have been joined together in marriage, but to that kind of union God instigated when only one man and one woman existed [Hb]. Making the reference abstract and general results in a stronger statement by including 'anything' joined together by God [Lns]. God's creation of mutually complementary sexes and the blessing he pronounced upon their union in Genesis 1:27–28 indicate that wedlock cannot just be dissolved at the discretion of a husband [Sw].
2. This pronoun refers directly to the man and the woman whom God has joined together [CEV, NCV].

QUESTION—Who is the 'man' who should not separate a husband and a wife?

1. 'Man' refers to the husband who is divorcing his wife [AB1, BECNT, BNTC, Hb, NAC, NICNT, NIGTC, Tay, TRT]. In Jewish practice, a divorce was only carried out by the husband [Tay, NAC, NICNT, NIGTC]. This directly refers to the man who is contemplating divorce [BECNT].
2. 'Man' refers to any human being [AB2; TEV].

3. 'Man' refers to any human authority [WBC; probably CEV, GW, NCV, NET, NRSV]. No human being should try to take apart what God has put together [WBC].

10:10 **And inside the house again the disciples were-asking him about this.**[a]
10:11 **And he-says to-them, "Whoever divorces**[b] **his wife and marries another (woman) commits-adultery**[c] **against her.**

LEXICON—a. οὗτος, αὕτη, τοῦτο (LN 92.29): 'this' [LN]. In this verse, the neuter form τούτου 'this' [AB2, BECNT, BNTC, Lns, NTC; WBC; GW, NASB, NET, NIV, REB] is also translated 'this matter' [ESV, NRSV, TEV], 'the matter' [AB1], 'the same matter' [KJV], 'what he had said' [CEV], 'the question of divorce' [NCV]. The phrase 'were asking him about this' is translated 'they brought up the subject again' [NLT]. This pronominal adjective refers to an entity regarded as a part of the discourse setting [LN].

b. aorist act. subj. of ἀπολύω (LN 34.78) (BAGD 2.a. p. 96): 'to divorce' [AB1, AB2, BAGD, BECNT, BNTC, LN, NTC, WBC; all versions except KJV], 'to put away' [KJV], 'to send away' [BAGD], 'to release' [Lns]. This verb literally means 'to send away, to separate from, to leave one another', but in the context of marriage it means to dissolve the marriage bond [LN].

c. pres. mid. indic. of μοιχάομαι, μοιχάω (LN 88.276) (BAGD 2. p. 526): 'to commit adultery' [LN]. The phrase μοιχᾶται ἐπ' αὐτήν 'commits/is-committing adultery against her' [AB2, BECNT, BNTC, WBC; ESV, KJV, NASB, NET, NIV, NLT, NRSV, REB] is also translated 'commits adultery against his wife' [TEV], 'is guilty of adultery against her' [NCV]. Since the idea of committing adultery with some other woman 'against' the true wife is difficult to translate, some translate it: 'commits adultery with her (the second wife)' [AB1], 'is made adulterous in regard to her' [Lns], 'is unfaithful to his wife' [CEV], 'is committing adultery' [GW]. This verb refers to the sexual intercourse of a man with a married woman other than his own spouse. From the standpoint of the NT, adultery was normally defined in terms of the married status of the woman involved in any such act. In other words, sexual intercourse of a married man with an unmarried woman would usually be regarded as πορνεία 'fornication' (88.271), but sexual intercourse of either an unmarried or a married man with someone else's wife was regarded as committing adultery by both the man and woman involved [LN]. A man who marries again after divorcing his wife, commits adultery against 'her,' the first wife [BAGD]. The translation that reads 'commits adultery *with* her' is explained to mean that the words '*with* her' refers to committing adultery with the wife of the second marriage, but that act of adultery is *against* the divorced wife [AB1].

QUESTION—What house were they inside of?
This refers to a house where Jesus and his disciples had found lodging at this time [Hb, Sw]. It was probably a house in one of the villages on the road to Jerusalem [Sw].

QUESTION—What were the disciples referring to when they asked Jesus about αὐτόν 'this'?
The pronominal adjective 'this' refers to the dialogue between the Pharisees and Jesus [BECNT, EBC, Hb, Gnd, My]. It refers to 'what he said' concerning the subject of divorce [TH, TRT].

QUESTION—What does the adverb πάλιν 'again' modify in verse 10?
1. This adverb modifies the implied verb 'were': 'And (when they were) inside the house again' [AB1, AB2, BECNT, EBC, Gnd, ICC, NIGTC; NET, NIV, REB]. The disciples had just heard about Jesus' verdict against divorce in Jesus' answer to the Pharisees in verse 5–9 and for the first time asked him to clarify some things about divorce [EBC, NIGTC].
2. This adverb modifies the following verb 'were asking' [Hb, Lns, My, NTC, Sw, Tay, TRT, WBC; ESV, KJV, NASB, NCV, NLT, NRSV; implied by TEV]: 'again the disciples were asking him about this'. After hearing Jesus' answer to the Pharisees, the disciples still had questions about divorce [Hb].
3. The adverb πάλιν 'again' is omitted in translation [CEV, GW].

QUESTION—What is meant by the man committing adultery ἐπ'αὐτήν 'against her'?
'Her' refers to the first woman, the wife whom the man had divorced, and the man is guilty of committing adultery *against* her [AB1, AB2, BECNT, BNTC, CGTC, Gnd, Hb, Lns, My, NAC, NCBC, NICNT, NIGTC, NTC, PNTC, Sw, Tay, TH, TRT, WBC]. This is as much adultery as if the husband had had intercourse with another woman during the time he was married to his first wife [NIGTC]. Since no formal procedure can break the first marriage, the second marriage is not effective and the man is committing adultery in his relationship with the second woman even though he has married her [ICC].

10:12 **And if she divorces her husband (and) marries another (man), she-commits-adultery.**

QUESTION—When was a Jewish woman allowed to divorce her husband?
Nowhere else in the Gospels is it assumed that a Jewish woman had the right to initiate a divorce. However, this was allowed by Roman law [ESVfn]. Jesus was preparing his disciples for their future world mission among Greeks and Romans [Hb].

QUESTION—Is it significant that the remarried woman μοιχᾶται 'commits adultery' while in verse 11 the remarried man μοιχᾶται ἐπ' αὐτήν 'commits adultery *against her*'?
This verse makes the same rule in the case of the wife [AB1, BNTC, NTC, Tay]. Because this case is equivalent to the previous verse about the husband

divorcing his wife and marrying another woman, the phrase 'she commits adultery' is to be filled out as 'she commits adultery against him' even though none of the translations have done so [Gnd, Lns].

DISCOURSE UNIT—10:13–16 [CBC, EBC, Hb, NICNT; CEV, ESV, GW, NASB, NCV, NET, NIV, NLT, NRSV, TEV]. The topic is the blessing of the children [EBC, Hb, NICNT], Jesus blesses the children [CBC; GW, NLT], Jesus blesses little children [CEV, NASB, NRSV, TEV], Let the children come to me [ESV], Jesus accepts children [NCV], Jesus and little children [NET], the little children and Jesus [NIV].

10:13 And they-were-bringing children to-him in-order-that he-might-touch[a] them. But his disciples rebuked[b] them.

TEXT—Manuscripts reading ἐπετίμησαν αὐτοῖς 'rebuked them' are given an A rating by GNT to indicate it was regarded to be certain. A variant reading is ἐπετίμων τοῖς προσφέρουσιν 'were rebuking the ones bringing to (him)' and it is followed by KJV. Another variant reading is ἐπετίμων τοῖς φέρουσιν 'they were rebuking the ones bringing'.

LEXICON—a. aorist mid. subj. of ἅπτομαι, ἅπτω (LN 24.73) (BAGD 2.b. p. 103): 'to touch' [AB1, AB2, BAGD, BECNT, BNTC, LN, Lns, NTC, WBC; ESV, KJV, NASB, NCV, NET, NIV, NRSV, REB]. The phrase 'in order that he might touch them' is translated 'for him to place his hands on them' [TEV], 'so he could touch and bless them' [NLT], 'so that he could bless them by placing his hands on them' [CEV], 'to have him hold them' [GW]. This verb means 'to touch,' and implies a relatively firm contact [LN]. This refers to laying his hands on the children for the purpose of blessing them [TH].

b. aorist act. indic. of ἐπιτιμάω (LN 33.419) (BAGD 1.a. p. 303): 'to rebuke' [AB1, AB2, BAGD, BECNT, LN, Lns, NTC, WBC; ESV, KJV, NASB, NIV, REB], 'to speak sternly' [NRSV], 'to reprove' [BAGD, BNTC], 'to scold' [NET, TEV]. The phrase 'rebuked them' is translated 'told them to stop' [NCV], 'told the people not to do that' [GW], 'scolded the parents for bothering him' [NLT], 'told the people to stop bothering him' [CEV]. This verb means to express strong disapproval of someone [LN].

QUESTION—Who were bringing children to Jesus?

This third person plural verb προσέφερον 'they were bringing' is the impersonal plural that means 'people were bringing' the children [TH, Tay]. Because the disciples were rebuking them for trying to bring their children to Jesus, the imperfect προσέφερον 'were bringing' is probably connative and means 'they were trying to bring' their children to Jesus [BECNT, Gnd, WBC]. The αὐτοῖς 'them' whom the disciples were rebuking is a masculine gender pronoun that includes both mothers and fathers [Hb, Lns, NIGTC, NTC, Tay, WBC]. 'They' could also include sisters and brothers [EBC, Hb, NICNT, Tay] and other close relatives [NTC]. The word παιδία 'children' can refer to children from eight days old to twelve years old [AB1, AB2,

BECNT, NAC, NCBC, Tay, TH, TRT], and the verb προσέφερον 'bringing' doesn't necessarily mean that they were carrying the children [AB2, BECNT, CGTC, NICNT] since it could include leading them to where Jesus was [BECNT]. These were probably small children since Jesus will take them in his arms in verse 16 [NAC, NICNT] and the parallel passage in Luke 18:15 uses the word βρέφη 'babies' to describe these children [AB1, AB2, CGTC, EBC, EGT, NCBC, NIGTC, NTC, TRT].

QUESTION—Why did these people want Jesus to touch their children?

They wanted Jesus to touch the children in order to bless them [AB1, BECNT, BNTC, CGTC, Gnd, Lns, My, NAC, NETfn, Tay, TH, NTC, TRT, WBC]. The touch would be on their heads [TRT]. The touch was a symbolic act that accompanied the blessing [ICC]. In verse 16 it is clear that this touch refers to laying his hands on the children as he blessed them [NIGTC]. Probably the blessing would be conveyed by his touch [BNTC]. The parallel passage in Matthew 19:13 says they wanted Jesus to put his hands on the children and pray for them [AB1, EGT, Hb, Lns]. Instead of a touch in order to bless them, one translation says that they brought their little children to Jesus in order to have him hold them [GW].

QUESTION—Who did the disciples rebuke and why did they do so?

The disciples rebuked the people who were bringing the children to Jesus [AB2, BECNT, CBC, Hb, ICC, NAC, NLTfn, NTC, TH], and probably told them, 'Don't do that!' [TH]. Jesus was probably inside the house since verse 14 says that Jesus finally *saw* what the disciples were doing [Lns]. Perhaps the disciples stood in the doorway of the house and used angry gestures to shoo away those who were approaching with children in their arms [NTC]. They thought the children might be disruptive and cause a distraction [BECNT, ESVfn]. The disciples probably thought they were protecting Jesus' privacy and were trying to shield him from needless interruptions [EBC]. They thought Jesus had more important matters to attended to than blessing little children [Hb, Lns]. The disciples didn't want to be bothered with children [NTC] and they didn't want Jesus to be bothered by such unimportant infants [NAC, NTC; CEV, NLT].

10:14 And having-seen (this) Jesus became-indignant[a] and said to-them, "Let[b] the children come to me, do- not -prevent[c] them, because to-(children/people)-such-as-these[d] is the kingdom of-God.

LEXICON—a. aorist act. indic. of ἀγανακτέω (LN 88.187) (BAGD p. 4): 'to be indignant' [BAGD, BECNT, BNTC, LN, Lns, NTC, WBC; ESV, NASB, NET, NIV, NRSV, REB], 'to be angry' [AB1, BAGD, LN; CEV, NLT, TEV], 'to be much displeased' [KJV], 'to become irritated' [GW], 'to be annoyed' [AB2], 'to be upset' [NCV]. This verb means to be indignant against what is judged to be wrong [LN]. The verb covers both Jesus' irritation at their failure to learn and his repugnance at their attitude [NIGTC]. 'Indignant' means 'to be aroused to anger' to such a level that one expresses his displeasure instead of just brooding about it [PNTC].

'Moved with indignation' is too strong for this verb, 'was much displeased' is better, and 'was annoyed' is better still [EGT].
b. aorist act. impera. of ἀφίημι (LN 13.140) (BAGD 4 p. 126): 'to let' [AB1, AB2, BAGD, BNTC, LN, Lns, NTC; CEV, ESV, NCV, NET, NIV, NLT, NRSV, REB, TEV], 'to permit' [BAGD, WBC; NASB], 'to allow' [BAGD, BECNT, LN], 'to suffer' [KJV], not explicit [GW]. This verb means to leave it up to someone to do something [LN].
c. pres. act. impera. of κωλύω (LN **13.146**) (BAGD 1. p. 461): 'to prevent' [BAGD, BECNT, BNTC, **LN**], 'to stop' [GW, NCV, NLT, NRSV, TEV], 'to try to stop' [AB1; CEV, NET, REB], 'to forbid' [AB2, WBC; KJV], 'to hinder' [BAGD, LN, Lns, NTC; ESV, NIV]. The two phrases 'Permit the children to come to me, do not hinder them' are translated 'Don't stop the children from coming to me' [GW]. This verb means to cause something not to happen [LN].
d. τοιοῦτος (LN 92.31) (BAGD 3.a.α. p. 821): 'such as these' [BAGD], 'of such a kind' [BAGD, LN], 'of a kind such as this' [LN]. The clause 'to such as these is the kingdom of God' is translated 'to such as these belongs the kingdom of God' [BECNT; similarly NTC; ESV], 'it is to such as these that the kingdom of God belongs' [NRSV], 'to such ones belong the dominion of God' [AB2], 'of such is the kingdom of God' [Lns; KJV; similarly WBC], 'the kingdom of God belongs to such as these' [NASB, NET, NIV, REB, TEV], 'the Kingdom of God is for such as these' [AB1], 'children like these are part of the kingdom of God' [GW], 'the kingdom of God belongs to people/those who are like these children' [NCV, NLT], 'it is to people like these that the kingdom belongs' [BNTC], 'people who are like these little children belong to the kingdom of God' [CEV], This pronominal adjective describes someone who is of such a kind as is identified in the context [LN].

QUESTION—How did Jesus see the disciples rebuking the people bringing the children?

From inside the house Jesus had seen the disciples rebuking the people [Sw]. Since Jesus had seen what had already happened, the disciples had succeeded in keeping the children away from him [Gnd].

QUESTION—Who are the ones who are 'such as these (children)'?
1. This refers to *children* such as these children [AB2, Gnd, NICNT, PNTC, Sw, Tay, WBC]. It means these children and others like them [AB2]. The children that the disciples were stopping belonged to the class of little ones who believed in Jesus just like those described in 9:42, and Jesus did not want them stopped from coming to him [Gnd].
2. This refers to *people* such as these children [BECNT, BNTC, CBC, CGTC, EBC, ESVfn, Hb, ICC, Lns, NAC, NCBC, NIGTC, NTC, TH]. The next verse talks of receiving the kingdom *like* a child, so it is evident that Jesus is speaking about the characteristics or qualities of children [TH]. Jesus was not thinking of children exclusively. These children were representative of all people who have a child's spirit of receptivity,

dependence, trustfulness [Hb], and humility [ICC]. The children represent all the people who are insignificant, weak, helpless, and dependent [NAC]. His disciples were to allow children to come to him because they represent all the people who share a child's status of insignificance [NIGTC]. The kingdom is promised to those who are obscure, trivial, unimportant, and weak and come empty-handed like a beggar [NCBC].

QUESTION—What is meant by the phrase τοιούτων ἐστὶν 'of such is' the kingdom of God?

It means the kingdom of God belongs to people like that [AB2, BNTC, BNTC, CGTC, Gnd, NICNT, NTC, TH; CEV, NCV, NET, NIV, NLT, NRSV, REB, TEV]. It does not imply that everyone must cultivate certain childlike qualities of personality in order to earn the right of entry into the kingdom [NCBC]. The kingdom belongs to such people because they receive it as a gift [CGTC, Tay]. They are the rightful recipients of the kingdom [AB1]. The kingdom is for such as these [AB1]. This passage illustrates how everyone is important to God, even those whom others regard as being insignificant [ESVfn].

10:15 Truly[a] I-say to-you, whoever does- not -receive[b] the kingdom of-God like[c] a-child, by-no-means may-enter[d] into it."

LEXICON—a. ἀμήν (LN 72.6) (BAGD 2. p. 45): 'truly' [BAGD, BECNT, BNTC, LN, WBC; ESV, NASB, NRSV, REB], 'indeed, it is true that' [LN], 'verily' [KJV], 'amen' [AB2, Lns]. The phrase 'truly I say to you' is also translated 'I tell you the truth' [NCV, NET, NIV, NLT], 'I assure you' [TEV], 'I promise you' [CEV], 'I can guarantee this truth' [GW], 'I solemnly declare to you' [NTC], 'in solemn truth I tell you' [AB1]. This particle makes a strong affirmation of what is declared [LN]. It is an assertive particle that begins a solemn declaration [BAGD]. The phrase 'truly I say to you' occurs at 3:28; 8:12; 9:1, 41; 10:15, 29; 11:23; 12:43; 13:30; 14:9, 18, 25, 30.

b. aorist mid. (deponent = act.) subj. of δέχομαι (LN 31.51) (BAGD 3.b. p. 177): 'to receive' [AB2, BECNT, BNTC, LN, Lns, NTC, WBC; all versions except CEV, NCV, REB], 'to accept' [AB1; CEV, NCV, REB]. This verb means to readily receive information and regard it as true [LN].

c. ὡς (LN 64.12) (BAGD I.2.a. p. 897): 'like, as' [LN]. The phrase 'as a child' [Lns, WBC] is also translated 'as a little child' [NTC; KJV, NRSV], 'like a child' [AB2, BECNT], 'like a little child' [BNTC; NIV], 'like a child will' [AB1; ESV, NASB, NET, NLT, REB, TEV], 'as a little child receives it' [GW], 'as if you were a little child' [NCV], 'the way a child does' [CEV]. This relatively weak conjunction indicates a relationship between events or states [LN].

d. aorist act. subj. of εἰσέρχομαι (LN 90.70) (BAGD 2.a. p. 233): 'to begin to experience, to come into an experience, to attain' [LN], 'to approve, to accept' [BAGD]. The clause 'by no means may enter into it' is translated 'will by no means enter it' [AB1], 'in no way shall enter into it' [Lns], 'will not enter it at all' [NASB], 'will/shall not enter it' [WBC; ESV; similarly KJV], 'will/shall never enter it' [AB2, BNTC, NTC; GW, NCV, NET, NIV, NLT, NRSV, NEB, TEV; similarly BECNT], 'you cannot get into it' [CEV], This verb means to begin to experience an event or state [LN].

QUESTION—What is meant by receiving the kingdom of God like a child?

To receive the kingdom of God means to accept the rule and authority of God [ICC, TH, TRT, WBC; CEV]. It means to become God's willing subject [NIGTC]. It means to receive God as one's King or ruler [TH]. This should be done in the same way that children would obey their parents without question and do whatever they are told [ICC]. The kingdom of God must be received as a gift from God in a simple, trusting faith just as a child receives a gift from a loved one [AB1, BECNT, Hb, NETfn, NICNT, NTC, Sw, Tay], without any sense of having earned it [AB1, NCBC], and with humility and trustfulness [Lns, Sw]. Children receive God's grace because of sheer neediness and not because of merit inherent in themselves [PNTC]. Children know that they are helpless and have no claim or merit [NIVfn]. Instead of comparing this with the way a child receives a gift, some translate this 'as a child receives the kingdom of God' [GW].

QUESTION—When does one enter the kingdom of God?

1. This kingdom is entered at the time of receiving it in this life [AB2, Gnd, Hb, Lns, NAC, NTC, Tay, TRT; probably CGTC, WBC]. We enter the kingdom through our response of faith and obedience [NAC]. Receiving the kingdom is an idiom meaning submitting to God's rule [TRT]. The kingdom is pictured as a society under God's rule, and a person becomes a member of that society by submitting to God's authority [Hb]. Entering the kingdom of God is about the same as entering eternal life when one is saved [NTC].

2. This kingdom will be entered in the future [AB1, BECNT, BNTC, Gnd, NICNT, NIGTC]. The reference to 'entering' the kingdom gives it a spatial meaning and implies that it will happen in the future [AB1, Gnd]. Receiving the kingdom seems to relate to a person's attitude and response towards what God demands in this life, but entering the kingdom seems to refer to one's eternal destiny, so one's reception of it now will be the means of entering that kingdom in the hereafter [NIGTC]. The kingdom has come in the ministry of Jesus and must be received now in order to experience its presence and benefits, but its consummation still lies in the future [BECNT]. The person who does not receive the kingdom now will not enter into it when it is finally established in the consummation of the kingdom [NICNT].

10:16 And having-taken- them -into-his-arms,[a] he-was-blessing[b] (them) placing[c] his hands on them.

LEXICON—a. aorist mid. (deponent = act.) participle of ἐναγκαλίζομαι (LN 34.63) (BAGD p. 261): 'to take in/into one's arms' [BAGD, NTC, WBC;

CEV, ESV, NASB, NCV, NET, NIV, NLT, TEV], 'to take up in one's arms' [Lns; KJV, NRSV], 'to put one's arms around' [AB1, BECNT, BNTC, **LN**; GW, REB], 'to embrace' [AB2, LN], 'to hug' [LN]. This verb means to put one's arms around someone as an expression of affection and concern [LN].

b. imperf. act. indic. of κατευλογέω (LN 33.470) (BAGD p. 422): 'to bless' [BAGD, LN; all translations]. This verb means to ask God to bestow his divine favor on someone [LN]. The imperfect tense is an iterative imperfect which indicates that Jesus was blessing the children one after another [Gnd].

c. pres. act. participle of τίθημι (LN 85.32) (BAGD I.1.a.β. p. 816): 'to put, to place' [BAGD, LN]. The clause 'he blessed them placing his hands on them' is translated 'he blessed them, laying his hands on them' [AB2, WBC; ESV], 'he began blessing them, laying his hands on them' [NASB], 'he tenderly blessed them one by one, laying his hands upon them' [NTC], 'he put his hands upon/on them, and blessed them' [KJV, NCV, NIV], 'he placed/laid his hands on them and blessed them' [NET, NRSV, REB], 'he placed his hands on their heads and blessed them' [NLT], 'he...placed his hands on each of them, and blessed them' [TEV], 'he laid his hands on them and blessed them [BNTC], 'having placed his hands upon them, he was blessing them [BECNT], 'he blessed them by placing his hands on them' [CEV, GW], 'he blessed them by laying his hands upon them' [AB1], 'he went on fervently blessing them, having placed his hands upon them' [Lns], 'he tenderly blessed them one by one, laying his hands upon them' [NTC]. This verb means to put or place in a particular location [LN].

QUESTION—Did Jesus take all of the children into his arms at the same time?

Jesus blessed the children individually one at a time [TRT]. The children were brought to Jesus one at a time and he took each one in his arms separately [EGT, Gnd, Hb, NTC, Sw, TH, TRT, WBC]. This embrace was a public demonstration of the child's acceptance and value in the kingdom [WBC]. Instead of just placing his hands on the babies while others held them, Jesus took them in his own arms as if they were his own children [Lns].

QUESTION—How did Jesus bless each child?

The participle τιθείς 'placing' indicates an accompanying circumstance as Jesus blessed the children [Gnd, Hb, Lns, NIGTC, NTC, TH; KJV, NCV, NET, NIV, NLT, NRSV, REB, TEV]. He blessed them as he put his hands on them. 'Placing his hands on them' describes the manner in which the blessing was administered [AB1, BECNT]. This touch was just a natural sign of association [NIGTC]. After Jesus hugged a child, he spoke a blessing while laying his hands on that child [Gnd]. As Jesus held the child close to his breast, he disengaged one hand to lay it upon the child's head while he pronounced the blessing [Hb]. Jesus took the child in one arm, placed his free hand upon the child's head and blessed him by uttering a brief prayer to the Father to bestow his blessing on that child [NTC]. According to the customs of that time, Jesus invoked God's blessing upon the children saying to each child, 'May God bless you' rather than saying 'I bless you' [TH].

DISCOURSE UNIT—10:17–31 [CBC, EBC; CEV, ESV, GW, NASB, NCV, NET, NIV, NRSV, TEV]. The topic is riches and the kingdom [EBC], eternal life in the kingdom [GW], the rich man [CEV, ESV, NET, NIV, NRSV, TEV], the rich young ruler [NASB], Jesus encounters a rich man [CBC], a rich young man's question [NCV].

DISCOURSE UNIT—10:17–27 [NICNT]. The topic is riches and the kingdom of God.

DISCOURSE UNIT—10:17–22 [Hb; NLT]. The topic is the rich man [NLT], a question concerning eternal life [Hb].

10:17 And (as) he was-going-out[a] on (the) road, one having-run and having-knelt-before him asked him. "Good[b] teacher, what must-I-do in-order-that I-may-inherit[c] eternal life?"

LEXICON—a. pres. mid./pass. (deponent = act.) participle of ἐκπορεύομαι (LN 15.40) (BAGD 1.c. p. 244): 'to go out of' [BAGD, LN], 'to depart out of, to leave from within' [LN]. The participial clause 'as/while he was going out on the road' [Lns] is also translated 'as he started out on the road' [NTC], 'as Jesus was coming out to the road' [GW], 'when he had gone out onto the road' [WBC], 'as he was starting/setting out on a/his journey' [AB1, BNTC; ESV, NASB, NRSV, REB], 'as he was setting out on the way' [AB2], 'as Jesus started on his way' [NIV], 'as Jesus was starting out on his way' [NET], 'as Jesus was starting out on his way again' [TEV], 'as Jesus was starting out on his way to Jerusalem' [NLT], 'as he was proceeding on the way' [BECNT], 'when he was gone forth into the way' [KJV], 'as Jesus started to leave' [NCV], 'he set out on a journey' [BAGD], 'Jesus was walking down a road' [CEV]. This verb means to move out of an enclosed or well-defined two or three-dimensional area [LN].
   b. ἀγαθός (LN 88.1) (BAGD 1.b.α. p. 3): 'good' [BAGD, LN; all translations]. This adjective refers to positive moral qualities of the most general nature [LN].
   c. aorist act. subj. of κληρονομέω (LN 57.131) (BAGD 2. p. 434): 'to inherit' [all translations except CEV, NCV, REB, TEV], 'to be given, to gain possession of' [LN], 'to receive' [BAGD, LN; TEV], 'to have' [CEV, NCV], 'to share in' [BAGD], 'to win' [REB]. This verb means to receive something of considerable value that has not been earned [LN].

QUESTION—When did this meeting occur?
The present tense of the participle 'going out' suggests that Jesus was in the act of leaving the house where he had blessed the little children [Hb, ICC, My, NTC, TRT, WBC]. Jesus was in the act of taking the road to the next village [Lns]. This pictures him as setting out on his way [CGTC]. He was

on his way to Jerusalem [PNTC], which is made explicit in verse 32 [CBC]. Verse 23 reveals that the disciples accompanied Jesus as he set out [TRT].

QUESTION—Who was the εἷς 'one' who ran up to Jesus and knelt before him?

Verse 22 reveals that this person was rich but Mark provides no other descriptive information about him as is done in Matt 19:22 where it describes his youth and in Luke 18:18 where it describes his political status [NIGTC].

QUESTION—What did this man mean when he said that Jesus was a 'good teacher'?

This expressed the young man's high regard for Jesus [EBC]. Although 'Teacher' occurs frequently in Mark, 'Good Teacher' is unusual [BECNT]. In this verse the adjective 'good' could mean that Jesus was a kind, beneficent, or generous teacher. He was not talking about the fact that Jesus was a good or capable teacher [TH]. This formal address from a kneeling position shows the man's deep respect for Jesus and his genuine earnestness to know the answer to his question. When he called Jesus 'good' he may have meant 'kind' or 'generous', or some other quality of goodness [NICNT]. He recognized the moral virtue of Jesus [Gnd]. Although 'good' was probably said sincerely, it was used with an imperfect standard of moral goodness since he regarded Jesus to be a merely human teacher [Sw].

QUESTION—What did the man mean by 'inheriting' eternal life?

This verb is often used in the sense of obtaining or having a portion of something, and the parallel account in Matthew 19:16 uses the verb ἔχω 'to have, to experience' eternal life [Lns]. Even though the verb may simply mean to obtain, acquire, or possess eternal life, its literal meaning 'to come into the inheritance of' supports the Jewish concept that because they are God's people, the people of Israel will receive 'eternal life' as a gift or inheritance from God. It does not at all imply that 'inherit' means that the life which is to be inherited is the life which has just been given up by someone else who died [TH]. The man wanted to know what work of righteousness he must do in order to merit eternal life [EBC]. He evidently thought there were conditions to be fulfilled beyond those set in the Jewish Law [NICNT, Tay]. 'Inheriting eternal life' is equivalent to 'entering the kingdom of God' [BNTC, ICC, NCBC], and the two phrases alternate in verses 23–25, 30 [BNTC]. We should not assume that this man used the term 'eternal life' with the same fullness of meaning it has in Christ's teaching [NTC]. The man's perception of eternal life relates to a life that is entered into at the resurrection and this does not indicate he was thinking of it as a possession to be had immediately as described in the Gospel of John [AB1]. The fuller meaning of eternal life as a present possession does not emerge in this story [Tay].

10:18 And Jesus said to-him, "Why do-you-call me good[a]? No-one (is) good except[b] one, God.

LEXICON—a. ἀγαθός (LN 88.1) (BAGD 1.b.α. p. 3): 'good' [BAGD, LN; all translations]. This adjective refers to having positive moral qualities of the most general nature [LN]. Jesus is referring to a moral goodness which is the implied equivalent of being 'perfect' when referring to God [BAGD, TH].

b. εἰ μή (LN 89.131): 'except that, but, however, instead, but only [LN]. The clause 'No one is good except one, God' [Lns, NTC, WBC] is also translated 'No one is good except/but God alone' [BECNT, BNTC; ESV, GW, NASB, NET, NIV, NRSV, REB, TEV; similarly AB1], 'Only God is good' [CEV, NCV], 'Only God is truly good' [NLT], 'There is nobody good except One, that is, God [AB2; similarly KJV]. This phrase indicates a contrast by designating an exception [LN].

QUESTION—What was Jesus' purpose in asking the rhetorical question, 'Why do you call me good?

This response by Jesus is an enigma, and there have been many different explanations given for the question and statement in this verse [BNTC, Tay]. Jesus knew that when the young man addressed him as 'good teacher' he was being very superficial. If the man had really believed that Jesus was good in the highest sense of the term, he would have obeyed Jesus' command in verse 21 [NTC]. Jesus isn't saying anything about his own goodness. He is telling the man to pause and think about what 'good' really means and not use the word lightly [Lns]. This man's idea of goodness is of the kind of goodness that is a man's achievement [CGTC].

QUESTION—What did Jesus mean by his statement, 'No one is good except one, God'?

The young man thought goodness was a personal moral attainment and regarded Jesus as one who had excelled in that attainment [Hb]. Pointing out that only God is absolutely good, Jesus lays the groundwork for showing the inadequacy of any person trying to keep God's commandments in order to inherit eternal life [Gnd, Hb]. Since only God is really good, perhaps Jesus wanted the man to consider the implication of calling Jesus 'good' [Hb, NETfn, WBC], and affirm the Godhead of Jesus rather than deny it [Lns]. Unless the young man was ready to acknowledge Jesus as God, it was not proper for him to address him as 'Good Teacher' [ESVfn]. But it is too subtle to see Jesus as affirming his own deity [CBC]. Others do not think that Jesus intended to pose the question of his own sinlessness or oneness with the Father. He was simply establishing the lordship of God here [NICNT]. Jesus is not implying that he himself is imperfect or less than good, his focus is on the God who made the covenant with Israel and whose commandments must be obeyed [WBC]. Only four commentaries take this to mean that Jesus was objecting to applying 'good' in the sense of 'perfect' to any human being, including himself, whose humanity was still subject to growth and trial [BECNT, CGTC, ICC, Tay]. The human goodness that develops like wisdom from childhood to manhood was possessed by Jesus [ICC].

10:19 **You-know the commandments: Do- not -murder, do- not -commit-adultery, do- not -steal, do- not -give-false-witness,[a] do- not -defraud,[b] honor[c] your father and mother."**

TEXT—Manuscripts reading μὴ ἀποστερήσῃς 'do not defraud' are given an A rating by GNT to indicate it was regarded to be certain. Another manuscript omits this phrase.

LEXICON—a. aorist act. subj. of ψευδομαρτυρέω (LN 33.271) (BAGD p. 892): 'to give false testimony' [BAGD, BECNT; GW, NET, NIV], 'to give false witness' [BNTC, LN], 'to bear false witness' [AB2, BAGD, Lns, NTC, WBC; ESV, KJV, NASB, NRSV], 'to give false evidence' [REB], 'to testify falsely' [LN; NLT], 'to perjure oneself' [AB1], 'to accuse anyone falsely' [TEV], 'to tell lies about others' [CEV], 'to tell lies about one's neighbor' [NCV]. This verb means to provide a false or untrue witness [LN].

b. aorist act. subj. of ἀποστερέω (LN **57.248**) (BAGD p. 99): 'to defraud' [AB1, AB2, BAGD, BECNT, BNTC, **LN**, NTC, WBC; ESV, KJV, NASB, NET, NIV, NRSV, REB], 'to steal' [BAGD], 'to cheat' [CEV, GW, NCV, NLT, TEV]. This verb means to take something from someone by deception or trickery [LN].

c. pres. act. impera. of τιμάω (LN 87.8) (BAGD 2. p. 817): 'to honor' [AB1, AB2, BAGD, BECNT, BNTC, LN, Lns, NTC, WBC; all versions except CEV], 'to respect' [LN; CEV], 'to revere' [BAGD]. This verb means to attribute high status to someone by honoring him [LN]. This word also occurs at 7:10.

QUESTION—Why are each of the commands addressed to a singular 'you'?

These are not OT commands given specifically to the young man Jesus was speaking to. They apply to all people and should be translated as general commands for everyone to obey, such as, 'A person must not do this,' 'You (plural) must not do this,' or 'No one must do this' [TRT].

QUESTION—Which commandments did Jesus quote?

The first four of the six commandments Jesus quotes are the sixth, seventh, eighth, and ninth commandments listed in Exodus 20:13–16, and those commands are about what a person must not do. Then instead of the tenth commandment, which is a long commandment about not coveting a neighbor's house, wife, servants, animals, or anything else belonging to the neighbor, Jesus gave the unexpected command, 'do not defraud'. Jesus ended his list by going back to the fifth commandment 'honor your father and mother'. Some commentaries point out that this fifth command is the only command in the first tablet of the Ten Commandments that deals with interpersonal relationships like the other commands Jesus listed [Gnd, WBC]. Most commentaries speculate about the reason for including the command 'Do not defraud'. Many think it is a substitute for the wordy tenth commandment against coveting [AB2, CBC, EBC, Sw, NCBC, NAC, NIGTC, TH, WBC] since fraud is a manifestation of coveting [EBC, NAC]. Some think it is an application of the eighth and ninth commandments [ESVfn, NICNT] or it gives another aspect of the eighth commandment 'do not steal' [BECNT, Gnd, TH]. Perhaps this commandment is included because a rich man often gains his wealth at the expense of the poor [PNTC]. There are even more speculations about why it is included in this list of commandments, but no satisfactory explanation has ever been given [BNTC].

10:20 And he said to-him, "Teacher, all these I-have-kept[a] from my youth.[b]"

LEXICON—a. aorist mid. indic. of φυλάσσω (LN 36.19) (BAGD 2.b. p. 868): 'to obey' [LN; CEV, GW, NCV, NLT, TEV], 'to wholeheartedly obey' [NET], 'to keep' [AB1, BAGD, LN; ESV, NASB, NIV, NRSV, REB], 'to observe' [AB2, BAGD, BECNT, BNTC, NTC, WBC; KJV], 'to follow' [BAGD]. This verb means to continue to obey orders or commandments [LN]. When referring to a commandment, the verb 'keep' means to observe or follow it [TH].

b. νεότης (LN 67.154) (BAGD p. 536): 'youth' [BAGD, LN], 'being young' [LN]. The phrase ἐκ νεότητός μου 'from/since my youth' [BECNT, BNTC, WBC; ESV, KJV, NET, NRSV] is also translated 'from my youth up' [AB2; NASB], 'since I was young' [NLT, TEV], 'since I was a child' [NTC], 'since I was a boy' [AB1; GW, NCV, NIV, REB], 'since I was a young man' [CEV]. This noun denotes a period of time when a person is young [LN]. Upon reaching the age of twelve, a Jewish boy assumed the yoke of the commandments and is held responsible for his actions from that time on [NICNT]. Others give the age of accountability to be thirteen [EBC, Gnd, TH, TRT].

QUESTION—Was this man speaking the truth?

He was claiming a clear conscience with regard to these commandments, and taken as rules of conduct, these commandments could be kept to the letter except for the positive requirement of honoring ones parents [NIGTC]. The deeper meaning and larger requirements of the Law were still hidden from him [Sw]. He spoke sincerely because he understood keeping the law to be a matter of external conformity [EBC].

10:21 And Jesus having-looked-at[a] him loved[b] him and said to-him, "One (thing) you lack.[c]

LEXICON—a. aorist act. participle of ἐμβλέπω (LN 24.9) (BAGD 1. p. 254): 'to look at' [AB2, BAGD, BECNT, NTC; all versions except CEV, KJV, TEV], 'to look closely at' [CEV], 'to look at steadily' [BNTC], 'to look straight at' [AB1, LN; TEV], 'to look upon' [Lns, WBC], 'to behold' [KJV], 'to look directly at' [LN], 'to fix one's gaze at' [BAGD]. This verb means to direct one's vision and attention to a particular object [LN]. The

verb is an intensified compound of the normal word for 'look' and means 'to look intently, to examine, to scrutinize' [PNTC].
  b. aorist act. indic. of ἀγαπάω (LN 25.43) (BAGD 1.b.α. p. 4): 'to love [BAGD, LN], 'to regard with affection' [LN]. The phrase 'loved him' [BECNT, BNTC, Lns, NTC, WBC; ESV, GW, KJV, NCV, NIV, NRSV] is also translated 'felt a love for him' [NASB; similarly NET], 'felt genuine love for him' [NLT], 'was moved with love for him' [AB2], '(looked straight at him) with love' [TEV], 'his heart warmed to him' [AB1; REB], 'liked him' [CEV]. At this point, Jesus began to love him [Hb, NTC]. This verb means to have love for someone based on sincere appreciation and high regard [LN]. Jesus had a profound admiration and regard for this young man [TH].
  c. pres. act. indic. of ὑστερέω (LN 13.21) (BAGD 1.d. p. 849): 'to lack' [BAGD], 'to fail to attain, to not attain, to be behind in' [LN]. The clause 'one thing you lack' [BECNT, BNTC, NTC; KJV, NASB, NIV, REB] is also translated 'you lack one thing' [BAGD, WBC; ESV, NET, NRSV], 'you're still missing one thing' [GW; similarly AB2], 'you need only one thing' [TEV], 'there is one thing wanting in you' [AB1], 'there's one thing you still need to do' [CEV], 'there is one more thing you need to do' [NCV], 'there is still one thing you haven't done' [NLT], 'one thing makes thee come behind' [Lns]. This verb means to fail in some measure to attain a certain state or condition [LN]. It means that there is still one thing he should do [TH].

QUESTION—What is the connection between Jesus looking at the young man and Jesus loving him?

Jesus first gave this man a searching and penetrating look in order to confirm the impression that his statement had made on him [ICC]. He admired him for not falling into gross outward sins and for seeking a solution to his problem [Lns]. Recognizing the man's sincerity, Jesus responded in love [EBC, Hb]. Jesus was so impressed that this man was genuinely seeking a right relationship with God that his heart warmed toward him [AB1]. This love was an inward impulse of admiring affection [Tay], a profound admiration and regard for him [TH]. After a supernatural diagnosis of this young man's character, Jesus developed a fatherly relationship with him [AB2]. This love that Jesus began to feel for the young man was not a mere emotional affection for him but a spiritual love that desired his highest welfare [Hb]. Three commentators suggest that the context implies that the words 'loved him' mean that Jesus put his arms around the man to show that he loved him [Gnd, TRT] or possibly hugged or held him by the shoulders as a sign of affection [WBC]. However, there is nothing in the text that indicates that this refers to such an action [EBC]. It doesn't refer to an embrace, attraction, or affection, but to a genuine love that was based on the man's need [NAC].

QUESTION—What was the one thing the young man lacked?
The one thing he lacked was not an additional personal virtue but the single-hearted devotion to God commanded by the first of the Ten Commandments [BECNT, CGTC, ESVfn, Hb, NLTfn]. He loved his riches more than he loved God [BECNT, NLTfn]. The one thing that prevented this man from having eternal life was the security he felt because of his wealth [EBC], so the command to sell all he possessed was appropriate to this particular situation [NICNT]. The one thing he lacked was compassion for people [WBC]. He lacked the self-sacrificing devotion that characterizes every true follower of Jesus [NCBC, NICNT]. Although adhering to the moral law was good and necessary, it was not a substitute for following Jesus [PNTC]. This 'one thing' to sell all that he has and give the proceeds to the poor was just the first step to inheriting eternal life because Jesus will now add that he must follow him. It is the act of following Jesus that will lead to eternal life [Tay].

Go, sell as-much-as[a] you have and give[b] to-the poor, and you-will-have treasure[c] in heaven, and (then) come, follow[d] me."

TEXT—Manuscripts reading δεῦρο ἀκολούθει μοι 'come follow me' are given an A rating by GNT to indicate it was regarded to be certain. A variant reading is δεῦρο ἀκολούθει μοι ἄρας τὸν σταυρόν 'come follow me having taken up the cross' and it is followed by KJV. Another variant reading is ἄρας τὸν σταυρόν σου δεῦρο ἀκολούθει μοι 'having taken up your cross come follow me'.

LEXICON—a. ὅσος (LN 59.7) (BAGD 2. p. 586): as much as, as many as' [BAGD, LN]. The phrase 'as much as you have' is translated 'all that you have' [AB1; ESV; similarly TEV], 'all you possess' [NASB], 'all your possessions' [NLT], 'everything you have' [BNTC; GW, NCV, NIV, REB], 'whatever you have' [AB2, BECNT, Lns, NTC; NET; similarly WBC; KJV], 'everything you own' [CEV], 'what you own' [NRSV]. This pronominal adjective pertains to a comparative quantity of objects or events [LN].

b. aorist act. impera. of δίδωμι (LN 57.71): 'to give' [LN]. The command 'give to the poor' [AB1, AB2, BECNT, Lns, WBC; ESV, KJV, NASB, NIV, REB] is also translated 'give the proceeds to the poor' [NTC], 'give the money to the poor' [BNTC; CEV, GW, NCV, NET, NLT, NRSV, TEV]. This verb means to give an object, usually something of value [LN]. The direct object of a verb was often omitted in Greek when it was clearly understood from the context, and the words 'the money' are implied in this instance [NETfn].

c. θησαυρός (LN 65.10) (BAGD 2.b.α. p. 361): 'treasure' [AB2, BAGD, BECNT, BNTC, LN, Lns, NTC, WBC; all versions except CEV, TEV], 'riches' [AB1, LN; CEV, TEV], 'wealth' [LN]. This noun denotes that which is of such exceptional value that it needs to be kept in a safe place [LN]. To have 'treasure in heaven' refers to this treasure as though it was deposited in heaven and would become available to the person after death [BAGD].

d. pres. act. impera. of ἀκολουθέω (LN 36.31): 'to follow, to be a disciple of someone' [LN]. The clause 'come, follow me' [BECNT, BNTC, NTC, WBC; ESV, KJV, NASB, NET, NIV, NLT, NRSV; similarly Lns] is also translated 'come and follow me' [AB1; NCV, REB, TEV], 'come on, follow me' [AB2], 'come with me' [CEV], 'follow me' [GW]. This verb means to be a follower or disciple of someone in the sense of adhering to the teachings or instructions of a leader and promoting his cause [LN].

QUESTION—What was the young man to give to the poor?

He was to give the proceeds from the sale of all of his possessions [BECNT, TH; CEV, GW, NCV, NET, NLT, NRSV, TEV]. In so doing he would get rid of what was keeping him from God and from inheriting eternal life [BECNT]. It is not implied that what was required by this particular rich young man is a requirement that should be applied to all believers [BECNT, EBC, Hb, NIVfn, NLTfn].

QUESTION—What is the treasure in heaven that he will have?

If he will fix his devotion on God instead of on his riches, he will gain God's approval and be assured of spiritual riches in future glory [Hb]. The full measure of all those blessings that are heavenly in character are reserved in heaven for all of God's children [NTC]. The young man had asked about eternal life in verse 17 [Gnd], so the 'treasure in heaven' specifically refers to eternal life [EBC, Gnd]. This promised treasure signifies either the gift of eternal life or salvation at the time the kingdom of God is revealed [NICNT, NIVfn].

QUESTION—How would the man follow Jesus after doing those things?

The present tense means 'be following me' and this was an invitation to a life of continuing fellowship with Jesus [Hb]. In the case of this young man it evidently means that he was to become one of Jesus' personal followers who traveled along with Jesus [ICC]. He was to follow Jesus on the journey Jesus was about to resume [BNTC].

10:22 But having-become-downcast/shocked[a] at the statement[b] he left grieving[c] because he-had many possessions.[d]

LEXICON—a. aorist act. participle of στυγνάζω (LN 25.286, 25.222) (BAGD 1. or 2.a. p. 771): 'to be downcast' [**LN (25.286)**], 'to look sad' [NET], 'to look gloomy' [LN], 'to look unhappy' [GW], 'to be crestfallen' [NTC], 'to be disheartened' [ESV], 'to be sad' [BECNT; KJV], 'to be very sad' [NCV], 'to be saddened' [NASB], 'to be gloomy' [BAGD (2.a.), Lns; CEV]. The phrase 'having become downcast' is translated 'the man's/his face fell' [AB1, BNTC; NIV, NLT, REB], 'his face falling' [WBC], 'the gloom spread over his face' [TEV]. Others take the alternative meaning of the verb: 'to be shocked' [BAGD (1.), LN (25.222); NRSV], 'to be appalled' [BAGD (1.), LN (25.222)], 'to be indignant' [AB2]. This verb means to experience an emotional state of both grief and discouragement that is overtly portrayed in one's face [LN (25.286)] or to experience an emotional state of great surprise because of something which appears incredible and alarming [LN (25.222)]. This refers to a man whose appearance shows that he is sad or gloomy [BAGD (2.a)] or who is shocked or appalled [BAGD (1.)].

b. λόγος (LN 33.98) (BAGD 1.a.γ. p. 477): 'statement' [BAGD, LN], 'declaration' [BAGD], 'word' [BAGD, LN], 'saying' [LN]. The phrase ἐπὶ τῷ λόγῳ 'at the statement' is translated 'at this statement' [BECNT; NET], 'by the statement' [ESV], 'at that saying' [KJV], 'at Jesus' word' [AB2], 'at these words' [BNTC; NASB, REB], 'because of these words' [NTC], 'at the/this word' [Lns, WBC], 'to hear Jesus say that' [NCV], 'When the man/he heard this' [AB1; NRSV, TEV], 'When the man heard that' [GW], 'When the man heard Jesus say this' [CEV], 'At this' [NIV, NLT]. This noun is a derivative of the verb λέγω 'to say' and denotes that which has been stated or said, its primary focus being on the content of the communication [LN]. It denotes a statement of definite content [BAGD].

c. pres. pass. participle of λυπέομαι, λυπέω (LN **25.274**) (BAGD 2.b. p 481): 'to be grieving' [AB2, BAGD, BECNT, WBC; NASB, NRSV], 'to be grieved' [KJV], 'to be aggrieved' [Lns], 'to be sad' [BAGD, LN; NLT], 'to be sad at heart' [BECNT, BNTC], 'to look unhappy' [GW], 'to be distressed' [AB1, BAGD], 'to be greatly distressed' [**LN**]. The phrase 'he left grieving' is translated 'he left sorrowfully' [NCV], 'he went away sorrowful' [NTC; ESV, NET], 'he went away sad' [CEV, NIV, TEV], 'he went away with a heavy heart' [REB]. This verb means to be sad because of what has happened or what one has done [LN].

d. κτῆμα (LN 57.15) (BAGD 1. p. 455): 'possession, property' [BAGD, LN]. The clause 'because/for he had many possessions' [BECNT, WBC; NLT, NRSV] is also translated 'for he had great possessions' [Lns; ESV, KJV], 'for he possessed much property' [NTC], 'for he was one who owned much property' [NASB], 'for he had great estates' [AB2], 'because he owned a lot of property' [GW], 'because he had great wealth' [NIV], 'for he was a man of great wealth' [BNTC; REB], 'for he was very wealthy' [AB1], 'because he was rich' [NCV], 'because/for he was very rich' [CEV, NET, TEV]. This noun is a derivative of κτάομαι 'to acquire' and denotes that which is owned or possessed, and it usually refers to land [LN]. It denotes property, a possession such as a field, a house, furniture, or any other kind of movable property. In later usage the noun became restricted to landed property, fields, or some piece of ground [BAGD].

QUESTION—Did the young man become downcast or did he become shocked?

1. He became downcast [BECNT, BNTC, CBC, EBC, EGT, Gnd, Hb, ICC, NICNT, NLTfn, NTC, PNTC, Sw, Tay, TH, WBC; all versions except NRSV]. He was sad and sullen [NTC]. He outwardly showed his sorrow and gloom [ICC]. This man's hopes were dashed, and his pain was visible

on his countenance [Sw]. There was an expression of deep gloom in his face [Hb]. His face fell, showing his disappointment and sorrow [NICNT].
2. He became shocked [NRSV] or indignant [AB2]. This attitude reverses the reverence that the young man showed when he knelt before Jesus in verse 17 [AB2].

QUESTION—Why did he leave Jesus at this point?

He felt great sorrow because of the unexpected demand Jesus had made and went away because he preferred his present earthly possessions to future possessions in heaven [Hb]. He was sorrowful because he realized that he had chosen earthly riches over the heavenly riches [BECNT]. To obey Jesus was too much of a risk for him to take [EBC, ICC]. The challenge was too great [BNTC].

QUESTION—What kind of possessions did this man have?

The words 'he had many possessions' reveal the kind of wealth he had [Gnd]. His wealth consisted of his possessions and real estate [PNTC]. He possessed property [Lns] consisting of estates and lands [Hb, NAC, Sw, Tay].

DISCOURSE UNIT—10:23–31 [Hb; NLT]. The topic is a discussion about wealth and reward [Hb], the rewards of discipleship [NLT].

10:23 And having-looked-around, Jesus says to his disciples, "How hard[a] (it is) for-the (ones) having wealth[b] to-enter[c] into the kingdom of God."

LEXICON—a. δυσκόλως (LN **22.32**) (BAGD 209): 'hard, difficult' [BAGD, LN], 'with difficulty' [LN]. The adverb δυσκόλως 'hardly' modifies the verb εἰσελεύσονται 'will enter' and is translated literally 'how hardly shall they…enter' [KJV], 'how with difficulty shall those…enter' [Lns]. All other translations adjust their translations to match the wording of the next verse in which the similar word δύσκολόν 'difficult' is an adjective modifying the supplied verb ἐστιν 'it is': 'how hard it is/will-be…to enter' [AB1, AB2, NTC; all versions except CEV, ESV, KJV], 'it's hard…to get into' [CEV], 'how difficult it will be…to enter' [BECNT, BNTC, WBC; ESV]. The adverb refers to the difficulty involved in accomplishing or doing something [LN].

b. χρῆμα [LN **57.31**] (BAGD 1. p. 885): 'wealth' [BAGD, LN], 'property' [BAGD], 'riches, abundance' [LN]. The phrase 'the (ones) having wealth' is translated 'those who have wealth' [WBC; ESV, NRSV], 'those who possess wealth' [NTC], 'those who are wealthy' [NASB], 'the wealthy' [REB], 'those who have riches' [AB1, BNTC; similarly BECNT; KJV], 'those who are rich' [**LN**], 'the rich' [AB2; NCV, NET, NIV, NLT], 'rich people' [CEV, GW, TEV]. This noun refers to economic resources and usually implies that there is an abundance of such assets [LN]. The word 'wealth' is more general than 'many possessions' in the preceding verse [Hb]. It can mean 'those who have much property' or 'those who are very rich' [TH]. It is a general term for 'monetary wealth' [PNTC]. The word 'wealth' is used instead of the 'many possessions' in the preceding verse since it refers to the money that would have come from the sale of his possessions [Gnd]. There seems to be no significant difference between the two terms since both refer to affluence [NIGTC].

c. fut. mid. (deponent = act.) indic. of εἰσέρχομαι (LN 15.93, 90.70) (BAGD 2.a. p. 233): 'to enter' [BAGD, LN (15.93); all translations except CEV], 'to get into' [CEV], 'to begin to experience, to attain' [LN (90.70)]. This verb means to move into a space [LN (15.93)] or to begin to experience an event or state [LN (90.70)]. This is a figurative use of 'to enter' and means 'to attain, to share in something, to come to enjoy something' [BAGD].

QUESTION—What was Jesus looking around to see?

This implies that the disciples were present while Jesus was talking with the young man [Gnd], and now Jesus turns around to look at the disciples standing around him [TH]. His eyes swept around the circle of the Twelve as he spoke to them about the incident they had witnessed [Sw]. Jesus was looking to see what impression his conversation with the rich man had made on them [EGT, Hb]. He wanted to impress upon them the significance of the young man's sorrowful departure and point out the difficulty of entering the kingdom of God [BNTC, NTC].

QUESTION—When does one enter the kingdom in the statement 'How hard it is…to enter into the kingdom of God'?

A similar question about the time of entering the kingdom was asked in verse 15 concerning Jesus' statement, 'Whoever does not *receive* the kingdom of God like a child, by no means may *enter* into it' and there was no clear consensus on the answer. In verse 17, a young man asked Jesus 'What must I do in order that I may *inherit* eternal life?' Jesus again responded by talking about *'entering into* the kingdom of God' in verses 23, 24, and 25. When the disciples ask the rhetorical question ' Who is able *to be saved*?' in verse 26, they are apparently convinced the time of entering the kingdom occurs when one is saved. Yet in verse 30 Jesus talks about *receiving* eternal life 'in the age to come'.

1. This refers to entering the form of the kingdom that is already present among them [BECNT, Hb, Lns, NAC, NTC, TRT, WBC]. The kingdom is pictured as a society under God's rule where a person becomes a member of that society by submitting to God's authority [Hb]. The kingdom has already come through the ministry of Jesus, and a person must enter this present form of the kingdom in order to experience its presence and benefits [BECNT]. While the blessings of the kingdom are to be received as a gift, we must enter the kingdom through our response of faith and obedience [NAC]. 'Receiving the kingdom' is an idiom for submitting to God's rule [TRT]. Entering the kingdom of God is about the same as entering eternal life at the time one is saved [NTC].

2. This refers to entering the future eschatological kingdom [AB1, NICNT, NIGTC, NTC, TH]. The reference to 'entering' the kingdom gives it a spatial meaning that implies it will happen in the future [AB1]. Even

though entering the kingdom includes becoming saved, the emphasis is on that future salvation when one becomes a partaker of ultimate bliss in the restored universe [NTC]. The person who does not receive the kingdom now will not enter into it when it is finally established in the consummation of the kingdom [NICNT]. This kind of life is the heritage that is entered at the time of the resurrection [AB1]. While *receiving* the kingdom seems to relate to a person's attitude and response towards what God demands in this life, *entering* the kingdom seems to refer to one's eternal destiny. One's reception of it now will be the means of entering that kingdom in the hereafter [NIGTC].

QUESTION—What makes it so hard for those who have wealth to enter the kingdom of God?

Wealth can be a dangerous instrument for reinforcing a person's self-sufficiency and independence from God [ESVfn, NICNT]. Too much wealth in the present age acts as a deterrent from preparing for the kingdom [WBC].

10:24 **And the disciples were-amazed**[a] **at his words. And Jesus again having-continued**[b] **says to-them, "Children,**[c] **how difficult it-is to-enter into the kingdom of-God.**

TEXT—Manuscripts reading πῶς δύσκολόν ἐστιν 'how difficult it is' are given an A rating by GNT to indicate it was regarded to be certain. A variant reading is πῶς δύσκολόν ἐστιν τους πεποιθότας ἐπὶ χρήμασιν 'how difficult it is for the (ones) trusting in riches' and it is followed by Hb, Lns; KJV.

LEXICON—a. perf. pass. indic. of θαμβέομαι, θαμβέω (LN 25.209) (BAGD 2. p. 350): 'to be amazed' [AB1, BAGD, BECNT, BNTC, LN, Lns; ESV, NASB, NCV, NIV, NLT, REB], 'to be astonished' [AB2, LN; KJV, NET], 'to be astounded' [BAGD], 'to be shocked' [CEV, TEV], 'to be stunned' [GW], 'to be startled' [NTC], 'to be perplexed' [NRSV]; 'to marvel' [WBC]. This verb means to experience astonishment as the result of some unusual event [LN]. They were surprised and could not entirely process what Jesus was saying [CBC]. This word occurs at 1:27; 10:24, 32.

b. aorist pass. (deponent = act.) participle of ἀποκρίνομαι (LN 33.28, 33.184) (BAGD 3. p. 93): 'to continue' [BAGD], 'to speak, to declare, to say' [LN (33.28)], 'to answer, to reply' [LN (33.184)]. The phrase 'again having continued says to them' is translated 'continued and said to them' [NTC], 'went on to say' [TEV], 'again answering, says to them' [Lns, WBC], 'again answered and said to them' [AB2; similarly KJV], 'again says to them in reply' [BECNT], 'answered again and said to them' [NASB]. Some consider the participle ἀποκριθεὶς 'having answered' to be redundant and do not translate it: 'again said to them' [NET], 'said to them again' [BNTC; ESV, GW, NRSV], 'again said' [AB1], 'said again' [NCV, NIV, NLT], 'told them again' [CEV], 'insisted' [REB]. This verb means to introduce or continue a somewhat formal discourse, and it

regularly occurs with λέγω 'to say' [LN (33.28)] or it means to respond to a question that asks for information [LN (33.184)]. It indicates the continuation of a discourse [BAGD].
  c. τέκνον (LN 9.46) (BAGD 2.b. p. 808): 'my child' [BAGD, LN], 'my dear friend, my dear man, my dear one, my dear lad' [LN]. It is translated 'children' [AB2, BNTC, Lns, NTC, WBC; ESV, GW, KJV, NASB, NET, NIV, NRSV, REB], 'my children' [NCV, TEV], 'dear children' [NLT], not explicit [CEV]. This noun is an extension of meaning of τέκνον 'child' and denotes a person of any age for whom there is a special relationship of endearment and association [LN]. The word is used figuratively to refer to a spiritual child in relation to his master [BAGD].
QUESTION—Why were the disciples amazed?
  They were amazed at the λόγοις 'words' Jesus spoke. The plural form 'words' refer to what Jesus had said to the young man and also to what he has just said to his disciples [Gnd]. The disciples had always thought of wealth as an advantage [Hb] and an indication of God's pleasure [BNTC]. They were amazed because Peter the fisherman and some of the others had possessions [ESVfn].
QUESTION—Why did Jesus call his disciples 'children'?
  This is an affectionate form of address [BECNT, Gnd, Hb]. Instead of just a way of showing his affection for his disciples, it could be that Jesus was taking the authoritative role of a father who has to explain something that his children had not grasped [Gnd].
QUESTION—Is it significant that the person entering the kingdom is not identified as being rich?
  1. This is now referring to anyone [AB2, BNTC, ICC, NAC, NCBC, NICNT, NIGTC, NTC, Sw, Tay, WBC]. It is a generalization [ICC, NIGTC]. Entry into the kingdom is difficult for everyone whether or not they are rich [WBC]. Although it is especially hard for a rich person, removing the qualifier ' a rich man' points out that it is hard for everyone to enter the kingdom of God regardless of their wealth [Sw, Tay].
  2. This still refers to rich men [Gnd, Hb, Lns; KJV]. This statement is still speaking about rich men and is probably an ellipsis which is to be filled in by the surrounding verses that are focused on rich men [Gnd]. The context argues against a generalization here. The manuscripts that add 'for the ones trusting in riches' are probably original [Hb, Lns].

10:25 It is easier (for) a camel to-go through the eye of-a needle than (for) a rich (person) to-enter into the kingdom of-God."
TEXT—Manuscripts reading κάμηλον 'camel' are given an A rating by GNT to indicate it was regarded to be certain. A variant reading is κάμιλον 'rope'.
QUESTION—Does this imply that a camel can actually go through the eye of a needle if it tries hard enough?
  This metaphor picks out the largest animal and the smallest opening in Palestine to vividly picture an impossibility [NICNT, TH]. It is a humorous

example of something being impossible [CGTC]. This was probably a popular proverb denoting that something was impossible [Hb]. The hyperbole of a large camel having to fit through the small eye of a needle emphasizes the fact that such a thing is humanly impossible [ESVfn]. It says that a rich man's entry into the kingdom would be even more difficult than for a camel to go through a needle's eye [Hb, Lns].

10:26 And they-were- exceedingly[a] -amazed,[b] saying to[c] themselves, "And who is-able[d] to-be-saved?"

TEXT—Manuscripts reading πρὸς ἑαυτούς 'to themselves' are given a B rating by GNT to indicate it was regarded to be almost certain. A variant reading is πρὸς αὐτόν 'to him' and it is followed by Lns, Tay; ESV, NASB.

LEXICON—a. περισσῶς (LN 78.31) (BAGD p. 651): 'exceedingly' [BAGD; ESV], 'beyond measure' [BAGD], 'very great, extremely, all the more, much greater' [LN]. See translations of this word in the preceding lexical item. This adverb indicates a degree which is considerably in excess of some point on an implied or explicit scale of extent [LN]. περισσῶς (LN 78.31) (BAGD p. 651): 'exceedingly' [BAGD; ESV], 'beyond measure' [BAGD], 'very great, extremely, all the more, much greater' [LN]. See translations of this word in the preceding lexical item. This adverb indicates a degree which is considerably in excess of some point on an implied or explicit scale of extent [LN].

b. imperf. pass. indic. of ἐκπλήσσομαι, ἐκπλήσσω (LN 25.219) (BAGD 2. p. 244): 'to be amazed, to be overwhelmed' [BAGD], 'to be greatly astounded' [LN]. The phrase οἱ περισσῶς ἐξεπλήσσοντο 'they were exceedingly amazed' is translated 'the disciples were completely amazed' [TEV], 'they were more amazed than ever' [AB1], 'Jesus' disciples/they were even more amazed' [AB2; CEV, NIV], 'this amazed his disciples more than ever' [GW], 'they were greatly astonished' [WBC], 'they were exceedingly astonished' [BECNT; ESV], 'they were even more astonished' [NASB, NET], 'they were greatly astounded' [NRSV], 'they were more astonished than ever' [BNTC; REB], 'the disciples were astounded' [NLT], 'they were astonished out of measure' [KJV], 'the followers were even more surprised' [NCV], 'they were beyond measure shocked' [Lns], 'shocked even more' [NTC]. This verb means to be so amazed that one is practically overwhelmed [LN]. The imperfect tense indicates the protracted feeling of their utter bewilderment [Hb]. This word occurs at 1:22; 6:2; 7:37; 10:26; 11:18

c. πρός (LN 90.58) (BAGD III.1.e. p. 710): 'to, with' [BAGD, LN]. The phrase λέγοντες πρὸς ἑαυτούς 'saying to themselves' [BECNT, WBC] is also translated 'saying among themselves' [AB2], 'said to one another' [AB1, BNTC; NET, NRSV, REB], 'said to each other' [NTC; NCV, NIV], 'they asked each other' [CEV, GW], 'asked one another' [TEV], 'they asked' [NLT], 'saying among themselves' [KJV]. Others follow a

different manuscript 'saying/said to him' [Lns; ESV, NASB]. This preposition indicates the experiencer of an event [LN].
d. pres. mid./pass. (deponent = act.) indic. of δύναμαι (LN 74.5): 'to be able to, can' [LN]. The clause 'And who is able to be saved?' [Lns] is also translated 'Then who can be saved?' [BECNT, BNTC, NTC, WBC; ESV, NASB, NCV, NET, NRSV, REB; similarly GW, KJV, NIV, TEV; similarly AB1, AB2], 'Then who in the world can be saved?' [NLT], 'How can anyone ever be saved?' [CEV]. This verb means to be able to do or to experience something [LN].

QUESTION—To whom did the disciples direct their questions?

The words λέγοντες πρὸς ἑαυτούς 'saying to themselves' could either mean 'saying within themselves' or 'among themselves' [AB2]. Who the disciples were addressing is uncertain [BNTC]. It probably means 'saying to one another' [AB2, Gnd] as it does in 9:10 [AB2]. It has the meaning 'saying to one another' [AB1, AB2, BNTC, NTC; CEV, GW, KJV, NCV, NET, NIV, NRSV, REB, TEV].

QUESTION—What is implied by their rhetorical question, 'And who is able to be saved?'

This shows they understood 'entering the kingdom' to mean the same as being saved and their question meant 'If a rich man can't be saved, then nobody can' [Hb, NTC, Tay]. Jesus had spoken about the difficulty for rich men to enter heaven in verse 23, and said it was just as difficult for all men in verse 24. So when Jesus seemed to indicate it was impossible for rich men to enter the kingdom of heaven in verse 25, they concluded that Jesus was now saying that no one could be saved [Lns, NTC]. Their question implies that what Jesus said couldn't be true [Lns]. A rich man possesses the leisure and means to perform many charitable acts and his wealth apparently witnesses to God's blessing and favor on him. So if it is impossible for such a man to be saved, how can anyone be saved? [BECNT].

QUESTION—What did they mean about being saved?

Being saved is synonymous with inheriting eternal life [NAC, TRT], having treasure in heaven [BECNT], entering the kingdom of God [BECNT, EBC, NAC, NCBC, NICNT, Tay, TRT], deliverance from hellfire [Gnd].

10:27 Having-looked-at[a] them, Jesus says, "For[b] men (this is) impossible,[c] but not for God. Because all (things) (are) possible[d] for God."

LEXICON—a. aorist act. participle of ἐμβλέπω (LN 24.9) (BAGD 1. p. 254): 'to look at' [AB1, AB2, BAGD, BECNT, Lns, WBC; all versions except KJV, NLT, TEV], 'to look at intently' [NLT], 'to look steadily at' [BNTC], 'to fasten one's eyes on' [NTC], 'to look straight at' [LN; TEV], 'to look upon' [KJV], 'to look directly at' [LN], 'to fix one's gaze at' [BAGD]. This verb means to direct one's vision and attention to a particular object [LN]. His look riveted their attention to his reply [Hb]. This word occurs at 10:21, 27.

b. παρά (LN 90.3) (BAGD II.2.e. p. 610): 'for' [AB1, BAGD, BECNT, BNTC, LN; GW, NET, NIV, NRSV, TEV], 'with' [AB2, LN, Lns, NTC, WBC; CEV, ESV, KJV, NASB], not explicit [NCV, NLT]. This preposition indicates a potential agent [LN].
c. ἀδύνατος (LN 71.3) (BAGD 2.a. p. 19): 'impossible' [BAGD, LN]. The phrase 'for men this/it is impossible' [AB1, BNTC; REB] is also translated 'with men impossible' [Lns], 'with men/man/people/humans this/it is impossible' [AB2, BECNT, WBC; ESV, KJV, NASB], 'for mortals it is impossible' [NRSV], 'there are some things that people cannot do' [CEV], 'this is something people cannot do' [NCV], 'this is impossible for human beings' [TEV], 'this is impossible for mere humans' [NET], 'humanly speaking, it is impossible' [NLT], 'it's impossible for people to save themselves' [GW]. This adjective pertains to something being impossible, presumably because of a lack of power to alter or control circumstances [LN].
d. δυνατός (LN 71.2) (BAGD 2.c. p. 209): 'possible' [BAGD, LN]. The clause 'all things are possible for God' [BECNT; NET] is also translated 'all things are possible with God' [AB2, Lns, WBC; ESV, NASB, NIV], 'for God all things are possible' [NRSV], 'with God all things are possible' [NTC; KJV], 'everything is possible with God' [NLT; similarly AB2], 'everything is possible for God' [BNTC; GW, REB, TEV], 'God can do all things' [NCV], 'God can do anything' [CEV]. This adjective pertains to something being possible and implies having the power or ability to alter or control circumstances [LN].

QUESTION—What is impossible for men but possible for God?
This refers to the process of being saved [Hb, TH]. No one can be saved by his own efforts, and God does for people what they cannot do for themselves [EBC]. This is true for rich and poor alike [Hb]. It is God who saves—not faith, not works, not any human endeavor [AB1]. This can be difficult to express in some languages and it could be filled out, 'People cannot save themselves, but God can save them.' An example of how a generic type of verb could be used is, 'men cannot do this, but God can save them' [TH].

QUESTION—What are the 'all things' that are possible for God?
This says that God can do 'anything' or 'all things' [TH]. God's power is unlimited, but it is understood that God does not do things that are contrary to his nature and 'all things' specifically relate to the things necessary for man's salvation in the context of this verse [Hb].

DISCOURSE UNIT—10:28-31 [NICNT]. The topic is the rewards of discipleship.

10:28 Peter began[a] to-say to-him, "Look,[b] we left[c] everything and have-followed[d] you."

LEXICON—a. aorist mid. indic. of ἄρχομαι (LN 68.1): 'to begin' [AB1, AB2, BECNT, LN, Lns, NLT, NTC, WBC; ESV, KJV, NASB, NET, NRSV], 'to commence' [LN]. The phrase ἄρξατο λέγειν 'began to say' is translated 'spoke up' [GW, TEV], 'said' [NCV, NIV, REB], 'replied' [CEV], 'asked' [BNTC]. This verb means to initiate an action [LN]. The aorist ἤρξατο 'began' with the infinitive λέγειν 'to say' has the same meaning as the imperfect verb 'was saying' [Tay]. 'Began' indicates that Peter intended to change the direction of the discussion [Hb].

b. ἰδού (LN 91.13) (BAGD 1.b.ε. p. 371): 'look' [AB1, AB2, BAGD, BECNT, LN, NTC; NCV, NET, NRSV, TEV], 'see' [ESV], 'behold' [BAGD, WBC; NASB], 'lo' [Lns; KJV], 'listen, pay attention' [LN], 'remember' [CEV], not explicit [GW, NIV, NLT]. 'Look' is translated 'What about us?' [BNTC; REB]. This demonstrative particle is a prompter of attention and serves to emphasize the statement that follows [LN]. It is used to emphasize the importance of something [BAGD]. This word does not imply a literal 'looking' at some object, but functions as an emphatic call for attention to what is being said [TH]. The word occurs at 1:2; 3:32; 4:3; 10:28, 33; 14:41, 42.

c. aorist act. indic. of ἀφίημι (LN 85.45) (BAGD 3.a. p. 126): 'to leave' [AB1, AB2, BAGD, BECNT, BNTC, LN, Lns, WBC; all versions except GW, NLT], 'to leave behind' [LN], 'to give up' [NTC; GW, NLT]. This verb means to let something be left behind at some place [LN]. The aorist tense looks back to the definite break they had made when they responded to Jesus' call to follow him [Hb]. This does not just refer to getting up and departing from a location, it also includes a renunciation of all that they possessed [TH]. The aorist tense points back to an accomplished fact [AB1, CBC, CGTC, EGT, Gnd, Tay].

d. perf. act. indic. of ἀκολουθέω (LN 36.31): 'to follow' [AB2, BECNT, BNTC, LN, Lns, NTC; ESV, KJV, NASB, NCV, NRSV, TEV], 'to be a disciple of' [LN]. The phrase 'and have followed you' [WBC] is also translated 'to follow you' [GW, NET, NIV, NLT, REB], 'to become your followers' [AB1], 'to be your followers' [CEV]. This verb means to be a follower or a disciple of someone by promoting the leader's cause and adhering to his teachings and instructions [LN]. The perfect tense stresses the fact that they were still following Jesus [AB1, CBC, CGTC, EGT, Gnd, Hb, Lns, Tay].

QUESTION—Why did Peter use the emphatic pronoun ἡμεῖς 'we'?

Peter drew attention to what he was going to say with 'look', and then emphasized the pronoun 'we' in order to make a contrast between the Twelve who had followed Jesus as disciples and the young man who had turned down Jesus' invitation to follow him [AB2, EBC, Hb, ICC, NICNT, PNTC, TH, TRT]. Peter was acting as the spokesman for the Twelve [CGTC, Gnd, NAC, NICNT, NIGTC].

QUESTION—What did Peter imply by his statement?

Peter was pointing out that the disciples had actually done what Jesus had asked the rich young man to do [BECNT, BNTC, Lns, NTC, WBC]. Some mention that there was a bit of exaggeration in Peter's claim since his break with home ties had not been complete as seen in 1:29; 3:9; 4:1, 36 [AB1,

AB2, NAC, NCBC, Tay], but another points out that even though Peter and Andrew still possessed a home (1:29) and a boat (3:9; 4:1, 36), their commitment to Jesus was total and whatever Jesus did tell them to leave, they did leave to follow him [BECNT]. The warnings about wealth which Jesus drew from the rich man's example didn't seem to apply to the Twelve and it seems that their place in the kingdom of God was already assured [NIGTC]. Matthew has recorded the implied question, 'What then shall we have?' (Matt. 19:27), showing that Peter was still thinking in terms of material riches rather than spiritual riches [EBC].

10:29 Jesus said, "Truly[a] I-say to-you(pl), there-is no-one who has-left house or brothers or sisters or mother or father or children or fields[b] for-my sake[c] and for-the-sake-of the good-news,

TEXT—Manuscripts reading ἢ μητέρα ἢ πατέρα ἢ τέκνα 'or mother, or father or children' are followed by GNT, which does not mention any variant reading. A variant reading is ἢ πατέρα ἢ μητέρα ἢ γυναῖκα ἢ τέκνα 'or father or mother or wife or children' and it is followed by KJV.

LEXICON—a. ἀμήν (LN 72.6) (BAGD 2. p. 45): 'truly' [AB1, BAGD, BECNT, BNTC, LN, WBC; ESV, NASB, NRSV, REB], 'indeed, it is true that' [LN], 'verily' [KJV], 'amen' [AB2, Lns]. The phrase 'truly I say to you' is also translated 'I tell you the truth' [NCV, NET, NIV], 'you can be sure that' [CEV], 'I can guarantee this truth' [GW], 'I solemnly declare to you' [NTC], 'yes' [NLT, TEV]. This particle makes a strong affirmation of what is being declared [LN]. It is an assertive particle that introduces something new by emphasizing its importance [BAGD]. The phrase 'truly I say to you' occurs at 3:28; 8:12; 9:1, 41; 10:15, 29; 11:23; 12:43; 13:30; 14:9, 18, 25, 30.

b. ἀγρός (LN 1.95) (BAGD 1. p. 14): 'field' [BAGD, LN]. The plural form is translated 'fields' [AB2, BECNT, Lns, NTC, WBC; GW, NET, NIV, NRSV, TEV], 'farms' [NASB, NCV], 'land' [AB1, BNTC, LN; CEV, REB], 'lands' [ESV, KJV], 'property' [NLT]. This denotes land that is under cultivation or is used for pasture [LN]. It is a plot of ground used mainly for agriculture and it is viewed primarily as a piece of property [BAGD].

c. ἕνεκεν, ἕνεκα (LN 90.43) (BAGD p. 264): 'for the sake of' [AB1, AB2, BAGD, BECNT, BNTC, LN, Lns, NTC, WBC; ESV, KJV, NASB, NET, NLT, NRSV, REB], 'for (me)' [CEV, NCV, NIV, TEV], 'because of' [BAGD, LN; GW], 'on account of' [BAGD]. This preposition indicates a participant constituting the reason for an event [LN].

QUESTION—What is the reason for the items in this list being connected by the conjunction ἢ 'or'?

The conjunction 'or' is not promising a reward for people unwilling to leave all they have in order to follow Jesus. The singular nouns are making allowance for the disciples whose 'all' does not include every item in the list. The parents of some may have died and some might not have any children

[Gnd] and only a few would have possessed land [NIGTC]. Not all of the disciples were required to leave everything listed here in order to follow Jesus [Hb, Lns]. The degree of renunciation should not be overstated. When Peter and his fellow disciples had left their nets to follow Jesus (1:16–20) the home owned by Peter and Andrew remained available for them (1:29) and was probably the house used by Jesus as his base in Capernaum. We should consider the reference to the leaving behind of family and possessions to be associated with the itinerant ministry of the disciples [NIGTC].

QUESTION—What is meant by leaving these relatives and things ἕνεκεν 'for the sake of' Jesus and the good news?

This could indicate either the *reason* a disciple had for leaving them, 'because of me and the good news' or the *purpose* for leaving them, 'for the benefit of me and the good news' [TH]. The disciples left home, relatives, and property because they were motivated by their love for Jesus and their desire to proclaim the good news [Hb].

10:30 **who will not receive a-hundredfold^a now in this era^b houses and brothers and sisters and mothers and children and fields, with persecutions,^c and in the age^d to-come eternal life.**

LEXICON—a. ἑκατονταπλασίων (LN 60.78) (BAGD p. 237): 'a hundredfold' [AB2, BAGD, Lns, NTC; ESV, KJV, NRSV], 'one hundredfold' [WBC], 'a hundred times as much' [AB2, LN; GW, NASB, NET, NIV, REB], 'a hundred times as many' [CEV, NLT], 'a hundred times more' [BECNT; NCV], 'a hundred times over' [BNTC], 'much more' [TEV]. This pronominal adjective refers to one hundred times as much in quantity [LN]. 'Hundredfold' is not to be understood literally but in the more general sense of a very abundant compensation [My].

b. καιρός (LN **67.145**) (BAGD 3. p. 395): 'era' [LN], 'age' [BAGD, LN]. The phrase νῦν ἐν τῷ καιρῷ τούτῳ 'now in this era' is translated 'now in this age' [NRSV], 'in this age' [NET, REB], 'in this present age' [AB1, BNTC; NIV, TEV], 'now in the present age' [NASB], 'in this present era' [**LN**], 'in this world' [CEV], 'here in this world' [NCV], 'now in this time' [AB2, BECNT, Lns, NTC, WBC; ESV, KJV], 'now' [NLT], 'here in this life' [GW]. This noun denotes an indefinite period of time that is probably related to a particular state of affairs [LN]. 'This era' refers to the period of time before the great day of judgment [NTC].

c. διωγμός (LN 39.45) (BAGD p. 201): 'persecution' [BAGD, LN]. The phrase 'with persecutions' [AB2, BECNT, BNTC, Lns, WBC; ESV, KJV, NRSV] is also translated 'and persecutions besides/as-well' [REB, TEV], 'along with persecutions/persecution' [NTC; GW, NASB, NLT], 'and persecutions, too' [AB1], 'all with persecutions' [NET], 'and with them, persecutions' [NIV], 'though they will be mistreated' [CEV], 'and with those things, they will also suffer for their belief' [NCV]. This noun denotes the type of persecution that is a systematic organized program to

      oppress and harass people [LN]. The term 'persecution' in the NT refers to religious persecution [CBC].
   d. αἰών (LN 67.143) (BAGD 2.b. p. 27): 'age' [BAGD, LN], 'era' [LN]. The phrase 'in the age to come' [AB1, BNTC, NTC; ESV, NASB, NET, NIV, NRSV, REB, TEV] is also translated 'in the coming age' [AB2, BECNT, WBC], 'in the age that is coming' [NCV], 'in the world to come' [CEV, GW, KJV, NLT], 'in the eon, the coming one' [Lns]. This noun denotes a unit of time that is a particular stage or period of history [LN]. It refers to a segment of time, and the phrase 'the age to come' refers either to the Messianic period or to all future time [BAGD].

QUESTION—What is being promised about receiving this list of things that have been given up for the sake of Jesus and the gospel in 'this era'?

    This should not be taken literally as if each disciple desired to have a hundred mothers and a hundred children of his own. This is about the extended family of the followers of Jesus [NIGTC]. It is about the fellowship that is found in the Christian community [BECNT, BNTC, WBC]. They can expect to enjoy fellowship with other believers and to find a welcome in the houses and lands of other believers [ESVfn]. Even if the disciples have to flee from their pursuers to a hundred different places, they will find a hundred different houses, families, and farms available to them through the hospitality of fellow believers. In fact they were already discovering such hospitality as they traveled about with Jesus [Gnd]. This is a promise for all true followers of Jesus and not just for the twelve disciples [NTC].

QUESTION—Why doesn't it include fathers?

    The believer already has a heavenly Father [BECNT]. God is the head of the new spiritual family [Gnd, NICNT, NIGTC].

QUESTION—What is meant by 'the age to come'?

    The terms 'this age' and 'the age to come' are derived from Jewish eschatology [Gnd, NICNT]. It is a Jewish rabbinical term [WBC]. The age to come is the heavenly eon that will begin at the end of the world after 'this era' has run its course [Lns].

QUESTION—Why does it say that 'eternal life' will be received in the age to come?

    Eternal life is the goal that the rich young man failed to obtain [BECNT, Gnd, NIGTC, NLTfn, WBC]. Mathew, Mark, and Luke speak of eternal life as something a person receives in the age to come. It is John who emphasizes the possibility of receiving eternal life in the present time [NETfn]. Although they already have eternal life in the present time, they will have a far more abundant and ever increasing measure of it in the age to come [NTC]. This refers to their entrance into the heavenly life [Lns].

10:31 But/and[a] many (that are) first[b] will-be last,[c] and the last (will be) first."

TEXT—Manuscripts reading οἱ ἔσχατοι 'the last' are given a C rating by GNT to indicate that choosing it over a variant text was difficult. A variant reading is ἔσχατοι 'last'.

LEXICON—a. δέ (LN 89.94, 89.124): 'but' [LN (89.124); all translations except Lns; NCV], 'and' [LN (89.93)], 'nevertheless' [Lns], not explicit [BNTC; NCV]. This conjunction indicates a contrast [LN (89.124)] or an additive relation [LN (89.93)].

b. πρῶτος (LN 87.45) (BAGD 1.c.β. p. 726): 'first' [BAGD, LN; all versions except NCV, NLT], 'foremost' [BAGD, LN], 'most important, most prominent' [BAGD], 'prominent, great, important, foremost' [LN]. The phrase 'who are first' is translated 'who have the highest place now' [NCV], 'who are the greatest now' [NLT]. This pronominal adjective refers to rank and implies special prominence and status because of high rank [LN (87.45)]. 'First' and 'last' do not refer to time but to rank [TH]. 'First' in this sense occurs at 9:35; 10:31, 44.

c. ἔσχατος (LN 87.66) (BAGD 2. p. 313): 'last' [BAGD, LN; all versions except NCV, NLT], 'least, most insignificant' [BAGD], 'lowest, least important' [LN]. The phrase 'will be last' is translated 'will have the lowest place in the future' [NCV], 'will be least important then' [CEV]. This adjective pertains to being in the lowest status [LN].

QUESTION—What is meant by being 'first' and 'last'?

The same saying is applied in different circumstances in Matthew 20:16 and Luke 13.30. The application of this saying in Mark is not clear [AB1, BNTC, CGTC, EBC, NICNT, NIGTC, NTC, Tay]. It is not possible to determine whether the conjunction δέ is the adversative 'but' or the explanatory 'for' [TH]. If it means 'and', it could make this verse a positive statement that reinforces the promise of verses 29–30, but if it means 'but', it could make this verse a warning against the presumption voiced by Peter in verse 28 where he asserted the superiority of the disciples over the rich man [NICNT, NIGTC]. None of the translations used in the lexicon have translated the conjunction δέ at the beginning of the verse to mean 'and'. This verse refers to the future when God will evaluate the lives of men and human values will be reversed [EBC]. It could be a warning against the self-seeking spirit that was behind Peter's comment about the Twelve leaving all to follow Jesus [EBC, Hb, My, NAC, NICNT, NIGTC, Sw]. The mere fact that these men were called first and were nearest to Jesus does not necessarily give them prominence or any exclusive right to the blessing promised by Jesus [ICC]. Jesus could be summarizing his teaching in verses 17–31 about the rich and powerful having the tables turned on them [EBC]. Perhaps this was a warning about the rich young man's attitude [NTC]. This contrasts the great difference between God's evaluation and humanity's evaluation [BECNT, TRT]. The 'first' are those who are highly regarded by others because of such things as their wealth, education, position, and prestige. But since God knows all hearts, he assigns many of such people to a lower position behind others and may even exclude some of them from heaven completely as described in Matthew 7:21–23 [NTC]. Some commentaries take being made 'last' to refer to being excluded from the kingdom of God [Gnd, Lns, TRT, WBC].

DISCOURSE UNIT—10:32–45 [NIGTC; NASB]. The topic is following Jesus in the way of the cross [NIGTC], Jesus' sufferings foretold [NASB].

DISCOURSE UNIT—10:32–34 [CBC, EBC, Hb, NICNT; CEV, GW, ESV, NCV, NET, NIV, NLT, NRSV, TEV]. The topic is the third announcement of the passion [Hb], the third prediction of the Passion [EBC], the third major prophecy of the passion [NICNT], Jesus foretells his death a third time [ESV], Jesus speaks a third time about his death [TEV], Jesus predicts his death again [CBC], Jesus again predicts his death [NIV], Jesus talks about his death [NCV], Jesus again talks about his death [CEV], for a third time Jesus foretells that he will die and come back to life [GW], a third time Jesus foretells his death and resurrection [NRSV], Jesus predicts his death and resurrection [NLT], the third prediction of Jesus' death and resurrection [NET].

10:32 And they were on the road going-up[a] to Jerusalem, and Jesus was going-on-ahead-of them, and they were amazed,[b] but/and the (ones) following-behind[c] were-afraid.[d]

TEXT—Manuscripts reading οἱ δὲ ἀκολουθοῦντες 'and the ones following' are followed by GNT, which does not mention any variant reading. A variant reading is καὶ ἀκολουθοῦντες 'and following (they were afraid)' and it is followed by KJV.

LEXICON—a. pres. act. participle of ἀναβαίνω (LN 15.101) (BAGD 1.a.α. p. 50): 'to go up' [AB1, AB2, BAGD, BECNT, LN, Lns, NTC; ESV, KJV, NASB, NET, NRSV, REB, TEV], 'to travel up' [BNTC], 'to ascend' [BAGD, LN, WBC], not explicit [CEV, GW, NCV, NIV, NLT]. This verb means to move up [LN]. The verb was regularly used to describe traveling to Jerusalem because of the city's greater height than the surrounding region. On this occasion they had not yet started their ascent from Jericho in the Jordan valley since they do not reach that town until verse 46 [TH]. Even though Jerusalem was not the highest point in all Israel, it was normal to speak of 'going up to Jerusalem' because the holy city was set upon a hill [CGTC, Hb, NICNT, WBC].

b. imperf. pass. indic. of θαμβέομαι, θαμβέω (LN 25.209) (BAGD 2. p. 350): 'to be amazed' [BAGD, BECNT, BNTC, LN, Lns, NTC, WBC; ESV, KJV, NASB, NCV, NET, NRSV], 'to be astonished' [AB2, **LN**; NIV], 'to be astounded' [BAGD], 'to be filled with alarm' [TEV], 'to be filled with awe' [NLT, REB], 'to be filled with wonder' [AB1], 'to be startled' [LN], 'to be confused' [CEV]. The phrase 'they were amazed' is translated 'his disciples were shocked that he was going to Jerusalem' [GW]. This verb means to experience astonishment as the result of some

unusual event [LN]. The imperfect tense describes a continuous state [Lns]. This word occurs at 1:27; 10:24, 32.
  c. pres. act. participle of ἀκολουθέω (LN 15.144): 'to follow, to come behind, to go behind' [LN]. The phrase 'but the ones following behind' is translated 'but those who followed' [NET; similarly WBC], 'but others in the crowd who followed' [NCV], 'but his other followers' [CEV], 'while those who followed' [NIV], 'while those who followed behind' [REB], 'and those who followed' [BNTC, NTC; ESV, NASB, NRSV; similarly AB2, BECNT], 'and those who followed behind' [AB1], 'and the people following behind' [NLT], 'moreover, those following' [Lns], 'the people who followed behind' [TEV], 'the others who followed' [GW], 'and as they followed' [KJV]. This verb means to come/go behind/after someone else [LN].
  d. imperf. pass. indic. of φοβέομαι (LN 25.252): 'to be afraid' [LN; all translations except NASB, NLT], 'to be fearful' [NASB], to be overwhelmed with fear' [NLT]. This verb means to be in a state of fear [LN].

QUESTION—Who are the referents of the 'they' who were on the road, the 'them' whom Jesus was going on ahead of, the 'they' who were amazed, and 'the ones' following behind who were afraid?

  1. Jesus and the twelve disciples were on the road. Jesus was going on ahead of the Twelve who were amazed [AB1, AB2, BECNT, CBC, CGTC, EBC, EGT, ESVfn, Hb, Lns, My, NAC, NCBC, NICNT, NIGTC, NLTfn, Sw, Tay, TH]. They were amazed that their Galilean ministry was to be finished so soon [AB1]. They were amazed that Jesus was determined to go to Jerusalem even though he knew of the danger that awaited him there [EBC, ESVfn, Hb, Lns, NIGTC]. Others think the ones who were afraid were another group of people following behind Jesus and the Twelve [EBC, Hb, NIGTC, Sw]. Some think that group was composed of other disciples of Jesus [AB2, BECNT, CGTC, ESVfn, Hb, Lns, NCBC, Tay]. They were afraid of what would happen to Jesus when he arrived in Jerusalem [CGTC, Lns]. They feared that they would also face hostility [BECNT, ESVfn]. Others think that this group was composed of ordinary fellow travelers who were on their way to Jerusalem at the same time [NIGTC, TH]. The people in this group intended to celebrate the Jewish feast at Jerusalem but they were afraid because they sensed something momentous was about to take place [EBC].
  2. Jesus and all the people mentioned in this verse were with him on the road to Jerusalem. Jesus was going on ahead of all of them. The twelve disciples followed after Jesus with the rest of the travelers behind them [BECNT, BNTC, Gnd, NTC, TRT]. The twelve disciples were amazed at the unwavering advance of their leader, but the wider circle of followers further behind were afraid [BECNT, NTC, TRT]. Their amazement was a reverential awe at Jesus' sense of destiny and his desire to fulfill God's

will [BECNT]. They feared the danger of being seen in the company of Jesus [NTC].
3. All of the people were amazed that Jesus would go on ahead of them toward the fate he had predicted for himself in Jerusalem. The twelve disciples were the ones 'following behind' Jesus because they were afraid to join him [Gnd].

And taking-aside[a] the Twelve again[b] he began to-tell them the (things) that-were[c] going-to-happen to-him.

LEXICON—a. aorist act. participle of παραλαμβάνω (LN 15.180) (BAGD 1. p. 619): 'to take aside' [AB1, BECNT, BNTC, LN, NTC, WBC; all versions except ESV, KJV], 'to take' [AB2, Lns; ESV, KJV]. This verb means to take or lead off to a private place [LN].

b. πάλιν (LN 67.55) (BAGD 1.a. p. 606): 'again' [AB2, BECNT, BNTC, LN, Lns, NTC, WBC; ESV, KJV, NASB, NCV, NET, NIV, NRSV], 'once again' [AB1; CEV, GW, REB, TEV], 'once more' [NLT], 'to bring back' [BAGD]. This adverb refers to a subsequent point of time involving repetition [LN]. Jesus 'brought the twelve back' after he had been separated from them for a time when he preceded them on the road [BAGD].

c. pres. act. participle of μέλλω (LN 71.36) (BAGD 1.c.δ. p. 501): 'must be, has to be' [LN], 'to be destined, must, will certainly' [BAGD]. The phrase τὰ μέλλοντα αὐτῷ συμβαίνειν 'the things that were going to happen to him' [TEV; similarly KJV] is also translated 'what was going to happen to him' [BNTC, NTC, WBC; CEV, GW, NASB, NET, NIV; similarly AB2; ESV, NRSV, REB], 'the impending things to happen to him' [Lns], 'what was to happen to him' [AB1], 'the things that were about to happen to him' [BECNT], 'what was about to happen in Jerusalem' [NCV], 'everything that was about to happen to him' [NLT]. This verb means to be inevitable with respect to future developments [LN]. It denotes an action that necessarily follows a divine decree [BAGD]. The participial form does not just mean the things 'that will happen in the future', but 'something that must take place' or 'something that is bound to happen' [TH].

QUESTION—Why does it say that Jesus took the Twelve aside 'again'?
The special mention of the Twelve implies there was a larger group that was not invited to hear what Jesus told the Twelve [Gnd, Hb]. Jesus gathered them around him to make clear the purpose of the journey which had been discussed earlier in less specific terms [NIC]. Jesus had taken various disciples apart as a separate group in 4:34; 7:17; 9:2, 28, and this is another occasion he took a group apart [WBC]. 'Again' refers back to the time in 9:35 that Jesus called these same disciples together to explain something to them [Gnd]. Another explanation is that Jesus gathered the Twelve around him to tell them something special after having walked ahead of them in silent meditation [Hb].

10:33 "Look,[a] we-are-going-up to Jerusalem, and the Son of-Man[b] will-be-delivered[c] to the chief–priests[d] and the scribes[e] and they-will-condemn[f] him to-death and will-deliver him to-the Gentiles[g]

LEXICON—a. ἰδού (LN 91.13) (BAGD 1.b.ε. p. 371): 'look' [AB2, BAGD, BNTC, LN; NCV, NET], 'behold' [BAGD, BECNT, WBC; KJV, NASB], 'see' [AB1; ESV, NRSV], 'listen' [LN, NTC; NLT, TEV], 'lo' [Lns], 'pay attention' [LN], not explicit [CEV, GW, NIV, REB]. This demonstrative particle is a prompter of attention and serves to emphasize the subsequent statement [LN]. It is used to emphasize the importance of something [BAGD, Hb]. This word is a command to pay attention to what is going to be said [TH]. The word occurs at 1:2; 3:32; 4:3; 10:28, 33; 14:41, 42.

b. υἱὸς τοῦ ἀνθρώπου (LN 9.3) (BAGD 2.e. p. 835): This title of Jesus is translated 'the Son of Man' [BAGD, LN; all translations except AB1], 'The Man' [AB1]. It is a title with Messianic implications that Jesus used to refer to himself [LN]. At that time Jewish teaching included a heavenly being who exercised Messianic functions such as judging the world and was described as the 'Son of Man' or just 'Man' [BAGD]. See 2:10 for a discussion of this title.

c. pres. pass. indic. of παραδίδωμι (LN 37.111) (BAGD 1.b. p. 614): 'to be handed over to' [AB1, BAGD, LN, NTC, WBC; CEV, NET, TEV], 'to be turned over to' [AB2, BAGD, LN; NCV], 'to be delivered to' [BNTC, Lns; NASB], 'to be delivered over to' [BECNT; ESV; similarly KJV], 'to be delivered to the control of' [LN], 'to be handed over to' [LN; NRSV, REB], 'to be betrayed to/by' [LN; GW, NIV, NLT]. This verb means to deliver a person into the control of someone else and involves either the handing over of a presumably guilty person for punishment by authorities or the handing over of an individual to an enemy who will presumably take undue advantage of the victim [LN]. This word occurs at 9:31; 10:33, 13:9, 11, 12; 15:1, 10, 15.

d. ἀρχιερεύς (LN 53.88) (BAGD 1.a. p. 112): The plural form is translated 'chief priests' [AB1, AB2, BECNT, BNTC, LN, NTC; CEV, ESV, GW, KJV, NASB, NET, NIV, NRSV, REB, TEV], 'high priests' [Lns], 'ruling priests' [WBC], 'leading priests' [NCV, NLT]. This noun denotes a principal priest who belongs to one of the high-priestly families [LN]. See this word at 8:31.

e. γραμματεύς (LN 53.94) (BAGD 2. p. 165): 'scribe' [AB1, AB2, BAGD, BECNT, BNTC, Lns, NTC, WBC; ESV, GW, KJV, NASB, NRSV, REB], 'a person learned in the Law' [LN], 'an expert in the Law/law' [BAGD, LN; NET], 'teacher of the Law/law' [NCV, NIV, TEV], 'teacher of the Law of Moses' [CEV], 'teacher of religious law' [NLT]. This noun denotes a recognized expert in Jewish law [LN]. This word occurs at 1:22; 2:6, 16; 3:22; 7:1, 5; 8:31; 9:11, 14; 10:33; 11:27; 12:28, 32, 38; 14:1, 43, 53; 15:1, 31.

f. fut. act. indic. of κατακρίνω (LN 56.31) (BAGD p. 412): 'to condemn' [AB1, AB2, BECNT, BNTC, LN, Lns, NTC, WBC; ESV, GW, KJV, NASB, NET, NIV, NRSV, REB, TEV], 'to sentence' [CEV, NLT], 'to render a verdict of guilt' [LN]. The clause 'they will condemn him to death' is translated 'they will say that he must die' [NCV]. This verb means to judge someone to be definitely guilty and subject to punishment [LN]. It indicates that there was going to be a trial [NTC].

g. ἔθνος (LN 11.37) (BAGD 2. p. 218): 'Gentiles' [AB2, BAGD, BECNT, BNTC, Lns, NTC; ESV, KJV, NASB, NET, NIV, NRSV, REB, TEV], 'foreigners' [AB1; CEV, GW], 'Romans' [NLT], 'heathen, pagans' [BAGD, LN], 'non-Jewish people' [NCV]. This noun only occurs in the plural and denotes those who do not belong to the Jewish or Christian faith [LN].

QUESTION—Who will deliver Jesus to the chief priests and scribes?

The passive form 'will be delivered' does not specify who will do this, but it will be revealed later that Judas is the one who will be involved in betraying Jesus to the Jewish solders who would then take Jesus to the Sanhedrin for trial [Lns, TH]. Others agree that the unnamed one is Judas who will hand Jesus over [Gnd, NIGTC, TRT]. Two think that the passive form is the 'divine passive' indicating that God is the one who will hand Jesus over [AB2, ESVfn].

QUESTION—Who were the chief priests and scribes?

The men who are designated as the chief priests and scribes were members of the Sanhedrin. As the highest council of the Jews, the Sanhedrin tried the most important cases involving Jewish law [ICC, NTC]. It will be this court that will condemn Jesus to death [BECNT, Lns] and turn him over to the Gentiles [BECNT]. The elders were also part of the Sanhedrin and perhaps they are not mentioned because they were the least important of the three groups [NTC, Sw], or perhaps this was done to stress the fact that Jesus would be handed over to the spiritual leaders of the Jews who should have known better [NTC].

QUESTION—Who are the ἔθνεσιν 'Gentiles" mentioned here?

The Jews considered all non-Jews to be pagan Gentiles, so this refers to the Jewish Sanhedrin delivering Jesus up to the Roman authorities [Hb, TH]. These Roman authorities were Pilate and those under his command [BECNT, Lns, NTC]. It was necessary to involve the Roman authorities if Jesus was to be put to death since only the Roman government had the authority to carry out executions [Hb, ICC, Lns, NTC].

10:34 and they-will-ridicule[a] him and spit on-him and whip[b] him and kill[c] (him), and after three days he-will-rise-again.[d]"

TEXT—Manuscripts reading μετὰ τρεῖς ἡμέρας 'after three days' are followed by GNT, which does not mention any variant reading. A variant reading is τῇ τρίτῃ ἡμέρᾳ 'on the third day' and it is followed by KJV.

LEXICON—a. fut. act. indic. of ἐμπαίζω (LN 33.406) (BAGD 1. p. 255): 'to ridicule' [BAGD, LN], 'to mock' [AB1, AB2, BAGD, BECNT, BNTC, LN, Lns, NTC, WBC; ESV, KJV, NASB, NET, NIV, NLT, NRSV; REB], 'to laugh at' [NCV], 'to make fun of' [BAGD; CEV, GW, TEV]. This verb means to make fun of someone by pretending that he is not what he is or by imitating him in a distorted manner [LN]. The Roman soldiers mocked him for his supposed claim to be a king [CGTC, ICC].
   b. fut. act. indic. of μαστιγόω (LN 19.9) (BAGD 1. p 495): 'to whip' [BAGD, LN; GW, TEV], 'to beat' [CEV], 'to beat with a-whip/whips' [LN; NCV], 'to flog' [AB1, BAGD, BNTC; ESV, NIV, NRSV, REB], 'to flog with a whip' [NLT], 'to flog severely' [NET], 'to scourge' [AB2, BAGD, BECNT, Lns, NTC, WBC; KJV, NASB]. This verb means to beat severely with a whip [LN]. This would be the usual beating given to those who have been condemned to death [BAGD].
   c. fut. act. indic. of ἀποκτείνω (LN 20.61): 'to kill' [LN; all translations except NCV], 'to crucify' [NCV]. This verb means to cause someone's death, normally by violent means whether with or without intent or legal justification [LN]. Scourging was an invariable accompaniment of crucifixion [BECNT, ICC. NICNT, NTC].
   d. fut. mid. indic. of ἀνίσταμαι, ἀνίστημι (LN 23.93) (BAGD 2.a. p. 70): 'to rise again' [Lns, NTC; KJV, NASB, NET, NLT, NRSV, REB], 'to arise' [AB2], 'to rise' [BAGD, BECNT; ESV, NIV], 'to rise up' [BNTC, WBC], 'to rise to life' [CEV, TEV], 'to rise to life again' [NCV], 'to come back to life' [LN; GW], 'to live again, to be resurrected' [LN], 'to be raised' [AB1]. This verb means to come back to life after having once died [LN]. The middle voice is always used in the active sense and this means 'he shall rise again' [Lns].

QUESTION—Who will ridicule, spit, whip, and kill Jesus?
   The subject of these plural verbs are the Gentiles [BECNT, CGTC, Gnd, Hb, Lns, My, NICNT, NIGTC, TH].

QUESTION—How would they kill Jesus?
   Even though 'kill' is not as specific as 'crucify' in Matt. 20:19, crucifixion was always used by the Roman authorities to execute Jews [Hb, Lns, ESV, NICNT].

QUESTION—What is meant by μετὰ τρεῖς ἡμέρας 'after three days?
   This has already been discussed at 8:31. The mention of three days in this verse indicates the quickness with which Jesus will rise [Gnd].

DISCOURSE UNIT—10:35–45 [CBC, EBC, Hb, NICNT; CEV, ESV, GW, NCV, NET, NIV, NLT, NRSV, TEV]. The topic is Jesus teaches about service [CBC], Jesus teaches about serving others [NLT], rank, precedence, and service [NICNT], the problem of position among the disciples [Hb], James and John make a request [GW], the request of James and John [EBC; CEV, ESV, NET, NIV, NRSV, TEV], two followers ask Jesus a favor [NCV].

10:35 And James and John the sons of-Zebedee approached[a] him saying to-him, "Teacher, we-want that you-do for-us what-ever we-ask of-you."
10:36 But he-said to-them, "What do-you-want[b] me to-do for-you?"

TEXT—In verse 35, manuscripts reading αἰτήσωμέν σε 'we ask of you' are followed by GNT, which does not mention any variant reading. A variant reading is αἰτήσωμέν 'we ask' and it is followed by KJV.

TEXT—In verse 36, manuscripts reading the grammatically irregular τί θέλετέ με ποιήσω 'what do you want me to do' are given a C rating by GNT to indicate that choosing it over a variant text was difficult. Variant readings are τί θέλετέ ποιήσω 'what do you want I should do', some manuscripts read τί θέλετε ποιῆσαι 'what do you want to do,' some manuscripts read τί θέλετέ με ποιῆσαι 'what do you want me to do,' some manuscripts read τί θέλετε ποιῆσαι με 'what do you want me to do,' some manuscripts and versions read τί ποιήσω 'what should I do.'

LEXICON—a. pres. mid./pass. (deponent = act.) indic. of προσπορεύομαι (LN 15.77) (BAGD p. 718): 'to approach' [AB1, BAGD, BNTC. **LN**, NTC, WBC; REB], 'to come up to' [AB2, BAGD; CEV, ESV, NASB], 'to come to' [BECNT, Lns; KJV, NCV, NET, NIV, TEV], 'to come forward to' [NRSV], 'to come over' [NLT], 'to go to' [GW], 'to move toward, to come near to' [LN]. This verb means to move toward a reference point [LN].

b. pres. act. indic. of θέλω (LN 25.1) (BAGD 1. p. 355): 'to want, to desire, to wish' [BAGD, LN]. The question Τί θέλετέ με ποιήσω ὑμῖν; 'What do you want me to do for you?' [AB2, BECNT, BNTC, NTC; ESV, GW, NASB, NCV, NET, NIV] is also translated 'What is it you want me to do for you?' [AB1; NRSV, REB], 'What do you wish that I might do for you?' [WBC; similarly Lns; KJV], 'What is your request?' [NLT], 'What is it?' [TEV], '(Jesus asked them) what they wanted' [CEV]. This verb means to desire to have or to experience something [LN].

QUESTION—Why does this account say James and John made the request when in the parallel account in Matthew 20:20–21, it says their mother made the request?

Mark may have omitted mentioning the intermediary of the request because the conversation is ultimately between Jesus and his two disciples and the reply made by Jesus is addressed to the brothers [BECNT].

QUESTION—What is implied by the question Jesus asked in return?

Jesus was resisting the demand made by the brothers [AB2]. He refused to sign a blank check [Gnd, NIGTC, NTC]. He wanted them to state their desire openly [Hb].

10:37 And they said to him, "Grant[a] to-us that we-may-sit one on-your right and one on-your left in your glory.[b]"

LEXICON—a. aorist act. impera. of δίδωμι (LN 13.142) (BAGD 1.b.β. p. 193): 'to grant' [AB2, BAGD, LN, Lns, NTC, WBC; ESV, KJV, NASB, NRSV], 'to let' [CEV, GW, NCV, NIV, TEV], 'to permit' [NET], 'to allow' [BNTC, LN; REB], 'to give the right (to do something) [AB1, BECNT]. This verb means to grant someone the opportunity or occasion to do something [LN].

b. δόξα (LN 79.18) (BAGD 1.a. p. 203): 'glory, splendor' [BAGD, LN]. The phrase ἐν τῇ δόξῃ σου 'in your glory' [AB2, BECNT, BNTC, Lns, NTC, WBC; ESV, GW, KJV, NASB, NET, NIV, NRSV, REB] is also translated 'in your glory in your kingdom' [NCV], 'in your triumph' [AB1], 'when you come into your glory' [CEV], 'when you sit on your glorious throne' [NLT], 'when you sit on your throne in your glorious Kingdom' [TEV]. This noun denotes the quality of a splendid, remarkable appearance [LN]. The quality of brightness, splendor, and radiance is widened to denote the glory of God in general [BAGD].

QUESTION—What is implied by their request to sit at the right and left sides of Jesus?

The idiom ἐκ δεξιῶν καθίζω 'to sit on the right side of' a ruler means to be granted a position of high status [LN (87.34)], and the idiom ἐξ ἀριστερῶν καθίζω 'to sit on the left side of' also means to be in a position of high status despite having a little less status than the right side [LN (87.35)]. Their request could be either for places of honor at the messianic banquet or for positions of eminence and authority when Jesus is enthroned as the eschatological supreme judge of the world [BECNT, BNTC, NCBC, NICNT, Tay]. This probably concerns the royal throne because they spoke of sitting at his side and not reclining as one would do at a banquet [BECNT, NIGTC]. Most think this refers to the places of honor on each side of the royal throne [BECNT, CGTC, EBC, ESVfn, Hb, Lns, NAC, NIGTC, NTC, PNTC, TRT]. They pictured Jesus as sitting upon his royal throne surrounded by all the disciples and high officials where James and John were occupying the two places of highest honor [Hb, NTC].

QUESTION—What is meant by the phrase ἐν τῇ δόξῃ σου 'in your glory'?

Because Jesus was the Messiah and he was on his way to Jerusalem, they thought he would reveal his messianic glory there [CGTC, EBC, ESVfn, Gnd, Hb, ICC, NAC, NICNT, NIGTC, PNTC, WBC]. This glory is that of the Messianic king [ICC]. Here the words 'in your glory' refers to Jesus' honor, dignity, and perhaps splendor [WBC]. In Matthew 20:20, it is worded ἐν τῇ βασιλείᾳ σου 'in your kingdom' [Lns, Sw]. Both 'Kingdom' and 'glory' represent the triumph of Jesus in the kingdom that the disciples had often heard Jesus speak about it as being very near [AB1].

10:38 But Jesus said to-them, "You-do- not -understand[a] what you-are-asking-for. Are-you-able to-drink the cup[b] that I drink or to-be-baptized (with) the baptism[c] that I am-baptized (with)?

LEXICON—a. pres. act. indic. of οἶδα (LN 32.4) (BAGD 1.f. p. 556): 'to understand, to comprehend' [LN], 'to understand' [LN; NCV, REB], 'to know' [AB1, AB2, BAGD, BECNT, BNTC, Lns, NTC, WBC; ESV, KJV, NASB, NET, NIV, NLT, NRSV, TEV], 'to really know' [CEV], 'to realize' [GW]. This verb means to comprehend the meaning of something, with the focus upon the resulting knowledge [LN].

b. ποτήριον (LN 24.81) (BAGD 2. p. 695): 'cup' [BAGD, LN], 'drinking vessel' [BAGD]. The clause δύνασθε πιεῖν τὸ ποτήριον ὃ ἐγὼ πίνω 'Are you able to drink the cup that I drink?' [NTC, WBC; ESV, NASB, NRSV; similarly NET] is also translated 'Are you able to drink the cup which I myself am drinking?' [Lns], 'Can you drink the cup that I drink?' [AB1, AB2, BNTC; REB; similarly KJV, NIV], 'Can you drink the cup that I'm going to drink?' [GW], 'Are you able to drink the cup that I am about to drink?' [BECNT], 'Are you able to drink from the cup that I must soon drink from?' [CEV], 'Can you drink the cup that I must drink?' [NCV], 'Can you drink the cup of suffering that I must drink?' [TEV], 'Are you able to drink from the bitter cup of suffering I am about to drink?' [NLT], 'Are you able to drink the cup of suffering that I must drink?' or 'Are you able to suffer as I must suffer?' [LN]. The phrase πίνω ποτήριον 'to drink a cup' is an idiom meaning to undergo a trying, and difficult experience [LN]. It can be used figuratively as an expression for one's destiny in either a good or bad sense, and in this verse it refers to undergoing a violent death [BAGD].

c. βάπτισμα (LN 24.82) (BAGD 3.c. p. 132): 'baptism' [BAGD, LN]. The clause ἢ τὸ βάπτισμα ὃ ἐγὼ βαπτίζομαι βαπτισθῆναι 'or to be baptized with the baptism with which I am baptized?' [BNTC, NTC, WBC; ESV, NASB; similarly Lns] is also translated 'or/and be baptized with the baptism that I am baptized with?' [AB2; KJV, NRSV; similarly NIV, REB], 'or be baptized as I must be baptized' [CEV], 'or be baptized with the baptism I experience?' [NET], 'or to be baptized with the baptism that I am about to be baptized?' [BECNT], 'Can you be baptized with the baptism that I'm going to receive?' [GW], 'Can you be baptized in the way I must suffer?' [TEV], 'And can you be baptized with the same kind of baptism that I must go through?' [NCV], 'Are you able to be baptized with the baptism of suffering I must be baptized with?' [NLT]. The phrase βάπτισμα απτίζομαι 'to be baptized with a baptism' is an idiom meaning to be overwhelmed by suffering or by undergoing some difficult experience or ordeal [LN]. It is used figuratively for martyrdom [BAGD]. This has a metaphorical sense of being overwhelmed by suffering and tribulation [TH].

QUESTION—What didn't these two disciples understand about their request to sit in the places of honor where Jesus would rule?

They didn't know that their request to participate in Jesus' glory was also a request to share in his painful destiny expressed by the images of the cup and baptism [NICNT, NIGTC, NTC], a destiny that belonged exclusively to the unique messianic mission of the Son of Man. Because this was impossible, the question in this verse calls for a negative answer [NICNT, NIGTC]. They would not have made their request if they had understood what the kingdom was really like and how its high places are bestowed [Lns].

QUESTION—How are the present tense verbs to be interpreted in the phrases ὃ ἐγὼ πίνω 'which I drink' and ὃ ἐγὼ βαπτίζομαι 'with which I am baptized'?
The present tense of these two verbs can be understood in three different ways [TH].
1. They are *futuristic presents*: are you able to drink the cup *which I am to drink* and to undergo the baptism with which *I am to be baptized?* [BECNT, CGTC, Gnd, Hb, ICC, LN (24.81), NIGTC, NTC, Sw, TH, TRT; CEV, GW, NCV, NLT, TEV]. It refers to the coming sufferings in Jerusalem that would culminate in his death [Hb]. It is a future that is already decided [NIGTC]. The tense emphasizes the nearness and certainty of the fulfillment of these events [Gnd].
2. These present tense verbs are *punctiliar present verbs* without any time references [possibly AB1, AB2, BNTC, NTC, WBC; ESV, KJV, NET, NASB, NIV, NRSV, REB]: are you able to drink *the cup I drink* and be baptized with *the baptism with which I am baptized*?
3. They are *linear presents*: are you able to drink the cup *I am now drinking* and the baptism *I am now undergoing?* [ICC, Lns, Sw, Tay]. The present tense indicates that this suffering has already begun [Tay]. Even though the Passion is chiefly in view, it refers to Jesus' incarnate life on earth [Sw].

QUESTION—What is the cup Jesus drinks?
To 'drink the cup' means to drink the contents of the cup [NTC, TH]. The cup is a metaphor for one's portion in life, whether it be good or bad [AB2]. Jesus was talking about the suffering he must go through [AB1, BECNT, BNTC, Gnd, Lns, NCBC, NIGTC, NLTfn, PNTC, Tay, TH, TRT, WBC; NLT, TEV], and death [BECNT, BNTC, PNTC, WBC]. Both the cup and the baptism represent martyrdom [My, NAC]. Another view is that it refers to the cup of God's wrath against sin [CGTC]. The question in verse 38 calls for a negative reply since the sufferings and death referred to by the two images of the cup and baptism belonged to the unique messianic mission of the Son of Man [NICNT]. It refers to the cup of God's wrath that will be poured out on Jesus when he bears that wrath in place of sinners [ESVfn].

QUESTION—What is the baptism with which Jesus is baptized?
This baptism is probably used figuratively of being flooded with calamities [BNTC, Tay]. It means to be overwhelmed by trouble [CGTC], agony [NTC], suffering [TRT; NLT] or some terrible fate [BECNT]. Jesus was referring to the suffering and death into which he would soon be plunged [BECNT, ESVfn, NGTC].

10:39 **And they-said to-him, "We-are-able." And Jesus said to-them, "The cup that I drink you-will-drink, and (with) the baptism (with) which I-am-baptized you-will be-baptized.**

QUESTION—Why did James and John think they were able?
They naively failed to understand what was involved in Jesus' sufferings [BNTC, EBC, Hb, Lns].

QUESTION—In what way will James and John drink the cup that Jesus drinks and be baptized with the baptism with which Jesus is baptized?

The rhetorical question in the previous verse implies that it is impossible for anyone else to share Jesus' unique role in redemptive suffering. However, James and John thought that the cup and the baptism represented a necessary hurdle of suffering that they must face as well [NIGTC]. They had failed to understand what all was involved in Jesus' sufferings, yet they too would have their own suffering to face [NIGTC]. Jesus prophesied that like himself they will endure great tribulation and suffering for the gospel [CGTC, EBC, Hb, ICC, NICNT], but without the redemptive character of Christ's own sufferings [CGTC, Hb]. Even though James was martyred, martyrdom is not necessarily meant [Tay].

10:40 **But to-sit on my right or on my left is not mine to-grant,^a but (it is) for-those (for whom) it-has-been-prepared.^b"**

TEXT—Manuscripts reading ἀλλ' οἷς 'but it is for those' are given an A rating by GNT to indicate it was regarded to be certain. A variant reading is ἄλλοις 'for others.'

TEXT—Manuscripts reading ἡτοίμασται 'it has been prepared' are given an A rating by GNT to indicate it was regarded to be certain. Variant readings are ἡτοίμασται ὑπὸ τοῦ πατρός μου 'it has been prepared by my Father' and one ancient manuscript reads ἡτοίμασται παρὰ τοῦ πατρός μου 'it has been prepared from my Father'.

LEXICON—a. aorist act. infin. of δίδωμι (LN 13.142) (BAGD 1.b.β. p. 193): 'to grant' [BAGD, LN], 'to allow' [LN]. The phrase οὐκ ἔστιν ἐμὸν δοῦναι 'is not mine to grant' [WBC; ESV, NRSV] is also translated 'is not for me to grant' [NTC; NIV, REB], 'is not mine to give' [AB1, AB2, BNTC; KJV, NASB, NET; similarly Lns], 'is not in my power to give' [BECNT], 'I don't have the authority to grant' [GW], 'I have no right to say who will' [NLT], 'I do not have the right to choose who' [TEV], 'I can not choose who' [NCV], 'it isn't for me to say who' [CEV]. This verb means to grant someone the opportunity or occasion to do something [LN]. This word also occurs at 10:37.

b. perf. pass. indic. of ἑτοιμάζω (LN 77.3) (BAGD 3. p. 316): 'to be prepared' [BAGD, LN], 'to be made ready' [LN]. The clause ἀλλ' οἷς ἡτοίμασται 'but it is for those for whom it has been prepared' [WBC; NASB, NRSV; AB2, NTC; ESV] is also translated 'It is for those for whom it has been prepared' [NET], 'but is for whom it is prepared' [Lns], 'but it shall be given to them for whom it is prepared' [KJV], 'that belongs to those for whom they have been prepared' [BNTC], 'but is reserved for those for whom it has been prepared' [BECNT], 'Those places belong to those for whom they have been prepared' [NCV, NIV], 'Those positions have already been prepared for certain people' [GW], 'it is for those to whom it has been assigned' [AB1], 'that honor is for those to whom it has already been assigned' [REB], 'It is God who will give these places to those for whom he has prepared them' [TEV], 'God has prepared those places for the ones he has chosen' [NLT], 'That is for God to decide' [CEV]. This verb means to cause to be ready [LN].

QUESTION—Why couldn't Jesus grant James and John permission to sit at his right and his left?

1. Jesus could not appoint anyone to those positions because God the Father is the one who does that [AB1, AB2, BECNT, CBC, CGTC, EBC, EGT, ESVfn, Hb, Lns, My, NAC, NCBC, NICNT, NLTfn, NIVfn, NTC, PNTC, Sw, TH, Tay, TRT; CEV, NLT, TEV]. The parallel passage in Matthew 20:13 states 'but it is for whom it has been prepared by my Father.' The perfect tense implies that the matter has already been decided [Hb]. The passive verb 'has been prepared' implies that God is the subject of the verb [AB2, BECNT, Hb, Lns, NICNT, NTC, TH]. God has already chosen people for those positions [CBC].
2. Jesus cannot appoint James and John because he has already chosen other people according to their qualifications [ICC, WBC]. A contrast is made between the persons involved, and this choice has already been made. Fitness, not influence, has decided the matter [WBC].

QUESTION—What does 'it' refer to in the final clause?

'It' refers to the prerogative to sit on the right and left [TH].

10:41 And having-heard, the ten became indignant[a] with James and John.

LEXICON—a. pres. act. infin. of ἀγανακτέω (LN **88.187**) (BAGD p. 4): 'to be indignant' [BAGD, **LN**], 'to be angry' [BAGD, LN], 'to be aroused' [BAGD]. The phrase ἤρξαντο ἀγανακτεῖν περὶ 'became indignant with' [NIV] is also translated 'began to be indignant at' [ESV], 'began to feel indignant with' [NASB], 'were indignant with' [REB; similarly NLT], 'became angry with' [NET, TEV], 'began to be angry with' [NCV, NRSV], 'were angry with' [CEV], 'were irritated with' [GW], 'began to be much displeased with' [KJV]. This verb means to be indignant against what is judged to be wrong [LN].

QUESTION—How did the other ten disciples hear about that request?

The participle ἀκούσαντες 'having heard' implies that the ten disciples were not present when James and John made their request [Hb, Tay], and it is not known how the other ten disciples heard about it [Hb].

QUESTION—Why did the ten disciples become indignant when they knew that James and John had made such a request?

They feared that the two brothers would secure some advantage over their own dignity [NICNT]. 'Began' suggests that their strong indignation against James and John was not allowed to continue for long, possibly because Jesus may have acted right away to arrest it [Hb, Lns, My].

10:42 And having-summoned[a] them Jesus says to-them, "You-know that the (ones) recognized[b] to-rule the Gentiles lord-it-over[c] them and the great-ones[d] of-them use-their-authority-over[e] them.

LEXICON—a. aorist mid. participle of προσκαλέομαι (LN 33.308): 'to summon' [BNTC,WBC], 'to call' [AB2, BECNT, LN, NTC; GW, NET, NRSV], 'to call to oneself' [LN; ESV, KJV, NASB, REB], 'to call together' [AB1; CEV, NCV, NIV, NLT, TEV], 'to call forward' [Lns]. This verb means to call to someone [LN].
   b. pres. act. participle of δοκέω (LN 87.42) (BAGD 2.b. p. 202): 'to suppose, to presume, to assume, to imagine, to believe, to think' [LN]. The phrase 'the ones recognized to rule the Gentiles' is translated 'those who are recognized as rulers of the Gentiles' [NASB, NET; similarly BECNT], 'those who are recognized as rulers among the foreigners' [AB1], 'they which are accounted to rule over the Gentiles' [KJV], 'those who are considered rulers of the Gentiles/heathen' [ESV, TEV], 'those who are regarded as rulers of the Gentiles' [NIV], 'the acknowledged rulers of nations' [GW], 'those reputed to rule the Gentiles' [Lns], 'those who are thought to rule over the Gentiles' [AB2], 'those who are supposed to rule over the Gentiles' [WBC], 'those who are supposed to be rulers among the Gentiles' [BNTC], 'the so-called rulers of the Gentiles' [NTC], 'those foreigners who call themselves kings' [CEV], 'the non-Jewish people have rulers' [NCV], 'the rulers in this world' [NLT], 'among the Gentiles those whom they recognize as their rulers' [NRSV], 'among the Gentiles the recognized rulers' [REB]. This verb means to regard something as presumably true, but without particular certainty [LN]. It means to be influential, to be recognized as being something [BAGD].
   c. pres. act. indic. of κατακυριεύω (LN 37.50) (BAGD p. 412): 'to lord it over, to rule over' [BAGD, LN], 'to rule, to govern, to reign over' [LN]. The phrase κατακυριεύουσιν αὐτῶν 'lord it over them' [AB2, BECNT, BNTC, Lns, NTC, WBC; ESV, NASB, NET, NIV, NRSV] is also translated 'lord it over their subjects/people' [AB1; NLT, REB], 'exercise lordship over them' [KJV], 'have absolute power over people' [GW], 'have power over them' [TEV], 'like to order their people around' [CEV], 'love to show their power over the people' [NCV]. This verb means to rule or reign over others, and in some contexts it implies 'lording it over others' [LN].
   d. μέγας (LN 87.22) (BAGD 2.b.α. p. 498): 'great' [BAGD, LN], 'important' [LN], 'the great men, those in high authority' [BAGD]. The phrase οἱ μεγάλοι αὐτῶν 'the great ones of them' is translated 'their great ones' [AB2, Lns, WBC; ESV, KJV, NRSV], 'their great men' [AB1, BECNT, NTC; NASB], 'their great leaders' [CEV], 'their important leaders' [NCV], 'the great' [REB], 'the leaders' [TEV], 'their officials' [GW], 'officials' [NLT], 'their high officials' [NIV], 'those in high positions' [BNTC; NET]. This adjective pertains to being great in terms

of status [LN]. It refers to those who have power and authority over others [CGTC].
e. pres. act. indic. of κατεξουσιάζω (LN 37.48) (BAGD p. 421): 'to exercise authority over someone' [BAGD], 'to rule, to govern, to reign over' [LN]. The phrase κατεξουσιάζουσιν αὐτῶν 'use their authority over them' [NET] is also translated 'exercise authority over them' [BECNT; ESV, NASB, NIV; similarly KJV], 'impose their authority' [AB1], 'make their authority felt' [REB], 'have complete authority' [TEV], 'have absolute authority over people' [GW], 'have power over them' [WBC], 'have full power over the people they rule' [CEV], 'exercise their authority over them' [Lns], 'love to use all their authority' [NCV], 'flaunt their authority over those under them' [NLT], 'oppress them' [AB2], 'make them feel the weight of their authority' [BNTC], 'keep them under their despotic power' [NTC], 'are tyrants over them' [NRSV]. This verb means to rule or reign over others and may imply lording it over others in some contexts [LN]. They exercise total control over the people [AB1].

QUESTION—Who were the 'them' whom Jesus summoned?

This refers to the ten indignant disciples if we assume that James and John were still present, but in any case, Jesus is now addressing all twelve of the disciples [Gnd, Hb]. All twelve were present [BNTC, NICNT, NIGTC]. The ten had reason to be offended, but all twelve needed the lesson Jesus would teach them [Hb].

QUESTION—What is meant by the phrase οἱ δοκοῦντες ἄρχειν 'the ones recognized to rule'?

This refers to the people who either pass for rulers or are esteemed as rulers [EGT]. It seems to be said in irony [AB1, BNTC, CGTC, Tay]. Perhaps it implies that their rule is only apparent and it is actually unreal in the eyes of God [BNTC]. Their power is as nothing compared to God's sovereignty [NCBC]. Another view is that it means they rightly have this reputation [Lns]. The Gentiles recognize them as their rulers [TRT]. Although many translate this expression as 'those who *appear* or *presume* to rule', this does not demand such a nuance. The same phrase occurs in Galatians 2:2, 5, 6 where it refers to the apostles in Jerusalem. Such authorities did rule, usually with a heavy hand [PNTC].

QUESTION—What is the difference between 'the ones recognized to rule' and 'the great ones of them'?

Neither term denotes a specific office. These are general terms for the ones who are in a position to impose their authority on others [NIGTC]. The two terms are synonymous for the sake of greater emphasis [Lns, NAC]. It could be making a distinction between the great lords in Rome and the petty rulers of Palestine and Syria [NICNT].

10:43 But it-is not so[a] among you. But whoever wants to-become-great[b] among you, must-be your servant.[c]

TEXT—Manuscripts reading ἐστιν 'it is' are given an A rating by GNT to indicate it was regarded to be certain. A variant reading is ἔσται 'it shall be' and it is followed by KJV.

LEXICON—a. οὕτως, οὕτω (LN 61.9) (BAGD 1.b. p. 597): 'so, thus' BAGD, LN], 'in this way' [LN]. The phrase οὐχ οὕτως δέ ἐστιν ἐν ὑμῖν 'But it is not so among you' [AB2; NRSV] is also translated 'But it is not this way among you' [NASB, NET], 'Not like that is it among you' [NTC; similarly Lns], 'This, however, is not the way it is among you' [TEV], 'But it is not to be so among you' [WBC; similarly BECNT], 'It is not to be that way with you' [BNTC], 'Not so with you' [NIV], 'That is not the way with you' [AB1], 'But among you it will be different' [NLT], 'But it shall not be so with you' [ESV; similarly REB], 'But that's not the way it's going to be among you' [GW], 'But so shall it not be among you' [KJV], 'But it should not be that way among you' [NCV], One translation makes this a command: 'But don't act like them' [CEV]. This adverb refers to that which precedes [LN]. The Greek is worded as a statement and not as a command [TH].

b. μέγας (LN 87.22) (BAGD 2.b.α. p. 498): 'great' [BAGD, LN; all translations except NLT], 'important' [LN]. The phrase 'But whoever wants to become great among you' is translated 'Whoever wants to be a leader among you' [NLT]. This adverb pertains to being great in terms of status [LN]. It refers to having a desire to have authority and to command others [TH].

c. διάκονος (LN 35.20) (BAGD 1.a. p. 184): 'servant' [BAGD, LN]. The clause 'must be your servant' [AB1, BNTC; ESV, NET, NRSV, NIV, NLT, REB] is also translated 'will/shall be your servant' [AB2, BECNT, WBC; GW NASB], 'let him be your servant' [NTC], 'he shall be your ministrant' [Lns], 'shall be your minister' [KJV], 'must serve all of you like a servant' [NCV], 'you must be the servant of the rest' [TEV], 'you must be the servant of all the others' [CEV]. Although being a servant is not as low as being a slave, it is a subordinate position to which the great ones of the world do not aspire [WBC].

QUESTION—In the statement 'But it is not so among you', what is the function of the present active verb ἐστιν 'it is'?

1. This verb is descriptive and refers to the present time [AB1, AB2, EBC, EGT, Gnd, Hb, ICC, Lns, NTC, PNTC, Sw, TH; NASB, NET, NIV, NRSV, TEV]: *It is not so among you.* It is stated as a present fact [Gnd, Hb, Lns, PNTC, TH]. Jesus had already inaugurated these new conditions of social life by example and teaching [Sw]. This ideal state is the essential principle of the kingdom of God even if the members of the kingdom have not yet reached it [EGT, ICC]. The conjunction δέ 'but' points to the contrast between the greatness operative in the Kingdom of

God and the greatness of the powerful ruling ones described in verse 42 [Gnd, Hb].
2. This verb is hortatory and refers to the future [BECNT, BNTC, NCBC, NICNT, WBC; CEV, ESV, GW, KJV, NCV, NLT, REB]: *It is not to be so among you!* What Jesus now commands his disciples is radically different from conventional wisdom [WBC]. Jesus contrasts the conduct of Gentile rulers with the service and sacrifice expected of discipleship [NICNT].

10:44 And whoever wants to-be-first[a] among you must-be slave[b] of-all.
LEXICON—a. πρῶτος (LN 87.45) (BAGD 1.c.β. p. 726): 'first' [BAGD; all translations except KJV, GW], 'most important' [BAGD; GW], most prominent' [BAGD], 'great, prominent, important' [LN], 'foremost' [BAGD, LN], 'the chiefest' [KJV]. This adjective pertains to being of high rank, and implies special prominence along with status [LN]. This is about having the ambition to attain the highest position among those who are 'great' [Hb].
  b. δοῦλος (LN 87.76) (BAGD 3. p. 205): 'slave' [BAGD, LN], 'servant' [BAGD]. The phrase ἔσται πάντων δοῦλος 'must be slave of all' [ESV, NIV, NRSV] is also translated 'must be the slave of all' [AB1, BNTC; NET, REB, TEV], 'shall be the slave of all' [AB2, BECNT, Lns; similarly WBC; NASB], 'must be the slave of everyone else' [NLT], 'will be a slave for everyone' [GW], 'must be everyone's slave' [CEV], 'must serve all of you like a slave' [NCV], 'let him be the humble attendant of all' [NTC], 'shall be servant of all' [KJV]. This noun denotes one who is a slave by becoming the property of an owner [LN].
QUESTION—What is the difference between being a διάκονος 'servant' in verse 43 and being a δοῦλος 'slave' in this verse?
  A slave has far less self-determination than a servant [NIGTC]. 'Slave' denotes a lower position than 'servant' and includes foregoing one's rights in order to serve others for Christ's sake [Hb]. 'Slave' intensifies the image. Being a servant is not as low as a slave, but it too is a subordinate position to which the world's great do not aspire [WBC]. *Servant* and *slave* function as synonymous parallelisms in these two verses [BECNT, CGTC, NTC]. The difference must not be pressed since the sense is the same [AB1].

10:45 Because even[a] the Son of-Man[b] did- not -come to-be-served[c] but to-serve and to-give his life (as) a-ransom[d] for[e] many."
LEXICON—a. καί (LN 89.93): 'even' [AB2, BECNT, LN, Lns, NTC; ESV, KJV, NASB, NET, NIV, NLT, TEV], 'and, and also, also, in addition' [LN], 'in the same way' [NCV], 'its the same way with' [GW], not explicit [AB1, BNTC, WBC; CEV, NRSV, REB]. This conjunction indicates an additive relationship that is not coordinate [LN].
  b. υἱὸς τοῦ ἀνθρώπου 'Son of Man' (LN 9.3) (BAGD 2.e. p. 835): This title of Jesus is translated 'the Son of Man' [BAGD, LN; all translations except AB1], 'The Man' [AB1]. It is a title with Messianic implications

that Jesus used concerning himself [LN]. At that time Jewish teaching included a heavenly being who was looked upon as a 'Son of Man' or 'Man' who exercised Messianic functions such as judging the world [BAGD]. See 2:10 for a discussion of this title.
  c. aorist pass. infin. of διακονέω (LN 35.19) (BAGD 2. p. 184): 'to be served' [AB1, AB2, BAGD, BECNT, BNTC, LN, NTC, WBC; all versions except CEV, GW, KJV], 'to be helped' [LN], 'to be ministered unto' [Lns; KJV]. The phrase 'did not come to be served' is translated 'didn't come so that others could serve him' [GW], 'did not come to be a slave master' [CEV]. This verb means to render assistance or help by performing certain duties that may often be of a humble or menial nature [LN].
  d. λύτρον (LN 37.130) (BAGD p. 482): 'ransom' [BAGD, LN], 'the price of release' [BAGD], 'the means of release' [LN]. The clause 'to give his life as a ransom for many/many-people' [AB1, AB2, BECNT, BNTC, WBC; ESV, GW, NCV, NET, NIV, NLT, REB; similarly KJV, NASB, NRSV] is also translated 'to give his life as a ransom in the place of many' [Lns, NTC], 'to give his life to redeem many people' [TEV], 'who will give his life to rescue many people' [CEV]. This noun denotes the means or instrument by which release or deliverance is made possible [LN].
  e. ἀντί (LN 90.37, 89.133) (BAGD 3. p. 73): 'for' [AB1, AB2, BAGD, BECNT, BNTC, LN (89.133, 90.37); all versions except CEV, TEV], 'on behalf of' [BAGD, LN (90.37), WBC], 'instead of' [LN (89.133)], 'in the place of' [Lns, NTC], not explicit [CEV, TEV]. This preposition indicates a participant who is benefited by an event, and it usually implies that some type of exchange or substitution is involved [LN (90.37)] or it indicates an alternative [LN (89.133)]. The meaning of ἀντί 'in place of' developed into 'for' or 'on behalf of' [BAGD]. Here it is used in conjunction with 'ransom' and means 'instead of' [EBC].

QUESTION—What is the function of the conjunction γάρ 'because'?
This indicates the reason for the rule Jesus has just laid down for his followers in verse 43. Not even Jesus himself was exempt from this rule [Hb] and Jesus is the greatest example of this principle [CGTC, EBC, Hb, ICC, NIGTC].

QUESTION—What is the purpose of the conjunction καί 'and' that begins the last phrase?
  1. This conjunction marks the climax of what Jesus came for [EBC, Hb, NIGTC]: he came to serve, *and he even gave his life as a ransom for many!* His coming resulted in giving his life as a ransom for many [EBC]. His death is the highest point of his service [Hb].
  2. This conjunction explains the preceding text and is equal to 'namely' [Hb, Lns, NICNT, NTC, TH]: he came to serve, *namely he came to give his life as a ransom for many.*

QUESTION—What is meant by Jesus coming to give his life 'as a ransom for many'?

The idea behind the metaphor of a ransom is that of paying a price to deliver someone from something [NICNT, NIGTC]. A ransom is the price that is paid to secure the release of prisoners or captives [Gnd, Hb, WBC]. Jesus does not explain the kind of slavery he has in mind nor does he specify to whom the ransom is paid [Gnd]. Some fill out the metaphor of paying a ransom by specifying that Jesus pays the ransom to the Father, not to Satan [Lns, NTC]. The Greek word does mean 'ransom', but the word had lost the meaning of a purchase price paid to someone and now had the meaning of 'redemption' or 'release' [EBC, TH]. The idea behind the metaphor emphasizes the substitutionary element in Jesus' death [EBC, Hb, ICC, NTC, TH]. Jesus didn't pay a purchase price to someone in this kind of ransom. He took the place of the many so that what should have happened to them happened to Jesus instead [EBC, NICNT]. It is based on Israel's release from the slavery of Egypt and on the passage in Isaiah 53:6 where it says 'the Lord has laid on him the iniquity of us all' [EBC]. The idea of Jesus' vicarious suffering can not be fully explained by any OT passage and must be understood from the actual history of his Passion [CGTC].

QUESTION—What is meant by the preposition ἀντὶ 'for' in the phrase 'for many?

1. Jesus gives his life 'instead of' or 'in place of' the people who would have had to give their own lives [BECNT, CGTC, EBC, ESVfn, Gnd, Hb, ICC, Lns, NAC, NICNT, NIGTC, NTC, PNTC, Tay, TH, TRT, WBC]. His life was a substitute in behalf of humanity [PNTC]. When Jesus takes the place of the many, what happens to him is what would have happened to them. The release brought about because of this offering overcomes man's alienation from God, his subjection to death, and his bondage to sin [EBC, NICNT].
2. Jesus gives his life 'for the sake of' or 'on behalf of' the lives of many people [NCBC].

QUESTION—What is meant by the word πολλῶν 'many'?

1. It has the inclusive meaning of 'all people' and contrasts a large number of people with the one person, Jesus, who gives his life as a ransom for all people [BECNT, EBC, CGTC, EBC, CGTC, Hb, ICC, LN, Lns, NAC, NCBC, NLTfn, NTC, PNTC, Tay, TH, TRT]. It is not correct to regard 'many' as a reference to only those who accept his redemption in faith since Jesus gave his life for all men [Lns]. In 1 Timothy 2:6 it says that Jesus 'gave himself as a ransom for *all* men'. Here in Mark Jesus appears to be emphasizing the contrast between the 'one (Jesus)' and the 'many' people he will give his life for and he does not intend the contrast to be between the words 'many' and 'all' [BECNT, NAC, PNTC. TRT] The question about whether the ransom is intended for the 'elect' or the 'the whole world' is not being addressed by Mark [BECNT]. Jesus offers his life on behalf of humanity [PNTC]. It is not saying that Jesus' life takes

the place of other lives that otherwise would have to be sacrificed in expiation of their sins. It means that that his life becomes the price by which anyone can be freed from bondage [ICC].
2. It has the exclusive meaning of a large number of people who are ransomed in contrast with other people who are not ransomed [AB1, AB2, ESVfn, NICNT, NTC]. The phrase for many' means 'in the place of many, but not all', and the 'many' includes people without any distinction as to race, nationality, class, age, sex, etc. [NTC]. The ransom was paid to God the Father who accepted it as the just payment for the sins of 'many', that is, of the many people who would be saved [ESVfn]. The 'many' are probably the members of the Christian community [AB1, AB2].

DISCOURSE UNIT—10:46-52 [CBC, EBC, Hb, NICNT, NIGTC; CEV, ESV, GW, NASB, NCV, NET, NIV, NLT, NRSV, TEV]. The topic is the second healing of a blind man [NIGTC], Jesus heals a blind man [NCV], the healing of the Jericho beggar [Hb], restoring the blind Bartimaeus's sight [EBC], Jesus heals blind Bartimaeus [CEV, ESV, TEV], Jesus heals the blind man Bartimaeus [CBC], Jesus heals Bartimaeus, a blind beggar [NLT], Jesus gives sight to Bartimaeus [GW], Bartimaeus receives his sight [NASB], the healing of blind Bartimaeus [NRSV], blind Bartimaeus receives his sight [NIV], healing blind Bartimaeus [NET], the faith of blind Bartimaeus [NICNT].

10:46 **And they-come to Jericho. And (as) he-was-leaving from Jericho with his disciples and a-large crowd, the son of Timaeus, Bartimaeus, a-blind beggar, was-sitting beside the road.**
QUESTION—Who are the people referred to by the verb ωρχονται 'they come'?
The plural subject of the verb 'they come' at least includes Jesus and his disciples [BECNT, Hb, NTC, Tay; CEV, NLT]. Because Jesus had taken aside the twelve disciples to speak with them privately in verse 32, there would have been a larger group than just the twelve disciples traveling with Jesus when 'they' arrived at Jericho [Gnd]. Some think the plural subject 'they' refers to Jesus, his twelve disciples, and a large crowd [BECNT, NIGTC, NTC, PNTC, Sw, Tay, TH, TRT, WBC]. The members of that crowd had probably been joining Jesus as he passed through Galilee and Perea [NTC]. The crowd consisted of pilgrims who had joined Jesus and his disciples on the trip to Jerusalem for the Feast of the Passover [EBC, Hb, NICNT]. Probably townspeople also had joined them as they passed through Jericho [Hb, NTC].
QUESTION—Why was Bartimaeus sitting beside the road?
This was a strategic location for this blind beggar since it gave him access to the traffic to and from Jerusalem. It was a trade route traveled by not only merchants but prosperous and pious people as well [WBC].

10:47 And having-heard that Jesus the Nazarene is-coming, he-began to-shout[a] and to-say, "Son of-David, Jesus, have-mercy[b] on-me!"

LEXICON—a. pres. act. infin. of κράζω (LN 33.83) (BAGD 2.a. p. 447): 'to shout' [LN], 'to call, to call out' [BAGD]. The phrase 'he began to shout and say' [AB2; NRSV] is also translated 'he began to cry out and say' [BECNT, WBC; ESV, KJV, NASB], 'he began to cry out, saying' [NTC], 'he began to yell and to say' [Lns], 'he began to shout' [AB1; GW, NCV, NET, NIV, NLT, REB, TEV], 'he began to cry out' [BNTC], 'he shouted' [CEV]. This verb means to shout or cry out [LN]. The blind man was unable to see where Jesus was but he hopefully shouted into the crowd [NIGTC].

  b. aorist act. impera. of ἐλεάω (LN 88.76) (BAGD 2.a. p. 249): 'to have mercy' [AB2, BAGD, BECNT, LN; all versions except CEV, REB], 'to have pity' [AB1, BNTC, WBC; CEV, REB], 'to take pity on' [NTC], 'to show mercy' [LN, Lns], 'to be merciful toward' [LN]. This verb means to show kindness or concern for someone in serious need [Gnd, LN].

QUESTION—Why did people tell the blind man that 'Jesus the Nazarene' was coming?

They used the ordinary personal name 'Jesus' but added 'the Nazarene' to single out this Jesus from the town of Nazareth from any other person who also had the name Jesus [BECNT, Lns, NIGTC,]. This was the Jesus who was the famous miracle-worker from Nazareth [Gnd, EBC].

QUESTION—Why did the blind man call Jesus 'Son of David'?

The title 'Son of David' was a Messianic title [AB1, BNTC, EBC, Hb, ICC, Lns, NICNT, NTC, Sw, Tay, WBC] that recalled the divine promises made to King David [Hb]. It indicates that Bartimaeus had heard about Jesus of Nazareth and believed that Jesus was able to heal him [NICNT]. Perhaps Bartimaeus had unusual spiritual insight as to whom Jesus was, or else he was simply aiming to gain his attention with the most flattering address he could think of [NICNT].

10:48 And many were-rebuking[a] him that he-should-be-silent. But much-more he-was-crying-out, "Son of David, have-mercy (on) me."

LEXICON—a. imperf. act. indic. of ἐπιτιμάω (LN 33.331) (BAGD 1. p. 303): 'to rebuke' [BAGD, LN; ESV], 'to reprove' [BAGD, LN], 'to command' [LN]. The phrase 'were rebuking him that he should be silent' is translated 'rebuked him, telling him to be silent' [ESV], 'rebuked him and told him to be quiet' [NIV], 'scolded him and told him to be quiet' [TEV], 'sternly ordered him to be quiet' [NRSV], 'were sternly telling him to be quiet' [NASB], 'warned the blind man to be quiet' [NCV], 'told the man to stop' [CEV], 'charged him that he should hold his peace' [KJV], 'scolded him to get him to be quiet' [NET], 'told him to be quiet' [GW], 'told him to hold his tongue' [REB], '"Be quiet!" many of the people yelled at him' [NLT]. This verb means to command with the implication of a threat [LN].

10:49 And having-stopped[a] Jesus said, "Summon[b] him." And they-summoned the blind-man saying, "Don't-be-afraid,[c] stand-up, he-is-summoning you." **10:50** And having-thrown-aside[d] his garment, and having-jumped-up[e] he came to Jesus.

LEXICON—a. aorist act. participle of ἵσταμαι, ἵστημι (LN 68.42) (BAGD II.1.a. p. 382): 'to stop' [BAGD, BECNT, BNTC, LN, NTC; all versions except KJV, NRSV], 'to stand still' [AB1, AB2, BAGD, Lns, WBC; KJV, NRSV]. This verb means to cease some type of movement [LN].
  b. aorist act. participle of φωνέω (LN 33.307) (BAGD 2.b. p. 870): 'to summon' [BAGD, LN], 'to call to oneself' [BAGD], 'to call' [LN]. The command 'Summon him' is translated 'Call him' [AB1, AB2, BECNT, BNTC, Lns, NTC, WBC; ESV, GW, NET, NIV, REB, TEV], 'Call him here' [NASB, NRSV], 'Call him over' [CEV], 'Tell him to come here' [NLT; similarly NCV], 'commanded him to be called' [KJV]. This verb means to communicate directly or indirectly to someone who is presumably at a distance in order to tell such a person to come [LN].
  c. pres. act. impera. of θαρσέω (LN 25.156) (BAGD p. 352): 'to not be afraid' [BAGD], 'to be courageous, to have courage' [BAGD, LN], 'to be bold' [LN], 'to be cheerful' [BAGD]. The command 'Don't be afraid' [CEV] is also translated 'Have courage' [NET], 'Take courage' [AB1; NASB, NTC; similarly BNTC; NET], 'Take heart' [BECNT; ESV, NRSV, REB], 'Be brave' [AB2], 'Be of good comfort' [KJV], 'Be of good cheer' [WBC], 'Cheer up' [Lns; GW, NCV, NIV, NLT, TEV]. This verb means to have confidence and firmness of purpose in the face of danger or testing [LN].
  d. aorist act. participle of ἀποβάλλω (LN 49.19): 'to throw off, to remove and throw aside' [LN]. The phrase ὁ ἀποβαλὼν τὸ ἱμάτιον αὐτοῦ 'having thrown aside his garment' is translated 'throwing off his garment' [AB2], 'throwing off his cloak' [ESV, NRSV; similarly **LN**; NET, REB, TEV], 'he threw off his himation' [AB1], 'throwing aside his cloak' [BNTC, WBC; NASB, NIV], 'threw aside his coat' [NLT], 'having thrown off his outer cloak' [BECNT], 'throwing aside his robe' [NTC], 'having thrown away his robe' [Lns], 'he threw off/aside his coat' [CEV, GW, NLT], 'casting away his garment' [KJV], 'left his coat there' [NCV]. This verb means to remove a piece of clothing quickly and cast it aside [LN].
  e. aorist act. participle of ἀναπηδάω (LN 15.241) (BAGD p. 59): 'to jump up' [AB1, BAGD, BECNT, BNTC, **LN**; CEV, GW, NASB, NCV, NET, NLT, TEV], 'to jump to one's feet' [NTC; NIV, REB], 'to get to one's feet' [WBC], 'to leap up' [AB2, LN, Lns], 'to spring up' [ESV, NRSV], 'to stand up' [BAGD], 'to rise' [KJV]. This verb means to leap or spring up, presumably from a seated position [LN].

QUESTION—Who did Jesus tell to summon the blind beggar and how did they do it?

The plural subject of the imperative verb Φωνήσατε 'summon' is not specified and it could refer to the disciples [TH], the large crowd of verse 48 [Hb], or the many people mentioned in verse 48 who had been telling the blind man to be silent [BECNT, EBC, Gnd, NIGTC]. The call was passed on to the front until it reached blind man [Sw].

QUESTION—Why did the beggar throw aside his garment?

He may have thrown aside his outer garment in order to run to Jesus faster [TH], or to avoid being entangled in it as he ran to Jesus [Hb, Lns],

10:51 And answering[a] him Jesus said, "What do-you-want me-to-do for-you?" And the blind-man said to-him, "Rabboni,[b] that I–might-see.[c]"

LEXICON—a. aorist pass. (deponent = act.) participle of ἀποκρίνομαι (LN 33.28) (BAGD 2. p. 93): 'to speak, to declare, to say' [LN]. The phrase 'answering him, Jesus said' [Lns; NASB] is also translated 'Jesus answered him and said' [AB2, WBC; similarly BECNT; KJV], 'in response Jesus said to him' [NTC], 'Jesus said to him' [AB1; ESV, NET, NRSV, REB], 'Jesus asked him' [BNTC; GW, NCV, NIV, TEV; similarly CEV, NLT]. This verb means to introduce or continue a somewhat formal discourse, and regularly occurs with λέγω 'to say' [LN (33.28)]. Jesus was responding to the situation and not just simply answering a question [NTC, WBC]. The phase 'having answered said' is an idiomatic expression for 'said' since no question had been asked [BECNT, Tay].

b. Ραββουνι (LN **33.247**) (BAGD p. 733): 'Rabboni' [Lns, NTC; NASB], Rabbouni' [AB2, BECNT], 'my rabbi' [NLT], 'my teacher' [**LN**; NRSV], 'my Master' [BAGD, WBC], 'my Lord' [BAGD], 'Rabbi' [AB1; ESV, NET, NIV, REB], 'Teacher' [GW, NCV, TEV], 'Master' [BNTC; CEV], 'Lord' [KJV]. This is a transliteration of the Palestinian Aramaic honorific title for a teacher of the Jewish Scriptures and its use implies an important personal relationship [LN]. The Aramaic form 'Rabboni' implies more reverence than the ordinary title 'Rabbi' [BECNT, BNTC, EGT, Gnd, Hb, ICC, Lns, NCBC]. This title is stronger than 'Rabbi' and means 'my Lord, my master' [AB1, CGTC, Tay]. Others say that this term is essentially no different from Rabbi [NIGTC]. Both Matthew and Luke use the Greek equivalent κύριος 'Lord' [AB2, Hb].

c. aorist act. subj. of ἀναβλέπω (LN 24.42) (BAGD 2.a.α. p. 51): 'to be able to see' [LN], 'to regain sight' [BAGD, LN]. The clause ἵνα ἀναβλέψω 'that I might see' [BECNT] is also translated 'that I might receive my sight' [KJV; similarly Lns], 'I want to see' [CEV, NCV, NIV, NLT]. Some indicate that he had once been able to see: 'that I might see again' [WBC], 'I want to see again' [AB1, GW, TEV], 'I want to regain my sight!' [Lns; NASB], 'I want my sight back' [REB], 'let me see again' [AB2, BNTC; NET, NRSV], 'let me recover my sight' [ESV]. This verb means to become able to see, either for the first time or again [BAGD, LN]. In the phrase ἵνα ἀναβλέψω 'that I might see', the conjunction ἵνα 'that' can indicate the content of the request '(I want) that I might see', or can be imperatival with the meaning 'Let me see!' [Gnd, TH].

QUESTION—Wasn't it clear what the blind man wanted?

Even though the blind man's need was obvious, Jesus asked the question so that Batimaeus would give expression to his need [CGTC, Hb, NICNT, Sw, Tay]. This question was intended to stimulate his faith [EBC, NICNT] by encouraging him to express it forthrightly [CGTC, ESVfn, NICNT]. Jesus might have implied, 'What do you want, alms or sight?' [EGT, Gnd].

QUESTION—Had Batimaeus ever been able to see?

1. The man had been able to see before he became blind and wanted to regain his sight [AB1, AB2, BECNT, BNTC, ICC, Lns, NETfn, NTC, Sw, Tay, WBC; ESV, GW, NASB, NET, REB, NRSV, TEV].
2. Other translations do not indicate that he had ever been able to see [BECNT, Hb, Lns; CEV, KJV, NCV, NIV, NLT].

10:52 And Jesus said to-him, "Go,ᵃ your faith has-healedᵇ you." And immediately he-could-see and he-was-followingᶜ him on the road.

LEXICON—a. pres. act. impera. of ὑπάγω (LN 15.52) (BAGD 1. p. 836): 'to go away' [BAGD, LN], 'to depart, to leave' [LN]. The command Ὕπαγε 'Go' [AB1, AB2, BECNT, BNTC, Lns, NTC, WBC; all versions except CEV, ESV, KJV] is also translated 'Be going!' [Lns], 'Go your way' [ESV, KJV], 'You may go' [CEV]. This verb means to depart from someone's presence [LN].

b. perf. act. indic. of σῴζω (LN 23.136) (BAGD 1.c. p. 798): 'to heal' [LN; NET, NIV, NLT, REB], 'to make the person well' [AB1, LN, NTC; ESV, GW, NASB, NRSV, TEV], 'to cure' [LN], 'to make whole' [KJV], 'to save, to free from disease' [BAGD]. The clause 'your faith has healed you' is translated 'you are healed because you believed' [NCV], 'your eyes are healed because of your faith' [CEV], 'your faith has saved you' [AB2, BECNT, BNTC; similarly Lns]. This verb means to cause someone to become well again after having been sick [LN]. In this context the word σῴζω 'to heal' refers to both physical healing and spiritual healing through the gift of salvation [BECNT, NAC].

c. imperf. act. indic. of ἀκολουθέω (LN 15.144): 'to follow' [AB1, AB2, BECNT, BNTC, LN, Lns, NTC; all versions except CEV], 'to go behind' [LN]. The clause 'he was following him on the road' is translated 'he went down the road with Jesus' [CEV]. This verb means to come or go behind or after someone [LN]. The imperfect tense is inceptive and indicates that he began to follow Jesus or it indicates a continuing action of following him [Hb].

QUESTION—What does the command 'Go' indicate?

This was not an abrupt dismissal, so it could be translated 'You may go.' [TH]. It simply means that the man is now cured and may go [NIGTC]. He didn't have to sit alongside the road begging any longer [Gnd]. Jesus dismissed the man as no longer needing his presence, and gave him the option to go on his way or to follow [Hb].

QUESTION—In what sense did this man follow Jesus 'on the road'?

1. This probably means that the man joined the crowd going up to the feast in Jerusalem, but it doesn't necessarily mean that he became a follower of Jesus in the sense of being a disciple [AB1, EBC, Gnd, Hb, NICNT, Sw]. He would want to go up to the Temple in order to offer a sacrifice of thanksgiving for receiving his sight [NICNT]. The large crowd of people who were on the road to Jerusalem did not qualify as being disciples of Jesus. Jesus did not require all believers to become the type of disciples who followed Jesus full time [Gnd].
2. This means that he became a follower or disciple of Jesus [AB2, BECNT, BNTC, CBC, CGTC, ESVfn, Lns, NAC, NCBC, NIGTC, NTC, PNTC, Tay, WBC]. Batimaeus joined with the other pilgrims on the road to Jerusalem, but it is likely that this implies that he had also become a disciple of Jesus [CGTC, ESVfn, NAC]. Batimaeus wanted to be on the road with Jesus along with the other disciples who regularly accompanied Jesus [Lns].

DISCOURSE UNIT—11:1–15:8 [NIGTC]. The topic is act three: Jerusalem.

DISCOURSE UNIT—11:1–13:37 [CBC, Hb, NICNT]. The topic is the ministry in Jerusalem [Hb, NICNT], conflict in Jerusalem and prediction of judgment [CBC].

DISCOURSE UNIT—11:1–12:44 [REB]. The topic is the challenge to Jerusalem.

DISCOURSE UNIT—11:1–26 [PNTC]. The topic is the barren temple.

DISCOURSE UNIT—11:1–25 [Hb, NIGTC]. The topic is preparatory events [Hb], throwing down the gauntlet [NIGTC].

DISCOURSE UNIT—11:1–14 [NASB, NCV]. The topic is the triumphal entry [NASB], Jesus enters Jerusalem as a king [NCV].

DISCOURSE UNIT—11:1–11 [CBC, Hb, NICNT; CEV, ESV, GW, NET, NIV, NLT, NRSV, TEV]. The topic is the entry into Jerusalem [NICNT], Jesus enters Jerusalem [CEV], the King comes to Jerusalem [GW], the entry into Jerusalem as Messiah [Hb], Jesus' triumphal entry [NLT], the triumphal entry [ESV, NET, NIV], Jesus' triumphal entry into Jerusalem [CBC; NRSV], the triumphant entry into Jerusalem [TEV].

11:1 And when they-drew-near to Jerusalem, to[a] Bethphage and Bethany, at[b] the Mount of-Olives, he-sends two of-his disciples **11:2** and he-says to-them, "Go into the village in-front[c] of-you, and immediately upon-entering into it you-will-find a-colt having-been tied,[d] on which no person has ever yet sat. Untie it and bring (it).

LEXICON—a. εἰς (LN 84.16) (BAGD 1.b. p. 228): 'to' [AB2, BECNT, Lns; ESV, GW], 'unto' [KJV], 'at' [NASB, NRSV], 'and they came to' [NTC; NCV, NIV], 'they came to the towns of' [NTC; NLT], 'and had reached' [BNTC], 'and when they reached' [AB1; REB; similarly Lns], 'near' [NET], 'near the towns of' [TEV], not explicit' [WBC; CEV]. This preposition indicates extension toward a special goal [LN].

b. πρός (LN 83.24): 'at' [AB1, BECNT, LN, WBC; ESV, GW, KJV, NET, NIV], 'by' [LN; ESV], 'near' [BNTC, NTC; CEV, NASB, NCV, NRSV], 'close by' [REB], 'unto' [KJV], 'toward' [AB2, Lns], 'on' [NLT]. This preposition indicates a position near another location or object [LN].

c. κατέναντι (LN 83.42) (BAGD 2.a. p. 421):, 'in front of, across from' [LN], 'before, opposite' [BAGD, LN]. The phrase 'the village in front of you' [ESV] is also translated 'the village ahead of you' [NET, NIV, NRSV], 'the next village' [CEV], 'the village opposite you' [AB2, BECNT, BNTC, Lns, NTC, WBC; NASB; similarly AB2; REB], 'the village over against you' [KJV], 'the village over there' [NLT], 'the town you can see there' [NCV]. 'Opposite you' is an unusual expression and could possibly refer to a village on the opposite side of a small ravine or valley [TH].

d. perf. pass. participle of δέω (LN 18.13) (BAGD 2. p. 178): to be tied' [BAGD, LN, Lns; ESV, KJV, NCV], 'to be tied up' [AB1, AB2, LN, NTC; TEV], 'to be tied there' [GW, NASB, NET, NIV, NLT, NRSV], 'to be tethered there' [BNTC; REB; similarly BECNT, WBC], not explicit [CEV]. This verb means to tie objects together [LN]. It means to tie to something [BAGD]. The colt would have been tethered to a post [TRT].

QUESTION—What was important about the villages of Bethphage and Bethany?

Just before the road from Jericho reaches Jerusalem it passes through the villages of Bethphage and Bethany which were located on the eastern slope of the Mount of Olives [BNTC, Hb]. Bethany was just two miles from Jerusalem, and Bethphage was less than a mile away [TH]. Some think the donkey was obtained in Bethany since the road leading up from Jericho first reaches Bethany [Gnd, ICC]. More think that Jesus and his disciples lodged in Bethany over the Sabbath day of rest [BECNT, Lns, NLTfn, PNTC], and then on their way to Jerusalem the next morning, Jesus paused to send two of his disciples on ahead to the village of Bethphage to obtain a donkey for his entry into Jerusalem [CGTC, EBC, Hb, Lns, My, NAC, NICNT, Sw, WBC].

QUESTION—What kind of animal was the colt and what is significant about it not having been previously ridden?

The colt was a young donkey [AB1, AB2, BECNT, CGTC, EBC, NAC, NIGTC, NIVfn, NTC, Tay, TH, TRT, WBC] as specified in Matthew 21:2 and John 12:15 [BECNT, CGTC, EBC, NAC, TRT]. There is an OT provision that an animal devoted to a sacred purpose must be one that has not been put to ordinary use (Numbers 19:2, Deuteronomy. 21:3, and 1 Samuel 6:7) [BNTC, CGTC, EBC, Hb, Lns, NAC, NCBC, NICNT, NIGTC, NTC, Sw]. Not having been trained for riding, this unbroken colt was accompanied by its mother to quiet it down as described in Matthew 21:2 [Hb].

11:3 And if someone says to-you, 'Why are-you-doing this?' say, 'The Lord/owner[a] has need of-it, and sends[b] it here again immediately.[c]' "

TEXT—Manuscripts reading αὐτὸν ἀποστέλλει πάλιν 'sends it again' are given a B rating by GNT to indicate it was regarded to be almost certain. Variant readings are αὐτὸν ἀποστέλλει 'he sends it' [KJV], and αὐτὸν ἀποστελεῖ 'he will send it'.

LEXICON—a. κύριος (LN 12.9, 57.12): 'Lord' [AB1, BECNT, LN (12.9), Lns, NTC, WBC; all versions except NCV, REB, TEV], 'Ruler, One who commands' [LN (12.9)], 'the Master' [BNTC; REB, TEV], 'its Master' [NCV], 'the master' [AB2], 'owner, master, lord' [LN (57.12)]. This noun is a title for God and for Christ, and it denotes the one who exercises supernatural authority over mankind [LN (12.9)] or it denotes someone who owns and controls property, servants, and slaves [LN (57.12)].

b. pres. act. indic. of ἀποστέλλω (LN 15.66) (BAGD 1.b.α. p. 98): 'to send' [BAGD, LN]. The phrase αὐτὸν ἀποστέλλει πάλιν ὧδε 'sends it here again' [WBC] is also translated 'sends him hither again' [Lns], 'will send it back here again' [AB2, BECNT], 'will send it back here' [ESV, NASB, NET, NIV, NRSV, REB], 'will send it back' [AB1, BNTC; TEV], 'will send it here' [GW; similarly KJV], 'will send it' [NCV], 'will return it' [NTC; NLT], 'will bring it back' [CEV]. This verb means to cause someone to depart for a particular purpose [LN]. This is a futuristic present tense, 'he is going to send it' [CGTC, Hb, NTC]. In connection with verbs of sending, the adverb πάλιν 'again' means to send something 'back' [BAGD].

c. εὐθύς (LN 67.53): 'immediately' [AB2, BECNT, LN, Lns, WBC; ESV, NASB, NRSV], 'right away' [AB1, LN], 'at once' [GW, NCV, TEV], 'without delay' [REB], 'straight away' [BNTC; similarly KJV], 'soon' [CEV, NET, NLT], 'shortly' [NTC; NIV], 'then' [LN]. This adverb indicates a point of time immediately subsequent to a previous point of time, with the actual interval of time depending upon the nature of the event and the manner in which the sequence is interpreted by the writer [LN]. This means that the animal would not be detained any longer than the occasion required [Sw].

QUESTION—Who was ὁ κύριος 'the Lord/owner' who had need of the colt?
1. This refers to the Lord Jesus [AB1, AB2, BECNT, BNTC, EBC, EGT, Gnd, Hb, ICC, Lns, NAC, NCBC, NTC, PNTC, Sw, TH, TRT, WBC; all versions]: *the Lord*. 'The Lord' is a common designation for Jesus in Luke and John, and Jesus would probably refer to himself in this way. The owner of the colt would understand the reference was to Jesus [Hb]. In Luke 19:33 it says the owners of the colt are the ones who questioned the disciples when they went to get it [EBC, TRT].
2. This refers to the owner of the colt [CGTC, NICNT, Tay]: *his owner*. It is unlikely that Jesus would refer to himself as 'the Lord', and it is reasonable to assume the owner of the colt was with Jesus at the time, and that would explain how Jesus knew about the colt. This interpretation is supported by the fact that the message was not sent to the owner but to anyone who might intervene [CGTC].
3. This refers to God [NIGTC]. Lord was the regular Jewish title for God, so this meant that the donkey was needed for God's service [NIGTC]

11:4 And they-left and found a-colt having-been-tied at[a] a-door outside[a] in the street,[b] and they-untie him.

LEXICON—a. πρός (LN 83.24) (BAGD III.7. p. 711): 'at' [BAGD, LN], 'by' [LN], 'near' [LN]. The phrase δεδεμένον πρὸς θύραν ἔξω ἐπὶ τοῦ ἀμφόδου 'having been tied at a door outside in the street' is translated 'tied at a/the door, outside in the street' [ESV, NASB, NET], 'tethered at a door outside in the street' [BECNT], 'tied by/near a door, outside in the street' [BNTC; NRSV], 'a tethered (colt) at the door, out in the open street' [WBC], 'tied up at a doorway/door outside in the street [AB1, AB2], 'tied near a door that faced the street' [CEV], 'in the street near the door of a house' [NCV], 'outside in the street, tied at a doorway' [NIV], 'outside in the street, tied up near the door' [NTC], 'outside in the street, tethered beside a door' [REB], 'standing in the street, tied outside the front door' [NLT], 'out in the street, tied to the door of a house' [TEV], 'It was tied to the door of a house' [GW], 'having been tied near the door outside on the way that leads around' [Lns], 'tied by the door without in a place where two ways met' [KJV]. This preposition indicates a position near another location or object [LN].

b. ἄμφοδον (LN 1.101) (BAGD p. 47): 'street' [BAGD, LN], 'city street' [LN]. See translations of this word in the preceding lexicon item. This noun denotes a thoroughfare within a city [LN]. The noun denotes a city quarter that is surrounded and crossed by streets, but it could be taken to refer to a street [BAGD]. This word only occurs here in the NT and some translations have taken it to refer to a place where roads come together, but this is not the meaning of the Greek word. The noun refers to the larger streets encircling the smaller quarters of a town where there are only small passageways between the houses [TH].

QUESTION—What was this door where the colt was tied?
It was the door of the owner of colt [Hb, Lns]. The better houses in the village were built around an open courtyard which had a passageway that led to the door that opened onto the street. The colt was standing outside of that door in the street [ICC, NTC]. The colt was tied *to* the door [GW, TEV], *at* the door [AB1, AB2, BECNT, WBC; ESV, NASB, NET, NIV], *near* the door [Gnd, Hb, Lns, NTC, TH; CEV, NCV, NRSV], *by* the door [BNTC; KJV], *beside* the door [REB], *outside* the door [NLT]. It would have been tied to a post [TRT].

11:5 And some of-the (people) standing there were-saying to-them, "What are-you-doing,^a untying the colt?" **11:6** And they told them just-as^b Jesus had-said, and they-permitted them. **11:7** And they-bring the colt to Jesus and they-threw-upon^c it their garments, and he-sat upon it.

LEXICON—a. pres. act. indic. of ποιέω (LN 42.7) (BAGD I.1.b.ε. p. 681): 'to do' [BAGD, LN], 'to act, to carry out, to accomplish, to perform' [LN]. The phrase Τί ποιεῖτε λύοντες 'What are you doing untying' [AB1, AB2, BECNT, BNTC, NTC, WBC; ESV, NASB, NET, NIV, NLT, NRSV, REB, TEV] is also translated 'What do ye, loosing' [Lns; KJV], 'What are you doing? Why are you untying' [NCV], 'Why are you untying' [CEV, GW]. This verb means to do or perform something, and it is a highly generic word for almost any type of activity [LN]. The question implies 'What right do you have to do that?' [Hb].
    b. καθώς (LN 64.14): 'just as' [AB1, BECNT; NASB, TEV], 'even as' [Lns; KJV], 'as' [AB2, BNTC, NTC, WBC; GW, NET, NIV, REB], 'what' [CEV, ESV, NRSV], 'what (Jesus had told them to say)' [NLT], 'the way (Jesus told them to answer)' [NCV]. This conjunction indicates a similarity in events and states [LN].
    c. pres. act. indic. of ἐπιβάλλω (LN 15.218) (BAGD 1.b. p. 289): 'to throw on' [LN]. 'to lay on, to put on' [BAGD]. The clause 'they threw upon it their garments' is translated 'they spread their outer garments upon it' [BNTC], 'they place their garments on it' [BECNT], 'they threw their cloaks/garments on/upon/over it' [WBC; ESV, NET, NIV, NLT, NRSV, TEV; similarly Lns; REB], 'they cast their garments on him' [KJV], 'they threw their himatia on it' [AB1], 'they put their clothes on it' [AB2], 'they put some of their clothes on its back' [CEV]. This verb means to throw something on something [LN].

QUESTION—Who threw their garments on the colt and why did they do that?
The disciples placed their outer garments on the colt in place of a saddle [BECNT, CGTC, EBC, Gnd, Hb, NICNT, NTC, Sw, TH, WBC]. Since there seems to be no shift in subjects, it refers to the two disciples who had brought the colt [Gnd]. In addition to the two disciples, some of the other disciples might have added their long outer robes across the back of the colt as a cushion for Jesus to sit on [Hb, Lns, NTC].

11:8 **And many spread their garments on the road, but others (spread) leafy-branches[a] having-cut (them) from the fields.**

TEXT—Manuscripts reading ἄλλοι δὲ στιβάδας κόψαντες ἐκ τῶν ἀγρῶν 'but others (spread) leafy branches having cut (them) from the fields' are followed by GNT, which does not mention any variant reading. A variant reading is ἄλλοι δὲ στοιβάδας ἔκοπτον ἐκ τῶν δένδρων, καὶ ἐστρώννυον εἰς τὴν ὁδόν 'but others cut leafy branches from the trees and were spreading them on the road' and it is followed by KJV.

LEXICON—a. στιβάς (LN **3.52**) (BAGD p. 768): 'leafy branch' [BAGD, LN], 'leaves' [BAGD]. The clause 'others spread leafy branches having cut them from the fields' is translated 'others, having cut off leafy branches from the fields, spread them' [BECNT], 'others spread leafy branches that/which they had cut from/in the fields [NTC; ESV, NASB, NLT, NRSV, similarly AB2], 'others spread branches they had cut in the fields' [NET, NIV], 'others cut branches/leafy-branches in the fields and spread them on the road' [GW, NCV, TEV], 'others went to cut branches from the fields' [CEV], 'others spread tall grass, cutting it from the fields; [WBC], 'others masses of leaves, having cut them out of the fields' [Lns], 'others, greenery cut from the fields' [BNTC], 'others spread greenery which they had cut in the fields' [REB], 'others spread brushwood which they had cut in the fields [AB1]. This noun denotes a leafy branch [LN]. The noun denotes a kind of bed or mattress made of straw, rushes, reeds, leaves, etc. [BAGD, NIGTC], but in this only occurrence in the NT it obviously refers to leaves or leafy branches [BAGD].

QUESTION—Why did people spread their garments on the road?
They spread their outer robes on the dusty road in order to carpet the way for Jesus as he came along riding on the colt [Hb]. It was an ancient practice for welcoming a new king [Hb].

QUESTION—What did other people spread on the road?
The word στιβάδας simply refers to unspecified vegetation and often referred to straw, rushes, leaves, and other material used for bedding [Hb, NIGTC]. This refers to straw cut from the fields [Gnd]. The parallel passage in Matthew 21:8 uses the word κλάδους 'branches from a tree' [Hb]. Leafy branches could easily be cut from a field nearby [EBC], and probably this refers to leafy branches cut from olive trees [TH]. They were not the palm leaves carried by the people who came out from Jerusalem to meet Jesus in John 12:19 [NCBC, NIVfn, TH, WBC]. Probably this was tall grass or even stalks of grain that could hardly be distinguishable from grass at this time of year [WBC]. However, two commentaries think that this does refer to palm branches [Lns, TRT]. With no main verb in this second clause, we can assume that once the vegetation was cut it was spread on the road like the clothes were [NIGTC, TH].

11:9 And the-ones going-in-front and the-ones following were-shouting, "Hosanna[a]! Blessed[b] (be/is) the (one) coming in (the) name[c] of-(the)-Lord.

LEXICON—a. ὡσαννά (LN 33.364) (BAGD p. 899): 'Hosanna!' [AB1, AB2, BAGD, BECNT, BNTC, LN, Lns, NTC, WBC; ESV, GW, KJV, NASB, NET, NIV, NRSV, REB], 'Praise God!' [NCV, NLT, TEV], 'Hooray!' [CEV]. This is a transliteration of an Aramaic expression meaning 'Help, I pray' or 'Save, I pray,' but it had become a strictly liturgical formula of praise, and here it was a shout of praise or adoration [LN].

  b. perf. pass. participle of εὐλογέω (LN 33.470) (BAGD 2.a. p. 322): 'to be blessed' [BAGD, LN]. The phrase 'blessed the one coming' [Lns] is translated as a prayer to God: 'God bless the one who comes' [CEV, NCV], 'God bless him who comes' [TEV], 'blessings on the one who comes' [NLT]. It is translated as a statement: 'blessed is the one coming' [BECNT, NTC], 'blessed is the one who comes' [AB1, BNTC, WBC; GW, NET, NRSV], 'blessed is he who comes' [AB2; ESV, KJV, NASB, NIV, REB]. This verb asks God to bestow his divine favor on someone [LN].

  c. ὄνομα (LN 33.126) (BAGD I.4.c.γ. p. 573): 'name' [BAGD, LN]. The phrase ἐν ὀνόματι κυρίου 'in the name of the Lord' [all translations except AB1, Lns], 'in the Lord's name' [AB1, Lns]. This noun denotes the proper name of a person or object [LN].

QUESTION—What did the people mean when they shouted 'Hosanna'?

1. This was an exclamation of praise to God [BECNT, BNTC, CBC, EBC, Hb, Lns, NAC, NCBC, NETfn, NICNT, NLTfn, TH, TRT, WBC; CEV, NCV, NLT, TEV]. It was a statement of joy and thanksgiving like the present day expression 'Praise the Lord!' [BECNT, NLTfn]. It was the customary greeting given to pilgrims who had come to Jerusalem for the feast [EBC, Hb, NCBC, NICNT]. It was a shout of welcome and expressed their great joy at the arrival of such a person as Jesus [TH]. Even though it is an acclamation of welcome in this verse, in the next verse it is an appeal for God's help to bring about the messianic deliverance they were expecting [EBC, Hb].

2. This was a prayer to God that he will save the Jewish nation [ICC, NTC, WBC]. Since it was addressed to God, the people were asking God to fulfill his promise of the deliverance of Israel through Jesus [ICC, WBC].

QUESTION—In what way is Jesus blessed?

With no verb included in the Greek text, this can be understood as a third person imperative 'blessed be' or as a third person declarative 'he is blessed' [TH].

1. This is a prayer that God will bless Jesus [ESVfn, NCBC, NLTfn, Sw, TH, TRT]: May God bless the one who comes.

2. This is a statement that God has blessed Jesus [BECNT, Hb, ICC, Lns, NTC, PNTC]: God has blessed the one who comes.

QUESTION—What is meant by Jesus 'coming in the name of the Lord'?

It means that Jesus has come as the representative of the Lord God [TH, TRT].

11:10 Blessed[a] (be/is) the coming kingdom of-our ancestor[b] David. Hosanna in the highest[c]."

TEXT—Manuscripts reading ἡ ἐρχομένη βασιλεία 'the coming kingdom' are followed by GNT, which does not mention any variant reading. A variant reading is ἡ ἐρχομένη βασιλεία ἐν ὀνόματι κυρίου 'the coming kingdom in the name of the Lord' and it is followed by KJV.

LEXICON—a. perf. pass. participle of εὐλογέω (LN 33.470) (BAGD 2.a. p. 322): 'to be blessed' [BAGD, LN]. The phrase 'Blessed be/is the coming kingdom' is translated as a prayer to God: 'Blessed be the kingdom' [KJV], 'Blessings on the coming kingdom' [NLT], 'God bless the coming kingdom' [CEV, TEV], 'God bless the kingdom (of our father David)! That kingdom is coming!' [NCV]. It is translated as a statement: 'Blessed is the coming kingdom' [NTC, WBC; ESV, NASB, NET, NIV, NRSV], 'Blessed is the kingdom…which is coming!' [REB], 'Blessed is (our ancestor David's) kingdom that is coming!' [GW]. This verb means to ask God to bestow his divine favor on someone [LN].

b. πατήρ (LN 10.20) (BAGD 1.b. p. 635): 'ancestor' [CEV, GW, NLT, NRSV], 'forefather' [LN], 'father' [NTC, WBC; ESV, KJV, NASB, NCV, NET, NIV, REB, TEV]. In this verse the noun 'father' denotes a person several preceding generations removed from the reference person [LN].

c. ὕψιστος (LN 1.13) (BAGD 1. p. 850): 'high, the world above, sky, heaven, on high' [LN], 'highest heaven' [BAGD]. The clause Ὡσαννὰ ἐν τοῖς ὑψίστοις 'Hosanna in the highest!' [NTC, WBC; ESV, KJV, NASB, NET, NIV] is also translated 'Hosanna in the highest heaven!' [GW, NRSV], 'Hosanna in the heavens!' [REB], 'Praise to God in heaven!' [NCV], 'Praise God in highest heaven!' [NLT], 'Praise be to God!' [TEV], 'Hooray for God in heaven above!' [CEV]. This pronominal adjective denotes a location above the earth that is associated with supernatural events or beings and there is no difference in meaning between the singular and plural forms of the word. The phrase ὡσαννὰ ἐν τοῖς ὑψίστοις 'hosanna in the highest' has been interpreted as a plea for salvation or deliverance from God who is in heaven. However, it seems preferable to understand 'hosanna' to simply be a shout of exclamation or praise meaning 'praise be to God' [LN]. The 'highest (places)' refers to heaven [TH].

QUESTION—What was the coming kingdom of David?

It was the messianic kingdom that was promised to David's descendant, Jesus [EBC, Hb]. They were now proclaiming the coming of the kingdom, not the king [EBC, NIGTC]. The kingdom's coming was no longer postponed [Hb]. The king is the coming one, Jesus, so his kingdom is the one that is coming [Lns]. This acknowledges Jesus to be the one who brings in the messianic kingdom [Hb].

QUESTION—What did the people mean when they shouted 'Hosanna in the highest places'?

'Hosanna' should be translated so that it is consistent with the way it was interpreted in verse 9 [TH].

1. This is a prayer that God will save the nation [CGTC, Hb, ICC, NICNT, Sw, Tay, WBC]. It means 'May our prayer for salvation be heard in heaven' [Hb].
2. This is an exclamation of praise [EBC, TH]. This shout of acclaim and thanksgiving is equivalent to shouting 'Praise be to God' or 'Let God be praised' [TH].

11:11 **And he-entered into Jerusalem into the temple[a] and having-looked-around[b] at-everything, the hour now being-late, he-went-out to Bethany with the twelve.**

LEXICON—a. ἱερόν (LN 7.16) (BAGD 2. p. 372): 'temple' [BAGD, LN]. This noun denotes a temple or sanctuary with its surrounding consecrated area [LN]. The temple in Jerusalem included the entire temple precinct with all of its buildings, courts, etc. In the following verses the action will take place in the Court of the Gentiles where merchants and money changers had their places of business [BAGD].

b. aorist mid. participle of περιβλέπομαι, περιβλέπω (LN 24.12) (BAGD 1. p. 646): 'to look around' [BAGD, LN]. This verb means to look around, though not necessarily in a complete circle [LN].

QUESTION—What was the point of looking around the temple at everything?

As the Lord of the temple, Jesus was inspecting its premises to determine whether the purpose intended by God was being fulfilled. This survey will provide the grounds for his actions the next day [NICNT].

QUESTION—What did Jesus go out of?

Jesus went out from both the temple precinct and the city [Hb].

DISCOURSE UNIT—11:12–25 [CBC]. The topic is Jesus curses the fig tree and clears the temple.

DISCOURSE UNIT—11:12–19 [NIV]. The topic is Jesus clears the temple.

DISCOURSE UNIT—11:12–14 [Hb; ESV, NICNT, CEV, GW, NET, NLT, NRSV, TEV]. The topic is Jesus puts a curse on a fig tree [CEV], Jesus curses the fig tree [ESV, GW, NLT, NRSV, TEV], the cursing of the fig tree [Hb; NET], the unproductive fig tree [NICNT].

11:12 And on-the next-day (when) they had-gone-out from Bethany, he-was-hungry. **11:13** And having-seen from a-distance a-fig-tree having-leaves he-went (to see) if perhaps he-would-find-anything on it. And having-come to it he-found nothing except leaves (because) it-was not the season (for) figs.

QUESTION—Why would Jesus have expected there might be figs on the tree if it was not yet the season for the figs to be ripe?

Although fig trees in Jerusalem usually have leaves by March or April, they do not produce figs until June [EBC, NICNT]. Jesus did not curse the tree because it had not produced fruit. This was an acted-out parable that explains the meaning of the cleansing of the temple [AB2, BECNT, BNTC, CGTC, EBC, ICC, NICNT, NIGTC, NTC, WBC]. The full leafed fig tree without fruit symbolizes the temple. and the temple with all its religious activities without spiritual fruit stands in danger of judgment [WBC]. Some think that the presence of the leaves on this particular fig tree was a sign that the tree already had fruit [EGT, Hb, ICC, Lns. NTC, Sw]. This particular tree must have had more abundant leaves than the other fig trees, hinting that it was ahead of the other fig trees in producing fruit [Hb, Sw].

11:14 And speaking[a] he said to-it, "No-longer into the age[b] no-one may-eat fruit[c] from you." And his disciples were-listening.

LEXICON—a. aorist pass. (deponent = act.) participle of ἀποκρίνομαι (LN 33.28) (BAGD 2. p. 93): 'to speak, to say, to declare' [LN], 'to speak up' [BAGD, Lns, NTC], 'to answer' [AB2, BECNT, WBC; KJV], not explicit [AB1, BNTC; all versions except KJV]. This verb means to introduce or to continue a somewhat formal discourse and it occurs regularly with the verb λέγω 'to say' [LN].

b. εἰς τὸν αἰῶνα (LN 67.95): The phrase εἰς τὸν αἰῶνα 'into the age' is translated ' (may no one) ever' [BNTC, WBC; all versions except CEV, KJV], 'ever again' [AB1, B2, BECNT], 'forever' [Lns; KJV], 'never' [NTC; CEV]. The phrase denotes an unlimited duration of time in regard to the future and can be translated 'always, forever, forever and ever, eternally' [LN].

c. καρπός (LN 3.33) (BAGD 1.a p. 404): 'fruit' [BAGD, LN; all translations]. This noun denotes any fruit part of plants [LN].

DISCOURSE UNIT—11:15–26 [NASB, NLT]. The topic is Jesus drives money changers from the temple [NASB], Jesus clears the temple [NLT].

DISCOURSE UNIT—11:15–19 [Hb, NICNT; CEV, GW, ESV, NCV, NET, NRSV, TEV]. The topic is Jesus goes to the temple [NCV, TEV], Jesus in the temple [CEV], the cleansing of the temple [Hb; NET], Jesus cleanses the temple [ESV, NRSV], Jesus throws out the money changers [GW], the expulsion of the merchants from the temple precincts [NICNT].

11:15 And they-come to Jerusalem. And having-entered into the temple he-began to-drive-out[a] the (people) selling and the (people) buying in the temple, and he-overturned[b] the tables of-the money-changers[c] and the chairs[d] of-the (people) selling the doves.

LEXICON—a. pres. act. infin. of ἐκβάλλω (LN 15.44) (BAGD 1. p. 237): 'to drive out' [AB1, BAGD, BNTC, **LN**, NTC, WBC; ESV, NASB, NET, NIV, NLT, NRSV, REB, TEV], 'to chase out' [CEV], 'to throw out' [AB2, Lns; GW, NCV], 'to cast out' [BECNT; KJV], 'to expel' [LN]. This verb means to cause someone to go out or leave, and it often involves the use of force [LN].

    b. aorist act. indic. of καταστρέφω (LN 16.18) (BAGD 1. p. 419): 'to overturn' [AB2, BAGD, BECNT, BNTC, LN, WBC; ESV, GW, NASB, NIV, NRSV, TEV], 'to overthrow' [KJV], 'to upset' [AB1, BAGD, LN, Lns; REB], 'to knock over' [NLT], 'to turn over' [LN; CEV, NCV, NET], 'to turn upside down' [NTC]. This verb means to cause something to be completely overturned [LN].

    c. κολλυβιστής (LN 57.205) (BAGD p. 442): 'money changer' [BAGD, LN; all translations except NCV], 'those who were exchanging different kinds of money' [NCV]. This noun denotes a person who exchanges currency for a different type of currency or for different values of the same currency [LN].

    d. καθέδρα (LN 6.111) (BAGD p. 388): 'chair' [BAGD, **LN**; GW, NET, NLT], 'seat' [AB1, AB2, BAGD, BECNT, BNTC, LN, Lns, NTC, WBC; ESV, KJV, NASB, NRSV, REB], 'stool' [LN; TEV], 'bench' [CEV, NCV, NIV].

QUESTION—What part of the temple precincts did Jesus and his disciples enter?

They entered the Court of the Gentiles where all of the commercial traffic mentioned in this verse was taking place [all commentaries]. It was called the Court of the Gentiles because Gentiles as well as Jews were allowed to enter this spacious outer courtyard. Only Jews were allowed to proceed beyond a high partition-wall to the interior parts of the Temple [NTC]. In the inner three sections of the Temple, Jewish women could go no farther than the Court of Women. The circumcised males could go on into the Court of the Israelites. Only priests were allowed to enter the innermost Court of the Priests which led directly into the temple proper where sacrifices were offered [Hb, PNTC]. The Court of the Gentiles seemed to have been turned into an oriental bazaar with numerous tables set up by merchants. There were also stalls filled with animals that were sold for sacrifices [NICNT]

QUESTION—What were the people selling and buying in the Court of the Gentiles?

Merchants sold the oil, wine, salt, and sacrificial animals that were required for the Temple sacrifices [ICC, NICNT, Sw, Tay, TH]. Many of the buyers were pilgrims who had come to the Temple to worship and offer sacrifices [Sw, TH]. Local worshippers also found it convenient to buy such things right there at the temple [Sw]. The trade in animals that had passed the criteria for sacrifice and the changing of money into the coins required by the temple treasury were necessary. Jesus' protest was not against the selling of such items, but against all of this business taking place inside the Temple [BECNT, NIGTC].

QUESTION—What did the moneychangers do?

Moneychangers sat at tables stacked with coins. Many of the worshippers did not have the Hebrew half shekel coins required for payment of the Temple taxes and so they had to exchange their Roman coins for the proper Hebrew coins [TH]. Starting on their twentieth birthday, every male Jew was required to pay a yearly half shekel towards the cost of the religious services in the Temple. Because foreign coins had idolatrous images engraved on them, they were not an acceptable means of payment. Charging a fee that was sometimes as high as ten percent, the money changers exchanged the Greek and Roman coins most people had for the required Hebrew coins [Hb]. They also changed money for the convenience of the numerous buyers and sellers in the Court of the Gentiles [ICC].

QUESTION—Why did merchants sell doves?

The sacrifice of a dove was required for the purification of women and for the cleansing of lepers [NICNT]. The poor were permitted to offer sacrifices of doves or pigeons instead of sheep and oxen [ICC, NICNT, TH, WBC].

QUESTION—How did Jesus drive these merchants out of the courtyard?

A previous cleansing of the temple is recorded in John 2:15 where Jesus had made a whip out of the cords that were lying about and used it to drive the merchants out of the courtyard. Perhaps he did this again [Lns, NTC]. Perhaps he inflicted blows on the merchants to drive them out of the courtyard [NICNT]. Given the huge size of the Court of the Gentiles, it is unlikely that Jesus brought the whole operation to a standstill [PNTC]. This verse says that Jesus ἤρξατο 'began' to drive these people out, but does not tell us that the whole huge courtyard area was left entirely empty of both buyers and sellers [NIGTC].

11:16 **And he-was- not -allowing**[a] **that anyone should-carry anything**[b] **through the temple.**

LEXICON—a. imperf. act. indic. of ἀφίημι (LN 13.140) (BAGD 4. p.126): 'to allow' [AB2, BAGD, BECNT. BNTC, LN, NTC; ESV, NCV, NIV], 'to let' [AB1, BAGD, LN; CEV, GW], 'to permit' [BAGD, Lns, WBC; NASB, NET], 'to suffer' [KJV]. The clause 'he was not allowing that anyone' is translated 'he stopped everyone from' [NLT]. This verb means to leave it to someone to do something [LN].

b. σκεῦος (LN 6.118) (BAGD 1.a. p. 754): 'thing' [BAGD], 'container, vessel' [LN]. It is translated 'anything' [**LN**; ESV, GW, NRSV, TEV], 'things' [CEV], 'a vessel' [BECNT, Lns, WBC; KJV], 'a container' [AB2], 'merchandise' [NTC; NASB, NET, NIV], 'goods' [AB1, BNTC; NCV, REB]. The verse is translated 'and he stopped everyone from using the Temple as a marketplace' [NLT]. This noun is a highly generic term for any kind of jar, bowl, basket, or vase [LN]. It denotes any object used for any purpose [BAGD].

QUESTION—What was wrong about carrying things through the Temple?
1. People were taking a shortcut through the Court of the Gentiles as they carried things between the Mount of Olives and the city of Jerusalem [AB1, BECNT, BNTC, CGTC, EBC, EGT, Hb, ICC, NCBC, NICNT, NIGTC, NTC, Sw, Tay, TH].
2. People were using the Court of the Gentiles as a marketplace for the things they sold or bought [CBC; NLT]: 'He stopped everyone from using the Temple as a marketplace' [NLT].

11:17 **And he-was-teaching[a] and saying to-them, "Is-it- not -written[b] 'My house shall-be-called[c] a-house of-prayer[d] (for) all the nations[e]'? But you have-made it a-den[f] of-robbers."**

LEXICON—a. imperf. act. indic. of διδάσκω (LN 33.224): 'to teach' [LN]. Most translations apply this reference to teaching directly to what Jesus says in this verse: 'then he taught the people, saying' [NCV; similarly CEV], 'he was teaching and saying to them' [AB2, BECNT, NTC, WBC; ESV], 'then he taught, saying unto them' [KJV], 'then he taught them by saying' [GW], 'he began to teach and say to them' [NASB], 'he began to teach them and said' [BNTC; NET, REB], 'he was teaching and saying' [NRSV], 'then he taught them' [AB1], 'he then taught the people' [TEV], 'he said to them' [NLT]. Some think the reference to his teaching covers more than what he told them in this verse [EGT, Hb, Lns, My, Tay]: 'he engaged in teaching and went on to say to them' [Lns], 'as he taught them, he said' [NIV]. This verb means to provide instruction in either a formal or informal setting [LN].

b. perf. pass. indic. of γράφω (LN 33.61) (BAGD 2.c. p. 166): 'to write' [BAGD, LN]. The phrase 'is it not written' [BECNT, BNTC, NTC, WBC; ESV, KJV, NASB, NET, NIV, NRSV] is also translated 'has it not been written' [AB2, Lns], 'does not scripture say' [REB], 'is it not said in Scripture' [AB1], 'it is written in the Scriptures' [NCV], 'Scripture says' [GW], 'the Scriptures say' [CEV], 'the Scriptures declare' [NLT], 'it is written in the Scriptures that' [TEV]. This is a formula for introducing quotations [BAGD]. This question anticipates a positive answer [TH].

c. fut. pass. indic. of καλέω (LN 33.129) (BAGD 1.a.β. p. 399): 'to be called' [BAGD, LN], 'to be named' [LN], 'to be designated' BAGD]. The verb κληθήσεται 'shall/will be called' [all translations except CEV] is also translated 'should be called' [CEV]. This verb means to speak of a person or object by means of a proper name [LN]. The phrase 'shall be called' is a Hebraism that means 'shall *be* (a house of prayer)' [TH].

d. προσευχή (LN 33.178) (BAGD 1, p. 713): 'prayer' [BAGD. LN]. The phrase οἶκος προσευχῆς 'a/the house of prayer' [all translations except CEV, NCV] is also translated 'a house for prayer' [NCV], 'a place of worship' [CEV]. This noun denotes a place where people customarily meet to pray [LN].

e. ἔθνος (LN 11.55) (BAGD 1. p. 218): 'nation, people' [BAGD, LN]. The plural form is translated 'nations' [AB1, AB2, BECNT, BNTC, Lns, NTC; all versions except NCV, TEV], 'people from all nations' [NCV], 'the people of all nations' [TEV], 'the Gentiles' [WBC]. This noun denotes the largest unit into which the people of the world are divided on the basis of their constituting a socio-political community [LN].

f. σπήλαιον (LN 1.57) (BAGD p. 762) 'den' [LN], 'cave, hideout' [BAGD, LN]. The phrase σπήλαιον λῃστῶν 'a den of robbers' [BECNT; ESV, NET, NIV, NLT, NRSV] is also translated 'a robbers' den' [BNTC, Lns, NTC; NASB], 'a den of thieves' [KJV], 'a den of brigands' [AB2], 'a cave of robbers' [WBC], 'a robbers' cave' [AB1; REB], 'a gathering place for thieves' [GW], 'a hideout for robbers' [NCV], 'a place where robbers hide' [CEV], 'a hideout for thieves' [TEV]. This noun denotes a cave or den that is generally large enough for at least temporary occupation by people. Such places were often used by refugees or thieves for habitation or refuge [LN]. A den is a cave that is used as a place in which to hide [TH].

QUESTION—Who were the people Jesus was teaching?

These unnamed people must be all the people who still remained in the Court of the Gentiles [BNTC]. Hundreds must have run to gather around Jesus when they saw that he had cleansed the courtyard [Lns]. The imperfect tense, 'he was teaching and saying' may suggest that this occurred while he was casting out the men who were guilty of making the temple a den of robbers [BECNT].

QUESTION—What OT passage is quoted?

The quotation is from the Septuagint Greek translation of Isaiah 56:7 [NICNT]. In that passage Yahweh is speaking, so the words 'my house' refers to God's house. Jesus was not claiming that the Temple was owned by him [TH]. This is translated 'It is written in the Scriptures that God said…' [TEV].

QUESTION—Where was this house of prayer?

Jesus was restoring the courtyard of the Gentiles to its proper purpose as a house of prayer [CGTC, EGT, Hb, Lns, Sw].

QUESTION—What is meant by making the courtyard 'a den of robbers'?

Robbers are those who take away possessions of others by force [TH]. The sales people and the money changers were no better than robbers when they overcharged the pilgrims. They thought they could safely sit in the Temple like robbers do in their dens [BECNT, EBC, Hb, Lns, Sw]. They thought their connections with the Temple would protect them from any penalties for cheating those who had come to make sacrifices [Hb, Lns]. In addition to robbing the people financially, the religious leaders were robbing them spiritually by stealing from them the opportunity to genuinely know God [NETfn]. By making it so difficult to pray in the Temple of the Gentiles, the

Jewish leaders were taking away the right to worship Israel's God from the Gentiles [EBC].

11:18 **And the chief-priests and the scribes heard (this/of-this) and they-were-looking-for**[a] **how they-might-kill**[b] **him because they-were-afraid**[c] **of him. Because the whole crowd was-amazed**[d] **at his teaching.**

LEXICON—a. imperf. act. indic. of ζητέω (LN 27.34) (BAGD 1.c. p. 339): 'to look for' [AB2, BNTC, NTC; CEV, GW, NIV, NRSV, REB, TEV], 'to search' [**LN**], 'to seek' [AB1, BAGD, BECNT, Lns, WBC; ESV, KJV, NASB], 'to try to find' [NCV], 'to consider' [BAGD; NET], 'to plan' [NLT], 'to investigate, to deliberate' [BAGD]. This verb means to attempt to learn something by careful investigation or searching [LN]. The imperfect tense 'they were looking for' refers to their continued deliberation [BECNT, Hb, NTC; NRSV]. Some take the imperfect to be inceptive, meaning 'they began to search' [Lns, CEV, NASB, NCV, NIV, NLT, TEV]. The adverb πῶς 'how' indicates that even though they had already decided that Jesus must be killed, they still needed to decide how to make it happen [Hb].

b. aorist act. subj. of ἀπόλλυμι (LN 20.31) (BAGD 1.a.α. p. 95): 'to kill' [AB1, NTC; CEV, GW, NCV, NIV, NLT, NRSV, TEV], 'to destroy' [AB2, BAGD, BECNT, BNTC, LN, Lns, WBC; ESV, KJV, NASB], 'to bring about his death' [REB], 'to assassinate' [NET]. This verb means to destroy or to cause the destruction of persons, objects, or institutions [LN].

c. imperf. pass. indic. of φοβέομαι (LN 25.252): 'to be afraid' [AB2, BNTC, LN, NTC; CEV, GW, NASB, NCV, NLT, NRSV, REB, TEV], 'to fear' [AB1, BECNT, LN, Lns, WBC; ESV, KJV, NET, NIV]. This verb means to be in a state of fearing [LN].

d. imperf. pass. indic. of ἐκπλήσσομαι (LN 25.219) (BAGD 2. p. 244): 'to be amazed' [BAGD; GW, NCV, NET, NIV, NLT, TEV], 'to be completely amazed' [CEV], 'to be overwhelmed' [AB2, BAGD], 'to be astonished' [BECNT, BNTC, Lns, NTC; ESV, KJV, NASB], 'to be greatly astounded' [LN], 'to be awestruck' [AB1], 'to be spellbound' [NRSV, REB], 'to be impressed' [WBC]. This verb means to be so amazed that one is practically overwhelmed [LN]. The imperfect tense indicates the protracted feeling of their utter bewilderment [Hb]. This word occurs at 1:22; 6:2; 7:37; 10:26; 11:18.

QUESTION—When did the chief priests and the scribes hear what Jesus said?
They personally heard Jesus say this [GW]. It doesn't have to mean that they were all present when Jesus made his statement and probably it just means 'they heard about what Jesus had said' [Sw, TH; NLT, REB].

QUESTION—Why did the authorities want to have Jesus killed?
The chief priests and the scribes constituted the main body of the Sanhedrim and they were the very ones who had sold the rights to sell in the Temple to the traders [ICC]. Jesus was directly challenging their authority when he

drove out the merchants whom they had authorized to be there. Jesus had no doubt cost those authorities a good deal of money. Besides that, their power and authority would be broken if Jesus managed to persuade the people to follow him [EBC]. Because the chief priests and the scribes feared Jesus' popularity with the crowds, they were looking for some way to get rid of him [TH].

11:19 **And when it-became late,[a] they-went outside the city.**

LEXICON—a. ὀψέ (LN 67.76) (BAGD 2. p. 601): 'late' [BAGD, LN], 'late in the day, that evening' [CEV]. The phrase 'when it became late' is translated in reference to that very evening: 'when evening came' [AB1, AB2, BECNT, BNTC; ESV, NASB, NET, NIV, NRSV, REB, TEV], 'that evening' [CEV, NCV, NLT], 'when even was come' [KJV]. It refers to more than one evening: 'every evening' [GW], 'whenever it got late' [Lns], 'whenever evening came' [WBC], 'whenever evening arrived' [NTC]. This adverb pertains to a point near the end of a day that is normally after sunset but before nightfall [LN].

QUESTION—Does the conjunction ὅταν 'when' refer to going out of the city that one day or going out of it several different days?
   1. This refers to the same day Jesus had cleansed the Temple [BNTC, CGTC, My, NICNT, TH; all versions except GW]: *when it became late they went outside the city.*
   2. This refers to several nights during that week. Each evening they would go outside the city [EGT, Hb, ICC, Lns, NIGTC, NTC, Sw, WBC; GW]: *whenever it became late, they would go outside the city.* From Monday night onward Jesus always left the city [Lns]. This was his practice during those first three days of Passion Week [Hb, Lns]. Jesus and his disciples could not find lodging in Jerusalem [WBC]. They either lodged with some friends of Jesus outside the city or they spent the night outside under the stars [NTC]. Probably they went back to nearby Bethany [Lns, NIGTC].

DISCOURSE UNIT—11:20–25 [Hb, NICNT; CEV, ESV, GW, NCV, NET, NIV, NRSV, TEV]. The topic is a lesson from the fig tree [CEV, TEV], the lesson from the withered fig tree [Hb; ESV, NRSV], the fig tree dries up [GW], the withered fig tree [NET, NIV], the withered fig tree, faith, and prayer [NICNT], the power of faith [NCV].

11:20 **And passing-by[a] early they-saw the fig-tree having-been-withered from[b] (the) roots.**

LEXICON—a. pres. mid./pass. (deponent = act.) participle of παραπορεύομαι (LN 15.28) (BAGD 1. p. 621): 'to pass by, to go by' [BAGD, LN]. The phrase καὶ παραπορευόμενοι πρωΐ 'and passing by early' is translated 'and passing by early in the morning' [AB2], 'and while passing by early in the morning' [BECNT, WBC], 'and passing by in the morning' [Lns], 'as they were-passing/passed by in the morning' [ESV, NASB], 'in the morning as they were-passing/passed by' [NTC; KJV, NET, NRSV], 'early in the morning, as they passed by' [AB1], 'early next morning, as they passed by' [BNTC; REB], 'in the morning, as they went along' [NIV], 'early next morning, as they walked along the road' [TEV], 'while Jesus and his disciples were walking early in the morning' [GW], 'the next morning as Jesus was passing by with his followers [NCV], 'as the disciples walked past the fig tree the next morning' [CEV], 'the next morning as they passed by the fig tree he had cursed' [NLT]. This verb means to move past a reference point [LN].

b. ἐκ (LN 90.16) (BAGD 2. p. 234): 'from' [BAGD, LN], 'out of, away from' [BAGD]. The phrase 'they saw the fig tree having-been-withered/withered from the roots' [AB2, NTC; NET, NIV] is also translated 'they saw the fig tree withered from the roots up' [BECNT, WBC; NASB], 'they saw the fig tree withered away to its roots' [ESV. NRSV, NRSV], 'they saw that the fig tree had withered from the roots up' [REB], 'the disciples noticed it had withered from the roots up' [NLT], 'they saw the fig tree having-dried/dried up from the roots' [Lns; KJV], 'they noticed that the fig tree was withered all the way down to the roots' [AB1], 'they noticed that it was completely dried up, roots and all' [CEV],'they saw that the fig tree had dried up' [GW], 'they saw the fig tree dry and dead, even to the roots' [NCV], 'they saw the fig tree. It was dead all the way down to its roots' [TEV]. This preposition indicates the source of an activity or state and it implies that something is proceeding from or out of that source [LN].

11:21 And having-remembered, Peter says to-him, "Rabbi,[a] look, the fig-tree that you cursed[b] has-withered.

LEXICON—a. ῥαββί (LN 33.246) (BAGD p. 733): 'rabbi' [AB1, AB2, BECNT, BNTC, LN, Lns, NTC, WBC; ESV, GW, NASB, NCV, NIV, NLT, REB, NRSV], 'teacher' [LN; CEV, NET, TEV], 'master' [KJV]. This noun is borrowed from Aramaic to denote a Jewish teacher and scholar who is recognized for his expertise in interpreting the Jewish Scriptures [LN]. It is an honorary title for the outstanding teachers of the law [BAGD]. This noun occurs at verses 9:5, 11.21, and 14:45.

b. aorist mid. (deponent = act.) indic. of καταράομαι (LN 33.471) (BAGD p. 417): 'to curse' [BAGD, LN; all versions except CEV], 'to put a curse on' [CEV]. This verb means to cause injury or harm by means of a statement regarded as having some supernatural power [LN].

QUESTION—What did Peter remember?

Some translations make explicit what Peter had remembered: 'what had happened' [AB1; REB, TEV], 'the tree' [NCV], 'Jesus' words' [BECNT, WBC], 'what Jesus had said' [GW], 'what Jesus had said to the tree' [CEV], 'what Jesus had said to the tree on the previous day' [NLT].

QUESTION—What is implied by Peter's statement?

Although Peter only stated the facts concerning the tree, he implied that he wondered how it could be that the tree could suddenly wither away and die [Hb].

11:22 **And answering/speaking,[a] Jesus says to-them, "Have faith in-God.**

TEXT—Manuscripts reading ἔχετε (understood as an imperative) 'Have' are given a B rating by GNT to indicate it was regarded to be almost certain. A variant reading is εἰ ἔχετε (understood as an indicative) 'if you have faith'

LEXICON—a. aorist pass. (deponent = act.) participle of ἀποκρίνομαι (LN 33.28, 33.184): 'to answer, to reply' [LN (33.184)], 'to speak, to say, to declare' [LN (33.28)]. The phrase ἀποκριθεὶς...λέγει 'answering/speaking...says' is translated 'answering...says' [Lns, WBC; KJV], 'answered and said/says' [AB2, BECNT], 'in response...said' [NTC], 'answered saying' [NASB], 'answered' [AB1, BNTC; ESV, NCV, NIV, NRSV, REB, TEV], 'said' [GW, NET, NLT], 'told' [CEV]. This verb means to respond to a question asking for information [LN (33.184)] or it occurs regularly with the verb λέγω 'to say' to introduce or continue a somewhat formal discourse [LN (33.28)].

QUESTION—What did Jesus mean when he said, 'Have faith in God'?

Jesus was now addressing the whole group of disciples since all of them had been surprised by the complete withering of the fig tree [Hb]. He answered the wonder in Peter's statement by explaining that God was the source of the amazing power that had been displayed when Jesus spoke to the fig tree. They could have the same kind of results as well if they also have faith in God [Hb. ICC]. This is not just faith in the general sense, but faith in God's miraculous help [NCNT]. Their faith must be in God since he is the source of power for performing miracles [EBC].

11:23 **Truly[a] I-say to-you(pl) that whoever says to-this mountain, 'Be-lifted-up[b] and be-thrown[c] into the sea' and does- not -doubt[d] in his heart but believes that what he-says will-happen, it-will-be[e] (done) for-him.**

TEXT—Manuscripts ending the verse with ἔσται αὐτῷ 'it will be for him' are followed by GNT, which does not mention any variant reading. A variant reading is ἔσται αὐτῷ ὃ ἐὰν εἴπῃ 'it will be for him whatever he may say' and it is followed by KJV.

LEXICON—a. ἀμήν (LN 72.6) (BAGD 2. p. 45): 'truly' [BAGD, BECNT, BNTC, LN, WBC; ESV, NASB, NRSV, REB], 'verily' [KJV], 'amen' [AB2, Lns], not explicit [CEV]. The phrase 'truly I say to you' is translated, 'indeed, it is true that' [LN], 'I tell you the truth' [NCV, NET, NIV, NLT], 'I assure you' [TEV], 'I can guarantee this truth' [GW], 'I solemnly declare to you' [NTC], 'in solemn truth I tell you' [AB1]. This particle makes a strong affirmation of what is declared [LN]. It is an assertive particle that begins a solemn declaration [BAGD]. The phrase 'truly I say to you' occurs at 3:28; 8:12; 9:1, 41; 10:15, 29; 11:23; 12:43; 13:30; 14:9, 18, 25, 30.

b. aorist pass. impera. of αἴρω (LN 15.203) (BAGD 1.a. p. 24): 'to be lifted up, to arise' [BAGD], 'to be carried away' [BAGD, LN], 'to be carried off, to be removed, to be taken away' [LN]. The command ἄρθητι 'be lifted up' [AB2, NTC; NET] is also translated 'may you be lifted up' [NLT], 'be lifted from your place' [REB], 'be it lifted from your place' [AB1], 'be taken up' [BECNT, BNTC, WBC; ESV, NASB, NRSV; similarly Lns], 'be uprooted' [GW], 'be thou removed' [KJV], 'go' [NCV, NIV], '(you can tell this mountain) to get up' [CEV]. '(whoever tells this hill) to get up' [TEV]. This verb means to lift up and carry (away) [LN]. The passive voice implies that God is the agent behind the actions [CBC, Hb, TRT]. Another view is that even though the two verbs 'be lifted up' and 'be thrown' are passive in form, they have the force of the middle voice: 'take and throw yourself into the sea' [TH].
c. aorist pass. impera. of βάλλω (LN 15.215) (BAGD 1.b. p. 131): 'to be thrown' [BAGD, LN]. The command 'be thrown into the sea' [AB1, Lns; ESV, GW, NET, NLT, NRSV] is also translated 'be cast into the sea' [AB2, BECNT, Lns, WBC; NASB; similarly KJV], 'be hurled into the sea' [BNTC; REB], 'throw yourself into the sea' [NIV], 'fall into the sea' [NCV], 'jump into the sea' [CEV], 'throw itself in the sea' [TEV]. This verb means to throw something [LN].
d. aorist pass. subj. of διακρίνομαι, διακρίνω (LN 31.37) (BAGD 2.b. p. 185): 'to doubt' [BAGD, LN], 'to waver' [BAGD], 'to be uncertain' [LN]. The phrase 'does not doubt in his heart' [AB2, BECNT, BNTC, NTC; ESV, NASB, NET, NIV, TEV] is also translated 'shall not doubt in his heart' [Lns; KJV], 'has no inner doubt' [AB1], 'has no inward doubts' [REB], 'who doesn't doubt' [GW], 'he should not waver in his heart' [WBC], 'but you must...have no doubt in your heart' [NLT], 'if you do not doubt in your heart' [NRSV], 'if you have no doubts in your mind' [NCV], 'don't doubt' [CEV]. This verb means to think that something may not be true or certain [LN].
e. fut. mid. (deponent = act.) indic. of εἰμί (LN 13.104): 'to be, to happen' [LN]. The phrase 'it will be done for him' [AB1, BECNT, WBC; ESV, GW, NET, NIV, REB, TEV] is also translated 'it will indeed be done for him' [NTC], 'it will be done' [BNTC], 'it will be his' [AB2], 'it will be granted him' [NASB], 'and it will happen' [NLT], 'and it will' [ESV], 'he shall have it' [Lns], 'he shall have (whatsoever he saith)' [KJV], 'it will be done for you' [NRSV], 'God will do it for you' [NCV]. In relation to an event, this verb means 'to occur' [LN].

QUESTION—What is meant by '*this* mountain' and did Jesus expect that someone would speak to it?

The adjective τούτῳ 'this' is significant. The words '*this* mountain' refers to the Mount of Olives [CGTC, EBC, ICC, Hb, Lns, NICNT, NIGTC, NTC, Sw, Tay]. Probably Jesus and his disciples were standing on the Mount of Olives at a place where they could see the Dead Sea in the distance [CGTC, EBC, Hb, Lns, NICNT, NIGTC, Sw, Tay]. Although this is a proverbial saying about doing difficult tasks without reference to any particular mountain, it is being applied to the temple mountain [AB2, BECNT, BNTC, NLTfn]. Jesus was speaking figuratively [CGTC, EBC, Hb, ICC, Lns, NTC, Tay, WBC] and used hyperbole [CGTC, NAC, NCBB, PNTC]. The sea in the saying could refer to any real or hypothetical sea [BECNT]. Neither Jesus nor his disciples ever removed actual mountains [Hb, ICC]. A mountain is used as a symbol for a great difficulty, so Jesus is saying that the greatest possible difficulty can be removed when a person has faith [EBC]. In response to faith, God will enable the disciples to do what seems to be impossible [CGTC, Hb, Lns, NIGTC, NTC]. The twelve disciples had already been doing things that would have been considered impossible when they had cast out demons and when Peter by faith had walked on the water [NTC]. The person who is praying can only have such assurance if he is sure that what he is asking is in harmony with the will of God and furthers God's purpose. This confidence is given by the Holy Spirit through the Word [Hb].

11:24 Because of-this^a I say to-you(pl), all things for which you pray and ask,^b believe that you-have-received^c (them), and it-will-be (so) for-you.

TEXT—Manuscripts reading ἐλάβετε 'you have received' are given an A rating by GNT to indicate it was regarded to be certain. A variant reading is λαμβάνετε 'you receive' and it is followed by KJV. Another variant reading is λήμψεσθε 'you will receive'.

LEXICON—a. The phrase διὰ τοῦτο 'because of this' is translated 'for this reason' [AB1, Lns, WBC; NET, TEV], 'therefore' [AB2, BECNT, BNTC, NTC; ESV, KJV, NASB, NIV], 'that's why' [GW], 'so' [NCV, NRSV], 'then' [REB], not explicit [CEV, NLT].
  b. pres. mid. indic. of αἰτέω (LN 33.163) (BAGD p. 26): 'to ask for, to demand' [BAGD, LN], 'to plead for' [LN]. The phrase 'all things for which you pray and ask' [NASB] is also translated 'all things whatsoever you pray and ask for' [BECNT], 'all that you pray and ask for' [WBC], 'everything you pray and ask for' [AB2], 'all things such as you go on praying for and asking for' [Lns], 'what things soever ye desire, when ye pray' [KJV], 'everything you ask for in prayer' [CEV], 'the things you ask for in prayer' [NCV], 'whatever you ask for in prayer' [AB1, BNTC. NTC; NIV, NRSV, REB], 'whatever you ask in prayer' [ESV], 'whatever you pray and ask for' [NET], 'whatever you pray for' [GW], 'when you pray and ask for something' [TEV], 'you can pray for anything' [NLT]. This verb means to ask for with urgency, even to the point of demanding [LN]. There really is no difference between 'pray' and 'ask for' in this verse, and it simply means 'ask for in prayer' [NTC].
  c. aorist act. indic. of λαμβάνω (LN 57.125): 'to receive' [LN]. The clause 'believe that you have already received them' [NASB] is also translated 'believe that you have received it' [AB1, AB2, BECNT, BNTC, WBC; ESV, NET, NIV, NRSV, REB, TEV], 'go on believing that you did receive them' [Lns], 'believe that you have received the things (you ask

for in prayer)' [NCV], 'believing that you received it' [NTC], 'have faith that you have already received whatsoever (you pray for)' [GW], 'if you believe that you've received it' [NLT], 'if only you have faith' [CEV]. This verb means to receive or accept an object or benefit for which the initiative rests with the giver [LN].

QUESTION—What is meant by the clause 'believe that you have received'?

The aorist tense 'you have received' has probably been used to represent the Semitic prophetic present tense and it expresses the certainty of a future action [BNTC, PNTC]. The future is so assured that it can be spoken of as already completed [PNTC]. Knowing that the petition is in God's will, faith accepts the answer as granted even though the actual bestowal is future [Hb]. Because this aorist is a rhetorical exaggeration of the immediateness of the answer, it antedates even the prayer in the mind of the petitioner [ICC]. This idiom expresses certainty and means 'you will definitely receive' [TRT].

11:25 **But/and whenever you-stand praying[a], forgive[b] if you-have something against someone, so-that your Father, who (is) in heaven, also may-forgive you your transgressions.[d]"**

LEXICON—a. pres. mid./pass. (deponent = act.) participle of προσεύχομαι (LN 33.178) (BAGD p. 714): 'to pray' [BAGD, LN; all translations], 'to speak to God' [LN]. This verb means to speak to or to make requests of God [LN].

b. pres. act. impera. of ἀφίημι (LN 40.8) (BAGD 2. p. 126): 'to forgive' [BAGD, LN; all translations except Lns], 'to pardon' [LN], 'to remit' [Lns]. The clause 'forgive if you have something against someone' is translated 'if you have a grievance against anyone, forgive him' [REB], 'if you are angry with someone, forgive him' [NCV], 'forgive anything you have against anyone' [GW], 'forgive whatever you have against anyone' [AB1], 'first forgive anyone you are holding a grudge against' [NLT]. Because a wrongdoing cannot be undone, 'to forgive' means that the guilt from that wrongdoing is pardoned and removed [LN]. The implied object of 'forgive' is the person against whom you have something [TH].

c. παράπτωμα (LN 88.297) (BAGD 2.b. p. 621): 'transgression' [AB1; NASB], 'sin' [BAGD, LN; CEV, NCV, NET, NIV, NLT], 'trespasses' [BECNT, Lns NTC], 'trespass' [ESV, KJV, NASB, NRSV], 'failure' [GW], 'wrongdoings' [BNTC], 'the wrongs you have done' [AB1; REB, TEV]. This noun denotes what a person has done in transgressing the will and law of God by some false step or failure [LN].

QUESTION—What is the function of the initial conjunction καί 'but, and'?

1. Καί means 'but' and adds an additional condition for the effective praying introduced in the preceding verse [BECNT, CBC, EBC, Hb, My, NAC, NICNT, NIGTC, NLTfn, PNTC, Sw]. The right to pray the prayer envisioned in verses 23 belongs only to brothers who are mutually reconciled and united [CBC, NICNT]. This verse extends the conditions

for effective prayer [NIGTC]. Faith and willingness to forgive are the two conditions of effectual prayer [EBC].

2. Καί means 'and' and it adds a comment about praying [CGTC, Gnd, ICC, NCBC, Tay]. The subject has changed from having faith in prayer in verse 24 to seeking God's forgiveness in prayer [ICC].

QUESTION—Why would someone stand up to pray?

Standing was the usual posture among Jewish people when praying [Hb, WBC]. The normal position for prayer was standing with one's face lifted up toward heaven [Sw], A person honored God by rising to stand in his presence [Lns]. A couple of translations leave out the Jewish custom of standing up in prayer: 'when you are praying' [NCV], 'whenever you pray' [GW].

QUESTION—What is meant by having something κατά 'against' a person?

That which is to be forgiven includes an actual sin or just something that our dislike causes us to hold against the person, no matter if that person is a believer or a nonbeliever [Hb]. It is translated 'you must forgive what others have done to you' [CEV], 'forgive anyone you are holding a grudge against' [NLT], and 'if you are angry with someone, forgive him' [NCV].

QUESTION—What transgressions are these that need to be forgiven?

This does not refer to the initial act of forgiveness that abolished the guilt of sin, but it is like the forgiveness of a father who restores fellowship with his child [WBC]. These are deviations from the path of truth and righteousness [NTC].

11:26 [[Omitted]]

TEXT—Manuscripts omitting this verse are given an A rating by GNT to indicate the omission was regarded to be certain. A variant reading is εἰ δὲ ὑμεῖς οὐκ ἀφίετε, οὐδὲ ὁ πατὴρ ὑμῶν ὁ ἐν τοῖς οὐρανοῖς ἀφήσει τὰ παραπτώματα ὑμῶν 'but if you do not forgive, neither will your Father in heaven forgive your transgressions' and it is followed by KJV. It is included in parentheses by AB1, and is bracketed by WBC and NASB. This is an insertion from Matthew 6:15 [EBC].

DISCOURSE UNIT—11:27–13:2 [NIGTC]. The topic is confrontation with the Jerusalem establishment.

DISCOURSE UNIT—11:27–12:44 [Hb, PNTC]. The topic is public teaching in Jerusalem [Hb], Jesus and the Sanhedrin [PNTC].

DISCOURSE UNIT—11:27–12:34 [Hb]. The topic is questions by the enemies.

DISCOURSE UNIT—11:27–12:12 [Hb]. The topic is the question of authority.

DISCOURSE UNIT—11:27–33 [CBC, Hb, NICNT; CEV, ESV, GW, NASB, NCV, NET, NIV, NLT, NRSV, TEV]. The topic is the authority of Jesus [NICNT; NET], the authority of Jesus challenged [ESV, NLT], the authority of

Jesus questioned [NIV, NRSV], the question about Jesus' authority [CEV, TEV], the question about the source of Jesus' authority [CBC], Jesus' authority questioned [NASB], Jesus' authority challenged [GW], leaders doubt Jesus' authority [NCV], questioners silenced [Hb].

11:27 And they-come again into Jerusalem. And (when) he was-walking-about in the temple, the chief-priests and the scribes and the elders[a] come to him. **11:28** And they-were saying to-him, "By what-kind-of[b] authority are-you-doing these (things)? Or who has-given you this authority[c] so-that you-may-do these (things)?"

LEXICON—a. πρεσβύτερος (LN 53.77) (BAGD 2.a.β. p. 700): 'elder' [BAGD, LN; all translations]. This noun denotes a person of responsibility and authority in matters of socio-religious concerns [LN]. It denotes an official who is a member of the particular group in the Sanhedrin called elders [BAGD]. This word occurs at 7:3, 5; 8:31; 11:27; 14:43, 53; 15:1.
- b. ποῖος (LN 58.30) (BAGD 2.a.γ. p. 684): 'what sort of, what kind of' [LN], 'which, what' [BAGD]. The phrase ἐν ποίᾳ ἐξουσίᾳ ταῦτα ποιεῖς; 'By what kind of authority are you doing these things' is translated 'By what authority are you doing these things?' [AB2, BECNT, BNTC, NTC; ESV, NASB, NET, NIV, NRSV; similarly AB2, WBC; KJV, NLT], 'By what authority are you acting like this?' [REB], 'What authority do you have to do these things?' [NCV], 'In connection with what authority art thou doing these things?' [Lns], 'What gives you the right to do these things?' [GW], 'What right do you have to do these things?' [CEV, TEV]. The interrogative pronoun 'what kind' is a reference to its class or kind [LN].
- c. ἐξουσία (LN 37.35) (BAGD 3. p. 278): 'authority to rule, right to control' [BAGD, LN]. The phrase ἢ τίς σοι ἔδωκεν τὴν ἐξουσίαν ἵνα ταῦτα ποιῇς; 'Or who has given you this authority so that you may do these things?' [AB2] is also translated 'and, "Who has given to you this authority, so that you may do these things?"' [WBC], 'Or who gave you this authority to do these-things/them?' [ESV, NASB, NET; similarly BECNT; KJV], 'who gave thee this authority so that thou dost these things?' [Lns], 'Who gave you authority to do them?' [AB1], 'And who gave you authority to do this?' [NIV], 'and who gave you the authority to do them?' [NTC; similarly NRSV], 'Who has-given/gave you authority to act in this way?' [BNTC; REB], 'Who gave you this authority?' [CEV, NCV], 'Who told you that you could do this?' [GW], 'Who gave you the right to do them?' [NLT], 'Who gave you such right?' [TEV]. This noun denotes the right to control or govern over others [LN].

QUESTION—Who came into the temple again?
Jesus and his disciples came into the temple again [Gnd, WBC]. They probably had spent the last two nights outside the city in the town of Bethany [Lns, NIGTC]. This was the third time they had come to the temple in Jerusalem. Jesus looked around in the temple on the first day (11:11), he

returned on the next day to drive out those who were buying and selling in the temple (11:15), and he returned to the temple on the third day only to be questioned by members of the Sanhedrin about his authority to drive out the people on the previous day [EGT].

QUESTION—Who were the men who came up to Jesus?

These men were representatives of the Sanhedrin [CGTC, Hb, Lns, NTC, Sw]. The fact that representatives from each of the three groups in the Jewish ruling council called the Sanhedrin were present and that emphasis was given to each of their groups with an article indicates the importance of this occasion [Hb]. Presumably only a few representatives of each of the three groups were present to question Jesus [CGTC, Hb, NICNT, NTC, TH, Tay].

QUESTION—Why did they ask Jesus 'by *what kind of* (ποίᾳ) authority' he was doing these things'?

This question was about the nature of Jesus' authority [Gnd, Hb, ICC, Sw]. They asked this questions in order to show that Jesus had no official priestly or scribal authority to do what he had done [EBC, ESVfn, Gnd, WBC]. They were questioning his legal rights to usurp their authority. The ruling priests in the temple had operational authority to authorize what went on there, and they were the ones who had authorized the activities of the buyers, sellers, and moneychangers. But they were subject to the broader legislative and judicial jurisdiction of the Sanhedrin, which in turn was subject to the ultimate authority of the high priest and his priestly associates [WBC]. Because he had not been authorized by the ruling priests to do that, was Jesus claiming prophetic, royal, or messianic authority? [Gnd]. They wanted to know if Jesus was acting on his own authority, perhaps as a prophet, when he cleansed the temple or if someone else had commissioned him to do so [NICNT].

QUESTION—Why did they add the second question, 'Who has given you this authority so that you may do these things'?

After asking about the nature of Jesus' authority, they now wanted the name of the person who had given him that authority [Hb, Tay]. Both questions are about Jesus' authority to do 'these things' and are essentially synonymous [BECNT]. The question 'who gave you this authority' merely restates the first question [ICC, Lns, NTC, WBC]. 'What authority' would be made plain when the author of this authority was named [Lns].

QUESTION—What were 'these things' Jesus was doing?

'These things' refer to the cleansing of the temple by throwing out the merchants [BECNT, BNTC, CGTC. EBC, Gnd, ICC, My, NICNT, NIGTC, Tay, WBC]. In the context of the temple precincts, 'these things' logically refer to what Jesus had done the preceding day in the Temple of the Gentile when he had interfered with the authority of these men [Sw WBC]. Their questions relate to the cleansing of the temple that had happened the day before, but also include the healing and teaching in the temple throughout his ministry [ESVfn, Lns]. 'These things' include Jesus' royal entry into Jerusalem, the cleansing of the temple, and the miracles he had performed in other towns [Lns, NTC]. A few think 'these things' refer to the whole career of Jesus [ESVfn, NCBC, NLTfn, Sw].

11:29 But Jesus said to-them, "I-will-ask you(pl) one question,[a] and you(pl)-answer[b] me and (then) I-will-tell you by what-kind-of authority I-do these (things).

LEXICON—a. λόγος (LN 33.98) (BAGD 1.a.β. p. 477): 'question' [AB1, BAGD, BECNT, BNTC, LN, NTC; all versions], 'thing' [AB2, NTC, WBC], 'statement, word, saying, message' LN]. This noun denotes that which has been stated or said, where the primary focus depends on the content of the communication [LN]. The exact translation of this noun depends on the context since it may take any one of many different forms [BAGD].

b. aorist pass. (deponent = act.) impera. of ἀποκρίνομαι (LN 33.184): 'to answer, to reply' [LN]. The clause καὶ ἀποκρίθητέ μοι καὶ 'and you answer me and' [AB2, BECNT] is also translated 'and do you answer me, and' [Lns], 'and you answer me, and then' [NASB], 'Answer me, and' [NTC; ESV, NET, NIV, NRSV; similarly KJV], 'Answer me, and then,' [GW], 'and if you give me an answer' [TEV], 'If you answer me' [BNTC, WBC; NCV], 'If you answer it' [CEV], 'and if you give me an answer' [AB1, REB], 'if you answer one question' [NLT]. This verb means to respond to a question that asks for information [LN]. The imperative voice demands an answer to his question since it would furnish the basis for his answer [Hb, NICNT]. The imperative verb followed by καί 'and' can be used in place of a conditional clause [AB2, CGTC, Gnd, NIGTC, Tay, TH, WBC].

11:30 The baptism of-John, was it from[a] heaven or from men? Answer[b] me."

LEXICON—a. ἐκ (LN 90.16) (BAGD 3.b. p. 235): 'from' [BAGD, LN]. The question 'The baptism of John, was it from heaven or from men?' [BECNT. Lns, NTC] is also translated 'The baptism of John, was it from heaven, or of men?' [KJV], 'John's baptism—was it from heaven or from men/people?' [NET, NIV], 'The baptism of John—was it from God, or from men?' [AB1; REB], 'The baptism of John—from heaven or from human beings?' [AB2], 'Was the baptism of John from heaven or from men?' [BNTC; ESV, NASB], 'Was the baptism of John from heaven or of human origin?' [WBC], 'Did the baptism of John come from heaven, or was it of human origin?' [NRSV], 'When John baptized people, was that authority from God or just from other people?' [NCV], 'Did John's authority to baptize come from heaven, or was it merely human?' [NLT], 'Did John's right to baptize come from heaven or from humans?' [GW], 'Who gave John the right to baptize? Was it God in heaven or merely some human being?' [CEV], 'Tell me, where did John's right to baptize come from: was it from God or from human beings?' [TEV]. This

preposition indicates the source of an activity or state and it implies that something proceeds from or out of that source [LN].
  b. aorist pass. (deponent = act.) impera. of ἀποκρίνομαι (LN 33.184): 'to answer, to reply' [LN]. The command ἀποκρίθητέ μοι 'Answer me' [AB1, AB2, BNTC, Lns, NTC, WBC; ESV, GW, KJV, NASB, NET, NLT, NRSV, REB] is also translated 'Tell me' [NCV, NIV, TEV], not explicit [CEV]. This verb means to respond to a question asking for information [LN]. The plain implication is that John's authority came from God [AB1]. This command is given in the confident manner of one who knows nobody can answer and will not even try [EGT].

QUESTION—What is meant by 'the baptism of John'?
John's ministry as a whole is symbolized by this reference to its distinctive feature of baptism [AB2, ESVfn, Hb, Lns, NAC, NCBC, NIGTC, Sw, Tay, TH]. Since this refers to the whole ministry of John the Baptist, it could be translated 'the baptism that John preached and administered.' If a language does not have the noun form for 'baptism,' the question could be worded 'Who sent John to baptize, God or men?' [TH].

QUESTION—What does the word οὐρανός 'heaven' refer to in this verse?
'Heaven is used as a synonym for 'God' [AB2, BAGD (3. p. 595), BECNT, CGTC, EBC, ESVfn, Hb, NAC, NCBC, NICNT, NIVfn, NTC, PNTC, Sw, Tay]. This was the characteristic Jewish substitution of the word 'heaven' for 'God' [Gnd]. In this verse οὐρανός 'heaven' is translated 'God in heaven' [CEV], 'God' [AB1; REB, TEV].

11:31 **And they-were discussing**[a] **with themselves saying, "If we-say, 'From heaven,' he-will-say, 'Then why did-you- not -believe him?'**

TEXT—Manuscripts reading διελογίζοντο 'they were discussing' are followed by GNT, which does not mention any variant reading. A variant reading is ἐλογίζοντο 'they were reasoning' and it is followed by KJV, NLT.

LEXICON—a. imperf. mid. or pass. (deponent = act.) indic. of διαλογίζομαι (LN 30.10, 33.158) (BAGD 2. p. 186): 'to discuss' [BAGD, LN (33.158)], 'to converse' [LN (33.158)], 'to argue' [BAGD], 'to think out carefully, to reason thoroughly, to consider carefully' [LN (30.10)]. The words διελογίζοντο πρὸς ἑαυτοὺς λέγοντες 'they were discussing with themselves saying' is translated 'they discussed it among themselves and said' [NIV], 'they discussed it with one another, saying' [ESV, NET], 'they talked it over among themselves' [NLT], 'they were reasoning with themselves, saying' [Lns; similarly KJV], 'they began reasoning among themselves, saying' [NASB; similarly NTC], 'they discussed this among themselves. They said' [GW; similarly BECNT, BNTC, WBC], 'they thought it over and said to each other' [CEV], 'they debated among themselves, saying' [AB2], 'They argued among themselves' [AB1], 'they argued with one another' [NRSV], 'they argued about Jesus' question, saying' [NCV], 'this set them arguing among themselves' [REB], 'they started to argue among themselves' [TEV]. This verb means to engage in some relatively detailed discussion of a matter [LN (33.158)] or to think or reason with thoroughness and completeness [LN (30.10)].

QUESTION—How were they διελογίζοντο πρὸς ἑαυτοὺς 'discussing *with* themselves'?

1. They discussed this among themselves [AB1, AB2, BECNT, BNTC, Lns, PNTC, TH, TRT, WBC; ESV, GW, NASB, NCV, NET, NIV, NLT, NRSV, REB, TEV]. They talked back and forth [TH]. It was a quiet discussion that went on among the authorities [Lns, WBC]. Since fear of the people determined their response, the context implies a private discussion of their predicament [WBC].
2. This refers to their unspoken thoughts as they considered the question [CGTC, EGT, Sw, Tay]. A discussion among themselves was scarcely possible in this setting. In the parallel account of Matthew 21:25, the wording διελογίζοντο ἐν ἑαυτοῖς 'they were discussing *in* themselves' confirms that they were not discussing it with each other as each individual came to the same conclusion [Sw].

QUESTION—Why didn't the authorities want to be asked the question, 'Then why did you not believe him?'?

1. The question was about believing that John's ministry and his baptism were ordained by God. If they said that they did believe that, then they should have already submitted themselves to John's baptism of repentance [BECNT, ESVfn, Hb. Lns, NAC, NTC, Tay, TRT, WBC]. But it was well known that the Sanhedrin had sent a committee to investigate John the Baptist because it had not believed his witness [Hb]. This discussion took place in the open temple court where a number of the pilgrims stood about listening to what was said. The authorities didn't want to face the consequences of having to explain why they had not believed John [Lns]. They didn't want to say that they did believe John since a follow-up question might have been, 'Why then do you not accept me as that one greater than John whom he foretold was coming?' [BECNT].
2. The question was about believing what John had said about Jesus. If they believed that John's ministry was authorized by God, they would have to accept what John had foretold about Jesus being the one who was greater than John. [AB2, BECNT, EBC, Gnd, NICNT, NLTfn, Tay]. If they acknowledged John's prophetic authority, they would be compelled to acknowledge that Jesus' authority came from God [NICNT]. That would make Jesus greater than even the Sanhedrin [Gnd].

11:32 But (if/shall-) we-say, 'From men'?"—they-were-afraid-of[a] the crowd. Because everyone held[b] that John really was a-prophet.[c]

TEXT—Manuscripts reading ὄχλον 'crowd' are followed by GNT, which does not mention any variant reading. A variant reading is λαόν 'people' and it is followed by KJV.

LEXICON—a. imperf. pass. indic. of φοβέομαι, φοβέω (LN 25.252) (BAGD 1.b.α. p. 863): 'to fear' [AB2, BAGD, BNTC, LN; KJV, NET, NIV], 'to

be afraid of' [AB1, BECNT, LN, Lns, NTC, WBC; CEV, ESV, GW, NASB, NCV, NRSV, REB, TEV]. The clause 'they were afraid of the crowd' is translated 'they were afraid of what the people would do' [NLT]. This verb means to be in a state of fearing [LN].
b. imperf. act. indic. of ἔχω [LN 31.1) (BAGD 1.5. p.333): 'to consider' [AB2, BAGD; NET], 'to believe' [NCV, NLT], 'to think' [CEV, GW], 'to hold a view, to have an opinion' [LN], 'to regard' [BECNT, LN, WBC], 'to consider' [AB2, LN; NASB], 'to hold' [AB1, BNTC, Lns, NTC; ESV, NIV, REB], 'to be convinced' [TEV], 'to regard' [NRSV], 'to count' [KJV]. This means to hold a view or to have an opinion with regard to something [LN]. Here 'to hold' has the sense of 'consider, look upon, view' [TH].
c. προφήτης (LN 53.79) (BAGD 2. p. 723):'prophet' [LN; all translations], 'inspired preacher' [LN]. This noun denotes one who proclaims inspired utterances on behalf of God. There is a tendency in a number of languages to translate this noun only in the sense of 'one who foretells the future', even though foretelling the future is only just one aspect of a prophet's function. In New Testament times the focus was upon the inspired utterance proclaimed on behalf of and on the authority of God. In a number of languages it is appropriate to translate it as 'one who speaks for God' [LN].

QUESTION—What kind of sentence is "But (if/shall) we say, 'From men'?"
1. It is a conditional clause with an implied 'if' [AB1, BECNT, BNTC, CGTC, EGT, Gnd, Lns, NICNT, NIGTC, Tay, TH, NTC, WBC; GW, NCV, NET, NIV, TEV]. One translation adds the implied main clause: "But if we say, 'From men,' then what will happen?' [GW]. The main clause of the condition is lacking since Mark immediately shifted to the reason for their unwillingness to give such an answer [NIGTC, TH, WBC].
2. It is a question, "But shall we say, 'From men'?"[AB2, CBC, Hb, ICC, My, Sw; ESV, KJV, NASB, NLT, NRSV, REB]. One translation reads, 'They were asking, "But do we dare say it was merely human?"' [NLT].
3. It is translated as a statement: 'We can't say that it was merely some human who gave John the right to baptize' [CEV].

QUESTION—What relationship is indicated by the conjunction γάρ 'because'?
This indicates the reason for their fear [Hb, NTC]. If they had denied that John was a prophet, the listening crowd would have regarded it to be blasphemy [NTC].

11:33 And answering Jesus they-say, "We-do- not -know." And Jesus says to-them, "Neither do-I-tell you by what authority[a] I-am-doing these (things)."

LEXICON—a. ἐξουσία (LN 37.35) (BAGD 3. p. 278); 'authority' [BAGD; all translations except CEV, GW, TEV], 'authority to rule, right to control' [LN], 'right' [TEV]. The phrase 'by what authority I am doing these things' is translated 'who gave me the right to do what I do' [CEV], 'why I have the right to do these things' [GW]. This noun denotes the right to control or govern over others [LN].

QUESTION—Why did they say 'We do not know'?

Their confession of ignorance was an attempt to evade the issue and implied that they had suspended their judgment [NICNT]. Their statement was tantamount to a refusal to answer Jesus' question [EBC]. This automatically disqualified them from judging Jesus' authority [Hb, NAC]QUESTION—Why did Jesus say that he would not tell them by what authority he was doing those things?

DISCOURSE UNIT—12:1–12 [CBC, Hb, NICNT; CEV, GW, ESV, NASB, NET, NIV, NLT, NRSV, TEV]. The topic is a story about a vineyard [GW], the parable of the tenants [ESV, NET, NIV], the parable of the tenants in the vineyard [TEV], the parable of the defiant tenants [NICNT], the parable of the wicked tenants [NRSV], the parable of the evil tenants [CBC], the parable of the vine-growers [NASB], the parable of the evil farmers [NLT], renters of a vineyard [CEV], a story about God's Son [NCV], questioners exposed [Hb].

12:1 **And he-began to-speak to-them in parables,**[a] **"A-man planted a-vineyard**[b] **and he-put-around (it) a-wall**[c] **and he-dug a-vat**[d] **and built a-tower**[e] **and he-leased**[f] **it to-farmers**[g] **and he-went-on-a-journey.**[h]

LEXICON—a. παραβολή (LN 33.15) (BAGD 2. p. 612): 'parable' [AB1, AB2, BAGD, BECNT, BNTC, LN, Lns, NTC, WBC; ESV, KJV, NASB, NET, NIV, NRSV, REB, TEV], 'illustration' [BAGD; GW], 'story' [CEV; NCV, NLT], 'figure, allegory, figure of speech' [LN]. This noun denotes a relatively short narrative with symbolic meaning [LN]. This word occurs at 3:23; 4:2, 10, 11, 13, 30, 33, 34; 7:17; 12:1, 12; 13:28.

b. ἀμπελών (LN 3.28) (BAGD p. 47): 'vineyard' [BAGD, LN; all translations], 'orchard of grapevines' [LN]. This noun refers to a number of grapevines growing in a garden or field. It could be described as 'a farm with grapevines' or 'a garden for grapes' [LN]. 'A man planted many plants which bore fruit' could be used in countries where grapes are unknown [TH].

c. φραγμός (LN 7.59) (BAGD 1. p. 865): 'wall' [AB1, BAGD, BNTC, LN; CEV, GW, NASB, NCV, NET, NIV, NLT, REB], 'fence' [AB2, BAGD, BECNT, **LN**, Lns, NTC, WBC; ESV, NRSV, TEV], 'hedge' [KJV]. This noun denotes a structure for enclosing an open area. Since the focus of this parable is on the function and not the form of the wall, a descriptive expression such as 'a barrier to surround a field' or 'a barrier to keep animals out of the field' might have to be used [LN]. It was probably a wall of unmortared stones [EBC, Hb, TH]. The wall marked the boundaries of the vineyard and it also protected the vineyard from marauders and wild animals [Hb].

d. ὑπολήνιον (LN **7.67**) (BAGD p. 845): 'trough' [BAGD], 'wine trough' [LN]; 'vat' [BAGD]. The clause 'and he dug a trough' is translated 'and he dug a wine trough' or 'and he dug a place where the juice of the grapes could be collected' [**LN**], 'and dug a trough for the winepress' [NTC], 'and dug a pit for a/its/the winepress' [BECNT; NET, NRSV], 'and dug a winepress-vat' [Lns], 'and made a vat for the winepress' [GW], 'and dug a vat under the winepress' [NASB], 'and dug/made a hole for a/the winepress' [AB1; NCV, TEV], 'and dug out a wine vat' [AB2], 'and hewed/dug out a winepress' [BNTC, WBC; REB], 'and digged a place for the winefat' [KJV], 'and dug a pit for the winepress' [ESV, NIV,], 'and dug a pit to crush the grapes in' [CEV], 'and dug a pit for pressing out the grape juice' [NLT]. This noun denotes a trough that is placed beneath a wine press in order to receive the grape juice as it is pressed out of the grapes [BAGD, LN].

e. πύργος (LN 7.23) (BAGD 1. p. 730): 'tower' [AB2, BAGD, BECNT, BNTC, LN, NTC; ESV, KJV, NASB, NCV], 'watchtower' [AB1, LN, Lns; GW, NET, NIV, NRSV, REB, TEV], 'lookout tower' [CEV, NLT]. This noun denotes a tall structure with a lookout station at the top. In the NT this term may designate any type of tower, whether employed for military purposes or used by watchmen protecting a harvest [LN]. This tower was made to protect the vineyard, but it also served as a shelter for the farmer [EBC]. It was usually an elevated platform made of stone [TH, TRT], where a watchman could keep watch over the vineyard [TRT].

f. aorist mid. indic. of ἐκδίδομαι, ἐκδίδωμι (LN 57.177) (BAGD p. 238): 'to lease' [BAGD, BECNT, LN, Lns, NTC, WBC; ESV, GW, NCV, NET, NLT, NRSV], 'to let out' [AB2, BAGD, BNTC, LN; KJV, REB], 'to rent' [NIV, TEV], 'to rent out' [AB1, LN; CEV, NASB]. This verb means to permit the use of property or assets in exchange for remuneration. In some languages it may be necessary to specify quite clearly the implications of 'renting out land', for example, 'he let farmers grow crops on his land in exchange for a part of the harvest' [LN].

g. γεωργός (LN 43.2) (BAGD 2. p. 157): 'farmer' [BAGD, LN; CEV, NCV, NIV], 'tenant' [BECNT, BNTC; ESV, NRSV, TEV], 'tenant farmer' [AB2, BAGD, WBC; NET, NLT], 'sharecropper' [NTC], 'vinedresser' [BAGD], 'vine-grower' [Lns; NASB, REB], 'winegrower' [AB1, 'vineyard worker' [GW], 'husbandman' [KJV]. This noun is a derivative of the verb γεωργέω 'to cultivate land' and denotes one who engages in agriculture or gardening [LN].

h. aorist act. indic. of ἀποδημέω (LN 15.47) (BAGD 1. p. 90): 'to go on a journey' [BAGD], 'to leave home on a journey, to be away from home on a journey' [LN]. The clause 'and he went on a journey' [AB1; NASB, NET] is also translated 'and went away on a journey' [NIV], 'and went on a trip' [GW], 'and left home on a trip' [TEV], 'and left for a trip' [NCV], 'and he departed' [BECNT, WBC], 'and went into/to another country' [ESV, NRSV], 'and moved to another country' [NLT], 'and went into a far country' [KJV], 'and went abroad' [AB2, BNTC, Lns, NTC; REB], 'and he left the country' [CEV]. This verb means to journey away from one's home or home country for a considerable period of time [LN]. The main point is that the owner was out of close touch with the men who were working his land. He was too far away to exercise close supervision and there was no easy way to communicate with them [TH].

12:2 And at-the time[a] he-sent a-slave[b] to the farmers in-order-that he-might-receive from the farmers a-part-of the harvest[c] of-the vineyard.

LEXICON—a. καιρός (LN 67.1) BAGD 2, p. 395): 'time, occasion' [LN], 'the right, proper, favorable time' [BAGD]. The phrase τῷ καιρῷ 'at the time' is translated 'at the right time' [GW], 'at the proper time' [AB2, NTC], 'in due course' [BECNT, WBC], 'at the season' [KJV; similarly Lns], 'at the proper season' [BNTC], 'at harvest time' [NET, NIV; similarly NASB], 'at the time of the grape harvest' [NLT], 'when it was harvest time' [CEV], 'when the season came' [AB1; ESV, NRSV, REB], 'when it was time for the grapes to be picked' [NCV], 'when the time came to gather the grapes' [TEV]. This noun denotes a point of time when an occasion for a particular event was to take place [LN]. The right time in this case would be the harvest time in the fifth year after planting the vineyard [TH].

b. δοῦλος (LN 87.76) (BAGD 1.a. p. 205): 'slave' [AB1, LN, Lns; NASB, NET, NRSV, TEV], 'servant' [AB2, BECNT, BNTC, NTC, WBC; CEV, ESV, GW, KJV, NCV, NASB, NLT, REB], 'bondservant' [LN]. This noun denotes one who is a slave in the sense of having become the property of a slave owner [LN].

c. καρπός (LN 43.15) (BAGD 1.a. p. 404): 'harvest, crop' [LN], 'fruit, produce' [BAGD]. The phrase ἀπὸ τῶν καρπῶν τοῦ ἀμπελῶνος 'a part of the harvest of the vineyard' is translated 'a portion/part of the fruit of the vineyard' [WBC; KJV], 'some of the fruits of the vineyard' [AB2, BECNT, Lns], 'a share of the grapes from the vineyard' [GW], 'his share of the vineyard's fruit' [NTC], 'his share of the produce of the vineyard' [NRSV], 'some of the fruit/product of the vineyard' [ESV, NASB, NIV], 'his portion of the crop' [NET], 'his share of the produce/grapes/crop/harvest' [AB1; CEV, NCV, NLT, REB, TEV]. This noun denotes that which is harvested [LN]. It refers to the percentage of the grape harvest that the tenants had agreed to pay the owner of the vineyard [BECNT, EBC]. An example of the contract the owner might have made is 'I will let you manage this vineyard and harvest its crop for yourselves provided that at the time of the vintage you give me the predetermined portion of the grapes' [NTC]. The rent would be paid in kind with grapes [AB2, BECNT, EBC, Hb, LN, NIGTC, NLTfn; ESV,GW, NET, NIV]. The payment might be in the form of grapes, raisins, or wine [Hb].

QUESTION—What kind of a δοῦλος 'slave' did the owner send to collect his share of the harvest?
This rich owner's slave would have been a person of consequence [NIGTC], and many translations call him a servant instead of a slave [AB2, BECNT, BNTC, NTC, WBC; CEV, ESV, GW, KJV, NCV, NASB, NLT, REB].

12:3 And having-grabbed[a] him they-beat[b] (him) and sent- (him) -away empty-handed.[c]

LEXICON—a. aorist act. participle of λαμβάνω (BAGD, LN 18.1) (BAGD 1.c. p. 464): 'to grab' [LN; NCV, NLT, TEV], 'to seize' [BNTC, NTC; NET, NIV, NRSV, REB], 'to take' [AB1, AB2, BECNT, Lns, WBC; ESV, GW, NASB], 'to take hold of' [BAGD, LN], 'to grasp' [LN], 'to catch' [KJV]. This verb means to take hold of something or someone, with or without force [LN].

b. aorist act. indic. of δέρω (LN 19.2) (BAGD 1. p. 175): 'to beat' [AB1, AB2, BAGD, BECNT, BNTC, LN, NTC, WBC; all versions except CEV, NLT, REB], 'to beat up' [CEV, NLT], 'to strike' [LN], 'to thrash' [REB], 'they hided (him)' [Lns]. This verb means to strike or beat repeatedly [LN].

c. κενός (LN **57.42**) (BAGD 1. p. 427): 'empty-handed' [BAGD, BECNT, BNTC, **LN**, Lns, WBC; NASB, NCV, NET, NIV, NLT, NRSV], 'empty' [AB2, LN, Lns; KJV], 'without anything/a thing' [LN; CEV, TEV], 'with nothing' [AB1; GW]. This adjective pertains to being without anything [LN].

12:4 And again he-sent to them another slave, and-that-one they-struck-on-the-head[a] and mistreated.[b] **12:5** And he-sent another, (and) that-one they-killed. And many others,[c] beating some, killing others.

TEXT—Manuscripts reading κἀκεῖνον ἐκεφαλίωσαν καὶ ἠτίμασαν 'that one they struck on the head and mistreated' are followed by GNT, which does not mention any variant reading. A variant reading is κἀκεῖνον λιθοβολήσαντες ἐκεφαλαίωσαν καὶ ἀπεστειλαν ἠτιμωμένον μτμωμενον 'and at him they cast stones and wounded him in the head, and sent him away shamefully handled' and it is followed by KJV.

LEXICON—a. aorist act. indic. of κεφαλιόω (LN 19.13) (BAGD p. 430): 'to strike on the head' [BAGD, BNTC, NTC, WBC; ESV, NET, NIV], 'to hit on the head' [GW, NCV], 'to beat on/over/about the head' [AB1, BECNT, LN; CEV, NLT, NRSV, REB, TEV], 'to wound in the head' [AB2, LN; NASB]. This verb means to beat someone on the head and implies that there are repeated blows [LN].

b. aorist act. indic. of ἀτιμάζω (LN **88.127**) (BAGD p. 120): 'to mistreat' [LN], 'to treat shamefully' [AB1, BAGD, BECNT, BNTC, **LN**; ESV, GW, NASB, NIV, TEV], 'to handle shamefully' [Lns], 'to treat outrageously' [NET, REB], 'to insult' [NLT, NRSV], 'to insult terribly' [CEV], 'to show no respect' [NCV], 'to dishonor' [AB2], 'to treat dishonorably' [WBC]. This verb means to treat someone in a shameful

and dishonorable manner [LN]. Since it refers to insult and disrespect, some have translated it 'they treated him as they should not have done' or 'they were very mean to him' [TH].
c. ἄλλος (LN 58.37): 'other' [LN]. The condensed clause καὶ πολλοὺς ἄλλους, 'And many others,' [AB2, BNTC, Lns, WBC; KJV] is translated with the focus on the owner sending others: 'he/the-man sent many others' [BECNT NTC; NCV, NIV], 'Then he sent many other servants' [GW], 'He kept sending servant after servant' [CEV], 'and many more as well, (of whom they beat some, and killed others)' [AB1], 'he sent many others (and they thrashed some and killed the rest)' [REB]. Others focus on how the people he sent were treated: 'And so it was with many others' [NRSV], 'And so with many others' [ESV, NASB], 'This happened to many others' [NET], 'and they treated many others the same way' [TEV], 'Others he sent were (either beaten or killed)' [NLT]. This pronominal adjective denotes that which is different than the item implied or identified in the context [LN].

12:6 **He- still^a -had one beloved^b son. Finally he-sent him to them, saying, "They-will-respect^c my son."**

TEXT—Manuscripts reading ἀγαπητόν 'beloved' are followed by GNT, which does not mention any variant reading. A variant reading is ἀγαπητόν αυτου 'his beloved' and it is followed by KJV.

LEXICON—a. ἔτι (LN 59.75, 67.128) (BAGD) 'still' [AB2; LN (67.128), BECNT, NTC], 'yet' [LN (67.128), Lns, WBC; KJV], 'in addition, besides' [LN (59.75)], not explicit [CEV]. The phrase 'he still had one' is translated 'he still had one other' [ESV; similarly NRSV], 'he had one left' [NET], 'he had one left to send' [NIV], 'he had one more person to send' [GW; similarly NASB], 'the man had one person left to send' [NCV], 'until there was only one left' [NLT], 'he had now only one to send' [AB1], 'he had now no one left to send except' [REB], 'the only one left to send was' [TEV]. This adverb indicates an extension of time up to and beyond an expected point [LN (67.128)] or it indicates the state of something being in addition to what already exists [LN (59.75)]. This means that he had yet one more he could send to the tenant farmers [WBC]. Sending his son underscores the serious view the owner of the vineyard took of the situation [EBC].

b. ἀγαπητός (LN 25.45) (BAGD 1. p. 6): 'beloved' [BAGD, LN WBC; ESV, NASB, NRSV, REB], 'his well beloved' [KJV], 'dear' [NET, TEV], 'whom he loved' [GW, NCV, NIV], 'whom he loved dearly' [NLT], 'he loved very much [CEV]. This adjective describes one who is loved [LN].

c. fut. pass. indic. of ἐντρέπομαι, ἐντρέπω (LN 87.11) (BAGD 2.b. p. 269): 'to respect' [BAGD, LN, WBC; all versions except KJV], 'to reverence' [KJV], 'to have regard for' [BAGD]. This verb means to show respect to a person on the basis of his high status [LN].

12:7 But those farmers said among[a] themselves, "This is the heir.[b] Come-on, let-us-kill him, and the inheritance[c] will-be ours."

LEXICON—a. πρός (LN 90.58) (BAGD III.1.e. p. 710): 'among' [BAGD], 'with' [LN], 'to' [BAGD, LN]. The phrase πρὸς ἑαυτοὺς 'among themselves' [AB2; KJV] is also translated 'to one another' [AB1, BECNT, BNTC; ESV, NASB, NET, NIV, NLT, NRSV, REB, TEV], 'to each other' [Lns, NTC; NCV], 'to themselves' [WBC; CEV], This preposition refers to an experience of an event [LN]. It was a mutual consultation among themselves [Hb].

b. κληρονόμος (LN **57.139**) (BAGD 1. p. 435): 'heir' [BAGD, LN]. The clause 'This is the heir' [AB1, AB2, BNTC, Lns, WBC; ESV, KJV, NASB, NET, NIV, NRSV, REB] is also translated 'he is the heir' [NTC], 'this is the heir to the property' [**LN**], 'Here comes the heir to this estate' [NLT], 'This is the owner's son' [TEV], 'Someday he will own the vineyard' [CEV], 'the son will inherit the vineyard' [NCV]. This noun denotes the person who inherits possessions [LN].

c. κληρονομία (LN 57.140) (BAGD 1. p. 435): 'inheritance' [BAGD, LN]. The clause 'the inheritance will/shall be ours' [BECNT, BNTC, NTC, WBC; ESV, KJV, NASB, NET, NIV, NRSV, REB] is also translated 'ours shall be the inheritance' [Lns], 'the inheritance will be our own' [AB2], 'it will be ours' [NCV], 'his/the property will be ours' [AB1; TEV], 'and get the estate for ourselves' [NLT], 'that way we can have it all for ourselves' [CEV]. This noun denotes that which is received from a deceased person [LN]. They thought that they would possess what the son would have gotten [TH].

QUESTION—What did they mean by the exhortation δεῦτε 'Come on'?

They were exhorting each other for group action with the idea being 'Let's get together' or 'Let's unite' [TH].

QUESTION—Why did these farmers think that they could inherit the property by killing the son of the landowner?

This may indicate that the farmers thought that the coming of the son meant that the owner had already died and the property would be ownerless if they killed the son. Since they were already working the property, the farmers thought they would be the first in line to reclaim it [EBC, Gnd, Hb, NICNT, TRT]. The tenants were acting irrationally [AB2, NCBC]. They foolishly forgot that the owner was still alive and would surely take vengeance [NTC]. This is about instinctive piracy rather than reasoned policy and should not be read in terms of formal legal claims [NIGTC]. The uncommon quality in an allegory is what makes it interesting [BECNT].

12:8 And having-seized[a] (him) they-killed him and threw[b] him out of the vineyard.

LEXICON—a. aorist act. participle of λαμβάνω (LN 18.1) (BAGD 1.c. p. 464): 'to seize' [AB1, AB2, BNTC; NET, NRSV, REB], 'to grab' [LN; CEV,

NLT, TEV], 'to take' [BAGD, BECNT, Lns, NTC, WBC; ESV, GW, KJV, NASB, NCV, NIV], 'to take hold of, to grasp' [LN]. This verb means to take hold of something or someone, with or without force [LN].
   b. aorist act. indic. of ἐκβάλλω (LN 15.220): 'to throw' [AB2, BNTC, LN; ESV, GW, NASB, NCV, NIV, NRSV], 'to cast' [BECNT, NTC, WBC; KJV]. The phrase 'threw him out' is translated 'threw his body out' [CEV, NET, NLT, TEV], 'flung his body out' [AB1; REB]. This verb means to throw something out of an area [LN].
QUESTION—What was their purpose in throwing his body out of the vineyard? Throwing his body out of the vineyard instead of burying it was a final indignity [BECNT, Hb, TH, WBC]. Instead of burying him, they left his body to rot [BNTC].

12:9 **What then will- the owner of the vineyard -do? He-will-come and destroy[a] the farmers and will-give the vineyard to-others.**
TEXT—a. fut. act. indic. of ἀπόλλυμι (LN 20.31) (BAGD 1.a.α. p. 95): 'to destroy' [AB2, BAGD, BECNT, LN, Lns, WBC; ESV, GW, KJV, NASB, NRSV], 'to put to death' [BAGD, BNTC; REB], 'to kill' [AB1, NTC; CEV, NCV, NET, NIV, NLT, TEV]. This verb means to destroy or to cause the destruction of persons, objects, or institutions [LN].
QUESTION—In what way will the owner give the vineyard to others?
   The owner will either rent the vineyard out to others or arrange to have other tenants take care of the vineyard [TH].

12:10 **And (have you) not read this Scripture,[a] '(The) stone[b] which the-ones building rejected,[c] this (one) has come-to-be the head[d] of-(the) corner.**
LEXICON—a. γραφή (LN 33.53) (BAGD 2.a. p. 166): 'Scripture' [LN, Lns, NTC, WBC; ESV, NASB, NCV], 'Scriptures' [CEV, NLT], 'scripture' [AB1, AB2, BECNT, BNTC; KJV, NET, NIV, NRSV, TEV], 'Scripture passage' [BAGD, LN; GW], 'text' [REB]. This noun denotes a particular passage of the OT [LN]. The singular form γραφὴν 'Scripture' refers to a particular passage in the OT and the quotation in verses 10–11 is exactly as it appears in the Septuagint Greek translation of Psalm 118: 22–23 [TH]. The Septuagint was the Bible of the Greek-speaking readers [BECNT].
   b. λίθος (LN 2.24) (BAGD 2. p. 474): 'stone' [BAGD, LN; all translations]. This noun denotes a piece of rock, whether it is shaped or natural [LN].
   c. aorist act. indic. of ἀποδοκιμάζω (LN 30.117) (BAGD 1. p. 90): 'to reject' [LN; all translations except CEV], 'to toss aside' [CEV], 'to regard as not worthy' [LN], 'to declare useless' [BAGD]. This verb means to judge something as not being worthy or genuine, and therefore something to be rejected [LN]. The verb indicates that the stone was regarded to be worthless or useless [TH].
   d. κεφαλή (LN 7.44) (BAGD 2.b. p. 430): 'cornerstone' [BAGD, LN], 'important stone' [LN]. The clause 'has come to be the head of the corner' is translated 'is/has-become the head of the corner' [AB2, BECNT, WBC;

KJV], 'became the corner head' [Lns], 'has-become/became the cornerstone' [NTC; ESV, GW, NCV, NET, NRSV], 'has-become/became the chief cornerstone' [BNTC; NASB], 'has now become the cornerstone' [NLT], 'has become the main corner-stone' [AB1; REB], 'has become the capstone' [NIV], 'is now the most important stone of all' [CEV]. The phrase κεφαλὴ γωνίας 'head of the corner' refers to either the cornerstone or capstone of a building that is essential to its construction [LN]. The noun 'head' is used figuratively to refer to the uppermost part, the end or point of something. It may be referring to the 'cornerstone' forming the farthest extension of the corner the building, or perhaps the 'keystone' or 'capstone' above the door [BAGD].

QUESTION—Was Jesus in doubt about whether or not they had read this Scripture passage?

This is a rhetorical question since Jesus knew that any ruling priest would have read Psalm 118 [WBC]. The form of his question implies that they had undoubtedly read this particular Scripture passage: 'Have you not even read this scripture?' [TH], 'You surely know that the Scriptures say…' [CEV]. It would be quite familiar to his audience [Hb].

QUESTION—What is the κεφαλὴν γωνίας 'the head of the corner'?

It is not clear whether the 'head of the corner' refers to a large cornerstone in the foundation of a building or the keystone of an arch [BNTC, NAC, Tay, TH, TRT].

1. This refers to the cornerstone of the building [AB1, CBC, NTC, PNTC, Sw; ESV, GW, NCV, NET, NLT, NRSV, REB]. It is a stone that binds two walls together [Hb, ICC], but it is uncertain whether it is placed at the bottom or the top of the corner [Hb]. The cornerstone governs every angle in the foundation and in the building itself [Lns].
2. This refers to a capstone [BECNT, NICNT; NIV, WBC]. This would be a capstone at the top of the building or a column that marks the completion of the building [BECNT]. This could be a capstone that completes an arch or the distinct top part of a pillar [WBC].
3. This is left open to either interpretation: 'the most important stone of all' [CEV].

12:11 This has-come from[a] the Lord, and it-is marvelous[b] in our eyes'?"

LEXICON—a. παρά (LN 90.14) (BAGD I.2. p. 609): 'from, by, of' [LN]. The clause 'this has come from the Lord' [AB2] is also translated 'from the Lord this came' [Lns], 'this came about from the Lord' [WBC; NASB], 'this is from the Lord' [NET], 'by the Lord this was done' [NTC], 'this is/was the Lord's doing' [AB1; KJV, NLT, NRSV], 'this is something the Lord has done' [CEV], 'this was done by the Lord' [TEV], 'the Lord has-done/did this' [GW, NCV, NIV], 'this was/is the Lord's doing' [BECNT; ESV, REB]. This preposition indicates the agentive source of an activity [LN]. It denotes the one who originates or directs something [BAGD].

b. θαυμαστός (LN 25.215) (BAGD 2. p. 352): 'marvelous' BAGD, LN], 'wonderful, remarkable' [BAGD, LN]. The clause 'it is marvelous in our eyes' [BNTC, Lns, WBC; ESV, KJV, NASB, NET, NIV] is also translated 'it is amazing in our eyes' [AB2; NRSV], 'it is amazing for us to see' [GW], 'it is wonderful in our eyes' [AB1, NTC; REB], 'it is wonderful to see' [NLT], 'what a wonderful sight it is' [TEV], 'it is wonderful to us' [NCV], 'it is amazing to us' [CEV]. This adjective refers to something that causes amazement and wonder [LN].

QUESTION—What was it that has come from the Lord?

1. The conditions needed for the rejected stone to become the head of the corner were brought about by the Lord God [AB1, BECNT, CGTC, Hb, Lns, Sw, Tay, TH, TRT, WBC; probably all versions]. The Lord did not make the builders reject the stone, but he did make the stone become the most important stone [TRT].
2. The corner stone came from the Lord God [ICC].

12:12 And they-were-wanting[a] to-arrest[b] him, and-yet[c] feared[d] the crowd, for they-knew that he-had-told the parable[e] against/about[f] them. And (so) leaving him they-went-away.

LEXICON—a. imperf. act. indic. of ζητέω (LN 68.60) (BAGD 2.b.γ. p. 339): 'to want' [AB2; GW, NCV, NET, NLT, NRSV, NRSV, REB], 'to seek' [BECNT, LN, Lns, WBC; ESV, KJV, NASB], 'to look for a way' [NIV], 'to try' [AB1, BNTC, LN, NTC; TEV], 'to desire, to wish' [BAGD]. This verb means to seek to do something, but without success [LN]. The imperfect tense ἐζήτουν 'they were wanting' to arrest Jesus indicates that they had been actively looking for a way to have Jesus arrested when he exposed their plot with the parable about the wicked farmers [Hb].

b. aorist act. infin. of κρατέω (LN 37.110) (BAGD 1.a. p. 448): 'to arrest' [AB1, AB2, BAGD, BECNT, BNTC, LN, Lns, NTC, WBC; all versions except KJV, NASB], 'to take into custody' [BAGD]: 'to seize' [LN; NASB], 'to lay hold of' [KJV]. The clause ἐζήτουν αὐτὸν κρατῆσαι 'were seeking to seize him' is translated 'they wanted to arrest him' [CEV]. This means that the authorities wanted to have soldiers carry out the arrest [TH].

c. καί (LN 89.92) (BAGD I.2.g. p. 392): 'and yet' [AB2, BAGD; NASB], 'but' [AB1, BECNT, BNTC, NTC, WBC; all versions except NASB], 'nevertheless, and in spite of that' [BAGD], 'and' [LN, Lns]. This preposition indicates a coordinate relationship [LN]. It emphasizes a surprising or unexpected fact [BAGD].

d. aorist pass. indic. of φοβέομαι, φοβέω (LN 25.252) (BAGD 1.b.α. p. 863): 'to fear' [AB2, BECNT, BNTC, LN, Lns, WBC; ESV, KJV, NASB, NET, NIV, NRSV], 'to be afraid' [AB1, BAGD, LN, NTC; CEV, GW, NCV, NIV, REB, TEV]. This verb means to be in a state of fear [LN].

e. παραβολή (LN 33.15) (BAGD 2. p. 612): 'parable' [AB1, AB2, BAGD, BECNT, BNTC, LN, Lns, NTC, WBC; all versions except CEV, GW, NCV], 'illustration' [BAGD; GW], 'figure, allegory' [LN], 'story' [NCV], not explicit [CEV]. This noun denotes a relatively short narrative that has symbolic meaning [LN]. This word occurs at 3:23; 4:2, 10, 11, 13, 30, 33, 34; 7:17; 12:1, 12; 13:28.

f. πρός (LN **90.25**, **90.33**) (BAGD III.5.a. p. 710): 'against' [AB1, AB2, BECNT, BNTC, **LN** (90.33), Lns, NTC; ESV, KJV, NASB, NET, NIV, NLT, NRSV, TEV], '(directed) at' [GW], '(aimed) at' [REB], 'to' [WBC], 'about' [**LN** (90.25); CEV, NCV], 'with reference to' [BAGD]. This preposition indicates opposition [LN (90.33)] or content [LN (90.25)].

QUESTION—Who were the people who wanted to arrest Jesus?

This refers to the chief priests, scribes, and elders of the Sanhedrin who had lost their argument with Jesus when they challenged his authority to cleanse the temple in 11:27–33 [BECNT, Lns, TH]. They wanted to have Jesus arrested, but they feared it would ignite a rebellion if they arrested him at this time when he was so popular with the crowds that filled the temple [WBC].

QUESTION—Who knew that Jesus had told the parable against the Sanhedrin?

1. The authorities wanted to arrest Jesus because *the authorities knew* that Jesus had told the parable against them. [AB1, Hb, BECNT, BNTC, CBC, CGTC, ICC, Lns, NIGTC, NTC, PNTC, Sw, TH. TRT; CEV, NCV, NIV, NLT, NRSV, REB, TEV]. Many reverse the order of the second and third clauses: 'And they were wanting to arrest him *because they knew that he had told the parable against them. Yet they were afraid of the crowd* and leaving him they went away' [AB1, BNTC, NTC; CEV, NCV, NIV, NLT, NRSV, REB, TEV]. One commentary fills out the compressed sentence this way: 'They were trying to arrest him (but could not yet because) they were afraid of the crowd since they knew (and were aware that the crowd also knew) that he had spoken this parable against them (so that the crowd was now more likely to take his side against them)' [NIGTC].

2. The authorities were afraid of the crowd because *the crowd knew* that Jesus had told the parable against the authorities [Gnd, My]. Although the authorities wanted to arrest Jesus, they were afraid that the crowd would take his arrest to be the fulfillment of the parable and would probably come to his support [My].

DISCOURSE UNIT—12:13–40 [NASB]. The topic is Jesus answers the Pharisees, Sadducees, and scribes.

DISCOURSE UNIT—12:13–17 [CBC, Hb, NICNT; CEV, ESV, GW, NCV, NET, NIV, NLT, NRSV, TEV]. The topic is a question about taxes [GW], the question about paying taxes [NRSV, TEV], the question concerning tribute [Hb, NICNT], paying taxes [CEV], a question concerning paying taxes to Caesar

[CBC], paying taxes to Caesar [ESV, NET, NIV], taxes for Caesar [NLT], is it right to pay taxes or not? [NCV].

12:13 And they-send to him some of-the Pharisees and the Herodians[a] in-order-that they-might-catch[b] him in-a-word.

LEXICON—a. Ἡρῳδιανοί [LN 11.87] (BAGD p. 348): 'Herodians' [AB2, BAGD, BECNT, BNTC, LN, Lns, NTC, WBC; ESV, KJV, NASB, NCV, NET, NIV, NRSV], 'men of Herod's party' [REB], 'members of Herod's party' [AB1; TEV], 'the followers of Herod' [LN], 'Herod's followers' [CEV, GW], 'supporters of Herod' [NLT]. This noun denotes the political followers of Herod the Great and his family [LN]. They were partisans of Herod the Great and his family [BAGD].

b. aorist act. subj. of ἀγρεύω (LN 27.30) (BAGD p. 13): 'to catch' [BAGD], 'to trap, to catch off guard' [LN]. The phrase ἀγρεύσωσιν λόγῳ 'they might catch him in a word' is translated 'to catch him in his words' [NTC; KJV, NIV], 'to catch him by means of a statement' [Lns], 'they might catch him in an unguarded statement' [BAGD], 'that they might trap him in his speech' [AB2, BECNT], 'to trap him with his own words' [NET], 'to trap him in what he said' [NRSV], 'to trap him in his talk' [AB1; ESV], 'to trap him in speaking' [BNTC], 'to trap him in a statement' [NASB], 'to trap him into saying the wrong thing' [GW], 'to trick Jesus/him into saying something wrong' [CEV, NCV], 'to trap Jesus into saying something for which he could be arrested' [NLT], 'trap him with a statement' [WBC], 'to trap him with questions' [LN; TEV], 'to trap him with a question' [REB]. This is a figurative extension of 'to hunt, to trap' and means to acquire information about an error or fault in order to cause harm or trouble [LN].

QUESTION—Who sent the Pharisees and Herodians?

The undefined verb ἀποστέλλουσιν 'they send' appears to refer to the baffled Sanhedrin members mentioned in verse 12 [BECNT, Gnd, My, NAC, NCBC, NIGTC]. However, it is not likely that the subject of the verb 'they send' is the 'they' of the previous verse [CGTC, TH]. It is more likely that it refers to the whole Sanhedrin or else some members of it [AB1, CGTC, Tay]. Matthew 22:15 says it was the Pharisees who concocted the scheme and sent their disciples along with the Herodians [Hb, Lns]. They were sent by certain members of the Sanhedrin or by leaders in their respective groups [NICNT].

QUESTION—Why were the Herodians involved in the delegation?

The Pharisees and the Herodians represented two sides to the question about taxes that will be proposed to Jesus [ICC, WBC]. The Pharisees were popular for their intense nationality and hatred of foreign rule while the Herodians were supporters of Herod, who owed what power he possessed to the Roman government. So whichever answer Jesus will give to the question will offend one of the sides in the delegation [ICC]. Both groups would probably have reluctantly voted for paying taxes because the *status quo* suited them better than open rebellion, but Jesus would lose popular support should he side with the government [BNTC].

QUESTION—What is meant by catching Jesus λόγῳ 'in a word'?
1. The 'word' refers to what Jesus will say when he answers their question [AB1, AB2, BECNT, BNTC, EBC, Gnd, Hb, Lns, NICNT, NTC, PNTC, TH, TRT; all versions except REB, TEV]. The delegation aimed to get Jesus to say something wrong [CEV].
2. The 'word' refers to what the delegation will ask Jesus [Hb, ICC, My, WBC; REB, TEV]. The primary reference is their cleverly devised question that will elicit from Jesus some statement they would be able to use against him [Hb].

12:14 And having-come they-say to-him, "Teacher, we-know that you-are truthful[a] and it-is- not -a-concern[b] to-you about anyone. Because you-do-not -look at (the) face[c] of-men, but on-the-basis-of truth[d] you-teach the way of-God.

LEXICON—a. ἀληθής (LN 88.39) (BAGD 1. p. 36): 'truthful' [AB2, BAGD, LN, Lns, NTC; NASB, NET], 'honest' [AB1, BAGD, BECNT, LN; CEV, NCV, NLT], 'true' [WBC; ESV, KJV], 'sincere' [BNTC; NRSV, REB], 'righteous' [BAGD], 'a person/man of integrity' [LN; NIV], 'you tell the truth' [GW, TEV]. This adjective pertains to being truthful and honest [LN].
  b. pres. act. indic. of μέλει (LN 30.39) (BAGD 2. p. 500): 'to be concerned about' [BAGD, LN], 'to think about' [LN]. The phrase οὐ μέλει σοι περὶ οὐδενός 'it is not a concern to you about anyone' is translated 'thou carest for no one' [Lns], 'you do not care about anyone's opinion' [ESV], 'you are not concerned with the opinion of others' [BECNT], 'another's opinion means nothing to you' [WBC], 'you do not court anyone's favor' [NET, REB; similarly AB1, BAGD, BNTC, NTC], 'you don't care what anyone thinks' [AB2], 'without worrying about what people think' [TEV], 'you are not afraid of what other people think about you' [NCV], 'you treat everyone with the same respect' [CEV], 'you are impartial' [NLT], 'you don't favor individuals' [GW], 'you are not swayed by men' [NIV], 'you show deference to no one' [NRSV], 'you defer to no one' [NASB], 'thou carest for no man' [KJV]. This verb means to think about something in such a way as to make an appropriate response [LN]. It doesn't mean that Jesus was indifferent to people, but that he was independent of their influence [Hb]. Jesus taught with strict justice and impartiality without fear of wounding anyone's sensibilities by the rigor of his teaching [TH].
  c. πρόσωπον (LN 30.120) (BAGD 1.c.β. p. 721): 'face' [BAGD, LN]. The clause οὐ βλέπεις εἰς πρόσωπον ἀνθρώπων 'you do not look into the face of men' is translated 'you don't look at the face of human beings' [AB2], 'thou dost not look on man's countenance' [Lns], 'you do not judge a person on the basis of outward appearance' [LN], 'thou regardest not the person of men' [KJV], 'you do not regard the position of people'

[WBC], 'you pay no attention to who they are' [NCV, NIV], 'you don't favor individuals because of who they are' [GW], 'you pay no attention to outward appearance' [AB1], 'you are not swayed by appearances' [ESV], 'you do not show partiality' [BECNT, BNTC], 'you show no partiality' [NET], 'you are not partial to anyone' [NTC], 'you do not regard people with partiality' [NRSV], 'you are not partial to any' [NASB], 'you don't play favorites' [NLT], 'whoever he may be' [REB], 'you treat everyone with the same respect' [CEV], 'you pay no attention to what people think' [TEV]. The idiom βλέπω εἰς πρόσωπον 'to see into the face' means 'to judge on the basis of appearance, to render a superficial judgment, to pay no attention to a person's status, to judge on the basis of reputation' [LN]. Jesus is impartial and is not influenced by a person's position, wealth, or power because he does not pay attention to their outward appearance [Hb].

d. ἀλήθεια (LN 70.4) (BAGD I.1.b.β. p. 286): 'truth' [BAGD, LN]. The phrase ἐπ' ἀληθείας 'on the basis of truth' [Lns] is also translated 'in accordance with the truth' [NET, NIV, NRSV], 'in truth' [KJV, NASB], 'truly' [ESV], 'truthfully' [AB2, BECNT, NTC; GW, NLT], 'in all sincerity' [REB], 'with sincerity' [BNTC], 'in all honesty' [AB1], 'actually, really' [LN]. The clause τὴν ὁδὸν τοῦ θεοῦ διδάσκεις 'on the basis of truth you teach the way of God' is translated 'you teach the truth about God's way' [NCV], 'you teach the truth about what God wants people to do' [CEV], 'you teach the truth about God's will for people' [TEV], 'you truly teach the way of God' [WBC]. The idiom ἐπ' ἀληθείας 'in truth, upon truth, according to truth' pertains to something being a real or actual event or state [LN].

QUESTION—Why did these enemies of Jesus start out by saying that he was truthful and paid no attention to the opinions of men?

They wanted to force him to face the issue they had decided upon by removing any argument he could make to evade their difficult question [NICNT].

Is-it-lawful[a] to-give a-poll-tax[b] to-Caesar[c] or not? Should-we-give or should-we- not -give?"

LEXICON—a. pres. act. indic. of ἔξεστι (LN 71.32) (BAGD 1. p. 275): 'to be permitted, to be proper, to be possible' [BAGD]. The phrase 'is it lawful to give' [BNTC; KJV] is also translated 'is it lawful to pay' [AB1, BECNT, LN, Lns, NTC, WBC; ESV, NASB, NRSV], 'is it against our Law to pay' [TEV], 'is it permissible to give' [AB2], 'are we permitted to pay' [REB], 'is it right to pay' [GW, NCV, NET, NIV, NLT], 'should we pay' [CEV]. This verb means to be obligatory [LN]. The question 'Is it lawful' assumes that the question must be decided in harmony with the demands of the Torah. Does that law permit it or not? [Hb]. This word could be translated 'in accordance with the law, right, proper', or even 'good' in the sense of being the correct thing to do [TH]. All of the other

uses of this verb in Mark in 2:24, 26; 3:4; 6:18; 10:2 have referred to what is permitted under divine law. The poll tax was mandatory under Roman law, so the question in this verse invites Jesus to claim divine sanction for opposing government law [NIGTC].
- b. κῆνσος (LN **57.180**) (BAGD p. 430): 'poll tax' [BAGD, LN, Lns, NTC; NASB, NET], 'tax' [BAGD, **LN**], 'taxes' [AB1; CEV, ESV, GW, NCV, NIV, NLT, NRSV, REB, TEV], 'tribute' [BNTC; KJV], 'tribute money' [AB2]. This noun denotes a tax paid by each adult male to the government [LN]. It was the annual head tax imposed by the Roman emperor for the imperial treasury [Hb]. The word 'tax' probably refers to a poll tax [BECNT, Hb, PNTC, Sw, Tay] or tribute money [EBC, NICNT].
- c. Καῖσαρ (LN 37.74) (BAGD p. 395): 'Caesar' [AB2, BAGD, BNTC, Lns, NTC; ESV, KJV, NASB, NCV, NET, NIV, NLT], 'Emperor' [BAGD, LN; CEV], 'emperor' [GW, NRSV], 'Roman emperor' [AB1; REB, TEV]. This is a title for the Roman Emperor [LN].

QUESTION—What was their purpose in asking Jesus this question?

They were not really seeking the truth on this issue, but were trying to trap Jesus with a tricky question they had come up with [BECNT]. The Jewish Zealots and other nationalists flatly refused to pay tribute money to the Roman emperor since they did not accept his right to rule. The Pharisees disliked the poll tax, although they did not actively oppose it. The Herodians had no objection to it [EBC]. Their trap is obvious. If Jesus sides with the nationalists, he can be denounced to the Roman authorities who will then arrest him for being a political agitator; if he sides with the government, he will lose his popular support [BECNT, BNTC, Gnd, NICNT, PNTC]. Whichever answer Jesus gives would bring an end to his popularity [BECNT].

QUESTION—Is the question Δῶμεν ἢ μὴ δῶμεν; 'Should we give or should we not give?' part of verse 14 or verse 15 in the Greek manuscripts?
1. This question ends verse 12:14 [AB1, AB2, BECNT, BNTC, GNT, Lns, NTC, WBC; CEV, ESV, GW, NET, TEV].
2. This question begins verse 12:15 [KJV, NASB, NCV, NIV, NLT, NRSV, REB].

12:15 But having-perceived[a] their hypocrisy[b] he said to-them, "Why are-you-testing[c] me? Bring me a-denarius[d] so-that I-may-look (at it)." **12:16** And they-brought (one). And he-says to-them, "Whose image[e] (is) this and (whose) inscription[f]?" And they-said to-him, "Caesar's."

LEXICON—a. perf. act. participle of οἶδα (LN 28.1) (BAGD 4. p. 556): 'to know' [BECNT, LN, Lns, WBC; CEV, ESV, KJV, NASB, NCV, NIV, NRSV], 'to know about' [LN], 'to be aware of' [NTC], 'to recognize' [BAGD; GW], 'to realize' [BNTC], 'to see' [AB2], 'to see through' [AB1; NET, NLT, REB, TEV], 'to understand' [BAGD]. This verb means to possess information about something [LN].

b. ὑπόκρισις (LN **88.227**) (BAGD p. 845): 'hypocrisy' [BAGD, BECNT, BNTC, **LN**, Lns, NTC, WBC; ESV, GW, KJV, NASB, NET, NIV, NLT, NRSV], 'duplicity' [REB], 'pretense' [BAGD, AB2], 'casuistry' [AB1], 'outward show' [BAGD], 'trick' [TEV]. The phrase αὐτῶν τὴν ὑπόκρισιν 'their hypocrisy' is translated 'what these men were really trying to do' [NCV], 'what they were up to' [CEV]. This noun denotes the giving of an impression of having certain purposes or motivations, while in reality having quite different ones [LN].

c. pres. act. indic. of πειράζω (LN 27.31) (BAGD 2.c. p. 640): 'to test' [AB2, BECNT, BNTC, WBC; GW, NASB, NET], 'to try to test' [CEV], 'to put to the test' [AB1, BAGD, NTC, WBC; ESV, NRSV], 'to try to trap' [LN; NCV, NIV, NLT], 'to attempt to catch in a mistake' [LN], 'to catch (me) out' [REB], 'to tempt' [Lns; KJV]. This verb means to obtain information to be used against a person by trying to cause someone to make a mistake [LN]. This word occurs at 1:13; 8:11; 10:2; 12:15.

d. δηνάριον (LN 6.75) (BAGD p. 179): 'denarius' [AB2, BAGD, BECNT, BNTC, LN, Lns, NTC, WBC; ESV, NASB, NET, NIV, NRSV], 'coin' [CEV, GW, NCV], 'Roman coin' [NLT], 'silver coin' [CEV], 'silver piece' [AB1; REB], 'penny' [KJV]. This noun denotes a silver Roman coin equivalent to a day's wage for a common laborer [LN].

e. εἰκών (LN 58.35) (BAGD 1.a. p. 222): 'image' [AB2, BAGD, BECNT, BNTC, LN, Lns, WBC; KJV, NCV, NET], 'likeness' [BAGD, LN, NTC; ESV, NASB], 'picture' [CEV, NLT], 'portrait' [AB1; NIV], 'face' [GW, TEV], 'head' [NRSV, REB]. This noun denotes that which has the same form as something else [LN].

f. ἐπιγραφή (LN 33.46) (BAGD p. 291): 'inscription' [AB2, BAGD, BECNT, BNTC, LN, NTC, WBC; ESV, NASB, NET, NIV, REB], 'writing' [LN], 'name' [CEV, GW, NCV, TEV], 'title' [NLT, NRSV], 'superscription' [AB1, Lns; KJV]. This noun denotes a brief notice used primarily for identification [LN].

QUESTION—What was the δηνάριον 'denarius' that Jesus specifically asked to see?

The denarius was a silver coin that was minted by the Roman government [TH]. At that time its value in Palestine was approximately one day's wage [WBC]. A denarius from the reign of the ruling emperor Tiberius pictures his head on one side with the inscription 'Tiberius Caesar Augustus, Son of the Divine Augustus'. On the reverse side he is shown seated on a throne clothed as a high priest with a diadem on his head with an inscription that reads "Highest Priest" [NTC]. The inscriptions would have been in Latin, the national language of the Roman Empire [TH]. The inscription was in raised letters [Hb]. A denarius was the only coin that was accepted for payment of the toll tax in Judea [NICNT].

QUESTION—Why did Jesus want to borrow a coin in order to look at it?

Even though Jesus had seen such coins before [BECNT, Hb], he made this request in order to direct everyone's attention to what appeared on the coin and what was written on it [NTC]. He intended to use it as a visual aid in answering their question [Hb].

12:17 And Jesus said to-them, "Give-back[a] to-Caesar the (things) of-Caesar and to-God the (things) of-God." And they-were-utterly-amazed[b] at him.

LEXICON—a. aorist act. impera. of ἀποδίδωμι (LN 57.153) (BAGD 1. p. 90): 'to give' [BAGD], 'to pay' [BAGD, LN], 'to render' [LN]. The clause τὰ Καίσαρος ἀπόδοτε Καίσαρι 'Give back to Caesar the things of Caesar' is translated 'Give to Caesar the things of Caesar' [WBC], 'Give to Caesar what is Caesar's' [NIV], 'Give to Caesar what belongs to Caesar' [BNTC; NLT], 'Give to the emperor the things that are the emperor's' [NRSV], 'Give the Emperor what belongs to the-Emperor/him' [CEV, GW], 'The things that belong to Caesar give to Caesar' [BECNT], 'Give to Caesar/the-emperor the things that are Caesar's/the-emperor's' [ESV, NCV, NET], 'Duly give the things of Caesar to Caesar' [Lns], 'Pay to Caesar the things of Caesar' [AB2], 'Pay Caesar what belongs to Caesar' [REB], 'Pay to the Emperor what belongs to the Emperor' [TEV], 'Then pay back to the emperor what belongs to him' [AB1], 'Render to Caesar the things that are Caesar's' [KJV, NASB], 'What is due to Caesar render to Caesar' [NTC]. This verb means to make a payment in response to an incurred obligation [LN]. The verb 'give' implies 'giving back what is due' [AB1]. In verse 14 the questioners had used the simple verb δίδωμι 'to give', but Jesus now uses the compound verb ἀποδίδωμι 'to give back or pay something which one owes as a debt', implying that they are under an obligation [CGTC].

b. imperf. act. indic. of ἐκθαυμάζω (LN **25.214**) (BAGD p. 240): 'to be utterly amazed' [BECNT; NET, NRSV], 'to be completely amazed' [NLT], 'to be totally amazed' [BNTC], 'to be very amazed' [**LN**], 'to be amazed' [AB2, NTC, WBC; CEV, NASB, NCV, NIV, TEV], 'to be completely taken aback' [REB], 'to be astounded' [AB1], 'to be surprised' [GW], 'to marvel' [Lns; ESV, KJV]. This verb means to wonder greatly or to be very much amazed [LN]. The verb ἐκθαυμάζω 'to be utterly amazed' is an intensive form of θαυμάζω 'to be amazed' [BECNT].

QUESTION—What did Jesus mean by his answer?

Jesus' answer was that each had a legitimate claim [AB1, BECNT, BNTC, CBC, CGTC, EBC, ICC, NAC, NCBC, NICNT, NIGTC, PNTC, Sw, Tay]. Their possession of a Roman coin indicated that they accepted the Roman Empire's economic system which obligated them to pay the taxes [BECNT, ICC, NAC, NICNT, NIGTC, PNTC]. The idea seems to be that 'the coin is Cesar's, so let him have his own' [Sw]. Their abiding obligation to God and their obligation to pay back their debt of things that belonged to Caesar are not in conflict [Hb]. They must pay both since both God and Caesar had legitimate claims on them [ICC]. Honoring God does not mean dishonoring

Caesar by refusing to pay for the privileges of a relatively orderly society, police protection, good roads, courts, etc. Jesus qualified his 'yes' to paying back by stating that the emperor should be given only what was his due. The divine honor claimed by the emperor must be refused since it was due to God alone. The Pharisees could not find any fault with this answer [NTC]. Jesus' answer was a clever evasion of the trap [WBC]. By giving an ambiguous answer, none of the parties could disagree with it. For the Zealot, what belonged to Caesar was nothing and what belonged to God was everything. For the moderate, what belonged to Caesar was tribute and what belonged to God was worship and fidelity to the covenant. Jesus probably intended to be ambiguous so that the problem of who should pay the toll tax would be left for the questioners [WBC].

QUESTION—Why were they so amazed at Jesus' answer?

They were amazed that Jesus did not fall into their trap [WBC]. They had not expected this kind of an answer [NTC]. Perhaps they were astonished at the authority of the reply, rather than its cleverness [BNTC]. Jesus had not only escaped their trap but had also thrown a flood of light on the problem [Hb, ICC].

DISCOURSE UNIT—12:18–27 [CBC, Hb, NICNT; CEV, ESV, GW, NCV, NET, NIV, NLT, NRSV, TEV]. The topic is marriage and the resurrection [NET], marriage at the resurrection [NIV], life in the future world [CEV], the dead come back to life [GW], the question about the resurrection [CBC, Hb, NICNT; NRSV], discussion about resurrection [NLT], the question about rising from death [TEV], the Sadducees ask about the resurrection [ESV], some Sadducees try to trick Jesus [NCV].

12:18 **And (some) Sadducees,ᵃ who say there-is no resurrection,ᵇ come to him, and they-were-questioning him saying,**

LEXICON—a. Σαδδουκαῖος (LN 11.48) (BAGD p. 739): 'Sadducee' [BAGD, LN; all translations]. This noun denotes a member of a politically influential Jewish party in Jerusalem that had control of certifying important political and religious positions. Their denial of the resurrection of the dead and their acceptance of only the first five books of the OT were not supported by the Pharisees. [LN]. Instead of being a religious party like the Pharisees, the Sadducees were an elite social class composed mostly of priests. As a party of traditionalists, they opposed any new religious teachings like the idea of the resurrection and the existence of angels [TH]. The clause 'who say there is no resurrection' refers to the Sadducees as a whole and not just the individuals who came to speak to Jesus [Hb, Sw, TH].

b. ἀνάστασις (LN 23.93) (BAGD 2.b. p. 60): 'resurrection' [AB1, AB2, BAGD, BECNT, BNTC, LN. Lns, NTC, WBC; ESV, KJV, NASB, NET, NIV, NLT, NRSV, REB]. The clause 'there is no resurrection' is translated 'people would not rise from the dead' [NCV], 'people will not rise from death' [TEV], 'people will never come back to life' [GW], 'did not believe that people would rise to life after death' [CEV]. This noun denotes the coming back to life of someone who had died [LN].

12:19 "Teacher, Moses wrote[a] for-us that if a-man's brother dies and leaves-behind[b] a-wife and leaves no child, his brother should-marry[c] the wife and raise-up[d] offspring[e] (for) his brother.

LEXICON—a. γράφω (LN 33.61): 'to write' [LN]. The phrase ἔγραψεν ἡμῖν 'wrote for us' [BECNT, BNTC, Lns, NTC, WBC; ESV, GW, NASB, NET, NIV, NRSV] is also translated 'wrote to us' [AB2], 'wrote unto us' [KJV], 'wrote that' [CEV, NCV], 'laid this/it down for us' [AB1; REB]. 'wrote this law for us' [TEV], 'gave us a law' [NLT]. This verb means 'to write' [LN].

  b. aorist act. subj. of καταλείπω (LN 85.65) (BAGD 1.b. p. 413): 'to leave behind' [BAGD, BECNT, LN, Lns, NTC, WBC; KJV, NASB], 'to leave' [AB1, AB2, BNTC, LN; all versions except CEV, KJV, NASB]. The clause 'if a brother of someone dies and leaves behind a wife' is translated 'if a married man dies and leaves behind a wife, his brother...' [CEV]. This verb means to cause someone to remain in a place when leaving [LN].

  c. aorist act. subj. of λαμβάνω (LN 57.55) (BAGD 1.c. p. 464): 'to take' [BAGD, LN], 'to acquire, to obtain' [LN]. The phrase λάβῃ ὁ ἀδελφὸς αὐτοῦ τὴν γυναῖκα 'his brother should marry the/his widow/wife' [CEV, GW, NASB, NLT] is also translated 'his brother must marry the widow' [AB1], 'his brother should take his/the wife' [AB2, BECNT, BNTC, WBC; KJV], 'let his brother take his wife' [Lns], 'the man must take the widow' [ESV], 'that man must marry the widow' [NTC; NET, NIV, NCV], 'the man shall marry the widow' [NRSV], 'that man's brother must marry the widow' [TEV], 'then the next should marry the widow' [REB]. This verb means to acquire possession of something [LN].

  d. aorist act. subj. of ἐξανίστημι (LN 23.59) (BAGD 1. p. 272): 'to raise up offspring' [BAGD], 'to be the father of, to procreate, to beget' [LN]. The phrase 'raise up offspring for his brother' [AB2, WBC; ESV] is also translated 'raise up seed for/unto his brother' [Lns; KJV], 'raise up children for his brother' [BECNT, BNTC, NTC, NRSV], 'raise up children to his brother' [NASB], 'have children for his brother' [GW, NCV, NIV], 'have a child who will carry on the brother's name' [NLT], 'raise up children on the brother's behalf' [AB1], 'must father children for his brother' [NET], 'they can have children who will be considered the dead man's children' [TEV], 'provide an heir for his brother' [REB], 'their first son would then be thought of as the son of the dead man' [CEV]. The idiom 'to raise up offspring' refers to the male role in causing the conception and birth of a child [LN]. 'Raise up' is used in the sense of begetting children and not in the modern sense of 'rearing' or 'bringing up' children [TH].

e. σπέρμα (LN 10.29) (BAGD 2.b. p. 762): 'offspring' [LN], 'posterity, descendants' [BAGD, LN], 'children' [BAGD]. See translations of this noun in the preceding lexical item. The noun is a figurative extension of meaning of 'seed' and denotes one's posterity where the emphasis is on the ancestor's role in founding the lineage [LN].

QUESTION—Where had the Sadducees read this command by Moses and who are the ἡμῖν 'us' he wrote it for?

The passage referred to here is a free rendering of Deut. 25:5–6. The pronoun 'us' refers to all Jews and not just the Sadducees [TH].

QUESTION—What was the purpose for this command?

This command was intended to provide the deceased brother with heirs who would preserve his name and inherit his property [BNTC]. This law would keep the family line from dying out and would prevent the family inheritance from being broken up. The firstborn son would be registered as the son of the dead brother [Hb, Lns, NTC].

QUESTION—How many children are referred to by the singular noun σπέρμα 'offspring' in this verse?

1. This includes all of the children resulting from the brother's marriage to the widow [AB1, AB2, BAGD, BECNT, BNTC, LN, TH; probably ESV, GW, NASB, NCV, NET, NIV, NRSV, TEV which use a plural form].
2. This refers only to the first son resulting from the marriage [probably CEV, NLT, REB which use a singular form].

12:20 There-were seven brothers. And the first took a-wife and dying[a] did-not -leave offspring. **12:21** And the second took her and he-died not having-left-behind offspring. And the third likewise.[b]

LEXICON—a. pres. act. participle of ἀποθνῄσκω (LN 23.99): 'to die' [LN; KJV]. The clause καὶ ἀποθνῄσκων οὐκ ἀφῆκεν σπέρμα 'and dying did not leave seed' [Lns] is also translated 'and dying, he left behind no offspring' [WBC], 'and died without leaving any children' [NIV], 'and died, leaving no children' [NASB, NCV], 'and then died without children' [NLT], 'but died without having children' [GW, TEV; similarly CEV], 'and when he died he had no children' [NET], 'and when he died left no offspring' [ESV; similarly AB2], 'and when he died left no children' [BECNT, BNTC, NTC; similarly NRSV], 'and died without issue' [REB], 'and died childless' [AB1]. This verb refers to the process of dying [TH]. This is a temporal participle meaning 'when he died' and the proper relationship with the following verb is 'he died without leaving...' [TH].

b. ὡσαύτως (LN 64.16) (BAGD p. 899): 'likewise' [BAGD], 'in the same way' [BAGD, LN], 'just as, in like manner' [LN], 'similarly' [BAGD]. The clause 'And the third likewise' [Lns, WBC; KJV, NASB, NRSV] is also translated 'and likewise the third' [NET], 'And the third did likewise' [BECNT; ESV], 'and the third similarly' [AB2], 'So did the third' [GW, REB; similarly BNTC, NTC], 'So too with the third' [AB1], 'It was the same with the third' [NIV], 'The same thing happened to/with the third brother' [CEV, NCV], 'Then the third brother married her' [NLT]. This adverb indicates a close similarity [LN].

QUESTION—Was this story about seven brothers factual?

This is a hypothetical case [BECNT, EBC, Gnd, NICNT, NIGTC, NTC, WBC]. Even though this story is probably fictional, it could be that they had heard of this extraordinary affair and seized upon it as a favorite weapon to further their views [Hb].

12:22 **And the seven did- not -leave offspring. Last of-all also the woman died.** **12:23** **In the resurrection when they-are-raised,**[a] **of-which of-them will-she-be the wife? Because the seven had her (as) wife."**

TEXT—In verse 23, manuscripts reading ἐν τῇ ἀναστάσει ὅταν ἀναστῶσιν 'in the resurrection when they arise' are given a C rating by GNT to indicate that choosing it over a variant text was difficult. Variant readings are ἐν τῇ οὖν ἀναστάσει ὅταν ἀναστῶσιν 'therefore in the resurrection when they arise', ἐν τῇ ἀναστάσει οὖν ὅταν ἀναστῶσιν 'in the resurrection therefore when they arise', ὅταν οὖν ἀναστῶσιν ἐν τῇ ἀναστάσει 'when therefore they arise in the resurrection', and ἐν τῇ ἀναστάσει 'in the resurrection', and some manuscripts read ἐν τῇ ἀναστάσει οὖν 'in the resurrection therefore'.

LEXICON—a. aorist act. subj. of ἀνίσταμαι (LN 23.93): 'to be resurrected, to come back to life, to live again' [LN]. The clause 'In the resurrection when they are raised' is translated 'In the resurrection, when they rise again' [ESV, NASB, NET], 'In the resurrection, when they rise' [AB2], 'In the resurrection therefore, when they shall rise' [KJV], 'Now, when all the dead rise to life on the day of resurrection' [TEV], 'In/at the resurrection, when they rise from the dead' [BECNT; REB], 'When the dead come back to life' [GW], 'At the resurrection' [NIV], 'In the resurrection' [AB1, BNTC, Lns, NTC, WBC; NLT, NRSV], 'when people rise from the dead' [NCV], 'When God raises people from death' [CEV]. This verb means to come back to life after having once died [LN].

QUESTION—What is the point of the question?

The Sadducees implied that when all of them had been resurrected, the woman would have seven husbands at the same time and thus violate the Mosaic law that required a woman to have only one husband at a time. Although a man might practice polygamy, a woman could not in the present life, and especially not in the resurrection! [Gnd]. It was unthinkable that all seven brothers could be her husbands at the same time in the present life, and even more implausible if there was a resurrection [Lns].

12:24 **Jesus said to-them, "(Is it) not because-of this you-are-mistaken,**[a] **not-knowing**[b] **the Scriptures nor the-power of-God?**

LEXICON—a. pres. pass. indic. of πλανάομαι, πλανάω (LN 31.67) (BAGD 2.c.γ. p. 665): 'to be mistaken' [AB1; GW, NASB, NLT], 'to be wrong' [BECNT, BNTC; ESV, NRSV, TEV], 'to be completely wrong' [CEV], 'to not understand' [NCV], 'to err' [KJV], 'to be in error' [NIV], 'to be

far from the truth' [REB], 'to be deceived' [AB2; NET], 'to deceive oneself' [Lns; NTC], 'to be misled' [BAGD, WBC], 'to wander about' [BAGD], 'to go astray' [BAGD, LN], 'to stray from the truth, to wander from the truth' [LN]. The verb πλανᾶσθεν literally means 'to wander about' (15.24), but it is used figuratively here to mean to no longer believe what is true and start believing what is false [LN]. They are mistaken in both judgment and speech [TH].
   b. perf. act. participle of οἶδα (LN 32.4): 'to understand, to comprehend' [LN]. The participial phrase μὴ εἰδότες 'not knowing' is translated 'you do not know' [AB1, AB2, BECNT; GW, NET, NIV, NLT, TEV; similarly Lns; KJV], 'knowing neither' [WBC], 'you know neither…' [NTC; ESV, NRSV, REB], 'don't you know' [NCV], 'you don't know anything about' [CEV], 'you do not understand' [NASB], 'you are ignorant of' [BNTC]. This verb means to comprehend the meaning of something [LN]. It is a causal participle that means 'because you do not know' [THQUESTION—What kind of a question did Jesus ask?

It was a rhetorical question that implies they were mistaken because they did not know the Scriptures or the power of God [Gnd, Hb, My, Sw, Tay].

QUESTION—Why didn't these Sadducees know the Scriptures?

They knew the contents of the Old Testament writings but failed to understand their true meaning [Hb]. They should have known that there is nothing in Deuteronomy 25:5 that makes it applicable to the life hereafter [Lns, NTC]. They should also have known that various OT passages did teach the resurrection of the body [Lns, NTC]. The resurrection is clearly taught in Isaiah 26:19; Ezekiel 37:1–14; Daniel 12:2; Psalms 16:9–11, 49:15, 73:23–26, and Job 19:26 [BECNT]. Marriage on earth is for the purpose of procreation and companionship, but there is no need for procreation in the resurrection because there will be no more death. Men will no longer marry, and women will no longer be given in marriage [BECNT].

QUESTION—Why didn't these Sadducees know the power of God?

They were limiting God's power to what they knew about their present life [BECNT]. They were denying the power of God to create life [BNTC]. They should have known God's plan for those raised from the dead does not include relationships defined by marriage [NTC].

12:25 Because when they-rise[a] from (the) dead, they- neither -marry nor are-they-given-in-marriage,[b] but they-are like[c] angels in heaven.

LEXICON—a. aorist act. subj. of ἀνίσταμα, ἀνίστημι (LN 23.93) (BAGD 2.a. p. 70): 'to rise' [BAGD], 'to come back to life, to live again, to be resurrected' [LN]. The phrase ὅταν ἐκ νεκρῶν ἀναστῶσιν 'when they/people rise from the dead' [BECNT, BNTC, WBC; ESV, NASB, NCV, NET, NRSV, REB; similarly Lns; KJV] is also translated 'when they rise from among the dead' [AB2], 'when the dead rise' [AB1, NTC; NIV, NLT], 'when the dead rise to life' [TEV], 'when the dead come back

to life' [GW], 'when God raises people to life' [CEV]. This verb means to come back to life after having once died [LN].
  b. pres. pass. indic. of γαμίζω (LN 34.72) (BAGD 1. or 2. p. 151): 'to give in marriage' [BAGD (1.), LN], 'to be given in marriage' [BAGD (2.)]. The phrase γαμίζονται 'are/be given in marriage' [BECNT, BNTC, Lns, NTC, WBC; ESV, KJV, NASB, NET, NIV, NLT, NRSV], 'are taken in marriage' [AB2], 'will be given to someone to marry' [NCV]. The clause 'they neither marry nor are they given in marriage' is translated 'they won't/don't/will-not marry' [CEV, GW, TEV], 'men do not marry, and women are not given in marriage' [AB1], 'men and women do not marry' [REB]. This verb means to cause a person to become married [LN].

QUESTION—What is the occasion when 'they' rise from the dead?
  The reference is impersonal and means 'when the dead rise' and not just when the seven brothers and the woman rise. It refers to the resurrection life after the dead are raised [Gnd, Hb, TH]. This refers to when their bodies shall rise up out of the graves [Lns]. It only concerns the resurrection of the righteous [AB1, Hb].

QUESTION—Who are the implied subjects of the two verbs in the statement, '*they* neither marry nor are *they* given in marriage'?
  This means that the men do not marry and the women are not given in marriage [Lns, TH].

QUESTION—In what respect will the people who rise from the dead be like angels 'in heaven'?
  The phrase 'in heaven' modifies the word 'angels', so the point is not that the risen dead will be in heaven like the angels. In this context it means that the risen dead will experience life with respect to sex and marriage in the same way that the heavenly angels do [BECNT, CGTC, Hb, ICC, NIGTC, Tay, TRT; NLT]. The risen people will not be angels, but they will be like angels in regard to sex and marriage [Lns, NTC]. Marriage will be a matter of the past [NTC]. Life will be like that of the angels where marriage will no longer exist as it does now [CGTC, EBC, ICC]. This does not mean that the Christians will be deprived of any meaningful relationships with believing family members and friends [NAC].

12:26 But concerning the dead that they-are-raised,[a] have-you- not -read in the book[b] of-Moses how at the bush[c] God spoke to-him saying, 'I[d] (am) the God of-Abraham and the God of-Isaac and the God of-Jacob'? 12:27 He is not (the) God of-dead (people) but of- living (people). You-are-mistaken[e] greatly."

TEXT—Manuscripts reading ὁ θεὸς Ἰσαὰκ καὶ ὁ θεὸς Ἰακώβ 'the God of Isaac and the God of Jacob' are given a C rating by GNT to indicate that choosing it over a variant text was difficult. A variant reading is θεὸς Ἰσαὰκ καὶ θεὸς Ἰακώβ 'God of Isaac and God of Jacob'.

LEXICON—a. pres. pass. indic. of ἐγείρω (LN 23.94) (BAGD 2.c. p. 215): 'to be raised' [AB1, AB2, BAGD, BECNT, WBC; CEV, ESV, NET, NLT,

NRSV, TEV], 'to be raised up' [Lns, NTC], 'to be raised to life, to be made to live again' [LN], 'to come back to life' [GW], 'to rise' [KJV, NCV, NIV], 'to rise again' [NASB], '(As for) the resurrection' [BNTC; REB]. This verb means to cause someone to live again after having once died [LN]. This passive voice in the present tense defines a general truth, but could have the force of a future tense [TH].

b. βίβλος (LN 33.52) (BAGD 1. p. 141): 'book' [BAGD, LN]. The phrase 'the book of Moses' [all translations except CEV, NCV, NLT] is also translated 'in the book in which Moses wrote' [NCV], 'the writings of Moses' [NLT], 'the story about Moses' [CEV]. This noun denotes the contents of a book [LN].

c. βάτος (LN 3.16) (BAGD p. 137): 'bush' [AB1, AB2, BNTC, LN, Lns, NTC, WBC; ESV, GW, KJV, NET, NIV, NRSV], 'thorn bush' [BAGD, LN]. The 'thorn bush' is identified in some translations: 'the burning bush' [BECNT; CEV, NASB, NCV, NLT, REB, TEV]. This noun denotes any type of thorn bush or shrub. Except for Luke 6:44 where it states that figs are not gathered from a thorn bush, all occurrences of this noun in the NT refer to the burning bush of Exodus 3:2 and some translations identify it here as the 'burning thorn bush' [LN].

d. ἐγώ (LN 92.1) (BAGD p. 217): 'I' [BAGD, LN]. The phrase 'I, the God of Abraham' is translated with a supplied verb: 'I am the God of Abraham' [all translations]. This pronoun is an emphatic reference to the subject of the sentence [BAGD, LN]. The Hebrew text that is quoted has no verb, which is normal in Hebrew. In the Septuagint Greek translation the verb εἰμι 'am' is supplied, showing that the translators took the words of God to Moses to be asserting God's abiding relationship to those patriarchs. The verb is supplied in the Greek translation of Matthew 22:32: Ἐγώ εἰμι ὁ θεὸς Ἀβραάμ '*I am the God* of Abraham' [Hb].

e. pres. pass. indic. of πλανάομαι, πλανάω (LN 31.67) (BAGD 2.c.γ. p. 665): to be mistaken, to deceive oneself' [BAGD], 'to go astray' [BAGD, LN], 'to stray from the truth, to wander from the truth' [LN]. The clause πολὺ πλανᾶσθε 'You are mistaken greatly' is translated 'You are greatly mistaken' [NASB], 'You are badly mistaken!' [GW, NET, NIV], 'you are very much mistaken' [BAGD], 'You are quite wrong' [ESV, NRSV], 'You have made a serious error' [NLT], 'ye therefore do greatly err' [KJV], 'You Sadducees are wrong!' [NCV], 'You Sadducees are all wrong' [CEV], 'You are completely wrong!' [TEV], 'You are very far from the truth' [REB]. This verb means to no longer believe what is true, but to start believing what is false [LN]. This verb also occurs at 12:24.

QUESTION—What type of question is being asked in verse 26?

It is a rhetorical question that assumes a positive answer [Hb, LN]. Some translate this as a statement: 'You know that in the story about Moses and the burning bush' [CEV], 'Surely you have read' [NCV].

QUESTION—What is meant by the phrase τῇ βίβλῳ Μωϋσέως 'the book of Moses'?

It means 'the book that Moses *wrote*,' and not 'the book that Moses possessed' as many translations seem to say. The book Moses wrote is the Pentateuch [Hb, TH], and the passage about Moses and the burning bush is in Exodus 3:2–6 [TH].

QUESTION—How were the Sadducees proved to be wrong?

Jesus cites the very words of God recorded in Exodus 3:6 where God said 'I am the God of Abraham and the God of Isaac and the God of Jacob.' Isaac and Jacob were the two other great patriarchs who had long since died when God spoke these words to Moses. Verse 27 makes the point that although their bodies had long since died, they were still alive in Moses' time, and we may be sure that in the Resurrection God will raise up their bodies to share in the blessedness of eternal life [EBC]. Since death did not break their spiritual relationship with God, they were still alive in the invisible world even though their bodies had died [Hb]. God is a God of people who are alive because even those who have died on earth are still alive with him in heaven [TRT].

DISCOURSE UNIT—12:28–40 [NCV]. The topic is the most important command.

DISCOURSE UNIT—12:28–34 [CBC, Hb, NICNT; CEV, ESV, GW, NET, NIV, NLT, NRSV, TEV]. The topic is the most important commandment [CBC; CEV, NLT], the first commandment [NRSV], the great commandment [ESV, TEV], the greatest commandment [NET, NIV], love God and your neighbor [GW], the question of the first commandment [Hb], the question concerning the great commandment [NICNT].

12:28 And having-approached, one of-the scribes[a] having heard them debating[b] (and) having-seen that he-answered them well,[c] asked him, "Which is (the) first[d] commandment of-all?"

LEXICON—a. γραμματεύς (LN 53.94): 'scribe' [AB1, AB2, BECNT, Lns, NTC, WBC; ESV, GW, KJV, NASB, NRSV, REB], 'a person learned in the Law' [LN], 'an expert in the Law/law' [LN; NET], 'a teacher of the Law/law' [BNTC; CEV, NCV, NIV, NIV, TEV], 'a teacher of religious law' [NLT], 'a teacher of the Law of Moses' [CEV]. This noun denotes a recognized expert in Jewish law [LN]. By the time the NT was written, the noun 'scribe' had changed from its original meaning of a copyist of the law to a biblical scholar who was an interpreter of the law and an expounder of tradition [TH]. The scribes studied, interpreted, and taught the Old Testament laws and the traditions that had developed from those laws [TRT]. This word occurs at 1:22; 2:6; 16; 3:22; 7:1, 5; 8:31; 9:11, 14; 10:33; 11:27; 12:28, 32, 38; 14:1, 43, 53; 15:1, 31.

b. pres. act. participle of συζητέω (LN 33.440) (BAGD 2. p. 775): 'to debate' [AB2, BAGD; NET, NIV], 'to dispute' [BAGD, BECNT, BNTC,

LN, Lns, WBC], 'to argue' [BAGD, NTC; CEV, NASB, NCV]. The phrase 'having heard them debating' is translated 'listening to the debate' [NLT], 'heard the discussion' [TEV], 'had heard all the discussion' [AB1], 'had been listening to these discussions' [REB], 'heard them disputing with one another' [ESV, NRSV], 'heard them reasoning together' [KJV], 'during the argument' [GW]. This verb means to express forceful differences of opinion without necessarily having a presumed goal of seeking a solution [LN].

c. καλῶς (LN 72.12) (BAGD 4.b. p. 401): 'well' [AB2, BAGD, BECNT, BNTC, NTC, WBC; ESV, GW, KJV, NASB, NET, NLT, NRSV, REB], 'correctly' [BAGD, LN], 'rightly' [LN], 'excellently' [Lns]. The phrase 'answered them well' is translated 'how well he answered' [AB1], 'give/had-given a good answer' [CEV, NIV, TEV], 'gave good answers to their questions' [NCV]. This adverb pertains to being accurate, right, and possibly even commendable [LN].

d. πρῶτος (LN 65.52) (BAGD 1.c.α. p. 726): 'most important' [BAGD, LN; CEV, ESV, GW, NCV, NET, NIV, NLT, TEV], 'foremost' [NTC; NASB], 'first' [AB1, AB2, BAGD, BECNT, BNTC, Lns, WBC; KJV, NRSV, REB]. This adjective describes something as exceeding everything else in importance [LN]. 'First' refers to the importance of the command and has nothing to do with the order in which God's commands were given [AB2, NIGTC, TRT]. It refers to the most fundamental one from which all the other commandments arise [BECNT, BNTC].

QUESTION—What debate had this scribe overheard?

The text is ambiguous. It could refer to the debate the scribes had with Jesus or to a debate the Sadducees might have had among themselves about the answer Jesus had given them. One of the alternative meanings must be chosen if the ambiguity cannot be retained [TH]. Many state that this refers to the debate between Jesus and the Sadducees [Gnd, Hb, Lns, NICNT, NIGTC, Sw, TRT, WBC; CEV, GW, NCV, TEV].

QUESTION—What is meant by the πρώτη 'first' commandment of all'?

'First' refers to the first in importance [AB1, AB2, Hb, NICNT, NIGTC, NTC, TRT, WBC; CEV, ESV, GW, NCV, NASB, NET, NIV, NLT, TEV]. Instead of asking about the most important law, the focus is on what sort of law is first of all [EGT, Hb, ICC, Lns, Sw], and what made a commandment of principal importance [Hb]. The wording could be taken to mean 'what sort of law' or just 'which Law'. But since Jesus names two laws as being first and second of all, he is asking, 'Which specific law must be rated as the first of all?' [Lns]. It refers to the most fundamental commandment from which all the other commandments arise [BECNT]. It refers to the basic principle from which the whole Law could be derived [BNTC].

12:29 Jesus answered, "(The) first is, 'Hear, Israel, (the) Lord our God is one Lord,[a] **12:30** and you(sg)-shall-love (the) Lord your God with all your heart[b] and with all your soul[c] and with all your mind[d] and with all your strength.[e]'

LEXICON—a. κύριος (LN 12.9) (BAGD 2.a. p. 459): 'Lord' [BAGD, LN], 'Ruler, One who commands' [LN]. The clause κύριος εἷς ἐστιν 'is one Lord' [Lns, WBC; KJV, NASB] is also translated 'the Lord is one' [NTC; ESV, NET, NIV, NRSV], 'is the one Lord' [BNTC; REB], 'is the only Lord' [GW, NCV, TEV], 'is the one and only Lord' [NLT]. The clause 'the Lord our God is one Lord' is translated 'You have only one Lord and God' [CEV]. This noun 'Lord' denotes the one who exercises supernatural authority over mankind and it is a title that can refer to both God and Christ [LN]. The Greek word Κύριος 'Lord' is the Septuagint rendering in Greek of the Hebrew tetragram YHWH for 'Yahweh' [Lns].

b. καρδία (LN 26.3) (BAGD 1.b.ζ. p. 404): 'heart' [BAGD, LN], 'inner self, mind' [LN]. The phrase ἐξ ὅλης τῆς καρδίας σου 'with all your heart' [AB1, BECNT, BNTC, NTC; all versions] is also translated 'with your whole heart' [WBC], 'out of your whole heart' [AB2, Lns]. This noun is a figurative extension of the meaning of καρδία 'heart' and denotes the causative source of a person's psychological life in its various aspects with a special emphasis upon one's thoughts [LN]. The heart is the seat of one's physical, spiritual, and mental life, and in this verse it is referring to one's love for the Lord [BAGD].

c. ψυχή (LN 26.4) (BAGD 1.b.γ. p. 893): 'soul' [BAGD], 'inner self, mind, thoughts, feelings, heart, being' [LN]. The phrase ἐξ ὅλης τῆς ψυχῆς 'with all your soul' [AB1, BECNT, BNTC, NTC; all versions] is also translated 'out of your whole soul' [AB2, Lns], 'with all your being' [AB1], 'with your whole life' [WBC]. This noun denotes the essence of life in terms of thinking, willing, and feeling. In this verse ψυχή 'soul' is contrasted with καρδία 'heart' and διάνοια 'mind'. Because of the three terms, some have insisted that there must be at least three quite different parts of the human personality. Others have concluded that they are only three different perspectives that one may employ in thinking about or describing human personality. Still others contend that the use of the three terms only emphasizes the totality of the human personality with no clear-cut distinctions to be made between them. Certainly the referents involve considerable overlapping. One could translate with complete justification this sequence as 'you shall love the Lord your God with all your heart and life and mind.' In many languages it is impossible to distinguish satisfactorily between 'heart' and 'mind', making it necessary to translate this as 'you shall love the Lord your God with all that you desire and with all that you think' or 'you must love the Lord your God with all your being' [LN]. As the seat and center of the inner life in its many and varied aspects, the soul is referring here to one's feelings and emotions in regard to loving God [BAGD].

d. διάνοια (LN 26.14) (BAGD 1. p. 187): 'mind' [BAGD, LN]. The phrase ἐξ ὅλης τῆς διανοίας σου 'with all your mind' [BECNT, BNTC, NTC; all versions] is also translated 'with your whole mind' [WBC], 'out of your whole mind' [AB2, Lns], 'with all your understanding' [AB1]. This noun denotes the psychological faculty of understanding, reasoning, thinking, and deciding [LN]. It refers to one's moral understanding in this verse [BAGD].

e. ἰσχύς (LN 74.8) (BAGD p. 383): 'strength' [BAGD, LN], 'capability' [LN]. The phrase ἐξ ὅλης τῆς ἰσχύος σου 'with all your strength' [AB1, BECNT, BNTC, LN, NTC; all versions] is also translated 'with your whole strength' [WBC], 'out of your whole strength' [AB2, Lns], 'with your whole being' [LN]. This noun denotes an exceptional capability. In a number of languages the expression 'to love the Lord with one's strength' in the sense of physical strength is meaningless, therefore it may be necessary to translate it 'love the Lord your God as completely as you can' [LN].

QUESTION—What passage in the OT is Jesus quoting?

Jesus answered the scribe by first quoting from Deuteronomy 6:4. The passage in Deuteronomy refers only to a person's heart, soul; and strength and Mark added the phrase καὶ ἐξ ὅλης τῆς διανοίας σου 'and with all your mind' [WBC]. The reference to heart, soul, mind, and strength must not be over-analyzed. This simply means that a man should love God with all the faculties with which God has endowed him [NTC]. The terms καρδία 'heart', ψυχή 'soul', διάνοια 'mind', and ἰσχύς 'strength' do not refer to completely different parts or aspects of human personality. They are combined in this verse to emphasize the totality of the individual. In some languages the equivalent way of expressing this comprehensive aspect of personality is 'love him completely with all you feel and all you think' [LN (74.8)].

12:31 (The) second (is) this, 'You(sg)-shall-love your neighbor[a] as yourself.' There-is no other commandment greater[b] than-these."

LEXICON—a. πλησίον (LN 11.19) (BAGD 1.b. p. 672): 'neighbor' [AB2, BECNT, BNTC, LN, Lns, NTC, WBC; all versions except CEV, GW, TEV], 'fellow man' [AB1]. The clause 'You shall love your neighbor as yourself' is translated 'Love your neighbor as you love yourself' [GW, TEV], 'Love others as much as you love yourself' [CEV]. This noun denotes a person who lives next to others and is part of the 'in-group' that an individual identifies with. Translating the singular noun πλησίον[β] 'neighbor' may pose a problem since the singular form may be understood in a specific rather than a generic sense and give rise to the question 'which neighbor?' Therefore, one must often translate this as 'you must love your neighbors as you love yourselves' or 'you must love other people as you love yourselves' [LN].

b. μείζων (LN 87.28): 'greater' [all translations except CEV, NCV, TEV], 'more important' [CEV, NCV, TEV], 'better, superior to' [LN]. This adjective pertains to having a higher status in comparison to something else [LN].

QUESTION—What passage in the OT is Jesus quoting?

This second command is quoted from the Septuagint Greek translation of Leviticus 19:18 [AB1, NLTfn, WBC].

QUESTION—How are the first commandment and the second commandment related to the scribe's question about which is the *first* commandment of all?

Even though the scribe was not asking for a second commandment, Jesus wanted to show that the first commandment was not just the first of many different commandments but was one of two connected commands that exhausted the concept of righteousness [ICC]. These two commandments are inseparable [CGTC, EBC, Hb, NICNT, PNTC]. The first commandment corresponded to the first table of the Decalogue that deals with a person's relationship with God and the second commandment corresponds to the second table of the Decalogue that deals with a person's relationships with fellow human beings [BECNT; NLTfn, WBC]. In a sense the two commands form a single command. All the other remaining 611 commands in the Law can be understood as an explication of this two-part command [BECNT, NICNT]. The 'greatest commandment of all' includes both of these commandments together [BECNT, CGTC, ICC, Lns, NLTfn, Sw]. These two commandments are ranked first and second in importance over all the other commandments [BECNT, ESVfn, TRT].

QUESTION—How is a person to 'love' one's neighbor as one's self?

This command to 'love' refers not just to the emotions felt toward others but also to the good deeds done for others [AB2]. This assumes that people do love themselves and that this kind of love should be extended to one's neighbor [BECNT].

12:32 And the scribe said to-him, "Well-done,ᵃ teacher, upon truthᵇ you-say that (he)-is one, and there-is not another besidesᶜ him.

TEXT—Manuscripts reading ὅτι εἷς ἐστιν 'that he is one' are followed by GNT, which does not mention any variant reading. A variant reading is ὅτι εἷς ἐστι Θεός 'that he is one God' and it is followed by KJV.

LEXICON—a. καλῶς (LN **65.23**) (BAGD 4.c. p. 401): 'fine, good, excellent' [LN], 'rightly, correctly' [BAGD], not explicit [CEV]. This adverb is translated as an exclamation: 'Well done' [**LN**; TEV], 'Well said' [AB2, BAGD, BECNT, BNTC, WBC; NIV, NLT, REB], 'that was well said' [GW], 'Well' [KJV], 'That was a good answer' [NCV], 'Right!' [NASB, NTC; NASB], 'Quite right' [BAGD], 'You are right' [AB1; ESV, NRSV], 'That is true' [BAGD; NET], 'excellently (didst thou say)' [Lns]. This adverb pertains to events that measure up to their intended purpose [LN].

b. ἀλήθεια [LN 72.2, 70.4] (BAGD 3. p. 36): 'truth' [BAGD, LN (72.2)]. The idiom ἐπ' ἀληθείας εἶπες 'upon truth you say' is translated 'you have truthfully/truly said/stated' [AB2, BECNT, NTC; ESV, NASB, NRSV], 'You have spoken the truth by saying' [NLT], 'You were right when you said' [NCV], 'you have rightly said' [AB1], 'You are right to-say/in-saying' [BNTC; NET, NIV, REB], 'you are certainly right to say' [CEV], 'In truth have you said' [WBC], 'thou hast said the truth' [KJV], 'didst thou say of a truth' [Lns], 'You've told the truth' [GW], 'It is true, as you say' [TEV]. The noun ἀλήθεια 'truth' refers to that which is true and thus in accordance with what actually happened' [LN (72.2)]. The idiom ἐπ' ἀληθείας 'upon truth' pertains to something as being a real or actual event and means 'actually, really' [LN (70.4)].

c. πλήν (LN 89.130) (BAGD 2. p. 669): 'besides' [AB2, WBC; ESV, GW, NASB, NCV, NET, NRSV; similarly AB1; REB], 'except' [BAGD, LN, Lns], 'than' [BECNT], 'but' [BNTC, LN, NTC; KJV, NIV, TEV]. The phrase 'there is not another besides him' is translated 'there is only one God and no other' [NLT], 'there is only one God' [CEV]. This preposition indicates contrast and implies the validity of something irrespective of other considerations [LN].

12:33 And to-love him with all the heart and with all the understanding[a] and with all the strength and to-love the neighbor as oneself is greater-than[b] all the whole-burnt-offerings[c] and sacrifices."

TEXT—After the clause ἐξ ὅλης τῆς συνέσεως 'with all the understanding' one manuscript includes the clause καὶ ἐξ ὅλης τῆς ψυχῆς 'and with all the soul' and it is followed by KJV.

LEXICON—a. σύνεσις (LN 32.26) (BAGD 1. p. 788): 'intelligence' [LN]. The phrase ἐξ ὅλης τῆς συνέσεως 'with all the/one's/your understanding' [AB1, BECNT; BNTC, NTC; ESV, GW, KJV, NASB, NIV, NLT, NRSV, REB], 'out of one's whole understanding' [AB2], 'from/with the whole understanding' [Lns, WBC], 'with all his/our/your mind' [CEV, NCV, NET, TEV]. This noun denotes intelligence [LN]. It denotes the faculty of comprehension, intelligence, acuteness, and shrewdness [BAGD].

b. περισσότερος (LN 78.31) (BAGD 2. p. 651): greater than' [AB2], 'much greater than' [BECNT], 'much more than' [BAGD, WBC; ESV, NASB], 'far more than' [AB1, BNTC, NTC; REB], 'more than' [KJV], 'more important than' [CEV, GW, NCV, NET, NIV, NLT, TEV], 'much more important than' [NRSV], 'all the more' [LN]. This comparative adjective indicates a degree that is considerably in excess of some point on an implied or explicit scale of extent [LN].

c. ὁλοκαύτωμα (LN 53.24) (BAGD 1. p. 564): 'whole burnt offering' [BAGD, LN]. The phrase πάντων τῶν ὁλοκαυτωμάτων καὶ θυσιῶν 'all whole burnt offerings and sacrifices' [BECNT, WBC; ESV, NRSV] is also translated 'all whole-burnt-offerings or sacrifice' [AB1], 'all burnt offerings and sacrifices' [AB2, KJV, GW, NASB, NET, NIV], 'any whole-offerings and sacrifices' [REB], 'all the sacrifices and offerings that we could possibly make' [CEV], 'all the animals and sacrifices we offer to God' [NCV], 'all the whole burnt offering and the slaughter sacrifices' [Lns], 'to offer all of the burnt offerings and sacrifices required by the law' [NLT], 'to offer on the altar animals and other sacrifices to God' [TEV]. This noun denotes an animal that has been sacrificed to God and is completely burned up on the altar [LN]. The phrase 'whole burnt offerings and sacrifices' was a set phrase that occurs more than one hundred times in the Septuagint Greek translation of the OT [WBC].

QUESTION—How did the scribe change what Jesus had said in verse 30?

The scribe omitted 'with all your soul' and changed 'with all your mind' to 'with all your understanding', but Mark does not attribute any significance to these minor differences [BECNT].

QUESTION—What is the difference between whole-burnt-offerings and sacrifices?

The compound noun ὁλοκαυτωμάτων 'whole-burnt-offerings' refers to offerings that were wholly consumed by fire [BECNT, NTC], and θυσιῶν 'sacrifices' probably refers to 'all other types of sacrifices' [NTC]. The word θυσιῶν 'sacrifices' refers to all animal and vegetable offerings or sacrifices [TH]. Together they refer to all of the altar offerings [Lns].

12:34 And Jesus, having-seen him that he-answered wisely,[a] said to-him, "You are not far[b] from the kingdom of God." And no-one was-daring[c] to-question him any-longer.

TEXT—Manuscripts reading ἰδὼν αὐτόν ὅτι 'having seen him that' are given a C rating by GNT to indicate that choosing it over a variant text was difficult. Other manuscripts read ἰδὼν αὐτόν ὅτι 'having seen that'. None of the translations use the combination ἰδὼν αὐτόν ὅτι 'having seen him that'. The phrase 'seeing him that' is a fairly common construction in Greek that lends emphasis to the displaced word. The equivalent in English is 'seeing that he' [TH].

LEXICON—a. νουνεχῶς (LN 32.29) (BAGD p. 544): 'wisely' [BAGD, BECNT, LN, NTC, WBC; ESV, GW, NCV, NIV, NRSV], 'intelligently' [AB2, Lns; NASB], 'thoughtfully' [AB1, BNTC; NET, REB], 'with understanding' [LN], 'discreetly' [KJV]. The phrase 'that he had answered wisely' is translated 'that the man had given a sensible answer' [CEV], 'how wise his answer was' [TEV], 'how much the man understood' [NLT]. This adverb pertains to having the ability to reason and understand [LN].

b. μακράν (LN 83.30) (BAGD 1.a.β. p. 487): 'far' [BAGD, LN; all translations except GW, NCV], 'too far' [GW]. The phrase 'not far from' is translated 'close to' [NCV]. This adverb refers to being at a relatively great distance from another position [LN]. 'Far' is used figuratively so that being 'not far from the kingdom' means to be almost ready to enter the kingdom [BAGD].

c. imperf. act. indic. of τολμάω (LN 25.161) (BAGD 1.a. p. 821): 'to dare' [BAGD, LN; all translations except NASB, NCV], 'to have the courage' [BAGD], 'to be brave enough' [BAGD; NCV], 'to venture' [NASB]. This verb means to be so bold as to challenge or defy possible danger or opposition [LN].

QUESTION—What is meant by being οὐ μακρὰν 'not far' from the kingdom of God?

Here the 'kingdom of God' is a condition or relationship into which one enters during the present time [TH]. By telling the scribe that he was not far from the kingdom of God, Jesus was urging him to take the next step and enter this kingdom [Lns]. The man was close to entering the ranks of those who have responded to the message of the kingdom. Perhaps all that remained for the scribe was the repentance that was required by both John the Baptist and Jesus [WBC]. He was not far from the kingdom of God in the sense that he was in the presence of the one who had brought the kingdom of God, and he understood the meaning and spirit of Jesus' teachings, and knew the way into the kingdom. But was his love for God so complete that he was willing to repent, believe in the gospel, leave everything, deny himself, take up his cross, and follow Jesus? His nearness and fate are left unresolved. [BECNT].

DISCOURSE UNIT—12:35–40 [Hb; NIV, NLT]. The topic is whose son is the Messiah? [NLT], whose son is the Christ? [NIV], a counterattack by Jesus [Hb].

DISCOURSE UNIT—12:35–37 [CBC, Hb, NICNT; CEV, ESV, NET, NRSV]. The topic is the Messiah: David's son and Lord [NET], the question about David's son [NICNT; NRSV], about David's son [CEV], whose son is the Christ? [ESV], a question about the Messiah [CBC], the question concerning the Messiah's sonship [Hb].

DISCOURSE UNIT—12:35–37a [GW, TEV]. The topic is the question about the Messiah [TEV], how can David's son be David's lord? [GW].

12:35 And speaking/answering[a] Jesus was-saying (while) teaching in the temple, "How can[b] the scribes say that the Messiah[c] is[d] (the) son of David?

LEXICON—a. aorist pass. (deponent = act.) participle of ἀποκρίνομαι (LN 33.28, 33.184) (BAGD 1. p. 93): 'to speak out' [LN (33.28)], 'to answer' [LN (33.184)], 'to reply' [LN BAGD (33.184)]. The clause 'speaking Jesus was saying while teaching in the temple' is translated 'Jesus began to say, as he taught in the temple' [NASB], 'As/while Jesus was-teaching/taught in the temple, he said/asked' [AB1, BNTC, WBC; CEV, ESV, NCV; similarly NLT], 'While Jesus was teaching in the temple courtyard, he asked' [GW; similarly NET, NIV, NRSV], 'As he taught in the temple, Jesus went on to say' [REB], 'As Jesus was teaching in the Temple, he asked the question' [TEV]. Since Jesus was still in the Temple courts, some translations take the verb ἀποκριθείς to have its usual meaning of 'to answer' (LN 33.28) and connect it with the preceding verses. Then the clause 'answering Jesus was saying' is translated: 'Jesus answered and said' [AB2; KJV], 'Jesus, answering, went on to say' [Lns], 'answering, Jesus was speaking' [WBC], 'Jesus, having answered the opponent's questions, (was teaching in the temple)' [BECNT]. This verb introduces or continues a somewhat formal discourse. It occurs regularly with the verb λέγω 'to say' [LN (33.28)] or it responds to a question asking for information [LN (33.184)].

b. πῶς (LN 92.16) (BAGD 1.a. p. 732): 'how can' [AB1, WBC; CEV, ESV, GW, NRSV, REB, TEV], 'how is it that' [BECNT, BNTC, LN; NASB, NET, NIV], 'how' [AB2, BAGD, LN, Lns, WBC; KJV], 'why do' [NCV, NLT]. This adverb is an interrogative reference to the means: 'by what means?' [LN]. It asks how something has come to be, and in this verse it means 'with what right?' [BAGD].

c. Χριστός (LN 53.82) (BAGD 1. p. 887): With the article it is translated 'the Messiah' [AB1, BAGD, BECNT, LN, WBC; CEV, GW, NLT, NRSV, REB, TEV], 'the Christ' [AB2, BAGD, BNTC, Lns, NTC; ESV, KJV, NASB, NCV, NET, NIV]. This noun literally means 'the one who has been anointed'. In the NT it is a title for Jesus who is 'the Messiah, the Christ'. In other contexts, especially when it is without an article, Χριστός functions as part of the name 'Jesus Christ' [LN]. This word occurs at 1:1; 8:29; 9:41; 12:35; 13:21; 14:61; 15:32.

d. pres. act. indic. of εἰμί (LN 13.4): 'to be' [LN]. The clause υἱὸς Δαυίδ ἐστιν 'is the son of David' [AB2, BECNT, BNTC, NTC; ESV, KJV, NASB, NCV, NIV, NLT, NRSV] is also translated 'is "son of David"' [AB1, WBC], 'is a son of David' [Lns; REB], 'is David's son' [GW, NET], 'will be the descendant of David' [TEV], 'will come from the family of King David' [CEV]. This verb means to be identical with someone [LN].

QESTION—What is meant by the Messiah being the 'son' of David?

As a messianic title, 'the Son of David' indicates that the Messiah would be of the lineage of David [TH]. The messianic promises in the OT refer to the Messiah as a 'branch' of David' and a 'branch from Jesse's stump'. In rabbinic literature, the Messiah was referred to as the 'Son of David' [BECNT]. The question does not deny the fact that the Messiah would be a descendant of David. It is asking, 'How can they say that the Messiah is *merely* the son of David?' [NTC] or 'in what sense is the Messiah the son of David?' [EBC].

12:36 David himself said by[a] the Holy Spirit, '(The) Lord[b] said to-my Lord, "Sit at the right[c] of me, until I put[d] your enemies under your feet."'

TEXT—Manuscripts reading ὑποκάτω τῶν ποδῶν σου 'under your feet' are given a C rating by GNT to indicate that choosing it over a variant text was difficult. A variant reading is ὑποπόδιον τῶν ποδῶν σου '(a) footstool of your feet' and it is followed by KJV.

MARK 12:36

LEXICON—a. ἐν (LN 90.6) (BAGD I.5.d. p. 260): 'by' [LN; KJV, NCV, NET, NIV, NRSV], 'in' [ESV, NASB]. The clause 'David himself said by the Holy Spirit' is translated 'David, guided by the Holy Spirit, said' [GW], 'David himself, speaking under the inspiration of the Holy Spirit' [NLT], 'The Holy Spirit inspired David to say' [TEV], 'The Holy Spirit had David say' [CEV], 'It was David himself who said, when inspired by the Holy Spirit' [REB]. This preposition indicates the agent and often implies that the agent is being used as an instrument [BAGD].

b. κύριος (LN 12.9) (BAGD 2.c.α. p. 459): 'Lord' [BAGD, LN]. The phrase εἶπεν κύριος τῷ κυρίῳ μου 'the Lord said to my Lord' [all translations except NET]. This is also translated using the lower case with the second lord to distinguish between the two: 'the Lord said to my lord' [NET]. This noun denotes one who exercises supernatural authority over mankind and it is a title either for God or for Christ [LN].

c. δεξιός (LN 82.8, 87.34): 'right, right side' (LN 82.8). The clause κάθου ἐκ δεξιῶν μου 'sit at the right of me' is translated 'sit at my right hand' [ESV, NASB, NET, NIV, NRSV, REB; similarly KJV], 'sit at my right side' [CEV], 'sit here at my right side' [TEV], 'sit by me at my right side' [NCV], 'sit in the place of honor at my right hand' [NLT], 'take the highest position in heaven' [GW]. The adjective δεξιός 'right' pertains to being to the right of some point of reference [LN (82.8)]. The idiom ἐκ δεξιῶν καθίζω 'to sit on the right side of' means to be in a position of high status and to sit on the right side of a ruler is to be granted a high position [LN (87.34)].

d. aorist act. subj. of τίθημι (LN 85.32) (BAGD I.1.a,β. p. 816): 'to put' [BAGD, LN] The clause 'until I put your enemies under/beneath your feet' [NASB, NET, NIV, NRSV, REB, TEV] is also translated 'until I make your enemies into a footstool for you' [CEV], 'until I humble your enemies beneath your feet' [NLT], 'until I put your enemies under your feet' [ESV], 'until I put your enemies under your control' [GW, NCV]. This verb means to put or place in a particular location [LN].

QUESTION—What Scripture passage is Jesus quoting?

The Greek text is an exact quotation from the Septuagint Greek translation of Psalm 110:1 except for the omission of the definite article before the first κύριος 'Lord', which has no affect on the meaning of the sentence [TH].

QUESTION—Who are the two 'Lords' involved in the clause 'The Lord said to my Lord'?

The same Greek word is used for two different Hebrew words. The first 'Lord' refers to *YHWH* 'Yahweh' (God) and the second 'Lord' refers to *la'dhoni* 'my Lord' (referring to the Messiah). However, the translation should be equivalent to the Greek text 'The Lord said to my Lord'. If translating the equivalent to the Greek text 'The Lord said to my Lord' is too ambiguous, the meaning could be conveyed by 'The Lord said to my Messiah' or 'God said to my Lord' [TH].

QUESTION—What is meant by putting his enemies under his feet?

After a battle, the conqueror would symbolize his power over the defeated enemy by placing his foot upon the neck of his enemy lying before him in the dust [TRT]. This refers to Messiah's enthronement in heaven that would follow his rejection by his enemies [Hb]. This battle was against the demonic powers of the spiritual world [NICNT]. Those reading Mark would probably think it refers to Jesus' triumph over sin and death by his death and resurrection and his coming to judge the world [BECNT].

12:37 **David himself calls him 'Lord', and how[a] is-he his son?"**

LEXICON—a. πόθεν (LN **89.86**) (BAGD 3. p. 680): 'how, in what manner' [LN], 'why, in what way' [BAGD]. The phrase καὶ πόθεν ἐστιν 'and how is he' [AB2] is also translated 'how can he/the-Messiah be' [CEV, NET, NLT, REB], 'how then can he be' [AB1, NTC; NIV], 'then how is he' [**LN**], 'so how is he' [BECNT, WBC; ESV], 'so how can he/the-Christ/the-Messiah be' [BNTC; GW, NCV, NRSV, TEV], 'so in what sense is he' [NASB], 'whence is he then' [KJV; similarly Lns]. This adverb indicates how something took place [LN].

QUESTION—What is the purpose of this question?

The question is ironic. The point is not to deny the Davidic descent of the Messiah, but to suggest that because David calls him 'lord', a much higher view of his origin is necessary [Tay]. The Messiah is not David's son *merely* in the sense of being his descendant. He is far more than that! [NTC]. They must have a higher view of the true nature of the Messiah in that he is more than a man [Hb]. It is assumed that the son of anyone is in some sense subordinate or even inferior to his father [WBC]. Another view is that since no father calls his own son 'lord' and David calls the Messiah 'lord', it is inappropriate to call him 'the Son of David' [AB2].

DISCOURSE UNIT—12:37b–40 [GW, TEV]. The topic is Jesus warns against the teachers of the Law [TEV], Jesus disapproves of the example set by the scribes [GW].

And the large crowd was-listening to-him gladly.[a]

LEXICON—a. ἡδέως (LN 25.129) (BAGD p. 343): 'gladly' [AB2, BAGD, BECNT, LN, Lns; ESV, KJV, TEV], 'happily' [LN], with pleasure' [WBC; NCV], 'with delight' [NET, NIV, NRSV], 'eagerly' [AB1, BNTC; REB]. The adverb is also translated as a verb: 'enjoyed' [NTC; CEV, GW, NASB]. This adverb pertains to experiencing happiness and is based primarily upon the pleasure derived from something [LN].

QUESTION—How does this sentence relate to its context?

If this is the concluding comment to only what immediately precedes it, then it serves to identify the common people with Jesus. They sensed the discomfort of the scribes and responded enthusiastically to Jesus' teaching. If this refers to Jesus' ministry in the Temple as a whole, then this is a

general comment upon the popular response to his extended ministry that has been summarized in the five conflict-stories in verses 13–37 [NICNT].
1. This is connected with the immediately preceding section [AB1, AB2, BECNT, BNTC, CBC, EBC, Gnd, Hb, ICC, Lns, My, NAC, NICNT, NIGTC, NTC, TRT, WBC; all versions except GW, REB, TEV]. The contrast is between the vast Passover crowd and the comparatively few Jewish leaders [Hb]. Apparently the crowd enjoyed seeing those so-called experts stumped [EBC].
2. This begins the following section [CGTC, NCBC, Sw, Tay; GW, REB, TEV]. Jesus is making a general statement [Tay].

DISCOURSE UNIT—12:38–44 [CBC]. The topic is: contrasting the scribes and a widow.

DISCOURSE UNIT—12:38–40 [Hb, NICNT; CEV, ESV, NET, NRSV]. The topic is Jesus' warnings about the experts in the Law [NET], Jesus denounces the scribes [NRSV], Jesus condemns the Pharisees and the teachers of the Law of Moses [CEV], the condemnation of the scribes [Hb], the warning concerning the scribes [NICNT], beware of the scribes [ESV].

12:38 And in his teaching, he-was-saying, "Beware[a] of the scribes, the-ones liking to-walk-about in long-robes and (liking) greetings[b] in the marketplaces **12:39** and seats-of-honor[c] in the synagogues and places of honor[d] at the banquets,[e]

LEXICON—a. pres. act. impera. of βλέπω (LN 27.58) (BAGD 6. p. 143): 'to beware of' [BAGD, BECNT, BNTC, LN, Lns, WBC; ESV, KJV, NASB, NCV, NLT, NRSV, REB], 'to watch out for' [AB1, AB2, LN; GW, NET, NIV, TEV], 'to be on guard against' [NTC], 'to guard against' [CEV]. This verb is a figurative extension of the verb 'to see' and means to notice carefully, to be ready to learn about future dangers, and to be prepared to respond appropriately [LN]. This is a warning to be on guard against the evil influence of the scribes [Hb].

b. ἀσπασμός (LN **33.20**) (BAGD 1. p. 117): 'greetings' [AB2, BAGD, BECNT, LN, WBC; ESV, NLT], 'respectful greetings' [NASB], 'elaborate greetings' [NET], 'deferential greetings' [AB1], 'salutations' [Lns; KJV], 'formal salutations' [NTC]. This noun is also translated as a verb: 'to be greeted' [LN; CEV, GW, NCV, NIV], 'to be greeted with respect' [NRSV, TEV], 'to be greeted respectfully' [REB], 'to be acknowledged' [BNTC]. This noun denotes a set phrase used as a part of the process of greeting someone [LN]. It is a formal salutation [BAGD].

c. πρωτοκαθεδρία (LN 87.18) (BAGD p. 725): 'place of honor, best seat' [BAGD, LN], 'seat of honor, best place' [LN]. Located in the synagogues, the noun πρωτοκαθεδρίας 'seats of honor' [BECNT; NLT] is also translated 'the best seats' [AB1; ESV, NET, NRSV], 'the chief seats' [NTC; KJV, NASB, REB], 'the most important seats' [NCV, NIV], 'the front seats' [AB1, BNTC; CEV, GW], 'the first seats' [AB2, Lns], 'the reserved seats' [TEV]. This noun denotes a seat that is to be occupied only by a person of particular importance [LN]. The choice seats were reserved for the dignitaries and honored guests who would be seated up in front facing the rest of the congregation [NICNT, NTC, WBC].

- d. πρωτοκλισία (LN 87.18) (BAGD p. 725): 'place of honor, best seat' [BAGD, LN], 'seat of honor, best place' [LN]. Located at the banquets, the noun πρωτοκλισίας 'the places of honor' [AB1, BECNT, BNTC, NTC, WBC; ESV, GW, NASB, NET, NIV, NRSV, REB] is also translated 'the best seats' [CEV], 'the most important seats' [NCV], 'the first couches' [AB2], 'the first reclining places' [Lns], 'the best places' [TEV], 'the head table' [NLT], 'the uppermost rooms' [KJV]. This noun has the same definition as πρωτοκαθεδρία in the preceding lexical item c [BAGD, LN].

QUESTION—Does the participle τῶν θελόντων 'the ones liking (to walk about in long robes, etc.)' refer only to the scribes who had those characteristics or to all the scribes as a class?

1. It is descriptive of the scribes as a class [AB1, BECNT, BNTC, NCBC, NIGTC; CEV, GW, NCV, NET, NIV, NLT; probably those translations that have a comma after the noun 'scribes': ESV, KJV, NRSV, REB, TEV].
2. It is restrictive and identifies which of the scribes to beware of [AB2, Hb, NAC, TH; NASB]: beware of those scribes who like to walk about, etc. Jesus was telling the people which kind of scribes they should not trust [Hb]. Jesus was not accusing all scribes of being like this [TH].

QUESTION—What were the στολαῖς 'long robes'?

The long robes were worn primarily by priests but probably by other religious men as well [WBC] They may not have been just the long flowing robes worn by religious men of high standing but also the distinguished garments worn by important men who wore them to announce their wealth [BECNT].

12:40 the-ones devouring[a] the houses of-the widows and for-a-pretense[b] praying long[c] (prayers). These will-receive (the) the greater condemnation."

LEXICON—a. pres. act. participle of κατεσθίω (LN 23.11, 57.247) (BAGD 2. p. 422): 'to devour' [AB2, BECNT, LN, Lns; ESV, NASB,], 'to eat up' [LN (23.11)], 'to appropriate dishonestly, to rob' [LN (57.247)]. The clause οἱ κατεσθίοντες τὰς οἰκίας τῶν χηρῶν 'the ones devouring the houses of widows' is translated 'those-who/who/they devour widow's houses' [NTC; ESV, KJV, NASB, NIV, NRSV], 'they devour the estates of widows' [WBC], 'they devour widow's property' [NET], 'They eat up the property of widows' [BNTC; similarly REB], 'they rob widows of their homes' [LN], 'they rob widows by taking their houses' [GW], 'But they cheat widows out of their homes' [CEV], 'As for those men who appropriate widow's houses' [AB1], 'But they cheat widows and steal their houses' [NCV], 'They take advantage of widows and rob them of

their homes' [TEV], 'Yet they shamelessly cheat widows out of their property' [NLT]. This verb means to devour something completely [LN (23.11)], and it is used figuratively in this verse to mean to take over the property of someone else by dishonest means [LN (57.247)]. To eat up widows' houses means to appropriate the houses illegally [BAGD]. The 'houses' they devour is a summary way of saying their belongings and their fortunes [TH].
- b. πρόφασις (LN 88.230) (BAGD 2. p. 722): 'pretense' [BAGD, LN], 'for a pretext; for appearance's sake' [BAGD]. The phrase προφάσει 'as/for a pretense' [AB2, Lns; ESV, KJV] is also translated 'in pretense' [WBC], 'for the sake of appearance' [NRSV], 'for appearance's sake' [AB1, BAGD; NASB, REB], 'for a pretext' [BAGD], 'to make themselves look good' [GW], 'try to make themselves look good' [NCV], 'as/for show' [BECNT, BNTC; NTC; NET, NIV], 'then make a show of' [TEV], 'just to show off' [CEV]. Their long prayers were used to make them look good [Gnd, NICNT] and served as a mask for their greed [EBC].
- c. κρίμα (LN 56.30) (BAGD 4.b. p. 450): 'condemnation' [BAGD, LN]. The clause 'These will receive the/a greater condemnation' [AB1, AB2, BNTC; ESV, NASB, NRSV; similarly BECNT] is also translated 'these shall receive the more abundant judgment' [Lns], 'these will receive the harsher judgment' [WBC], 'they will receive a greater punishment' [NCV], 'these shall receive greater damnation' [KJV], 'these men will receive a more severe punishment' [NET], 'they shall receive a heavier sentence' [NTC], 'will receive a sentence all the more severe' [REB], 'They will be punished most of all' [CEV], 'Their punishment will be all the worse!' [TEV], 'Such men will be punished most severely' [NIV], 'The scribes will receive the most severe punishment' [GW], 'Because of this, they will be more severely punished' [NLT]. This verb denotes the condemnation of a person who is judged to be guilty and liable to punishment [LN]. It refers to a sentence of condemnation and may include the subsequent punishment as well [BAGD]. On the day of judgment they will receive a more severe sentence from God [TH]. The punishment will be greater than the punishment they would have received if they had made no pretences of piety [Hb, ICC].

QUESTION—How did the scribes 'devour' the houses of widows?

Since it is uncertain what this expression means, commentaries list many possibilities. It is clear, however, that the scribes were in some way taking financial advantage of the vulnerable and needy widows [BECNT].

QUESTION—How is the phrase καὶ προφάσει 'and for a pretense' to be connected?
- 1. It is to be connected with the action preceding it since the lengthy prayers were for the purpose of deceiving the widows [AB1, BECNT, BNTC, EGT, Hb, NIGTC, Sw]. Presumably these prayers were made for the widows with the purpose of getting money from them [EGT]. Perhaps there was a payment from the widows for the prayers of the scribes

[NIGTC]. As a pretended expression of their love for God, their real aim was to win the esteem of their victims [Hb]. They preyed upon needy widows while clothing their behavior with a religious veneer [BECNT].

2. Their lengthy prayers were for the purpose of deceiving people in general [BAGD, CBC, ICC, Lns, NICNT, Tay, TH, WBC; CEV]. They did so for appearance's sake [BAGD]. To cover up their taking advantage of the widows, they publicly prayed to impress men [ICC, Lns; GW NASB, NCV, NLT, NRSV, REB, TEV]. By enhancing their status through implied piety, they could then take advantage of less influential people such as the widows [WBC]. This additional accusation is that the scribes made their public prayers an opportunity to appear deeply pious in order to win the esteem of men [NICNT].

DISCOURSE UNIT—12:41–44 [Hb, NICNT; CEV, ESV, GW, NASB, NCV, NET, NIV, NLT, NRSV, TEV]. The topic is a widow's offering [CEV, ESV, NET, NIV, NLT, NRSV, TEV], the widow who gave everything [NICNT], a widow's contribution [GW], the widow's mite [NASB], commendation of the widow's giving [Hb], true giving [NCV].

12:41 And having-sat-down opposite[a] the offering-box,[b] he was-observing how the crowd was-putting copper-money[c] into the offering-box. And many rich-people were-putting-in much (money).[d]

TEXT—Manuscripts reading καθίσας κατέναντι τοῦ γαζοθυλακίου 'having sat down opposite the treasury' are given a B rating by GNT to indicate that the text is almost certain. A variant reading is καθίσα ὁ Ἰησοῦς κατέναντι τοῦ γαζοθυλακίου 'Jesus having sat down opposite the treasury' and it is followed by KJV. Other variant readings are κατέναντι τοῦ γαζοθυλακίου καθεζόμενος ὁ Ἰησοῦς 'Jesus sitting opposite the treasury', and ἑστὼς ὁ Ἰησοῦς κατέναντι τοῦ γαζοθυλακίου 'Jesus standing opposite the treasury'.

LEXICON—a. κατέναντι (LN 83.42) (BAGD 2.a. p. 421): 'opposite' [AB2, BAGD, BECNT, BNTC, LN, NTC, WBC; ESV, NASB, NET, NIV, NRSV, REB], 'over against' [Lns; KJV], 'in front of, before, across from' [LN], 'facing' [GW], 'near' [CEV, NCV, NLT, TEV], 'by' [AB1]. This preposition refers to a position opposite another position [LN]. Jesus sat down on a bench where he could watch the people bring their offerings to put them in one of the thirteen trumpet-shaped boxes that were used for that purpose [EBC, NICNT].

b. γαζοφυλάκιον (LN 6.141) (BAGD p. 149): 'offering box' [LN, WBC; CEV, NET], 'temple offering box' [GW], 'contribution box' [BAGD], 'collection box in the temple' [NLT], 'Temple money box' [NCV], 'treasury' [AB1, AB2, BECNT, BNTC, NTC, WBC; ESV, KJV, NASB, NRSV], 'Temple treasury' [REB, TEV], 'treasury chest' [Lns], 'the place where the offerings were put' [NIV]. This noun denotes a large box in which offerings were placed [LN]. This was probably one of the thirteen contribution boxes or receptacles that were in the form of trumpets with broad bases and narrow openings at the top. They were placed under the colonnade in the Court of the Women which may also have been known as the 'treasury' [TH]. Each of the thirteen receptacles for receiving religious and charitable contributions bore an inscription indicating what the money would be used for [Hb].

c. χαλκός (LN **6.72**) (BAGD 2. p. 875): 'copper coins' [BAGD, **LN**], 'bronze money' [LN], 'money' [BAGD; all translations except Lns; CEV, NET], 'coins' [Lns; NET], 'small change, [BAGD], 'gifts' [CEV]. This noun denotes a coin of bronze or copper that had little value [LN]. This word refers to the copper money given by most people at the temple but does not refer to money in general [My]. Later papyrus usage shows that this word denoted money generally. While the majority of the givers would only have copper coins to offer, the rich people made their offerings in silver coins [Hb].

d. πολύς (LN 59.11) (BAGD I.1.a.α. p. 687): 'much' [BAGD, LN, Lns; KJV], 'large amounts' [AB2, BECNT, NTC; GW, NET, NIV, NLT, REB], 'large sums' [AB1, BNTC, WBC; ESV, NASB, NRSV], 'large sums of money' [NCV], 'a lot of money' [CEV, TEV]. This pronominal adjective indicates a relatively large quantity [LN].

12:42 And having-come, one poor widow put-in two *leptas*,[a] which is a-*kodrantes*.[b]

LEXICON—a. λεπτόν, λεπτός (LN 6.79) (BAGD 2. p. 472): 'lepton' [AB2, LN, Lns], 'copper coin' [AB1; NET], 'a small/little copper coin' [BAGD; ESV, NASB, NCV, NRSV, TEV], 'a very small copper coin' [NTC; NIV], 'a small coin' [BECNT, **LN**, WBC; GW, NLT], 'a tiny coin' [BNTC], 'a coin' [CEV; REB], 'a mite' [KJV]. This noun denotes a copper coin worth 1/2 of a *quadron* or 1/128 of a *denarius*. In practically all instances, references to a *lepton* may be made in terms of 'a very small coin', 'a coin with very little value', or 'money that was not worth very much' [LN]. The *lepton* was the smallest Jewish coin in circulation [TH]. The fact that this poor widow gave two *leptas* is significant since she could easily have kept one for herself [BNTC, EGT, NICNT, Sw].

b. κοδράντης (LN 6.78) (BAGD p. 437): 'quadrans' [AB2, LN, Lns], 'penny' [BECNT, BNTC, LN, WBC; ESV, NET, NRSV, REB, TEV], 'a fraction of a penny' [NTC; NIV], 'a farthing' [KJV], 'a cent' [NASB], 'a few cents/pennies' [CEV, NCV], 'less than a cent' [AB1; GW], not explicit [NLT]. This noun denotes a Roman copper coin worth 1/4 of an *assarion* or 1/64 of a *denarius* [LN]. Mark gives the value of the two Hebrew *leptons* for the benefit of his Roman readers [EBC, Gnd, Hb, ICC, NICNT, Sw, TH].

12:43 And having-summoned his disciples, he said to-them, "Truly I-say to-you that this poor widow has-put-in more-than[a] all the ones-putting-into the offering-box."

LEXICON—a. πλεῖον (LN 78.28): 'more than, to a greater degree, even more' [LN]. The clause πλεῖον πάντων ἔβαλεν τῶν βαλλόντων εἰς τὸ γαζοφυλάκιον is literally 'more than all have put in, the ones who are putting into the offering-box' and it is translated 'has put in more than all those who are contributing to the offering-box/treasury' [ESV, NRSV], 'has given more than all the others who are making contributions' [NLT], 'threw in more than all those throwing into the treasury chest' [Lns], 'gave more than all those who are contributing to the treasury' [AB1], 'has thrown in more than all of those who have been throwing into the treasury' [AB2], 'put in more than all the contributors to the treasury' [NASB], 'put in more than all the others who contributed money into the treasury' [BECNT], 'has put in more than all those who are contributing to the treasury' [NRSV], 'has thrown in more than all who have contributed to the treasury' [BNTC], 'has put more into/in the offering-box/treasury than all the others' [NET, NIV, TEV], 'has put-in/given more than all the others' [CEV, GW], 'gave more than all those rich people' [NCV], 'dropped more into the treasury than all the others' [NTC], 'has given more than all those giving to the treasury' [REB], 'has cast in more money than all who cast money into the offering box' [WBC], 'hath cast more in, than all they which have cast into the treasury' [KJV]. This pronominal adjective indicates a degree which surpasses in some manner a point on a scale of extent [LN].

QUESTION—In what way did the poor widow put more into the offering box than the other people?

It was not the amount of the gift but the heart of the giver that mattered most [NTC]. Because the poor widow gave all she had and the rich people gave from their surplus, God considered the widow's contribution to be a greater offering [ESVfn]. 'More than all' does not deny the value of their gifts, but insists that *they all gave less* than the widow. Jesus' words may even mean '*more than all those put together*' [Hb]. It is the quality of the gift that makes it more [Lns]. All of the others gave in their superfluity while she gave all she had to live on [Sw, Tay]. This could be taken in either a distributive sense meaning 'she gave more than any of them,' or in a collective sense meaning 'she gave more than all of them put together.' The contrast between the single widow and the group of rich people is not focused on the quantity that was given but on the quantity that was retained [AB2]. What this poor widow has put in the offering-box surpasses all that the rest have put in [TH]. Her offering was more than all the gifts of others both in proportion and the spirit in which she gave it. It was in the latter that she was richer than all of them [EBC].

12:44 Because they-all put-in from their abounding,^a but from her need^b she-has-put-in as-much-as she-had—all she-had to-live-on.^c"

LEXICON—a. pres. act. participle of περισσεύω (LN 59.52) (BAGD 1.a.β. p. 650): 'to abound, to be in abundance, to be a lot of, to exist in a large quantity, to be left over' [LN]. The clause 'from their abounding' is translated 'from their superfluity' [AB1], 'from/out-of their abundance' [AB2, BECNT, NTC, WBC; CEV, ESV, NRSV; similarly KJV], 'out of their surplus' [BNTC; NASB], 'out of their wealth' [NET, NIV], 'the others...had more than enough' [REB], 'what they could spare' [GW], 'what they had to spare' [TEV], 'what they did not need' [CEV, NCV], 'what is over and above to them' [Lns], 'a tiny part of their surplus' [NLT]. This verb is a derivative of περισσός 'abundant' and means to be or exist in abundance. It implies being considerably more than what would be expected [LN].

b. ὑστέρησις (LN 57.37) (BAGD p. 849): 'need' [LN]. The clause ἐκ τῆς ὑστερήσεως αὐτῆς 'from her need' is translated 'out of her need' [BNTC], 'out of her poverty' [AB1, BECNT; ESV, NASB, NET, NIV, NRSV], 'out of her scarcity' [AB2], 'out-of/in her poverty' [NTC; GW], 'poor as she is' [NLT, TEV], 'of/from her want' [Lns, WBC; KJV], 'with less than enough' [REB], 'she/this-woman is very poor' [CEV, NCV], This noun denotes what is lacking or needed [LN].

c. βίος (LN 57.18) (BAGD 3. p. 142): 'possessions, property, livelihood' [LN], 'means of substance, worldly goods' [BAGD]. The clause ὅλον τὸν βίον αὐτῆς 'all/everything she had to live on' [AB1, BECNT, BNTC, LN; all versions except CEV, KJV, NET] is also translated 'everything she had' [NET], 'her whole living' [AB2, Lns, NTC], 'even all her living' [KJV], 'her whole life' [WBC], 'now she doesn't have a cent to live on' [CEV]. This noun denotes the resources which one has as a means of living [LN].

QUESTION—What is the function of this verse?

Jesus is explaining the reason he had for setting such a high value on the poor widow's gift [Lns]. Proportionally the widow gave the most [Hb].

DISCOURSE UNIT—13:1–37 [CBC, Hb, NICNT, PNTC; NCV, NLT, REB]. The topic is the Olivet discourse [NICNT], an eschatological discourse to the disciples [Hb], watchfulness in tribulation and triumph [PNTC], Jesus foretells the future [NLT], the temple will be destroyed [NCV], the destruction of the temple and the return of the Son of Man [CBC], warnings about the end [REB].

DISCOURSE UNIT—13:1–31 [NIV]. The topic is the signs of the end of the age.

DISCOURSE UNIT—13:1–30 [GW]. The topic is Jesus teaches disciples on the mount of Olives.

DISCOURSE UNIT—13:1–23 [NASB]. The topic is the things to come.

DISCOURSE UNIT—13:1-8 [NRSV]. The topic is the destruction of the temple foretold.

DISCOURSE UNIT—13:1-2 [Hb; CEV, ESV, NET, TEV]. The topic is the prediction about the temple [Hb], Jesus foretells destruction of the temple [ESV], Jesus speaks of the destruction of the temple [TEV], the temple will be destroyed [CEV], the destruction of the temple [NET].

13:1 **And (as) he was-going-out[a] of the temple, one of-his disciples says to-him, "Teacher, look![b] What-sort-of[c] stones and what-sort-of[c] buildings!"**

LEXICON—a. pres. mid./pass. (deponent = act.) participle of ἐκπορεύομαι (LN **15.40**) (BAGD 244): 'to go out' [BAGD, LN], 'to depart, to leave from within' [LN]. The clause 'as he was going out of the temple' is translated 'As he came/went out of the temple' [WBC; ESV, KJV, NRSV], 'As he was coming/going out of the temple/Temple' [AB2, NTC; NASB], 'And as he (Jesus) was proceeding out of the temple' [BECNT], 'While he is going out of the Temple' [Lns]. 'As he/Jesus was leaving the temple/Temple' [AB1; CEV, NCV, NIV, NLT, REB, TEV; similarly BNTC], 'When he had gone out of the Temple' [**LN**]. Some are more specific about the location in the temple complex: 'As Jesus was going out of the temple courtyard' [GW], 'Now as Jesus was going out of the temple courts' [NET]. This verb means to move out of an enclosed or well defined two or three-dimensional area [LN].

b. ἴδε (LN 91.13) (BAGD 1. p. 369): 'look, listen, pay attention' [LN], 'see' [BAGD]. Some translate ἴδε 'look' as a separate exclamation: 'Teacher, look! Such stones…!' [AB2], 'Look, Teacher! How big the stones are!' [NCV], 'Look, Teacher! What massive stones!' [NIV], 'Look, Teacher, what large/huge stones…!' [BNTC, NTC; NRSV, REB], 'Look, Teacher! What wonderful stones…!' [TEV], 'Teacher, behold, what wonderful stones!' [WBC], 'Look, Teacher, what wonderful stones…!' [ESV], 'Rabbi, look—what great stones…! [AB1], 'Teacher, see, what stones…!' [Lns]. Others translate ἴδε 'look' as the main verb of the sentence: 'Teacher, look at these beautiful stones' [CEV], 'Teacher, behold what wonderful stones…!' [NASB], 'Teacher, look what (huge) stones…!' [BECNT], 'Teacher, look at these huge/tremendous stones…!' [GW, NET], 'Teacher, look at the impressive stones in the walls' [NLT], 'Master, see what manner of stones…are here!' [KJV]. This interjection is a prompter of attention that also serves to emphasize the statement following it [LN]. It points out something the speaker wants to draw attention to [BAGD].

c. ποταπός (LN 58.30) (BAGD 1.a. p. 695): 'what sort of, what kind of' [BAGD, LN], 'what manner of' [KJV], 'what' [Lns], 'such' [AB2]. Sometimes the context calls for the meaning 'how great, how wonderful' [BAGD]. In regard to the stones, ποταπός refers to them being 'massive' [NIV], 'big' [NCV], 'large' [NRSV], 'huge' [BECNT, BNTC; GW, REB], 'great' [AB1], 'tremendous' [NET], 'wonderful' [WBC; ESV,

NASB, TEV], 'beautiful' [CEV], 'impressive' [NLT]. In regard to the buildings, ποταπός refers to them being 'wonderful' [AB1, BNTC, WBC; CEV, ESV, NASB, TEV], 'beautiful' [BECNT; GW, NCV], 'fine' [REB], 'magnificent' [NIV, NLT], 'tremendous' [NET], 'large' [NRSV].

QUESTION—What was impressive about the walls and buildings of the Temple complex?

Some of the surviving stones in the retaining wall weigh fifty tons or more. One is forty feet long and weighs about three hundred tons. The walls towered more than eighty feet above the roadways that circled the structure [AB2]. In addition to the building itself, the temple area included porticoes and clustered courts that were flanked by beautiful colonnades. This temple area took up about one-sixth of the city of Jerusalem [EBC]. It dominated the Kidron gorge as an object of dazzling beauty and appeared to be like a mountain of white marble decorated with gold [NICNT].

13:2 And Jesus said to him, "Do-you-see these great[a] buildings? There-will-not be-left[b] here a-stone upon a-stone that will- not -be-thrown-down.[c]"

TEXT—Manuscripts reading μὴ ἀφεθῇ ὧδε 'there will not be left here' are given a B rating by GNT to indicate it was regarded to be almost certain. A variant reading is μὴ ἀφεθῇ 'there will not be left' and it is followed by KJV, REB.

LEXICON—a. μέγας (LN 79.123) (BAGD 1.a. p. 497): 'great' [BAGD, LN; all translations except CEV, GW], 'huge' [CEV], 'large' [BAGD, LN; GW], 'big' [LN]. This adjective describes something as being of a large size relative to the norm for that class of objects [LN].

b. aorist pass. subj. of ἀφίημι (LN 85.62) (3.a. p. 126): 'to be left, to be allowed to remain' [LN], 'to be left standing' [BAGD]. The clause 'there will not be left here a stone upon a stone' is translated 'there surely won't be left a stone upon a stone' [AB2; similarly Lns], 'not one stone will be left here upon another' [WBC; NRSV; similarly NIV, REB], 'there will not be left one stone upon another' [ESV, KJV], 'there will not be left here one stone upon another' [BECNT, NTC], 'there will not be one stone left here on another' [BNTC], 'not one stone will be left upon/on/on-top-of another' [NASB, NCV, NET, NLT], 'not one of these stones will be left on top of another' [GW], 'not one/a-single stone here will be left in its place' [CEV, TEV]. This verb means to permit something to stay in place [LN]. The double negative of the phrase οὐ μὴ 'not not' is an emphatic '*not* (be left)' [TH], and it stresses the certainty of the fulfillment of Jesus' words [Hb].

c. aorist pass. subj. of καταλύω (LN 20.54) (BAGD 1.a. p. 414): 'to be thrown down' [BECNT, BNTC, NTC, WBC; ESV, KJV, NIV, NRSV, REB, TEV], 'to be thrown down to the ground' [NCV], 'to be torn down' [LN; CEV, GW, NASB, NET], 'to be dislodged' [Lns], 'to be destroyed' [LN], 'to be completely demolished' [NLT]. This verb means to destroy something completely by tearing it down and dismantling it [LN].

QUESTION—Why did Jesus ask his disciples if they could see the great buildings of the temple?'

Jesus asked this question in order to fix their attention on the material structure of the buildings [Hb]. He did this in order to prepare them for the astonishing announcement he would make [EGT, Hb].

QUESTION—What will happen to the stones?

This means that no two joining stones will be left standing together. It indicates how thorough the destruction of the temple will be [TH]. It is hyperbolical statement used to emphasize the totality of the predicted destruction [NTC]. This prediction was fulfilled when Jerusalem was destroyed by the Roman soldiers in A.D. 70. After fire had raged through the Temple precincts, Titus ordered that the Temple buildings be leveled to the ground [NICNT].

DISCOURSE UNIT—13:3–35 [NIGTC]. The topic is the explanatory discourse: the end of the old order.

DISCOURSE UNIT—13:3–13 [CEV, ESV, TEV]. The topic is the signs of the close of the age [ESV], a warning about trouble [CEV], troubles and persecutions [TEV].

DISCOURSE UNIT—13:3–8 [NET]. The topic is the signs of the end of the age.

DISCOURSE UNIT—13:3–4 [Hb]. The topic is the question by four disciples.

13:3 And (as) he was-sitting on the Mount of-Olives opposite the temple, Peter and James and John and Andrew were-questioning him privately,[a] **13:4** "Tell us, when will- these (things) -happen,[b] and what (will be) the sign[c] when all these (things) are-about to-be-accomplished[d]?"

LEXICON—a. κατ' ἰδίαν (LN 28.67). The idiom κατ' ἰδίαν 'according to that which is private' is translated 'privately' [AB1, AB2, BECNT, BNTC, LN, NTC; all versions except CEV, NCV, TEV], 'in private' [Lns, WBC; CEV, TEV]. The clause '…were questioning him privately' is translated 'Later…he was alone with Peter, James, John, and Andrew. They asked Jesus…' [NCV]. This idiom refers to something occurring in a private setting so as to keep it from being known publicly [LN]. This idiom occurs at 4:34; 6:31; 7:33; 9:2, 28; 13:3.

b. fut. middle (deponent = act.) indic. of εἰμί (LN 13.104): 'to happen' [AB1, BNTC, LN, NTC; CEV, GW, NCV, NET, NIV, NLT, REB], 'to be' [AB2, BECNT, LN, Lns, WBC; ESV, KJV, NASB, NRSV, TEV]. This verb means to occur in regard to some event [LN].

c. σημεῖον (LN 33.477) (BAGD 1. p. 747): 'sign' [LN; all translations except TEV]. The phrase τί τὸ σημεῖον 'what will be the sign' is translated 'what will happen to show that the time has come' [TEV]. This noun denotes an event that is regarded to have some special meaning [LN].

d. pres. pass. infin. of συντελέω (LN 68.22) (BAGD 1. or 2. p. 792): 'to be accomplished, to be ended' [LN], 'to be completed, to be finished' [BAGD, LN], 'to be brought to an end' [BAGD]. The clause 'when all these things are about to be accomplished' [BECNT, NTC, WBC; ESV; similarly Lns] is also translated 'when all these things will be accomplished' [AB2], 'that all these things are about to be accomplished' [NRSV], 'that they/all-these-things are about to take place' [CEV, NET], 'that these/all-these things are about to be fulfilled' [NLT, REB], 'that they are all about to be fulfilled' [NIV], 'when all these things are going to be fulfilled' [NASB], 'when the fulfillment of all these things is near' [AB1], 'when all these things shall be fulfilled' [KJV], 'that all these things are about to be fulfilled' [BNTC], 'that they are going to happen' [NCV], 'the time has come for all these things to take place' [TEV], 'when all of this will come to an end' [GW]. This verb means to bring an activity to a successful finish [LN].

QUESTION—Why is the singular verb ἐπηρώτα 'he was questioning' translated 'Peter and James and John and Andrew *were* questioning'?

The subject of this singular verb must be Peter who was acting as spokesman for this group of four disciples [NIGTC]. All of the translations include all four as the subject of the verb.

QUESTION—What is meant by the four disciples questioning Jesus 'privately'?

1. These four disciples were the only ones who were with Jesus [AB2, BNTC, CBC, EBC, Gnd, NICNT, NIGTC, PNTC, Sw, Tay, WBC]. The other eight disciples remained at a distance [Sw].
2. These four disciples were talking with Jesus somewhere away from the crowd [Hb, Lns, NTC]. The parallel passage in Matthew 24:3 says '*the disciples* came to him privately' and Luke 21:7 merely states '*they* asked him'. Although 'privately' means that this took place away from the crowd, it is not known if all of the Twelve were there [Hb]. This was probably done in private with the rest of the disciples listening to what Jesus said [Lns].

QUESTION—What is meant by 'all these things' in the second question?

1. This second question refers to the coming of the Messiah at the close of the age (AB2, BNTC, CGTC, EBC, ESVfn, Gnd, Hb, Lns, NAC, NTC, PNTC]. It is an abbreviated account of what is stated more fully in Matthew 24:3 where the disciples ask 'Tell us when these things will be, and what will be the sign of your coming and of the close of the age?' [CGTC, NTC, Tay]. What the disciples meant by 'the sign' was the sign of Jesus' own coming at the end of the world [Lns]. The disciples thought of the destruction of the temple as one of the events that accompanied the end of the age. So they wanted a sign by which they would know that the destruction of the temple was about to occur and that the end of the age was approaching [EBC]. The destruction of Jerusalem functions as a foreshadowing of the final judgment that will occur when Jesus returns [ESVfn].

2. This second question also refers to the destruction of the temple [BECNT, ICC, NICNT, NIGTC, TH, WBC]. The plural 'these things' refers to different aspects of the same event [BECNT]. The first question asks when the destruction of the temple precincts will take place and the second question asks about signs that will indicate when that would happen [WBC].

DISCOURSE UNIT—13:5–37 [Hb]. The topic is a prophetic answer to the disciples.

DISCOURSE UNIT—13:5–13 [Hb]. The topic is about warnings to the disciples.

13:5 And Jesus began[a] to-say to-them, "Watch-out[b] lest someone deceives[c] you. **13:6** Many will come in my name[d] saying, 'I am[e] (he)!' and they-will-deceive many.

LEXICON—a. aorist mid. indic. of ἄρχομαι (LN 68.1): 'to begin' [LN; ESV, KJV, NASB, NCV, NET, NRSV], 'to commence' [LN]. The phrase 'began to say to them' [AB2, BECNT, Lns, NTC] is also translated 'began to speak to them' [WBC], 'began to tell them' [BNTC], 'said to them' [NIV, TEV], 'answered them' [GW; similarly CEV], 'began' [AB1; REB], 'replied' [NLT]. This verb means to initiate an action, process, or state of being [LN]. The words 'began to say' is a common construction used twenty-six times in Mark [BECNT].

b. pres. act. impera. of βλέπω (LN 27.58) (BAGD 6. p. 143): 'to watch out' [BAGD, BECNT, LN, WBC; CEV, NET, NIV, TEV], 'to look out' [AB2], 'to be on guard' [BNTC; REB], 'to be careful' [GW, NCV], 'to see that' [ESV], 'to see to it' [Lns; NASB], 'to beware' [BAGD, LN; NRSV], 'to pay attention' [LN], 'to take care' [AB1, NTC], 'to take heed' [KJV]. His warning is translated 'Don't let anyone mislead you' [NLT]. This is a figurative extension of meaning of the verb 'to see' and means to be ready to learn about future dangers or needs and to be prepared to respond appropriately [LN].

c. aorist act. subj. of πλανάω (LN 31.8) (BAGD 1.b. p. 665): 'to deceive' [BAGD, LN, Lns, NTC; GW, KJV, NIV], 'to mislead' [AB1, BAGD, BNTC, LN, WBC; NASB, NET, NLT, REB], 'to lead astray' [AB2, BECNT; ESV, NRSV], 'to fool' [CEV, NCV, TEV]. This is a figurative extension of meaning of the verb 'to cause to wander off the path' and means to cause someone to hold a wrong view and thus be mistaken [LN].

d. ὄνομα (LN 33.126) (BAGD I.4.c.ε. p. 573): 'name' [BAGD, LN]. The clause 'will come in my name' [AB2, BECNT, BNTC, Lns, NTC, WBC; ESV, KJV, NASB, NET, NCV, NLT, NRSV] is also translated 'will come using my name' [AB1, BAGD; GW, NCV], 'will come claiming my name' [REB], 'claiming to speak for me' [TEV], 'will claim to be me' [CEV]. This noun denotes the proper name of a person [LN]. The context

seems to demand the meaning 'representing to be me' (or 'as though they were I') since they will also say 'I am he' [TH].
- e. pres. act. indic. of εἰμί (LN 13.4) (BAGD II.5 p. 224): 'to be' [LN]. The statement Ἐγώ εἰμι 'I am he' [AB1, AB2, BECNT, BNTC, NTC, WBC; ESV, GW, NASB, NET, NIV, NRSV, REB, TEV] is also translated 'I myself am he' [Lns], 'I am the One' [NCV], 'I am the Messiah' [NLT], 'I am Christ' [KJV], 'they will use my name' [CEV]. This verb means to be identical with someone or something [LN]. The predicate must be understood from the context [BAGD]. This is a claim to be the Messiah [EBC, NICNT, TH, WBC] and Matthew 24:5 makes this explicit: Ἐγώ εἰμι ὁ Χριστός 'I am the Messiah' [Hb].

QUESTION—Who are the many people who will come ἐπὶ τῷ ὀνόματί μου 'in my name'?
  1. They are the people who will falsely claim to be the Messiah [AB1, BECNT, BNTC, CGTC, EBC, Gnd, Hb, ICC, NCBC, NAC, NICNT, NIGTC, NTC, TH, WBC; CEV, GW, NCV, REB]. The interpretation depends upon the nuance expressed in the related phrases 'in my name' and 'I am he'. A person coming 'in my name' would ordinarily mean a person claiming to be sent by Jesus. But when that person immediately says 'I am he', then 'in my name' signifies that such a person is claming for himself the title and authority that properly belongs only to Jesus [NICNT]. The name they will claim will be 'Christ' [BNTC, Gnd]. Even though they would not claim to be Jesus returning to earth, they would claim his title of 'Messiah' [ICC].
  2. It means that such people are claiming to speak for Jesus [TEV].

13:7 But when you hear of-wars and rumors[a] of-wars, do- not -be-troubled.[b] It-is-necessary (for these things) to-occur, but the end[c] (is) not-yet.

TEXT—Manuscripts reading δεῖ γενέσθαι 'It is necessary (for these things) to occur' are followed by GNT which does not mention any variant reading. A variant reading is δεῖ γὰρ γενέσθαι 'for it is necessary (for these things) to occur' and it is followed by KJV.

LEXICON—a. ἀκοή (LN 33.213) (BAGD 2.a. p. 31): 'rumors' [AB2, BAGD, BNTC, Lns, NTC, WBC; ESV, GW, KJV, NASB, NET, NIV, NRSV, REB], 'reports' [BAGD, BECNT, LN], 'news, information' [LN], 'threats' [CEV, NLT]. The phrase 'reports of wars' is translated 'stories of wars that are coming' [NCV], 'news of battles far away' [TEV], 'the noises of war' [AB1]. This noun denotes the content of the news that is heard [LN].
  b. pres. pass. impera. of θροέομαι, θροέω (LN 25.262) (BAGD p. 364): 'to be alarmed' [AB1, BNTC, LN, Lns, WBC; ESV, GW, NET, NIV, NRSV, REB], 'to be troubled' [BECNT; KJV, TEV], 'to be disturbed' [AB2, BAGD, NTC], 'to be frightened' [BAGD; NASB], 'to be afraid' [CEV,

NCV], 'to be startled' [LN], 'to panic' [NLT]. This verb means to be in a state of fear that is associated with surprise [LN].
  c. τέλος (LN 67.66) (BAGD 1.b. p. 811): 'end' [AB2, BAGD, BECNT, LN, Lns, NTC WBC; ESV, KJV, NASB], 'End' [BNTC], 'the end of the age' [AB1]. The phrase 'the end is not yet' is translated 'the end is still to come' [NET, NIV, NRSV, REB], 'they do not mean that the end has come' [GW, TEV], 'that isn't the end' [CEV], 'the end won't follow immediately' [NLT], '(these things must happen) before the end comes' [NCV]. This noun denotes a point of time that marks the end of a duration of time [LN]. It refers to the final act in the cosmic drama [BAGD].

QUESTION—What is meant by ἀκοὰς 'reports' of wars?
  1. This refers to rumors of wars which may begin in the future [CGTC, EGT, Hb, NICNT, Sw; CEV, CEV, NCV, NLT]. It refers to a widespread expectation of wars [Hb].
  2. This refers to news about wars already in progress [BECNT, Lns, TH, WBC; TEV]. These are the reports of actual battles far away [TH].

QUESTION—Why is it necessary that these battles occur?
  Wars have not been preordained by God's decree but are the inevitable consequences of human depravity which God permits in his eschatological program for this world [Hb]. Since wars are always happening, they should not be construed as signs [ICC]. Wars fall within the eschatological purpose of God which includes both judgment and salvation [CGTC]. God controls the historic destinies of nations [NICNT, Tay].

QUESTION—When was the end to come?
  In verse 4, the disciples were primarily concerned about the end of Jerusalem with their questions about when these things would be completed. Yet a more distant end may also be in view [Sw]. If verses 5–23 deal only with the destruction of Jerusalem, then 'the end' refers to the end of God's judgment on Jerusalem. It is more likely that it refers to both the destruction of Jerusalem and the end of the age [EBC]. It refers to the end of the age [AB1, CBC, Hb, TH, TRT].

13:8 For nation[a] will-be-raised-up[b] against nation, and kingdom[c] against kingdom. There-will-be earthquakes in various[d] places (and) there-will-be famines.[e] These (things) are (the) beginning of (the) birth-pains.[f]

TEXT—Manuscripts reading λιμοί 'famines' are given an A rating by GNT to indicate it was regarded to be certain. A variant reading is λιμοὶ καὶ ταραχαί 'famines and tumults' and it is followed by KJV.

LEXICON—a. ἔθνος (LN 11.55) (BAGD 1. p. 218): 'nation' [BAGD, LN; all translations except TEV], 'country' [TEV]. This noun denotes the largest unit into which the people of the world are divided on the basis of their constituting a socio-political community [LN].
  b. fut. pass. indic. of ἐγείρομαι, ἐγείρω (LN 55.2) (BAGD 2.d. p. 215): 'to rise in arms' [BAGD], 'to rise up in arms against, to make war against' [LN]. The clause 'nation will be raised/raised-up against nation' [AB1,

WBC] is also translated 'nation will/shall rise/rise-up against nation' [BECNT, BNTC, Lns; ESV, KJV, NASB, NIV, NRSV], 'nation will rise up in arms against nation' [NET], 'nation will fight against nation' [GW], 'nations will fight against other nations' [NCV], 'one nation will make war against another nation' [AB1], 'nation will go to war against nation' [NLT, REB], 'nations (and kingdoms) will go to war against each other' [CEV], 'countries will fight each other' [TEV]. This verb means to go to war against someone [LN].

c. βασιλεία (LN 1.82) (BAGD 2. p. 135): 'kingdom' [BAGD, LN; all translations except AB2], 'dominion' [AB2]. This noun denotes an area or district ruled by a king [LN].

d. κατά (LN **89.90**) (BAGD II.1.a. p. 406): 'throughout' [LN]. The phrase κατὰ τόπους 'in various places' [AB1, BECNT, WBC; ESV, GW, NASB, NET, NIV, NRSV] is also translated 'in many places' [CEV, REB], 'in different places' [NCV], 'in divers places' [KJV], 'from place to place' [Lns], 'in place after place' [AB2, BAGD, **LN**], 'in many parts of the world' [NLT], 'everywhere' [BNTC; TEV]. This preposition indicates distributive relations, whether of place, time, or number [LN].

e. λιμός (LN 23.33) (BAGD 2. p. 475): 'famine' [BAGD, LN; all translations except CEV, NCV], 'hunger' [LN]. The clause 'there will be famines' is translated 'there will be times when there is no food for people to eat' [NCV], 'people will starve to death' [CEV]. This noun denotes a widespread lack of food over a considerable period of time that results in hunger for many people [LN].

f. ὠδίν (LN 24.87) (BAGD 2.d. p. 895): 'birth pain(s)' [BAGD], 'great pain' [BAGD, LN]. The clause 'These are the beginning of the birth/labor pains' [AB2; similarly BECNT, BNTC, Lns, WBC; NIV] is also translated 'These things are merely/but the beginning of birth pangs' [AB1, NTC; NASB, NET; similarly NRSV], 'These things are like the first pains of childbirth' [TEV], 'But this is only the first of the birth pains, with many more to come' [NLT], 'But this is just the beginning of troubles' [CEV], 'These are the beginnings of sorrows' [KJV], 'These things are like the first pains when something new is about to be born' [NCV], 'These are only the beginning pains of the end' [GW], 'These are the first birth-pangs of the new age' [REB]. This noun denotes the pain that a mother suffers in childbirth [TH]. It is a figurative extension of 'birth pain' and means to suffer intensely [LN].

QUESTION—What is implied by calling such sufferings 'birth pains'?

The metaphor of birth pains describes the increase in frequency and duration of those events [ESVfn]. In the OT the pangs of birth are a recurring image of divine judgment, often in the context of God's eschatological action [NICNT]. Although the image of childbirth primarily focuses on the calamities preceding the coming of the Messiah, it also includes the event that they usher in [CGTC, ICC, WBC]. Even as the birth pangs of a woman ultimately ends in birth, so the birth pangs described in verses 7–8 will ultimately be followed by the desecration of Jerusalem. However, in the more distant future the Son of Man (verse 26) will come to gather God's elect (verse 27) [BECNT]. The sufferings will be intensified in the end time, but those sufferings will be the 'birth pangs' for the birth of the Messianic kingdom of peace [Hb].

DISCOURSE UNIT—13:9–13 [NET, NRSV]. The topic is persecution is foretold [NRSV], the persecution of disciples [NET].

13:9 But you, watch-out-for[a] yourselves. They-will-hand- you -over to city-councils[b] and in synagogues[c] you-will-be-beaten and you-will-stand before governors[d] and kings for-(the)-sake[e] of-me as a-testimony[f] to-them.

LEXICON—a. pres. act. impera. of βλέπω (LN 27.58) (BAGD 6. p. 143): 'to watch out for, to beware of' [BAGD, LN], 'to pay attention to' [LN]. The phrase βλέπετε ὑμεῖς ἑαυτούς 'you, watch out for yourselves' is translated 'As for yourselves, watch out!' [BECNT], 'as for yourselves, beware' [NRSV], 'As for you, be on your guard' [AB1; REB; similarly BNTC], 'You yourselves must watch out' [TEV], 'you, look to yourselves' [AB2], 'you on your part see to yourselves!' [Lns], 'You must watch out for yourselves' [NET], 'watch out for yourselves' [WBC], 'take heed to yourselves' [KJV], 'You must be careful' [NCV], 'You must be on your guard' [NIV], 'Be on your guard!' [NTC; CEV, ESV, GW, NASB], 'When these things begin to happen, watch out!' [NLT]. This verb means to be ready to learn about future dangers or needs and be prepared to respond to them appropriately [LN]. It means to be aware of the danger to which they will be exposed [TH]. This is the same command that was given in verse 5.

b. συνέδριον (LN 11.79) (BAGD 3, p. 786): 'council' [AB1, AB2, BECNT, Lns, NTC, WBC; ESV, KJV, NET, NRSV], 'local council' [BAGD; NIV, NLT], 'city council, council of judges' [LN], 'court' [BNTC; CEV, NASB, NCV, REB, TEV], 'Jewish court' [GW]. This noun denotes a socio-political group acting as a judicial council. In parts of the world where a 'city council' is primarily legislative rather than judicial, a better translation would be 'the council which will judge you' or 'before a group of men who will decide whether you have done right or wrong' [LN]. The plural form refers to councils in general [WBC]. They are religious courts made up of the elders of the synagogues who were assembled to exercise their disciplinary powers [EBC].

c. συναγωγή (LN 7.20) (BAGD 2.a. p. 782): The plural form is translated 'synagogues' [BAGD, LN; all translations except CEV], 'meeting places' [CEV], 'places of assembly' [BAGD]. This noun denotes an assembly building that was associated with religious activity. Normally the building was used for Jewish worship and for the teaching of the Law [LN]. Even though the synagogues were primarily used for worship, the local councils also used the building for their own sessions [Hb, Sw].

d. ἡγεμών (LN 37.83) (BAGD 2. p. 343): 'governor' [BAGD, BECNT, BNTC, LN, Lns, NTC, WBC; all versions except CEV, KJV, TEV], 'ruler' [AB1, AB2; CEV, KJV, TEV]. This noun denotes a person who ruled over a minor Roman province [LN]. The governor was the imperial governor for a province [BAGD].

e. ἕνεκεν or ἕνεκα (LN 89.31) (BAGD p. 264): 'for the sake of, because of, on account of' [BAGD, LN]. The clause ἕνεκεν ἐμοῦ 'for my sake' [AB2, BNTC, WBC; ESV, KJV, NASB, TEV] is also translated 'because of me' [AB1, BECNT; CEV, GW, NET, NRSV], 'on account of me' [Lns; NIV], 'on my account' [NTC; REB], 'because you are my followers' [NLT], 'This will happen to you because you follow me' [NCV]. This preposition indicates cause or reason, and often implies purpose in the sense of 'for the sake of' [LN].

f. μαρτύριον (LN 33.262, 33.264) (BAGD 1.a. p. 493): 'testimony' [BAGD, LN], 'witness' [LN]. The clause εἰς μαρτύριον αὐτοῖς 'as/for a testimony to them' [Lns, NTC; NASB, NRSV] is also translated 'to bear testimony to them' [BNTC], 'as a-witness/witnesses to them' [AB2; NET, NIV], 'for a witness to them' [BECNT], 'to testify to them' [GW], 'to testify before them' [AB1], 'to testify in their presence' [REB], 'to give testimony to them' [WBC], 'to bear witness before them' [ESV], 'to tell them about me' [NCV], 'to tell about your faith' [CEV], 'to tell them the Good News' [TEV], 'But this will be your opportunity to tell them about me' [NLT]. Instead of giving a testimony to them, one translation takes it to mean that the testimony is given against them: 'for a testimony against them' [KJV]. This noun denotes the content of what is witnessed or said [LN].

QUESTION—What are the disciples to watch out for?

This warning is given to prepare them to faithfully endure the persecution rather than tell them how to escape it [BECNT, NIGTC]. They must be on the watch that they not lose their faith and perish when it happens [Lns]. The disciples are warned to be alert against any thoughtless or unworthy actions during the persecution [Hb].

QUESTION—Who are the people who will hand the disciples over to the city councils?

The implied 'they' of the verb παραδώσουσιν 'they will hand over' is a general reference to the people who will persecute Jesus' followers NIGTC, TRT]. It means 'people will deliver you over' or 'you will be delivered over' [TRT].

QUESTION—What is meant by the second occurrence of the preposition εἰς in the statements 'They will hand you over εἰς (to) city councils and εἰς (to/in) synagogues you will be beaten'?

1. The second preposition refers to a separate event: They will hand you over **to** city councils, and **in** synagogues you will be beaten [AB2, BECNT, BNTC, CGTC, EBC, Hb, Lns, NIGTC, NTC, Sw, Tay NTC, WBC; all

versions]. In the Koine Greek, the preposition εἰς was freely used in place of ἐν 'in' [Tay, WBC].
2. The second preposition joins the city councils: They will deliver you **to** city councils and **to** synagogues. You will be beaten [EGT, ICC, My].

QUESTION—What will the disciples go through for the sake of Jesus?

The disciples will experience rejection and punishment because of their association with Jesus [NICNT] and their loyalty to him [Hb].

QUESTION—In what way will the disciples give a testimony to them?

When they are brought before governors and kings to be examined, they will have the opportunity to declare their faith in Christ before those governors and kings [PNTC], to explain the whole course of the gospel [Lns], and to witness for Christ [NCBC].

13:10 And first[a] the Good-News[b] must be-proclaimed[c] to all the nations.[d]

LEXICON—a. πρῶτος (LN 60.46) (BAGD 2.a. p. 726): 'first' [AB1, AB2, BAGD, BECNT, BNTC, LN, Lns, NTC, NTC, WBC; ESV, GW, KJV, NASB, NET, NIV, NLT, NRSV]. The phrase καὶ...πρῶτον 'and first' is translated 'But before these things happen' [NCV], 'But before the end comes' [CEV, TEV], 'Before the end' [REB]. This adverb means first in a series involving time [LN]. 'First' indicates that the consummation cannot come until this condition has been satisfied [NICNT].

b. εὐαγγέλιον (LN 33.217) (BAGD 1.c. p. 318): 'the good-news/Good-News' [AB2, BAGD, BNTC; CEV, GW, NCV, NLT, NRSV], 'the gospel' [BECNT, LN, Lns, NTC, WBC; ESV, KJV, NASB, NET, NIV, REB, TEV], 'the Proclamation' [AB1]. This noun denotes the content of good news, and in the NT it is the gospel about Jesus [LN].

c. aorist pass. infin. of κηρύσσω (LN 33.256) (BAGD 2.b.β. p. 431): 'to be proclaimed' [WBC; ESV, NRSV, REB], 'to be preached' [AB2, BECNT, BNTC, LN, Lns, NTC; CEV, NASB, NET, NIV, NLT, TEV], 'to be announced, to be made known' [BAGD], 'to be made' [AB1], 'to be told' [NCV], 'to be spread' [GW], 'to be published' [KJV]. This verb means to publicly announce religious truths and principles while urging acceptance and compliance [LN]. It refers to the proclamation of contemporary preachers [BAGD].

d. ἔθνος (LN 11.55, 11.37) (BAGD 1. p. 218): 'nation, people' [BAGD, LN (11.55)], and the phrase τὰ ἔθνη 'the nations' is translated 'the heathen, the pagans' [LN (11.37)]. The phrase εἰς πάντα τὰ ἔθνη 'to all the nations' [AB1, AB2, WBC; ESV, NASB, NET; similarly Lns] is also translated 'to all nations' [BNTC; CEV, GW, NIV, NLT, NRSV, REB], 'in all the nations' [BECNT], 'among all nations' [KJV], 'to all people/peoples' [NCV, TEV]. This noun denotes the largest unit into which the people of the world are divided on the basis of their constituting a socio-political community [LN (11.55)], and the phrase τὰ ἔθνη 'the nations' has an extended reference to those who do not belong to the Jewish or Christian faith [LN (11.37)].

QUESTION—What is meant by the good news being preached πρῶτον 'first'?
1. 'First' means before the end of this age. This refers to proclaiming the Good News to all the nations of the world before the second coming of Jesus [AB2, BNTC, CGTC, EBC, Hb, Lns, NCBC, NICNT, NIGTC, NTC, Sw]. This announcement assures the disciples that the Kingdom of God cannot be impeded by any local persecution in Palestine or elsewhere [NIGTC]. All nations will have the opportunity to accept the gospel [CGTC]. The world will not end until the gospel has been taken to the uttermost part of the earth [Lns].
2. 'First' means before the destruction of the city of Jerusalem. This refers to proclaiming the Good News throughout the Roman world by A.D. 60. [BECNT, Gnd]. Paul wrote in Romans 16:26 and Colossians 1:6, 23 that the gospel had been 'made known' to all nations, which implies this requirement was already fulfilled before the destruction of the temple [BECNT]. 'First' means before the end. Paul's letters and the Book of Acts let us know that by the tine Mark wrote his gospel, Jesus' prediction of the prior evangelization of 'all nations' had already been fulfilled (Romans 1:5, 8–17; 11:11–36; 15:14–21, 26; Ephesians 2:11–3:21; Colossians 1:6, 23, 27; 1 Timothy 3:16). The prediction of international evangelism implies that we are to understand that the governors and kings represent the Gentiles, and the Jewish courts and synagogues included those scattered throughout the dispersion of the Jews beyond Israel. [Gnd].

13:11 And when they-arrest you[a] (and) hand-(you)-over,[b] do- not -be-worried-beforehand (about) what you-might-say, but whatever is-given[c] to-you in that hour, this you-shall-say, because you- yourselves -are not the-ones speaking but the Holy Spirit.
TEXT—Manuscripts reading τί λαλήσητε 'what you might say' are followed by GNT which does not mention any variant reading. A variant reading is τί λαλήσητε, μεδὲ μελετᾶτε 'what you might say, nor be anxious' and it is followed by KJV.
LEXICON—a. pres. act. subj. of ἄγω (LN 15.165) (BAGD 2. p. 14): 'to arrest, to lead away, to take into custody' [BAGD], 'to bring, to lead' [LN]. The phrase ὅταν ἄγωσιν ὑμᾶς 'when they arrest you' [AB1, AB2; NASB, NET] is also translated 'when/whenever you are arrested' [NTC; CEV, NCV, NIV, NLT, REB, TEV], 'when they hand you over' [BNTC], 'when/whenever they bring you' [Lns], 'when they shall lead you' [KJV], 'when they take you away' [GW], 'when they lead you to trial' [BECNT, WBC], 'when they bring you to trial' [ESV, NRSV]. This verb means to direct or guide the movement of an object without special regard for the point of departure or goal [LN]. This is a legal use of the word [BAGD]. It means to arrest someone [TH]. 'Lead' pictures them as arrested persons on the way to be handed over to the judge [Hb].

b. pres. act. participle of παραδίδωμι (LN 37.111) (BAGD 1.b. p. 614): 'to hand over' [BAGD, LN], 'to turn over to' [LN]. The phrase 'handing you over' is translated 'and hand you over' [NASB, NRSV; similarly BECNT], 'to hand you over to the authorities' [CEV, GW], 'and turn you over' [AB2], 'and deliver you over' [ESV], 'delivering you up' [Lns, WBC; similarly KJV], 'and deliver you up to trial' [AB1], 'and hand you over for trial' [NET], 'and brought to trial' [NIV], 'and taken to trial' [NTC], 'and stand trial' [NLT], 'and put on trial' [REB], 'and taken to court' [TEV; similarly BNTC], 'and judged' [NCV]. This verb means to deliver a person into the control of someone else. It refers to handing over a presumably guilty person for punishment by the authorities [LN]. It refers to handing over someone into the custody of some official [BAGD]. It refers to handing someone over to the authorities to be tried [TH].

c. aorist pass. subj. of δίδωμι (LN 13.142): 'to be granted' [LN]. The phrase 'whatever is given you' [AB1, AB2, BECNT, NTC, WBC; ESV, NASB, NET, NIV, NRSV; similarly Lns; KJV] is also translated 'whatever is then given to you' [TEV], 'whatever is given you/to-you to say' [CEV, GW, NCV, REB; similarly BNTC], 'say what God tells you' [NLT]. This verb means to grant someone the opportunity or occasion to do something [LN]. This implies that it is given by God [LN].

QUESTION—How is this verse connected with what precedes it?

Verse 9 finished with Jesus telling them 'They will hand you over to city councils... and you will stand before governors and kings for my sake as a testimony to them'. Verse 11 now picks up from where verse 9 left off [BECNT, NIGTC, WBC].

QUESTION—Why would they be worried about what to say before the authorities?

Since they were primarily concerned with the honor of Christ and the gospel, they might worry more about making mistakes that could injure the Lord's cause than how they might defend themselves to escape any penalties [Lns]. This is not about their own defense but about giving testimony to the kingdom [ICC]. Since these disciples were uneducated with no formal academic background, they needed this assurance [WBC]. The Holy Spirit will remind them of everything Jesus had said to them [NTC]. Others think that since the disciples would be the ones on trial, this concerns speaking for their own defense [EBC, NICNT, NIGTC, Tay]. The Holy Spirit will reveal the appropriate words to speak right when they need them [EBC], and premeditation would be impossible [Sw]. Jesus is not prohibiting thinking about what to say but alleviating the anxious worry that accompanies it [Hb, Tay].

13:12 And brother will-hand-over brother to death[a], and father (his) child. And children will-rise-up[b] against parents and put- them -to-death.[c]

LEXICON—a. θάνατος (LN 23.99) (BAGD 1.b.a. p. 351): 'death' [BAGD, LN]. The phrase παραδώσει εἰς θάνατον 'will hand over to death' [GW,

NET, REB] is also translated 'will hand over to be put to death' [TEV], 'will turn over to death' [AB2], 'will deliver over to death' [BECNT; ESV], 'will deliver up to death' [Lns, NTC], 'will deliver to death' [WBC], 'will give to be killed' [NCV], 'will betray to death' [AB1, BNTC; KJV, NASB, NIV, NLT, NRSV]. The clause 'And brother will hand over brother to death' is translated 'Brothers and sisters will betray each other and have each other put to death' [CEV].

b. fut. mid. indic. of ἐπανίσταμα, ἐπανίστημι (LN **39.34**) (BAGD p. 283): 'to rise up' [BAGD, LN], 'to rebel against, to revolt, to engage in insurrection' [LN]. The phrase ἐπαναστήσονται ἐπί 'will rise up against' [AB2, BAGD, BECNT, BNTC, **LN**, Lns, NTC, WBC; KJV, NASB] is also translated 'will rise against' [ESV, NET, NRSV], 'will turn against' [AB1; CEV, REB, TEV], 'will rebel against' [**LN**; GW, NIV, NLT], 'will fight against' [NCV]. This verb means to rise up in open defiance of authority with the presumed intention to overthrow that authority or to act in complete opposition to its demands [LN].

c. fut. act. indic. of θανατόω (LN 20.65) (BAGD 1. p. 351): 'to put to death' [BAGD], 'to kill, to execute' [LN]. The clause καὶ θανατώσουσιν αὐτούς 'and put/will-put them to death' [BNTC, WBC] is also translated 'and have them put to death' [AB2, BECNT; ESV, NASB, NET, NIV, NRSV, TEV], 'and cause them to be put to death' [KJV, NCV], 'and will-kill/kill them' [NTC; GW], 'and hand them over to be killed' [AB1], 'and have them killed' [CEV], 'and cause them to be killed' [NLT], 'and will bring them to death' [Lns], 'and send them to their death' [REB]. This verb means to deprive a person of life, and it implies that it is the result of condemnation by legal or quasi-legal procedures [LN]. This means to bring about their deaths rather than 'to kill them' [CGTC]. When it is reported to the authorities that they are Christians, the authorities will then put them to death. [Hb]. The person who unjustly causes someone to be put to death is just as guilty as if he had committed the act with his own hands [NTC].

QUESTION—What is the motive for such actions against members of one's own families?

The motive for betrayal from within the family may be fanatical hatred of the gospel [EBC, CGTC, NICNT] or the desire to save one's own life by betraying others [CGTC, NICNT]. These are frightful cases of denunciation in pagan courts [Lns]. It doesn't mean that all brothers, fathers, and children will be involved [TRT].

13:13 And you-will-be hated by every-one because-of my name.[a] But the (person) having-endured[b] to (the) end, this (one) will-be-saved.[c]

LEXICON—a. ὄνομα (LN 33.126) (BAGD I.4.c.α. p. 572): 'name' BAGD, LN]. The phrase διὰ τὸ ὄνομά μου 'because of my name' [BECNT, Lns; NASB, NET, NRSV] is also translated 'on account of my name' [WBC], 'because you bear my name' [BAGD], 'for my name's sake' [NTC; ESV,

KJV], 'for the sake of my name' [AB2], 'for my sake' [BNTC], 'because of me' [AB1; CEV, NIV, TEV], 'because you follow me' [NCV], 'because you are my followers' [NLT], 'because you are committed to me' [GW], 'for your allegiance to me' [REB]. This noun denotes the proper name of a person [LN]. 'Because of my name' is a synonym for 'because of me' [BECNT].

    b. aorist act. participle of ὑπομένω (LN 25.175) (BAGD 2. p. 845): 'to endure, to bear up, to demonstrate endurance, to put up with' [LN]. The phrase ὑπομείνας εἰς τέλος 'having endured to the end' is translated 'did/shall endure to the end' [Lns; KJV], 'endures to the end' [AB2, NTC, WBC; ESV, GW, NASB, NET, NLT, NRSV, REB], 'perseveres unto the end' [BECNT], 'stands firm to the end' [NIV], 'holds out to the End' [BNTC], 'holds out to the end' [AB1, TEV], 'keep their faith until the end' [NCV], 'keep on being faithful right up to the end' [CEV]. This verb means to continue to bear up in spite of difficulties and suffering [LN]. It means to stand one's ground, to hold out, to endure trouble, affliction, or persecution. [BAGD].

    c. fut. pass. indic. of σῴζω (LN 21.18, 21.27) (BAGD 2.b. p. 798): 'to be saved' [BAGD, LN (21.27); all translations], 'to be delivered, to be rescued, to be made safe' [LN (21.18)], 'to attain salvation' [BAGD]. This verb means to rescue from danger and to restore to a former state of safety and well being [LN (21.18)] or to cause someone to experience divine salvation [LN (21.27)].

QUESTION—What is meant by being hated ὑπὸ πάντων 'by everyone'?

'Everyone' is hyperbole for *many* people [TRT]. It means to be hated by people in general, regardless of rank, station, race, nationality, sex, or age [NTC]. It means every segment of society: the authorities, citizens, and even members of one's own family [BECNT, NTC, WBC]. Because the world hates Christ, it also hates his representatives [NTC].

QUESTION—What is meant by enduring εἰς τέλος 'to the end'?

    1. For each disciple this persecution will last until death when he leaves this earthly scene [CBC, EBC, NTC, Sw, TH, WBC]. This testing will be one of the features of the last times when not all will stand the test. However, he who does endure to the end of his life because of his genuine faith will be saved [EBC]. It means until the end of the period of persecution [Lns, NTC, Tay].

    2. Because 'to the end' was a standard expression of 'forever' and there is no expectation that this hostility will be overcome, it means 'right through, forever' without any specific τέλος 'end' in sight. It simply means to endure whatever may come without giving up [NIGTC]. It does not refer to either the end of the age or the end of life. It is about total endurance without wavering [NAC].

QUESTION—In what way will that person σωθήσεται 'be saved'?

This refers to final eschatological salvation [CGTC, Hb, Lns, NTC, TH, Tay, Sw, WBC], spiritual salvation, final salvation [NAC].

DISCOURSE UNIT—13:14–27 [Hb]. The topic is the signs of the end and the advent.

DISCOURSE UNIT—13:14–23 [Hb; CEV, ESV, NET, NRSV, TEV]. The topic is the end-time crisis [Hb], the horrible thing [CEV], the abomination of desolation [ESV, NET], the desolating sacrilege [NRSV], the awful horror [TEV].

13:14 **And when you(pl) see the abomination^a of-desolation^b having-stood where he/it-should not (be) [(let) the (one) who-is-reading understand^c] then the (ones) in Judea must-flee^d to the mountains.**

TEXT—Manuscripts reading ἐρημώσεως ἑστηκότα 'desolation having stood' are followed by GNT which does not mention any variant reading. A variant reading is ἐρημώσεως τὸ πηθὲν ὑπὸ Δανιὴλ τοῦ προφήτου ἑστηκότα 'desolation that was spoken of by Daniel the prophet having stood' and it is followed by KJV.

LEXICON—a. βδέλυγμα (LN 25.187) (BAGD 3. p. 138): 'abomination, detestable thing' [BAGD], 'what is detestable, what is abhorrent' [LN (25.187)]. Additional translations of this word are listed in the next lexicon item. This noun denotes that which is utterly detestable and abhorrent [LN]. The 'abomination' refers to something repugnant to God [EBC].

b. ἐρήμωσις (LN 20.41, 53.38) (BAGD p. 309): 'desolation' [LN (20.41)], 'devastation, destruction' [BAGD, LN], 'depopulation' [BAGD]. The phrase τὸ βδέλυγμα τῆς ἐρημώσεως 'the abomination of desolation' [AB2, BECNT, BNTC, Lns, WBC; ESV, KJV, NASB, NET, REB] is also translated 'the abomination that causes desolation' [NIV], 'the Abominable Desecration' [AB1], 'an abomination which desolates, a horrible thing which defiles' [LN (53.38)], 'the disgusting thing that will cause destruction' [GW], 'the sacrilegious object that causes desecration' [NLT], 'the desolating sacrilege' [NTC; NRSV], 'the destroying terror' [NCV], 'that "Horrible Thing"' [CEV], 'The Awful Horror' [TEV]. The phrase τὸ βδέλυγμα τῆς ἐρημώσεως 'the detestable thing of desolation' is derived from Hebrew and denotes an abomination (referring to either an object or an event) which defiles a holy place, casing it to be abandoned and left desolate. In some languages, it may be necessary to translate βδέλυγμα 'detestable' using a phrase such as 'that which God detests' or 'that which God hates' or even 'that which causes God's anger'. The term ἐρημώσεως 'desolation' may then be translated as 'that which causes people to abandon' or 'that which causes something to be deserted'. In some languages, the entire phrase may be translated as 'that which God detests and which causes something to be abandoned or left-desolate' [LN (53.38)]. The genitive phrase τῆς ἐρημώσεως 'of desolation' suggests the holy and pious worshippers have vacated the temple, leaving it deserted and desolate because of the abomination [EBC].

c. pres act. impera. of νοέω (LN 32.2) (BAGD 2. p. 540): 'to understand, to perceive, to gain insight into, to comprehend' [LN], 'to consider, to take note of, to think over' [BAGD]. The inserted clause 'let the (one) who is reading understand' [WBC; similarly KJV, NTC] is also translated 'let the reader understand' [AB1, AB2, BECNT, BNTC; ESV, NASB, NET, NIV, NRSV, REB], 'let the reader take note' [GW], 'he that reads let him understand' [Lns], 'Reader, pay attention!' [NLT], 'Everyone who reads this must try to understand!' [CEV], 'You who read this should understand what it means' [NCV], 'Note to the reader: understand what this means' [TEV]. This verb means to comprehend something on the basis of careful thought and consideration [LN].

d. pres. act. impera/of φεύγω (LN 15.61) (BAGD 1. p. 855): 'to flee' [AB2, BAGD, BECNT, BNTC, LN, Lns, NTC, WBC; ESV, GW, KJV, NASB, NET, NIV, NLT], 'to run away' [NCV, NLT, TEV], 'to run' [LN; CEV], 'to take to (the hills)' [AB1; REB], 'to seek safety in flight' [BAGD]. This verb means to move quickly from a point or area in order to avoid presumed danger or difficulty [LN].

QUESTION—What is meant by the phrase 'the abomination of desolation'?

This terminology is borrowed from Daniel 9:27, 11:31, and 12:11 [EBC, NICNT, NIGTC]. Daniel's prophecy is usually considered to have been fulfilled in 167 B.C. when a representative of Antiochus IV profaned the altar of burnt offering in the temple of Jerusalem [EBC, TRT]. Antiochus erected an altar in the temple to worship Zeus, the chief god of the Greeks [TRT]. Even though the word βδέλυγμα 'abomination' is a neuter noun that would normally be referred to as 'it', the following participle ἑστηκότα 'having stood' is masculine, suggesting that the abomination refers to a person [EBC]. Some take the following third person active verb δεῖ 'should' as also being masculine: 'where *he* should not be' [AB1, AB2, BECNT, BNTC, NCBC, NICNT, NIGTC NTC, WBC; ESV, NLT, REB, TEV]. Others refer to the neuter gender of the noun 'abomination: 'where *it* should not be' [BNTC, Lns; CEV, GW, KJV, NASB, NCV, NET, NIV, NRSV].

QUESTION—When will this next 'abomination of desolation' happen?

1. This refers to what will happen before the fall of Jerusalem in A.D. 70 [AB2, BECNT, EBC, ICC, Lns, NICNT, NIGTC, NTC Sw]. This warning points to the coming of the Roman army flying the military standards that the Jews considered to be idolatrous and an abomination [EBC, ICC, Lns, NICNT, NIGTC, NTC Sw]. The people in Judea must escape to the mountains when that army appears [NIGTC]. Since the people living inside the besieged city of Jerusalem would be unable to flee, these verses must apply to those living in the countryside of Judea who would still be able to flee [NIGTC].

2. This refers to a future event at the end of this age when the Antichrist will profane the holy temple by taking his seat in God's temple and by proclaiming himself to be God (2 Thessalonians 2:4) [CGTC, Hb, WBC].

The abomination is the personal Antichrist in a reestablished Jewish temple [Hb].

3. This refers to both of the above events [BNTC, EBC, NAC]. This is the kind of prophetic passage in which two events are viewed as if they were but one. It moves beyond the destruction of Jerusalem to the Parousia and the end of all things since the two events belong together, the first heralding the other [BNTC, NAC]. The 'abomination that causes desolation' had already occurred in the Maccabean period. This warning refers to a second occurrence of an abomination when the Roman army appears with its military standard that the Jews considered to be idolatrous and to a third occurrence when the Antichrist appears at the end times [EBC].

QUESTION—Who is making the parenthetical comment 'let the one reading understand'?

1. This is Mark's comment to his readers [CGTC, BECNT, BNTC, EBC, EGT, Hb, ICC, NAC, NCBC, NICNT, NIGTC, NTC, TH, WBC; all versions]. Mark advises his readers that one must read Daniel to understand what is happening [WBC].
2. This is a comment by Jesus to those listening to him. Jesus parenthetically comments 'He that reads (Daniel's statement about the abomination of desolation), let him understand' [Lns].

13:15 And the (one) on the housetop^a is- not -to-go-down^b nor to-enter to-take^c anything out-of his house. **13:16** And the (one) in the field is- not -to-turn back to-get his garment.

TEXT—Manuscripts reading μὴ καταβάτω 'is not to go down' are followed by GNT which does not mention any variant reading. A variant reading is μὴ καταβάτω εἰς τὴν οἰκίαν 'is not to go down into the house' and it is followed by KJV.

LEXICON—a. δῶμα (LN 7.51) (BAGD p. 210): 'housetop' [BAGD, BECNT, LN, Lns, NTC, WBC; ESV, NASB, KJV, NRSV], 'roof' [AB1, AB2, BAGD, BNTC; CEV, GW, NCV, NET, NIV, REB], 'roof of a house' [TEV], 'the deck of a roof' [NLT]. This noun denotes the area on the top of a flat-roof house. The roofs referred to in the NT generally had flat tops made of pounded dirt that was sometimes mixed with lime or stone. [LN].

b. aorist act. impera. of καταβαίνω (LN 15.107) (BAGD 1.a.α. p. 408): 'to go down, to come down' [BAGD, LN], 'to move down, to descend' [LN]. The words μὴ καταβάτω μηδὲ εἰσελθάτω ἆραί τι 'is not to go down nor to go in to take anything' is translated 'let him...not come down, nor enter to take anything out' [WBC], 'let him not go down nor go inside to remove something out' [Lns], 'must not go down, or go in to get anything' [NASB], 'must not come down or go inside to take anything' [NET], 'must not go down or enter...to take anything away' [NRSV], 'let him ...not go down or enter (his house) to get something out' [NTC], 'let not the person...come down or go in to get anything' [AB2], 'let no one…go down or enter…to take anything' [NIV], 'must not go down or go inside to get anything' [NCV], 'let (the one)…not go down, nor enter (his house), to take anything out' [ESV], 'let him…not go down (into the house), neither enter therein, to take any thing' [KJV]. Some translations explicitly connect the two actions of coming down and entering the house: 'must not go down to enter to get anything' [BECNT], 'must not go down to fetch anything out' [REB; similarly BNTC], 'should not come down to get anything out' [GW], 'must not go down…to pack' [NLT], 'he must not come into the house to take anything out' [AB1], 'don't go inside to get anything' [CEV], 'must not lose time by going down…to get anything to take along' [TEV]. This verb means to move down, irrespective of the gradient [LN].

c. aorist act. impera' of ἐπιστρέφω (LN 15.90) (BAGD 1.b.α. p. 301): 'to turn back' [AB2, BAGD, BECNT, BNTC; ESV, GW, KJV, NASB, NET, NRSV, REB], 'to go back' [NTC; CEV, NCV, NIV, CEV], 'to come back' [AB1], 'to return' [LN, WBC; NLT], 'to turn to the rear' [Lns]. This verb means to go back toward or to some point or area [LN].

QUESTION—Why would someone be up on the housetop?
People spent much of their leisure time on the flat roofs of their houses, especially in the cool of the evening. They reached the rooftop by outside steps [TH]. People used their rooftops for relaxing, sleeping, praying, and storing goods [AB2].

QUESTION—Does the instruction for the man on the housetop 'not to go down' mean that he is to remain on the housetop?
The man on the housetop certainly must go down to the ground in order to flee. Because the two verbs μὴ καταβάτω μηδὲ εἰσελθάτω 'is not to go down nor to go in' are closely connected, they mean that the man is not to come down from the housetop and then take the time to enter his house to get something from inside it [CGTC]. This is an order for the man to get down to the ground and immediately flee to the hills without taking the time to go into the house to get some of his belongings [TH]. The danger would be so great that people should flee without even stopping to gather up their possessions [WBC].

QUESTION—Why would the field worker be concerned about taking time to get his garment?
Although the outer garment was not needed while working in the field, it would be highly desirable at night [CGTC, Hb]. It might have been left in another corner of the field [NICNT] or at home [ICC, Lns; TEV]. Any delay might mean being captured, turned back, or perhaps killed [NTC].

13:17 And woe[a] to-the (ones) having (a child) in (the) womb and the (ones) nursing in those days. **13:18** But pray that it- not -happen in-winter.

TEXT—Manuscripts reading μὴ γένηται 'it not happen' are followed by GNT which does not mention any variant reading. A variant reading is μὴ γένηται ἡ φυγὴ ὑμῶν 'your flight not happen' and it is followed by KJV.

LEXICON—a. οὐαί (LN 22.9) (BAGD 1.a. p. 591): 'woe, alas!' [BAGD], 'how disastrous, how terrible' [LN]. The phrase 'woe to' [BECNT, Lns, NTC, WBC; KJV, NASB, NET, NRSV] is also translated 'alas for' [AB1, AB2, BNTC; ESV, REB], 'how horrible it will be for' [GW], 'how terrible it will be for' [NCV, NLT, TEV], 'it will be an awful time for' [CEV], 'how dreadful it will be for' [NIV]. This exclamatory particle indicates a state of intense hardship or distress. In languages where there is no noun for 'disaster', the meaning of the Greek term can be expressed as 'how greatly one will suffer' or 'what terrible pain will come to one' [LN]. It denotes pain or displeasure [BAGD]. 'Woe' is an expression of pity, not condemnation [Hb].

b. aorist mid. (deponent = act.) subjunctive of γινομαι (LN 13.107): 'to happen, to occur' [LN]. The phrase ἵνα μὴ γένηται 'that it not happen' is translated 'that it won't happen' [CEV, NET], 'that it does not happen' [BNTC], 'that it might/may not happen/occur' [AB1, AB2, Lns, NTC, WBC; ESV, NASB], 'that these things will not happen' [NCV, TEV], 'that it may not come' [REB], 'that this will not take place' [NIV; similarly BECNT], 'that it will/may not be' [GW, NRSV], 'that your flight will not be' [NLT; similarly KJV]. This verb means 'to happen' and implies that what happens is different from some previous state [LN]. Keeping warm in the countryside is a problem that makes traveling in the winter more difficult [WBC].

QUESTION—Why are these women singled out?

Women who are pregnant and women who are nursing their children cannot just drop their burdens and run. They will face greater danger than others [WBC].

QUESTION—What are they supposed to pray will not happen in winter?

This refers to the time of their flight [AB1, AB2, BNTC, CBC, CGTC, EBC, Lns, NAC, NCBC, NTC, Sw, Tay, TH, WBC; KJV, NLT]. Matthew 24:20 explicitly states that they should pray that their flight does not happen in the winter.

13:19 Because in-those days there-will-be trouble[a] such as has- not -happened since (the) beginning of (the) creation[b] that God created until now, and-never will-happen (again).

LEXICON—a. θλῖψις (LN 22.2) (BAGD 1. p. 362): 'trouble' [LN; NCV, TEV], 'tribulation' [AB2, BAGD, BECNT, Lns, NTC, WBC; ESV, NASB], 'suffering' [LN; NET, NRSV], 'misery' [GW], 'distress' [AB1, BNTC; NIV, REB], 'anguish' [NLT], 'persecution' [LN], 'affliction' [BAGD; KJV], 'time of suffering' [CEV]. This noun denotes trouble that involves direct suffering [LN]. Those days of trouble will be one long tribulation of dire pressure and continuing distress caused by outward circumstances [Hb, My].

b. κτίσις (LN 42.35) (BAGD 1.b.β. p. 456): 'the creation' [AB1, AB2, BAGD, BECNT, LN, Lns, NTC, WBC; ESV, KJV, NASB, NET, NRSV], 'the beginning of the world' [BAGD, BNTC]. The clause 'since the beginning of the creation that God created' is translated 'since/from the beginning when God created the world' [LN; NIV; similarly TEV], 'since the beginning of the world which God created' [REB], 'since the beginning, when God made the world' [NCV], 'since God created the world' [CEV, NLT], 'from the beginning of God's creation' [GW]. This noun denotes something that has been made or created, and is used exclusively in the NT for God's activity in creation [LN]. It refers to the sum total of everything created [BAGD].

QUESTION—What is the function of the initial conjunction ἵνα 'because'?

This introduces the reason why the flight was so urgent [Lns, NICNT].

QUESTION—What is the coming trouble, and in what way will it be greater than any trouble that has ever happened before it or will happen after it?

1. This is a hyperbolic statement referring to the coming destruction of Jerusalem and how terrible it will be [BECNT, NICNT, NLTfn]. The severity of the distress caused by the destruction of Jerusalem is vividly suggested through Semitic hyperbole [NICNT, NLTfn]. The use of hyperbolic language is far more expressive than any scientific or statistical language. Because the words 'and never will be' imply that time will continue on after the event, so it does not refer to the great tribulation that precedes the last days [BECNT].

2. This refers to the coming destruction of Jerusalem and the terribleness of it is described as a fact [Gnd, Lns, NIGTC, Sw]. Since flight is no longer described as an option in this verse, it seems to refer to the siege in Jerusalem rather than the general distress of Judea [NIGTC].

3. This refers to the final tribulation that will occur just before the second coming of Christ [AB1, BNTC, CGTC, EBC, ESVfn, Hb, NAC, NCBC, NETfn, NTC, PNTC, Tay, WBC]. Because this assertion is too emphatic to refer to just a siege, it clearly refers to the eschatological event that is the final and greatest tribulation in all history [Hb, Tay]. Though partially fulfilled in the great stress that occurred at the fall of Jerusalem in A.D. 70, this looks forward to the Great Tribulation that will precede the end of this age [EBC]. The reference to 'the chosen' in the next verse seems to point to the saved during the days of the Great Tribulation just prior to Christ's return [WBC].

13:20 **And unless (the) Lord decreased[a] the days, not any person[b] would have-been-saved.[c] But on-account-of the chosen-ones[d] whom he-chose, he decreased the days.**

LEXICON—a. aorist act. indic. of κολοβόω (LN 59.71): 'to decrease, to reduce in number' [LN], 'to cut short' [AB1, NTC; ESV, NET, NIV, NRSV], 'to shorten' [AB2, BECNT, LN, Lns, WBC; KJV, NASB], 'to make short' [NCV]. The phrase 'decreased the days' is translated 'reduced the number of those days' [TEV], 'reduce that time' [GW], 'shortened the time' [BNTC], 'shortens the time of calamity' [NLT], ' cut short that time of troubles' [REB], 'make the time shorter' [CEV]. This verb means to cause something to be reduced in number [LN]. It means to reduce the number of days of the tribulation but not the length of each day [ICC, NTC]. The Lord shortened the period of tribulation [NICNT, WBC]. The whole verse conforms to the Hebrew prophetic style by speaking of the matter as if it were in the past [TH].

b. σάρξ (LN 9.11) (BAGD 3. p. 743): 'person' [BAGD, LN; NLT], 'human' [WBC], 'human being' [AB1, LN; ESV], 'flesh' [AB2, Lns; KJV], 'life' [NASB]. The phrase 'not any person' is translated 'not a single person' [NLT], 'no one' [BECNT, BNTC, NTC; CEV, GW, NCV, NET, NIV, NRSV], 'nobody' [TEV], 'no living thing' [REB]. This noun is a figurative extension of the meaning of σάρξα 'flesh' and refers to a human as a physical being [LN].

c. aorist pass. indic. of σῴζω (LN 21.18) (BAGD 1.a. p. 798): 'to be saved' [AB2, BAGD, BECNT, BNTC, Lns, NTC; ESV, GW, KJV, NASB, NET, NRSV], 'to be delivered, to be rescued, to be made safe' [LN], 'to be left alive' [CEV], 'to go on living' [NCV], 'to survive' [AB1, WBC; NIV, NLT, REB, TEV]. This verb means to rescue from danger and to restore to a former state of safety and well-being [LN]. It means to save from physical death [BAGD, NICNT, TRT]. In this context it means to escape, to survive, to live through something [TH].

d. ἐκλεκτός (LN 30.93) (BAGD 1.b. p. 242): 'the chosen' [BAGD, LN]. The phrase τοὺς ἐκλεκτοὺς οὓς ἐξελέξατο 'the chosen ones whom he chose' [AB2] is also translated, 'the elect, whom he chose/has-chosen' [AB1, BNTC, WBC; ESV, NASB, NET, NIV, NRSV; similarly KJV], 'the elect, whom he elected for himself' [Lns, NTC; similarly BECNT], 'his chosen and special ones' [CEV], 'his own, whom he has chosen' [REB], 'those whom God has chosen' [GW], 'the people he has chosen' [NCV], 'his chosen ones/people' [NLT, TEV]. This pronominal adjective denotes a person has been chosen [LN]. In this context it refers to the Christians, the followers of Jesus [BECNT, TH].

QUESTION—Who is the κύριος 'Lord'?
'Lord' refers to the Lord God [TH].

13:21 And then if someone says to-you, 'Look, here (is) the Messiah![a]' 'Look, there (he is)!', do- not -believe (it/him). **13:22** Because false-Messiahs[b] and false-prophets will-be-raised-up[c] and they-will-perform signs[d] and wonders so-as to-deceive,[e] if possible, the chosen-ones.

LEXICON—a. Χριστός (LN 53.82) (BAGD 1. p. 887): With the article, it is translated 'the Messiah' [AB1, BAGD, BECNT, LN, WBC; CEV, GW, NLT, NRSV, REB, TEV], 'the Christ' [AB2, BAGD, BNTC, Lns, NTC; ESV, KJV, NASB, NCV, NET, NIV]. This noun means 'the one who has been anointed'. In the NT, it is a title for Jesus who is 'the Messiah, the Christ'. In other contexts, especially when it is without an article,

Χριστός functions as part of the name 'Jesus Christ' [LN]. This word occurs at 1:1; 8:29; 9:41; 12:35; 13:21; 14:61; 15:32.
b. ψευδόχριστος (LN 53.84) (BAGD p. 892): The plural form is translated 'false Messiahs' [BAGD, LN; CEV, TEV], 'false messiahs' [BECNT, WBC; NET, NLT, NRSV], 'pseudo-messiahs' [AB1], 'false Christs' [AB2, BNTC, LN, Lns, NTC; KJV, NASB, NCV, NIV], 'false christs' [ESV, GW], 'imposters claming to be messiahs' [REB]. This noun denotes one who claims to be the Messiah but isn't [LN].
c. fut. pass. indic. of ἐγείρω (LN 13.83) (BAGD 2.e. p. 215): 'to be raised up' [AB2, LN, WBC], 'to rise up' [NLT], 'to arise' [BECNT, Lns, NTC; ESV, NASB], 'to rise' [KJV], 'to appear' [BAGD, BNTC; GW, NET, NIV, NRSV, TEV], 'to arrive on the scene' [AB1], 'to come' [CEV, NCV, REB]. This verb means to come into existence [LN].
d. σημεῖον (LN 33.477) (BAGD 2.b. p. 748): 'sign' [BAGD, LN]. The phrase δώσουσιν σημεῖα 'will perform signs' [BNTC, NTC; ESV, NET, NIV, NLT] is also translated 'will produce/give/furnish/offer signs' [AB1, AB2, LN, WBC; NRSV, REB], 'will perform miracles' [TEV], 'will perform great wonders' [NCV], 'will work miraculous signs' [GW], 'will work miracles' [CEV], 'will/shall show signs' [KJV, NASB]. This noun refers to an event that has a special meaning [LN]. It refers to a sign consisting of a wonder or miracle worked by Satan or his agents [BAGD].
e. pres. act. infin. of ἀποπλανάω (LN 31.11): 'to deceive' [BECNT, LN, WBC; GW, NET, NIV, NLT, TEV], 'to lead astray' [AB2, Lns; ESV, NASB, NRSV], 'to mislead' [AB1, BNTC, **LN,** NTC; REB], 'to seduce' [KJV], 'to try to fool' [CEV, NCV], 'to cause others to have completely wrong views' [LN]. This verb means to cause others to go astray in regard to their beliefs or views [LN].

QUESTION—Who is making the two statements?
1. The same person makes both statements: 'If someone says to you, "Look, here is the Messiah!" *or if he says*, "Look, there he is!" don't believe it' [TH; KJV, NASB, NET].
2. Different people make the statements: 'If someone says to you "Look, here is the Messiah!" *or if another says*, "Look, there he is!" don't believe it' [NCV].

QUESTION—Is it possible to deceive the chosen ones?
1. Even though the aim is to deceive believers and lead them astray, the addition 'if possible' indicates that they will not succeed [EBC, ESVfn, Gnd, Hb, Lns, NAC, NIGTC, NTC, WBC]. God will protect his own people so that they will not believe in a false messiah or prophet [ESVfn].
2. This means that there is a possibility that they may succeed in leading some astray [BNTC, Sw, TRT]. It does not indicate whether or not the false messiahs will succeed in deceiving some of the elect. The point is that they will try to deceive the disciples and they may or may not succeed in individual cases [TRT].

13:23 But you(pl) beware.[a] I-have-forewarned[b] you (concerning) all (things).

LEXICON—a. pres. act. impera. of βλέπω (LN 27.58): 'to beware' [LN, WBC], 'to be on guard' [AB1, NTC; CEV, ESV, GW, NIV, REB, TEV], 'to be alert' [NRSV], 'to look/watch out' [AB2, BECNT, LN; NLT], 'to pay attention' [LN], 'to take heed' [KJV, NASB], 'to be careful' [NCV, NET], 'to see to it' [Lns]. This is a figurative extension of the verb 'to see' and means to be ready to learn about future dangers and be prepared to respond appropriately [LN].

b. perf. act. indic. of προλέγω (LN 33.281): 'to forewarn' [REB], 'to foretell' [AB2; KJV], 'to tell ahead of time' [LN, NTC; NET, NIV, TEV], 'to warn ahead of time' [NLT], 'to predict' [LN], 'to warn/tell beforehand' [AB1, BECNT; ESV], 'to tell in advance' [NASB], 'to tell/warn before it happens' [GW, NCV], 'to already tell' [NRSV], 'to tell now' [CEV]. This verb means to say in advance what is going to happen [LN].

DISCOURSE UNIT—13:24–37 [NASB]. The topic is the return of Christ.

DISCOURSE UNIT—13:24–27 [Hb; CEV, ESV, NET, NRSV, TEV]. The topic is the coming of the Son of Man [ESV, NRSV, TEV], the arrival of the Son of Man [NET], when the Son of Man appears [CEV], the return of the Son of man [Hb].

13:24 But in the days after that trouble the sun will-be-darkened,[a] and the moon will- not -give its light, **13:25** and the stars will-be falling from the sky, and the powers,[b] the-ones in the skies, will-be-shaken.[c]

TEXT—In verse 25, manuscripts reading ἔσονται ἐκ τοῦ οὐρανοῦ πίπτοντες 'will be falling from the sky' are followed by GNT which does not mention any variant reading. A variant reading is ἔσονται ἐκ πίπτοντες 'will be falling' and it is followed by KJV.

LEXICON—a. fut. pass. indic. of σκοτίζομαι (LN 14.55) (BAGD 1. p. 757): 'to be darkened' [AB1, AB2, BAGD, BECNT, BNTC, NTC, WBC; ESV, KJV, NASB, NET, NIV, NLT, NRSV, REB], 'to become dark' [BAGD, LN; CEV], 'to grow dark' [NCV, TEV], 'to turn dark' [GW], 'to be made dark' [Lns]. This verb means to change from a condition of being light to being dark [LN]. It means that the sun will become dark in the sense that it will not shine [TH].

b. δύναμις (LN 12.44) (BAGD 5. p. 208): 'power' [BAGD, LN], 'authority, lordship, ruler, wicked force' [LN], The phrase αἱ δυνάμεις αἱ ἐν τοῖς οὐρανοῖς 'the powers, the ones in the skies' is translated 'the powers in the sky' [CEV], 'the powers in the heavens' [BECNT, Lns, WBC; ESV, NET, NLT, NRSV], 'the powers that are in heaven' [KJV], 'the powers that are in the heavens' [NTC; NASB], 'the powers of the heavens' [AB1, AB2; NCV], 'the powers in space' [TEV], 'the powers of the universe' [GW], 'the celestial powers' [BNTC; REB], 'the heavenly bodies' [NIV]. This noun denotes a supernatural power having some particular role in

controlling the destiny and activities of human beings [LN]. This refers to the heavenly bodies as though they are the armies of heaven [BAGD]. The term τοῖς οὐρανοῖς 'the heavens' refers to the sky, not to the abode of God [TH].
  c. fut. pass. indic. of σαλεύω (LN 16.7) (BAGD 1. p. 740): 'to be shaken' [BAGD, LN; all translations except TEV], 'to be driven from their courses' [TEV]. This verb means to cause something to move back and forth rapidly, often violently [LN].

QUESTION—Why does this verse begin with the conjunction ἀλλά 'but'?

This indicates a contrast with the trouble described in verses 19–23 [BECNT, NICNT, TH]. 'There will be false messianic figures where Jerusalem is judged. Do not be misled by them. *But* when the Messiah actually appears, his coming will be like this…' [NICNT]. This marks the transition from the supreme distress described in 19–23 to an abrupt and full deliverance when the Son of Man appears [BECNT, CGTC, NTC].

QUESTION—What time is indicted by the reference to 'the days after that trouble'?

The proposition 'after' refers to the sequence of two events and does not indicate how much time will transpire between them [TH]. The days of tribulation will come to an end, and the final event will occur at some undisclosed time afterwards [Lns]. 'In the days after' could refer to any time after the events of verses 5–23 [NLTfn]. This is speaking of the end times [EBC] that lead up to the second coming of Christ [CBC, CGT, Gnd, EBC, ESVfn, Hb. NAC, NICNT, NIGTC, PNTC, Tay].

QUESTION—What is meant by the 'powers in the skies'?

'The stars will fall' and 'the powers will be shaken' could be a parallelism that refers to just one event or it could refer to two different events. Some think 'powers' is another way of referring to the sun, moon, stars, and planets. Others think the 'powers' refer to spiritual forces that control those things [TRT]. In accordance with Hebrew parallelism these heavenly powers may simply be the stars themselves or the evil spirits who were thought to rule the heavenly bodies [Hb, Tay, TH].
  1. The reference to 'the powers in the sky' refers to the stars in the sky [AB2, BAGD, BNTC, EBC, EGT, ICC, Lns, NTC, Sw, Tay; NIV]. The 'powers' probably summarizes the preceding references to the sun, moon, and stars [NTC]. Whatever holds the heavenly bodies in their orbits and enables the sun, moon, and stars to light the earth will give way [Lns].
  2. The heavens probably were considered to be the abode of heavenly forces and their 'shaking' indicates distress in the spiritual realm [NETfn].

13:26 And then (they)-will-see the Son of-Man[a] coming in/on clouds[b] with great power[c] and glory.

LEXICON—a. υἱὸς τοῦ ἀνθρώπου 'Son of Man' (LN 9.3) (BAGD 2.e. p. 835): This title of Jesus is translated 'the Son of Man' [BAGD, LN; all translations except AB1], 'The Man' [AB1]. It is a title with Messianic implications that Jesus used concerning himself [LN]. Jewish teaching of that era included a heavenly being called the 'Son of Man' or 'Man' who exercised Messianic functions such as judging the world [BAGD]. See 2:10 for a discussion of this title.

b. νεφέλη (LN 1.34) (BAGD p. 536): 'cloud' [BAGD, LN]. The phrase ἐρχόμενον ἐν νεφέλαις 'coming in clouds' [AB1, AB2, BECNT, Lns, NTC, WBC; ESV, GW, NASB, NCV, NIV, NRSV] is also translated 'coming in the clouds' [BNTC; CEV, KJV, REB], 'arriving in the clouds' [NET, TEV], 'coming on the clouds' [NLT]. It is natural to think that they will see the Son of Man coming *towards* them [BNTC].

c. δύναμις (LN 76.1): 'power' [LN]. The phrase μετὰ δυνάμεως πολλῆς καὶ δόξης is translated 'with great power and glory' [all translations]. This noun denotes the potentiality to exert force in performing some function [LN]. Christ's 'power' is his omnipotence, and his 'glory' is the sum of all his divine attributes [Lns].

QUESTION—How is this verse connected with the Old Testament?

Jesus describes his coming almost entirely from the Old Testament scriptures [CGTC, EBC]. The terminology is taken from Daniel 7:13–14 in which the seer beholds 'one like a son of man' coming 'with clouds' and being presented to the 'Ancient of Days' who bestows his own authority, glory, and dominion upon him [AB2].

QUESTION—Who will see the Son of Man coming?

Everyone will see him coming [CGTC, NTC, WBC]. 'They' refers to all the living inhabitants of the earth. The world will have been plunged into darkness when the Son of Man comes out of heaven in supernatural brilliancy and glory [Lns]. The indefinite plural 'will see' is often used in the Aramaic language for the simple passive: 'And then the Son of Man will be seen' [NICNT].

QUESTION—What is meant by the Son of Man coming ἐν ἐκλεκτοὺς 'in/on clouds'?

1. The phrase 'coming *in* clouds' indicates the divinity of the Son of Man [AB1, AB2, BNTC, Hb, ICC, NCBC, PNTC, TH]. The presence of God manifests itself 'in a cloud' as in Ex. 34:5, Lev. 16:2, and Num. 11:25 [TH]. Clouds in the OT often symbolize the presence and glory of God [Hb, PNTC]. The clouds are an outward symbol of God's dignity and honor [AB1]. Because clouds frequently accompany visible manifestations of God, this cloud indicates that the Son of Man is a divine person [AB2]. The clouds are not to be taken literally. This means that the kingdom that is to be setup is from heaven [ICC].

2. The phrase 'coming *on* clouds' pictures the clouds as being the vehicle on which the Son of Man will arrive to earth [BAGD, Lns, NICNT, Tay; NLT]. He comes in a celestial chariot of clouds [NICNT, Lns]. His divine origin is suggested by his arrival on the clouds [Tay].

13:27 And then he-will-send the angels and gather his chosen-ones[a] from the four winds,[b] from (the) end of-the-earth to (the) end of-(the)-sky.[c]

TEXT—Manuscripts reading τοὺς ἐκλεκτοὺς αὐτοῦ 'his chosen ones' are given a C rating by GNT to indicate that choosing it over a variant text was difficult. A variant reading is τοὺς ἐκλεκτοὺς 'the chosen ones' and it is followed by AB1, BNTC.

LEXICON—a. ἐκλεκτός (LN 30.93) (BAGD 1.b. p. 242): 'chosen' [BAGD, LN]. The phrase τοὺς ἐκλεκτοὺς ἐκλεκτοὺς αὐτοῦ 'his chosen ones/people' [AB2; CEV, NCV, NLT] is also translated 'his chosen' [REB], 'the chosen' [AB1], 'his elect' [BECNT, Lns, NTC, WBC; ESV, KJV, NASB, NET, NIV, NRSV], 'the elect' [BNTC], 'God's chosen people' [TEV], 'those whom God has chosen' [GW]. This pronominal adjective denotes a person who has been chosen [LN].

b. ἄνεμος (LN 14.4) (BAGD 1.b. p. 64): 'wind' [BAGD, LN]. The phrase ἐκ τῶν τεσσάρων ἀνέδμων 'from the four winds' [AB2, BECNT, BNTC, Lns, NTC, WBC; ESV, KJV, NASB, NET, NIV, NRSV, REB] is also translated 'from all over the world' [NLT], 'all around the earth' [NCV]. Some translations leave out this difficult idiom about the four winds since the following idiom has the same meaning [AB1; CEV, GW, TEV]. This noun denotes air that is rapidly moving [LN]. The phrase 'from the four winds' means from all directions [BNTC], from everywhere [NTC].

c. οὐρανός (LN 1.5) (BAGD 1.a.b. p. 594): 'sky' [LN], 'heaven' [BAGD]. The clause ἀπ' ἄκρου γῆς ἕως ἄκρου οὐρανοῦ 'from the end of the earth to the end of the sky' is translated 'from the end/ends of the earth to the end/ends of heaven' [AB2, BECNT, BNTC, Lns; ESV, NET, NRSV; similarly NIV], 'from the corner of the earth to the corner of heaven' [WBC], 'from the farthest end of the earth to the farthest end of heaven' [NASB], 'from farthest reach of earth to farthest reach of heaven' [NTC], 'from the most uttermost part of the earth to the uttermost part of heaven' [KJV], 'from the farthest ends of the earth and heaven' [NLT], 'from every part of the earth and from every part of heaven' [NCV], 'from the farthest bounds of earth to the farthest bounds of heaven' [AB1; REB], 'from one end of the world to the other' [TEV], 'from every direction under the sky' [GW], 'from all over the earth' [CEV]. The noun οὐρανός 'sky' denotes the space above the earth. In this verse it refers to the vault arching high over the earth from one horizon to another that contains the sun, moon, and stars [LN]. The unique combination 'from the end of the earth to the end of the sky' means from the extremity of the earth to the extremity of the heavens. The Jewish concept of the universe underlying this idiom is that heaven is a half circle overarching the earth where earth and sky meet at their two extremes. It simply means 'from one end of the world to the other' [TH]. It does not include everywhere in heaven. It reflects the fact that the earth and the sky appear to meet at the horizon and just means 'from everywhere all over the earth' [TRT].

QUESTION—Where did the angels come from?

These angels will accompany Jesus when he comes 'with great power and glory' and Jesus will send them to gather up all of the elect [Lns, NTC].

QUESTION—Who are the 'chosen ones' who will be gathered by the angels?

His chosen ones are the people who believe in him [BECNT, NLTfn] and follow him [NLTfn]. The identity of the chosen ones referred to in this verse depends upon one's eschatological views. Some think this refers to the resurrection of everyone who has ever believed in Jesus [Lns, NTC]. Others think it refers only to those believers who have come though the Great Tribulation. Others think it refers only to those of the church who will emerge from the Great Tribulation. Others think it refers only to the Jewish believers who have been won to faith in Christ as their Messiah during the Great Tribulation [Hb]

DISCOURSE UNIT—13:28–37 [Hb]. The topic is the concluding instructions.

DISCOURSE UNIT—13:28–31 [CEV, ESV, NET, NRSV, TEV]. The topic is a lesson from a fig tree [CEV, ESV], the lesson of the fig tree [NRSV, TEV], the parable of the fig tree [NET].

13:28 **And learn**[a] **the parable from the fig-tree: when its branch already has-become tender**[b] **and puts-forth its leaves, you know that summer is near.** **13:29** **So also you, when you see these (things) happening, know that (he/it) is near, at (the) gates.**[c]

LEXICON—a. aorist act. impera. of μανθάνω (LN 27.12) (BAGD 1. p. 490): 'to learn, to be instructed, to be taught' [TH]. The phrase μάθετε τὴν παραβολήν 'learn the/a parable' [AB2, Lns, WBC; KJV, NASB] is also translated 'learn this parable' [NET], 'learn this/a lesson' [AB1, BNTC, NTC; CEV, ESV, NCV, NIV, NLT, NRSV, REB], 'learn the lesson of the parable' [BECNT], 'learn from the story of' [GW], '(let the fig tree) teach you a lesson' [TEV]. This verb means to acquire information as the result of being instructed [LN].

b. ἁπαλός (LN 79.101) (BAGD p. 80): 'tender' [AB1, AB2, BAGD, BECNT, BNTC, LN, Lns, NTC, WBC; ESV, GW, KJV, NASB, NET, NRSV]. The clause 'when its branch already has become tender' is translated 'when its twigs get tender' [NIV], 'when its tender shoots appear' [REB], 'when its branches bud' [NLT], 'when its branches sprout' [BAGD; CEV], 'when its branches become green and soft/tender' [NCV, TEV]. This adjective indicates that something is tender in the sense that it yields readily to pressure [LN]. In the springtime the sap rises through the limbs to make the branch tender and causes the leaves to sprout [TH].

c. θύρα (LN 7.49, 67.58) (BAGD 2.a. p. 365): 'gate' [LN (7.49)], 'door' [BAGD, LN (7.49)]. The clause ἐγγύς ἐστιν ἐπὶ θύραις '(he/it) is near, at the gates' is translated in reference to the Son of Man: 'he is near, at the gates' [WBC], 'he is near, at the very door/gates' [AB1, BNTC; ESV, NRSV], 'he is near, right at the door' [NASB, NET; similarly AB2; GW], 'his return is very near, right at the door' [NLT]. Others translate it in reference to the time of a coming event: 'the time is near, ready to begin' [TEV], 'the time is near, ready to come' [NCV], 'the time has almost come' [CEV], 'the end is near, at the very door' [REB], 'it is near, right at the door' [NIV], 'it is near, at the doors' [Lns], 'it is near, at the very gates' [BECNT, NTC], 'it is nigh, even at the door' [KJV]. This noun denotes the door to a house or building and often appears in a plural form to designate double doors or gates [LN (7.49)]. The idiom ἐπὶ θύραις 'at the gates/doors' refers to a point in time subsequent to another point in time and indicates imminence so that the subsequent event is regarded as almost begun [LN (67.58)].

QUESTION—Is verse 29 a statement or a command?
1. It is a statement [AB1, AB2, BECNT, BNTC, EBC, NTC, NIGTC, WBC; CEV, ESV, GW, NCV, NIV, NLT, NRSV, REB, TEV]: 'When you see these things happening, you will know that…'.
2. It is a command [Gnd, Hb, ICC, Lns, NTC, Tay, TH; KJV, NASB, NET]: 'When you see these things happening, then know that…' Jesus was urging them to realize what is happening [Hb]. It is a command for them to understand the meaning of what they will see [Gnd].

QUESTION—When they see ταῦτα 'these things' happening, what is it that they will see?

The reference to 'these things' indicates that the parable was an addition to a preceding account, but it is not clear about what things Mark had in mind [BNTC]. 'These things' could be the signs listed in verses 5–23 that precede the destruction of Jerusalem and/or the signs listed in verses 24–25 that precede the end of the age [NIVfn].
1. They will see the signs leading up to the coming destruction of Jerusalem [AB2, BECNT, CGTC, EBC, EGT, Gnd, ICC, NAC, NICNT, NIGTC, NTC]. The parallel statement in verse 30 clearly refers to verses 4–20 [NICNT]. When they see the abomination of desolation standing where he/it should not (verses 14–23), they will know the fall of Jerusalem is near [BECNT, CGTC, Gnd, NAC, PNTC].
2. When they see the signs in the heavens described in verses 24–25, then they will know that the Son of Man mentioned in verses 26–27 will soon come in the clouds with great power and glory [AB1, BNTC, CBC, Gnd, Lns, NIVfn, Tay, TH; ESV, GW, NASB, NET, NLT, NRSV].
3. This refers to all of the various predictions in verses 5–27 [Lns, WBC]. Jesus expected that all of these things will take place within the span of a single generation [WBC]. We are always to be ready since all the signs have occurred again and again [Lns].

13:30 Truly[a] I-say to-you that this generation[b] will- not -pass-away[c] until all these-things happen. **13:31** Heaven and earth will-pass-away, but my words will- not -pass-away.[d]

LEXICON—a. ἀμήν (LN 72.6) (BAGD 2. p. 45): 'truly' [BAGD, BECNT, BNTC, LN, WBC; ESV, NASB, NRSV, REB], 'indeed, it is true that' [LN], 'verily' [KJV], 'amen' [AB2, Lns]. The phrase 'truly I say to you' is translated 'I tell you the truth' [NCV, NET, NIV, NLT], 'I can guarantee this truth' [GW], 'I solemnly declare to you' [NTC], 'in truth I tell you' [AB1], 'you can be sure' [CEV], not explicit [TEV]. This particle makes a strong affirmation of what is declared [LN]. It is an assertive particle that begins a solemn declaration [BAGD]. The phrase 'truly I say to you' occurs at 3:28; 8:12; 9:1, 41; 10:15, 29; 11:23; 12:43; 13:30; 14:9, 18, 25, 30.

b. γενεά (LN 10.4 or 11.4) (BAGD 2. p. 154): 'generation, contemporaries' [BAGD], 'people of the same kind' [LN (10.4)], 'people of the same time, those of the same generation' [LN (11.4)]. The phrase ἡ γενεὰ αὕτη 'this generation' [AB1, AB2, BECNT, BNTC, Lns, NTC, WBC; ESV, GW, KJV, NASB, NET, NLT, NRSV] is also translated 'the present generation' [REB], 'some of the people of this generation' [CEV], 'the people now living' [TEV], 'the people of this time' [NCV]. This noun denotes an ethnic group exhibiting cultural similarities [LN (10.4)] or people living at the same time and belonging to the same reproductive age-class [LN (11.4)].

c. aorist act. subj. of παρέρχομαι (LN 13.93, 67.85) (BAGD 1.b.α. p. 626): 'to pass away [AB1, AB2, BAGD, LN (13.93)], 'to come to an end' [BAGD], 'to cease to exist' [LN (13.93)]. The clause 'will not pass away' [BNTC, NTC, WBC; ESV, NASB, NET, NRSV] is also translated 'will in no way pass away' [BECNT], 'shall not pass' [KJV], 'will not pass from the scene' [NLT], 'will not disappear' [GW], 'will still be alive' [CEV], 'will live (to see it all)' [REB], 'all these things will happen while the people of this time are still living' [NLT]. This verb means to go out of existence [LN (13.93)] or to mark the passage of time with the focus upon its completion [LN (67.83)].

d. fut. mid. (deponent = act.) indic. of παρέρχομαι (LN 13.93) (BAGD 1.b.α. p. 626): 'to pass away' [BAGD, LN]. The clause 'my words will not pass away' [BNTC, WBC; ESV, KJV, NASB, NET, NIV, NRSV] is also translated 'my words will never pass away' [AB1, AB2, BECNT, NTC; REB, TEV], 'my words shall in no wise pass away' [Lns], 'my words will never disappear' [GW, NLT], 'the words I have said will never be destroyed' [NCV], 'my words will last forever' [CEV]. This verb means to go out of existence [LN (13.93)]. His words will never stop being dependable prophecy [TH].

QUESTION—What are 'these things' and who are the people of ἡ γενεὰ αὕτη 'this generation' who will not pass away?
1. 'These things' refer to the events leading up to the destruction of Jerusalem [AB2, BECNT, EBC, EGT, Hb, Gnd, ICC, NAC, NICNT, NIGTC, PNTC, Tay, TH]. The people referred to by 'this generation' are obviously Jesus' contemporaries [BECNT, TH, WBC]. It means 'all these things' will happen during the lifetime of his generation [TH, WBC]. 'This generation' could refer to the disciples who are alive while Jesus was speaking, and 'all these things' refers to the beginning of the sufferings described in verses 3–13. [ESVfn]. Both verse 4 and verses 29–30 use 'these things' and 'all these things' to describe the predicted destruction of Jerusalem in verse 2 [BECNT].
2. 'These things' concern the events leading up to the future second coming of Christ [CGTC, Hb, Lns]. If 'all these things' refers to the future coming of the Son of Man, then 'this generation' cannot refer to the people who were alive during the ministry of Jesus. Therefore 'this generation' must refer either to (1) the continued existence throughout the centuries of the whole human race, the Jewish people, or the Christian community, or (2) the last generation living at the end time [NLTfn]. It refers to that future wicked generation that will actually see the beginning of those eschatological events [Hb]. It could mean that the same type of Jew that Jesus was contending with will still be present all the way up to the Second Coming [Lns]. The generation that sees the signs of the end will also see the end itself since all the events connected with the end will happen in rapid succession [NETfn].
3. 'These things' concern all the things Jesus predicted in this chapter [NTC, TNTC, WBC]. 'This generation' might mean 'this type of generation' and refer to the generation of wicked humanity. Then it would mean that humanity will not perish because God will redeem it [NETfn]. The phrase 'this generation' could refer to (1) this generation of believers throughout the entire present age, (2) this evil generation that will remain until Christ returns to establish his kingdom, or (3) the Jewish people who will not pass away until Christ returns [ESVfn]. This 'generation' refers to the Jewish race, and the phrase 'all these things' covers the entire dispensation, including even the final tribulation and the Lord's glorious return [NTC].

QUESTION—What words of Jesus will not pass away?
It could refer to all his teachings as a whole [Hb, NAC, WBC], to what he taught in verses 5–30, or to what he had said in the preceding verse [WBC]. Jesus is giving his personal guarantee to the truthfulness of what he said in verse 30, but what 'words' will not pass away is not made explicit. It could refer to what he said in verses 28–30, the entire apocalyptic discourse, or all of his teachings [BECNT]. The words of Jesus that will not pass away include everything he said and not just what was written in verse 30 [Lns].

QUESTION—How will heaven and earth pass away?
'Heaven' refers to the sky in this verse, and it means that the whole created universe will come to an end [TH]. In spite of their present stability, heaven and earth will come to the end of their present state of existence [Hb]. The word 'pass away' doesn't specify whether it refers to annihilation, sinking back into nothingness, or being transformed to a different state of existence [LN]. It implies that there will be a glorious renewal [NTC].

DISCOURSE UNIT—13:32–37 [CEV, ESV, GW, NET, NIV, NRSV, TEV]. The topic is that no one knows when the earth and the heavens will disappear [GW], no one knows the day or time [CEV], no one knows that day or hour [ESV, TEV], the day and hour are unknown [NIV], the necessity for watchfulness [NRSV], be ready! [NET].

13:32 **But concerning that day or the hour no-one knows, neither the angels in heaven nor the Son, only the Father (knows).**
QUESTION—How is this verse connected with its context?
   1. It begins the following paragraph [AB1, BECNT, BNTC, EBC, Gnd, Lns, NAC, NICNT, NIGTC, PNTC; CEV, ESV, GW, NCV, NET, NIV, NLT, NRSV, TEV].
   2. It ends the preceding paragraph [AB2, Hb, Sw, WBC; NASB].
   3. It is a separate paragraph [REB].
QUESTION—What does 'that day or hour' refer to?
It refers to that day and hour when the Son of Man will appear in glory and power (verse 26) [AB1, AB2, BECNT, BNTC, CBC, CGTC, EBC, Hb, Lns, My, NAC, NICNT, NIGTC, NTC, NTC, PNTC, Sw, Tay, WBC]. The adversative 'but' sets this verse in contrast to the preceding subject of 'these things' where it refers to the fall of Jerusalem. The words 'day' and 'hour' are often charged with eschatological meaning in the Bible and the end is shrouded in mystery [PNTC]. The mention of the day and the hour is simply a way of saying that no one knows the precise moment when the time will come [TH]. Although the series of events preceding Christ's return have been described, the precise moment has not been specified [EBC, NTC].

13:33 **Watch,ᵃ be-alertᵇ because you(pl)-know not when the time is.**
TEXT—Manuscripts reading ἀγρυπνεῖτε 'be alert' are given a B rating by GNT to indicate it was regarded to be almost certain. A variant reading is ἀγρυπνεῖτε καὶ προσεύχεσθε 'be alert and be praying' and it is followed by KJV.
LEXICON—a. pres. act. impera. of βλέπω (LN 27.58) (BAGD 4.a. p. 143): 'to watch' [AB1], 'to watch out' [BECNT LN, WBC; CEV, NET], 'to be on watch' [TEV], 'to look out' [AB2], 'to be on guard' [BNTC, NTC; ESV, NIV, NLT, REB], 'to be careful' [GW, NCV], 'to take heed' [KJV, NASB], 'to take care' [BAGD], 'to beware' [LN; NRSV], 'to pay attention' [LN], 'to be wakeful' [Lns]. This verb is a figurative extension of the meaning of the verb 'to see' and means to be ready to learn about

future dangers or needs. It implies being prepared to respond appropriately [LN]. The present tense of the command indicates that this watching is to be continuous [Lns].

b. pres. act. impera. of ἀγρυπνέω (LN **27.57**) (BAGD 1. p. 14): 'to be alert' [AB1, BECNT, BNTC, **LN**, WBC; NIV, TEV], 'to stay/keep alert' [NET, NLT, NRSV], 'to not fall asleep' [AB2], 'to always be alert' [NCV], 'to keep on the alert' [NASB], 'to be ready' [CEV], 'to be on the lookout for, to be vigilant' [LN], 'to watch' [GW, KJV], 'to keep watch' [NTC; REB], 'to be/keep awake' [BAGD; ESV], 'to be praying' [Lns]. This verb is a figurative extension of the meaning 'to keep oneself awake' that means to make an effort to learn about what might be a potential future threat [LN]. Their need for constant vigilance is because they do not know when the time will come [BNTC].

QUESTION—What is the function of the command to 'watch and be alert'?

This command is the keynote of the entire paragraph. If Jesus himself does not know the time of the Parousia (verse 32), the disciples must realize their own ignorance of when it will happen and always be prepared for it [EBC, Sw]. The connections with the following parable are: 'No one knows that day or that hour' (verse 32), 'you know not when the time is' (verse 33), and 'for you do not know when the lord of the household comes' (verse 35) [NICNT].

13:34 **(It is) like a-man (who) is-gone on-a-journey,**[a] **having-left his house and having-given to his slaves authority,**[b] **(assigning) to-each his work,**[c] **and he-commanded the doorkeeper that he-keep-alert.**[d]

LEXICON—a. ἀπόδημος (LN 85.22) (BAGD p. 90): 'to go on a journey' [BECNT; ESV, NET, NRSV], 'to be on a journey' [AB1, WBC], 'to go on a trip' [GW, NCV, TEV], 'to go on a long trip' [NLT], 'to go abroad' [Lns], 'to be away on a journey' [BAGD, LN, NTC; NASB], 'to be away from home' [AB1, BNTC], 'to go away' [NIV], 'to go away for a while' [CEV], 'to be away from home' [LN; REB], 'to take a far journey' [KJV]. This adjective pertains to being away from where one usually resides [LN].

b. ἐξουσία (LN 37.35) (BAGD 3. p. 278): 'authority' [BAGD, LN], 'right to control' [LN]. The phrase 'to give authority to' [AB2, BECNT, Lns, WBC; KJV] is also translated 'to put in charge' [BNTC, NTC; ESV, GW, NASB, NET, NIV, NRSV, REB], 'to leave in charge' [AB1; TEV], 'to place in charge of everything' [CEV], 'to let (his servants) take care of it' [NCV], not explicit [NLT]. This noun denotes the right to control or govern over others [LN].

c. ἔργον (LN 42.42) (BAGD 2. p. 308): 'work, task' [BAGD, LN]. The clause 'assigning to each his work' [NET] is also translated 'assigning to each (one) his task' [NTC; NASB], 'giving each his task' [BNTC], 'giving each one a special job to do' [NCV], 'gave instructions about the work they were to do' [NLT], 'after giving to each one his own work to do' [TEV], 'he assigned work to each one' [GW], 'to each (one) his work' [AB2, Lns, WBC], 'to each one for his work' [BECNT], 'and to every man his work' [KJV], 'each with his work' [ESV, NRSV], 'each with his own work to do' [AB1; REB], 'each with his assigned task' [NIV], 'he tells each one of them what to do' [CEV]. This noun denotes that which one normally does [LN]. The clause 'having given his slaves authority, assigning to each his work' is translated 'giving the responsibility to his servants, to each one his particular work to do' [LN (42.42)].

d. pres. act. subj. of γρηγορέω (LN 27.56) (BAGD 1. p. 167): 'to be alert' [LN; GW], 'to keep/stay alert' [CEV, NET], 'to keep on the alert' [NTC], 'to stay on the alert' [NASB], 'to keep/stay awake' [AB2, BAGD; ESV, REB], 'to watch' [AB1, BECNT, Lns; KJV], 'to keep watch' [BNTC, WBC; NIV, TEV], 'to be on the watch' [NRSV], 'to be watchful' [LN; NCV], 'to watch for his return' [NLT], 'to be vigilant' [LN]. This is a figurative extension of the verb 'to stay awake' and it means to be in continuous readiness and alertness [LN].

13:35 Therefore you-be-alert because you-do- not -know when the owner[a] of-the house comes,[b] whether evening[c] or midnight[d] or cockcrow[e] or early,[f] **13:36** lest having-come suddenly[g] he finds you sleeping.

LEXICON—a. κύριος (LN 57.12) (BAGD 1.a.α. p. 459): 'owner' [BAGD, LN; GW, NCV, NET, NIV], 'master' [BAGD, LN; CEV, ESV, KJV, NASB, NLT, NRSV, REB, TEV], 'lord' [LN]. This noun denotes one who owns and controls his property, servants, and slaves. It has important supplementary semantic components of high status and respect [LN].

b. pres. mid./pass. (deponent = act.) indic. of ἔρχομαι (LN 15.81): 'to come' [LN; ESV, KJV, NASB, NRSV, REB, TEV], 'to come back' [CEV, NCV, NIV], 'to return' [GW, NET, NLT]. This verb means to move toward or up to the reference point of the viewpoint character or event [LN].

c. ὀψέ (LN 67.197) (BAGD 2. p. 601): 'evening' [LN; REB, TEV], 'in the evening' [CEV, ESV, GW, NASB, NCV, NIV, NLT, NRSV], 'during evening' [NET], 'at even' [KJV]. This adjective refers to the period after sunset but before darkness [LN].

d. μεσονύκτιον (67.75) (BAGD p. 507): 'midnight' [BAGD, LN; REB], 'at midnight' [all translations except REB]. This noun denotes the midpoint of the night. In some languages this may be described as 'when the night is half over' or 'when the night is cut in half' [LN].

e. ἀλεκτοροφωνία (LN 67.198) (BAGD p. 35): 'cockcrow' [LN; REB], 'when the cock crows' [LN], 'the crowing of a cock' [BAGD], 'at the cockcrowing' [KJV], 'at cockcrow' [NRSV], 'when the rooster crows' [ESV, NASB, NET, NIV], 'before dawn' [CEV, NLT, TEV], 'at dawn' [GW], 'in the morning while it is still dark' [NCV]. This noun means 'cockcrow' which is the name of the third Roman watch during the night [LN].

f. πρωΐ, πρωΐα (LN 67.187) (BAGD p. 723): 'early morning' [BAGD, LN], 'early dawn' [REB], 'at dawn' [NET, NIV, NRSV], 'at daybreak' [NLT], 'in the morning' [CEV, ESV, GW, KJV, NASB], 'at sunrise' [TEV], 'when the sun rises' [NCV]. This adjective refers to the early part of the daylight period [LN].
   g. ἐξαίφνης (LN 67.113) (BAGD p. 272): 'suddenly' [BAGD, LN; all versions except NLT], 'at once, immediately' [LN], 'unexpectedly' [BAGD], 'without warning' [NLT]. This adverb pertains to an extremely short period of time between a state or event and the subsequent state or event. In a number of contexts there is the implication of unexpectedness, but this seems to be a derivative of the context as a whole and not a part of the meaning of the lexical item [LN].

QUESTION—Who is Jesus telling to be alert
   Jesus is now applying the parable in verse 34 to his disciples by making no distinction between the doorkeeper and the other servants. The doorkeeper's need to keep alert applies to all of the disciples who must keep alert for the coming of the Lord [Hb]. This command applies to the four disciples mentioned in verse 3 [EBC].

QUESTION—What distinguishes the four different times listed here?
   These refer to the four divisions of the nighttime used by the Roman military to divide the nighttime into four watches of three hours each, beginning at 6:00 P.M. and ending at 6:00 A.M. [TH].

13:37 And what I-say to-you, I-say to-everyone, "Be alert."

QUESTION—Who are the people included in the pronoun ὑμῖν 'you'?
   Jesus was speaking with Peter, James, John, and Andrew (verses 3–5) [CGTC, EBC, WBC].

QUESTION—Who are the people included in the pronoun πᾶσιν 'everyone'?
   This includes the whole Christian church throughout the Last Times and not just the four disciples he was addressing in verse 5 [CGTC, EBC, NIGTC, WBC]. The question of the date of the destruction of the temple was directly relevant to only a limited number of disciples living in that generation, but the changed perspective of the concluding verses has widened the relevance of his teaching to all of his present disciples and all those who become his disciples in the future since all must live with the prospect of an unexpected parousia [NIGTC].

DISCOURSE UNIT—14:1–16:8 [CBC]. The topic is the king of the Jews executed for blasphemy, confessed as God's Son, and vindicated by God.

DISCOURSE UNIT—14:1–15:47 [Hb, NICNT; REB]. The topic is the trial and crucifixion of Jesus [REB], the passion narrative [NICNT], the self-sacrifice of the Servant [Hb].

DISCOURSE UNIT—14:1–72 [PNTC]. The topic is the abandonment of Jesus.

DISCOURSE UNIT—14:1-11 [Hb, NIGTC; NASB, NIV]. The topic is setting the scene for the Passion [NIGTC], foes and friends of Jesus [Hb], death plot and anointing [NASB], Jesus anointed at Bethany [NIV].

DISCOURSE UNIT—14:1-9 [NLT]. The topic is Jesus is anointed at Bethany.

DISCOURSE UNIT—14:1-2 [CBC, Hb, NICNT; CEV, ESV, GW, NCV, NET, NRSV, TEV]. The topic is a plot to kill Jesus [CEV, ESV, GW, NRSV], the plan to kill Jesus [NCV], the plotting of the Sanhedrin [Hb], the plot to arrest Jesus [CBC], the plot to seize Jesus [NICNT], the plot against Jesus [NET, TEV].

14:1 **Now the Passover^a and the (Festival of) Unleavened-Bread^b were two days away. And the chief-priests and the scribes were-seeking how having-seized (him) by deceit^c they-might-kill him.**

LEXICON—a. πάσχα (LN 51.6) (BAGD 1. p. 633): 'the Passover' [AB2, BAGD, BECNT, LN, Lns, WBC; CEV, GW, ESV, NASB, NCV, NET, NIV, NRSV], 'Passover' [AB1; NLT], 'the Passover festival' [BAGD, LN], 'the Festival of Passover' [BNTC; REB, TEV], 'the feast of the Passover' [NTC; KJV]. This noun denotes the Jewish festival commemorating the deliverance of Jews from Egypt [LN]. It was celebrated on the 14th day of the month of Nisan [BAGD]. The festival commemorated the time when the angel of the Lord passed over the homes of the Hebrews as he killed the firstborn sons in the Egyptian homes [NIVfn].

b. ἄζυμος (LN 5.13) (BAGD 1.b. p 20): 'unleavened, without yeast' [LN]. The phrase τὰ ἄζυμα 'the Unleavened Bread' [AB1; NASB] is also translated 'the Festival of Unleavened Bread' [BAGD, Lns, WBC; GW, NLT, NRSV], 'the Feast of Unleavened Bread' [AB2, BECNT; ESV, KJV, NCV, NET, NIV], 'the Festival of Thin Bread' [CEV]. Some translations indicate that the two festivals were essentially just one long celebration: 'the Festival of Passover and Unleavened Bread' [BNTC; REB, TEV], 'the feast of the Passover and Unleavened Bread' [NTC]. The word 'unleavened (bread)' refers to bread made without yeast' or 'bread which does not rise'. The expression 'the days of unleavened bread' may be rendered as 'the days when people ate bread that had no yeast'. This term is used in reference to the feast or festival of Unleavened Bread' [LN]. The Festival of Unleavened Bread immediately followed the Passover and lasted for seven days [NICfn].

c. δόλος (LN 88.154) (BAGD p. 203): 'deceit, cunning' [BAGD], 'trick' [NTC], 'subterfuge' [BECNT], 'stealth' [BNTC, WBC; NASB, NET, NRSV], 'craft' [Lns; KJV], 'treachery' [BAGD, LN]. The clause 'were seeking how having seized him by deceit they might kill him' is translated 'were planning how they could sneak around and have Jesus arrested and put to death' [CEV], 'were seeking how to arrest him by stealth and kill him' [ESV], 'were seeking how they might stealthily seize and kill him' [AB2], 'were looking for some sly way to arrest Jesus and kill him'

[NIV], 'were looking for a way to arrest Jesus secretly and put him to death' [AB1], 'were still looking for an opportunity to capture Jesus secretly and kill him' [NLT], 'were trying to devise some scheme to seize him and put him to death' [REB], 'were trying to find a trick to arrest Jesus and kill him' [NCV], 'were looking for some underhanded way to arrest Jesus and to kill him' [GW], 'were looking for a way to arrest Jesus secretly and put him to death' [TEV]. This noun denotes deception by using trickery and falsehood [LN]. They hoped to take Jesus into custody by surprise and without a public show of force [WBC]. Seizing Jesus openly would have caused a riot [BECNT].

QUESTION—Who were the 'chief-priests and scribes' involved in the plan to kill Jesus?

This does not refer to every chief-priest and scribe in the country. This was a way of referring to the whole Sanhedrin by mentioning the two principal classes of Jewish authorities that composed it [ICC]. It was probably an unofficial meeting that involved all the members of the Sanhedrin [Hb, Sw].

14:2 For they-were-saying, "Not during the festival,[a] lest there-be a-riot[b] of-the people."

LEXICON—a. ἑορτή (LN 51.2) (BAGD p. 280): 'festival' [BAGD, BNTC, LN, Lns; NASB, NRSV], 'feast' [AB2, BAGD, BECNT, LN, NTC, WBC; ESV, KJV, NET]. The clause 'Not at the festival' is translated 'But not during the Feast' [NIV], 'But not during the Passover celebration' [NLT], 'It must not be during the festival' [REB], 'We must not do it during the festival/feast' [CEV, NCV, TEV], 'We shouldn't arrest him during the Festival' [GW], 'But not in the presence of the festival crowd' [AB1]. This noun denotes the events associated with celebrating a festival or feast [LN].

b. θόρυβος (LN 39.42) (BAGD 3.b.p. 363): 'riot' [AB1, BECNT, LN, WBC; GW, NASB, NCV, NET, NRSV, TEV], 'disturbance' [AB2], 'tumult' [Lns], 'turmoil, excitement' [BAGD], 'uproar' [BAGD, NTC; ESV, KJV]. The noun is also translated as a verb: 'to riot' [BNTC; CEV, NIV, NLT], 'to have rioting' [REB]. This noun denotes the disorderly behavior of the people who are violently opposing their authorities [LN]. It refers to the noise and confusion of an excited crowd [BAGD]. The population of Jerusalem would have increased from about 50,000 to a few hundred thousand during the two festivals [NIVfn].

QUESTION—What relationship is indicated by the conjunction γάρ 'for'?

This presents the reason why the Sanhedrin was seeking for a way to seize Jesus in secret [CGTC]. They did not dare to act openly against Jesus [Hb].

DISCOURSE UNIT—14:3–9 [CBC, Hb, NICNT; CEV, ESV, GW, NCV, NET, NRSV, TEV]. The topic is: At Bethany [CEV], the anointing at Bethany [CBC, Hb, NICNT; NRSV], Jesus is anointed at Bethany [ESV, TEV], Jesus' anointing [NET], a woman with perfume for Jesus [NCV], a woman prepares Jesus' body for the tomb [GW].

14:3 And while he was in Bethany at the house of-Simon the Leper, as he was reclining[a] (at the table), a-woman came having an-alabaster-jar[b] of-perfume'[c] (made from) expensive pure nard.[d] (And) having-broken the alabaster-jar she-poured-(it)-on his head.

LEXICON—a. pres. mid./pass. (deponent = act) participle of κατάκειμαι (LN 17.23) (BAGD 3. p. 411): 'to recline' [AB2, BAGD, LN, WBC]. The phrase 'reclining at (the) table' [Lns, NTC; ESV, NAS, NET, NIV] is also translated 'was sitting there' [GW], 'as he sat at table' [NRSV, REB], 'while he was at the table' [AB1], 'as he sat at meat' [KJV], 'was eating' [CEV, NCV, NLT, TEV]. This verb means to be in a reclining position as one eats [LN].

b. ἀλάβαστρον (LN 6.131) (BAGD p. 34): 'alabaster jar' [AB1, AB2, BECNT, BNTC, LN, NTC; NCV, NET, NIV, NLT, NRSV, TEV], 'alabaster vial' [Lns; NASB], 'alabaster flask' [BAGD, WBC; ESV], 'alabaster box' [KJV], 'bottle' [CEV, GW, REB]. This noun denotes a jar made of alabaster stone. The alabaster jar normally had a rather long neck that was broken off when the contents were to be used. It served primarily as a container for precious substances such as perfumes. In translating 'alabaster jar' many translators have simply used a term meaning 'jar' or 'flask' and then added a descriptive qualifier such as 'made of alabaster stone, made of valuable stone, made of a valuable stone called alabaster' [LN].

c. μύρον (LN 6.205) (BAGD p. 30): 'perfume' [AB1, AB2, BAGD, BNTC, LN, Lns, NTC; all versions except ESV, KJV, NET], 'perfumed oil' [LN], 'aromatic oil' [NET], 'ointment' [BAGD, BECNT, WBC; ESV, KJV]. This noun denotes an expensive ointment that is strongly aromatic [LN]. In some languages, the word for 'ointment' or 'oil' may give a wrong impression since the perfume poured on Jesus' head would have rapidly evaporated and left only a lovely odor without an oily stain [Lns].

d. νάρδος (LN **6.210**) (BAGD 2. p. 534): 'nard' [AB1, AB2, BECNT, BNTC, Lns, NTC, WBC; all versions except KJV, CEV], 'spikenard' [KJV], 'perfume of nard' [**LN**], 'oil of nard' [BAGD, LN], not explicit [CEV]. This noun denotes an aromatic oil extracted from a plant called nard. Translators normally borrow the term 'nard' and employ some type of classifier such as 'a perfume called nard' or 'a sweet-smelling substance, nard' [LN]. This perfume was extracted from the dried root of a Himalayan plant and was called nard [NTC].

QUESTION—When did this event occur?
1. This occurred on Tuesday evening after Jesus had returned to Bethany to spend the night [BECNT, BNTC, Hb, Sw, WBC].
2. Mark now interrupts his account to go back to the preceding Saturday evening when a supper was given in honor of Jesus at Bethany [CBC, CGTC, ESV, Lns, NAC, NIVfn, NTC, PNTC, Sw]. This incident is placed out of order so that the woman's love and devotion to Jesus can be

contrasted with both the hatred of the religious leaders in verses 1–2 and the betrayal of Judas that follows in verses 10–11 [ESV, NIVfn].

QUESTION—Who was Simon 'the Leper'?

The origin of Simon's nickname is unknown [Hb]. Apparently Simon the Leper was the host. Since lepers were traditionally isolated from society to prevent the spread of the disease, he must have already been healed from his leprosy, possibly by Jesus himself [BECNT, Hb, Lns, TRT]. This was the home of 'Simon, who once had leprosy' [CEV].

QUESTION—Why did the woman break the alabaster jar and pour the nard on Jesus' head?

She forcefully snapped the narrow neck of the flask in order to quickly pour out the entire contents on his head. This was a common treatment of a festive guest [Hb]. This act expressed the woman's devotion to Jesus [NICNT].

14:4 But being-indignant[a] some (were saying) among/to themselves, "For what (reason) has this waste of-perfume happened?[b] **14:5** For this perfume might-have-been sold for more than three hundred denarii[c] and (the money) given to-the poor." And they were-reproaching[d] her.

TEXT—In verse 14:5, manuscripts reading τοῦτο τὸ μύρονν 'this perfume' are followed by GNT which does not mention any variant reading. A variant reading is τοῦτο 'this' and it is followed by KJV.

LEXICON—a. pres. act. participle of ἀγανακτέω (LN 88.187) (BAGD p. 44): 'to be indignant' [AB1, AB2, BECNT, BNTC, LN, Lns, NTC, WBC; ESV, KJV, NASB, NET, NIV, NLT, REB], 'to be irritated' [GW], 'to be angry' [LN; CEV, NRSV, TEV], 'to be upset' [NCV]. This verb means to be indignant about something that is judged to be wrong [LN].

b. ἀπώλεια (LN **65.14**) (BAGD 1. p. 104): 'waste' [AB2, BAGD, **LN**, Lns, NTC, WBC; CEV, KJV, NET, NIV, REB, TEV]. This noun is also translated as a verb: 'to be wasted' [BECNT; ESV, GW, NRSV], 'to waste' [AB1, BNTC; NCV, NET, NLT]. This noun denotes an action demonstrating complete disregard for the value of something. In some languages this question could be translated 'Why did she not think about the value of the perfume?' [LN].

c. δηνάριον (LN 6.75) (BAGD p. 179): 'denarius (singular), denarii (plural)' [AB1, AB2, BECNT, BNTC, LN, Lns, WBC; ESV, NASB, NRSV, REB], 'silver coin' [CEV, NET, TEV], 'pence' [KJV]. The phrase 'more than three hundred denarii' is also translated 'more than a year's wages' [NTC; NIV], 'a year's wages' [NLT], 'worth a full year's work' [NCV], 'a high price' [GW]. This noun denotes a Roman silver coin equivalent to the day's wage of a common laborer [LN].

d. imperf. mid./pass. (deponent = act.) indic. of ἐμβριμάομαι (LN **33.421**) (BAGD p. 254): 'to reproach' [WBC], 'to scold' [BNTC, LN, Lns; NRSV, REB], 'to scold harshly' [NLT], 'to rebuke harshly' [NIV], 'to denounce harshly' [**LN**], 'to criticize harshly' [TEV], 'to say cruel things' [CEV], 'to say very unkind things' [GW], 'to berate' [BECNT], 'to grumble at' [NTC], 'to murmur against' [KJV], 'to speak angrily to' [NET], 'to be angry with' [NCV], 'to be outraged at' [AB2]. This verb means to exhibit irritation or even anger while expressing a harsh reproof [LN].

QUESTION—Who were these indignant people and how were they saying this? They were some of the guests [BECNT; CEV]. The parallel passage in Matthew 26:6 says that these indignant people were the disciples, and that is probably implied here [AB2, CGTC, EBC, Hb, NAC, NICNT, NIGTC, NTC, WBC]. They are identified as the disciples in Matthew 26:8 and Judas Iscariot is singled out in John 12:4 [NIVfn]. It could also include outsiders [BNTC].

1. They were saying this to one another [AB2, BECNT, BNTC, NIVfn, NTC, TH; CEV, GW, NASB, NCV, NET, NIV, NLT, NRSV, REB, TEV].
2. They were just thinking this [ICC, WBC; KJV, ESV]. Each kept his indignation to himself [ICC; KJV].

14:6 But Jesus said, "Let her (alone). Why are-you causing her troubles[a]? She-has-done a-good deed[b] to me. **14:7** For[c] you- always -have the poor (people) with you and whenever you-want, you-can do good[d] to-them, but me you-do- not always -have.[e]

LEXICON—a. κόπος (LN 22.7) (BAGD 1. p. 443): 'trouble' [BAGD, LN], 'distress' [LN], The question τί αὐτῇ κόπους παρέχετε; 'Why are you causing her troubles?' is translated 'Why are you causing her trouble?' [AB1], 'Why are you troubling her?' [BECNT], 'Why make trouble for her?' [REB], 'Why do you trouble her?' [ESV, NRSV; similarly KJV, NCV], 'Why do you give her trouble?' [WBC], 'Why are you distressing her?' [Lns], 'Why are you bothering her?' [AB2, NTC; CEV, GW, NET, NIV, TEV; similarly BNTC, NASB], 'Why criticize her?' [NLT]. This noun denotes a state characterized by troubling circumstances [LN].

b. ἔργον (LN 42.12) (BAGD 1.c.β. p. 308): 'deed' [BAGD, LN], 'act' [LN]. The phrase καλὸν ἔργον 'a good deed' [AB2] is also translated 'a good thing' [BECNT; NLT], 'a fine thing' [BNTC; REB], 'a beautiful thing' [NTC, WBC; CEV, ESV, GW, NASB, NIV, NTC], 'a fine and beautiful thing' [TEV], 'an excellent thing' [NCV], 'a noble thing' [AB1], 'a good service' [NET, NRSV], 'an excellent work' [Lns], 'a good work' [KJV]. This noun denotes that which is done and it may focus on the energy or the effort involved [LN].

c. γάρ (LN 89.23): 'for' [AB2, BECNT, BNTC, LN, Lns, NTC, WBC; ESV, KJV, NASB, NET, NRSV], 'because' [LN], not explicit [AB1; CEV, GW, NCV, NIV, NLT, REB, TEV]. This conjunction indicates the cause or reason between events [LN].

d. εὖ (LN 88.6) (BAGD p. 317): 'good, beneficial' [LN], 'well' [BAGD]. The phrase αὐτοῖς εὖ ποιῆσαι 'you can do good to them' [AB1, BNTC, LN, NTC; NASB] is also translated 'you can do good for them' [ESV,

NET], 'you can do something good for them' [BECNT, WBC], 'you can do them good' [AB2], 'you can give to them' [CEV], 'you can help them' [GW, NCV, NIV, NLT, REB, TEV], 'you can show kindness to them' [NRSV], 'you are able to treat them well' [Lns], 'you can/may do them good' [AB1; KJV]. This adverb refers to that which is good in the sense of being beneficial [LN].

e. ἔχω (LN 57.1) (BAGD I.3 p. 333): 'to have' [BAGD, LN]. The clause 'But me you do-not/won't always have' [AB2, WBC; similarly KJV] is also translated 'but me you have not always' [Lns, NTC], 'but me you will not always have with you' [BECNT], 'but you do not always have me' [BNTC; NASB], 'But you will not always have me' [AB1; ESV, NCV, NET, NIV, NLT, NRSV, REB, TEV], 'But you will/do not always have me with you' [GW], 'But you won't always have me here with you' [CEV]. This verb means to have with oneself or to have in one's company [BAGD].

QUESTION—Did Jesus expect these men to give a reason why they were criticizing the woman who anointed Jesus?

This was a rhetorical question that implied their criticism of the woman was unreasonable and had caused her a needless difficulty [TH]. His question implied that those who were criticizing her could not justify their complaint [Lns].

QUESTION—What is the function of the conjunction γάρ 'for' at the beginning of verse 7?

This indicates that Jesus was going to vindicate the woman's action [Hb].

14:8 She has done what she could. She-has-anointed^a my body beforehand for burial.

LEXICON—a. aorist act. infin. of μυρίζω (LN 6.206) (BAGD p. 529): 'to anoint' [AB1, AB2, BECNT, BNTC, Lns, NTC, WBC; ESV, KJV, NASB, NCV, NET, NLT, NRSV, REB], 'to pour perfume on' [CEV, GW, NIV, TEV], 'to anoint with perfume, to anoint for burial' [LN]. This verb is a derivative of the noun μύρον 'perfume' and means to anoint with perfumed oil [LN].

QUESTION—In what way did this woman do all she could for his burial?

Since this was the only opportunity to serve Jesus that appeared to be open to her, she acted on it [Hb]. It was the only service within her power [EGT, Tay]. Not only was her gift an expression of generous self-forgetting love, it was especially appropriate since the Messiah was soon to die and be buried [CGTC, NICNT]. Even though she was not aware of Jesus' approaching death, she did have a greater sensitivity to what was about to happen to Jesus than the twelve disciples did [EBC].

14:9 And truly[a] I-say to-you, wherever the good-news is proclaimed in (the) whole world, what this (woman) did will- also -be-told in memory[b] of-her."

LEXICON—a. ἀμήν (LN 72.6) (BAGD 2. p. 45): 'truly' [BAGD, BECNT, BNTC, LN, WBC; ESV, NASB, NRSV, REB], 'indeed, it is true that' [LN], 'verily' [KJV], 'amen' [AB2, Lns]. The phrase 'truly I say to you' is translated 'you may be sure' [CEV], 'I tell you the truth' [NCV, NET, NIV, NLT], 'I assure you' [TEV], 'I can guarantee this truth' [GW], 'I solemnly assure you' [NTC], 'in solemn truth I tell you' [AB1]. This particle makes a strong affirmation of what is declared [LN]. It is an assertive particle that begins a solemn declaration [BAGD]. The phrase 'truly I say to you' occurs at 3:28; 8:12; 9:1, 41; 10:15, 29; 11:23; 12:43; 13:30; 14:9, 18, 25, 30.

b. μνημόσυνον (LN **29.12**) (BAGD p. 525): 'memory' [BAGD], 'something to cause people to remember, a memorial, in memory of' [LN]. The clause λαληθήσεται εἰς μνημόσυνον αὐτῆς 'will also be told in memory of her' [**LN**, NTC; ESV, GW, NET, NIV, TEV] is also translated 'will also be spoken of in memory of her' [NASB; similarly BECNT], 'will be told as her memorial' [AB1, BNTC; REB], 'will also be spoken of, as a memorial for her' [AB2], 'also…shall be spoken of for a memorial of her' [KJV; similarly Lns], 'will be told in remembrance of her' [NRSV], 'will also be spoken of in her memory' [WBC], 'will be told, and people will remember her' [NCV], 'will be remembered and discussed' [NLT], 'people will remember (what she has done). And they will tell others' [CEV]. This noun is derived from the verb ἀναμιμνήσκω 'to think about again, to remember' and denotes that which is designed to cause people to remember something [LN]. The phrase 'in memory of her' could be recast as a verb phrase: 'tell so that people will remember her' or 'tell so that her name shall be remembered' [TH].

DISCOURSE UNIT—14:10–11 [CBC, Hb, NICNT; CEV, ESV, GW, NCV, NET, NLT, NRSV, TEV]. The topic is the plan to betray Jesus [NET], Judas plans to betray Jesus [GW], Judas agrees to betray Jesus [NLT, NRSV, TEV], Judas to betray Jesus [ESV], Judas betrays Jesus [CBC], the betrayal by Judas [NICNT], Judas and the chief priests [CEV], the treachery of Judas [Hb], Judas become an enemy of Jesus [NCV].

14:10 And Judas Iscariot, one of-the Twelve,[a] went to the chief-priests in-order-that he-might-betray[b] him to-them. **14:11** And having-heard (this), they rejoiced and promised to-give him money.[c] And he-was-seeking how he-might-betray him at-an-opportune-time.[d]

LEXICON—a. δώδεκα (LN 60.21): 'twelve' [LN]. The phrase τῶν δώδεκα 'the Twelve' [AB1, AB2, BECNT, BNTC, Lns, WBC; NIV, NRSV] is also translated 'the twelve' [NTC; ESV, KJV, NASB, NET, NRSV], 'the twelve disciples' [CEV, GW, NCV, NLT, TEV]. The phrase 'the Twelve' is not simply a number, it was the title given to the twelve disciples [TH].

b. aorist act. subj. of παραδίδωμι (LN 37.111) (BAGD 1.b. p. 614): 'to betray' [BNTC, LN; all versions except CEV, NCV], 'to hand over' [AB1, BAGD, LN, NTC, WBC; NCV], 'to deliver' [BECNT, Lns], 'to turn over (to)' [AB2, BAGD, LN]. The clause 'in order that he might betray him to them' is translated 'and offered to help them arrest Jesus' [CEV]. This verb means to deliver a person into the control of someone else, and it involves either the handing over of a presumably guilty person for punishment by authorities or the handing over of an individual to an enemy who will presumably take undue advantage of the victim [LN].

c. ἀργύριον (LN 6.73) (BAGD 2.b. p. 104): 'money' [BAGD; all translations except Lns, CEV], 'silver money' [BAGD, LN], 'silver coin' [LN], 'silver' [Lns]. The phrase 'to give him money' is translated 'to pay him' [CEV]. Judas was given thirty pieces of silver as specified in Matthew 26:15 [NETfn].

d. εὐκαίρως (LN **67.6**) (BAGD p. 321): 'favorable, good' [LN], 'conveniently' [BAGD]. This adverb is connected with the verb παραδοῖ 'he might betray': 'he might conveniently betray him' [KJV], 'betray him at an opportune time' [NASB], 'hand him over at an opportune moment' [WBC], 'might deliver him in a timely way' [Lns]. Many connect it with the verb ἐζήτει 'he was seeking': 'he was seeking how he might find the right time' [AB2], 'he was looking for an opportunity' [NTC; similarly AB1, BECNT, BNTC, ESV, NIV, NLT, NRSV, REB], 'he started looking for a good chance' [CEV, TEV; similarly GW], 'he began looking for the best time' [NET; similarly NCV], 'he was seeking how he might find the right time' [AB2]. This adverb refers to a favorable occasion for some event [LN]. This probably refers to waiting for a situation where Jesus would be away from the crowds of people who usually followed him [TRT].

DISCOURSE UNIT—14:12–42 [NIGTC]. The topic is the last hours with the disciples.

DISCOURSE UNIT—14:12–26 [CBC; NIV, NLT]. The topic is the Lord's supper [NIV], the last supper [CBC; NLT].

DISCOURSE UNIT—14:12–25 [Hb]. The topic is the Passover observance.

DISCOURSE UNIT—14:12–21 [CEV, ESV, NASB, NCV, NET, NRSV, TEV]. The topic is Jesus eats with his disciples [CEV], Jesus eats the Passover meal [NCV], Jesus eats the Passover meal with his disciples [TEV], the Passover with the disciples [ESV, NRSV], the Passover [NET], the last Passover [NASB].

DISCOURSE UNIT—14:12–17 [GW]. The topic is the preparations for the Passover.

DISCOURSE UNIT—14:12–16 [Hb, NICNT]. The topic is the preparation for the Passover [Hb], preparation of the meal [NICNT].

14:12 And on (the) first day of-the (Festival of)-Unleavened-Bread, when the Passover-(lamb)[a] was-being-sacrificed,[b] his disciples say to-him, "Where do-you-want us to-go and prepare for you to-eat the Passover-(meal)[c]?"

LEXICON—a. πάσχα (LN 4.27) (BAGD 2. p. 633): 'the Passover lamb' [BAGD, BECNT, LN, NTC, WBC; all versions except KJV, TEV], 'the Passover lambs' [AB1], 'the passover lambs' [BNTC], 'The Passover' [AB2, Lns], 'the passover' [KJV], 'the lambs for the Passover meal' [TEV]. This noun denotes a specially selected lamb (or it has a collective sense and refers to all such lambs) that is killed and eaten during the festival commemorating the departure of Israel from Egypt. The word πάσχα is borrowed from Hebrew and has three different meanings which refer to different aspects of the Passover. In a context which speaks of 'the Passover taking place', it refers to the festival (51.6). When paired with a term such as ἑτοιμάζειν 'to prepare', the word πάσχα means the Passover meal. When the word is used with terms meaning 'to kill' or 'to sacrifice', the meaning is the Passover lamb. It is often impossible to use a phrase such as 'Passover lamb', since a literal rendering may suggest 'a lamb that passes over' or 'a lamb that someone has passed over' in the sense of 'ridden over' or 'neglected'. To avoid any misunderstanding, the phrase must be expanded in many languages to read 'the lamb that is eaten at the Passover Festival' or 'the lamb associated with the Festival that celebrates the passing over'. Even expanding the phrase 'passing over' to refer specifically to the passing over of the angel of death may not be sufficient if a literal rendering could be misunderstood as merely 'flying above' the Israelites. Therefore, it may be necessary to use an expression roughly equivalent to 'passing by'. In some cases, it may be better to use a short, though somewhat obscure, expression in the text and then provide a full explanation in a marginal note or glossary [LN].
  b. imperf. act. indic. of θύω (LN 53.19) (BAGD 2. p. 367): 'to sacrifice' [AB2, BECNT, LN, Lns, NTC; ESV, NASB, NCV, NET, NIV, NLT, NRSV], 'to slaughter' [BAGD, BNTC, WBC; REB], 'to kill' [AB1, BAGD; CEV, GW, KJV, TEV]. This verb means to slaughter an animal in a ritual manner as a sacrifice to deity [LN].
  c. πάσχα (LN 51.7) (BAGD 3. p. 633): 'the Passover' [AB2, BECNT, BNTC, Lns, WBC; ESV, KJV, NASB, NET, NIV, NRSV, REB], 'the Passover meal' [AB1, BAGD, LN; CEV, GW, NCV, NLT, TEV], 'the Passover Supper' [NTC]. This noun denotes the Passover meal eaten in connection with the Passover festival [LN].

QUESTION—How would the disciples prepare the Passover meal?
Preparation involved procuring and preparing the lamb, making arrangements for a room for the feast, and then procuring unleavened cakes, wine, water, bitter herbs, and crushed fruit moistened with vinegar [Hb].

QUESTION—What did Jesus' disciples mean when they said 'that *you* may eat the Passover'?

They mentioned only Jesus eating the Passover meal because he was their master, but they would naturally be eating with him [Lns]. Jesus would be the host, and it is assumed that they would eat with him [Hb].

14:13 And he sends two of his disciples and says to-them, "Go into the city, and a-man will-meet you carrying a-jar[a] of-water. Follow him **14:14** and wherever he-enters say to-the owner[b] of (the) house, 'The teacher says, "Where is my guest-room[c] where I-may-eat the Passover-(meal) with my disciples?"'

TEXT—In verse 14, manuscripts reading τὸ κατάλυμά μου 'my guest room' are followed by GNT which does not mention any variant reading. A variant reading is τὸ κατάλυμά 'the guest room' and it is followed by KJV.

LEXICON—a. κεράμιον (LN **6.128**) (BAGD p. 428): 'jar' [AB1, BAGD, BECNT, BNTC, LN, NTC, WBC; CEV, ESV, NCV, NEV, NIV, NRSV, REB, TEV], 'jug' [GW], 'vessel' [**LN**], 'pitcher' [KJV, NASB, NLT], 'a ceramic water jar' [AB2], 'an earthenware vessel' [BAGD; similarly Lns]. This noun denotes an earthenware container [LN]. This jar would normally be carried on one's head [TH].

b. οἰκοδεσπότης (LN 57.14) (BAGD p. 558): 'owner of the house' [BECNT, NTC, WBC; NASB, NCV, NET, NIV, NRSV, TEV], 'master of the house' [AB2, BAGD; ESV], 'master of the household' [LN], 'houselord' [Lns], 'householder' [AB1, BNTC; REB], 'goodman of the house' [KJV], 'owner' [CEV, GW, NLT]. This noun denotes one who owns and manages a household that includes his family, servants, and slaves [LN]. It refers to the owner of the house [TH].

c. κατάλυμα (LN **7.30**) (BAGD p. 414): 'guest room' [BAGD], 'room' [LN], 'dining room' [BAGD, **LN**], 'quarters' [LN]. The phrase τὸ κατάλυμά μου 'my guest room' [AB1, BECNT, Lns, NTC, WBC; ESV, NASB, NCV, NET, NIV, NRSV] is also translated 'my room' [BNTC], 'my lodging' [AB2], 'the guestchamber' [KJV], 'a/the room' [CEV, REB, TEV]. This noun denotes a room in a relatively large structure [LN].

QUESTION—What city does this refer to?

The city was Jerusalem [AB1, Hb, Sw, Tay, TH]. They were presently in the town of Bethany, which was about two miles from the city of Jerusalem [Hb, Sw].

QUESTION—How were they to find and follow a man carrying a jar of water?

Since women were normally the ones who carried water in jars, a man carrying a jar of water would stand out [AB1, BECNT, CGTC, EBC, NICNT, NIGTC, Tay]. A man carrying the jar was probably a prearranged sign [AB1, BECNT, CGTC, EBC, NICNT, NIGTC] and he would be the one who would lead them to the house where the owner had a guest room for Jesus [EBC]. The two disciples were to go along with that man [AB1, TH]. Either Jesus had made prior arrangements with friends in Jerusalem to avoid the Jewish authorities or the encounter would be a miraculous work of God [ESVfn]. This arrangement had probably been made in order to keep it a secret where Jesus and his disciples would be celebrating the Passover meal [NIVfn, WBC]. Jesus had kept the householder's name and the location of the house secret so that Judas would not know where the Passover Supper would be taking place [Lns]. Some think it might be an instance of Jesus' supernatural knowledge of events [ICC, Gnd, Hb, Lns, NAC].

QUESTION—What did Jesus mean when he said '*my* guest-room'?

The translation should not imply that Jesus owned a part of the house. Here it could mean 'a guest room for me', 'a room where I may be a guest', or just 'a room where I am to eat' [TH]. It probably means that Jesus had made arrangements to use a room in the house for the Passover meal [AB1, BECNT, CGTC, TRT].

14:15 And he will-show you a-large upstairs-room^a furnished^b (and) ready,^c and there prepare^d (the meal) for-us." **14:16** And the disciples went-out^e and they-came into the city and found (things) just-as he-had-told them, and they-prepared the Passover (meal).

TEXT—In verse 16, manuscripts reading οἱ μαθηταί 'the disciples' are followed by GNT which does not mention any variant reading. A variant reading is οἱ μαθηταί αὐτοῦ 'his disciples' and it is followed by KJV.

LEXICON—a. ἀνάγαιον (LN 7.27) (BAGD p. 51): 'an upstairs room' [AB1, BNTC, LN; REB, TEV], 'an upper room' [AB2, BECNT, Lns, NTC, WBC; ESV, KJV, NASB, NIV], 'a room upstairs' [BAGD; NCV, NET, NRSV]. The clause 'will show you a large upstairs room' is translated 'will take you upstairs and show you a large room' [CEV, GW], 'will take you upstairs to a large room' [NLT]. This noun denotes a room on the level above the ground floor. It is the 'second story' in American usage, but the 'first story' in most other languages [LN].

b. perf. pass. participle of στρώννυμι (LN 46.9) (BAGD p. 771): 'to be furnished' [AB2, BECNT, BNTC, LN, NTC, WBC; CEV, ESV, GW, KJV, NASB, NCV, NET, NIV, NRSV], 'to be arranged' [LN], 'to be set up' [NLT], 'to be fixed up' [TEV], 'to be set out' [REB]. The clause 'having been furnished and prepared' is translated 'that is already set up' [NLT], 'set out in readiness' [REB], 'already furnished' [AB1], 'the room will be completely furnished' [GW], 'spread with couches ready' [Lns]. This verb means to fit out or arrange a room in a suitable manner by providing it with the necessary furniture [LN]. It refers to preparing a room for a banquet [BAGD]. 'Furnished' probably means that the room had already been furnished with couches for reclining at a low table [CGTC, EGT, ICC, Lns, NTC].

c. ἕτοιμος (LN 77.2) (BAGD 1. p. 316): 'ready' [BAGD, BECNT, BNTC, LN, NTC, WBC; CEV, ESV, NASB, NCV, NET, NIV, NRSV], 'in readiness' [REB], 'prepared' [AB2, LN; KJV], 'furnished' [BECNT; TEV], not explicit [GW, NLT]. This adjective refers to being in a state of

readiness [LN]. In this context, it refers to a dining room being put into readiness [BAGD]. It means the room was ready to be used [CEV]. It was all ready to be used for the Passover meal [Hb].
   d. aorist act. impera. of ἑτοιμάζω (LN 77.3) (BAGD 1. p. 316): 'to prepare' [AB2, BNTC, LN, WBC; CEV, ESV, NASB, NCV, NLT], 'to make preparations' [AB1; NET, NIV, NRSV, REB], 'to make ready' [BECNT, LN, Lns, NTC; KJV], 'to get ready' [GW, TEV]. This verb means to cause something to be ready [LN]. Because the room had already been prepared for company [Hb], this refers to preparing the Passover meal [BAGD, Hb; CEV, NLT]. They were preparing for the coming of Jesus and the other disciples [BNTC].
   e. aorist act. indic. of ἐξέρχομαι (LN 15.40): 'to go out' [AB2, LN, Lns, WBC; NASB], 'to go' [NTC], 'to set out' [AB1, BECNT; ESV, NRSV], 'to set off' [BNTC], 'to leave' [GW, NCV, NET, NIV, TEV], 'to go forth/off' [KJV, REB], 'to depart out of, to leave from within' [LN]. The clause 'went out and they came into the city' is translated 'went into the city' [CEV, NLT]. This verb means to move out of an enclosed or well-defined two or three-dimensional area [LN]. They left the place where Jesus and his disciples had been staying outside the city. Jesus and the other disciples would wait there until the Passover meal was ready [Hb].

QUESTION—How did they prepare the Passover meal?
   The two disciples set out the unleavened bread and the wine, prepared the bitter herbs and sauces, and roasted the Passover lamb [NICNT]. The passover lamb would have to be slaughtered, cleaned, and roasted [BECNT].

DISCOURSE UNIT—14:17–21 [Hb, NICNT]. The topic is the announcement of the betrayal.

14:17 And evening having come,[a] he-comes[b] with the Twelve.

LEXICON—a. aorist middle (deponent = act.) participle of γίνομαι (LN 13.107) (BAGD I.1.b.γ. p. 158): 'to come to be' [BAGD, LN], 'to happen, to occur' [LN]. The phrase 'evening having come' is translated 'when evening came' [BECNT, Lns; GW, NIV], 'when it was evening' [AB1, AB2, BNTC, NTC, WBC; ESV, NASB, NET, NRSV, TEV], 'in the evening' [KJV, NCV, NLT, REB], 'that evening' [CEV]. This verb means 'to happen' and implies that what happens is different than a previous state [LN].
   b. pres. mid./pass. (deponent = act.) indic. of ἔρχομαι (LN 15.7): 'to come' [AB2, BNTC, Lns; ESV, KJV, NASB, NET, NET, NRSV, REB, TEV], 'to arrive' [AB1, BECNT, Lns, NTC; GW, NIV, NLT], 'to go' [LN], not explicit [CEV]. This verb means to move from one place to another [LN].

QUESTION—What is significant about the evening having come?
   This was Thursday evening, the beginning of the Jewish Friday [Lns]. The 15th day of Nissan had now begun and the Passover meal was always celebrated on this evening [AB1, BNTC, ESVfn, Hb].

QUESTION—How could Jesus come with the twelve disciples when he had already sent two of them ahead to prepare the upper room for the Passover meal?

> The term the 'Twelve' was a fixed expression for the select group of disciples that accompanied Jesus regardless of the exact number of those disciples in focus. In 1 Corinthians 15:5 it says that after Jesus' resurrection he was seen by Peter and then by the 'Twelve' even though at that time Judas had not yet been replaced and there were only a total of eleven disciples constituting the 'Twelve'. Furthermore, the two disciples preparing the meal could have returned with news that all was ready [NAC].
> 1. Jesus came with all twelve of his disciples [EBC, Hb, TRT, and probably those who translate this as 'the twelve disciples: NTC; KJV, NLT, TEV]. This suggests that the two disciples who had prepared the meal in Jerusalem had returned to Bethany so that all twelve members of the 'Twelve' would be accompanying Jesus when he entered Jerusalem that evening [EBC].
> 2. Jesus came with the rest of the 'Twelve' [BECNT, NIGTC, NLTfn, TH]. The 'Twelve' is a title for the twelve disciples Jesus had picked to accompany him [TH]. Here 'the Twelve' refers to the remaining ten disciples who had not gone to prepare the Passover meal [BECNT].

DISCOURSE UNIT—14:18–21 [GW]. The topic is Jesus knows who will betray him.

14:18 And (while) they-were reclining[a] and eating Jesus said, "Truly I-say to-you that one of you will-betray[b] me, the (one) eating with me."

LEXICON—a. pres. mid./pass. participle (deponent = act.) participle of ἀνάκειμαι (LN 17.23) (BAGD 2. p. 55): 'to recline' [AB2, BECNT, Lns, LN, WBC], 'to sit down to eat, to eat' [LN], 'to recline at the table' [AB1, NTC; ESV, NASB, NIV], 'to sit at table' [BNTC], 'to be at table' [LN; GW, NET, NLT], 'to dine' [BAGD, LN], 'to sit' [KJV]. The clause ἀνακειμένων αὐτῶν καὶ ἐσθιόντων 'while they were reclining and eating' is translated 'when they had taken their places and were eating' [NRSV], 'as they sat at supper' [REB], 'while Jesus and the twelve disciples were eating together' [CEV], 'while they were all eating' [NCV], 'while they were at the table eating' [TEV]. This verb means to be in a reclining position while one eats [LN]. Just like other banquet meals, the Passover was eaten in a reclining position [NLTfn]. This refers to their recumbent posture on couches arranged around the table [Hb].

b. fut. act. indic. of παραδίδωμι (LN 37.111) (BAGD 1.b. p. 614): 'to betray' [BAGD, LN; all translations except AB2, Lns], 'to deliver up' [Lns], 'to turn someone over' [AB2]. This verb means to deliver a person into the control of someone else and can refer to either handing over a presumably guilty person for punishment by authorities or handing over an individual to an enemy who will presumably take undue advantage of the victim [LN].

QUESTION—Who is being pointed out by the clause 'the one eating with me'? The definite article ὁ 'the (one)' simply indicates that the traitor was present in the group gathered around the table [AB1, BECNT, BNTC, EBC, Gnd, Hb, Lns, NICNT; NTC, TH, TRT, WBC]. Jesus is not specifying who will be the traitor but is focusing on the treachery of the act [ICC, Tay]. The identity of the traitor did not seem to be particularly evident to the others around the table since they all seemed to regard themselves as candidates [TH].

14:19 **They-began to-be-sorrowful**[a] **and to-say to-him one by one, "(Surely) not**[b] **I?"** **14:20** **And he-said to-them, "One of-the Twelve, the (one) dipping**[c] **with me into the bowl.**

TEXT—Manuscripts reading Μήτι ἐγώ; '(Surely) not I?' are followed by GNT which does not mention any variant reading. A variant reading is Μήτι ἐγώ; καὶ ἄλλος, Μήτι ἐγώ; '"(Surely) not I?" and another, "(Surely) not I?"' and it is followed by KJV.

LEXICON—a. pres. pass. infin. of λυπέομαι, λυπέω (LN 25.274) (BAGD 2.b. p. 481): 'to be sorrowful' [AB1, BAGD; ESV, KJV], 'to be sad' [BAGD, LN; CEV], 'to be saddened' [NIV], 'to be very sad' [NCV], 'to feel hurt' [GW], 'to be grieved' [AB2, Lns, WBC; NASB], 'to be distressed' [BAGD, BECNT, BNTC, LN, NTC; NET, NRSV, REB], 'to be greatly distressed' [NLT], 'to be upset' [TEV]. This verb mean to be sad because of what has happened or what one has done [LN].

b. μήτι (LN 69.16) (BAGD p. 520): '(surely) not' [LN]. The question 'Μήτι ἐγώ; 'Surely not I?' [NTC; NASB, NET, NIV, NRSV; similarly Lns] is also translated 'Surely it is not I, is it?' [BECNT], 'Surely you do not mean me?' [BNTC; REB], 'Surely you don't mean me, do you?' [TEV], 'You don't mean me, do you?' [GW], 'Am I the one?' [NLT], 'I am not the one, am I?' [NCV], 'It is not I/me, is it?' [AB1, AB2, WBC], 'Is it I?' [ESV, KJV]. This question is also translated as an emphatic statement: 'You surely do not mean me!' [CEV]. Even though this question usually suggests a negative answer, it could also be used in questions in which the questioner is in doubt about the answer [BAGD].

c. pres. mid. participle of ἐμβάπτω (LN 47.11) (BAGD p. 254): 'to dip' [AB2, BAGD, BNTC, LN, Lns, WBC; KJV, NASB, REB]. The participle 'dipping' is also translated 'dipping bread' [AB1; ESV, NRSV; similarly NCV, NIV, TEV], 'dipping his hand' [GW; similarly NET]. The clause 'dipping with me into the bowl' is translated 'who is eating from this dish/bowl with me' [CEV, NLT], 'who is eating with me' [BECNT; NTC]. This verb means to dip an object in a liquid [LN].

QUESTION—Why did each disciple ask Jesus this question? The disciples knew of nothing in their own thoughts that would lead to an act of betrayal, yet it must be true since Jesus had said it would happen [Hb, Lns]. Except for Judas, it was an honest question that was prompted by fear and lack of confidence in one's own spiritual and moral strength [EBC]. The fact that the question was asked at all shows their self-doubt [NICTC]. The form of their question called for a negative answer as they each asked for a reassuring denial from Jesus [CBC, Hb, LN]. Each hoped that Jesus would say, 'No, it is not you' [BECNT]. Their question simply requests Jesus to confirm their loyalty [TH].

QUESTION—What is meant by 'dipping into the bowl'?

Dipping food in bowls of sauces and relishes was a common feature of meals [AB2]. This probably refers to dipping bread and bitter herbs into a bowl of stewed fruit on the table [NICNT].

QUESTION—Who is the traitor who is dipping into the bowl with Jesus?

1. This does not identify the traitor [AB2, BECNT, BNTC, CBC, CGTC, EBC, Gnd, Hb, Lns, NAC, NCBC, NIGTC, NTC, Tay, WBC]. Neither 'the one eating with me' nor 'the one dipping with me' is meant to single out Judas. There would have been a reaction from the other disciples if Jesus had openly identified Judas to be his future betrayer [AB2]. It refers only to 'one' of the twelve without naming him [Lns, NTC]. There were other disciples present in the room besides the Twelve, so the presence of the article ὁ 'the (one)' means 'not just one of my disciples, but one of the Twelve, indeed one who even dips into the bowl with me' [PNTC, WBC].

2. This identifies the traitor to be Judas [AB1]. The presence of the article ὁ 'the (one)' seems to indicate that Judas was then reaching out his food to dip it in the bowl [AB1].

14:21 For the Son of Man[a] will-die/go[b] just-as it-has-been-written about him, but woe[c] to that man by whom the Son of Man is-betrayed. (It would have been) better (for) that man if he-had- not -been-born."

LEXICON—a. υἱὸς τοῦ ἀνθρώπου 'Son of Man' (LN 9.3) (BAGD 2.e. p. 835): This title of Jesus is translated 'the Son of Man' [BAGD, LN; all translations except AB1], 'The Man' [AB1]. It is a title with Messianic implications that Jesus used concerning himself [LN]. At that time Jewish teaching included a heavenly being who was looked upon as a 'Son of Man' or 'Man' who exercised Messianic functions such as judging the world [BAGD]. See 2:10 for a discussion of this title.

b. pres. act. indic. of ὑπάγω (LN **23.101**) (BAGD 3. p. 837): 'to die' [**LN**; CEV, GW, NCV, NLT, TEV], 'to leave this life' [LN], 'to go' [BAGD, BECNT, BNTC, NTC, WBC; ESV, KJV, NASB, NET, NIV, NRSV, REB], 'to go away' [AB2, Lns], 'to go the way appointed for him' [AB1]. This is a figurative extension meaning of the verb 'to go, to depart' and it refers to departing from life [LN]. It is a euphemism for dying [BAGD]. 'Go' obviously refers to death [TH].

c. οὐαί (LN 22.9) (BAGD 1.a. p. 591): 'woe' [BAGD, BECNT, BNTC, LN, Lns, NTC, WBC; ESV, KJV, NASB, NET, NIV, NRSV], 'alas' [AB1, AB2, BAGD; REB], 'disaster, horror' [LN]. The phrase 'woe to' is translated 'it is going to be terrible for' [CEV], 'how terrible it will be' [NCV, NLT, similarly TEV], 'how horrible it will be' [GW]. This interjection denotes a state of intense hardship or distress [LN]. It is a cry of commiseration [TH]. Jesus is not making a threat but is expressing his sorrow and pity for the traitor [CGTC, Hb, Tay].

QUESTION—What is meant by the initial conjunction ὅτι 'for'?

'For' indicates that the traitor's action was part of a divine plan, yet that does not lessen his responsibility for the part he plays in bringing about Jesus' death [Hb, NICNT, NIGTC].

QUESTION—Where is the death of Jesus written about in the OT?

This will fulfill what was written in Psalm 41:9, 'Even my close friend in whom I trusted, who ate my bread, has lifted his heel against me' [ESV, WBC]. This brings to mind Psalm 22, Isaiah 51, and the symbolism of the whole OT sacrificial system [Hb].

QUESTION—Why did Jesus say 'woe' to the traitor?

'Woe' is not a malediction but a lament of frustrated love [Hb]. The final sentence gives the reason for saying 'woe' to the one who betrays the Son of Man. It would be better for that man if he had not been born at all than to have been born and do such a deed that brings him to such an end [Lns, TH].

DISCOURSE UNIT—14:22–31 [NASB]. The topic is the Lord's supper.

DISCOURSE UNIT—14:22–26 [NICNT; CEV, GW, NCV, NET, TEV]. The topic is the Lord's Supper [CEV, GW, NCV, NET, TEV], the institution of the Lord's supper [NICNT].

DISCOURSE UNIT—14:22–25 [Hb; ESV, NRSV]. The topic is the institution of the Lord's Supper.

14:22 And as- they -were-eating, having-taken[a] bread (and) having-given-thanks,[b] he-broke[c] (it) and gave (it) to-them and said, "Take (it), this is my body."

TEXT—Manuscripts reading Λάβετε 'Take it' are followed by GNT which does not mention any variant reading. A variant reading is Λάβετε, φάγετε 'Take it, eat it' and it is followed by KJV.

LEXICON—a. aorist act. participle of λαμβάνω (LN 18.1) (BAGD 1.a. p. 464): 'to take' [all translations except CEV], 'to take hold of' [BAGD, LN], 'to take in the hand' [BAGD]. The phrase 'having taken bread' is translated 'took some bread in his hands' [CEV]. This verb means to take hold of something [LN]. Jesus took the bread from the table [TH]. This bread was one of the thin unleavened Passover cakes that were on their table [Hb].

b. aorist act. participle of εὐλογέω (LN 33.356, 33.470) (BAGD 1. or 2.b. p. 322): 'to give thanks' [AB1, BAGD (2.b.), NTC; NET, NIV], 'to thank God for it' [NCV], 'to give a prayer of thanks' [TEV], 'to praise God for it' [BNTC; similarly LN (33.356)], 'to bless (it/the bread)' [AB2, LN (33.470), Lns, WBC; CEV, ESV, GW, KJV, NLT, NRSV], 'to bless God for it' [BECNT], 'after a blessing [NASB], 'to say the blessing' [REB], 'to consecrate' [BAGD (2.b.)]. This verb means to speak of something in favorable terms [LN (33.356)] or to ask God to bestow his divine favor on something [LN (33.470)]. It means to give thanks and praise [BAGD (1.)] or to call down God's gracious power on something, thus causing it be consecrated [BAGD (2.b.)]. The Jewish blessing spoken over the bread would have been: 'Blessed be thou, O Lord our God, king of the world, who causes bread to come forth from the earth'. As in 6:41, it refers to the act of blessing God, that is, of praising God. This verb has the same function as εὐχαριστήσας '(having taken a cup and) having given thanks' in verse 23 [TH]. The two Greek words εὐλογήσας in verse 22 and εὐχαριστήσας in verse 23 are both equivalent to the Hebrew verb *barak* 'to bless' or 'to praise' God [EBC], and some translations simply say that Jesus thanked God for the bread in this verse and thanked God for the wine in the next verse [AB1, BAGD (2.b.), NCV, NTC; NET, NIV, TEV].

c. aorist act. indic. of κλάω (LN 19.34) (BAGD p. 433): 'to break' [BAGD, LN; all translations except NLT], 'to break in pieces' [NLT]. This verb means to break any object into two or more parts, but it is only used in the NT to describe the breaking of bread [LN]. Jesus broke the bread into pieces [TH]. The family head would keep breaking off pieces of bread to be passed around the table until everyone had a piece [NICNT].

QUESTION—What did Jesus mean when he said 'This is my body'?

The adjective 'this' refers to the broken loaf of bread [AB1]. The gospels do not give any command for the repetition of the supper, nor for its continuance as a church institution, but that is implied in 1 Corinthians 11:25 [ICC]. The four views concerning the elements in the Lord's Supper are (1) *transubstantiation:* upon consecration the bread and wine become the real body and blood of Christ, (2) *consubstantiation:* the body and blood of Christ are mysteriously and supernaturally united with the unchanged elements, (3) *spiritual presence:* the natural elements are instrumentally used to convey the spiritual presence of Christ to the partaker through faith, and (4) *symbolic:* the elements commemorate the sacrificial work of Christ with the value to the participant being the spiritual blessings received during the proceedings [Hb]. Regardless of what interpretation is taken, the translation must faithfully represent the plain meaning of the words in the text [TH].

14:23 And having-taken a-cup (and) having-given-thanks,[a] he-gave (it) to-them, and everyone drank from it. **14:24** And he-said to-them, "This is my blood of-the covenant,[b] the (blood) poured-out[c] for many.

TEXT—In verse 24, manuscripts reading τῆς διαθήκης 'of the covenant' are given an A rating by GNT to indicate it was regarded to be certain. A variant reading is τὸ τῆς καινῆς διαθήκης 'the one of the new covenant' and it is followed by KJV.

LEXICON—a. aorist act. participle of εὐχαριστέω (LN 33.349) (BAGD 2. p. 328): 'to give thanks' [AB1, AB2, BAGD, BECNT, LN, NTC, WBC; ESV, KJV, NASB, NET, NIV, NRSV], 'to speak a prayer of thanks-giving' [GW], 'to bless' [Lns]. The clause 'having given thanks' is translated 'having offered thanks to God' [REB], 'gave thanks to God' [BNTC; CEV, NLT, TEV], 'and thanked God for it' [NCV]. This verb means to express gratitude for benefits or blessings [LN].

b. διαθήκη (LN 34.44) (BAGD 2. p. 183): 'covenant' [AB1, AB2, BAGD, BECNT, BNTC, LN, NTC, WBC; ESV, NASB, NET, NIV, NRSV, REB], 'testament' [Lns; KJV], 'pact' [LN]. The clause 'This is my blood of the covenant' is translated 'This is the blood which is the new agreement that God makes with his people' [NCV], 'This is my blood, the blood of the promise' [GW], 'This is my blood…, my blood which seals God's covenant' [TEV], 'This is my blood, which confirms the covenant between God and his people' [NLT], 'This is my blood…and with it God makes his agreement' [CEV]. This noun denotes the verbal content of an agreement between two persons that specifies reciprocal benefits and responsibilities [LN]. It is a declaration of one person's will and not the result of any agreement between two parties. It is a declaration of the will of God who unilaterally determined the conditions of that covenant [BAGD]. God's covenant with mankind is a one-sided peace treaty or agreement where God is the one who made the promises and set the conditions for the covenant. God made it for the benefit of mankind and breaking it has serious consequences [TRT].

c. pres. pass. participle of ἐκχύννομαι, ἐκχέω (LN 23.112) (BAGD 1. p. 247): 'to be poured out' [AB1, AB2, BAGD, BECNT, BNTC, Lns, NTC, WBC; all versions except KJV, NLT, REB], 'to be shed' [BAGD; KJV, REB]. The clause 'the (blood) poured out for many' is translated 'It is poured out as a sacrifice for many' [NLT]. The phrase τὸ ἐκχυννόμενον 'the (blood) poured out' is an idiom that refers to dying as a sacrifice [LN]. It refers to Jesus' death in which his blood is shed for the benefit of many [BAGD]. In accordance with Aramaic usage, the participle should be taken as having a future force 'the blood which will be poured out'. 'Poured out' is not used in the sense of pouring blood from a glass. It refers to the shedding of Jesus' own blood, and some languages may have to translate this as 'coming out', 'running out', or 'gushing out' [TH]. Jesus' blood is what sealed and established God's new covenant with mankind and made any other sacrifices unnecessary. The mention that his blood is 'poured out' is an idiom that means it was 'sacrificed' [TRT].

QUESTION—What was in the cup that Jesus thanked God for and then passed on to his disciples?

The cup contained wine [TH]. Jesus gave thanks to God for what was in the cup and not for the cup itself [Lns]. Some translations specify what was in the cup: 'a cup of wine' [CEV, NLT]. A single cup filled with wine was passed around to all the disciples so that each one could drink some of it [Lns, NICNT, TH].

QUESTION—What did Jesus mean by calling the cup of wine the 'blood of the covenant'?
>This phrase probably reflects the wording of Exodus 24:8, 'Behold the blood of the covenant…which the Lord has made with you'. The 'blood of the covenant' means 'the blood that ratifies (or seals) the covenant' [Tay, TH]. Jesus is reinterpreting the symbolism of the Passover meal to indicate the presence of a new era [NETfn]. In Exodus 24:6–8 the Old Covenant had been ratified by the sprinkling of the sacrificial blood of animals, but God's New Covenant with people will be established by Jesus' death [CGTC, Sw].

QUESTION—Who is included in the πολλῶν 'many' for whom Jesus' blood is to be poured out?
>See the discussion of a similar reference to 'many' in 10:45 where it says 'the Son of Man came…to give his life as a ransom for many'.
>1. It has the inclusive meaning of 'all the many people everywhere' and not just the eleven disciples partaking in the Passover meal [BECNT, BNTC, EBC, Lns, NAC, NLTfn]. It refers to all people, who are many in number [NAC].
>2. The 'many' people are all of the people who will be saved by his blood in contrast with other people who will not be saved [AB1, AB2, Hb, NICNT, NIGTC, NTC].

14:25 Truly I-say to-you that no-longer by no means will-I-drink of the fruit[a] of the vine until that day when I-drink it new/anew[b] in the Kingdom of-God."

TEXT—Manuscripts reading οὐκέτι οὐ μὴ πίω 'no longer by no means will I drink' are given a C rating by GNT to indicate that choosing it over a variant text was difficult. Variant readings are οὐ μὴ πίω 'by no means will I drink', οὐ μὴ προσθῶ πεῖν 'by no means will I add to drink', οὐκέτι οὐ προσθῶ πιεῖν 'no longer I will not add to drink', and οὐκέτι οὐ μὴ προσθῶμεν πιεῖν 'no longer by no means will we add to drink'.

LEXICON—a. γένημα (LN 13.49) (BAGD p. 155): 'fruit' [AB2, BAGD, BECNT, BNTC, Lns, NTC, WBC; ESV, KJV, NASB, NCV, NET, NIV, NRSV, REB], 'product' [BAGD, LN], 'yield' [LN]. The phrase τοῦ γενήματος τῆς ἀμπέλου 'of the fruit of the vine' is translated 'wine' [CEV, GW, NLT, TEV]. This noun denotes that which is the product or result of something [LN].
>b. καινός (LN 67.115) (BAGD 3.b. p. 394): 'new' [BAGD, BECNT, BNTC, LN, Lns, NTC, WBC; ESV, KJV, NASB, NCV, NET, NLT, NRSV, REB], 'new wine' [AB1, LN, NTC; CEV, GW, TEV], 'recent' [LN], 'anew' [AB2; NIV]. As an adjective it pertains to having been in existence for only a short time [LN].

QUESTION—How will Jesus drink the wine in the Kingdom of God?
>To drink wine καινός 'new/anew' is ambiguous and can be interpreted adjectivally to describe αὐτό 'it' (the fruit of the vine) or adverbially to indicate when he will drink it [BECNT].

1. This is to be taken adjectivally to describe the fruit of the vine as being new [AB1, BECNT, Hb, ICC, Lns, NIGTC, NTC; CEV, GW, TEV]. 'New' denotes newness in quality and points to the spiritual character of that feast [Hb]. 'New' is compared with what is old [Lns]. It will be a new kind of wine [ICC].
2. This is to be taken adverbially to indicate when Jesus will drink it anew [AB2, EBC, Gnd, NICNT, Sw, WBC; NIV]. The wording is literally 'when it I drink new' and this favors taking καινόν 'new' to be functioning as an adverb, 'when I drink it anew' [Gnd]. Then it will not be the old Jesus but the 'new' Jesus who will drink it in the kingdom [WBC]. He will drink it with a new redeemed community in the kingdom of God [EBC, NICNT].

QUESTION—When will Jesus drink the wine in the Kingdom of God?

This anticipates that glorious day when believers will share the 'new' wine and food of the messianic banquet with Jesus [BECNT]. It looks forward to the future eschatological day when the kingdom will be established in all its glory. Drinking wine in the kingdom metaphorically describes the kingdom in terms of a messianic banquet where Jesus will be the host. The present tense 'I drink' indicates that the feast will not be a single event but a continuing feast [Hb].

DISCOURSE UNIT—14:26–52 [Hb]. The topic is the garden of Gethsemane.

DISCOURSE UNIT—14:26–31 [Hb; ESV, NRSV]. The topic is Jesus foretells Peter's denial [ESV], Peter's denial foretold [NRSV], revelation on the way to the garden. [Hb].

14:26 And having-sung-a-hymn[a] they-went-out to the Mount of-Olives.

LEXICON—a. aorist act. participle of ὑμνέω (LN 33.113) (BAGD 2. p. 836): 'to sing a hymn' [BAGD, LN; all translations except BECNT; REB], 'to sing the Passover hymn' [REB], 'to sing a song of praise' [LN], 'to sing' [BECNT]. This verb means to sing a song associated with religion and worship [LN]. It was a song of praise, thanksgiving, and trust [NTC]. At the end of the Jewish Passover, Psalms 115–118 would usually be sung [BECNT, ICC, PNTC, TEV].

QUESTION—What is the function of this verse?
1. This verse provides the ending for the preceding section [CBC, EBC, NAC, NICNT, NTC, TRT; CEV, GW, NCV, NET, NIV, NLT, NRSV, TEV]. The hymns were a fitting conclusion to the blessings enjoyed at the Lord's Supper [NTC].
2. It begins a new section [AB1, AB2, BECNT, BNT, CGTC, Gnd, ICC, NCBC, NIGTC, PNTC, Sw, Tay, WBC; ESV]. It provides the setting for the next topic [WBC]. It is best understood as beginning a new section since in Mark the geographical and chronological changes usually serve as introductions to what follows rather than as conclusions to what precedes [BECNT].

3. This verse is transitional and should be a separate paragraph since it marks the conclusion of the upper room events and also leads to the scene in the garden [Hb].

DISCOURSE UNIT—14:27–31 [CBC, NICNT; CEV, GW, NCV, NET, NIV, NLT, TEV]. The topic is the revelation on the way to the garden [Hb], Jesus predicts Peter's denial [GW, NIV, NLT, TEV], the prediction of Peter's denial [NET], Peter's denial predicted [CBC], the prophecy of failure and denial [NICNT], Peter's promise [CEV], Jesus' followers will leave him [NCV].

14:27 And Jesus says to-them, "All of you will-fall-away,[a] because it-has-been-written, 'I-will-strike-down[b] the shepherd and the sheep will-be-scattered.'[c] **14:28** But after I am-raised[d] I-will-go-before you into Galilee."

TEXT—In verse 27, manuscripts reading σκανδαλισθήσεσθε 'you will fall away' are followed by GNT which does not mention any variant reading. A variant reading is σκανδαλισθήσεσθε ἐν ἐμοὶ ἐν τῇ νυκτὶ ταύτῃ 'you will fall away because of me this very night' and it is followed by KJV.

LEXICON—a. fut. pass. indic. of σκανδαλίζομαι (LN 31.77) (BAGD 1.a. p. 752): 'to fall away' [BAGD, BECNT, BNTC, NTC, WBC; ESV, NASB, NET, NIV], 'to abandon (me)' [GW], 'to desert (me)' [NLT], 'to be deserters' [NRSV], 'to reject (me)' [CEV], 'to run away and leave (me)' [TEV], 'to be trapped' [Lns], 'to be tripped up' [AB2], 'to stumble' [AB1], 'to stumble in one's faith' [NCV], 'to lose faith' [REB], 'to cease believing, to give up believing' [LN], 'to be offended' [KJV], 'to be led into sin, to be caused to sin' [BAGD]. This is a figurative extension of meaning of the verb 'to fall into a trap' and it means to give up believing what is right and to let oneself believe what is false [LN]. In this context it probably means either 'turn away from me' or 'turn against me' [TH].

b. fut. act. indic. of πατάσσω (LN 20.73) (BAGD 1.a. p. 634): 'to strike down' [AB1, BAGD, LN, NTC; CEV, NASB], 'to strike' [AB2, BECNT, BNTC, WBC; ESV, GW, NET, NIV, NLT, NRSV, REB], 'to smite' [Lns; KJV], 'to slay' [BAGD, LN], 'to kill' [NCV, TEV]. This verb means to slay by means of a mortal blow [LN].

c. fut. pass. indic. of διασπείρω (LN 15.136) (BAGD p. 188): 'to be scattered' [BAGD, LN; all translations except Lns; NCV], 'to be scattered wide' [Lns], 'to scatter' [NCV], 'to be caused to disperse' [LN]. This verb means to cause a group or a gathering to disperse or scatter, sometimes with an emphasis on the distributive nature of the scattering when each goes in a different direction [LN]. This verb does not necessarily imply an active agent [TH].

d. aorist pass. infin. of ἐγείρω (LN 23.94) (BAGD 2.c. p. 215): 'to be raised' [BAGD, BNTC, NTC; NASB, NET, NLT; similarly NIV], 'to be raised up' [AB1, AB2, Lns, WBC; NRSV], 'to be raised to life' [LN; CEV, ESV, TEV], 'to be brought back to life' [GW], 'to be made to live again' [LN], 'to arise' [KJV], 'to rise up' [BECNT], 'to rise from the dead' [NCV]. This verb means to cause someone to live again after having once

264   MARK 14:27–28

died [LN]. This refers to when God raises Jesus up by causing him to live again [TH].

QUESTION—What is meant by the disciples σκανδαλισθήσεσθε 'falling away'?

Even though there are a variety of opinions, the final answer should probably be based on the quotation that immediately follows [EBC, NIGTC]. It doesn't mean that the disciples will lose their faith in Jesus, but that their courage will fail and they will forsake him [EBC]. They will defect from Jesus in the face of trial and persecution [NICNT]. They will be overwhelmed by what happens to Jesus that very night when he is suddenly arrested and put on trial [Hb, Lns]. They will be overwhelmed by what will happen to Jesus that night. It will stagger their faith and shake their confidence that Jesus really is the Messiah [Hb]. It refers to when they run away and leave him [TEV]. Since John 13:13 tells us Judas had already left at this point, Jesus was only talking to the eleven remaining disciples [TRT].

QUESTION—Where is the OT passage quoted by Jesus?

The prophecy that all the disciples will fall away is supported by this quotation from Zechariah 13:7 [NICNT]. In this quotation, God is the speaker and the verb 'to strike down' means 'to kill' the shepherd [TH]. The shepherd in Zechariah is probably the king and the sheep are probably the people in his kingdom [ICC].

QUESTION—Why does verse 28 begin with ἀλλά 'but'?

It indicates that their falling away in verse 27 is not the end of the story [BECNT]. Verse 28 counter-balances the prophecy about the disciples deserting Jesus with the promise of a coming reunion in Galilee that will follow the resurrection [NICNT].

QUESTION—What is meant by Jesus going 'before' his disciples into Galilee?

Jesus will go on ahead and already be there when they arrive [BECNT, NTC; NLT]. Jesus will not lead the disciples to Galilee, but when they get to Galilee they will find that he has already arrived ahead of them. This refers to an exceptional meeting in Galilee that was not recorded by Mark [Hb]. Most think that this refers to Jesus' resurrection appearance to his disciples recorded in 16:7 [TH].

14:29 **And Peter said to-him, "Even if everyone will-fall-away, yet I (will) not." 14:30 And Jesus says to-him, "Truly I-say to-you that today,[a] this very night, before a-rooster crows twice, you will-deny[b] me three (times)."**

TEXT—In verse 30, manuscripts reading πρὶν ἢ δὶς ἀλέκτορα φωνῆσαι, which is literally 'before than twice (a) rooster crows' are given a C rating by GNT to indicate that choosing it over a variant text was difficult. Variant readings are πρὶν ἀλέκτορα φωνῆσαι 'before a rooster crows' and πρὶν ἀλέκτορα δὶς φωνῆσαι 'before a rooster twice crows'.

LEXICON—a. σήμερον (LN 67.205) (BAGD p. 749): 'today' [LN]. The words σήμερον ταύτῃ τῇ νυκτὶ 'today, this very night' [BECNT, WBC; NET] are also translated 'this day, this very night' [NRSV; similarly Lns], 'today–yes, tonight' [NIV], 'today–yes, this very night' [NTC], 'today, in this night' [AB2], 'this day, even in this night' [KJV]. The Jewish 'today' would last all through the night and all the next day until sunset, and since the rooster would crow after midnight others translate the words 'today, this very night' as 'this very night' [AB1, BNTC; CEV, ESV, NASB, NLT, REB], 'tonight' [GW, NCV, TEV]. This adverb refers to the same day as the day of a discourse [LN].

b. fut. mid. (deponent = act.) indic. of ἀπαρνέομαι (LN 33.277) (BAGD p. 81): 'to deny' [AB2, BAGD, BECNT, BNTC, LN, Lns, NTC, WBC; ESV, KJV, NASB, NET, NRSV], 'to disown' [AB1; NIV, REB]. The phrase 'you will deny me' is translated 'you will deny...that you even know me' [NLT], 'you will say...that you do not know me' [CEV, GW, NCV, TEV]. This verb means to say that one does not know about or is in any way related to a particular person or event [LN]. This refers to disowning Jesus in the sense of refusing to admit any prior knowledge of Jesus [TH].

14:31 And emphatically[a] he-was-saying, "If it-is-necessary[b] (for) me to-die for-you, by-no-means will-I-deny you." And also each-one said the same-thing.

LEXICON—a. ἐκπερισσῶς (LN **78.31**) (BAGD p. 243): 'emphatically' [BNTC; ESV, NET, NIV, NLT], 'even more emphatically' [**LN**], 'with great emphasis' [BAGD, NTC], 'even more strongly' [TEV], 'very strongly' [GW], 'vehemently' [AB1, AB2, BECNT, WBC; NRSV], 'more vehemently' [KJV], 'exceedingly' [Lns], 'insistently' [NASB]. This is also translated as a verb phrase: 'he insisted' [NCV, REB], 'was so sure of himself' [CEV]. This adverb indicates a degree that is considerably in excess of some point on an implied or explicit scale of extent [LN]. Peter repeatedly affirmed his boast [EGT, Hb, Lns, Sw, Tay, WBC].

b. pres. act. subj. of δεῖ (LN 71.34) (BAGD 4. p. 172): 'to be necessary' [LN, Lns], 'to have to' [AB1, AB2, BNTC, NTC, WBC; CEV, GW, NASB, NIV, NLT, REB, TEV], 'must' [BAGD, Lns; ESV, NET, NRSV], 'should' [KJV], not explicit [NCV]. This verb means to be that which must necessarily take place, often with the implication of inevitability [LN].

DISCOURSE UNIT—14:32–42 [CBC, Hb, NICNT; CEV, ESV, GW, NASB, NCV, NET, NIV, NLT, NRSV, TEV]. The topic is Jesus prays [CEV], Jesus prays in Gethsemane [ESV, NLT, NRSV, TEV], Jesus prays in the garden of Gethsemane [GW], Jesus in Gethsemane [CBC; NASB], Gethsemane [NICNT; NET, NIV], Jesus prays alone [NCV], agony in the garden [Hb].

14:32 And they-come to a-place named Gethsemane and he-says to his disciples, "Sit-down here while I-pray." **14:33** And he-takes Peter and James and John with him and he-began to-be-distressed[a] and troubled.[b]

14:34 And he-says to-them, "My soul[c] is very-sorrowful to-the-point of-death. Remain here and stay-awake/keep-alert.[d]"

LEXICON—a. pres. pass. infin. of ἐκθαμβέομαι, ἐκθαμβέω (LN 25.210) (BAGD p. 240): 'to be distressed' [AB1, BAGD, WBC; ESV, GW, NASB, NET, NIV, NRSV], 'to be/feel distressed' [BECNT; GW], 'to be overwhelmed [AB2], 'to be sad' [CEV, NCV], 'to be troubled' [BNTC[, 'to be deeply troubled' [NLT], 'to be greatly upset' [Lns], 'to be sore amazed' [KJV], 'to be amazed, to be astounded, to be alarmed' [LN], 'to be filled/overwhelmed with horror' [NTC; REB]. This verb means to be greatly astounded and may be used with either positive or negative reactions [LN].

b. pres. act. infin. of ἀδημονέω (LN 25.247) (BAGD p. 16): 'to be troubled' [BAGD, BECNT, BNTC, LN, WBC; CEV, ESV, NASB, NCV, NIV], 'to be distressed' [BAGD, BNTC, LN; NET, NLT], 'to be full of dread' [AB1], 'to be anguished' [GW], 'to be filled/overwhelmed with anguish' [NTC; REB, TEV], 'to be anxious' [AB2], 'to be in anxiety' [BAGD], 'to be agitated' [NRSV], 'to be worried' [Lns], 'to be heavy' [KJV]. This verb means to be distressed and troubled [LN].

c. ψυχή (LN 26.4) (BAGD 1.b.g. p. 893): 'soul' [AB2, BECNT, Lns, WBC; ESV, KJV, NASB, NIV, NET, NLT], 'heart' [NCV], 'I' [NRSV], 'inner self, mind, thought, feelings, heart, being' [LN]. The clause 'My soul is very sorrowful to the point of death' is translated 'My anguish is so great that I feel as if I'm dying' [GW], 'I am so sad that I feel as if I am dying' [CEV], 'I am overwhelmed with sorrow to the point of death' [NTC], 'My heart is overwhelmed with grief and is ready to break' [BNTC], 'My sorrow is so great that it almost overwhelms me' [AB1], 'The sorrow in my heart is so great that it almost crushes me' [TEV], 'My heart is ready to break with grief' [REB]. This noun denotes the essence of life in terms of thinking, willing, and feeling. In passages like this, it refers to the entire being of a person, and it may very well be rendered as 'my sorrow is so great it almost kills me' [LN]. The soul represents the seat and center of the inner life, and here it refers to one's feelings and emotions [BAGD].

d. pres. act. impera. of γρηγορέω (LN 23.72 or LN 27.56) (BAGD 1. p. 167): 'to be awake' [BAGD], 'to stay awake' [LN (23.72); GW, REB], 'to keep awake' [AB2, BAGD, NTC; CEV, NRSV]. Others take it to mean 'to be watchful' [LN (27.56)], 'to watch' [AB1, BECNT, Lns, WBC; ESV, KJV, NCV], 'to keep watch' [BNTC; NASB, NIV, NLT, TEV], 'to be alert' [LN (27.56)], 'to stay alert' [NET], 'to be vigilant' [LN (27.56)]. This verb means to remain awake because of the need for continued alertness [LN (23.72)], or it means to be in continuous readiness and alertness [LN (27.56)]. It means to be awake or to stay awake. It can be used figuratively to mean 'to be on the alert, to be watchful' [BAGD].

QUESTION—What is meant by the verb ἤρξατο 'began' in connection with the following two verbs 'to be distressed' and 'to be troubled' and what caused Jesus to react this way?

The verb 'began' gives a picture of an ever-increasing terror and agitation [AB1]. The extremely acute emotion described by the two verbs together includes a combination of bewilderment, fear, uncertainty, and anxiety [EBC]. The two expressions add emphasis to the description of Jesus' agony [BECNT]. Having already foreseen his coming death, Jesus was feeling the horror of that coming ordeal. It was not a physical fear, but the pressure of the sin of the world upon his sinless soul along with the knowledge of what that will involve [Hb]. Jesus was horrified at the prospect of the alienation from God entailed in being judged for the sins of mankind [NICNT].

14:35 And having-gone-forth a-little he-fell[a] to the ground and prayed that if it-is possible, the hour[b] might-pass-away from him. **14:36** And he-was-saying, "Abba[c] Father, all-things (are) possible for-you. Take-away this cup[d] from me. Yet not what I-want but what you (want)."

LEXICON—a. perf. act. indic. of πίπτω (LN 17.22) (BAGD 1.b.α. p. 659): 'to fall' [AB2, BECNT, Lns, WBC; ESV, GW, KJV, NASB, NCV, NIV, NLT], 'to fall down' [BAGD, LN], 'to prostrate oneself' [AB1, LN], 'to throw oneself' [BNTC, NTC; NET, NRSV, REB, TEV], 'to kneel down' [CEV]. This verb means to prostrate oneself before someone in supplication [LN]. It means to fall down to the ground as a sign of devotion, especially when approaching someone with a petition [BAGD].

    b. ὥρα (LN 67.1) (BAGD 3. p. 896): 'hour' [AB1, AB2, BECNT, BNTC, Lns, NTC, WBC; ESV, KJV, NASB, NIV, NET, NRSV, REB], 'the awful hour' [NLT], 'time, occasion' [LN]. The clause 'the hour might pass away from him' is translated 'he might not have to suffer what was ahead of him' [GW], 'he would not have this time of suffering' [NCV], 'he would not have to go through that time of suffering' [TEV]. The clause 'was praying that if it is possible, the hour might pass away from him' is translated 'prayed, "Father, if it is possible, don't let this happen to me"' [CEV]. This noun denotes a point in time consisting of an occasion for a particular event [LN]. It refers to the time when something takes place [BAGD].

    c. αββα (LN 12.12) (BAGD p. 1): 'abba' [BAGD, LN]. The phrase Αββα ὁ πατήρ 'Abba, Father' [BECNT, BNTC, Lns, NTC, WBC; ESV, KJV, NIV, NET, NLT, NRSV, REB] is also translated 'Abba, Father!' [NCV], 'Abba! Father!' [GW, NASB], 'Abba, my Father' [AB1], 'Father, my Father' [TEV], 'Abba (Father)' [AB2], 'Father' [CEV]. The word αββα is the Greek transliteration of the Aramaic word that means 'father' [LN].

    d. ποτήριον (LN 6.121; 90.97) (BAGD 2. p. 693): 'cup' [BAGD, LN (6.121)], 'drinking vessel' [BAGD]. The clause 'Take away this cup from me' [BECNT; KJV, REB; similarly BNTC; NET] is also translated 'Take this cup from me' [AB2; NIV], 'Remove this cup from me' [AB, Lns,

NTC, WBC; ESV, NASB, NRSV], 'Take away this cup of suffering' [NCV], 'Take this cup of suffering away from me' [GW, TEV], 'Please take this cup of suffering away from me' [NLT], 'Don't make me suffer by having to drink from this cup' [CEV]. The noun ποτήριον 'cup' denotes an object from which one may drink [LN (6.121)]. The phrase 'take away this cup from' is an idiom that means to prevent someone from undergoing a trying experience, and here it means 'take this cup of suffering from me' or 'do not make me undergo this suffering' [LN 90.97].

QUESTION—Did Jesus actually address his heavenly Father with both the Aramaic and Greek words for 'Father'?

The word Αββα 'Abba' is the Aramaic intimate form for 'father' and means something like 'Daddy'. The Jews did not address God in this way because they thought it would be disrespectful. However, it was natural for Jesus to use it since he was the unique Son of God and was on the most intimate terms with him [EBC].

1. Jesus was praying in Aramaic and only used the Aramaic word Αββα to address God, his Father [AB1, AB2, BECNT, EGT, ICC, Lns, NAC, NCBC, NIGTC, NTC, PNTC, Tay, TH].
1.1 Mark made the point that Jesus used the intimate term 'Abba' for 'father', and then Mark added the Greek word πατήρ 'Father' for the benefit of his Greek readers [AB2, BECNT, Lns, NAC, NTC, PNTC].
1.2 Jesus only used the word 'Abba', but in translating this into Greek, Mark used the combination 'Abba, Father' that Greek-speaking Christians were then using in their prayers to God [AB1, EGT, ICC, Lns, NCBC, NIGTC, Tay, TH].
2. Jesus used both the Aramaic and the Greek words in his prayer [BNTC, CGTC, EBC, Hb, NICNT, WBC]. Because Jesus was bilingual, his deep emotional state may have impelled him to use both terms [Hb].

QUESTION—What 'hour' did Jesus want to pass away from him?

The text does not specify what 'this hour' refers to and several explanations have been given. It may be the 'hour' in verse 35 that refers to the foreseeable events that include his betrayal, arrest, and execution as a condemned criminal [NICNT, WBC]. It may be the appointed time for his sacrificial death [Hb, NTC]. His petition was that if there were a possibility for him to complete his messianic mission without a sacrificial death, he desired that [Hb].

QUESTION—What does the 'cup' refer to?

It is the same cup of wrath of God that is referred to in 10:38–39 [EBC, NAC, NICNT, NIGTC, TH]. 'Cup' is regularly used in the OT as a metaphor for punishment and judgment [EBC, NICNT, NIGTC]. It refers to the suffering Jesus will experience [BECNT, NTC, TH] and complete abandonment [NTC]. It refers to both his suffering and his death [Lns, NCBC].

14:37 And he-comes and finds them sleeping. And he says to Peter, "Simon, are-you-asleep? Were-you- not -able to-stay-awake^a one hour?"

LEXICON—a. pres. act. impera. of γρηγορέω (LN 23.72 or 27.56) (BAGD 1. p. 167): 'to be awake' [BAGD], 'to stay awake' [LN (23.72), NTC; CEV, GW, NCV, NET, REB, TEV], 'to keep awake' [AB2, BAGD; NRSV]. Others take it to mean 'to be watchful' [LN (27.56)], 'to watch' [AB1, BECNT, Lns, WBC; ESV, KJV, NIV, NLT], 'to keep watch' [BNTC; NASB], 'to be alert' [LN (27.56)], 'to be vigilant' [LN (27.56)]. This verb means to remain awake because of the need for continued alertness [LN (23.72)] or it is a figurative extension of meaning of staying awake, and means to be in continuous readiness and alertness to learn something [LN (27.56)]. It means to be awake or keep awake. It can be used figuratively and mean 'to be on the alert, to be watchful' [BAGD].

QUESTION—Why did Jesus single out Peter using his other name 'Simon'?

Jesus probably singled out Peter because he was the person who had boasted earlier of his fidelity to Jesus [EBC, NICNT]. This is the first use of the name Simon in Mark since 3:16. Apparently Jesus intended to remind him that he was not living up to the meaning of his new name Πέτρος 'Peter' (the Rock) [AB2, EGT, Hb, Lns, Sw].

QUESTION—What did Jesus intend to communicate by asking Simon if he was asleep?

This was a rhetorical question expressing Jesus' pain and disappointment to find Peter sleeping [Hb]. It was a gentle reprimand [NTC].

14:38 Stay-awake(pl) and pray(pl) that/so-that^a you(pl)- not -come into temptation.^b Indeed the spirit^c (is) willing but (the) flesh^d (is) weak."

LEXICON—a. ἵνα (LN 90.22, 89.59): 'that' [AB1, BECNT, BNTC, LN (90.22), NTC, WBC; all versions except NCV, NIV, NLT], '(pray) for' [NCV]. It is also translated with the meaning 'so that' [AB2, LN (89.59); NIV, NLT], 'lest' [Lns], 'in order to, for the purpose of' [LN (89.59)]. This conjunction indicates the content of discourse, particularly if and when purpose is implied [LN (90.22)] or it indicates the purpose for events and states [LN (89.59)].

b. πειρασμός (LN 88.308) (BAGD 2.b. p. 641): 'temptation' [BAGD, BECNT, BNTC, LN]. The phase 'come into temptation' [WBC; NASB] is also translated 'give into temptation' [NLT], 'fall into temptation' [NIV, NET, TEV], 'enter into temptation' [Lns, NTC; ESV, KJV], 'enter into testing' [AB2], 'come into the time of trial' [NRSV], '(for strength against) temptation' [NCV], 'may be spared the test' [AB1; REB], '(be) tempted' [GW], '(be) tested' [CEV]. The phrase 'come into temptation' means 'yield to temptation' in this verse [EBC].

c. πνεῦμα (LN 26.9) (BAGD 3.b. p. 67): 'spirit' [BAGD, LN], 'spiritual nature, inner being' [LN]. The clause τὸ πνεῦμα πρόθυμον 'the spirit is willing' [AB1, AB2, BECNT, BNTC, WBC; ESV, NASB, NIV, NET, NLT, NRSV, REB, TEV] is also translated 'the spirit is ready' [KJV], 'the spirit is eager' [Lns; NTC], 'the spirit wants to do what is right' [NCV], 'you want to do what is right' [GW]. This noun denotes the non-material, psychological faculty that is potentially sensitive and responsive to God [LN]. The spirit is the source and seat of insight, feeling, and will [BAGD].

d. σάρξ (LN 26.7) (BAGD 7. p. 744): 'flesh' [BAGD], 'human nature, human aspects' [LN]. The clause ἡ σὰρξ ἀσθενής 'the flesh is weak' [AB1, AB2, BECNT, BNTC, Lns, NTC, WBC; ESV, KJV, NASB, NET, NRSV, REB, TEV] is also translated 'the body is weak [NCV, NIV, NLT], 'you are weak' [CEV, GW]. This noun denotes the psychological aspect of human nature that contrasts with the spiritual nature. The typical human reasoning and desires of human nature are being differentiated from human thoughts and behaviors that relate to God and the spiritual life [LN].

QUESTION—What is the function of the conjunction ἵνα 'that' which follows the commands 'stay awake and pray'.

1. It indicates the content of what they are to pray about [AB1, BECNT, BNTC, CGTC, NTC, Tay, WBC; all versions except NIC, NIV, NLT]. This expresses the content of the prayer [CGTC]. It concerns the temptation of denying Jesus [BECNT].
2. It indicates the purpose for staying awake and praying [AB2, Hb, ICC, Lns, NICNT, NIGTC, Sw, WBC; NIV, NLT]. This conjunction depends upon both imperatives and states the purpose of their watching and praying [Lns]. The object of their wakefulness and prayer is not to find strength to withstand temptation but to resist any temptation to be disloyal [NIGTC]. Their attitude of alertness and prayer will enable them to escape the temptation to believe that Jesus is not the Messiah [Hb]. Alertness was necessary in order to enable them to continue in prayer so that they would be able to resist the temptation to think that Jesus was not really the Messiah [Hb]. This is the temptation to abandon the cause to which Jesus has called his disciples [WBC].

QUESTION—What is meant by the statement 'the spirit is willing but the flesh is weak'?

Their spirits are contrasted with their human bodies and its natural feelings [AB1, BAGD, BECNT, BNTC, ICC, NCBC, NTC, Sw, TH]. The spirit is the human spirit that is fickle and all too often faithless [WBC]. The contrast is between the will and the inferior feelings such as fear, anxiety, etc. that are attributed to the 'flesh' [TH]. The spirit is the spiritual part of a person, and the flesh is the weak and debased lower nature [ICC]. The word 'spirit' refers to a person's human nature considered from the aspect of its relation to God, while 'flesh' refers to the human nature considered from the aspect of its frailty. In this case, there was a battle between their spirits and their flesh. Their spirits were eager to do what was right and remain on guard against temptation, but their weakly flesh was prone to yield to Satan's desires [NTC]. It does not say what the spirit is willing to do. It could mean that their spirits might be willing to resist 'temptation' since Jesus had just mentionedin the preceding sentence, bur it could mean that their spirits might be willing to 'watch' since that is what Jesus had originally asked them to do [TRT].

14:39 And again having-gone-away he-prayed saying the same word.[a]

TEXT—Manuscripts reading τὸν αὐτὸν λόγον εἰπών 'saying the same word' are followed by GNT which does not mention any variant reading. A variant reading omits the phrase.

LEXICON—a. λόγος (LN 33.98) (BAGD 1.a.β. p. 477): 'word, statement, saying, message' [LN]. Since the noun λόγον 'word' has the singular form in this verse, the phrase τὸν αὐτὸν λόγο 'the same word' is translated 'the same thing' [AB2, BECNT, Lns, NTC, WBC; NCV, NIV, NET], 'the same prayer' [CEV], 'the same prayer as before' [GW]. Some pluralize the singular form for the English translation: 'the same words' [BNTC; ESV, KJV, NASB, NRSV, TEV], and one simply says that 'he went away and prayed' [REB]. This noun denotes that which has been stated or said where the primary focus is on the content of the communication [LN]. The term λόγος 'word' may take any one of many different forms, so the translation depends on the context [BAGD]. This is Jesus' second prayer [Gnd]. The singular noun phrase 'the same word' does not denote a verbatim repetition but a prayer to the same effect [Hb].

14:40 And again having-come he-found them sleeping[a] because their eyes were-heavy,[b] and they did- not -know what they-might-say-to/answer[c] him.

LEXICON—a. pres. act. participle of καθεύδω (LN 23.66) (BAGD 1. p. 388): 'to sleep' [AB1, AB2, BAGD, BECNT, BNTC, LN, Lns, WBC; CEV, ESV, NASB, NET, NIV, NLT, NRSV], 'to be asleep' [LN, NTC; GW, KJV, NCV, REB, TEV]. This verb refers to the state of being asleep [LN].

b. pres. pass. participle of καταβαρύνομαι (LN 23.69) (BAGD p. 408): 'to weigh heavily' [BAGD], 'to have become very sleepy, to be very sleepy' [LN]. The phrase 'their eyes were (very) heavy' [AB1, BECNT, BNTC, WBC; ESV,.KJV, NASB, NCV, NIV, NRSV, REB] is also translated 'their eyes were weighed down' [AB2, Lns], 'their eyes were weighed down with sleep' [NTC], 'they could not keep their eyes open' [CEV, GW, NET, NLT, TEV], 'they were exceedingly sleepy' [LN]. The idiom 'the eyes were heavy' means to be exceedingly sleepy [LN]. It means they were so sleepy that they could not keep their eyes open [Hb].

c. aorist pass. (deponent = act.) subj. of ἀποκρίνομαι (LN 33.28, 33.184) (BAGD 1. p. 93): 'to say' [BECNT, LN (33.28); CEV, GW, NCV, NIV, NLT, NRSV, TEV], 'to answer' [AB1, AB2, BAGD, BNTC, LN (33.184), Lns, NTC, WBC; ESV, KJV, NASB, REB], 'to tell' [NET], 'to reply' [BAGD, LN (33.184)]. This verb means either to introduce or to continue a somewhat formal discourse [LN (33.28)] or to respond to a question asking for information [LN (33.184)]. This verb does not always mean 'to answer' an implied previous question. It may simply mean 'to say' [TH]. They were probably so embarrassed and ashamed they didn't know what to say to him [EBC].

14:41 And he-comes a-third (time) and says to-them, "You-are -asleep and resting?/! Enough!ᵃ The hourᵇ has-come. Look, the Son of-Man is-being deliveredᶜ into the hands of-sinners. **14:42** Get-up, let-us-go. Look, the one-delivering me has-drawn-near."

TEXT—Manuscripts reading ἀπέχει ἦλθεν ἡ ὥρα 'it is enough; the hour has come' are given a B rating by GNT to indicate it was regarded to be almost certain. Variant readings are ἀπέχει τὸ τέλος καὶ ἡ ὥρα 'the end and the hour is enough', ἀπέχει ἡ ὥρα 'the hour is enough', ἀπέχει τὸ τέλος ἦλθεν ἡ ὥρα 'the end is enough; the hour has come', and ὅτι ἦλθεν ἡ ὥρα 'because the hour has come'.

LEXICON—a. pres. act. indic. of ἀπέχω (LN **59.47**) (BAGD 1 p. 85): 'to be enough, to be sufficient' [LN]. The clause ἀπέχει 'Enough!' [AB2, BNTC, **LN**, NTC; NIV, NRSV, REB, TEV] is also translated 'Enough of that!' [CEV, NET], 'It is enough' [BAGD, Lns, NTC; ESV, KJV NASB], 'But no' [NLT], 'That's enough' [NCV], 'Is it far off? (The hour has come!)' [WBC], 'It's all over' [GW], 'It (the money) is paid' [BECNT]. This verb means to mark the point at which the duration of a state or process is enough. In a number of languages the equivalent of 'Enough!' would be 'that is the end' or 'you must stop sleeping now' [LN]. This refers to their sleeping [TRT].

b. ὥρα (LN 67.1) (BAGD 3. p. 896): 'hour' [AB1, AB2, BECNT, BNTC, Lns, WBC; ESV, KJV, NASB, NET, NIV, NRSV, REB, TEV], 'time' [BAGD, LN; CEV, GW, NCV, NLT], 'occasion' [LN], not explicit [NTC]. This noun denotes a point in time consisting of an occasion for a particular event [LN].

c. pres. pass. indic. of παραδίδωμι (LN 37.12, 37.111) (BAGD 1.b. p. 614): 'to be delivered' [BECNT, LN (37.111), WBC], 'to be handed over' [AB1, BAGD, BNTC, LN (37.111); CEV, GW, NCV, TEV], 'to be turned over to' [AB2, LN (37.111)], 'to be betrayed' [Lns, LN (37.111), NTC; ESV, KJV, NASB, NET, NIV, NLT, NRSV, REB]. This verb means to deliver a person into the control of someone else by handing over a presumably guilty person for punishment or by handing over an individual to an enemy who will presumably take undue advantage of the victim [LN (37.111)]. The idiom παραδίδωμι εἰς χεῖρας 'to give into the hands' means to deliver a person into the control of others and could be translated 'will hand him over to be arrested' or 'will cause him to be taken into custody' [LN (37.12)].

QUESTION—What is the function of the declaration, Καθεύδετε τὸ λοιπὸν καὶ ἀναπαύεσθε 'You are asleep and resting?/!'

1. It is a question that indicates surprise: 'Are you asleep and resting?' [AB2, BECNT, BNTC, CGTC, EBC, Tay, TH; all versions except REB], 'Still

asleep? Still resting?' [REB]. This rhetorical question indicates a certain amount of surprise or irony [TH].
2. It is a command that might be serious or sarcastic [ICC, Lns, My, NIGTC, NTC, Sw; KJV]: 'Go ahead and sleep. Have your rest' [NLT], 'You might as well sleep now' [GW]. Since Jesus had finished praying, he no longer needs them to stay awake [NIGTC]. This is said with irony since Jesus immediately makes two announcements that would drive all trace of sleep from their eyes [Lns].

QUESTION—What is ἀπέχει 'enough'?
It doesn't tell us what was enough and many scholars have despaired of coming to a solution [BECNT, EBC, NIGTC, NTC].
1. It is enough sleep and now it is time for the disciples to be awake [BNTC, Hb, Lns, NIGTC, TH, TRT]. Jesus tells them 'Enough of that!' [TH]. Perhaps we are to assume that after Jesus told them to go to asleep, a short time later sounds were heard that indicated the approach of the arresting party and he had to countermand his permission to sleep [NIGTC].
2. The common monetary use of the term is intended: 'He (Judas) is paid!' [BECNT].

QUESTION—What hour has come?
The hour refers to the time when Jesus will be given into the hands of sinners [BNTC, ESVfn, Lns, NICNT, TRT].

QUESTION—Where did Jesus want them to go?
He wanted them to accompany him as he went to meet his approaching enemies [BECNT, BNTC, Hb, NTC, TH, TRT, WBC].

DISCOURSE UNIT—14:43–15:15 [NIGTC]. The topic is the arrest and trials of Jesus.

DISCOURSE UNIT—14:43–52 [CBC, NICNT; CEV, GW, NASB, NCV, NET, NIV, NLT, NRSV, TEV]. The topic is the arrest of Jesus [TEV], Jesus is arrested [CEV, GW, NCV, NIV], Jesus is betrayed and arrested [CBC; NLT], betrayal and arrest [NASB, NET], the betrayal and arrest of Jesus [NICNT; NRSV].

DISCOURSE UNIT—14:43–50 [Hb; ESV]. The topic is the betrayal and arrest of Jesus.

14:43 And immediately while he is-speaking, Judas, one of the twelve, arrives from[a] the chief-priests and the scribes and the elders, and with him (came) a-crowd[b] with swords and clubs. **14:44** Now the-one betraying[c] him had-given a-signal to them saying, 'Whoever I-kiss, he is (the one). Arrest[d] him and take-(him)-away securely.[e]"

TEXT—In verse 43, the manuscripts reading ὄχλος 'a crowd' are followed by GNT which does not mention any variant reading. A variant reading is ὄχλος πολύς 'a large crowd' and it is followed by KJV.
LEXICON—a. παρά (LN 90.14) (BAGD I.1. p. 609): 'from' [AB1, AB2, BAGD, BECNT, LN, Lns, NTC; ESV, GW, KJV, NASB, NCV, NIV,

NRSV]. Instead of a direct connection with the verb 'arrives', some insert the verb 'sent': '(sent) from' [WBC], '(sent) by' [BNTC; CEV, NET, NLT, REB, TEV]. This preposition indicates the agentive source of an activity [LN].
b. ὄχλος (LN 11.1): 'a crowd' [AB1, AB2, BECNT, BNTC, LN, NTC, WBC; ESV, GW, NASB, NET, NIV, NRSV, REB, TEV], 'a multitude' [LN, Lns], 'a crowd of men' [NLT], 'a mob of men' [CEV], 'many people' [NCV], 'a great multitude' [KJV]. This noun denotes a fairly large group of people who are assembled for some purpose. When a language has no term corresponding to 'crowd', a potential replacement is 'many people' or 'many men and women' [LN].
c. pres. act. participle of παραδίδωμι (LN 37.111) (BAGD 1.b. p. 614): 'to betray' [BECNT, LN, Lns, NTC, WBC; KJV, NASB], 'to turn over to (someone)' [AB2, BAGD, LN], 'to hand over' [BAGD, LN]. The phrase ὁ παραδιδούς 'the one betraying' is translated: 'the betrayer' [ESV, NET, NIV, NRSV, REB, TEV], '(his) betrayer' [BNTC], 'the traitor' [AB1; GW, NLT], 'Judas' [CEV, NCV]. This verb means to deliver a person into the control of someone else [LN].
d. aorist act. impera. of κρατέω (LN 37.110) (BAGD 1.a. p. 448): 'to arrest' [BAGD, Lns; CEV, GW, NCV, NET, NIV, NLT, NRSV, TEV], 'to take into custody' [BAGD], 'to take' [KJV], 'to seize' [AB1, AB2, BECNT, BNTC, LN, WBC; NASB, ESV, REB], 'to grab' [NTC]. This verb literally means 'to lay hands on' and is used as an idiom for taking a person into custody for alleged illegal activity [LN].
e. ἀσφαλῶς (LN 21.10) (BAGD 1. p. 119): 'securely' [AB2, BAGD, BECNT, LN], 'safely' [AB1, Lns; KJV, REB], 'under guard' [BAGD, BNTC, NTC, WBC; ESV, NASB, NCV, NET, NIV, NLT, NRSV, TEV]. This is also translated as a clause: 'guard him closely' [GW], 'tie him up tight' [CEV]. This adverb normally refers to a state of safety and security that causes one to be free from danger. When referring to prisoners; however, it refers not to their safety but to the security needed to guard them and to eliminate any danger they might escape [LN].

QUESTION—Why is Judas again identified as being 'one of the twelve'?
By repeating what was described in verse 10, the tragic element of the situation is being emphasized [Hb, ICC].

QUESTION—Who comprised the ὄχλος 'crowd' that accompanied Judas?
Even though Mark does not specify who was in the armed crowd, they must have been the Jewish temple guards since they came from the Temple authorities and Jesus states in verse 49 that they could have arrested him many times while he was teaching in the temple [NIGTC]. This arresting party was probably composed of the Temple police who were assigned the task of maintaining public order beyond the Temple precincts. A large squad was neither necessary nor practical since it was imperative that an uproar be avoided [AB2, BECNT, NICNT].

QUESTION—Why would Judas kiss Jesus when he went up to him?

Greeting another man by kissing him on the cheek was a normal way of greeting someone in that culture [NIGTC, TH]. In some cultures, it may be necessary to include the purpose of the kiss with something like 'whoever I greet by kissing him' [TH].

14:45 **And having-come, immediately approaching him he-says "Rabbi."ᵃ And he-kissed him.** **14:46** **And they-laidᵇ their hands on-him and arrestedᶜ him.**

TEXT—Manuscripts reading Ῥαββί 'Rabbi' are followed by GNT which does not mention any variant reading. A variant reading is Ῥαββί ῥαββί 'Rabbi, rabbi' and it is followed by KJV.

LEXICON—a. ῥαββί (LN 33.246) (BAGD p. 733): 'rabbi' [AB1, AB2, BECNT, BNTC, LN, Lns, NTC, WBC; ESV, GW, NASB, NIV, NLT, REB, NRSV], 'teacher' [LN; CEV, NCV, NET, TEV], 'master' [KJV]. This noun is borrowed from Aramaic to denote a Jewish teacher and scholar who is recognized for his expertise in interpreting the Jewish Scriptures [LN]. It is an honorary title for the outstanding teachers of the law [BAGD]. This noun occurs at verses 9:5, 11:21, and 14:45.

b. aorist act. indic. of ἐπιβάλλω (LN 85.51) (BAGD 1.b. p. 289): 'to lay on, to put on' [BAGD, LN], 'to place on' [LN]. The clause 'they laid (their) hands on him [AB2, BNTC, NTC, WBC; ESV, KJV, NASB, NRSV] is also translated 'they threw their hands upon him' [Lns], 'some men took hold of Jesus' [GW; similarly NET], 'they held him tight' [TEV], 'the men seized Jesus' [NIV; similarly REB], '(they) grabbed him/Jesus' [AB1; CEV, NLT]. The idiom ἐπιβάλλω τὰς χεῖρας 'to lay hands on' refers to taking a person into custody for alleged illegal activity, and has the same meaning as 'to seize, to arrest' [LN (37.120)].

c. aorist act. indic. of κρατέω (LN 18.6) (BAGD1.a p. 448]: 'to arrest' [BAGD, Lns, WBC; CEV, GW, NCV, NET, NIV, NLT, NRSV, TEV], 'to take' [KJV], 'to take into custody' [AB2, BAGD], 'to apprehend' [BAGD], 'to seize' [BECNT, LN, WBC; ESV, NASB], 'to hold onto' [LN], 'to hold tight' [TEV], 'to hold fast' [BNTC, REB]. This verb means to hold on to an object [LN].

14:47 **And one of-those standing-by, having-drawn his sword, struck the slave of-the high-priest and cut-off his ear.**

QUESTION—Who was the man who drew his sword?

Mark does not identify him, but Matthew 20:51 says that he was one of the Twelve, and John 18:10 says that he was Simon Peter [Hb].

QUESTION—Why did he cut off the man's ear?

When he tried to split the man's head wide open, only the ear was sheared off because the slave probably dodged and used his heavy shoulder armor to stop the sword from doing any other damage. Mark says nothing about how Jesus healed that slave's ear [Lns]. Mark uses the diminutive form ὠτάριον 'ear', so perhaps only the lobe was cut off. That would explain why Luke says that Jesus healed the ear instead of replacing it [EBC].

QUESTION—Why was the slave of the high priest present with the soldiers?

The definite article '*the* slave' points out his distinctive position. He probably was the personal slave of the high priest, Caiaphas, and had been sent with the soldiers to bring back a report about everything that happens [Hb, Lns].

14:48 And speaking, Jesus said to-them, "Have-you-come-out with swords and clubs to arrest[a] me, as (you would) against a robber[b]? 14:49 Every day I-was with you in the temple teaching, and you-did- not -arrest[c] me. But in-order-that the Scriptures should-be-fulfilled...[d]" 14:50 And having-left him, (they) all fled.

LEXICON—a. aorist act. infin. of συλλαμβάνω (LN 37.109) (BAGD 1.a.α. p. 776): 'to arrest' [BAGD, LN; CEV, GW, NASB, NET, NLT, NRSV, REB], 'to seize' [BAGD, LN], 'to capture' [ESV, NIV, TEV], 'to catch' [LN], 'to take' [LN, WBC; KJV], 'to get' [NCV]. This verb means to seize someone and take him somewhere [LN].

b. λῃστής (LN 57.240) (BAGD 2. p. 473): 'robber' [BAGD, Lns; ESV, NASB, REB], 'bandit' [NRSV], 'criminal' [CEV, GW, NCV], 'outlaw' [NET, TEV], 'thief' [KJV], 'highwayman' [BAGD, LN], 'insurrectionist' [WBC], 'dangerous revolutionary' [NLT]. One translation begins the question, 'Am I leading a rebellion (that you have come out with...)?' [NIV]. This noun denotes someone who robs by force and violence [LN].

c. aorist act. indic. of κρατέω (LN 37.110) (BAGD 1.a. p. 448): 'to arrest' [BAGD, LN; CEV, GW, NCV, NET, NIV, NLT, NRSV, TEV], 'to seize' [LN; ESV, NASB], 'to lay hands on (me)' [REB], 'to take' [WBC; KJV], 'to take into custody, to apprehend' [BAGD]. This verb means to take a person into custody for alleged illegal activity [LN].

d. The unfinished sentence ἀλλ' ἵνα πληρωθῶσιν αἱ γραφαί 'But in order that the Scriptures may/should be fulfilled...' [AB2, Lns, WBC] is incomplete, but apparently the thought is 'You did not arrest me then, in order that the scriptures might be fulfilled' [Hb]. Matthew 26:56 has a full sentence that some translations repeat in part in order to make a sentence here in Mark: 'But *this has taken place* to fulfill the Scriptures' [NASB], 'But this happened/has-happened so that the scriptures would be fulfilled' [NTC; NET], 'But all these things have happened to make the Scriptures come true' [NCV], 'But these things are happening to fulfill what the Scriptures say about me' [NLT], 'But let it be in order that the Scriptures may be fulfilled' [BECNT]. All the other translations in Mark are presented as complete sentences: 'But let the Scriptures be fulfilled' [AB1, BNTC; ESV, NRSV, REB], 'But the Scriptures must be fulfilled' [KJV, NIV], 'But the Scriptures must come true' [TEV], 'But what the Scriptures say must come true' [CEV, GW].

QUESTION—Who were all the people who left Jesus and fled?

Some translations explicitly say that it was all the disciples of Jesus that fled [AB1, BNTC; GW, NCV, NET, NLT, REB, TEV].

DISCOURSE UNIT—14:51–52 [Hb; ESV]. The topic is a young man flees [ESV], the young man who fled [Hb].

14:51 **And a-certain young-man was following him wearing nothing but a-linen-cloth**[a] **about his naked (body). And they-tried-to-seize**[b] **him. 14:52 But leaving-behind the linen cloth, he ran-away naked.**

TEXT—Manuscripts reading καὶ κρατοῦσιν αὐτόν 'And they tried to seize him' are followed by GNT which does not mention any variant reading. A variant reading is καὶ κρατοῦσιν αὐτόν οἱ νεανίσκοι 'and the young men tried to seize him' and it is followed by KJV.

LEXICON—a. σινδών (LN 6.155) (BAGD 2. p. 751): 'a linen cloth' [AB1, AB2, BAGD, BNTC, LN, Lns, NTC; CEV, ESV, KJV, NCV, NET, NRSV, REB, TEV], 'a linen sheet' [WBC; GW, NASB], 'a linen garment' [BECNT; NIV], 'a long linen shirt' [NLT]. This noun denotes a linen cloth of good quality. For languages where there is no term for linen, many translators have used 'fine cloth' or 'good cloth' to make sure the emphasis is on the quality of the cloth and not the material from which it is made. [LN]. This linen cloth refers to a tunic or shirt that was the only garment worn by the youth who was following Jesus unless he had just wrapped a linen sheet about his body [BAGD].

b. pres. act. indic. of κρατέω (LN 18.6, 37.110) (BAGD 1.a. p. 448): 'to seize' [AB1, AB2, BECNT, BNTC, LN (18.6, 37.110), NTC, WBC; ESV, NASB, NIV, REB], 'to grab' [CEV, NCV, NLT], 'to catch hold of' [NRSV], 'to lay hold of' [KJV], 'to hold on to' [LN (18.6)], 'to arrest' [BAGD, LN (37.110), Lns; GW, NET, TEV], 'to take into custody, to apprehend' [BAGD]. This verb means to hold on to an object [LN (18.6)] or to take a person into custody for alleged illegal activity [LN (37.110)].

QUESTION—What was the linen cloth that the young man was wearing?

1. He only had a linen sheet around him [EGT, Hb, ICC, NAC, NTC, Tay, WBC; GW, NASB]. This was a sheet he had quickly wrapped around him when he was awakened by the noise of the crowd passing by his house [ICC].
2. He was wearing a linen garment [AB1, BECNT, BNTC, CGTC, EBC, My, NICNT, NIV, NLT, NTC, Sw]. It may mean that he was wearing nothing except a linen tunic [TH]. After being roused from his sleep by the noise and excitement, he only had enough time to put on a short tunic [AB1]. He was wearing a linen sleeping garment [My]. It was a loin cloth [AB2].

QUESTION—Who tried to seize the young man?

'They' refers to the group who had come out against Jesus [TH]. They were the men who were leading Jesus away [Hb]. Evidently this young man betrayed his interest in Jesus by following along after them [Lns]. When some men in the group tried to capture the young man, their hands only got a good hold on the linen cloth as he fled away [Hb].

DISCOURSE UNIT—14:53–15:20a [Hb]. The topic is the trials of Jesus.

DISCOURSE UNIT—14:53–65 [CBC, Hb, NICNT; CEV, ESV, GW, NASB, NCV, NET, NIV, NLT, NRSV, TEV]. The topic is Jesus being questioned by the council [CEV], the Jewish leaders examine Jesus [CBC], Jesus before the council [ESV, NLT, NRSV, TEV], Jesus before the leaders [NCV], a 'trial' before the Sanhedrin [Hb], before the Sanhedrin [NIV], Jesus before his accusers [NASB], the trial in front of the Jewish council [GW], condemned by the Sanhedrin [NET], the proceedings of the Sanhedrin [NICNT].

14:53 **And they-led-away Jesus to the high-priest, and all the chief-priests and the elders and the scribes gathered-together.** **14:54** **And Peter had-followed him at a-distance, right into the courtyard of-the high-priest, and he-was-sitting with the guards[a] and was-warming-himself at (the) light (of the fire).[b]**

TEXT—In verse 53, manuscripts reading συνέρχονται 'gathered together' are followed by GNT which does not mention any variant reading. A variant reading is συνέρχονται αὐτῷ 'gathered together to him' and it is followed by KJV.

LEXICON—a. ὑπηρέτης (LN 35.20) (BAGD p. 842): 'guards' [all versions except KJV, NASB, REB], 'officers' [NTC, WBC; NASB], 'servants' [BAGD, BECNT, LN; KJV], 'attendants' [AB1, AB2, BNTC; REB], 'helpers, assistants' [BAGD], 'underlings' [Lns]. This noun denotes a person who renders service. In the NT it refers to someone who is employed, and it can refer to many diverse types of servants, such as attendants to a king, officers of the Sanhedrin, attendants of magistrates, and Jewish Temple guards [LN].

b. φῶς (LN 14.36; 2.5) (BAGD 1.b.α. p. 872): 'light' (LN (14.36)], 'fire, bonfire' [BAGD, LN (2.5)]. The phrase πρὸς τὸ φῶς 'at the light' [AB2] is also translated 'near the light' [Lns], 'facing the glow of a fire' [GW], 'at the fire' [AB1, BECNT; ESV, NASB, KJV, NIV, NRSV, REB], 'by the fire' [BNTC, WBC; NCV, NET, NLT, TEV], 'near the fire' [NTC], 'beside a fire' [CEV]. This noun denotes 'light' in contrast with darkness, and it is usually used in relationship to some source of light such as the sun, moon, fire, or lamp [LN (14.36)], or this noun denotes a pile or heap of burning material [LN (2.5)]. The phrase πρὸς τὸ φῶς 'at the light' means 'at the light of the fire' [TH].

QUESTION—What prompted the chief priests, elders, and scribes to gather together?

When it was certain that Jesus had been arrested, the high priest quickly sent messengers to summon all seventy members of the Sanhedrin to a meeting [Hb]. The chief priests, elders, and scribes referred to here were the men who constituted the Sanhedrin, and they made up the supreme Jewish court of law that the high priest presided over [NICNT]. What Mark probably intended to communicate by 'entire' is that enough of them were present to constitute a quorum [EBC, NICNT].

QUESTION—Why did Peter go into the courtyard of the high priest?

Peter hoped to learn about the fate of his teacher and friend who had been taken to the High Priest. He was trying to be inconspicuous among the throng of officers and servants who were warming themselves in the uncovered courtyard outside of the high priest's house [WBC].

14:55 **And the chief-priests and (the) entire Sanhedrin were-seeking a-testimony[a] against Jesus in-order to-execute[b] him, and they-were not finding (any) 14:56 because many were-testifying-falsely[c] against him, and the testimonies were not the-same.**

LEXICON—a. μαρτυρία (LN **33.264**) (BAGD 2.a. p. 493): 'testimony' [AB2, BAGD, BECNT, **LN**, WBC; ESV, GW, NASB, NRSV], 'evidence' [AB1, BNTC, NTC; NET, NIV, NLT, REB, TEV], 'witness' [LN, Lns; KJV]. The phrase ἐζήτουν κατὰ τοῦ Ἰησοῦ μαρτυρίαν 'were seeking a testimony against Jesus' is translated 'tried to find someone to accuse Jesus of a crime' [CEV], 'tried to find something that Jesus had done wrong' [NCV]. This noun denotes the content of what someone witnesses to or says. Some languages require the content of the testimony or the witness to be identified with phrases like 'they tried to find someone who would testify against Jesus' or 'they tried to say something against Jesus' [LN]. This refers to a testimony that is given in court [BAGD]. Even though they had decided that Jesus must be put to death, they needed incriminating evidence that would convince the Roman governor [Hb, Lns, NTC, WBC].

b. aorist act. infin. of θανατόω (LN 20.65) (BAGD 1. p. 351): 'to execute' [LN; GW], 'to put to death' [BAGD; all translations except AB2; GW, NCV, REB], 'to kill' [AB2, BAGD, LN; NCV], 'to warrant a death sentence' [REB]. This verb means to deprive a person of life with the implication that it is the result of a condemnation by legal or quasi-legal procedures [LN].

c. imperf. act. indic. of ψευδομαρτυρέω (LN **33.271**) (BAGD p. 892): 'to give false witness/testimony' [BAGD, BECNT, **LN**, WBC; GW, NASB, NET, NRSV], 'to give perjured testimony' [AB1], 'to give false evidence' [BNTC; REB], 'to bear false witness' [AB2, BAGD, NTC; ESV, KJV], 'to testify falsely' [LN; NIV], 'to witness falsely' [LN], 'to tell false things' [NCV], 'to tell lies' [CEV, TEV]. The clause 'many were testifying falsely against him' is translated 'many false witnesses spoke against him' [NLT]. This verb means to provide a false or untrue witness. A person who gives false witness may deceive by pretending to have been an eyewitness to an event or by saying something that is not true. [LN].

QUESTION—What prevented the Sanhedrin from using the testimonies of the witnesses?

The Jewish judicial procedure required each witness to present their evidence individually before the judges and the accused. If any differences were identified in their individual dispositions, all of the affected testimonies would then be ruled inadmissible as evidence no matter how trivial those differences might be [NICNT]. According to Numbers 35:39 and Deuteronomy 17:6; 19:15, the agreement of two or three witnesses was required [CGTC, EBC, Hb, Lns], and it was apparent that those who appeared as witnesses against Jesus were giving false testimonies [Hb]. The objective of the Sanhedrin was to produce evidence that could justify the desired guilty verdict without any regard for the truth [NLTfn].

14:57 And having-stood-up, some were-testifying-falsely against him saying, **14:58** "We heard him say, 'I will-tear-down[a] this man-made[b] temple and within[c] three days I-will-build another (that is) not-man-made.'" **14:59** And not-even-then (did they give) the same testimony.

LEXICON—a. fut. act. indic. of καταλύω (LN 20.54) (BAGD 1.b.α. p. 414): 'to tear down' [AB1, LN; CEV, GW, TEV], 'to pull down' [REB], 'to destroy' [AB2, BAGD, BECNT, BNTC, LN, Lns, NTC, WBC; ESV, KJV, NASB, NCV, NET, NIV, NLT, NRSV], 'to demolish' [BAGD]. This verb means to destroy something completely by tearing it down or dismantling it [LN].
  b. χειροποίητος (LN 42.32) (BAGD p. 880): 'man-made' [LN], 'made by humans' [GW], 'made by man' [NIV], 'made by human hands' [BAGD, LN, NTC], 'made with human hands' [BNTC; NLT], 'made by hands' [AB2], 'made with hands' [BECNT, WBC; ESV, KJV, NASB, NET, NRSV, REB], 'built with hands' [Lns], 'that people made' [NCV], 'which men have made' [TEV], 'this man-made (temple)' [AB1], '(this temple) that we built' [CEV]. This adjective pertains to what has been made by a human [LN].
  c. διά (LN **67.136**) (BAGD A.II.1.b. p. 180): 'within' [AB2, BAGD, **LN**; KJV], 'during, in the course of' [BAGD, LN], 'in' [AB1, BNTC, NTC; CEV, ESV, GW, NASB, NET, NIV, NLT, NRSV, REB], 'after' [BECNT, Lns, WBC; TEV], 'later' [NCV]. This preposition indicates the extent of time within a unit [LN].

QUESTION—What is meant by 'this man-made temple'?

It refers to the temple building itself, not the whole temple complex [Lns, TH].

QUESTION—Had Jesus ever said that he would destroy the temple?

Jesus had never said 'I will destroy this temple'. John 2:19 records the statement he made about the destruction of a temple two years prior when he said 'destroy this temple and in three days I will raise it'. But he was referring to his own body and not the temple building in Jerusalem [EBC, Hb, Lns, NICNT]. Perhaps these witnesses remembered that Jesus had once talked about the destruction of a temple and wrongly connected that with his statement in Mark 13:2 where he predicted the destruction of the Jerusalem temple [ESV].

QUESTION—Why did the testimonies of the witnesses fail to validate the charge against Jesus?

The witnesses did not agree on what Jesus had done [EBC, NIV, TEV]. The witnesses may have broken down under examination or may have contradicted one another in regard to details [Sw]. The charge against Jesus was not validated because the testimonies of the witnesses were inconsistent [EBC].

14:60 And having-stood-up in (their) midst,[a] the high-priest questioned Jesus, saying, "Why do-you- not -speak[b]? What is it that these men are-testifying-against[c] you?"

LEXICON—a. μέσος (LN 83.10) (BAGD 2. p. 507): 'in their/the midst' [BECNT, LN (83.10), Lns, WBC; ESV, KJV], 'in the middle' [AB2, BAGD, LN], 'in the center' [GW], 'in the presence of everybody' [AB1], 'before them' [NCV, NET, NIV, NLT, NRSV], 'in front of them' [TEV], 'in the council' [CEV], 'came forward' [BNTC, NTC; NASB], not explicit [REB]. This pronominal adjective refers to the middle of an area [LN]. The high priest stood up in the midst of the council [WBC]. By standing up and taking center stage, the high priest signaled that the hearing had reached its decisive phase [NIGTC]. Because the testimonies of the witnesses had not secured the desired result, the presiding justice was now going to interrogate Jesus himself [NICNT].

b. pres. mid. or pass. (deponent = act) indic. of ἀποκρίνομαι (LN 33.28): 'to speak' [LN]. The question Οὐκ ἀποκρίνῃ οὐδὲν 'Why do you not speak?' is translated 'Have you no answer to make?' [ESV; similarly Lns; KJV, NASB, NET, NRSV], 'Have you nothing to reply?' [BNTC], 'Aren't you going to answer?' [NCV, NIV], 'Are you not answering anything?' [BECNT], 'You don't answer?' [NTC], 'You make no reply?' [AB2], 'Are you not going to reply?' [WBC], 'Why don't you say something in your own defense?' [CEV], 'What do you have to say for yourself?' [NLT]. Some combine both of the high priest's questions: 'Don't you have any answer to what these men testify against you?' [GW], 'Have you no answer to the accusations that these witnesses bring against you?' [REB], 'Have you no reply/answer to the accusations they bring against you?' [AB1; TEV]. This verb means to introduce or to continue a somewhat formal discourse [LN]. The belligerent high priest was trying to goad Jesus into saying something that could be used against him [Hb].

c. pres. act. indic. of καταμαρτυρέω (LN 33.269) (BAGD p. 4.14): 'to testify against' [BAGD, LN], 'to witness against' [LN]. The clause 'What is it that these men are-testifying/witness against you?' [BNTC, NTC; NASB; similarly ESV, NET, NRSV] is also translated 'What is this testimony that these men are bringing against you?' [NIV], 'What are these men witnessing/testifying against you?' [BECNT, Lns, WBC], 'Don't you hear the charges they are making against you?' [CEV], 'Don't you have something to say about their charges against you?' [NCV], 'Well, aren't you going to answer these charges?' [NLT], 'What is it which these witness against thee?' [KJV]. This verb means to witness against someone or some statement [LN].

14:61 But he-remained-silent and did- not -answer. Again the high-priest questioned him and says to-him, "Are you the Messiah,[a] the Son of the Blessed-One[b]?"

LEXICON—a. Χριστός (LN 53.82) (BAGD 1. p. 887): With the article, it is translated 'the Messiah' [AB1, BAGD, BECNT, LN, WBC; CEV, GW, NLT, NRSV, REB, TEV], 'the Christ' [AB2, BAGD, BNTC, Lns, NTC; ESV, KJV, NASB, NCV, NET, NIV]. This noun means 'the one who has been anointed'. In the NT it is a title for Jesus who is 'the Messiah, the Christ'. In other contexts, especially when it is without an article, Χριστός functions as part of the name 'Jesus Christ' [LN]. This word occurs at 1:1; 8:29; 9:41; 12:35; 13:21; 14:61; 15:32.

b. εὐλογητός (LN 33.362) (BAGD p. 322): 'the One who should be praised' [LN]. The phrase ὁ υἱὸς τοῦ εὐλογητοῦ 'the Son of the Blessed One' [AB1, AB2; GW, NASB, NET, NIV, NLT, NRSV, REB] is also translated 'the Son of the Blessed' [BECNT, BNTC, Lns, NTC; ESV, KJV], 'the son of the Blessed' [WBC], 'the Son of the Blessed God' [TEV], 'the Son of the blessed God' [NCV], 'the Son of the glorious God' [CEV]. This title is a derivative of the verb εὐλογέωα 'to praise' and pertains to being worthy of praise or commendation [LN]. The title 'Blessed' is a circumlocution to avoid saying 'God', and reflects the Jewish reverence for the name of God [BECNT, Hb].

QUESTION—What was the high priest asking Jesus about?

1. In the combination 'the Messiah, the Son of the Blessed One', the second clause 'son of God' was only used by NT Jewish scholars in a messianic sense, so it stands in apposition to the first. The question is simply asking Jesus if he claimed to be 'the Messiah' and does not address his deity [AB1, AB2, BNTC, EBC, ICC, ESVfn, NICNT].
2. In the combination 'the Messiah, the Son of the Blessed One', the first clause refers to a claim to be the Messiah and the second clause refers to a claim of deity [BECNT, CGTC, Gnd, Hb, Lns, NAC, NIGTC, NTC, PNTC, Sw, WBC]. The reference to Jesus as the 'Son of God' has been used twice by God (1:11 and 9:7) and twice by demons (3:11 and 5:7). The only time Jesus referred to himself as the Son of God was in a private audience with his disciples in 13:32. Jesus is thought to have presented himself in both of these capacities in order to describe two different aspects of his claim to special authority [NIGTC].

14:62 And Jesus said, "I am,ª and you(pl)-will-see the Son of-Manᵇ sitting at (the) right (hand) of-the Powerᶜ and coming with the clouds of-heaven.ᵈ"

LEXICON—a. pres. act. indic. of εἰμί (LN 13.4) (BAGD II.5. p. 224): 'to be' [BAGD, LN]. The statement Ἐγώ εἰμι 'I am' [all translations except CEV, GW, NLT] is also translated 'I AM' [NLT], 'Yes, I am' [CEV, GW]. This verb means to be identical with someone [LN].

  b. υἱὸς τοῦ ἀνθρώπου (LN 9.3) (BAGD 2.e. p. 835): This title of Jesus is translated 'the Son of Man' [BAGD, LN; all translations except AB1], 'The Man' [AB1]. It is a title with Messianic implications that Jesus used concerning himself [LN]. Jewish teaching at that time included a heavenly being who was looked upon as a 'Son of Man' or 'Man' who exercised Messianic functions such as judging the world [BAGD]. See 2:10 for a discussion of this title.

  c. δύναμις (LN 12.44) (BAGD 1. p. 207): 'power' [BAGD, LN], 'might, strength' [BAGD]. The designation τῆς δυνάμεως 'the Power' [AB2, NTC, WBC; NET, NRSV] is also translated 'Power' [BECNT; ESV, NASB], 'power' [AB1, BNTC, Lns; KJV], 'God All-Powerful' [CEV], 'God, the powerful One' [NCV], 'the Almighty' [REB, TEV], 'the Mighty One' [NIV]. The clause 'sitting at the right hand of the Power' is translated 'seated in the place of power at God's right hand' [NLT], 'in the highest position in heaven' [GW]. This noun denotes power and in this verse it refers to supernatural power that functions as a figurative extension of meaning of θρόνοςa 'throne' [LN]. 'Power' was a recognized circumlocution for God [AB2, BECNT, Hb, NICNT, TRT]. If the words 'the right hand of the Power' are unintelligible in a language, the meaning can be expressed as 'the right hand of God who has power' [TH].

  d. οὐρανός (LN 1.5) (BAGD 1.d. p. 504): 'cloud' [BAGD, LN]. The phrase ἐρχόμενον μετὰ τῶν νεφελῶν τοῦ οὐρανοῦ 'coming with the clouds of heaven' [AB2, BECNT, BNTC, Lns, NTC, WBC; CEV, ESV, GW, NASB, NET, NRSV, REB, TEV] is also translated 'coming in the clouds of heaven' [KJV], 'coming on the clouds of heaven' [NIV, NLT], 'coming on the clouds in the sky' [NCV]. This noun denotes the space above the earth, including the vault arching high over the earth from one horizon to another, as well as the sun, moon, and stars [LN]. 'Coming *with* the clouds' is similar to the statement in 13:26 where Jesus said, 'They will see the Son of Man coming *in/on* clouds with great power and glory.' Both verses refer to Daniel 7:13, where the Hebrew text says the Son of man came 'with' the clouds and the Septuagint Greek translation says 'on' the clouds [TH].

QUESTION—What did Jesus mean when he answered Ἐγώ εἰμι 'I am'?

  This is a simple assertion and not an allusion to the divine name 'I AM' [BECNT, EBC, Hb, LN, Lns, NICNT, NTC, PNTC, WBC]. It means 'I am indeed the Christ, the Son of the Blessed' [NTC]. The words 'I am' may imply a subtle allusion to the divine self-revelation in Exodus 3:14–15 where

God says to Moses, 'I am who I am'…Say this to the people of Israel, 'I am has sent me to you'. When languages require some type of predicate compliment for the words 'I am', this type of allusion is difficult to reproduce and Jesus' reply will need to be translated as an affirmative 'Yes' or as a declaration such as 'I am the Messiah' [TH].

QUESTION—When will the Son of Man be sitting at the right hand of the 'Power'?

This refers to the exaltation of Christ to the right hand of God after his resurrection [BECNT, EBC, NICNT, NTC]. They will see the Son of Man whenever he comes as Judge, whether it be during their lifetime or when they are raised for the last judgment after their deaths [CGTC, Gnd]. Those who are now judging Christ will see him enthroned at God's right hand, invested with power and majesty in his position as their eschatological Judge. It is then that he will be unveiled as the Anointed of God [NICNT]. These very men will see Jesus' glorification by the miracles that occur at the crucifixion, in his resurrection, and in every other manifestation of his power [Lns]. Jesus' sovereignty began to become visible to these men with the powerful growth of the NT church and the demise of Jerusalem and its temple as the focus of God's rule on earth [NIGTC]. They will see evidence of his advancing kingdom in the world [ICC].

QUESTION—When will Jesus come with the clouds of heaven?

1. This refers to their perception of his power and judgment during their lifetimes [ICC, Lns, My, NIGTC, Tay]. The conjunction καί 'and' beginning this clause is not to be interpreted as a coming to earth since that is not suggested by either Daniel or Mark. Instead of indicating a time break between the two metaphors, each expresses in their distinctive ways the same concept of a sovereign authority [NIGTC].
2. This refers to the Second Coming of Jesus [BECNT, CGTC, EBC, EGT, Gnd, Hb, NICNT, NTC, Sw, WBC]. Revelation 1:7 expands on it by saying: 'Look, he is coming with the clouds, and every eye will see him, even those who pierced him' [EBC], and that coming in judgment will occur at the end of history [BECNT]. Jesus will return to judge his enemies as the figure depicted in Daniel's vision who is seated at the right hand of God in the divine chariot-throne [WBC].

14:63 **And having-torn his clothes,[a] the high-priest says, "What further need do-we-have of-witnesses? 14:64 You heard the blasphemy.[b] How does-it-seem to-you(pl)?" And they all condemned him to-be deserving of-death.**

LEXICON—a. χιτών (LN 6.162) (BAGD p. 882): 'clothes' [AB1, BAGD, BNTC, NTC; KJV, NASB, NCV, NET, NIV, NRSV], 'clothing, apparel' [LN], 'garments' [AB2, BECNT; ESV], 'robes' [WBC; REB, TEV], 'tunics' [Lns]. The clause 'having torn his clothes' is translated' 'ripped his robe apart' [CEV], 'tore his clothes in horror' [GW], 'tore his clothing to show his horror' [NLT]. This noun denotes any kind of clothing [LN].

The gesture of tearing one's garments was indicative of sorrow or horror. In the case of this judicial proceeding, the high priest was indulging in a formal ceremonial act that was minutely prescribed by tradition [TH]. It was a formal judicial act, and not an act of uncontrolled rage [BECNT].

b. βλασφημία (LN 33.401) (BAGD 2.b. p. 143): 'blasphemy' [LN, Lns, NTC; all translations except CEV, GW, NCV], 'serious insult' [LN], 'evil speech against God' [BAGD]. The phrase 'the blasphemy' is translated 'say these things against God' [NCV], 'claim to be God' [CEV], 'dishonor God' [GW]. This noun denotes the content of a defamation [LN].

14:65 And some began to-spit-on him, and to-cover his face and strike him and to-say to-him, "Prophesy[a]!" And the guards[b] received[c] him with-slaps.

TEXT—Manuscripts reading αὐτῷ 'him' are given an A rating by GNT to indicate it was regarded to be certain. Variant readings are τῷ προσώπῳ αὐτοῦ 'his face' and αὐτοῦ τῷ προσώπῳ 'his face'.

TEXT—Manuscripts reading Προφήτευσον 'Prophesy!' are given a B rating by GNT to indicate it was regarded to be almost certain. Other variant readings are Προφήτευσον ἡμῖν 'Prophesy to us', Προφήτευσον ἡμῖν, Χριστέ 'Prophesy to us, Christ', Προφήτευσον ἡμῖν, Χριστέ, τίς ἐστιν ὁ παίσας σε 'Prophesy to us, Christ, who is the one having struck you?', and Προφήτευσον ἡμῖν, τίς ἐστιν ὁ παίσας σε 'Prophesy to us, who is the one having struck you?'.

TEXT—Manuscripts reading ἔλαβον 'received' are followed by GNT which does not mention any variant reading. A variant reading is εβαλλον 'struck' and it is followed by KJV.

LEXICON—a. aorist act. impera. of προφητεύω (LN 33.459) (BAGD 2. p. 723): 'to prophesy' [LN], 'to make inspired utterances' [LN], 'to prophetically reveal what is hidden' [BAGD]. The command Προφήτευσον 'Prophesy!' [AB1, AB2, BECNT, BNTC, Lns, NTC, WBC; ESV, GW, KJV, NASB, NET, NIV, NRSV, REB] is also translated 'Prophesy to us' [NLT], 'Prove you are a prophet!' [NCV], 'Tell us who hit you!' [CEV], 'Guess who hit you' [TEV]. This verb means to speak under the influence of divine inspiration, with or without reference to future events [LN].

b. ὑπηρέτης (LN 35.20) (BAGD p. 842): 'guard' [BECNT; all versions except KJV, NASB, REB], 'officer' [NTC, WBC; NASB], 'servant' [BAGD, LN; KJV], 'attendant' [AB1, AB2, BNTC; REB], 'underling' [Lns], 'helper, assistant' [BAGD]. This noun denotes a person who renders service. It is used to refer to many diverse types of servants, such as attendants to a king, officers of the Sanhedrin, attendants of magistrates, and the Jewish Temple guards [LN].

c. aorist act. indic. of λαμβάνω (LN 90.85) (BAGD 1.e.α. p. 464): 'to receive' [BAGD], 'to take' [BAGD, LN]. The clause ῥαπίσμασιν αὐτὸν ἔλαβον 'received him with slaps' [AB2, WBC] is also translated 'received him with slaps in the face' [NASB], 'received him with blows' [BECNT; NTC; ESV], 'received him with blows in the face' [Lns], 'took charge of Jesus and beat him' [CEV], 'took him over and beat him' [NRSV], 'took him and beat him' [NET, NIV], 'took him and slapped him' [GW, TEV], 'set on him with blows' [AB1], 'led Jesus away and beat him' [NCV], 'slapped him in the face' [BNTC; REB], 'did strike him with the palms of their hands' [KJV], 'slapped him as they took him away' [NLT]. This verb means to cause to experience something that is usually something grievous. In this verse, 'made him experience slapping' means 'the guards slapped him'. A more literal translation of this verse could be 'the guards took him and slapped him' [LN]. This is a colloquial expression for 'the servants treated him with blows' [BAGD]. It means that they beat him up [TH].

QUESTION—Who were the τινες 'some' who began to spit on Jesus and strike him?

This refers to the members of the Sanhedrin [EBC, EGT, Gnd, Hb, My, NTC, WBC]. The guards were not involved in this since they would not take custody of Jesus until later [EBC]. To spit on someone's face was the strongest and grossest form of personal insult [Hb, Lns, NIGTC].

QUESTION—Why did they cover Jesus' face?

They threw a cloth over Jesus' head so they could jeeringly ask him to use his prophetic powers to identify who was hitting him with their clenched fists [Hb, Lns]. The parallels in Mathew 26:68 and Luke 22:64 make it clear that they were challenging Jesus to name who it was that was striking him [NIGTC, TH].

DISCOURSE UNIT—14:66–72 [CBC, Hb, NICNT; CEV, ESV, GW, NASB, NCV, NET, NIV, NLT, NRSV, TEV]. The topic is Peter's denials [CBC; NASB, NET], Peter's denial of Jesus [NICNT], Peter denies Jesus [ESV, GW, NLT, NRSV, TEV], Peter says he doesn't know Jesus [CEV, NCV], Peter disowns Jesus [NIV], three denials by Peter [Hb].

14:66 And (as) Peter was below in the courtyard, one of-the servant-girls^a of-the high-priest, comes, 14:67 and seeing Peter warming-himself, she-looked-at him and said, "You also were with the Nazarene, Jesus." 14:68 But he-denied (it), saying, "I neither know nor understand^b what you are-talking-about." And he-went-out into the gateway^c and a-rooster crowed.

TEXT—In verse 68, manuscripts including the clause καὶ ἀλέκτωρ ἐφώνησεν 'and a rooster crowed' are given a C rating by GNT to indicate that its inclusion was a difficult decision. Some manuscripts omit the phrase.

LEXICON—a. παιδίσκη (LN 87.83) (BAGD p. 604): 'servant girl' [BAGD, BNTC, NTC; CEV, ESV, NASB, NCV, NIV, NLT, NRSV, REB], 'servant woman' [TEV], 'female servant' [BECNT; GW], 'maid' [AB1, BAGD, Lns; KJV], 'maid servant' [WBC], 'female slave' [BAGD], 'slave girl' [AB2, LN; NET]. This noun denotes a female slave [LN]. She was one of the high priest's servant maids [Sw]. She may have been the person

MARK 14:66–68   287

who admitted Peter at the courtyard gate [Hb]. John 18:16 says that she was the doorkeeper [NIVfn].
b. pres. mid. or pass. (deponent = act.) indic. of ἐπίσταμαι (LN 32.3) (BAGD 1. p. 300): 'to understand' [BAGD, LN], 'to be aware of, to really know' [LN]. The clause 'I neither/don't know nor/or understand' [AB2, BECNT, NTC, WBC; ESV, NASB, NCV, NIV, NIV, NRSV; similarly BNTC, Lns; KJV, TEV] is also translated 'I don't know (him) and I don't understand' [GW], 'I don't know (what you're talking about). I don't have any idea (what you mean)' [CEV], 'I know nothing, I have no idea' [REB], 'I know nothing, I do not understand what you mean' [AB1], 'I don't even understand what you're talking about' [NET], 'I don't know what you are talking about' [NLT]. This verb means to have or gain insight where the focus is on the process [LN]. It is doubtful whether any distinction can be made between the two verbs 'know' and 'understand'. Some suggest the meaning is 'I neither know him, nor understand what you mean', but that requires reading into the verse the personal pronoun 'him' which is not necessarily implied [LN]. The combination was an expression used in Jewish law courts for a formal legal denial [NTCfn].
c. προαύλιον (LN 7.37) (BAGD p. 702): 'gateway' [LN; ESV, NET], 'forecourt' [AB1, AB2, BAGD, LN, Lns, WBC; NRSV, REB], 'porch' [BNTC; KJV, NASB]. The phrase 'into the gateway' [**LN**] is also translated 'into the entryway' [BECNT, NTC; NIV, NLT], 'into the passageway' [TEV], 'to the entrance' [GW], 'out to the gate' [CEV], 'out in front of the building' [**LN**], 'toward the entrance of the courtyard' [NCV]. This noun denotes the area in front of an entrance to a building [LN]. It is the place in front of the house [BAGD]. He went out of the courtyard into the passageway leading to the gate [Lns, TH].

QUESTION—What is implied by the accusation 'You also were with the Nazarene, Jesus'?

The emphatic 'the Nazarene' shows contempt for anyone from Nazareth [Hb]. The servant girl had probably seen Peter accompany Jesus in the streets of Jerusalem or in the temple earlier in the week [EGT].

14:69 And having-seen him, the servant-girl again began to-say to-the (ones) standing-by, "This-one is (one) of them." **14:70** But again he denied (it). And after a-little (while) the (ones) standing-by were- again -saying to-Peter, "Truly you-are (one) of them because you-are a-Galilean." **14:71** And he-began to-curse[a] and to-swear,[b] "I-do- not -know this man of-whom you-speak."

LEXICON—a. pres. act. infin. of ἀναθεματίζω (LN **33.472**) (BAGD 2. p. 54): 'to curse' [BAGD, BECNT, BNTC, **LN**, Lns, NTC, WBC; CEV, GW, KJV, NASB, NET, NRSV, REB], 'to call down curses' [AB2]. The clause ἤρξατο ἀναθεματίζειν 'he began to curse' is translated 'he began to invoke a curse upon himself' [AB1; ESV], 'he began to place a curse on himself' [NCV], 'he began to call down curses on himself' [NIV]. The clause 'he began to curse and to swear' is translated 'Peter swore, "A curse on me if I'm lying"' [NLT], 'Peter said, "I swear that I am telling the truth! May God punish me if I am not!"' [TEV]. The verb means to invoke divine harm if what is said is not true or if one does not carry out what has been promised [LN]. The verb means 'to devote to destruction' and the speaker would say, 'May I be accursed if what I say is not true' [TH].

b. pres. act. infin. of ὀμνύω (LN 33.463) (BAGD p. 566): 'to swear' [AB2, BAGD, BNTC, LN, Lns, NTC, WBC; CEV, ESV, KJV, NASB, NCV, NIV, NLT], 'to swear with an oath' [GW, NET; similarly BECNT], 'to declare with an oath' [REB], 'to swear an oath' [NRSV], 'to make an oath' [BAGD, LN], 'to put oneself under oath' [AB1]. This verb means to affirm the truth of a statement by calling on a divine being to execute sanctions against the person if the statement in question is not true [LN]. Paul swore that he did not know the man of whom they spoke [Tay; NIV].

QUESTION—Was this the same servant girl referred to in verse 66?

1. This was the same servant girl [Hb, ICC, Lns, My, NICNT, Sw, TH, Tay, WBC]. The definite article '*the* servant girl' identifies her as the same girl who had challenged him by the fire. Either she had returned to her post as the doorkeeper or she had maliciously followed Peter. Since Matthew mentions 'another maid' (26:71) and Luke mentions 'another (man)' (22:58), it is clear that she was not the only one that was challenging Peter at this time [Hb].
2. This was a different servant girl [NTC].

QUESTION—Where was Peter when the people standing by him began talking to him again in verse 70?

Luke 22:59 reports this happened about an hour later. Having been refused exit at the door, Peter had then returned to the open courtyard and tried to lose himself in the crowd [NTC]. By now Peter's identity had become a matter of general discussion [Hb].

QUESTION—What made the people in verse 70 convinced that Peter was one of the 'them'?

The people would have known that Jesus and Peter were from the Galilee Province because the people from Galilee spoke with a distinctive accent [TRT].

QUESTION—Who is the object of Peter's curse in verse 71?

1. Peter was calling down a curse on himself if he was not telling the truth [AB1, BNTC, CBC, CGTC, Hb, ICC, Lns, NAC, NICNT, NIGTC, NTC, Sw, Tay, TH, TRT; ESV, NCV, NIV, NLT, TEV]. Peter was putting himself under oath in order to emphasize the fact that he was telling the truth [TRT]. Peter called down the curse of God upon himself if he were not telling the truth [Hb]. Peter swore that he didn't know the man they were talking about and reinforced it by calling a curse on himself if it wasn't true [EBC].

2. Peter was calling down a curse on Jesus [AB2, BECNT, Gnd]. Since Peter has been asked about his association with Jesus, the object of Peter's curse is probably Jesus, whose name may have been suppressed for reverential reasons [AB2]. Cursing can refer to calling a curse upon oneself if one is lying or will not fulfill a promise (Acts 23:12, 14, 21). But in this context the object is likely Jesus: 'And he began to curse Jesus' [BECNT].

14:72 And immediately a rooster crowed for a-second (time). And Peter remembered the word[a] that Jesus had-said to-him, "Before a-rooster crows twice, you-will-deny[b] me three (times)." And he-began[c] to-cry.

TEXT—Manuscripts reading εὐθὺς 'immediately' are followed by GNT which does not mention any variant reading. A variant reading omits this word and it is followed by KJV.

TEXT—Manuscripts reading καὶ ἐπιβαλὼν ἔκλαιεν 'and having broken down he began to weep' are given a B rating by GNT to indicate it was regarded to be almost certain. A variant reading is καὶ ἤρξατο κλαίειν 'and he began to weep' and it is followed by CEV, GW, NASB. Another variant reading is καὶ ἐξελθὼν ἔξω ἔκλαυσεν πικρῶς 'and having gone outside he wept bitterly'.

LEXICON—a. ῥῆμα (LN 33.98) (BAGD 1. p. 735): 'word' [AB2, BAGD, LN, NTC, WBC; KJV, NIV, NLT], 'saying' [BAGD, BECNT, LN], 'message, statement' [LN], 'utterances' [Lns], 'that which is said, saying' [BAGD]. The phrase 'remembered the word that' is translated 'remembered that' [CEV, GW, NRSV], 'remembered how' [BNTC; ESV, NASB, REB, TEV], 'remembered what' [NCV, NET]. This noun denotes that which has been stated or said [LN].

b. fut. mid. (deponent= act) indic. of ἀπαρνέομαι (LN 33.277) (BAGD p. 81): 'to deny' [BAGD, LN]. See translations of this word in verse 30. This verb means to say that one does not know about or is in any way related to a person or event [LN].

c. aorist act. participle of ἐπιβάλλω (LN 30.7, 68.5) (BAGD 2.b. p. 290): Because of the uncertain meaning of the word ἐπιβαλὼν (literally 'to throw on') in this context, the clause ἐπιβαλὼν ἔκλαιεν' is translated in various ways: 'he began to cry' [LN (68.5)], 'he began to weep' [WBC; NASB], 'Peter started crying' [CEV], 'he broke into tears' [AB1], 'he burst into tears' [REB], 'Peter began to cry very hard' [GW]. Other translations are: 'he broke down and wept/cried' [ESV, NET, NIV, NLT, NRSV, TEV], 'he threw himself down and wept' [BNTC], 'when he reflected on this he wept' [NTC], 'when he thought thereon, he wept' [KJV], 'when he thought-of/reflected-on it he cried' [LN (68.5)], 'as he thought seriously about this, he cried' [LN (30.7)], 'Peter lost control of himself and began to cry' [NCV], 'having fallen to it, he began to weep' [Lns], 'rushing outside, he wept' [AB2], 'having rushed out, he began to weep' [BECNT]. This verb means to begin an activity with a special emphasis upon the inception or possibly the suddenness with which the event takes place [LN (68.5)] or it means to give careful consideration to various implications of an issue [LN (30.7)]. There is no agreement on how to translate this verb [AB1, BNTC, CGTC, EBC, Gnd, Hb, NAC, NCBC, NIGTC, Tay, TH, NTC, Lns, WBC]. It may mean: (1) he began to cry, (2) he burst into tears, (3) he thought on it and wept, (4) he covered his head and wept, (5) he threw himself on the ground and wept, (6) he dashed out crying. With such a display of different translations no final certainty can be reached [TH].

DISCOURSE UNIT—15:1–8 [PNTC]. The topic is the cross and the empty tomb.

DISCOURSE UNIT—15:1–15 [CBC, Hb, NICNT; NASB, NIV, NLT]. The topic is the trial before Pilate [Hb], Jesus' trial before Pilate [CBC; NLT], Jesus before Pilate [NASB, NIV], the trial of Jesus before Pilate's tribunal [NICNT].

DISCOURSE UNIT—15:1–5 [CEV, ESV, GW, NCV, NET, NRSV, TEV]. The topic is Pilate questions Jesus [CEV, GW, NCV], Jesus delivered to Pilate [ESV], Jesus brought before Pilate [NET], Jesus before Pilate [NRSV, TEV].

15:1 **And as-soon-as it-was-morning, the chief-priests held a-consultation[a] with the elders and scribes and (the) entire Council. Then having-bound Jesus, they-led-(him)-away[b] and turned-(him)-over[c] to-Pilate.**

LEXICON—a. συμβούλιον (LN 30.71) (BAGD 1. p. 778): 'consultation' [BAGD, BNTC, LN, WBC; ESV, KJV, NASB, NRSV], 'conference' [LN]. The phrase 'held a consultation' is translated 'met' [TEV], 'met together' [CEV], 'met to discuss their next step' [NLT], 'made their plans' [REB; similarly BECNT], 'having taken council' [AB2], 'came to a decision' [GW], 'reached a decision' [AB1; NIV], 'after forming a plan' [NET], 'passed a resolution' [Lns, NTC], 'decided what to do with Jesus' [NCV]. This noun denotes a joint planning session to devise a course of common action, often with a harmful or evil purpose in mind [LN].

b. aorist act. indic. of ἀποφέρω (LN 15.177) (BAGD 1.a.β. p. 101): 'to lead away' [BAGD, LN; all translations except Lns, WBC; CEV, KJV], 'to lead off' [LN; CEV], 'to take away [LN], 'to carry away' [Lns, WBC; KJV]. This verb means to lead or take away from a particular place [LN]. Although the verb can mean 'to carry' and can imply that Jesus' feet were bound so that he could not walk, that meaning might be taking the language too literally [WBC].

c. aorist act. indic. of παραδίδωμι (LN 37.111) (BAGD 1.b. p. 614): 'to turn over (to)' [AB2, BAGD, LN; NCV], 'to hand over' [AB1, BAGD, BECNT, BNTC, LN, WBC; GW, NET, NIV, NRSV, REB, TEV], 'to deliver' [LN, Lns, NTC; ESV, KJV, NASB], 'to take' [NLT], not explicit [CEV]. This verb means to deliver a person into the control of someone else and here it refers to the handing over of a presumably guilty person for punishment by the authorities [LN].

QUESTION—Who were the members of the 'entire Council'?
The 'entire Counsel' refers to the Sanhedrin [ESVfn]. This note is added to indicate it was a very important meeting [EGT].
1. It refers to the rest of the Sanhedrin [AB2, TH]. If the translation implies that the chief priests, elders, and scribes were not members of the Council, it could be translated 'and *all the rest of* the members of the Council' [TH].
2. It refers to the preceding list of its members [AB1, NTC; NLT, REB]: 'that is, the entire Sanhedrin' [NTC].

QUESTION—Who was Pilate?
Even though this is the first mention of Pilate, Mark felt no need to add any further identification because his readers would have already known the historical facts involving Pilate [Hb]. Pontius Pilate was the Roman governor of Judea from AD 20–30. Even though he was based in Caesarea, he stayed in Jerusalem during the Passover celebrations [NLTfn]. Only a Roman authority such as Pilate had the right to execute a person convicted of a capital crime [ESVfn].

15:2 And Pilate questioned him, "Are you the King of-the Jews?" And answering him he-says, "You say^a (so)."

LEXICON—a. pres. act. indic. of λέγω (LN 33.69) (BAGD II.1.e. p. 469): 'to say' [LN], 'to maintain' [BAGD]. Jesus' answer Σὺ λέγει 'You say' is translated 'You say so' [BNTC; NET, NRSV], 'You are saying so' [BECNT], 'You say it' [WBC; KJV; similarly AB2, Lns], 'You have said so' [ESV], 'So you say' [TEV], 'You have said it' [NLT], 'You said it' [NTC], 'That is what you maintain' [BAGD], 'Those are your words' [CEV, NCV], 'The words are yours' [AB1, REB], 'It is as you say' [NASB], 'Yes, it is as you say' [NIV], 'Yes, I am' [GW]. This verb means to speak or talk where the focus is upon the content of what is said [LN].

QUESTION—Why did Pilate ask Jesus if he was the king of the Jews?
Although the Jewish authorities wanted to have Jesus executed for the crime of blasphemy, they knew Pilate would not want to be involved in purely religious crimes. So they had accused Jesus of claiming to be the king of the Jews, a crime that challenged Caesar's rule and would compel the Roman government to execute Jesus [ESVfn].

QUESTION—What did Jesus mean when he replied, 'You say so'?
Jesus' words have been taken as being a denial, a noncommittal response, or a firm acknowledgment. A denial is inconsistent with the facts. If Jesus was using a Hebrew idiom, it was the regular way of confirmation. But since the answer was in Greek, it could be a qualified assent, 'Yes, but not with your exact meaning' and imply that his answer was open to further discussion [Hb]. Pilate had asked the question 'Are *you* the King of the Jews' with a touch of mockery suggesting that he had anticipated meeting someone more impressive. So Jesus replied in kind and said '*You* say it' to emphasize that it was Pilate's choice of words and not his own. Jesus really was 'the king of

the Jews' so he did not deny that identification, but it was not his preferred self-designation [WBC]. His answer means 'It is as you have stated' because in Matthew 26:25 his answer is a clear affirmation, ἐγώ εἰμι 'I am' [NTC]. Despite giving a positive reply, Jesus also implied that his understanding of the title was not the same as Pilate's [BECNT]. The question does not lend itself to a plain yes or no answer. Jesus meant that he would have posed the question differently [AB1]. Jesus' answer meant 'Yes I am the king of the Jews, but your concept of what that means and mine are poles apart' [EBC].

15:3 **And the chief-priests were accusing him much/of-many-things.**[a]

TEXT—Manuscripts ending this verse with πολλά 'much/of many things' are followed by GNT which does not mention any variant reading. A variant reading ends the verse δέ οὐδέν ἀποκρίνατος 'but he answered nothing' and it is followed by AB1; KJV.

LEXICON—a. πολύς (LN 59.1 or 59.11) (BAGD I.2.b.β. p. 688): This word is either adverbial (much, insistently, strongly) or adjectival of (many things) [TH]. It is adverbial and modifies the verb: They were accusing him 'much' [WBC], 'repeatedly' [NET], 'harshly' [NASB], 'greatly, loudly, often' [BAGD], 'brought many accusations against him' [BNTC], 'were-bringing/brought many charges against Jesus/him' [AB1; CEV, REB]. It is adjectival and modifies an implied direct object of the verb: They were accusing him 'of many things' [AB2, BECNT, Lns, NTC; GW, ESV, KJV, NCV, NIV, NRSV, TEV], 'of many crimes' [NLT]. This word can function as an adverb and refer to the upper range of a scale of extent: 'great, greatly, much, a great deal' [LN (59.1)] or as an adjective and refer to a relatively large quantity of objects or events 'many, a great deal of, a great number of' [LN (59.11)]. Luke 23:2 mentions three of their accusations against Jesus: he stirs up trouble among the people, he keeps them from paying taxes to the emperor, and he says that he is Messiah, a king. Pilate was most interested in the third accusation since he asked Jesus about it in verse 2 [EBC].

15:4 **And again Pilate questioned him, saying, "Do you- not -answer**[a] **anything? See how-many (things) they-are-accusing**[b] **you (of)."** **15:5** **But Jesus made no-further answer, so-that Pilate was-amazed.**[c]

TEXT—In verse 4, manuscripts reading κατηγοροῦσιν 'they are accusing' are followed by GNT which does not mention any variant reading. A variant reading is καταμαρτυροῦσιν 'they witness against' and it is followed by KJV.

LEXICON—a. pres. mid./pass. (deponent = act.) indic. of ἀποκρίνομαι (LN 33.184): 'to answer' [LN], 'to reply' [LN]. The clause Οὐ ἀποκρίνῃ οὐδέν; 'Do you not answer anything?' is translated 'Do you answer nothing?' [WBC; similarly Lns; KJV], 'Are you not answering at all?' [BECNT; similarly NTC], 'Do you not answer?' [NASB], 'Don't you have any answer?' [GW], 'Have you no answer to make?' [AB1; ESV; similarly NRSV], 'Aren't you going to answer them?' [NLT; similarly

NCV, NIV, TEV], 'Don't you have anything to say?' [CEV; similarly NET], 'Have you nothing to say in your defense?' [REB], 'Have you nothing to reply?' [BNTC], 'You make no reply?' [AB2]. This verb means to respond to a question that is asking for information [LN].
  b. pres. act. indic. of κατηγορέω (LN 33.427) (BAGD 1.a. p. 423): 'to accuse, to bring charges' [BAGD, LN]. The clause 'See how many things they are accusing you of' [BECNT; NIV; similarly Lns] is also translated 'See how many charges they are bringing against you!' [NET; similarly ESV, NRSV, REB], 'You see how many charges they bring against you!' [AB1], 'Look how many accusations they're bringing against you!' [GW, NASB; similarly AB1, BNTC], 'Look how much they accuse you!' [WBC], 'You can see that they are accusing you of many things' [NCV], 'See what great things they are charging you with!' [AB2], 'Don't you hear what crimes they say you have done?' [CEV], 'You hear how many accustions they are bringing against you' [NTC], 'Listen to all their accusations!' [TEV], 'What about all these charges they are bringing against you?' [NLT]. This verb means to bring serious charges or accusations against someone [LN].
  c. pres. act. infin. of θαυμάζω (LN 25.213) (BAGD 1.a.α. p. 352): 'to be amazed' [AB2, LN, NTC, WBC; CEV, ESV, NASB, NET, NIV, NRSV, TEV], 'to be astonished' [BAGD; similarly REB], 'to be surprised' [GW, NCV; similarly NLT], 'to wonder' [BAGD, LN, Lns], 'to marvel' [BAGD, BECNT, BNTC, LN; KJV]. This verb is also translated as a noun: '(to Pilate's) amazement' [AB1]. This verb means to wonder or marvel at some event or object [LN].
QUESTION—What amazed Pilate?
  Pilate had expected the usual protestations of innocence [Hb]. He was disinclined to believe that Jesus was guilty [NICNT, NIGTC].

DISCOURSE UNIT—15:6–20 [CBC, NICNT; NCV]. The topic is the mocking of Jesus [NICNT], the soldiers mock Jesus [CBC], Peter tries to free Jesus [NCV].

DISCOURSE UNIT—15:6–15 [CEV, ESV, GW, NET, NRSV, TEV]. The topic is Jesus is sentenced to death [TEV], Pilate delivers Jesus to be crucified [ESV], Pilate hands Jesus over to be crucified [NRSV], the death sentence [CEV], the crowd rejects Jesus [GW], Jesus and Barabbas [NET].

15:6 Now (at) every festival he-would-release[a] for-them (any) one prisoner whom they-requested. **15:7** And the (man) named Barabbas had been imprisoned with the rebels[b] who(pl) had committed murder during the insurrection.[c]
  LEXICON—a. imperf. act. indic. of ἀπολύω (LN 37.127) (BAGD 1. p. 96): 'to release' [AB1, AB2, BAGD, BECNT, BNTC, LN, Lns, NTC, WBC; ESV, KJV, NASB, NET, NIV, NLT, NRSV, REB], 'to set free' [BAGD, LN; CEV, TEV], 'to free' [GW, NCV], 'to pardon' [BAGD]. This verb

means to release from control and set free. It's highly generic meaning is applicable to a wide variety of circumstances that include confinement, political domination, sin, and sickness [LN]. The imperfect tense indicates a habitual action [BECNT, Hb, Lns, TH]. He did this every year [TH].
- b. στασιαστής (LN 39.37) (BAGD p. 764): 'rebel' [AB1, AB2, BAGD, BECNT, BNTC, LN, Lns, WBC; ESV, GW, NCV, NET, NRSV, REB, TEV], 'insurrectionist' [AB2, LN, Lns; NASB, NIV], '(one that) had made insurrection' [KJV], 'revolutionary' [BAGD; NLT], not explicit [CEV]. This noun denotes a person who engages in insurrection [LN]. It refers to those who fight against the government [TH].
- c. στάσις (LN 39.34) (BAGD 2. p. 764): 'insurrection' [AB2, Lns, NTC; ESV, KJV, NASB, NET, NRSV], 'rebellion' [AB1, BAGD, BECNT, LN, WBC], 'uprising' [BAGD, BNTC; NIV, NLT], 'revolt' [BAGD], 'rising' [REB], 'riot' [BAGD; CEV, GW, NCV, TEV]. This noun denotes a defiance of authority that is done with the intention of overthrowing it or acting in complete opposition to its demands [LN].

QUESTION—Did a prisoner release like this happen at any other festival during the year?

It only happened at the annual Passover festival [Hb, Lns, TH]. John 18:39 specifies that it was a Passover custom [NIGTC].

QUESTION—What insurrection were Barabbas and the other rebels involved in?

Nothing is known about that particular uprising even though Mark speaks of '*the* insurrection' as though it had been well known. Insurrections were constantly happening during that time of Roman rule [NICNT]. Since those rebels were still in prison, it would have been a fairly recent insurrection [EGT, Lns, My].

QUESTION—Was Barabbas the one who had committed the murder?

The pronominal adjective 'who' is plural. The willingness of Pilate to release Barabbas suggests he was not the rebel who had actually committed the murder [BNTC, WBC].

15:8 And having-come-up, the crowd began to-ask[a] (Pilate to do) as he-usually-did for-them.

TEXT—Manuscripts reading ἀναβάς 'having come up' are given a B rating by GNT to indicate it was regarded to be almost certain. A variant reading is ἀναβοήσας 'having cried out' and it is followed by KJV.

LEXICON—a. pres. mid. infin. of αἰτέω (LN 33.163) (BAGD p. 26): 'to ask for, to demand' [BAGD, LN], 'to plead for' [LN], 'to request' [WBC]. The unfinished phrase ἤρξατο αἰτεῖσθαι 'began to ask' is translated, 'began to ask Pilate/him to do…' [AB1; ESV, NASB, NRSV], 'began to ask that he would/should do…' [BECNT, BNTC], 'began to ask him to act' [AB2], 'asked Pilate to do…' [NTC; GW, NIV], 'began to desire him to do…' [KJV], 'began to ask him to free a prisoner' [NCV], 'began to ask Pilate to release a prisoner for them' [NET], 'asked Pilate to set a prisoner free' [CEV], 'asked him to release a prisoner' [NLT], 'began to ask Pilate (for the usual favor)' [TEV; similarly REB], 'began to ask for themselves (as he was used to do for them)' [Lns]. This verb means to ask for something with urgency, even to the point of demanding [LN].

15:9 **And Pilate answered them, saying, "Do you-want (that) I-should-release[a] to-you the King of-the Jews?"** **15:10** **For he-knew that because-of envy[b] the chief-priests had-turned-over (Jesus) to-him.**

LEXICON—a. aorist act. subj. of ἀπολύω (LN 37.127): 'to release' [AB2, BECNT, BNTC, LN, Lns, NTC, WBC; ESV, KJV, NASB, NCV, NIV, NLT, NRSV, REB], 'to free' [CEV, GW, NCV], 'to set free' [AB1; TEV]. This verb means to release from one's control or to set free [LN].

b. φθόνος (LN 88.160) (BAGD p. 857): 'envy' [AB2, BAGD, BECNT, BNTC, LN, Lns, NTC, WBC; ESV, KJV, NASB, NET, NIV, NLT], 'jealousy' [BAGD, LN; NRSV], 'malice' [AB1; REB]. It is also translated as a verb: 'to be jealous' [CEV, GW, NCV, TEV]. This noun denotes the state of ill will someone has toward another who has either a real or presumed advantage over him [LN].

QUESTION—Why did Pilate ask the crowd this question?

Pilate presented the 'King of the Jews' as his candidate to release prior to getting any feedback from the crowd [NICNT]. He wanted to find out if the crowd also wanted Jesus executed or if that desire was confined to the few ruling priests who had charged him [WBC]. He knew there was no just cause for the plot of the Jewish leaders to put Jesus to death. The chief priests wanted Jesus executed because they envied his fame and his many followers [NTC].

15:11 **But the chief-priests stirred-up[a] the crowd so-that he-would-release Barabbas for-them instead (of Jesus).**

LEXICON—a. aorist act. indic. of ἀνασείω (LN 39.44) (BAGD p. 60): 'to stir up' [BAGD, BECNT, BNTC, LN, Lns, WBC; ESV, GW, NET, NIV, NLT, NRSV], 'to incite' [AB1, BAGD; REB], 'to start a riot, to cause an uproar' [LN]. The clause 'stirred up the crowd' is translated 'stirred up the crowd to ask' [AB2; NASB, TEV], 'had persuaded the people to ask' [NCV], 'stirred up the mob to get him to' [NTC], 'told the crowd' [CEV], 'moved the people' [KJV]. This verb means to cause people to riot against something [LN].

QUESTION—How did the chief priests stir up the crowd?

There was probably a time interval between the presentation of which candidates could be released and the call for the crowd's vote [Lns, Sw]. Mathew 27:19 describes an urgent message that Pilate received from his wife that probably was the cause of the time interval [Hb]. While Herod was gone, the chief priests sent their men throughout the crowd to get them to ask for the release of Barabbas instead of Jesus [Lns, NICNT]. Some think that Barabbas may already have been the people's choice [EBC, NIGTC].

15:12 And answering/speaking[a] Pilate again said to-them, "What then do you-want (that) I-should-do (with the one) whom you-call the King of the Jews?" **15:13** And again they-shouted,[b] "Crucify[c] him!"

TEXT—In verse 12, manuscripts reading θέλετε ποιήσω 'do you want I should do' are given a C rating by GNT to indicate that choosing it over a variant text was difficult. A variant reading is θέλετε ἵνα ποιήσω 'do you wish that I should do' and it is followed by KJV. Another variant reading is ποιήσω 'should I do'.

TEXT—Manuscripts reading ὃν λέγετε 'whom you call' are given a C rating by GNT to indicate that choosing it over a variant text was difficult. A variant reading omits the phrase.

LEXICON—a. aorist pass. (deponent = act.) participle of ἀποκρίνομαι (LN 33.28, 33.184): 'to answer, to reply' [LN (33.28)] or 'to speak, to declare, to say' [**LN** (33.28)]. Some take this to be an answer to an implied question: 'again answering said/was-saying to them' [Lns, WBC], 'again answered them, saying' [AB2], 'answering again...said to them' [NASB], 'answered and said again unto them' [KJV], 'replying, said to them' [NTC]. Others take it to be a simple introduction to Pilate's question: 'spoke to them again' [AB1; NET, NRSV, REB], 'spoke again to the crowd' [TEV], 'again was saying to them' [BECNT], 'again said to them' [ESV], 'again asked them' [GW], 'asked them again' [BNTC], 'asked the crowd again' [NCV], 'asked them' [NIV, NLT], 'asked the crowd' [CEV]. This verb means to respond to a question asking for information [LN (33.184)] or to introduce or continue a somewhat formal discourse. It occurs regularly with λέγωα 'to say' [LN (33.28)]. Because this is actually a question posed by Pilate, the verb 'said' may need to be translated 'asked' [TH].

b. aorist act. indic. of κράζω (LN 33.83) (BAGD 2.a. p. 447): 'to shout' [AB1, LN, Lns, NTC, WBC; all versions except CEV, ESV, KJV], 'to cry out' [AB2, BECNT; ESV, KJV], 'to yell' [Lns; CEV], 'to call out' [BAGD, LN]. This verb means to shout or cry out [LN].

c. aorist act. impera. of σταυρόω (LN 20.76) (BAGD p. 765): 'to crucify' [AB1, AB2, BAGD, BECNT, LN, NTC, WBC; all versions except CEV], 'to nail to a cross' [BAGD; CEV]. This verb means to execute by nailing to a cross. For languages where there is no technical term or phrase meaning 'to crucify', a phrase such as 'to nail to a cross bar', 'to nail up on wood', or even 'to nail up high' can be used [LN].

15:14 But Pilate said to-them, "Why? What evil[a] has he done?" But they shouted all the more, "Crucify him!"

LEXICON—a. κακός (LN 88.106) (BAGD 1.c. p. 397): 'evil' [BAGD, BECNT, BNTC, LN, Lns, WBC; ESV, KJV. NASB, NRSV], 'wrong' [AB2; GW, NCV, NET, REB], 'crime' [BAGD; CEV, NIV, NLT, TEV], 'harm' [AB1], 'wickedness, badness' [LN]. The adjectival pronominal form refers to the quality of wickedness and implies that it is something that is harmful and damaging [LN]. It refers to being guilty of doing an evil deed or a bad thing [TH].

QUESTION—What did Pilate mean by his question?

This is probably a rhetorical question that really means 'He didn't do anything wrong!' [TRT]. It is a final attempt to save Jesus [EBC]. It is actually a negation of their surprising demand [Hb]. It was a protest that no sufficient cause had been demonstrated and was a challenge to the crowd to name a reasonable crime that merited this punishment [NICNT]. Luke 23:22 adds that the governor had found nothing to warrant the death penalty [AB2].

15:15 So desiring to-satisfy[a] the crowd, Pilate released[b] Barabbas for/to them, and (after) having-had- (Jesus) -flogged,[c] he-handed-over[d] Jesus in-order-that he-be-crucified.

LEXICON—a. The idiom τὸ ἱκανὸν ποιῆσαι 'to do what is enough' [LN 25.96] is translated 'to satisfy' [AB2, BECNT, BNTC, NTC, WBC; ESV, GW, NASB, NET, NIV, NRSV, REB], 'to please' [AB1, LN; CEV, NCV, TEV], 'to pacify' [NLT], 'to content' [KJV], 'to do enough for' [Lns]. The idiom τὸ ἱκανὸν ποιῆσαι 'to do what is enough' means to cause someone to be pleased by doing what will satisfy him [LN 25.96].

b. aorist act. indic. of ἀπολύω (LN 37.127): 'to release' [LN]. The phrase ἀπέλυσεν αὐτοῖς 'released for (the crowd)' [AB2, BNTC; ESV; KJV, NASB, NET, NRSV] is also translated 'freed for (them)' [GW, NCV], 'released to (the crowd)' [AB2, BECNT, Lns, NTC, WBC; KJV, NIV, NLT], 'released' [AB1], 'set free' [CEV, TEV]. This verb means to release from one's control [LN].

c. aorist act. participle of φραγελλόω (LN 19.9) (BAGD p. 865): 'to flog' [AB1, AB2, BAGD, BNTC, NTC; NET, NIV, NRSV], 'to flog with a lead-tipped whip [NLT], 'to scourge' [BAGD, BECNT, Lns, WBC; KJV, NASB], 'to whip' [LN; GW, TEV], 'to beat with a whip' [LN; CEV, NCV]. This verb means to severely beat someone with a whip [LN]. It was a severe punishment inflicted on slaves and provincials after a sentence of death had been pronounced on them [BAGD]. Even though the aorist participle 'having flogged him' indicates that Jesus was flogged before Pilate handed him over, the translation should not suggest that Pilate personally flogged Jesus [TH].

d. aorist act. indic. of παραδίδωμι (LN 37.111) (BAGD 1.b p. 615): 'to hand over' [AB1, BAGD, BNTC, LN, NTC, WBC; GW, NASB, NCV, NET, NIV, NRSV, TEV], 'to turn over' [AB2, BAGD, LN; NLT], 'to give up' [BAGD, LN], 'to deliver' [BECNT, Lns; ESV, KJV], not explicit [CEV]. This verb means to deliver a person into the control of someone else [LN]. This is a condensed expression concerning handing Jesus over to the soldiers so that they could nail him to a cross [TH]. Jesus is not actually crucified until verse 24 [TRT].

QUESTION—Why was Jesus flogged before being crucified?

Flogging was part of the procedure in most cases of crucifixion [ICC]. The whip was made of several pieces of leather that had pieces of bone and lead embedded near the ends. The Romans first stripped the victim and tied his hands above his head to a post. Usually two men, one on each side of the victim, did the flogging [EBC]. This severe scourging caused Jesus to break down under the weight of the cross and it also accelerated his death [Lns, NTC].

DISCOURSE UNIT—15:16–47 [NIGTC]. The topic is the arrest and trials of Jesus.

DISCOURSE UNIT—15:16–21 [CEV, NASB]. The topic is the soldiers make fun of Jesus [CEV], Jesus is mocked [NASB].

DISCOURSE UNIT—15:16–20 [CBC; ESV, NET, NIV, NLT, NRSV, TEV]. The topic is the soldiers mock Jesus [CBC; NIV, NLT, NRSV], Jesus is mocked [ESV, NET], the soldiers make fun of Jesus [TEV].

DISCOURSE UNIT—15:16–20a [Hb]. The topic is mockery by the soldiers.

DISCOURSE UNIT—15:16–19 [GW]. The topic is the soldiers make fun of Jesus.

15:16 And the soldiers led- him -away (to) inside the courtyard/palace,[a] which is the Praetorium[b], and they-call-together the whole battalion.[c]

LEXICON—a. αὐλή (LN 7.6 or LN 7.56) (BAGD 4. p. 121): 'dwelling, palace, mansion' [LN (7.6)], 'courtyard' [LN 7.56]. See translations of this word in the next lexicon item. This noun denotes any dwelling that has an interior courtyard [LN (7.6)], or it denotes a walled enclosure used to enclose human activity [LN (7.56)]. This refers to the court of a prince [BAGD, TH], and then to 'palace [BAGD].

b. πραιτώριον (LN 7.7) (BAGD p. 697): 'praetorium' [BAGD, LN], 'palace, fortress' [LN]. The clause τῆς αὐλῆς, ὅ ἐστιν πραιτώριον 'the courtyard/palace, which is the Praetorium' is translated 'the courtyard, which is the praetorium' [Lns], 'the courtyard–that is, of the praetorium' [AB2], 'the courtyard of the governor's headquarters (called the Praetorium)' [NLT], 'the palace (that is, the Praetorium)' [BECNT, BNTC; NASB, NIV], 'the hall, called Praetorium' [KJV], 'the governor's palace (called the Praetorium)' [NCV], 'the governor's residence, the Praetorium' [REB], 'the palace, which is the Praetorium' [WBC], 'the courtyard–that is, the governor's headquarters' [AB1], 'the courtyard of the palace (that is, the governor's palace)' [NRSV], 'the palace, that is, the governor's headquarters' [ESV, NTC], 'the palace (that is, the governor's residence)' [NET], 'the courtyard of the governor's palace' [TEV], 'the courtyard of the palace' [GW], 'the courtyard of the fortress' [CEV]. This noun denotes a governor's official residence which may be a palace or a fortress. This word may be translated 'the palace where the governor lived' or 'the large dwelling where the ruler lived' [LN]. It denotes a governor's official residence [BAGD]. The 'Praetorium' was the name for this particular palace in Jerusalem [AB2, BECNT, BNTC, EBC, Lns, WBC; KJV, NASB, NCV, NIV, NLT, REB].

c. σπεῖρα (LN 55.9) (BAGD p. 761): 'battalion' [WBC; ESV], 'troop' [GW], 'cohort' [AB2, BECNT, LN, Lns; NRSV, NRSV], 'band' [KJV], 'regiment' [NLT], 'company' [AB1, BNTC; REB, TEV], 'company of soldiers' [NIV], 'band of soldiers' [LN], '(the rest of the) troops' [CEV], '(all the other) soldiers' [NCV]. This noun normally denotes a Roman military unit of about six hundred soldiers, but the soldiers often traveled in smaller groups that were still referred to as battalions [LN]. The whole battalion of six hundred men at full strength was there, and its presence assumes that Jesus was a rebel against Rome [ESVfn]. The designation 'battalion' is probably loosely used to refer to only those soldiers immediately at hand [CGTC, EBC, NIGTC, Sw, Tay, TH]. A large number of soldiers participated in the mockery [Hb].

QUESTION—Where did the soldiers take Jesus?

1. They took Jesus to the courtyard [A1, AB2, Gnd, EBC, ICC, Lns, Sw; CEV, NLT, TEV]. They took Jesus to the αὐλῆς 'courtyard', the same word used in 14:54 where Peter followed Jesus into the αὐλῆς 'courtyard' of the high priest and in 14:66 where Peter returned to that αὐλῆς 'courtyard'. This time Jesus was taken to another αὐλῆς 'courtyard', an open courtyard in Herod's palace. The view that the term αὐλῆς now means 'palace' instead 0f 'courtyard is due to Mark's addition ὅ ἐστιν πραιτώριον 'which is the Praetorium'. Apparently Mark was loosely equating the two [Hb]. It is possible that the courtyard (αὐλῆς) was known as the 'Praetorium' because it was the most public part of the palace [EBC, Sw].

2. They took Jesus to the palace [BECNT, BNTC, ICC, NAC, NCBC, NIGTC, NTC, WBC; ESV, NASB, NCV, NET, NIV], Here αὐλῆς means a house or palace [NTC]. It is translated 'palace' because of the explanatory clause, 'that is, the Praetorium' [EBC, ICC, NAC]. Although the added comment 'which is the Praetorium' might refer to the governor's headquarters as a whole, it probably is used in the limited sense of 'guardroom or 'barracks' [NIGTC].

15:17 And they clothe him (in) purple-cloth[a] and after-twisting-together[b] a-crown[c] of thorns,[d] they place it on him.

LEXICON—a. πορφύρα (LN 6.169) (BAGD p. 694): 'purple' [AB1, BNTC, Lns, WBC; KJV, NASB, GW, REB], 'purple robe' [BECNT, NTC; CEV, NCV, NIV, NLT, TEV], 'purple cloak' [ESV, NCV, NRSV], 'purple garment/clothes' [AB2, BAGD], 'purple cloth' [LN]. This noun denotes a reddish-purple cloth that was dyed with a substance obtained from the murex shellfish [LN]. This noun refers to purple cloth, but it is also used to describe the red garment the soldiers put on Jesus [BAGD]. In Mark this word could refer to an expensive purple robe that a king might wear. Mathew 27:27 explains that both the crown of thorns and the red military cloak were being used to mock Jesus [NIGTC]. It probably was a cast-off and faded rag that had enough color left to suggest a royal purple robe [EBC, Sw].

b. aorist act. participle of πλέκω (LN 49.27) (BAGD p. 667): 'to twist together' [ESV, NIV], 'to twist' [NASB, GW, NRSV], 'to weave together' [WBC], 'to weave' [AB2; BAGD, BECNT, **LN**, NTC; NLT], 'to plait' [AB1, BAGD, BNTC, Lns; KJV, REB], 'to braid' [LN; NET], 'to make' [CEV, NCV, TEV]. This verb means to interlace strands by braiding or weaving them [LN].

c. στέφανος (LN 6.192) (BAGD 1. p. 767): 'crown' [BAGD, LN; all translations], 'wreath' [BAGD, LN]. This noun denotes a wreath made of foliage or precious metals that was formed to resemble foliage and was worn as a symbol of honor or high office. In order to do justice to the cultural relevance of such a wreath, it may be important to add some type of marginal note [LN].

d. ἀκάνθινος (LN 3.18) (BAGD p. 29): 'thorny' [BAGD, BECNT, BNTC, LN, Lns], 'thorny branches' [NCV, TEV], 'of thorns' [AB2, **LN**; ESV, KJV, NASB, NET, NIV, REB], 'thorns' [NTC, WBC; GW, NRSV], 'thorn branch' [AB1; CEV, NLT]. This adjective is a derivative of ἄκανθα 'thorn plant' and pertains to being made of thorns. It may be necessary to indicate that the 'crown of thorns' was not just made of thorns but included the branches of a thorny bush [LN]. It refers to the twigs of the thorn bush and not exclusively to the thorns themselves [ICC].

QUESTION—What is meant by the statement 'they clothed him'?

Some think it means that they exchanged whatever Jesus was wearing for this purple robe in order to mock him. In verse 20 it tells how they took the purple from him and put on his own clothes [TH]. Matthew 27:28 says that they stripped Jesus and put a scarlet robe on him [NTC]. Some think that after Jesus was brought into the courtyard naked, the soldiers clothed him in a robe in order to mock him [Lns, NICNT]. Jesus was naked when the soldiers took him into the courtyard because his clothes were laying in a little heap on the outside where he had been stripped for the scourging [Lns].

QUESTION—What is important about the color of the cloth?

The purple cloak probably refers to an old military cloak whose red color suggested royalty [ESVfn, NETfn, NIVfn, WBC]. This ugly scarlet cloak was to serve as the royal purple mantle that was worn by kings on state occasions [Lns].

QUESTION—Why is the στέφανος 'wreath' made of thorns called a διάδημα 'crown' in the translations?

The soldiers did this to mock Jesus' claim to be a king, and the crown of thorns represented the crown on the heads of the rulers portrayed on the coins [NETfn]. The traditional understanding is that this refers to a crown made from a thorn bush that was intended to torture Jesus. Others think that verses 17–19 indicate that it involves not so much physical torture but humiliation, and that the thorns may have radiated outwards from Jesus' head [BECNT]. They pressed a crown made of thorny twigs on his head as an act of cruelty and disrespect for the 'king of the Jews' [NTC] or the crown of thorns was simply part of Jesus' mock attire and not intended to cause any additional physical discomfort [NICNT].

15:18 **And they-began to-greet**ᵃ **him, "Hail,**ᵇ **King of the Jews!"**
LEXICON—a. pres. mid./pass. (deponent = act.) infin. of ἀσπάζομαι (LN 33.20) (BAGD 1.a. p. 117): 'to greet' [BAGD, Lns; GW], 'to salute' [AB1, AB2, BECNT, BNTC, NTC, WBC; ESV, KJV, NET, NRSV, REB, TEV], 'to call out to' [NCV, NIV], 'to acclaim' [NASB]. The clause 'they began to greet him' is translated 'they saluted him and taunted' [NLT], 'they made fun of Jesus and shouted' [CEV]. This verb means to employ certain set phrases as a part of the process of greeting [LN]. Here it refers to an act of homage given to a king [BAGD].
  b. pres. act. impera. of χαίρω (LN 33.22) (BAGD 2.a. p. 874): 'Hail' [AB1, AB2, BAGD, BECNT, BNTC, LN, Lns, NTC, WBC; ESV, KJV, NASB, NCV, NET, NIV, NRSV, REB], 'long live (the King)' [GW, TEV], 'hey, you' [CEV], 'greetings' [LN]. This verb means to use a formalized expression of greeting that implies a wish for happiness on the part of the person being greeted. The functional equivalent in Spanish would be 'que viva'. In traditional English one might employ an expression such as 'long live!' [LN].
QUESTION—Why did the soldiers greet Jesus in this way?
  They were pretending to recognize Jesus' regal claim [NICNT]. Their salute imitated the Latin imperial greeting 'Hail, Caesar!' [BECNT, WBC]. They were ridiculing his kingly claims [BECNT, Hb]. They thought it was a great joke that this gentle Jew claimed to be a king [EBC].

15:19 **And they-were-beating him (on) the head with-a-reed**ᵃ **and they-were-spitting on-him, and kneeling-down, they-were-prostrating-themselves-before**ᵇ **him.**
LEXICON—a. κάλαμος (LN **3.55**) (BAGD 2. p. 398): 'reed' [BECNT, **LN**, Lns, WBC; ESV, KJV, NASB, NRSV], 'stick' [AB1, NTC; CEV, GW, NCV, TEV], 'reed stick' [NLT], 'stalk' [BAGD], 'staff' [BAGD; NET, NIV], 'cane' [AB2, BNTC], 'the head of a stick' [REB]. This noun denotes the stalk of a reed plant. To avoid the impression that the instrument used to strike Jesus was some flimsy or fragile stalk of a plant, it may be necessary to use a phrase such as 'heavy reed' or 'strong reed' [LN].
  b. imperf. act. indic. of προσκυνέω (LN **17.21**) (BAGD 5. p. 717): 'to prostrate oneself before (someone)' [BAGD, **LN**], 'to worship, to do obeisance to, to do reverence to' [BAGD]. The clause 'kneeling down they were prostrating themselves before him' is translated 'kneeling down

(in mockery) they were paying homage to him' [BECNT], 'having bent the knees, kept making obeisance to him' [Lns], 'on bended knees doing him homage' [NTC], 'fell on their knees in homage to him' [AB1], 'falling on their knees, did obeisance to him' [BNTC], 'bowing on their knees and worshipping him' [NCV; similarly KJV], 'bowing their knees, they were doing homage to him' [WBC], 'bending the knee and bowing down to him' [AB2], 'falling on their knees, they paid homage to him' [NIV], 'fell on their knees and bowed down to him' [TEV], 'kneeling and bowing before him' [NASB], 'dropped to their knees in mock worship' [NLT], 'kneeling/knelt down in homage to him' [ESV, NRSV], 'knelt-down/knelt and paid homage to him' [NET, REB], 'knelt down and pretended to worship him' [CEV], 'kneeling in front of him with false humility' [GW]. This verb means to prostrate oneself before someone as an act of reverence, fear, or supplication [LN]. This is semantically very complex in that it indicates not only a body position but also an attitude and activity of reverence or honor. Only one of the semantic elements needs to be selected to effectively convey the meaning. For example, translations for this verse could be 'they knelt before him and worshiped him in a mocking way' or 'they knelt before him and prostrated themselves before him' [LN].

QUESTION—What was the purpose of the reed?

The reed represented a scepter that was primarily used to deride Jesus but not used to increase his pain [WBC]. Matthew 27:29 describes how they initially forced Jesus to hold the staff as a mock scepter [EBC]. Others think that buffeting the exhausted prisoner with rods and with the fists was mere brutality [NICNT]. The reed was used to pound the crown of thorns deeper into his flesh [TH].

DISCOURSE UNIT—15:20–32 [GW]. The topic is the crucifixion.

15:20 And when they-had-ridiculed[a] him, they-took-off[b] of-him the purple-cloth and clothed him (in) his(own) garments.

LEXICON—a. aorist act. indic. of ἐμπαίζω (LN 33.406) (BAGD 1. p. 255): 'to ridicule' [BAGD, LN], 'to mock' [BAGD, LN], 'to make fun of' [BAGD]. The clause 'when they had ridiculed him' is translated 'when they finished/had-finished mocking him' [BNTC, Lns, NTC; NET], 'when/after they had mocked him' [AB, BECNT, WBC; ESV, KJV, NASB, NIV; similarly NRSV], 'when they/the-soldiers had finished making fun of him/Jesus' [CEV, GW], 'when they had finished their mockery' [AB1; REB], 'when they finally tired of mocking him' [NLT], 'when they had finished making fun of him' [TEV], 'after they finished' [NCV]. This verb means to make fun of someone by pretending that he is not what he is or by imitating him in a distorted manner [LN].

b. aorist act. indic. of ἐκδύω (LN 49.18) (BAGD 1. p. 239): 'to take off' [AB2, BAGD, BECNT, LN, Lns, NTC; CEV, GW, KJV, NASB, NCV,

NIV, NLT, TEV], 'to strip' [AB1, BAGD, BNTC, LN, WBC; ESV, NET, NRSV, REB]. This verb means to remove clothing from the body [LN].

DISCOURSE UNIT—15:20b–41 [Hb]. The topic is the account of the crucifixion.

DISCOURSE UNIT—15:20b–22 [Hb]. The topic is the road to Golgotha.

And they lead- him -out[a] so-that they-might-crucify him.
LEXICON—a. pres. act. indic. of ἐξάγω (LN 15.174) (BAGD 1. p. 271): 'to lead out' [AB2, BAGD, BECNT, BNTC, LN, Lns, WBC; all versions except CEV, NET, NLT], 'to take out' [AB1], 'to lead off' [CEV], 'to lead away' [NTC; NET, NLT], 'to bring out' [BAGD], 'to bring forth' [LN]. This verb means to lead or bring out of a structure or area [LN].

DISCOURSE UNIT—15:21–39 [CBC]. The topic is Jesus' crucifixion and death.

DISCOURSE UNIT—15:21–32 [NICNT; ESV, NCV, NET, NIV, NLT, NRSV, TEV]. The topic is Jesus is crucified [NCV, TEV], the crucifixion [ESV, NET, NIV, NLT], the crucifixion of Jesus [NICNT; NRSV].

15:21 **And they-requisitioned[a] a-man passing-by, Simon of Cyrene, the father of-Alexander and Rufus, who-was-coming-in from the country,[b] in-order-that he-carry his cross.[c]**
LEXICON—a. pres. act. indic. of ἀγγαρεύω (LN 37.34) (BAGD p. 6): 'to requisition' [BAGD], 'to impress' [Lns], 'to press into service' [AB2, BAGD, **LN**; NASB, REB], 'to compel' [AB1, BECNT, BNTC, LN, WBC; ESV, KJV, NRSV], 'to force' [NTC; CEV, GW, NCV, NET, NIV, NLT, TEV]. This verb means to force a civilian to carry a load for some distance. In the NT times Roman soldiers had the authority to enforce such service [LN].
b. ἀγρός (LN 1.87) (BAGD 2. p. 14): 'country' [AB1, AB2, BAGD, BECNT, BNTC, Lns, NTC, WBC; ESV, KJV, NASB, NET, NIV, NRSV, REB, TEV], 'countryside' [LN; NLT], 'fields' [NCV, NCV], 'rural area' [LN], 'a farm' [CEV], 'his home in the country' [GW]. This noun denotes a rural area in contrast with a population center [LN]. This denotes the country as opposed to the city or village [BAGD].
c. σταυρός (LN 6.27) (BAGD 1. p. 765): 'cross' [BAGD, LN; all translations]. This noun denotes a pole stuck into the ground in an upright position with a crosspiece attached to its upper part. In some receptor languages where the term for a cross simply means 'crossbeam' or 'crossed poles' it is important to avoid any suggestion of crossed sticks in the form of X instead of a cross consisting of an upright pole with a horizontal beam [LN].

QUESTION—Who requisitioned Simon to carry the cross?
The pronoun 'they' refers only to the centurion and his assistants who had been assigned to carry out Pilate's orders and not all of the soldiers who had been participating in the mockery [Hb].

QUESTION—Why did Jesus need to have his cross carried by someone else?
Although Jesus had started out carrying his cross (John 19:17), the pain caused by the heavy beam pressing against the lacerated skin and muscles of his shoulders along with the loss of blood had weakened him so that he could not go on carrying the heavy crossbeam [EBC]. The words τὸν σταυρὸν αὐτοῦ 'his cross' refers to the complete cross and all translations use the word 'cross'. Some commentaries mention that the men who were condemned to die by crucifixion were customarily required to carry only the heavy wooden crosspiece on which they were to be nailed and that is what Jesus was probably carrying [AB1, BNTC, CGTC, EBC, NICNT, NIGTC, TH]. Just the crosspiece would usually weigh thirty or forty pounds [EBC]. The crosspiece would then be fixed to the upright post at the place of execution [BNTC].

QUESTION—Who was Simon and why does it mention his two sons, Alexander and Rufus?
Simon was no doubt a Jew on his way to the city of Jerusalem for the Passover celebration. Perhaps his two sons are mentioned because they had become well known to the Roman church by the time this was written [EBC, ESVfn].

DISCOURSE UNIT—15:22–41 [NASB]. The topic is the crucifixion.

DISCOURSE UNIT—15:22–32 [CEV]. The topic is Jesus is nailed to a cross.

15:22 And they-bring him to the place (called) Golgotha, which being-translated[a] means "Place of-a-Skull."

LEXICON—a. pres. pass. participle of μεθερμηνεύω (LN 33.145) (BAGD p. 498): 'to be translated' [AB2, BAGD, LN, Lns, NTC; NASB, NET], 'to be interpreted' [LN; KJV], not explicit [AB1, BECNT, BNTC, WBC; all versions except KJV, NASB, NET]. This verb means to translate from one language to another language [LN].

QUESTION—Why was this place called the 'Place of a Skull'?
'Golgotha' is a translation of the Aramaic word for skull. The history behind the naming of this site is not documented [EBC]. Some think the name 'skull' was probably derived from the shape of the bare round hill which resembled a human skull [BECNT, BNTC, Hb, ICC, NAC, NICNT, Sw]. Executions were performed outside the city on a hill that was named the 'Place of-a-Skull' either because of its skull-like shape or because it was a customary place of executions [AB1, CGTC, NIGTC, NTC, TH, TRT]. There is no universally accepted explanation [TH]. It is possible that both conjectures contain an element of truth [AB2].

DISCOURSE UNIT—15:23–32 [Hb]. The topic is the crucifixion and the first three hours.

15:23 And they-tried-to-give him wine mixed-with-myrrh,[a] but he did-not-take[b] (it).

LEXICON—a. perf. pass. participle of σμυρνίζω (LN 6.204) (BAGD p. 759): 'mixed with myrrh' [BECNT, WBC; ESV, NASB, NCV, NET, NIV, NRSV], 'treated with myrrh' [BAGD], 'made like myrrh' [Lns], 'flavored with myrrh' [NTC], 'mingled with myrrh' [KJV], 'drugged with myrrh' [BNTC; NLT], 'myrrhed (wine)' [AB2], 'drugged (wine)' [AB1; REB], 'mixed with a drug called myrrh' [GW, TEV], 'mixed with a drug to ease the pain' [CEV]. The phrase ἐσμυρνισμένον 'wine mixed with myrrh' usually must be translated into a phrase such as 'wine which has been mixed with a drug called myrrh' or 'wine mixed with a drug to reduce pain'. If an abbreviated phrase such as 'myrrhed wine' is used, then an explanation of its function should be included in a marginal note [LN].

b. aorist act. indic. of λαμβάνω (LN 57.125) (BAGD 1.a. p. 464): 'to take' [AB1, BAGD, BECNT, BNTC, Lns, WBC; ESV, GW, NASB, NET, NIV, NRSV, REB], 'to receive' [LN; KJV], 'to accept' [AB2, LN, NTC], 'to drink' [CEV]. This is also translated 'he refused' [NCV, NLT], 'Jesus would not drink it' [TEV]. This verb means to receive or accept an object or benefit where the initiative rests with the giver but where the attention is focused on the receiver [LN].

QUESTION—Who were the people who tried to give Jesus the wine treated with myrrh?
1. They could have been some women from Jerusalem who were Jewish sympathizers [BECNT, BNTC]. The noblewomen of Jerusalem used to donate this drugged wine by bringing it to those being executed [BECNT].
2. They were the Roman soldiers [BECNT, Lns, NTC, WBC]. The 'they' who offer it to Jesus are probably the Roman solders mentioned in verse 16 since they are the antecedent for all the subsequent 'they(s)' in verses 16b–22 [BECNT, NTC]. Since there is no evidence that myrrh had analgesic properties, it is difficult to interpret this offer as an act of mercy. Probably the soldiers were offering Jesus what they called the 'finest of wines' to the 'King of the Jews' as part of their ongoing mockery [WBC].

15:24 And they-crucify[a] him and divide[b] his garments, casting a-lot[c] for them, (to determine who) would-get what. **15:25** And it-was (the) third[d] hour when they crucified him.

LEXICON—a. pres. act. indic. of σταυρόω (LN 20.76) (BAGD 1. p. 765): 'to crucify' [BAGD, LN; all translations except CEV, NLT, REB], 'to nail to a/the cross' [CEV, NLT], 'to fasten to the cross' [REB]. Literally 'to hang on a tree', this verb is an idiom that means to execute by nailing to a cross. For most receptor languages, there is no equivalent term or phrase meaning 'to crucify', so an expression such as 'to nail to a cross bar', 'to nail up on wood', or even 'to nail up high' must be used [LN]. Jesus' hands were nailed above the wrist onto the horizontal beam of the cross, and one foot was placed on top of the other to be nailed to the vertical beam [ESVfn].

b. pres. mid. indic. of διαμερίζω (LN 57.89) (BAGD 1.b. p. 186): 'to divide' [AB1, AB2, BAGD, BECNT, LN, NTC, WBC; NET, NLT, NRSV, TEV], 'to divide up' [KJV, NIV], 'to divide among them/themselves' [ESV, GW, NCV], 'to distribute' [BAGD, LN], 'to apportion' [Lns], 'to share out' [BNTC; REB], 'to part' [KJV], not explicit [CEV]. This verb means to distribute objects to a series of persons [LN].

c. κλῆρος (LN 6.219) (BAGD 1. p. 435): 'lot' [BAGD, LN]. The phrase 'casting a lot' is translated 'casting lots' [AB1, AB2, BECNT, BNTC, Lns, NTC, WBC; ESV, KJV, NRSV, REB], 'throwing/cast lots' [NCV, NIV], 'throwing/threw dice' [GW, NET, NLT, TEV], 'gambled' [CEV]. This noun denotes a specially marked pebble, piece of pottery, or stick used to make decisions based upon chance. Considering both form and function, the closest equivalent of 'lot' is frequently a term that refers to dice [LN].

d. τρίτος (LN 60.50) (BAGD 2. p. 896): 'third' [LN]. The phrase ὥρα τρίτη 'the third hour' [AB2, BECNT, BNTC, Lns, NTC, WBC; ESV, KJV, NIV] is also translated 'nine o'clock in the morning' [NCV, NET, NLT, NRSV, TEV], 'nine in the morning' [AB1; GW, REB], 'about nine o'clock in the morning' [CEV]. This temporal adjective refers to the third in a series. In reference to time, the 'third hour' is nine o'clock in the morning [LN].

QUESTION—What garments did the soldiers cast a lot for?

Jesus' clothes probably included a robe, a long T-shirt-like garment called a tunic, a cloth belt, sandals, and perhaps a head covering [NICNT, TRT]. They were his headgear, sandals, belt, and outer garment [NTC]. A common way of casting lots was to place lots in a helmet and then shake them until one fell out. Another way was to reach into the helmet to draw out a lot. In the case of a more valuable object such as a tunic, only one of the four lots would be marked to win [Lns].

15:26 **And the inscription[a] of-the charge (against) him had been-written-over (him), "The King of-the Jews."** **15:27** **And with him they-crucify two robbers,[c] one on (the) right and one on (the) left of-him.**

LEXICON—a. ἐπιγραφή (LN 33.46) (BAGD p. 291): 'inscription' [AB1, AB2, BAGD, BECNT, BNTC, LN, WBC; ESV, NASB, NET, NRSV, REB], 'superscription' [Lns, NTC; KJV], 'writing' [LN], 'written notice' [NIV], 'notice' [GW, TEV], 'sign' [NCV, NLT]. The phrase 'the inscription of the charge' is translated 'a sign that told why he was nailed there' [CEV]. This noun denotes a brief notice used primarily for identification [LN].

b. perf. pass. participle of ἐπιγράφω (LN 33.65) (BAGD 1. p. 291): 'to-be-written on' [LN], 'to write in/on' [BAGD]. The phrase ἐπιγεγραμμένη 'had been written' is translated to indicate the content of what was inscribed: 'the inscription/superscription...read' [AB1, BECNT, BNTC, NTC; ESV, NASB, NET, NRSV, REB], 'the written notice...read' [NIV], 'the inscription...was' [WBC], 'the inscription...was inscribed' [AB2], 'It read' [CEV, GW, NLT], 'the notice...said' [TEV], 'a sign with this charge...written on it' [NCV]. Others translate it to indicate the location of the inscription: 'the inscription...placed over him' [BAGD], 'the superscription...was written over' [KJV], 'there was the superscription... written above' [Lns]. This verb means to write on a surface [LN].

c. λῃστής (LN 57.240) (BAGD 1. p. 473): 'robber' [BAGD, LN, NTC; ESV, NASB, NCV, NIV, REB], 'highwayman' [BAGD, LN], 'criminal' [CEV, GW], 'bandit' [AB1, BAGD, BECNT, BNTC; NRSV, TEV], 'outlaw' [NET], 'thief' [KJV], 'rebel' [WBC]; 'revolutionary' [NLT]. This noun denotes someone who robs by force and violence [LN]. Although the normal meaning is 'robbers', it is used here to refer to 'insurrectionists' [EBC, NICNT] or 'revolutionaries' [NIGTC].

QUESTION—Where was the charge against Jesus 'written'?

The charge was written *on* a tablet [LN, TH; all versions except VEV, NLT]. It simply means that it was written on a tablet and does not necessarily imply the inscription was written *over* Jesus in the sense that it was affixed to the cross above his head [TH]. The tablet on which the charge was written was attached to the cross *above* Jesus' head [BAGD, Hb, Lns; CEV, NLT].

15:28 [[Omitted]]

TEXT—Manuscripts omitting this verse are given a B rating by GNT to indicate the omission was regarded to be almost certain. A variant reading is 'And the scripture was fulfilled, which says, "And he was numbered with the transgressors."' and it is supported by KJV. It is enclosed in brackets by AB1 and NASB.

15:29 **And the-ones passing-by were-ridiculing**[a] **him, shaking**[b] **their heads and saying, "Aha!**[c] **You who are-going-to-destroy the temple and build (it) in three days, 15:30 save yourself by-coming-down from the cross!"**

LEXICON—a. imperf. act. indic. of βλασφημέω (LN 33.400) (BAGD 2.b.δ. p. 142): 'to ridicule' [WBC], 'to jeer at someone' [REB], 'to deride' [ESV, NRSV], 'to defame' [LN; NET], 'to hurl abuse on someone' [NASB], 'to revile' [LN], 'to insult' [GW, NCV], 'to rail on someone' [KJV], 'to shout abuse' [NLT], 'to fling/hurl insults at someone' [AB1, BNTC; NIV, TEV], 'to say terrible things about someone' [CEV], 'to blaspheme' [AB2, BAGD, BECNT, LN, Lns, NTC]. This verb means to speak against people or divine beings in such a way as to harm or injure their reputation [LN]. Here the word has the sense of derision, insult, and slander [TH]. Since it is directed against a man, it was not 'irreverent speech' directed against God [NIGTC, TH]. Others regard it to be blasphemy [AB2, BAGD, BECNT, Hb, LN, Lns, NTC, PNTC] because even though they did not realize it, they were mocking the very Son of God [Hb, NTC].

b. pres. act. participle of κινέω (LN **16.2**) (BAGD 2.a. p. 432): 'to shake' [AB1, AB2, BAGD, BECNT, BNTC, **LN**, Lns, NTC; CEV, GW, NCV, NET, NIV, NLT, NRSV, TEV], 'to wag' [WBC; ESV, KJV, NASB, REB]. This verb means to set something in motion where the nature of movement is dependent on the object in question (e.g., 'to shake one's head'). Derision and scorn is signified by the shaking of the head in this verse, but other gestures such as pointing with the finger, throwing back the head, or shrugging the shoulders may be necessary to convey the same meaning in other languages. In some languages shaking the head from side to side means assent, while nodding shows opposition [LN]. This was an OT gesture of scorn and derision [Hb, TRT]. This action indicated both their contempt and arrogance [NTC].

c. οὐά (LN **33.411**) (BAGD p. 591): 'Aha!' [AB1, BAGD, BNTC, **LN**, NTC; ESV, NET, NRSV, TEV], 'Ha!' [AB1, BECNT, Lns WBC; CEV, NASB, NLT], 'Ah,' [KJV], 'So!' [NIV], 'Bravo!' [REB], 'What a joke!' [GW], not implicit [NCV]. This interjection is an exclamation of mocking and ridicule. If an interjection or exclamatory expression to indicate ridicule does not exist in a language, this verse can be translated 'now what about you, you who are going to destroy the sanctuary and in three days build it up again!' [LN]. One should not translate this as 'Aha!' if the same meaning will not be conveyed in the new language [TRT].

QUESTION—Who was passing by?

They were people who were on their way somewhere else when they stopped long enough to take in the scene [NTC]. They could have been country people on their way to Jerusalem or city people whose business called them into the country [NTC]. These were people who had started out from the city and were just passing by [AB1, BECNT, Lns] since people who came from a distance would not have known some of the details of the night trial [Lns]. The crucifixion had attracted a large crowd of people traveling on the road [Hb, NICNT]. Their scornful allusion to the words of Jesus concerning the destruction of the Temple indicates that they were members of the Sanhedrin or court attendants who had been privileged to sit in on the hearings [NICNT].

15:31 And also the chief-priests, along with the scribes, were-mocking[a] (him) among themselves, saying, "He saved others, he-is- not -able-to-save himself! **15:32** Let- the Messiah, the king of-Israel, -come-down now from the cross so-that we-may-see and believe." And those who-were-crucified with him were-also-insulting[b] him.

LEXICON—a. pres. act. participle of ἐμπαίζω (LN 33.406) (BAGD 1. p. 255): 'to mock' [AB2, BAGD, BECNT, LN, Lns, NTC, WBC; ESV, KJV, NASB, NET, NIV, NLT, NRSV], 'to ridicule' [BAGD, BNTC, LN], 'to make fun of' [BAGD, LN; CEV, GW, NCV, TEV], 'to jest' [REB], 'to

joke' [AB1]. This verb means to make fun of someone by pretending that he is not what he is or by imitating him in a distorted manner [LN]. Their mocking was probably heard by Jesus [EBC].
   b. imperf. act. indic. of ὀνειδίζω (LN 33.389, 33.422) (BAGD 1. p. 570): 'to insult' [AB1, LN (33.389); GW, NASB, NCV, TEV], 'to taunt' [NRSV, REB], 'to say cruel things' [CEV], 'to revile' [BAGD, BNTC, WBC; ESV, KJV], 'to ridicule' [BNTC; NLT], 'to reprimand' [LN (33.422)], 'to reproach' [BAGD, LN (33.422), Lns], 'to rail against' [AB2], 'to speak abusively' [NET], 'to heap insult upon someone' [BAGD, NTC; NIV]. This verb means to speak disparagingly of a person in a manner which is not justified [LN (33.389)] or to reproach someone with the implication that he was evidently to blame [LN (33.422)].

QUESTION—How is the verb σῴζω 'to save' to be understood in the statement, 'He saved others, he is not able to save himself'?

It means even though Jesus saved others from diseases, he was not able to use that same power to save himself from dying. Their point was that if that power had now deserted him, the source of that power was clearly not from God [Hb]. While they unconsciously bore witness to his miraculous powers when they said he saved others, they did not understand that Jesus had the power to save himself but could not because his messianic mission made his death necessary for man's redemption [EBC]. The implication is that he has saved no one else, no matter what had been rumored of him [WBC].

DISCOURSE UNIT—15:33–41 [NICNT; CEV, ESV, GW, NCV, NET, NIV, NLT, NRSV, TEV]. The topic is Jesus dies on the cross [GW], Jesus dies [NCV], the death of Jesus [NICNT; CEV, ESV, NIV, NLT, NRSV, TEV], Jesus' death [NET].

DISCOURSE UNIT—15:33–39 [Hb]. The topic is the last three hours and death.

15:33 And when (the) sixth hour[a] had-come, there was darkness[b] over the whole land until the ninth hour. **15:34** And at-the ninth hour Jesus cried-out with a-loud voice, "Eloi, Eloi, lema sabachthani?" which being-translated means, "My God, my God, why have-you-forsaken[c] me?"

TEXT—Manuscripts reading εἰς τί ἐγκατέλιπές με 'for what (why) have you forsaken me?' are given a B rating by GNT to indicate it was regarded to be almost certain. Variant readings are εἰς τί με ἐγκατέλιπες 'for what (why) have you forsaken me?' and some manuscripts read εἰς τί ὠνείδισάς με 'for what (why) have you reproached me?

LEXICON—a. ὥρα (LN 67.199) (BAGD 2.b. p. 896): 'hour' [AB2, BAGD, BNTC, LN, Lns, NTC, WBC; ESV, KJV, NASB, NIV]. This noun denotes the twelfth part of a day that is measured from sunrise to sunset. The actual length of an hour would vary throughout the year, but the hours on any given day were always divided into equal lengths of time [LN]. The sixth hour is also translated 'at noon' [GW, NCV, NLT, TEV], 'about noon' [CEV], 'when it was noon' [NET, NRSV], 'at midday' [AB1; REB]. The following ninth hour is translated 'three o'clock' [GW, NRSV, NLT, TEV], 'three in the afternoon' [AB1; NET, NRSV, REB], 'around three o'clock' [CEV, NET], '(and the darkness) lasted for three hours' [NCV].

b. σκότος (LN 14.53) (BAGD 1. p. 757): 'darkness' [BAGD, LN]. The phrase 'there was darkness over the whole land' [NTC; ESV, KJV] is also translated 'darkness came upon/over the whole land' [BECNT; GW, NET, NIV, NRSV], 'darkness fell over/across the whole land' [BNTC, WBC; NASB, NLT, REB], 'a darkness fell over all the land' [AB1], 'the whole country was covered with darkness' [TEV], 'the whole country became dark' [NCV], 'the sky turned dark' [ESV], 'there was darkness over the whole earth' [AB2], 'a darkness came on the whole earth' [Lns]. This noun denotes a condition resulting from the partial or complete absence of light [LN]. This was not a solar eclipse. The darkness represented lament and divine judgment [ESVfn].

c. aorist act. indic. of ἐγκαταλείπω (LN 35.54) (BAGD 2. p. 215): 'to forsake' [AB1, BAGD, BECNT, LN, NTC; ESV, KJV, NASB, NET, NIV, NRSV, REB], 'to abandon' [AB2, BAGD, BNTC, WBC; GW, NLT, TEV], 'to desert' [BAGD, LN; CEV], 'to reject' [NCV]. This verb means to desert or forsake a person. [LN].

QUESTION—How much land was included in the ὅλος 'whole' land?
1. It refers to the land of Judea [BECNT, BNTC, EBC, Hb, NIGTC]. This darkness symbolizes the judgment coming upon the land of Israel [BECNT, BNTC], but both the darkness and the judgment will be real [BECNT].
2. It refers to the whole earth [AB2, Lns].

15:35 And some of the bystanders having-heard, said, "Look! he is calling for-Elijah" **15:36** And someone ran and filled a-sponge with-sour-wine,[a] put it on a-reed-stalk, and gave-it to-him to-drink, saying, "Wait/Leave (him/me)-alone[b] let-us-see if Elijah comes to-take- him -down."

LEXICON—a. ὄξος (LN 6.201) (BAGD p. 574): 'sour wine' [BAGD, BECNT, BNTC, LN, Lns, NTC; ESV, NASB, NET, NLT, NRSV, REB], 'cheap wine' [TEV], 'wine' [CEV], 'wine vinegar' [NIV], 'vinegar' [AB1, AB2, WBC; GW, KJV, NCV]. This noun denotes a cheap sour wine. It was a favorite beverage of the poor people that was relatively effective in quenching one's thirst [LN].

b. aorist act. impera. of ἀφίημι (LN 13.140) (BAGD 4. p. 126): 'to let' [BAGD, LN], 'to allow' [LN]. The imperative Ἄφετε is translated 'Wait' [BECNT; ESV, NLT, NRSV, TEV], 'Let's wait' [CEV], 'Let alone' [KJV], 'Leave him alone!' [NET, NIV], 'Allow/permit me' [NTC, WBC], 'Let me be!' [AB2], not explicit [GW, NASB, NCV, REB]. The combination Ἄφετε ἴδωμεν is taken as a unit: 'Oh, do let us see' [AB1], 'Let us see' [BNTC, Lns]. This verb means to leave it up to someone to do something and implies distancing oneself from the event [LN]. It is unclear whether the offer of wine was an act of kindness or an act of mockery. A few think the man said 'Wait, let us see if Elijah comes to take him down' intending this as an act of kindness but the majority think the man did not really think Elijah would appear and was mocking Jesus [BECNT].

QUESTION—Why did the bystanders think Jesus was calling for Elijah?

The ignorant bystanders mistook the first words of Jesus' cry 'Eloi, Eloi' to be a cry for Elijah who was thought to be the forerunner and helper of the Messiah [EBC].

15:37 **And Jesus, having-given**[a] **a-loud cry, died.**[b]

LEXICON—a. aorist act. participle of ἀφίημι (LN 90.50) (BAGD 1.a.β. p. 125): 'to give, to produce, to make' [LN], 'to utter' [BAGD]. The clause 'having given a loud cry' [AB2] is also translated 'gave a loud cry' [AB1, BNTC, LN; NRSV, REB], 'uttered a loud cry' [ESV, NASB], 'uttered another loud cry' [NLT], 'having let out a loud cry' [BECNT], 'after letting out a loud cry' [WBC], 'with a loud cry' [LN; NTC; NIV, TEV], 'cried out in a loud voice' [GW, KJV, NCV, NET], 'let out a great voice' [Lns], 'shouted' [CEV]. This verb indicates an agent relation with numerable events [LN].

b. aorist act, indic. of ἐκπνέω (LN 23.103) (BAGD p. 244): 'to die' [AB1, BAGD, BNTC, LN; CEV, GW, NCV, REB, TEV], 'to expire' [AB2, BECNT, Lns, WBC], 'to breathe out one's last' [LN; ESV, NASB, NLT], 'to breath one's last' [NTC; NET, NIV], 'to give up the ghost' [KJV], 'to breath out the life or the soul' [BAGD]. This verb is a figurative extension of 'to breathe out' and it means to engage in the final act of dying [LN].

QUESTION—What was the reason for the loud cry?

This shout indicated the moment of his death [WBC]. He died with an unusual show of strength [TRT]. It was a shout of victory that anticipated the triumph of the Resurrection. It was definitely not the last gasp of a dying man [EBC]. It was a cry of victory [ESVfn, Hb]. John 19:30 reads 'he said "It is finished" and he bowed his head and gave up his spirit' [ESVfn, Hb]. This shout shows that he died voluntarily and did not just let his life ebb away [NTC].

15:38 **And the curtain**[a] **of-the temple was-torn**[b] **in two, from top to bottom.**

LEXICON—a. καταπέτασμα (LN 6.160) (BAGD p. 416): 'curtain' [BAGD, LN; all translations except AB2, WBC; KJV, NASB], 'drape' [LN], 'veil' [AB2, LN, WBC; KJV, NASB]. This noun denotes a hanging cloth over an opening [LN].

b. aorist pass. indic. of σχίζω (LN 19.27) (BAGD 1.b. p. 797): 'to be torn' [LN; all translations except AB2, BECNT, Lns; KJV, GW], 'to be split' [BAGD, BECNT, LN; GW], 'to be ripped' [AB2], 'to be rent' [Lns], 'to be rent in twain' [KJV], 'to be divided, to be torn apart' [BAGD]. This verb means to split or to tear an object into at least two parts [LN].

QUESTION—Which of the two temple curtains was torn in two?
1. This was the curtain that separated the innermost Holy of Holies from the rest of the Temple [AB1, AB2, BNTC, CGTC, EBC, ESVfn, Hb, ICC, Lns, NAC, NIVfn, NTC, Sw, TH, WBC]. The inner curtain described in Exodus 26:31–33, 35 was instantly torn when Jesus died [NTC, WBC]. The torn inner curtain between the Holy Place and the Most Holy Place indicated that access to God was no longer provided by temple sacrifices but by the unique sacrifice of Jesus [ESVfn].
2. This was the outer curtain that separated the Temple proper from the courtyard. Josephus describes this curtain as a magnificent tapestry eighty feet tall [NICNT, PNTC]. The tearing of this curtain would function as a public sign comparable to the darkness that covered the land. Jesus' death and the destruction of the formal structures of Judaism were inseparably bound together [NICNT].

QUESTION—What is significant about the curtain being completely torn in two from top to bottom?

This signifies that this act come from God [AB2]. The rip was a precursor to the demolition of the Temple by the Romans forty years after Jesus' death [AB1, AB2].

15:39 And the centurion,[a] who-was standing-there on the opposite (side)[b] of-him/of-the-cross, having-seen that thus[c] he-died, said, "Truly this man was the Son of-God."

TEXT—Manuscripts reading ὅτι οὕτως ἐξέπνευσεν 'that thus he died' are given a C rating by GNT to indicate that choosing it over a variant text was difficult. A variant reading is ὅτι οὕτως κράξας ἐξέπνευσεν 'that thus having cried he died', and it is followed by KJV and perhaps by AB1, NTC, NIV.

LEXICON—a. κεντυρίων (LN 55.16) (BAGD p. 428): 'centurion' [AB1, AB2, BECNT, BNTC, LN, Lns, NTC, WBC; ESV, KJV, NASB, NET, NIV, NRSV, REB], 'captain' [LN], 'officer' [GW], 'army officer' [NCV, TEV], 'Roman officer' [NLT], 'Roman army officer' [CEV]. This noun denotes a Roman officer in command of about one hundred men [LN].

b. ἐξ ἐναντίας (LN 83.42): The phrase ἐξ ἐναντίας 'on the opposite side' is translated 'opposite him' [AB1, AB2, BECNT, BNTC, WBC], 'in front of him/Jesus' [CEV, NET, NIV], 'right in front of him' [NASB], 'facing him/Jesus' [NTC; ESV, GW, NLT, NRSV], 'over against him' [Lns; KJV, REB]. Other translations refer to the cross: 'in front of the cross' [TEV], 'standing in front of the cross' [NCV], 'opposite the cross' [LN]. This phrase refers to a position over against an object or other position [LN].

c. οὕτως (LN 61.9): 'thus, so' [LN]. The phrase οὕτως ἐξέπνευσεν 'thus he died' is translated 'how he died' [Lns; CEV, NET, NLT, REB], 'how Jesus had died' [TEV], 'he expired thus' [Lns], 'he expired in this manner' [AB2, BECNT], 'in this way he breathed his last' [ESV, NRSV], 'how he gave up his spirit' [GW], 'that he had died in this way' [WBC], 'the way he breathed his last' [NASB], 'what happened when Jesus died' [NCV], 'how he (cried out and) died' [AB1], 'he thus (cried out and) died' [NTC], 'he (so cried out, and) gave up the ghost' [KJV], '(heard his cry and) saw how he died' [NIV]. This adverb refers to that which precedes [LN]. For the verb ἐκπνέω 'to die' see lexicon item b in verse 37.

DISCOURSE UNIT—15:40–47 [CBC]. The topic is Jesus' burial.

DISCOURSE UNIT—15:40–41 [Hb]. The topic is the women watching from afar.

15:40 And there-were also (some) women looking-on from a-distance, among whom (were) both Mary the Magdalene[a] and Mary the mother of-James the younger and of-Joses and Salome. **15:41** When he-was in Galilee, they were-following[b] him and ministering[c] to him, and (there were also) many other (women) who had-come-up-with him to Jerusalem.

LEXICON—a. Μαγδαληνή (LN 93.242) (BAGD p. 484): The name Μαρία ἡ Μαγδαληνή 'Mary the Magdalene' [AB2, Lns] is also translated 'Mary Magdalene' [BAGD, LN; all translations except AB1, AB2, Lns, GW, REB], 'Mary from Magdala' [GW], 'Mary of Magdala' [AB1; REB]. This noun identifies Mary, 'a woman of Magdala' [LN]. This refers to a specific Mary who was from the town of Magdala [BAGD]. The articular adjective, '*the* Magdalene' singles out this Mary from any other Mary who was a follower of Jesus [Hb]. The town of Magdala was near Tiberias on the west shore of the Lake of Galilee. The only thing known about her is that she had seven demons driven out of her by Jesus [TH].

b. imperf. act. indic. of ἀκολουθέω (LN 36.31): 'to follow' [LN; all translations except CEV, NLT], 'to be a follower' [CEV, NLT], 'to be a disciple of' [LN]. This verb means to be a follower or a disciple of someone in the sense of adhering to the teachings or instructions of the leader and in promoting the cause of that leader [LN]. Here 'follow' has the sense of 'accompany' [TH].

c. imperf. act. indic. of διακονέω (LN 35.37) (BAGD 2. p. 184): 'to minister to' [BAGD, BECNT, Lns; ESV, KJV, NASB], 'to minister to his needs' [NTC], 'to care for his needs' [NIV, NLT], 'to support' [GW], 'to give support' [NET], 'to help' [CEV, NCV, TEV], 'to serve' [AB2, BAGD, WBC], 'to wait on' [AB1], 'to take care of' [LN], 'to look after' [BNTC; REB], 'to provide for' [NRSV]. This verb means to take care of someone by rendering humble service to that person [LN]. Some translations might need to specify what they probably did, such as serving food [TH, TRT], washing clothes, and perhaps giving financial support [TRT]. These women that followed Jesus from place to place were not just devout listeners but were also ministering to him by sharing their resources [Hb].

DISCOURSE UNIT—15:42–47 [Hb, NICNT; CEV, ESV, GW, NASB, NCV, NET, NIV, NLT, NRSV, TEV]. The topic is Jesus is buried [CEV, ESV, GW, NASB, NCV], the burial of Jesus [NICNT; NRSV, TEV], Jesus' burial [NET, NIV, NLT], the burial of the body [Hb].

15:42 And when evening already had-come, since it-was the Day-of-Preparation,[a] which is the day before the Sabbath, **15:43** Joseph the-one from Arimathea, a prominent[b] member of the Council, who was himself looking-forward-to[c] the kingdom of God, taking-courage,[d] went-in to Pilate and asked (for) the body of Jesus.

LEXICON—a. παρασκευή (LN 67.201) (BAGD p. 622): 'Day of Preparation/preparation' [BAGD, BECNT, LN, WBC; ESV, NET, NLT, NRSV, REB], 'Preparation/preparation day' [AB1, AB2, Lns, NTC; NASB, NCV, NIV], 'Preparation/preparation' [BNTC; KJV], not explicit [GW]. The phrase 'it was the Day of Preparation' is translated 'the Jewish people were getting ready for that sacred day' [CEV]. This noun denotes a day on which preparations were made for a sacred day or feast day. This word was so often used in conjunction with Friday that it actually became the present-day Greek term for Friday [LN]. It was Friday, the day on which everything had to be prepared for the Sabbath when no work would be permitted [BAGD].

  b. εὐσχήμων (LN 87.33) (BAGD 2. p. 327): 'prominent' [AB2, BAGD, Lns; NASB, NIV], 'important' [GW, NCV], 'of high standing or repute' [BAGD], 'respected' [AB1, BECNT, WBC; ESV, NRSV, REB], 'highly respected' [CEV], 'highly regarded' [NET], 'esteemed' [**LN**], 'influential' [BNTC], 'distinguished' [NTC], 'honorable' [KJV], 'honored' [LN; NLT]. This adjective pertains to having special prestige or honor [LN].

  c. pres. mid. or pass. (deponent = act.) participle of προσδέχομαι (**LN** 85.60) (BAGD 2.b. p. 712): 'to wait for' [BAGD, BNTC, **LN**, NTC; CEV, NASB, GW, KJV, NCV, NIV, NLT], 'to wait expectantly' [NRSV], 'to await' [LN, Lns], 'to eagerly await' [BECNT], 'to expect' [AB2, BAGD, WBC], 'to look forward to' [NET, REB], 'to look for' [AB1; ESV]. This verb means to remain in a place and/or state with expectancy concerning a future event [LN].

  d. aorist act. participle of τολμάω (LN 25.161) (BAGD 2. p. 822): 'to dare' [**LN**, Lns], 'to be bold' [WBC; GW, KJV, NET, NIV, NRSV], 'to take a risk' [NLT], 'to take courage' [ESV], 'to gather up courage' [NASB], 'to summon up courage' [BNTC, NTC], 'to pluck up courage' [AB2], 'to be courageous' [BAGD, BECNT], 'to be brave' [AB1; CEV, NCV, REB]. This verb means to be bold enough to challenge or defy possible danger or opposition [LN]. His request was daring because it was essentially a confession of his commitment to the condemned and crucified Jesus [CGTC, Hb].

QUESTION—How was this still the day of preparation if 'evening already had come'?

1. Even though the words 'when evening had come' would ordinarily mean it was after sunset, this must refer to the approach of evening since it seems that everything Joseph did took place between the time Jesus died at 3:00 P.M. and sunset at 6:00 P.M. when the Sabbath began [TH]. What Mark intended to communicate was that the day's end was fast approaching since it was already between 4:00 and 5:00 P.M [WBC]. Some translate this 'as evening approached' [BNTC, EBC; NIV, NLT], 'it was toward evening' [TEV].
2. The ancient Hebrews broke up the evening into two stages with the first beginning at 3 P.M. in what we currently call the 'afternoon' and the second at 6 P.M. Since a Jew would not have asked for the body of Jesus if the Sabbath had already begun, the words 'when evening already had come' must refer to the first stage of the evening [NTC]. Jesus was buried before sundown, so 'evening' in this verse must refer to the 'first evening' from mid afternoon to sunset and not the second evening from sunset to dark [Hb, Lns, NTC].
3. The usage of the word 'evening' here refers to a window of time of several hours on either side of sundown [NAC, NCBC, Tay].

15:44 And Pilate was-amazed[a] that (Jesus)-had-died already, and having-summoned[b] the centurion, he-asked him whether[c] (Jesus) had-died already. **15:45** And having-found-out from the centurion, he-granted[d] Joseph the dead-body.

LEXICON—a. aorist act. indic. of θαυμάζω (LN 25.213) (BAGD 1.a.γ. p. 352): 'to be amazed, to marvel' [LN], 'to wonder' [BAGD, LN]. The phrase ἐθαύμασεν εἰ 'was amazed that' [NCV] is also translated 'was astonished that' [BNTC], 'was surprised that' [WBC; NET], 'was surprised to hear that' [AB1, NTC; CEV, ESV, NIV, REB, TEV], 'couldn't believe that' [NLT], 'marveled that' [BECNT], 'wondered if' [GW, NASB, NRSV], 'wondered whether' [AB Lns], 'marveled if' [KJV]. This verb means to wonder or marvel at some event or object [LN].

b. aorist mid. participle of προσκαλέομαι, προσκαλέω (LN 33.308) (BAGD 1.a. p. 715): 'to summon' [AB2, NTC, WBC; ESV, GW, NASB, NIV, NRSV], 'to send for' [AB1, BNTC; REB], 'to call to oneself' [BAGD, LN, Lns; KJV], 'to call' [BECNT, LN; NCV, NET, TEV], 'to call for' [NLT], 'to call in' [CEV]. This verb means to call to someone [LN].

c. εἰ (LN 90.26) (BAGD V.2.a. p. 219): 'whether' [AB2, BAGD, BNTC, LN, Lns, NTC; ESV, KJV, NASB, NRSV], 'if' [BECNT, LN, WBC; CEV, GW, NCV, NET, NIV, NLT, TEV], 'that' [LN; REB], not explicit [AB1]. This means 'whether' in indirect questions [BAGD].

d. aorist mid. (deponent = act.) indic. of δωρέομαι (LN 57.83) (BAGD p. 210): 'to grant' [AB2, BECNT, BNTC, LN, NTC; ESV, NASB, NRSV], 'to let' [CEV, GW], 'to give' [AB1, BAGD, LN, WBC; KJV, NET, NIV], 'to give leave to' [REB], 'to present to' [Lns], 'to tell (Joseph he could)' [NCV, NLT, TEV]. This verb means to give an object or benefit to someone with the probable implication of formality [LN].

15:46 And having-bought a-linen-cloth[a] (and) having- taken- him -down,[b] he-wrapped (him) in the linen-cloth and put him in a-tomb[c] which was cut[d] from rock. And he-rolled a-stone against the entrance of-the tomb. **15:47** And Mary Magdalene and Mary the (mother) of Joses were watching where he has-been-laid.

LEXICON—a. σινδών (LN 6.155) (BAGD 1. p. 751): 'linen cloth' [AB2, BAGD, BECNT, LN, Lns, NTC; CEV, GW, NASB, NCV, NET, NIV, NRSV], 'a linen sheet' [AB1, BNTC; REB, TEV], 'a long sheet of linen cloth' [NLT], 'a linen shroud' [WBC; ESV], 'fine linen' [KJV]. This noun denotes linen cloth of good quality [LN].

b. aorist act. participle of καθαιρέω (LN 15.199) (BAGD p. 386): 'to take down' [AB1, AB2, BAGD, LN, Lns, NTC, WBC; ESV, KJV, NASB, NET, NIV, NRSV, TEV]. The phrase 'having taken him down' is translated 'took him down from the cross' [BECNT, BNTC; REB], 'took the/Jesus' body down from the cross' [CEV, GW, NCV, NCV]. This verb means to bring something down from one point to another [LN].

c. μνημεῖον (LN 7.75) (BAGD 2. p. 524): 'tomb' [AB1, AB2, BAGD, BECNT, BNTC, LN, Lns, NTC, WBC; all versions except KJV], 'grave' [BAGD, LN], 'sepulcher' [KJV]. This noun denotes a construction for the burial of the dead [LN].

d. perf. pass. participle of λατομέω (LN 19.25) (BAGD 1. p. 467): 'to cut rock' [LN], 'to hew out rock' [BAGD, LN]. The clause 'cut from rock' is translated 'cut into solid rock' [CEV], 'cut out of the rock' [AB1, BECNT, BNTC, NTC, WBC; ESV, GW, NET, NIV, NLT, REB], 'hewn out-of-a/in-the rock' [AB2, Lns; KJV, NASB, NRSV], 'dug out of solid rock' [TEV], 'cut out of a wall of rock' [NCV]. This verb means to shape rock by cutting it either internally or externally. In some languages important distinctions are made in terms for cutting rock depending upon the type of activity. For example, shaping of rock by cutting, the quarrying of rock from an outcrop, the hewing of an area inside the outcropping of a rock, or making a cave-like structure hewn into rock [LN]. It means to hew out of the rock [BAGD].

QUESTION—Did Joseph take care of Jesus' body all by himself?

Mark does not mention anyone assisting Joseph in all the actions described here, but Joseph would have needed help in removing the body from the cross, preparing it for burial, and carrying it to the place of burial. Because he was a rich man, he probably had his servants help him [EBC, NICNT].

QUESTION—What was the point of rolling a stone against the entrance of the tomb?

Tombs cut out of large rocks were closed by rolling a stone against the entrance. The stone might be a flat stone disc that rolled in a sloped channel or simply a large rock that could be rolled in front of the entrance [EBC].

DISCOURSE UNIT—16:1–20 [Hb]. The topic is the resurrection of the Servant.

DISCOURSE UNIT—16:1–13 [NASB]. The topic is the resurrection.

DISCOURSE UNIT—16:1–8 [CBC, Hb, NICNT, NIGTC; CEV, ESV, GW, NCV, NET, NIV, NLT, NRSV, REB, TEV]. The topic is the empty tomb [NIGTC], Jesus is alive [CEV], Jesus comes back to life [GW], Jesus rises from the dead [NCV], the resurrection [ESV, NET, NIV, NLT, TEV], the resurrection of Jesus [CBC; NICNT; NRSV, REB], women coming to the empty tomb [Hb].

16:1 **And the Sabbath having-passed, Mary the Magdalene and Mary the (mother) of James and Salome bought spices^a in-order-that having-come they-might-anoint^b him.**

TEXT—Manuscripts reading διαγενομένου τοῦ σαββάτου...καὶ Σαλώμη ἠγόρασαν 'the Sabbath having passed...and Salome bought' are given an A rating by GNT to indicate it was regarded to be certain. Variant readings are διαγενομένου τοῦ σαββάτου...καὶ Σαλώμη πορευθεῖσαι ἠγόρασαν 'the Sabbath having passed...and Salome having gone bought' and πορευθεῖσαι ἠγόρασαν 'having gone bought'.

LEXICON—a. ἄρωμα (LN **6.207**) (BAGD 114): 'spices' [AB2, BAGD, BECNT, BNTC, Lns, NTC, WBC; CEV, ESV, GW, NASB, NIV, NRSV, TEV], 'sweet spices' [KJV], 'sweet smelling spices' [NCV], 'aromatic spices' [NET], 'burial spices' [NLT], 'aromatic oils' [AB1; REB], 'aromatic salves' [**LN**], 'perfumed ointment' [LN]. This noun denotes aromatic oils or salves that were used especially for embalming the dead. This word's equivalent in some languages is 'sweet-smelling herbs, good-smelling leaves, perfumed oil' [LN]. It refers to substances like myrrh that were sweet smelling enough to cover the smell of a decaying body. It is important to not give the impression they were going to embalm Jesus' body or that they were simply using food spices [TRT].

b. aorist act. subj. of ἀλείφω (LN 47.14) (BAGD 1. p. 35): 'to anoint (him/Jesus)' [AB1, AB2, BAGD, BECNT, BNTC, LN, Lns, NTC, WBC; ESV, GW, KJV, NASB, NET, NRSV, REB], 'to anoint (his body)' [BECNT; NIV, NLT, TEV], 'to put on (his body)' [CEV, NCV]. This verb means to anoint with a liquid that is normally oil or perfume [LN].

QUESTION—Who were these women?

These are the three women who are named in 15:40. The two women named Mary were also watching where the body was being placed in the tomb in 15:47 [Tay].

QUESTION—Why did the women buy spices to anoint Jesus' body at that time?

The women had to wait until the shops opened for a few hours of brisk trade after the Sabbath had ended [Hb]. The first day of the week began at the same time the Sabbath was ending at 6:00 PM [TH]. Apparently they wanted to anoint Jesus' body with the fragrant ointments as an expression of their love for him [EBC, Hb, Sw, WBC]. Their desire to 'anoint' him probably means they planned to pour the oil over his head [NICNT] or his body [BECN, BNTC, EBC, Lns, NTC, WBC; NIV, NLT, TEV]. These spices were probably used to reduce the stench of a decomposing body, but they did not help in preserving it [WBC]. Apparently they planned to anoint the body now since Joseph of Arimathea had not done that when he hurriedly buried the body just before the Sabbath began [BECNT, NIGTC, WBC].

16:2 **And very early on the first (day) of-the week, they come to the tomb when the sun had-risen.** **16:3** **And they-were-saying to one-another, "Who will-roll away the stone from the entrance to-the tomb for us?"** **16:4** **And having-looked-up, they-see that the stone had-been-rolled-away, because it-was very large.**

TEXT—In 16:2, manuscripts reading ἀνατείλαντος τοῦ ἡλίου 'the sun had risen' are given an A rating by GNT to indicate it was regarded to be certain. Variant readings are ἔτι ἀνατείλαντος τοῦ ἡλίου 'the sun already having risen' and ἀνατέλλοντος τοῦ ἡλίου 'the sun rising'.

QUESTION—What is the function of the final clause in verse 4, ἦν γὰρ μέγας σφόδρα 'because it was very large'?

1. The conjunction γάρ means 'because' and explains the reason for something [AB2, BECNT, Hb, ICC, NTC, TH, WBC; KJV].
    1.1 This clause explains why the women had been concerned earlier about rolling the stone aside [AB2, BECNT, ICC, NTC, WBC], and one translates it: 'They had been alarmed about the stone for it was very large' [NTC].
    1.2 This assumes that they were still some distance away when they looked up and the reason they could already see that the stone had been rolled away was because of the stone's large size [Hb, TH].
2. The conjunction γάρ simply makes an additional comment about the size of the stone: 'And it was a huge stone!' [CEV], 'It was a very large stone' [GW, TEV; similarly ESV], 'which was very large' [NET, NIV, NLT, NRSV], 'big/huge as it was' [AB1, REB].

16:5 **And having-gone into the tomb, they-saw a-young-man clothed[a] (in) a-white robe,[b] sitting on the right and they-were-amazed.[c]**

LEXICON—a. perf. mid. participle of περιβάλλω (LN 49.3) (BAGD 1.b.α. p. 646): 'to be clothed' [BECNT, LN; KJV, NLT], 'to be dressed' [AB2, NTC, WBC; ESV, GW, NET, NIV, NRSV], 'to wear' [AB1, BAGD, BNTC; NASB, NCV, REB, TEV], 'in' [CEV], 'to have thrown around him' [Lns]. This verb means to put on clothes [LN].

b. στολή (LN **6.174**) (BAGD 769): 'robe' [BAGD; all translations except KJV], 'long robe' [**LN**], 'long flowing robe' [BAGD], 'long garment' [KJV]. This noun denotes a long flowing robe [LN].

c. aorist pass. indic. of ἐκθαμβέομαι (LN 25.210) (BAGD p. 240): 'to be amazed' [LN; NASB], 'to be utterly amazed' [BECNT], 'to be astounded' [AB2, BNTC, LN; NCV], 'to be dumbfounded' [REB], 'to be alarmed' [BAGD, **LN**, NTC], 'to be distressed' [WBC; CEV, ESV, NET, NIV, NLT, NRSV, TEV], 'to be afraid' [AB1, LN, Lns], 'to be affrighted' [KJV], 'to be panic-stricken' [GW]. This verb means to be greatly astounded [LN].

QUESTION—Who was the young man?

Although Mark does not identify the young man as an angel, the long white robe suggests it and Matthew 28:2 confirms it [EBC]. The translation should follow the text and call him a 'young man' even though the circumstances would imply that this young man they saw wearing a white robe was really an angel [TH].

QUESTION—Where was the young man seated?

The statement 'sitting on the right' means that when the women entered the tomb, he was sitting to their right [Hb]. The translation must not imply that the young man was sitting on the right side of a corpse [TH].

16:6 And he-says to-them, "Do- not -be-alarmed. You-are-seeking Jesus the Nazarene,ª the-one having-been-crucified. He-has-been-raised,ᵇ Look,ᶜ (here is) the place where they-laidᵈ him.

LEXICON—a. Ναζαρηνός (LN 93.537) (BAGD p. 532): 'Nazarene' [BAGD, LN]. The phrase 'Jesus the Nazarene' [AB2, Lns, NTC, WBC; NASB, NET, NIV] is also translated 'Jesus of Nazareth' [AB1, BECNT, BNTC; ESV, KJV, NLT, NRSV, REB, TEV], 'Jesus from Nazareth' [CEV, GW, NCV]. This adjective is a derivative of the town Ναζαρέθ 'Nazareth' and refers to a person who either lived in Nazareth or was a native of that town [LN]. In 14:67, Jesus is referred to as τοῦ Ναζαρηνοῦ Ἰησοῦ 'the Nazarene, Jesus'.

b. aorist pass. indic. of ἐγείρω (LN 23.94): 'to be raised to life, to be made to live again' [LN]. The clause ἠγέρθη 'he has been raised' [AB1, AB2, BNTC, WBC; NET, NIV, NRSV, REB, TEV] is also translated 'God has raised him to life' [CEV], 'he has been brought back to life' [GW]. Others translate this as an active verb: 'he has risen' [BECNT, NTC; ESV, NASB; similarly KJV], 'he has/is risen from the dead' [NCV, NLT], 'he arose' [Lns]. This verb means to cause someone to live again after having once died [LN]. This is the divine passive that indicates Jesus was raised by God [NETfn].

c. ἴδε (LN 91.13) (BAGD 3. p. 369): 'look, listen, pay attention' [LN], 'here is' [BAGD]. The phrase ἴδε ὁ τόπος 'Look, here/there is the place' [AB1, BNTC; NTC; NCV, NET, NRSV, REB, TEV] is also translated 'Look, this is where' [NLT], 'Look at the place' [GW], 'See the place' [AB2,

BECNT, Lns; ESV, NIV], 'Behold the place' [WBC; KJV], 'Behold, here is the place' [NASB], 'You can see the place' [CEV]. This particle is a prompter of attention that also serves to emphasize the following statement [LN].
   d. aorist act. indic. of τίθημι (LN 85.32) (BAGD I.1.a.α. p. 815): 'to lay' [BAGD], 'to put, to place' [BAGD, LN]. The phrase 'where they laid him/his-body' [AB1, AB2, BECNT, BNTC, Lns, NTC, WBC; all versions except CEV, TEV] is also translated 'where they put his body' [CEV], 'where he was placed' [TEV]. This verb means to put or place something in a particular location [LN].

16:7 **But go tell his disciples and Peter, 'He-is-going-ahead[a] of-you into Galilee. There you-will-see him, just-as he-told you.'"**
LEXICON—a. pres. act. impera. of προάγω (LN 15.142) (BAGD 2.b. p. 702): 'to go prior to, to go away beforehand' [LN], 'to go before someone' [BAGD]. The phrase Προάγει ὑμᾶς 'He is-going/will-go ahead of you' [BECNT, NTC; CEV, NASB, NLT, NCV, NET, NIV, NRSV, REB, TEV] is also translated 'He is-going/going-on before you' [AB1, AB2, BNTC, Lns, WBC; ESV; similarly GW], 'He is-going/goes before you [Lns, WBC; KJV]. This verb means to go on ahead, to precede others [LN].
QUESTION—Why is Peter's name mentioned separately?
   This does not mean Peter was no longer a disciple because of his denial but that he needed the restoring effect of this announcement more than the other disciples because his faith had been shaken the most [ICC]. It means 'and in particular Peter' [Sw]. God graciously provided for Peter's special needs through the words of the angel [EBC]. Peter is singled out because he had denied Jesus in 14:66–72 [EBC, NTC]. This is a message of assurance that Peter was still included in the circle of the disciples in spite of his denials [Hb].

16:8 **And having-gone-out they-fled[a] from the tomb because trembling[b] and astonishment[c] had-seized[d] them, and they-said nothing to-anyone because they-were-afraid.[e]**
LEXICON—a. aorist act. indic. of φεύγω (LN 15.61) (BAGD 1. p. 855): 'to flee' [AB2, BAGD, BECNT, BNTC, LN, Lns, NTC, WBC; ESV, KJV, NASB, NIV, NLT, NRSV], 'to run away' [LN; GW, NCV, REB], 'to run' [AB1; CEV, NET, TEV], 'to seek safety in flight' [BAGD]. This verb means to move quickly away from a point or area in order to avoid some presumed danger or difficulty [LN].
   b. τρόμος (LN 16.6) (BAGD p. 827): 'trembling' [BAGD, LN], 'quivering' [BAGD]. This noun denotes a state of trembling from fear [BAGD, LN]. See the translations of this noun in lexicon item d.
   c. ἔκστασις (LN 25.217) (BAGD 1. p. 245): 'astonishment' [BAGD, LN], 'amazement' [LN], 'confusion' [BAGD]. This noun denotes a state of such intense amazement that one is at the point of being beside himself

MARK 16:8 321

with astonishment [LN]. See the translations of this noun in lexicon item d.

d. imperf. act. indic. of ἔχω (LN 90.65) (BAGD I.1.d. p. 332): 'to be seized with' [BAGD], 'to experience, to have' [LN]. The clause εἶχεν αὐτὰς τρόμος καὶ ἔκστασις 'trembling and astonishment had seized/taken-hold-of them' [AB2, BECNT; ESV] is also translated 'terror and bewilderment/amazement had seized them' [NET, NRSV], 'shock and trembling had overwhelmed/gripped them' [GW, NASB], 'trembling and amazement held/were-holding/had-taken-hold-of them' [Lns, NTC, WBC], 'they trembled and were amazed' [KJV], 'trembling with amazement' [REB], 'overcome by trembling and terror' [BNTC], 'beside themselves with trembling and awe' [AB1], 'were confused and shaking all over' [CEV], 'were confused and shaking with fear' [NCV], '(ran from the tomb) distressed and terrified' [TEV], '(fled) trembling and bewildered' [NIV, NLT]. This verb means to experience some state or condition [LN].

e. imperf. pass. indic. of φοβέομαι, φοβέω (LN 25.252) (BAGD 1.a. p. 862 or 2.a. p. 863): 'to be afraid' [AB1, AB2, BECNT, BNTC, LN, Lns, NTC; all versions except NLT], 'to be frightened' [NLT]. The verb ἐφοβοῦντο 'they were afraid' is also translated 'they were too afraid (to tell anyone)' [CEV]. This verb means to be in a state of fearing something [LN]. This verb could mean 'to fear' in the sense of being frightened [BAGD (1.a)] or 'to fear' in the sense of being reverent [BAGD (2.a.)].

QUESTION—What were the women afraid of?

They were in a state of reverential awe because of the angel's message [AB1, AB2, BECNT, ESV fn, Hb, Lns, WBC; ESV, KJV]. Their trembling and astonishment reflected their awe at being eyewitnesses to an act of God [EBC, ESVfn, LN]. Others think this means that their fear and astonishment caused them to flee from the tomb [NTC]. When their confrontation with the angel proved to be too much, the women fled away bewildered and trembling [EBC].

QUESTION—Did the women ever tell anyone?

Mark meant they were only silent in the immediate aftermath of this event [CGTC, ESVfn]. After they had collected their wits, they did a lot of talking [EBC]. Mathew 28:8 says that they left the tomb μετὰ φόβου καὶ χαρᾶς μεγάλης 'with fear and great joy' as they ran to tell Jesus' disciples [BECNT, Hb, Lns]. When Jesus appeared to these women soon after they had left the tomb (Mathew 28:9-10), it probably removed any lingering fear that they had to tell the disciples the angel's message. Luke 24:9-11 tells us that no one believed the women when they communicated the angel's message to the disciples after returning from the tomb [TRT].

[[16:9–20]]

The most reliable manuscripts of the Gospel of Mark end with verse 8. Verses 9–20 constitute a 'Longer Ending' that was appended to the Gospel of Mark sometime between A.D. 100 and 140. Erasmus used these later manuscripts with the 'Longer Ending' when preparing his Greek New Testament in 1560, so it has been included in the *Textus Receptus* and all subsequent editions of the Greek New Testaments. Modern editions of the Greek New Testament isolate this 'Longer Ending' in an appendix by putting it in brackets. Any modern translation should indicate by some means that the Longer Ending is not part of the original Gospel of Mark [TH]. These verses are not included in AB2, BECNT, NAC, NICNT, and NIGTC.

DISCOURSE UNIT—16:9–20 [GW]. The topic is Jesus appears to his followers.

DISCOURSE UNIT—16:9–14 [Hb]. The topic is the appearings of Jesus.

DISCOURSE UNIT—16:9–13 [NCV]. The topic is some followers see Jesus.

DISCOURSE UNIT—16:9–11 [CEV, ESV, NRSV, TEV]. The topic is Jesus appears to Mary Magdalene.

16:9 And having-risen[a] early on-(the) first (day) of-the week, he-appeared[b] first to-Mary Magdalene, from whom he-had-cast-out[c] seven demons.[d]

LEXICON—a. aorist act. participle of ἀνίσταμαι (LN 23.93) (BAGD 2.a. p. 70): 'to rise' [BAGD, BNTC, Lns, NTC, WBC; ESV, KJV, NASB, NET, NIV, NRSV], 'to rise to life' [CEV], 'to rise from the dead' [NCV, NLT, REB, TEV], 'to come back to life' [LN; GW], 'to be raised' [AB1], 'to be resurrected, to live again' [LN]. This noun means to come back to life after having once died [LN]. It means 'having risen (from the dead)' [TH].

b. aorist pass. indic. of φαίνομαι (LN 24.18) (BAGD 2.c. p. 852): 'to appear' [BAGD, BNTC, LN, Lns, NTC, WBC; all versions except NCV, NLT], 'to become visible' [LN], 'to show oneself' [NCV], 'to be seen by' [NLT]. This verb means to become visible to someone. In a number of languages the equivalent of 'appeared to' would simply be 'came to' [LN]. This could be rendered as 'showed himself to' or 'caused her to see him' [TH]. This means that he made himself visible to Mary [Hb].

c. pluperfect act. indic, of ἐκβάλλω [LN 53.102) (BAGD 1.p. 237): 'to cast out' [LN, Lns, NTC, WBC; ESV, KJV, NASB, NLT, NRSV], 'to exorcise' [LN], 'to expel' [BAGD], 'to drive out' [BAGD, BNTC; NET, NIV, REB, TEV], 'to force out' [CEV, GW, NCV]. This verb means to cause a demon to no longer possess or control a person [LN]. The pluperfect describes an action completed in the past [TH]. In reference to 'casting out' demons, this verb occurs at 1:34, 39; 3:15, 22, 23; 6:13; 7:26; 9:18, 28, 38; 16:9, 17.

d. δαιμόνιον (LN 12.37): 'demon' [BAGD, LN, Lns, NTC, WBC; NASB; all versions except KJV], 'evil spirit' [LN], 'devil' [KJV]. This noun denotes an evil supernatural being or spirit [LN].

16:10 She went (and) and told the-ones who-had-been with him as they-were-mourning[a] and weeping.[b] **16:11** When they-heard (her say) that he-was-alive and had-been-seen by her, they-did-not-believe (it).

LEXICON—a. pres. act. participle of πενθέω (LN 25.142) (BAGD 1. p. 642): 'to mourn' [AB1, BAGD, BNTC, Lns, NTC, WBC; all versions except GW, NCV, NLT], 'to be sad' [BAGD, LN; NCV], 'to grieve' [BAGD, LN; GW, NLT], 'to weep (for)' [LN]. This verb means to experience sadness or grief as the result of depressing circumstances [LN].

b. pres. act. participle of κλαίω (LN 25.138) (BAGD 1. p. 433): 'to weep' [BAGD, BNTC, LN, Lns, NTC, WBC; ESV, NASB, KJV, NET, NIV, NLT, NRSV], 'to cry' [BAGD; CEV, GW, NCV, TEV], 'to be in tears' [AB1], 'to wail, to lament' [LN], 'to be sorrowful' [REB]. This verb means to weep or wail where the emphasis is on the noise accompanying the weeping [LN].

DISCOURSE UNIT—16:12–13 [CEV, ESV, NRSV, TEV]. The topic is Jesus appears to two disciples [CEV, ESV, NRSV], Jesus appears to two followers [TEV].

16:12 And after this he-appeared in a-different form[a] to-two of them as-they-were-walking in[b] (the) country. **16:13** And-they went-back and told the rest, but they-did-not believe (them).

LEXICON—a. μορφή (LN **58.15**) (BAGD p. 528): 'form, outward appearance' [BAGD], 'visual form, appearance' [LN]. The clause ἐν ἑτέρᾳ μορφῇ 'in a different form' [LN, NTC; NASB, NET, NIV, NLT, REB] is also translated 'in another form' [AB1, BNTC, Lns, WBC; CEV, ESV, KJV, NRSV], 'in a different manner' [TEV], 'He did not look as he usually did' [GW], 'but he did not look the same as before' [NCV]. This noun denotes the visual form of something [LN].

b. εἰς (LN 83.13, 84.22) (BAGD 1.a.α. p. 228): 'in' [BAGD, LN (83.13)], 'into' [BAGD, LN (84.22)]. The phrase εἰς ἀγρόν 'in the country' [WBC; NCV, NIV] is also translated 'into the country' [AB1, BNTC, NTC; ESV, KJV, NLT, NRSV, REB], 'to the country' [NET], 'on their way to the country' [NASB, TEV], 'to their home in the country' [GW], 'as they were on their way out of the city' [CEV]. This preposition indicates a position defined as being within certain limits (LN 83.13)] or it refers to an extension toward a goal that is inside an area [LN 84.22)]. The context implies that it was a journey from Jerusalem out to the neighboring rural region [TH].

QUESTION—What is meant by Jesus appearing in 'a different form'?

1. Jesus appeared to be a different person than the Jesus that these two disciples on the road to Emmaus knew so well (see Luke 24:13–35) [AB1, BNTC, CBC, CGTC, EBC, Hb, ICC, Lns, My, NCBC, NTC, PNTC, Sw, Tay, WBC].
2. Jesus appeared in a form different from the one in which he appeared to Mary [TH].

DISCOURSE UNIT—16:14–20 [ESV, NASB, TEV]. The topic is the great commission [ESV], the disciples commissioned [NASB], Jesus talks to the Apostles [NCV].

DISCOURSE UNIT—16:14–18 [CEV, NRSV, TEV]. The topic is Jesus appears to the eleven [TEV], Jesus commissions the disciples [NRSV], what Jesus' followers must do [CEV].

16:14 And later he-appeared[a] to-the Eleven themselves as they-were-reclining-at-table, and he-reproached[b] (them) for their unbelief and hardness-of-heart,[c] because they-had- not -believed those who-had-seen him (after) he-had-been-raised-to-life.[d]

LEXICON—a. aorist pass. indic. of φανερόω (LN 24.19) (BAGD 2.b.β. p. 853): 'to appear' [BAGD, BNTC, LN, WBC; all version except NCV], 'to show one's self' [AB1; NCV], 'to be manifested' [Lns], 'to become visible, to be seen' [LN]. This verb means to make oneself visible [LN].

b. aorist act. indic. of ὀνειδίζω (LN 33.422) (BAGD 2. p. 570): 'to reproach' [BAGD, BNTC, LN, WBC; NASB, REB], 'to rebuke' [AB1; ESV, NET, NIV, NLT], 'to criticize' [NCV], 'to reprimand' [LN], 'to scold' [CEV, TEV], 'to upbraid' [Lns; KJV, NRSV], 'to put to shame' [GW]. This verb means to reproach someone who is to blame for something [LN].

c. σκληροκαρδία (LN 88.224) (BAGD p. 756): This noun literally refers to someone being 'uncircumcised in heart and ears'. It is an idiom for someone who is obdurate and obstinate [LN]. It refers to 'hardness of heart' [BAGD, BNTC, NTC, WBC; ESV, KJV, NASB, NET], 'stubbornness' [BAGD, LN; CEV, GW, NIV, NLT NRSV, TEV], 'being completely unyielding' [LN], 'heart stiffness' [Lns], 'refusal to believe' [NCV], 'incredulity' [REB], 'obstinacy' [BAGD], 'obduracy' [AB1].

d. perf. pass. participle of ἐγείρω (LN 23.94): 'to be raised to life, to be made to live again' [LN]. This passive form is translated 'as having arisen' [Lns], 'had been raised' [AB1, BNTC], 'had been raised from the dead' [NLT, REB], 'had been raised to life' [CEV], '(had seen him) resurrected' [NET], '(had seen him) risen' [WBC], '(had seen him) alive' [GW, TEV]. Others take this verb to be active in meaning: 'had risen' [ESV, NASB, NIV, NRSV], 'had risen from the dead' [NCV], 'was risen' [KJV]. This verb means to cause someone to live again after having once died [LN].

DISCOURSE UNIT—16:15–18 [Hb]. The topic is the commission to his followers.

16:15 And he-said to-them, "Go into all the world (and) preach[a] the good-news to every creature.[b] **16:16** The-one having-believed and been-baptized will-be-saved, but the-one not having-believed will-be-condemned.[c]

LEXICON—a. aorist act. imperf. of κηρύσσω (LN 33.256) (BAGD 2.b.β. p. 431): 'to preach' [LN, NTC, WBC; CEV, KJV, NASB, NET, NIV,

NLT, TEV], 'to proclaim' [BAGD, BNTC; ESV, NRSV, REB], 'to tell' [GW, NCV], 'to herald' [Lns], 'to make the Proclamation' [AB1]. This verb means to publicly announce religious truths and principles while urging acceptance and compliance [LN].
  b. κτίσις (LN 42.38) (BAGD 1.b.β. p. 456): 'creature' [LN], 'creation' [BAGD, LN]. The phrase πάσῃ τῇ κτίσει 'every creature' [WBC; KJV, NET] is also translated 'the whole creation' [AB1, BNTC, Lns, NTC; ESV, NRSV, REB], 'all creation' [NASB, NIV], 'all people' [TEV], 'everyone' [CEV, GW, NCV, NLT]. This noun denotes that which has been created [BAGD, LN]. This noun does not refer to the general act of creation but to what has been created and is probably pointing to the special creation of mankind [CGTC, Hb, Lns, TH].
  c. fut. pass. indic. of κατακρίνω (LN 56.31) (BAGD p. 412): 'to be condemned' [AB2, BAGD, BNTC, LN, Lns, NTC, WBC; all versions except KJV, NCV], 'to be damned' [KJV], 'to be punished' [NCV]. This verb means to judge someone to be definitely guilty and subject to punishment [LN]. 'Condemned' is more than 'being judged'. It is used in a theological sense and refers to being condemned at the Day of Judgment [TH].
QUESTION—How close is this account connected with the preceding verse?
  The strange contrast to the stern reproof in the previous verse and the introductory phrase 'and he said to them' means these instructions were probably given at a later time [Sw].
QUESTION—How are 'believing' and 'being baptized' connected?
  A single definite article joins the two verbs 'having believed and been baptized' and it could be translated 'the baptized believer' [TH]. It connects the inward reception of the gospel by faith with the outward testimony to that faith in baptism [Hb].

16:17 And these signs[a] will-accompany[b] those who-believe: in[c] my name they-will-cast-out demons, they-will-speak in-new[d] tongues, **16:18** and with their hands they-will-pick-up snakes, and-if they-drink any deadly-poison in-no-way will-it-harm them, they-will-place[e] (their) hands on (the) sick, and they-will-be well."

LEXICON—a. σημεῖον (LN 33.477) (BAGD 2.a. p. 748): 'signs' [AB1, BAGD, BNTC, LN, Lns, NTC, WBC; ESV, KJV, NASB, NET, NIV, NRSV], 'miraculous signs' [GW, NLT], 'miracles' [REB, TEV], 'wonderful things' [CEV]. The clause 'these signs will accompany those who believe' is translated 'those who believe will be able to do these things as proof: (they will…)' [NCV]. This noun denotes an event that is regarded to have a special meaning [LN]. It refers to a sign consisting of a miracle [BAGD].
  b. fut. act. indic. of παρακολουθέω (LN **13.113**) (BAGD 1. p. 619): 'to accompany' [BAGD, BNTC, **LN**, NTC, WBC; ESV, GW, NASB, NET, NIV, NLT, NRSV], 'to happen along with, to happen at the same time' [LN], 'to follow' [AB1, Lns; KJV], not explicit [CEV, NCV, REB, TEV].

This verb means to happen in conjunction with some other happening [LN].

c. ἐν (LN 89.76): 'by means of, through, by' [LN]. The phrase 'in my name' [AB1, BNTC, Lns, NTC, WBC; ESV, KJV, NASB, NET, NIV, NLT, REB, TEV] is also translated 'by using my name' [CEV, NRSV], 'will use my name' [NCV], 'they will use the power and authority of my name' [GW]. This preposition indicates the means by which one event makes another event possible [LN]. The signs will be granted when they invoke his power as his representatives [Hb].

d. καινός (LN 28.33) (BAGD 2. p. 394): 'unknown' [BAGD], 'previously unknown, new, previously unheard of' LN]. The phrase γλώσσαις... καιναῖς 'in/with new tongues' [Lns, NTC, WBC; ESV, KJV, NASB, NET, NIV, NRSV] is also translated 'in new languages' [NCV, NLT], 'new languages' [CEV, GW], 'in strange tongues' [BNTC; REB, TEV], 'will have the gift of tongues' [AB1]. The adjective 'new' pertains to not being well known previously but being significant [LN]. Since this is the only time speaking in tongues is mentioned in the Gospels, it seems to reflect a post-Pentecost situation [EBC].

e. fut. act. indic. of ἐπιτίθημι (LN 85.51) (BAGD 1.a.α. p. 303): 'to put on, to lay on' [AB1, BAGD, LN, BNTC, WBC; ESV, KJV, NASB, NRSV, REB], 'to place on' [LN, Lns, NTC; CEV, GW, NET, NIV, NLT, TEV], 'to touch' [NCV]. This verb means to place something on something [LN].

QUESTION—Will every believer in Jesus be able to do these things?

This promise does not say that 'all' individuals will experience these signs in their personal lives. They are given to the church collectively so that the miraculous signs can be the authenticating credentials of the apostolic message that indicates the presence of the living Christ working through his messengers who are mentioned in verse 20 [Hb].

QUESTION—Why would they pick up snakes and drink a deadly poison?

Jesus is not telling his disciples to do such things. He is talking about situations where they are forced to pick up poisonous snakes, forced to drink deadly poison, or accidentally do either one [TRT].

DISCOURSE UNIT—16:19–20 [Hb; CEV, NRSV, TEV]. The topic is Jesus returns to heaven [CEV], the ascension of Jesus [Hb; NRSV], Jesus is taken up to heaven [TEV].

16:19 Then the Lord Jesus, after he-had-spoken to-them, was-taken-up[a] into heaven, and sat-down at (the) right (hand) of-God.

TEXT—Manuscripts reading κύριος Ἰησοῦς 'Lord Jesus' are followed by GNT which does not mention any variant reading. A variant reading is κύριος 'Lord' and it is followed by KJV.

LEXICON—a. aorist pass. indic. of ἀναλαμβάνω (LN 15.203) (BAGD 1. p. 56): 'to be taken up' [AB2, BAGD, BNTC, NTC, WBC; ESV, NET, NIV, NLT, NRSV, REB, TEV], 'to be taken back up' [CEV], 'to be taken away' [LN], 'to be taken' [GW], 'to be carried up' [NCV], 'to be received up' [Lns; KJV, NASB]. This verb means to lift up and carry something away from some location [LN]. The passive sense means that it was the Father who drew his Son to himself [NTC, TH].

QUESTION—Who was Jesus speaking to?

The translation should be clear that Jesus was speaking to his disciples [TH].

QUESTION—What is the significance of Jesus sitting down at the right hand of God?

The phrase ἐκ δεξιῶν καθίζω 'to sit on the right side of' is an idiom for being in a position of high status [LN 87.34].

16:20 **And those having-gone-forth preached everywhere, while the Lord worked-with (them), confirming[a] the message through the accompanying signs.**

TEXT—Manuscripts ending this verse with the word σημείων. 'signs.' are followed by GNT which does not mention any variant reading. A variant reading adds a closing word to the book: Ἀμήν 'Amen' and it is followed by KJV.

LEXICON—a. pres. act. participle of βεβαιόω (LN 28.44) (BAGD 1. p. 138): 'to confirm' [AB1, BAGD, BNTC, LN, Lns, NTC, WBC; all versions except CEV, NCV, TEV], 'to prove' [CEV, NCV, TV], 'to verify, to prove to be true and certain' [LN]. This verb means to cause something to be known as certain [LN (28.44)].

QUESTION—Who are σημείων 'those' who had gone out to preach everywhere?

They were Jesus' disciples who presumably had left from Jerusalem [TH].

QUESTION—What were the accompanying signs?

They are probably the signs that are mentioned in verses 17–18 [TH].